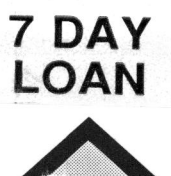
KITAJ

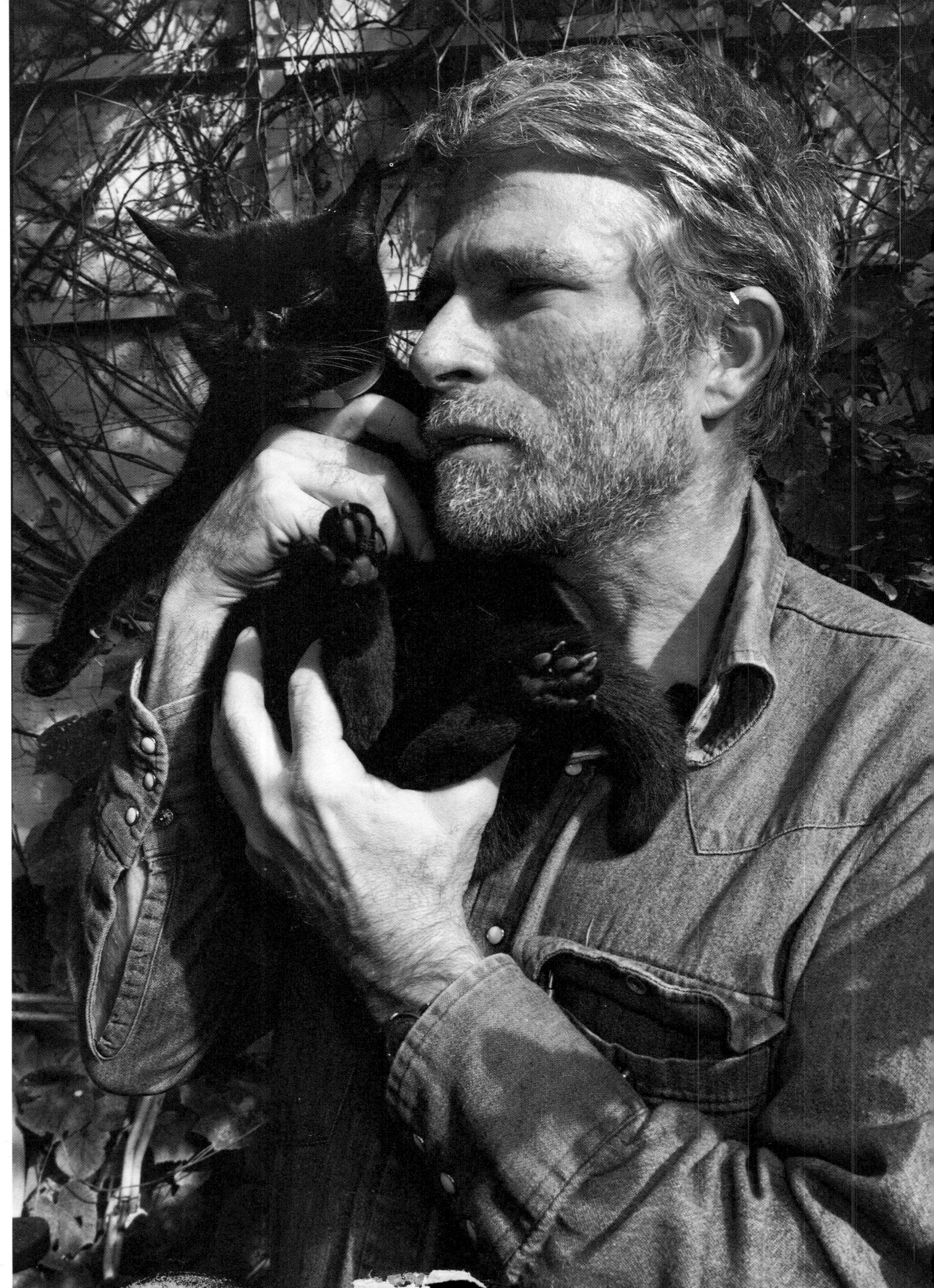

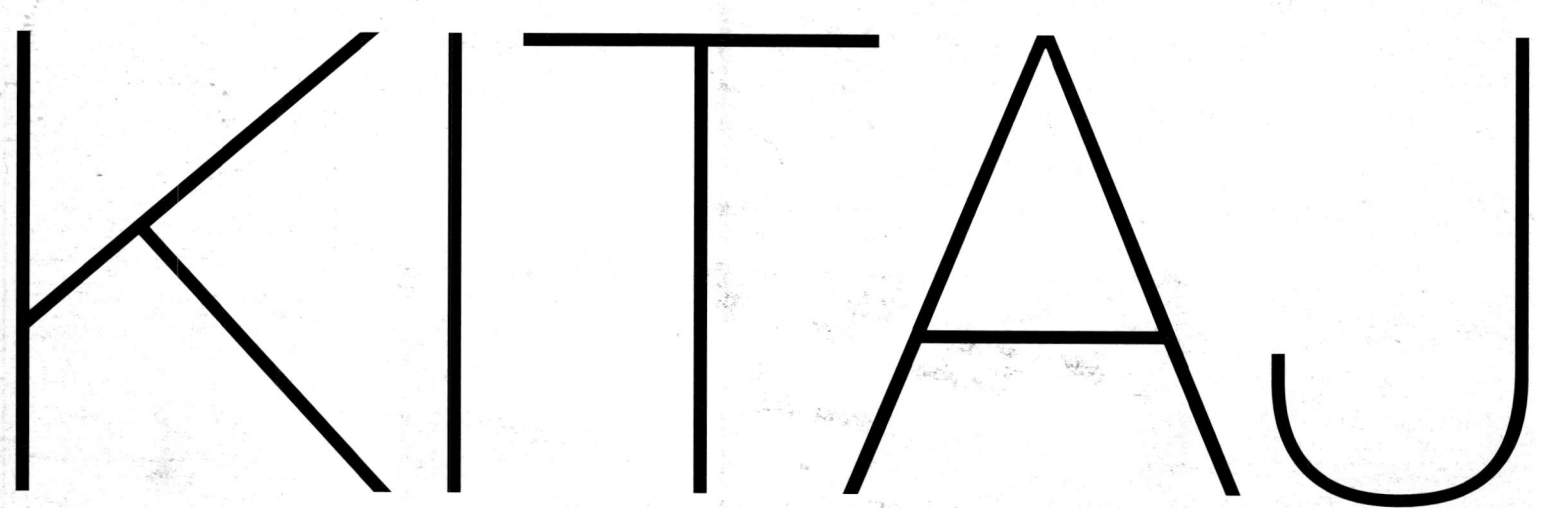

KITAJ

MARCO LIVINGSTONE

To my Parents

Frontispiece: Portrait of Kitaj, 1983, by Lee Friedlander

Phaidon Press Limited
Regent's Wharf
All Saints Street
London N1 9PA

First published as *R.B. Kitaj,* 1985
Revised and expanded edition 1992
Reprinted 1994
Third edition (revised and expanded) 1999

© 1985, 1992, 1999 Phaidon Press Limited

The publishers wish to acknowledge
the help of Marlborough Fine Art
(London) Ltd in the preparation of
this book.

A CIP catalogue record of this book
is available from the British Library

ISBN 0 7148 3891 8

Text set in Monotype Bembo 11 on 14pt
Printed in Hong Kong

CONTENTS

PREFACE

It is nearly a decade since I first met R.B. Kitaj, thanks to an introduction from my tutor, John Golding. In the intervening years I have had the good fortune of maintaining contact with the artist, an exchange of ideas and information which has been especially close in the two years since I was commissioned to write this study. The immense and revealing correspondence by which we have conducted a series of interviews on diverse aspects of the painter's work forms, in a real sense, the very core of this book. It is to Kitaj himself, therefore, that I express my first and most profound thanks, for the honesty, frankness and thoughtful care with which he has so patiently answered my many questions and by means of which he has helped unravel both the intimate circumstances of his life and the complex implications of his work.

Marlborough Fine Art, London, have greatly simplified my task in making available their complete photographic documentation of the artist's pictures, as well as their press files and published items which would otherwise have been difficult to trace. My thanks especially to Geoffrey Parton, for giving me early access to the list of paintings and drawings compiled by him for inclusion in this volume, and for showing me works by the artist in store at the gallery. I am grateful, likewise, to the staff of the Tate Gallery Print Department and to other public bodies and individuals who over the years have allowed me to look at works in their collections.

The chapter concerning Kitaj's early work, *Certain Forms of Association*, is closely based on my article, 'Iconology as Theme in the Early Work of R.B. Kitaj', published in the July 1980 issue of the *Burlington Magazine*. I am much obliged to Richard Shone and his colleagues at the *Burlington* for granting me permission to re-use this material.

I might not have taken on this project at all had it not been for the support of David Pears, until recently Chairman of the Museum of Modern Art Oxford, and of David Elliott, its Director, who together with the Museum's Council of Management generously granted me time in which to complete my writing. To them and to all my colleagues at the Museum I should like to express my warm appreciation.

MARCO LIVINGSTONE   *Oxford, July 1984*

Preface to the Third Edition

The seven years that have lapsed since the publication of the first revised edition of this book have been momentous but also tragic ones in Kitaj's life. The prospect of his Tate Gallery retrospective in 1994 stimulated him to produce an unusually large number of new works in a far looser and more spontaneous style, but the exhibition, while widely admired, was also the subject of vicious personal attacks. The death of the artist's wife, the American painter Sandra Fisher, only two weeks after the close of that show was the final blow. Feeling that London was now also dead for him, he returned in summer 1997 to the United States, where he has opened a new chapter in his life. It is this entire period that is the subject of the new chapter in this third edition, to which a new section of plates has also been added. The updating of the bibliography and the conversion of many illustrations from black and white into colour make this the definitive edition of the monograph.

MARCO LIVINGSTONE   *London, May 1999*

INTRODUCTION

The first half-century of R.B. Kitaj's life has all the makings of a novel, filled with incident and romance, with memorable personal encounters and different cultures. The intricacies of his experiences, together with the artist's constant practice of reinventing himself – dramatizing his changing situation by devising new self-images and by identifying with people he has known, with artists and writers whose work and lives have caught his imagination, and even with figures from the realm of fiction – provide in themselves a worthy subject and one that would go far to explain the context of his work as a painter. The intimate snatches of autobiography that Kitaj has conveyed to me in our constant correspondence over the past two years must, however, remain as fragments within this study of his art.

'As you may guess,' Kitaj wrote as we embarked on our course of written interviews, 'I'm always keen to confound the very widespread idea among our art people that *nothing* matters but the damned *thing* itself and that thing has to "work", as if there could be any real agreement about what "works" and what does not. Even artists I most admire, many dear friends, really shy away from making connections between art and what may be called *the life*, one's life ... Not me.'[1] On a separate occasion, however, he warned against taking too much account of what he himself had said in earlier interviews, admitting that 'My pictures had and have secret lives ... and so there were things I did not tell, a lot of stuff I did not say back then which I'm saying now. Also, what I did say was not always well put and was tempered by the secret lives of various pictures. I intend to continue, by the way, allowing forms of secret life to paintings I'm working on right now because it excites me to do that, which excitement can't be all bad, can it?'

Kitaj's contradictory but related impulses towards self-confession on the one hand and, on the other, towards secrecy and ambiguity lie at the root of his art. The work's intimacy and wide range of reference offer points of access, which are, however, often made impenetrable by their frequently private and esoteric nature. Kitaj from the beginning has distrusted the notion, prevalent in our time, that a work of art can be totally self-sufficient and that it can communicate its meaning almost at once without the benefit of additional information; even those forms of painting most rigorously dedicated to questions of perception are modified by the viewer's knowledge of their philosophical standpoint and theoretical intentions and by their place within the history of the avant-garde. Rather than simply accepting that his work, like that of other artists, will be viewed in different ways according to the frame of reference of whoever sees it, Kitaj has sought to incorporate intellectual, emotional and sensual forms of experience into his pictures so that everybody can find the point of entry most pertinent to his or her own personality, knowledge and experience.

Inevitably there will be aspects of certain pictures and perhaps some of Kitaj's general concerns that will remain unclear to those viewers who lack the motivation to make their own investigations. There is a real danger of an artist putting off his prospective audience by making their task as demanding as his own, as I know from my own frustrations in trying to understand the poetry of one of Kitaj's earlier exemplars, Ezra Pound. For their part, Kitaj's pictures, when I first came to know them, seemed threatening in their difficulty and in their constant allusions to historical and political figures and to literature with which I was not always familiar. Even now I must confess that I am unable – even unwilling – to follow Kitaj in the full diversity of his intellectual and cultural explorations, for they do not all touch me in the same way. My experience and intellectual preoccupations, after all, are not identical to his. But an instance of the power of Kitaj's work – assumed by some of its detractors to appeal primarily to literary minds – is the hold it has had over me, by no means a conventionally 'bookish' person, for more than a decade now. Kitaj's work has long prompted me to extend my knowledge through reading and to reconsider the implications of the art of our time in the context of earlier art. Gradually, and, I must admit, with Kitaj's help as well as by my own investigations, I have experienced the pleasure of deciphering plausible meanings of particular pictures, always keeping in mind the possibility of other, equally convincing, interpretations or contexts in which the works could usefully be viewed.

Kitaj has consistently used all means at his disposal to ensure that the life of his pictures should not be circumscribed by the period of time in which they were made. The pictures generally have a long gestation, formulated by a mixture of impulses which reinforce one another while controlling excesses in any particular direction: the structuring of a picture is as likely to arise from free association from the subconscious, a legacy of Kitaj's grounding in Surrealism, as from a deliberate urge to integrate found images, direct observations from life, personal circumstances and subjects drawn from sources in art, literature and history. The significance of a painting or drawing can change even for the artist because of the complex relationship between conscious intention and subconscious impulse, just as events in one's own life can be reinterpreted through recourse to memory and later experience. It is an issue that interests Kitaj greatly:

Flaubert liked to identify what he called an 'unconscious poetics' which brings work into being. I believe that pictures have many lives and selves and intentions ... I am a revisionist. The ancient injunction – *Remember!* – has become a force in my life and pictures and, like other sublimations, has always been there I guess. I try to recover that remembrance of past things. I tend to refuse the notion that pictures should just linger and be left to their autonomous moment. It is never so. They *can* be taken up again and they always are in history. For one thing, they can be taken up again physically ... I've tried to reclaim pictures to work on or cut up and sometimes I've been able to do that. I would destroy many of my pictures if I were allowed to. Instead, I content myself with seeking out what interests me or/and what I like about them and also *remembering*, in the spirit of the great Midrashic traditions (I've only recently discovered) which for thousands of years have sought meanings other than literal ones in spiritual texts long past.

As a Young Man

Kitaj was born Ronald Brooks in Cleveland, Ohio, on 29 October 1932. He never knew his Hungarian father – 'a nice guy, I'm told, a drifter who loved horses and books' – who left when Kitaj was aged about one and died in California a decade later. His mother, Jeanne Brooks, raised him alone, working first as a secretary in a steel mill and later as a schoolteacher; the daughter of Russian Jews, she married for the second time in 1941, taking as her husband a Viennese Jew named Dr Walter Kitaj, whose foreign background, like that of his mother, who came to live with them after the War, 'was a striking infusion and counterpoint in my otherwise rather normal American youth'.

Characteristically, Kitaj cites two novels as indicative of the milieu in which he was raised: *Studs Lonigan*, the first of James T. Farrell's trilogy, which he read in his early 'teens and in which he recognized his own experience of big city life, and Edward Dahlberg's *Because I Was Flesh*, 'a Portrait of the Artist as a Young Jew', to use Kitaj's description, in which many years later he discovered an even more accurate mirror of his own youth.[2] The happiest memories of the ten years that Kitaj spent in Cleveland are of the art classes that he attended as a small child in the Cleveland Museum of Art and of the favourite pictures that linger with him to this day: Albert Ryder's *Race Track (Death*

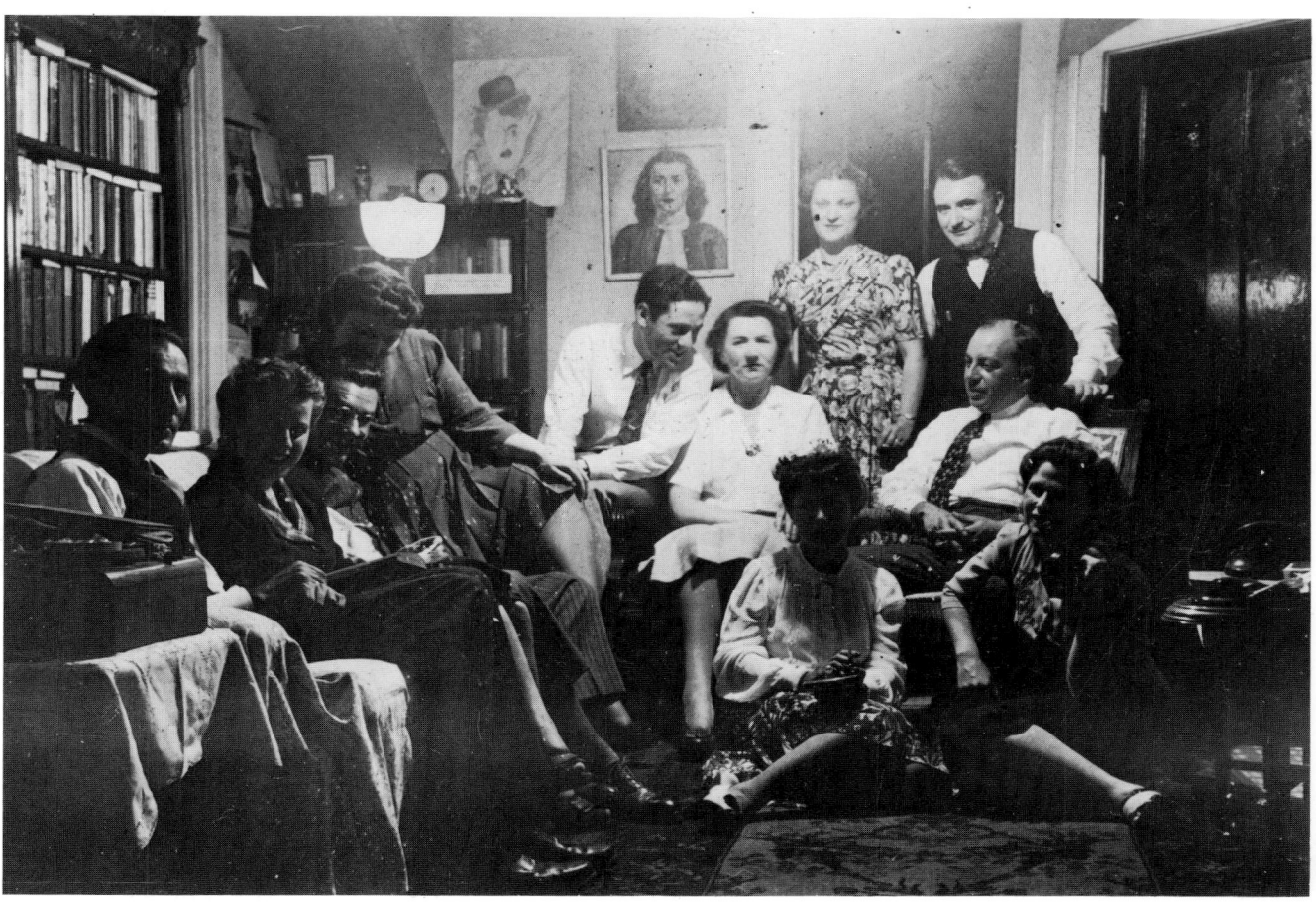

Fig. 1. Photograph of Joe Singer's apartment, Cleveland, Ohio, in the late 1930s. Jeanne Brooks is on the far right, Dr Kitaj in the centre, and Joe Singer is standing.

on a Pale Horse), John Singleton Copley's *Portrait of Nathaniel Hurd*, El Greco's *Holy Family*, and Jacopo Bassano's *Lazarus and the Rich Man*, a picture that appeared to him as 'a tantalizing study in humiliation and persecution' and which produced in him one of his earliest sexual *frissons*. During the War years Kitaj made regular visits back to Cleveland to see his grandparents, encountering Picasso's blue period masterpiece *La Vie* (1903), which was acquired in 1945 by the Museum and which remains a favourite picture of his.

'Above all there was drawing. I was always a little old kid mad about drawing and although there were times I would have settled for a career in baseball or at sea later on, I never wanted to do anything other than art – and long before Freud's claim that it was really about fame, money and the love of women could take hold of me (I think).' Describing the 'agnostic, left-liberal milieu' in which he was brought up and in which 'political and literary instincts and turmoil colored and overwhelmed more stable or traditional absolutes', Kitaj points to the combination of forces that from the beginning helped shape his ambitions for art: 'Not to labor the point much more, my earliest years knew a confluence of art and books and political life overshadowed by the distant storm in Europe.'

In 1942 Kitaj's stepfather got a job as a research chemist in Troy, a small town in upstate New York, and it was there that Kitaj spent the subsequent six years.

Troy was heavily Irish Catholic and I would huddle with the others to hail Mary before baseball, basketball and boxing. Troy was a lot of sport, pals who endure as close friends to this day, the beautiful Hudson River Valley, refugees, the death of Mr Roosevelt (a big thing), the Truman years and the end of the war (another big thing), more refugees (and by that, I mean – very much *in* our lives), the McCarthy era and the blooming of an ever newer political soul in me, cruising cars for girls (almost untouchable Catholic girls), the discovery of a modern literature (Whitman, early Joyce, Hemingway, Hart Crane) … and somehow, beyond the girls and movies and refugees there was always to be art, always drawing, always going to be an artist. I didn't have the Cleveland Museum any more so my focus switched to art books and one of the unsung art-class-rooms of America – *Life* magazine. *Life* was always jam-packed with terrific reproductions in full color. I've always kept these reproductions. I use them every week of my life. They are tattered, treasured survivors pinned to my walls and stuffed into folders.

On leaving high school, his head 'brim full of Thomas Wolfe and Conrad and O'Neill's *Long Voyage Home*', Kitaj hitch-hiked to New York in the company of his closest friend, Jim Whiton, and with him signed on as a messman on a Norwegian ship called SS Corona, headed for Havana and Mexican ports. This was to be the first of a series of voyages that Kitaj was to make over the following four years, alternating with periods of training at the Cooper Union Institute and at the Academy in Vienna. Kitaj's time as a merchant seaman, often spent on what was referred to as the 'Romance Run' on ships of the Moore-McCormack Line – Santos, Rio de Janeiro, Montevideo and Buenos Aires – had a lasting effect on him. On the one hand it was a period of intense reading, with Kafka and Borges among those whose writings he consumed as part of his daily routine; on the other, it pushed him headlong into maturity while intensifying his taste for romantic adventure. 'Port life', he recalls, 'has marked me in many ways, sexually and otherwise, and themes for an art can be traced there.' The memory of his introduction to brothel life in Havana on his first voyage at the age of seventeen lingers with him still, and it is to this area of experience, which has insinuated itself into his pictures over the years, that he continued to pin his ambitions for a type of painting that would synthesize his achievements, as Cézanne did in his late *Bathers* or Picasso in the *Demoiselles d'Avignon*. In 1990 he produced two paintings, *The First Time (Havana, 1949)* (pl. 177) and *The Second Time (Vera Cruz, 1949)*, in which for the first time he explicitly rendered precisely these events from his early life.

Kitaj arrived at the Cooper Union in the autumn of 1950, excited at the prospect of living in New York but resistant to the Abstract Expressionist ethos, which then held sway. Though he admired De Kooning and took notice of contemporary developments in painting, his secret ambition – admittedly unfulfilled – was to paint like Hans Memling.

Nevertheless, I would, for better and often for worse, become rather addicted to the surreal–dada–symbolist strain in our modern art which I haven't been able to get off my back yet. There were remarkable teachers there and memorable students. The Cosmopolitanism of the place was, in retrospect, its distinguishing aspect for me and I suppose, come to think of it, it is the Cosmopolitan nature of Modernism which I find most attractive still.

He pays tribute to the teaching of Sydney Delevante, 'a genuine early American modernist of the surreal–symbolist persuasion', but perhaps the most profound part of his education took place outside the school in the bookshops along 4th Avenue. 'I had discovered Pound and Eliot and Joyce and Kafka and an innate bibliomania was rekindled there as it would be, on and off, manic and depressive through my life, feeding and bloating the pictures I would do.'

In the autumn of 1951 Kitaj passed through Paris on his way to Vienna, which he recalls as being very much as shown in Carol Reed's 1949 film *The Third Man*. He registered at the Akademie, where Klimt and Schiele had been students at the turn of the century, and entered the studios of Albert Paris von Gütersloh, who himself had been a friend of Schiele. He drew regularly from the figure and also produced watercolours and drawings of the bombed ruins of the Opera and of the Danube Canal in the Russian zone; none of these, however, seems to have survived. In the anatomical dissection class that he attended he met an American girl from Cleveland, Elsi Roessler, whom he began courting and whom he married in the following winter after his return to New York.

In 1953 Kitaj and his bride returned to Vienna and then travelled on through North

Africa and Spain, spending the winter in what was then the quiet port of San Felíu de Guixols. It was during that first stay in this town, to which he made several return visits during the fifties before beginning his regular pilgrimages there in the summer of 1962, that Kitaj met José Vicente Roma, 'an extraordinary man who would become one of my many brothers and a very great influence on my life'.

Having made his last journey to sea, Kitaj was conscripted into the American Army in 1956 and was posted to AFCE headquarters at Fontainebleau, where he drew pictures of the latest Russian tanks and installations for war games. He lived with his wife at Thoméry sur Seine, a town set in the forest near many of the sites painted by the Impressionists, and at the weekends they generally drove into Paris. On finishing his duty as an enlisted man, he decided to avail himself of the further art training offered at two British colleges under the terms of the American G.I. Bill, choosing the Ruskin School of Drawing and Fine Art at Oxford in favour of Edinburgh. He and his wife made the journey by car.

It was a lonely drive because Suez had just been invaded and there was no petrol to be had in Europe. I had a supply in cans from the Army and I was just about the only car on the road. I had just read the two volumes of Will Rothenstein's *Men and Memories* and so I knew something of the life I was driving into.

Certain Forms of Association

By the time Kitaj arrived in Oxford at the beginning of 1958, aged twenty-five, he had led several lives and educated himself about a considerable range of art, politics and literature. An indication of the diversity of his artistic interests alone can be gleaned from his recollections of *Life* magazine:

First, it was where a lot of us saw mainstream modernism for the first time if one didn't live in N.Y. – Picasso to Pollock in technicolor. But also there were alternative conventions which many artists of a certain age must carry somewhere in the back of their mind. Along with the great European Moderns were pages and pages of what I guess you could call American Romantic art, swerving from downright realism to surrealism and symbolism: Blakelock, Eilshemius and the magnificent Albert Ryder; Eakins and Homer (best of breed); the Ashcan School; Hopper, Marsh, Soyer, Bishop, Bellows, Tchelitchew and Ivan Albright; I first saw Arthur Dove there and O'Keeffe, Marin, Nadelman, Cornell and Marsden Hartley, as well as the Romantic Surreal roots of abstraction in Gorky, Pollock, De Kooning and Rothko ... I could go on and on because these pictures, first in reproduction, and a few years later in N.Y. in the flesh, are printed inside me.

It was above all to the Surrealist tradition, however, that the young Kitaj looked for guidance. Referring to himself even today as 'a grandchild of Surrealism', he openly acknowledged the parentage as early as 1961, when he appropriated the title of his mysteriously wispy canvas, *Certain Forms of Association Neglected Before* (pl. 17), from André Breton's first Surrealist Manifesto of 1924:

ENCYCLOPEDIA. *Philosophy*. Surrealism is based on the belief in the superior reality of certain forms of association neglected before, in the omnipotence of dream, in the disinterested play of thought.[3]

It is telling that it was to Breton's second definition of Surrealism, as a philosophy or frame of mind rather than as a technical method of 'psychic automatism' as outlined in the first, that Kitaj made reference, since from the start he was a neo-Surrealist in attitude rather than a follower of orthodox Surrealist painting.[4] The intuitive means by which Kitaj composed his pictures in the early sixties found further sustenance in the artist's encounter, later in the decade, with Carl Gustav Jung's concept of the 'active imagination', by which, as Kitaj explains, 'consciousness is only an agent noting what comes up in one's fantasy as it arises … One is instructed (by C.G.J.) to be "uncritical" of these fantasies, to actually *write them down*, as if describing a dream or a play, *without editing* or criticism! This was a revelation for me because I'd been in the habit of painting like that anyway.'

The deliberate scattering of attention across the surface of Kitaj's early paintings provides an inducement for the mind to wander, focusing attention randomly on specific images as an equivalent to the mind's habit of jumping suddenly from vague reverie to a specific idea. At a time when much 'advanced' painting was marked by a reductive tendency for the sake of visual and emotional impact, Kitaj found it truer to his own experience to incorporate in his work as many different kinds of complexity as he could. The fragmentary nature of the early paintings, their stylistic jumps and clues to further meanings, far from threatening their coherence, provided an apt visual metaphor of the diversity both of modern culture and of the artist's own background.

One aspect of Surrealist method that was of use to Kitaj in establishing his own practice of picture-making was that of collage – as exemplified by the composite engravings such as *Une Semaine de Bonté* (1934) by Max Ernst – which provided a means of bringing together surprising and thought-provoking conjunctions of images.[5] Much of Kitaj's earlier work was collage-based, either literally in the incorporation of pasted additions to the paintings and in the composition of the screenprints from various types of ready-made material, or, obliquely, in the translation of a number of sources onto a single surface painted or drawn entirely by hand.

At Oxford Kitaj encountered Edgar Wind, the University's first Professor of Art History and a leading scholar in the field of iconographic studies established by Aby Warburg;[6] at the same time he came across the *Journals of the Warburg and Courtauld Institutes* in the Ashmolean Library, journals which he soon began to collect for his own use as source material. For Kitaj this newly-discovered material, with its fascinating juxtapositions and its persuasive thesis on the capacity of images to give form to ideas, provided both an extension of, and complement to, his devotion to Surrealism. 'Warburg', in his view, 'was like a Surrealist: he tried to bring odd things together like Breton did: "Magic and logic flowering on the same tree". Somehow the two strains came together.' He recognized, moreover, a direct connection between Surrealism and iconographic studies, for instance in the 'Warburg-type' material published in the American Surrealist magazine *View* in the 1940s:

Iconological studies had caught my interest by the time I was eighteen or so in New York. I had read into Panofsky long before I heard of Wind. You see, it was the *weirdness*, the unfamiliar ring of so much of the 'art' they would use to illustrate their theses … If you were a young romantic like I was, having been drawn inexorably to modernist Surrealism and arcane Duchampism as a precocious teenager, these studies, with their fabulous visual models and sources in ancient engravings, broadsheets, emblem-books, incunabula, were like buried treasure! Like a latter-day Student of Prague, stumbling into an alchemist's library … akin to Breton and Kafka and Borges, all of whom, in those days, danced in my brain. So – one of the first turn-ons had been purely *visual* … appropriate, after all, for a painter …

But, of course, there were, for me, ideological discoveries in those obscure readings … It dawned on me that here were people who had spent their lives re-connecting pictures to the worlds from which they came.

The paintings that Kitaj began after transferring to the Royal College of Art in London in the autumn of 1959 were in many instances based directly on illustrated essays in the *Journals of the Warburg and Courtauld Institutes*. A paper by Rudolf Wittkower entitled 'Marvels of the East', concerning the monstrous races and animals invented by the Greeks as sublimations of instinctive fears, provided Kitaj with imagery for *Pariah* (1960, pl. 21), *Welcome Every Dread Delight* (1962) and *Isaac Babel Riding with Budyonny* (1962, pl. 34).[7] Not only were the profuse illustrations that accompanied this article attractively bizarre, they also provided a meeting ground between iconology and Surrealism through psychology. In another Warburg Journal article Kitaj discovered the late medieval figure of Nobody, represented as a man with padlocked mouth, a symbol of Society's tendency to create a scapegoat on which to blame its ills.[8] Kitaj seems to have been attracted to the idea of resurrecting an image which had finally died out after centuries of use and endless transmutations in popular illustrations, so it emerges as the protagonist of paintings such as *Yamhill* (1961) and *Notes towards a Definition of Nobody* (1961, pl. 41).

The figure of Nobody, his mouth forcibly shut as a sign of his inability to defend himself, was treated by Kitaj largely as a symbol of political rebellion, as was *Pariah* (pl. 21), in whose facial features one critic has detected reference to the 'exiles of visionary socialism' such as Herzen or Bakunin, who make their appearance in *The Red Banquet* (1960, pl. 9).[9] Indeed the roots of Socialism and themes of political martyrdom are major preoccupations of the artist as early as *The Murder of Rosa Luxemburg* (1960, pl. 30), a painting about which he has recently written one of his most revealing essays.[10] In retrospect, however, the twin themes of exile and of guilt borne for unknown deeds carry strong echoes of the equally mysterious fate endured by the protagonists of Kafka's novels, a connection that Kitaj agrees has some foundation, even though it may have been subconscious at the time.[11] The painful sense of being cut off from communion with one's fellow men is one that re-emerged in the figures with hearing-aids who feature as protagonists in various paintings of the mid-seventies, though in both cases there is the suggestion that sight can heal the suffering caused by silence, that communication by visual means can go some way toward eliminating the barriers of speech.

In his work of the early sixties, in a way unparalleled in the art of his contemporaries, Kitaj made use of the written word. An anxiety that visual means alone could prove insufficient led him to append handwritten or printed material within the picture itself as a means of clarifying its theme, for instance in the collaged note on *The Red Banquet* , in the captions that accompany the images in *Reflections on Violence* (pl. 15), and in the handwritten 'bibliography' attached to the surface of *Specimen Musings of a Democrat* (pl. 12). Kitaj was particularly keen to connect his pictures with the literary material that supplied him with some of his ideas, drily noting in an essay published in 1964 that 'some books have pictures and some pictures have books'.[12] Many of these references were listed in footnotes in the catalogues of his first two one-man exhibitions in 1963-5, a practice that he discontinued for several years out of impatience with the frequent misinterpretations of his motives but that he has begun to take up again in a new way: witness the artist's texts published in the present volume. Citing as a precedent the elaboration of themes by means of footnotes in T.S. Eliot's *The Waste Land*, Kitaj likewise suggested to the viewer the possibility of delving deeper into the significance of the images he was using or of exploring ideas at a tangent of the central subject.[13] Kitaj explained in his 1964 essay that even after the paintings had left his studio they could be retitled or have further texts associated with them as a way to 'carry on his dialogue with his work' and to 'help to leave the question of "finishing" a painting open'.[14] These are practices that Kitaj still favours, while continuing to express his doubts about their role in his work.

Picture-making as a form of communication is the implicit theme of *Erasmus Variations* (pl. 1), painted in Oxford in 1958 and regarded by Kitaj as one of his first substantial pictures. The imagery and format alike are adapted from a plate in a book on Desiderius Erasmus illustrating a sequence of doodles made by the philosopher in the margin of one of his manuscripts.[15] Some of the images, notably in the top left, are obscured by smudging, so that clarification is achieved only through comparison with the source. These scribbles of cartoon-like simplicity seem slight and of no great formal

Fig. 2. Doodles by Erasmus in the margin of one of
his manuscripts, from Erasmus of Rotterdam by
J. Huizinga, Plate V.

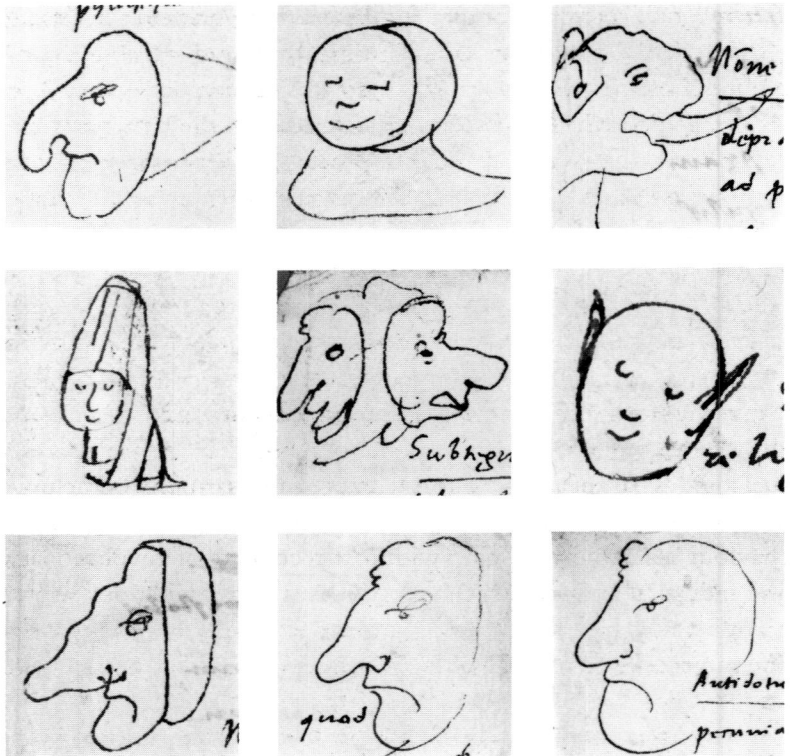

interest, but once their identity is known they take on a talismanic quality as autographic
examples revealing the workings of a great thinker's mind. We are thus presented with
a historical prefiguration of the Surrealist method of automatic writing as the key to true
thought 'in the absence of any control exercised by reason', as defined by Breton in the
First Surrealist Manifesto of 1924. Kitaj was aware of the persistence of this interpretation of handwriting as an agent capable of revealing personality in the Abstract
Expressionist concept of 'gesture', and makes the historical connection explicit by
quoting the style and technique from De Kooning, style and image thus reinforcing each
other in conveying the theme.

Kitaj extended this notion of images as a kind of visual writing by quoting American
Indian pictographs in several paintings in 1960–2. The author of the 1893 Smithsonian
Institution study from which Kitaj borrowed his material defined picture-writing as a
form of notation which aims at 'expressing thoughts or noting facts which at first were
confined to the portrayal of natural or artificial objects'.[16] In *The Bells of Hell* (1960, pl.
26) Kitaj quotes literally from the illustrations in the Smithsonian report in order to
produce a modern version of a historical narrative picture, one that deals with an actual
event – the decimation of Custer's cavalry at the Battle of the Little Big Horn – both
through the eyes of contemporary witnesses and from the perspective of an artist living
a century later.

The references to pictographs tie up with Warburg's visit to the American Indians in
1895–6, described by Fritz Saxl as 'a journey to the archetypes', during which he formed
his conclusions on the persistence of visual symbols in 'the social memory'.[17] As a specific
example Saxl cited the Indian representation of lightning in the form of a snake, an image
that is found in Kitaj's *The Red Banquet* (1960, pl. 9) both in the rain-clouds and in the
snake-like form of the pictograph-derived figure at the far right. The imagery of this
painting, in fact, derives largely from illustrations to Saxl's *Lectures*, particularly from the
discussion concerning the interrelationship of art and science as the meeting of two separate realms of facts, 'the world of rational experience and that of magic'.[18] In Kitaj's
painting there is a deliberate disjunction between the revolutionary mid-nineteenth-
century figures and the Modernist setting of a Le Corbusier villa in which they are put,

which echoes Saxl's free range of references united by theme. Kitaj painted the setting from a photograph in Saxl, where it was paired with a painting by Salvador Dalí as a contrast between logic and irrationality, the two primary forces of human behaviour. The relationship of figures to setting, to which our attention is directed in the Kitaj painting, is also discussed by Saxl, who explains the development of perspective in the Renaissance as a method of imposing a mathematical construction of space on reality. Likewise Saxl states that the belief that 'nature is governed by rational conditions' directed the search for an abstract system of proportion to describe the human body, seen in extreme form in the geometric figure studies of the thirteenth-century architect Villard d'Honnecourt; these are quoted by Kitaj in the diagrammatic skeleton near the centre of the picture.[19]

Kitaj's intention in quoting from such sources is not to impress or dazzle the viewer but rather to deal with a complex of themes in an economical but open-ended fashion: the urge towards a visual logic as part of a larger effort to express the harmony of the universe, the coining of symbols as a means of grasping difficult concepts, and the inconsistencies of human behaviour all come into play within the context of revolutionary activities, encompassing industrial and scientific evolution as well as aspirations which are fundamentally Romantic. The handwritten note attached to the lower-left provides a lead in identifying the subject, the figures, the architecture and the literary source on which the scene is based.[20]

American Indian pictographs are referred to once more in *Reflections on Violence* (1962, pl. 15) in the two panels along the lower-right edge, this time with the source identified in a caption above the image. Other textual material, including a newspaper cutting headed 'When nuns may use birth control', is scattered across the surface, interspersed with images of varying legibility around a number of themes suggested by Sorel's book of the same title.[21] The organization of the picture in a seemingly random scatter directs the eye not to any one image but to their interrelationships, a vivid instance of a compositional technique which Kitaj used to term 'plural energies'. The more clearly-defined grid structure of *Specimen Musings of a Democrat* (1961, pl. 12), although reminiscent of some of Robert Rauschenberg's paintings of the mid-fifties – themselves adaptations of Abstract Expressionism to a figurative context – was, in fact, based on an alphabet table devised by the thirteenth-century Catalan logician Ramón Lull, which Kitaj discovered in yet another article in the Warburg Journals. Just as Lull drew up a system in which 'ten questions are to be asked of the "subjects" with which the Art deals', Kitaj planned to show the modifications of selected image-types by six influences.[22] Although he then added other image-types and changed the number of categories, the chart-like organization was maintained and many of the subject headings listed in the 'bibliography' (three rows across, four up) were later taken up in other paintings. Conventional compositional methods and illusionary space were dispensed with, since the painting could support itself on its own internal logic. Form and structure themselves thus became carriers of meaning.

Specimen Musings, both in its subject matter and in the source that triggered it off, represented a meeting-point for some of Kitaj's most passionate concerns: Socialist politics and anarchism; Catalonia, to which he was becoming increasingly attached; the Spanish Civil War and its implications for the American leftist milieu in which he was raised. 'Spain meant a lot to me', he recalls simply. 'It was the focus of a tremendous romance for me in its civil war against fascism (...). I had been raised in a milieu for which Spain was a place of destiny. (...) I was so very moved to be journeying through that defeated land.'

Kennst Du das Land? (pl. 22), painted in London in 1962, is referred to by Kitaj as his 'ikon for that sentimental journey'; the personal significance of the picture is indicated by the fact that he bought it back years later to hang it in his home. The picture deals with the Spanish Civil War not simply as an isolated historical occurrence but as a more general indication of the tragic consequences of human frailty. The romantic views of foreigners towards other countries is revealed with self-conscious irony in the borrowing of the title from Goethe, transposed by Kitaj from Italy to Spain.[23] Style and image, in turn, are quoted from Goya as a means of commenting on the disservice of certain Spaniards to their country and as a reminder of the continual undercurrent of political rebellion in Spain as exemplified by one of her greatest artists.[24] The Spanish Civil War theme is central to other paintings of the period, such as *Interior/Dan Chatterton's House* (pl. 14) painted in the summer of 1962 at San Felíu; the logic, as Kitaj recalls it now, was that 'Dan Chatterton was a legendary anarchist and Catalonia had been the hotbed of anarchism.' *Junta* (pl. 31), on which the artist himself expands in a separate essay in this book, deals more directly with Durruti and other Spanish anarchists; as far as the artist can remember, this picture, too, was begun in that summer at San Felíu.

In dealing with the recent past rather than with the present, Kitaj establishes a historical distance which allows him to idealize and romanticize his political impulses, just as he has done by identifying with compassionate socialism rather than Marxism, which has never interested him. 'Yes, I *am* a romantic' Kitaj admits. 'Romance provides some of my happiest times: sexual romance, the romance of picturemaking, the romance in books, the romance of big city streets and political-historical romance.' He rightly maintains, however, that the implications of the recent events on which he has touched are still with us today and that, moreover, a certain amount of historical distance can help to produce a more lasting statement. 'Tolstoy wrote maybe the greatest novel ever written about wars that were fought 30 years before he was born. Three-quarters of the greatest paintings ever painted may've been painted "about" quite ancient events (Crucifixions and all that) or about "rumoured" events or downright fantasy, like Titian's *Marsyas* we've just had in London, maybe my favorite easel painting ever.' As to his own political views, he maintains that he has 'always been more drawn to certain persons (people I know or people I read about) than to ideology' adding that in spite of a certain disenchantment he continues to believe that the promise of socialism is still with us.

Socialism was always another word for compassion in my life, but obviously freighted and complicated by all kinds of history. I hope always to be unreconstructed as to compassion but as to the performance of institutional Socialism in most of its guises (as well as institutional Religion et al), I remain at best unimpressed and at worst (Gulag) disgusted and fearful. The only good thing I can think of about our experience of Socialism is the often very brief hope it offers to very poor people and some of the reforms which persist (such as National Health and Social Security systems) long after many other hopes are either bashed against a bloody wall or just dissolve in a grey 'life' of mediocrity, slogans and gloom.

Kitaj's excursions into historic events, it is fair to say, thus betray his own personality and outlook rather than giving an objective picture of our era. He recognizes that in speaking for himself about matters to which he is passionately and intimately committed, he is more likely to be speaking also on behalf of others than if he set himself up to make grandiose abstract statements.

Kitaj early acknowledged that poetry and literature served as an essential backdrop to his work as a painter. He prefaced the catalogue to his first one-man exhibition in 1963 with a citation from Horace which succinctly defined his ambition – 'as in painting, so it is in poetry' – and remarked in an interview two years later that 'For me, books are what trees are for the landscape painter.'[25] Although it could be said that poetry was a more significant source for Kitaj's art in the sixties than it has been in subsequent years, the artist himself is the first to point out that such hard-and-fast divisions make little sense in the case of a man whose 'book-craze' and 'false-scholarship' have led him to devour an enormous range of writing. Kitaj today explains that it is the great writers such as

Baudelaire, Tolstoy, Dickens, Dostoyevsky and Kafka, as well as the transcendent painters, by whom he sets his ambition, but adds that 'It is because one is that ambitious (foolishly) that one pushes through smaller doors (Pound, Benjamin, Babel) where one detects an opening through to a corridor, all one's own, down which, maybe, someday, a passage may lead to an ante-chamber to the main rooms in the Castle!'

It was, in fact, in a picture inspired by T.S. Eliot, *Tarot Variations* (1958, pl. 4), painted at Oxford at about the same time as *Erasmus Variations* (pl. 1), that Kitaj first glimpsed the possibilities for his own highly personal form of picture-making. Painted from Tarot cards, the real subject of the picture is rooted in *The Waste Land*, specifically in the first section, 'The Burial of the Dead', in which Tarot images are treated as archetypes of the past. The picture, however, is no more an illustration of the poem than was to be the case many years later with *If Not, Not* (1975-6, pl. 92), which took the same poem as one of its sources. Though Kitaj used to read deeply into both Eliot and Pound and has always acknowledged the profound ways in which they affected his thinking – for better and, as he himself has admitted, sometimes for worse, in the difficulties created by their private and arcane frames of reference – it is an influence which has permeated his work as a whole rather than one which can be pin-pointed in particular pictures. 'Pound's great advice was enough: that demarcation he spoke of between a symbol which in effect exhausts its references and a sign or mark of something which constantly renews its reference. Poems etc. act as signs in my experience, often not "understood".'[26]

Just as Kitaj took political and historical themes as a means of expressing his own world view, so he felt free to make literary sources serve him rather than making himself a slave to particular texts. Both linear narrative and conventional logic were dispensed with, and Kitaj often brought in sources that were historically unrelated but which helped to elaborate his own theme or the mood that he sought to convey. Such was the case with *Tedeum* (pl. 71), based on a photograph of a New York stage production of Sartre's *No Exit* just after the War, but incorporating at the right an image of Goethe as a giant figure.[27] 'The Goethe figure in *Tedeum*', Kitaj explains, 'adds a Romantic image of transcendental stasis (someone seen from the back, in a room, gazing out the window) to a picture "about" tedium, discontent ... *ennui* ... The lovely Sickert by that name was on my mind in those days also.'

It would be fruitless, too, to seek in *Isaac Babel Riding with Budyonny* a direct parallel to the *Red Cavalry* stories. The painting has only the most general connection with the stories in its sense of violence and chaotic movement and in its military and equestrian imagery; it relates more closely to Babel himself and to the Revolutionary circumstances from which he drew his inspiration, and in that sense qualifies more as a portrait or as an icon of Kitaj's own standpoint as a young leftist and a Jew than as an illustration of a literary text.[28]

The imagery of Kitaj's early paintings is of such seductive complexity and mysterious force that it can easily dominate one's attention, as it has mine in these pages. It is in the imagery, moreover, that the greatest problems of decoding lie, thus necessitating what might appear to be an undue amount of explication at the expense of the formal and technical procedures by which the paintings were made. The ways that Kitaj devised for applying paint in his early work are as varied as the sources of his imagery: brushed on impulsively over bare canvas, applied thinly as a glaze of colour, worked up to a physical density with the addition of collage elements, or treated as a concise form of line drawing, the latter being of particular use in translating an image from a ready-made source. Techniques borrowed from Abstract Expressionism, Surrealism, the example of Robert Rauschenberg[29] and of Francis Bacon all come into play, but with such a high degree of self-consciousness that it would be misleading to speak here of 'influence'. Kitaj, in effect, was quoting technique as well as style – jumping suddenly from one idiom to another, each often possessed of its own historical associations – in largely the same spirit in which he borrowed much of his imagery: as a means of appropriating whatever he found of interest, of extending his range and of declaring the possibility of speaking in whatever voice was most suited to the things he wished to communicate on any particular occasion.

Kitaj has periodically expressed regret, particularly in recent years, about the impenetrability of much of his work, but he is unrepentant about the ambiguities and mysteries that will linger in his paintings no matter how often they are 'explained' by him or by others. Mystery is a quality that he cherishes in the art of the past as well as a characteristic of much twentieth-century art, literature and music, which often presupposes on the part of the audience a prior knowledge of the artist's terms of reference. Kitaj cites in his support the writings of William Empson:

I used to dip into his wonderful books and poems from my Oxford days. His *Seven Types of Ambiguity* had an influence on me. One of his types allows for the poet (artist) to *find* his intention in the course of writing (read – painting), to *discover* his idea after he's begun. This is *very* important for my own work. Why should *I* not discover intentions, ideas, meanings long after, it occurred to me ...

Kitaj holds, as ever, to Empson's view that 'The machinations of ambiguity are among the very roots of poetry.'[30]

An American in England

When Kitaj began his studies at the Ruskin School in Oxford at the beginning of 1958, he was excited by the prospect of living in England and conscious of the history of Americans who had preceded him there or to Europe generally: Henry James, Gertrude Stein, Pound, Eliot, Hemingway, Whistler, John Singer Sargent among others. He could have had little idea, however, that the country was to become his permanent home, for if he had not been accepted at London's Royal College of Art in the autumn of 1959 he might well have returned to the United States at that time. In the event, the sense of estrangement, of being an outsider caught between two cultures, has given him the sharp perspective as well as the bitter-sweet sense of loss which can be traced through all his work.

My sense of national belonging (...) is both confused and not confused. I feel very 'American' ... always will ... The American language and culture and one's childhood secures that belonging and it is sustained by deep American friendships and interests and always renewed contact with America; nothing much in American life escapes my notice one way or another.

I seem to belong, now, to England and to London after all these years ... but I can say without hesitation that I don't fit in here and never will in any comfortable way. I've noticed that some exiles do become very English and Some Do Not. I won't name names. The Jewish Thing is also so complex ... it will have tempered much for me ... the life, the art, the American times, the English passage .... Even those periods in my youth when I didn't *feel* like a Jew, of course.

Kitaj's introduction to British life happily met his expectations. He was pleased by Oxford and by the quiet school's academic insistence on life drawing as part of the daily routine. A group of about a dozen drawings from this period, and a similar number of small life paintings done as part of the course, are still in the artist's hands. The best of them, such as the pencil drawing of *Miss Ivy Cavendish* (1958, pl. 2), are characterized by marks that look bold, almost reckless, but which were in fact the product of an intense and prolonged period of scrutiny of four or five hours a day for two or three days. Kitaj now bitterly regrets that he did not continue the practice of drawing on a regular basis

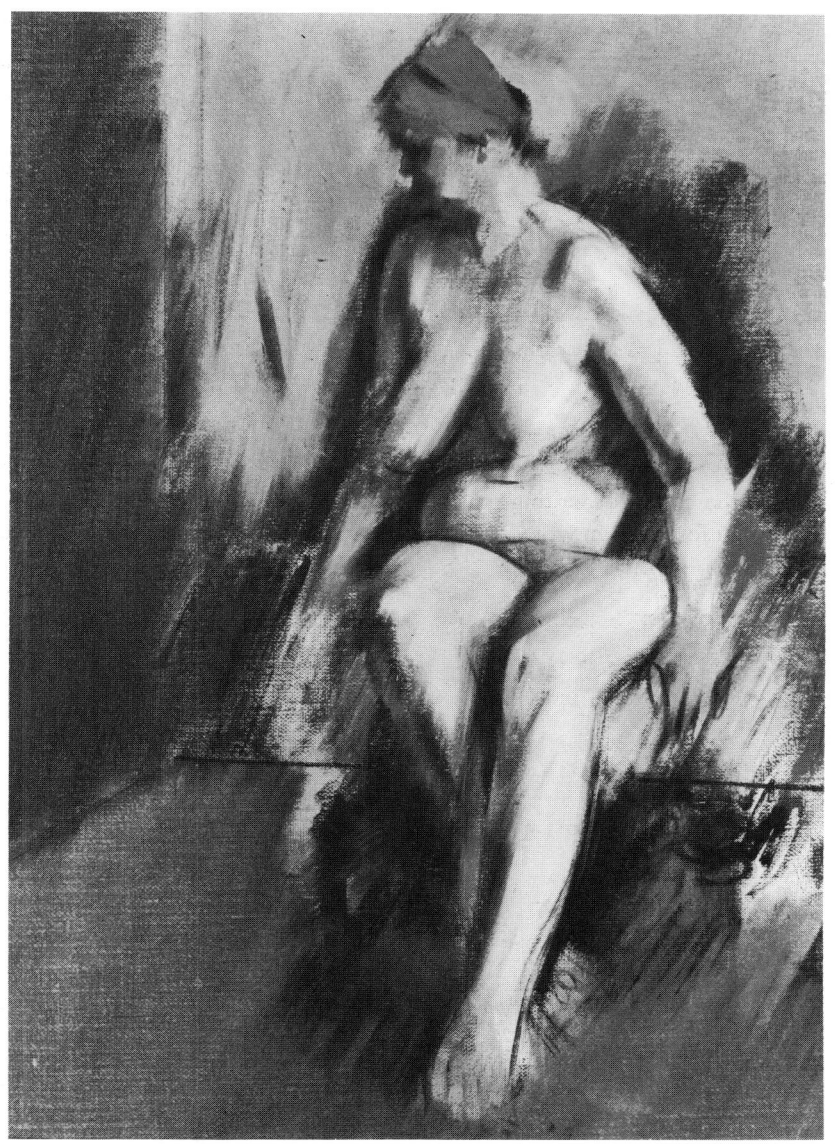

during the decade following his departure from the Royal College in the summer of 1961, but regards his time at the Ruskin, along with his previous training in New York and Vienna, as essential background to the work he is doing today, with its strong emphasis on drawing.

In the autumn of 1959 Kitaj moved to London to begin a post-graduate course at the Royal College, where he met and befriended another student in his year, David Hockney, who was to become a lifelong and intimate associate. His influence on Hockney and on other students at the College such as Derek Boshier, Patrick Caulfield, Allen Jones and Peter Phillips, all of whom were to make a considerable impact as Pop artists on leaving the College in 1962, is a subject in itself but one which would take us beyond the realm of the present discussion.[31] Kitaj, apart from the unwanted confusion of being identified with a movement for which he had little sympathy, was hardly changed by the Royal College experience, in part because he was in his late twenties by the time he arrived there, already well-entrenched in his own forms of picture-making, and in part because his presence at the College under the terms of the G.I. Bill allowed him to go his own way rather than follow the prescribed course. The students in Kitaj's year were fiercely independent; in fact it was Kitaj himself to whom some of the liveliest of them looked for guidance. What seems to have been more important for Kitaj was the opportunity he now had to live in London.

I liked Oxford very much but I was happy I got a place at the Royal College and I was anxious to live in a great city again and to learn London, a dream of my youth. I couldn't have thought beyond the College … I'm really a big-city boy through and through and I would always seek what Flaubert called its 'bitter undertaste'. When that's lacking, I miss it and look for it.

As a student, Kitaj lived with his wife and new-born son on Pickwick Road in Dulwich Village, a suburb of South London, later moving around the corner to a bigger house near the Dulwich College Picture Gallery, on Burbage Road, where they remained until 1967. During this period Kitaj taught briefly during 1961-3 at Ealing Technical College and at Camberwell School of Art and Crafts, where he gave a life drawing class in the department headed by Robert Medley, and from 1963 until 1967 he did occasional day visits at the Slade School of Fine Art on the invitation of William Coldstream. It was largely a time of consolidation for Kitaj – giving himself to his paintings, on which he has always worked slowly – and of family life, with the adoption of a daughter of Indian extraction, Dominie Lee, in 1964. Summers, from 1962 onwards, were generally spent in San Felíu, the Catalonian town which Kitaj first visited with his wife nine years earlier and in which he was to buy a house in 1972.[32]

In February 1963 came Kitaj's first one-man exhibition at Marlborough Fine Art in London. The headline with which *The Times* preceded their glowing review – 'An Eagerly Awaited First Exhibition'[33] – was indicative of the immediate success which greeted the thirty-year old painter, a success marked, too, by the purchase of *Isaac Babel Riding with Budyonny* (pl. 34) by the Tate Gallery. The praise and encouragement, Kitaj agrees, helped drive him on to produce work of ever-growing ambition and scope.

The Age of Mechanical Reproduction

A new grandeur of conception, boldness of idiom and clarity of image characterize the paintings that Kitaj began to produce in 1964. Still relying on his intuition, the artist continued to explore the themes which had interested him – poetry, history, heroes and villains – replacing, however, the tentative nature of his earlier statements with a far more transparent sense of purpose. The sense of painted collage and of intentionally jarring juxtapositions of image and style remain, for instance, a vital ingredient of paintings such as *Erie Shore* (pl. 43) and *Walter Lippmann* (pl. 40), both of 1966, but the images are now phrased in a much harder language and pieced together with a graphic precision as part of an overall surface design. The Surrealist element, moreover, attains a subtlety and eloquence beyond that of the previous pictures, the unexpected unfolding gradually as in the case of *Where the Railroad Leaves the Sea* (pl. 36): the composition at first sight appears virtually symmetrical, but on closer inspection all manner of inconsistencies begin to emerge, culminating in the almost shocking recognition that the arm of the man draped around his lover is not visually attached to his own body. One person is literally depicted 'giving himself' to another, a poignant image of the loss of self by which we recognize love. The figures that in Kitaj's previous paintings had tended to be mere ciphers – even when treated on a fairly large scale, as in *Nietzsche's Moustache* (1962, pl. 25) – take on a more convincing corporeal reality, still expressed in largely graphic terms, allowing Kitaj to effect distortions of human anatomy as expressive in their own way as were those of Ingres more than a century earlier.

Kitaj's pictures continued then, as they do now, to have 'secret lives'. Without being told, for instance, one would have no means of knowing that *Where the Railroad Leaves the Sea* took as its setting the end of the line at San Felíu of a now defunct railroad from Gerona. This private significance, however, enriches the meaning of the image rather than interfering with it. Evidence, moreover, now begins to be incorporated within the paintings themselves of the elements that are the cause of their enigmatic and often disturbing air, as in *Apotheosis of Groundlessness* (1964, pl. 18), an apparently straightforward architectural image which achieves its sense of shifting weightlessness through the simple device of multiple viewpoints. It would be inaccurate to maintain that Kitaj's work in the mid-sixties suddenly became easily comprehensible; the subject matter of the more complex pictures needs to be teased out as much as before, and many of the works require at least a title or further clue for their meaning to be unravelled. What is true, however, is that Kitaj was now sufficiently at ease to be able to vary the tone and nature of his work by shifting from visual and conceptual complexity to a much more direct and down to earth approach. He has spoken of his desire to be like a 'switch hitter' in terms of painting, an apt metaphor for an artist who in 1967 was to paint a delightfully direct series of pictures on a subject always dear to his heart: baseball. The tone of these pictures, which declare his lifelong love of a popular sport, is an appropriately humble and unpretentious one.

A tiny canvas of 1965 called *The Rival Poet* provides a vivid instance of the balance between the straightforward and the difficult, which continued to mark Kitaj's work. Like two other canvases of that year, *They Went* and *Alone*, it is but a section of a much larger work, *Primer of Motives (Intuitions of Irregularity)*, which Kitaj had painted in New York and then destroyed, keeping only these three pieces. Kitaj says of it:

I have no memory of what the original picture meant, although the title would suggest a compendium. It is, on the one hand, the compendious nature of certain modern poets and writers which has interested me: Joyce, Pound, Eliot, Mann, Benjamin, Ashbery, Duncan, et al ... those who try to get the whole world in, and, on the other hand, I love the more intimate, confessional ones like Creeley, Lowell, Emily Dickinson, et al... whose world-view is more in their own mirror. The picture would seem to have been an anthology of irregular, intuitive (freely associated, that is) parts ... the motivating principle being, I would guess, that of *collage* as a free-verse game to play in art.

Kitaj's decision to give a new identity to his *Rival Poet* by removing the image from its original context brings to mind two of the artist's constant practices over the years: that of recycling images, including figures, from one picture to another – their identity shifting according to context – and that of reproducing in his catalogues details from the pictures in such a way as to suggest that, removed from their customary context, they have the potential of another life. The faces and figures thus treated strike a familiar chord, but it is a haunting and surprising form of familiarity; one senses them not merely as segments of a larger whole but also as different views or reconstructions of a single character, altered in memory. These practices, which have allowed Kitaj's characters to adopt, or at least to feign, another life, were to have great bearing on Kitaj's plans in the mid-seventies to create a stock of characters equivalent in visual terms to those found in works of fiction.[34]

The separate strands of poetry to which Kitaj refers – the 'confessional' and the 'compendious' – were paid tribute in two canvases produced in 1964. One of these, *An Urban Old Man, Who Never Looked at the Sea, Except Perhaps Once*, is an imaginary portrait of Constantin Cavafy in Alexandria; the title of the picture was a description of the poet that the artist had read, though he no longer recalls the source. Years later Kitaj was to paint another reverie about Cavafy, *Smyrna Greek (Nikos)* (1976-7, pl. 122). Kitaj's interest is as much in the man as in his poetry; or to be more accurate, he has chosen to portray the poet and his work in terms of his melancholic personality and of the circumstances of his life. The confessional aspect of Cavafy's poetry is alluring to Kitaj and pertinent to his own work, particularly in the suggestion that the most intimate, even sordid, experiences, can be retrieved morally through their transformation into art. It is a theme on which Cavafy touched in many of his poems, such as 'Their Beginning', in which, having described the feelings of guilt occasioned by a furtive sexual encounter, he concludes:

But for the artist how his life has gained.
Tomorrow, the next day or years after will be written
The lines of strength that here had their beginning.[35]

The second portrait of 1964, *Aureolin* (pl. 39), which emerged also as a screenprint called *Yaller Bird* in the same year, after a line in a translation by Ezra Pound, is of the American poet Jonathan Williams, whom Kitaj had met in 1962 or 1963 at a poetry-reading in a pub in Dulwich Village. Williams, who to this day continues to divide his time between North Carolina and Dentdale, Cumbria, is also a major publisher of contemporary poetry through his Jargon Press. 'I was hooked on Pound, Eliot and their crowd when I met Jonathan Williams,' recalls Kitaj, 'but it was *he* who led me to post-Pound American poetry and particularly to Olson, Creeley and Duncan (all of whom he'd published when they were unknown).' Kitaj was later to pay homage to this younger generation of poets, some of whom, like Creeley, Duncan and Ashbery, were to become close friends, in a series of screenprints produced from 1966 until 1969, now known collectively as *Some Poets*.[36] In the meantime a group of poems by Williams, which he was to publish in 1966 as *Mahler*, started Kitaj off on another series of screen-prints, *Mahler Becomes Politics, Beisbol*, which he began in 1964 and completed in 1967.[37]

As important as poetry may have been to Kitaj during the sixties, it was by no means his only or even his most important source. Ready-made visual material continued to exercise his imagination. The paintings of historical subjects, such as *The Murder of Rosa Luxemburg* (pl. 30) and *Kennst Du das Land?* (pl. 22), were often charged with the sense of actuality which one associates with documentary photographs printed in newspapers and magazines; the association, deliberately played on, lends credence to the scenes as accounts of real events. By 1962, in *Good News for Incunabulists* (pl. 33), Kitaj was to base an entire composition on a photograph by Edward Steichen of a stage production of *The Front Page*.[38]

Given Kitaj's immersion in photographic material and reproductions of all kinds, as well as his introduction in 1963 to screenprinting – as a way of recycling ready-made images by means of photo-mechanical reproduction, in editions which made his work more generally available – he was well-prepared to absorb the writings of Walter Benjamin, which he came across in the mid-sixties. Benjamin, of whom Kitaj produced an intimate and introspective lithographic portrait in 1966, became an exemplar at once, recalls the artist, 'because of the impossible-to-categorize quality of his creative, highly fragmented texts'. Although it was not until the early seventies that Kitaj began work on two major paintings about this German Jewish writer, the views expressed by Benjamin in essays such as 'The Work of Art in the Age of Mechanical Reproduction' (1936) had a more immediate bearing on the paintings that Kitaj was already producing. What better example than Kitaj's own work could there be for Benjamin's thesis that the position of the artist had been irreparably changed by the introduction of mechanical repro-duction, which, in making possible the wide dissemination of images, threatened the sovereignty of the unique work of art just as the cinema was seducing the public away from painting?[39]

'Movies, and particularly frame-enlargements, have been in my work what engrav-ings and such were for artists in the distant past, what printed illustrations were for painters like Manet and Van Gogh, what photographs were for Degas and Cézanne and later for Sickert and Bacon … no more and no less.' Kitaj is quick to admit that he envies the scope of the cinema and its sense of modern life, but he stresses that this is only one force among many in his work and that there is a distinction between those films that have acted upon him generally and the isolated cases in which he has based an image on a film still.

The film references in Kitaj's paintings of the mid-sixties onwards can be as tentative as the appropriation of a title, as in *Shanghai Gestures* (1968), or they can go so far as to inform the very format and composition of a major work such as *Walter Lippmann* (1966, pl. 40).[40] The latter includes what could be construed as episodes of a ruptured narrative: the man holding a drink, Kitaj later recalled, had as one of its sources the actor Robert Donat; the confrontation in the background between a pretty girl under lamplight and a trench-coated man in shadow, a paraphrase of an archetypal romantic scene from Hollywood films, was to reappear as a separate subject in subsequent pictures such as *Little Romance I* (1969, pl. 54) and *The Street (A Life)* (1975, pl. 136), once known under the title *Femme du Peuple II*.[41] A cinematic sense likewise informs more modest pictures of this period, such as *Screenplay* (1967), the punning title of which defined painting as a realization of a concept that could be regarded as its text and also as a screen on which an image is projected, with a further pun arising from the openwork 'Moorish/Matissean' screens which inspired the framing device. The central landscape image was derived from a photograph by Bill Brandt of Top Withens, the windswept site in Yorkshire traditionally identified as Emily Brontë's Wuthering Heights.[42]

As if consciously resisting the threat of depersonalization that is implicit in the use of found material and images produced by machine, Kitaj during this period developed a highly personal facture and graphic style. Abrupt changes of pace remain an essential device, but the inventory-like assemblage of images of the early sixties paintings increasingly gives way to a more homogeneous and illusionistic space. There is a new generosity of scale even in the small canvases, which allows for easier legibility of the image, an urge to make contact with the spectator further aided by the strong descriptive contours, surfaces paradoxically dry and restrained but seductively tactile, and juxtapositions of hot and acid colours as surprising and compelling as the conjunctions of images.

In spite of Kitaj's harsh self-indictment, it could truthfully be said that he never stopped drawing during the sixties. On the one hand he produced several groups of tiny canvases, which, though executed in oil, he himself regarded as drawings: works such as *In the Social Memory* (1964) and *His Cult of the Fragment* (1964); the baseball pictures of 1967 and portraits of friends such as Hockney, Francis Bacon and a group of contemporary poets; plus the occasional photographically derived portraits of historical figures such as *Unity Mitford* (1968, pl. 44) and *La Pasionaria* (1969, pl. 51). The paintings themselves made independent drawings largely superfluous because, with few exceptions, they were essentially graphic in nature, their structure built up through drawing in quite a traditional manner. Kitaj explained in an interview with Maurice Tuchman published in 1965 that he rarely worked from drawings in building up a painting and that the composition as a whole was rarely clear in his mind to begin with.[43]

Just as Kitaj's technical control was reaching a new level of assurance, so his grasp of the subjects that most concerned him achieved at this time a far greater sense of purpose. This is not to say, however, that the meaning was necessarily any more self-evident. *A Disciple of Bernstein and Kautsky* (1964), for instance, takes as its title a phrase that the Chinese used to describe Khrushchev, but this is used not to 'explain' the image of the aviator – mysterious enough in itself – but to add to it another level of enigma. The relationship of image to title here, Kitaj recalls, was like that of *An Andalusian Dog* to the film made in 1928 by Luis Buñuel and Salvador Dalí; the Surrealist romance was still very much to the fore. Yet the impulse to ambiguity for its own sake was beginning to fade, making way for the directness of the baseball pictures and the small portrait studies. Private meanings linger still in a painting such as *Little Slum Picture* (1968, pl. 48) – which incorporates references to Barcelona's red light district, the 'Barrio Chino', where Kitaj had been looking for a flat – but the scene itself is sufficiently familiar for the viewer to

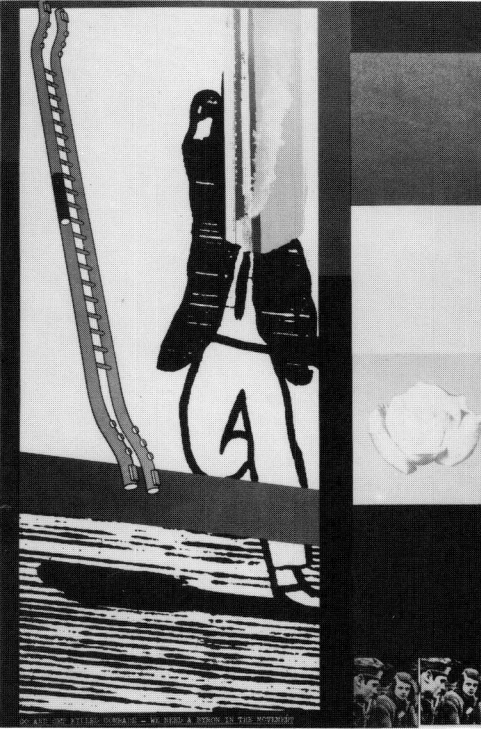

Fig. 4. Go and Get Killed Comrade – We Need a Byron in the Movement, 1966, from *Malher Becomes Politics, Beisbol*. Screenprint, 32 x 21⅞ in (81.3 x 55.6 cm.).

be able to relate it to his or her own experience without knowledge of this biographical context. *Synchromy with F.B. – General of Hot Desire* (1968-9, pl. 47) similarly contains certain conjunctions of image, the meanings of which are not readily apparent, but these serve to embellish what in the first instance is a clear statement of homage to a painter Kitaj has long admired, Francis Bacon. One needs only the most basic familiarity with Bacon's work and its homosexual eroticism to appreciate the mischievous inclusion of a disturbingly disjointed and overtly sexual female nude. What continues to come over most powerfully is the massive presence of the figures themselves, nearly life-size and enveloped in an environment of luscious colour.

Kitaj's treatment of political themes in paintings such as *The Ohio Gang* (pl. 53) and *Dismantling the Red Tent* (pl. 29), both produced in 1964, remains allusive in terms of imagery but is more powerful than ever in evoking the mood of the time. Criminality, thuggery, games of power and control, corruption and moral degeneracy have been all too current in our century; it hardly matters whether one reads into *The Ohio Gang* references to low-life gangsterism or treats it as a metaphor of Fascism, for in either case it captures a general malaise of our time. Even in dealing more openly with contemporary events – as is the case with *Dismantling the Red Tent*, an allusion to the assassination of President Kennedy in 1963, or *Juan de la Cruz* (pl. 61), a bitter icon of the Vietnam War – Kitaj's concern is to go beyond documenting a historical situation in order to contemplate its wider significance as a manifestation of human weakness, wickedness and failure. As if to make the general application abundantly clear, Kitaj brings in deliberately anachronistic elements such as the late nineteenth-century etching by Alphonse Legros that is collaged onto the surface of the *Red Tent* as a complement to the main scene, or the scene of rape and piracy on high seas that occurs in the background of *Juan de la Cruz*. Here the disruption of both style and tone has a similar function in the depiction of the rapist as a cartoon figure, disturbingly at odds with the violent situation itself.

Erie Shore (1966, pl. 43), inspired by a newspaper account of the death by pollution of Lake Erie, incorporates what the artist terms 'psycho-dramatic links to a dream of Ohio boyhood', literally depicted at the far right of the canvas, within the context of 'a kind of allegorical, hardly explainable apocalypse'. The derivation of certain images from pre-existent sources – the falling figures at the extreme left, for example, are taken from an engraving by Gustave Doré – hardly seems to matter here, so overwhelming is the anxiety and sense of loss that the picture as a whole conveys. Difficult and puzzling as this and other pictures of the mid-sixties remain, one could ask for no better evidence of the strides that Kitaj was making to convey to his audience a coherent and compelling world view.

Unsettled Years

Life was never quite the same for Kitaj after his first solo exhibition. Welcome as it may have been to be the object of critical enthusiasm and commercial success, the pressures to become a public figure and to concentrate on the work at hand in the studio, knowing that there was a waiting list for pictures not yet completed, were rather more difficult to bear. Kitaj in 1964 found himself for the first, but by no means the last, time in the role of polemicist, delivering slide lectures in Cambridge, Oxford and London, and invitations to take part in group exhibitions began to multiply.[44]

In February 1965 Kitaj had his second one-man show, this time at Marlborough-Gerson Gallery in New York. The reception was more mixed than in London, but Alfred H. Barr Jr. purchased *The Ohio Gang* (pl. 53) for the Museum of Modern Art, New York, and later in the year Maurice Tuchman was curator of Kitaj's first museum show for the Los Angeles County Museum of Art. In the autumn of 1967 Kitaj accepted a Visiting Professorship at Berkeley, California. 'Apart from my saddening marriage, it was a memorable year of baseball and American poetry and the three terrific Bay Cities and I fell in love with all the kids I taught and my "art" got subsumed in all that, which may not have been such a bad pause after all.' Kitaj saw much of Hockney, who had just moved back to Los Angeles after a spell of teaching at Berkeley; he also befriended the poet Robert Duncan and his companion, the painter Jess Collins, and visited Creeley in New Mexico.

Kitaj returned to England only to experience the death of his wife in 1969, a traumatic event about which he is still loath to speak. With his children he returned to North America, staying in Los Angeles until 1971.

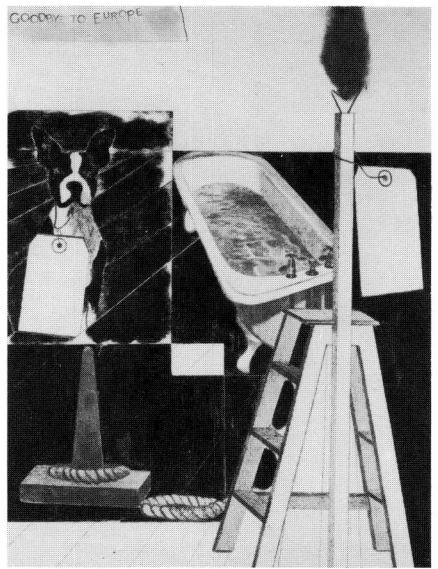

Fig. 5. Goodbye to Europe, 1969. *Cat. no. 123.*

I'd accepted another professorship at UCLA for the school year. We took a house right in old Hollywood, overlooking the Sunset Strip, and lived a crazy year during which I began to devote myself to raising the children. I only had two morning classes and I tried to work in a studio they gave me but I couldn't work well. The children were my real life. Lem and I visited some of the great old directors like John Ford and Renoir, Mamoulian, Milestone and Billy Wilder. I sketched them for a painting I never made about Hollywood, but I really did those visits for Lem. It was a year jampacked with friends, for which I was grateful. Lee Friedlander was teaching there that year and we've been very close ever since. I admire him greatly and lose myself in the poetry of photography whenever I'm with him. For the Art and Technology show, I did a lithograph at Gemini, where I met a beautiful young woman, Sandra Fisher, working there as Ken Tyler's assistant. We were both otherwise involved at the time, but she was destined to change my life.

In 1970 a retrospective exhibition of Kitaj's paintings was organized by the Kestner Gesellschaft, Hannover, which was then toured to the Boymans-van Beuningen Museum in Rotterdam; a selection from this exhibition was subsequently shown at Marlborough Fine Art in London. Kitaj does not remember how he felt about this opportunity to reassess his past production. As so often happens with such projects, however, the mental and physical energies expended in looking over previous work, combined in Kitaj's case with the upheavals in his private life, seem not to have spurred him to work with renewed vigour but rather to have created a temporary sense of confusion about his future direction. It should come as no surprise that it was precisely during the period 1969-71 that Kitaj 'committed my most extreme acts of ordinary modernity' – two series of screenprints, *In Our Time* (1969) and *A Day Book* (1971), and the objects produced in relation to the Art and Technology project organized in 1969 by the Los Angeles County Museum of Art – and that it was the least productive period in his life as far as painting was concerned.[45] Life and work alike, however, would soon be looking up again.

In Our Time

In Our Time (1969), subtitled 'Covers for a small library after the life for the most part', was the main project on which Kitaj occupied himself in the year of his wife's death. Taken as a whole, the set is a vivid record of the artist's preoccupations and as such is also a useful key to his paintings and drawings. Though he remains fonder of some of the prints in this series than of many of the collage-based screenprints that he produced earlier in the decade, he admits that they constitute his most blatant excursions into 'Duchampism' and that he has reservations about them, too. 'They're like first drafts', he says now. 'I'm not really reconciled to them. I'd like to destroy two-fifths of them and eventually I will do that to proofs in my possession.'

Much of Kitaj's time during the unsettled period of the late sixties and early seventies was spent on printmaking projects. Most of these, like the portfolio *A Day Book* (1971), on which Kitaj collaborated with the poet Robert Creeley, were in the form of screenprints made with the assistance of Chris Prater, 'surely the world's greatest screenprinter'.[46] Prater acted both as a technician, translating the artist's ideas into printed form, and as a collaborator with a creative as well as a practical role.[47] Kitaj's substantial body of graphic work, though much admired, is regarded by the artist himself as an area of only peripheral interest in the context of his work as a whole.

When Kitaj's confidence as a painter returned in 1972, it was thanks in some measure to his friendship with the young American painter Sandra Fisher, whom he had met again in London in the previous year. He turned for guidance to his own large figure paintings of 1967-8, such as *Juan de la Cruz* (pl. 61) and *Synchromy with F.B.* (pl. 47), seeking through expansiveness of scale and lusciousness of colour to support the powerful human presences conjured by line. The first completed canvases, a series of full-length figures of *Superman* (pls. 66 and 68), *Batman* (pl 67) and *Bill at Sunset* (pl. 65), reveal a chastened sensibility, one bent not just on the study of heroic failures, as had been the case from the early sixties, or on the elevation of popular figures to a nobility of status, as in the baseball portraits of 1967, but dwelling on pretence and on false roles. Kitaj put much of himself into these paintings, so that what appears to be light-hearted, even flippant, on the surface – sweet colour and references to comic strips – only half-conceals an underlying tone of bitterness and despair.

Superman (1973, pl. 66 and 68) appears in a half-way state between 'mild-mannered Clark Kent' and his powerful alter-ego, but what comes across of the figure is his intense vulnerability. It was based on a drawing of the comic book hero by a psychotic child. The rather sinister-looking *Batman* (1973, pl. 67) bears an even more tenuous relation to its comic book source, as it was derived instead from a portrait of Beethoven taking a walk; he appears to be hiding his identity behind a mask not for the greater good of humanity but for the sheer malicious pleasure of deceit. These single figure studies, encased in compositions of a simplicity heretofore unknown in Kitaj's work, remain mysterious and enigmatic. Perhaps because they themselves seem to be lost in their thoughts, they lead us in turn to ponder their identities, their frames of mind and their future actions.

It was in this group of single figure paintings that Kitaj began to formulate a plan that was to have major repercussions on his subsequent work: that of devising characters as a novelist would, suggesting that their fictional lives might continue beyond the confines of the canvas or the page.[48] In an interview published four years later, Kitaj remarked: 'I like the idea that it might be possible to invent a figure, a character, in a picture the way novelists have been able to do – a memorable character like the people you remember out of Dickens, Dostoyevsky, Tolstoy.'[49] The challenge is one which continues to pre-occupy him. 'If the pictured character were to last and stick in people's minds, he adds today, 'it would be a *visual* triumph, an achievement of the terms of painting.'

Superman and *Batman* were rather anomalous figures for Kitaj to tackle, but he was soon to begin populating his pictures with characters of his own invention. The first of these was Bill, derived from a movie still which Kitaj can no longer locate: an image, assumed by the artist to be the self-portrait of a tramp, crudely drawn on the side of an American railroad boxcar. The attraction of the image may subconsciously be linked to Kitaj's reveries about the drifter father he never knew, but it also has connotations of an imaginary self-portrait set in the future: 'I often imagine I may end up as a tramp myself or more likely as a refugee.' First pictured in *Bill at Sunset* (1973, pl. 65), the character reappears in the background of another painting of the same year, *Kenneth Anger and Michael Powell* (pl. 62).

Kitaj cites as a visual precedent for the scheme of character inventions, which he instigated in the seventies, the work of Honoré Daumier, and, in particular, individuals such as Ratapoil and Macaire, who recur in Daumier's pictures and sculpture as police spies and agitators.[50]

Discovering these characters, invented not by a novelist but by a painter/sculptor/draftsman was another of those happy shocks of recognition because the very idea had been haunting me for years (…). I've known Ratapoil all my life but never knew his details, the sense of him, until maybe the early seventies. In any case, I'm happy to credit Daumier with a major kick in the ass.

Also in the back of Kitaj's mind must have been the example of Manet, whose prints he had begun to collect by this time and whose paintings of the early 1860s likewise played with the idea of a stock of characters that reappeared from one picture to another. The reaction of Manet's contemporaries to such transpositions in his work, recounted by George Heard Hamilton, bears a curious resemblance to the accusations that have been directed at Kitaj:

What made his paintings seem so strange and peculiar to his contemporaries was the grotesque character of contemporary scenes arranged in imitation of the grand manner. The compositions of Velázquez and Goya, of Titian, Tintoretto, and Raphael, had been contemporary in their day and had arisen logically out of situations within their own experience. An air of masquerade or worse was the inevitable result when men and women of the 1860s posed in attitudes originally determined by other customs and costumes. Here are to be found the reasons for their hesitation, felt even by those who were inclined to admire Manet … it accounts for Baudelaire's remark that Manet had been 'touched by romanticism from birth'. They were bewildered by his failure to create an art wholly of his own time.[51]

Kitaj's imaginative compositions of the period such as *The Man of the Woods and the Cat of the Mountains* (1973, pl. 53) and *Pacific Coast Highway (Across the Pacific)* (1973, pl. 63), though dreamlike in atmosphere and heavy with a sense of allegory, have a weight and conviction equivalent to that of scenes of real people, thanks to a large degree to the sheer physical presence and emphatic sense of personality with which the figure inventions were now endowed. The representations of actual people, in turn, may include elements of fantasy, as in the intrusion of Kitaj's invented alter-ego Bill into the double portrait of film directors Kenneth Anger and Michael Powell (1973, pl. œ).[52] Scenes from life straightforwardly depicted may, moreover, have an underlying symbolic intention. This is the case with *To Live in Peace (The Singers)* (1973-4, pl. 73), a representation of an Easter feast celebrated by a group of the artist's close friends in Catalonia at the time that Franco was still in power: an image of tranquillity and an emblem of the quiet rebellion possible even in the shadow of Fascism.

The complex text that Kitaj assembled for his major painting of this period, *The Autumn of Central Paris (After Walter Benjamin)* (1972-3, pl. 57), when it was shown in London in 1977, provides manifest evidence of his continuing devotion to the 'picture puzzle'.[53] Set in a Parisian café in the autumn of 1940, a time that witnessed not only Benjamin's suicide but the fall of France to the Nazis, this canvas represents a meeting point for the many strands of Kitaj's interest for which Benjamin has been the most eloquent exemplar. The figures act as signs representing different segments of society. The man with the pickaxe, for example, who is painted red and who reappears in Pacific Coast Highway, still trampled underfoot, stands for the labourer obediently going about his work. The man with the hearing-aid, identified in Kitaj's text as 'the police spy/secret agent', could be taken as an image of the artist himself – he was advised to wear a hearing-aid in the late sixties and had been doing so since the mid-seventies – in the guise of an intruder who listens in on the lives of others. Such a role was, indeed, taken on by figures in later paintings such as *If Not, Not* (1975-6, pl. 92) – the witness in the lower left is not, as is often assumed, T.S. Eliot – and *The Jew Etc.* (1976-9, pl. 97). The subject of the 'café as open-air interior', which Kitaj appropriated from Benjamin, itself has strong associations and precedents in the history of painting, particularly in the work of Manet, Degas and the Impressionists, highly appropriate for this Parisian scene. Even the format of the picture carries meaning, as the artist himself is the first to point out, in its associations with film posters, with collage and with Benjamin's notion of the 'barricade'.

The Autumn of Central Paris and the accompanying *Arcades (After Walter Benjamin)* (1972-4, pl. 46) summarize and give form to many aspects of Benjamin's thought with which Kitaj has felt the greatest affinity. Most evident are the parallels with the essayist's obsession with fragments and with quotation; with his probing of the Baudelairean spirit; with his ambivalent role as an assimilated Jew; with his views on the isolation and loss of self of the city-dweller; and with the image of the city's streets as the corridors inside a house, at once anonymous and intimate.[54] The derivation of certain images, though, remains tangential and idiosyncratic.[55] Kitaj says simply that he finds whatever he needs for his pictures, whatever seems relevant to his concept or to his formal terms, and he cites in his support a comment ascribed to Picasso: 'If I don't have red, I use blue.'

Though the sources may remain abstruse, Kitaj's ability to transcend them so that what matters in the end is not the derivation of a picture, but its physical presence and its emotional and intellectual dimensions, is nowhere more evident than in *The Man of the Woods and the Cat of the Mountains* (pl. 53). The sources of this picture are many and include a portrait of the novelist George Sand – which perversely, perhaps, served as the model for the man's face – and a still from an early Soviet film, Ermler's *Fragment of an Empire*; the scene as a whole was based on an early nineteenth-century satirical engraving attributed to Thomas Lane.[56] Having used these sources to start him off, however, Kitaj develops in his painting a narrative and theme of his own. A dusky atmosphere fills the room, but outside things seem to be coming to life, suggesting a glimmer of hope. The gentle gaze that the man of the woods directs to the cat of the mountains, and the poignant manner with which he clutches her hand, suggests that a more benevolent future may lie in companionship. It is not, perhaps, far-fetched to interpret the image as a private gesture of the artist's romantic attachment and commitment to Sandra Fisher, nor to attribute the cautious optimism that begins to appear in Kitaj's work to the security of their relationship.

Towards a Better Life

The Better Life announced by Kitaj in one of the prints of the *In Our Time* portfolio, in 1969, began to materialize for him only two years later, when two events occurred: the purchase, on his return from California, of a large house in London, and the renewed contact with Sandra Fisher, destined to become his companion and eventually his wife. Herself a painter, she has had major repercussions on Kitaj's life and work, not only by giving him moral support but also by encouraging him to draw again. Kitaj has likewise been sustained during these years by his close friendships with other artists who are too numerous to mention, many of them in some way connected to the 'School of London' to which Kitaj was to pay tribute in the *Human Clay* exhibition in 1976.[57] Above all there has been the sense of solidarity with his closest friend from the Royal College days, David Hockney, whom he visited frequently during the latter's stay in Paris from 1973 until 1975 and with whom he has maintained a constant and intimate correspondence over the years. When one takes into account, too, Kitaj's friendship with the poets already mentioned and with figures from the British literary world, there begins to emerge a sense of the rich artistic milieu within which he has produced his work. Ambitious art, as Kitaj himself maintains, requires a strong context. 'A lot of good and regular art gets made because of who you talk to', he remarks. 'No one is immune to human contact, and art is not made in a vacuum. History is full of flourishing milieux in which all kinds of people act upon one another. Who is terrific and who is less terrific gets sorted out often after death.'

It was in 1974, during one of his visits to Hockney in Paris, that Kitaj experienced the pastels of Degas as a sudden revelation of major significance for his own art. 'Sandra had begun to work in pastel', he explains today, 'but I used to discourage her, saying it was not an accurate enough medium. She didn't listen and persisted ahead of me.' The drawings in the collection of the Petit Palais made a particular impression on him and set him on an almost fanatical course of re-education as a draftsman which he maintains with great intensity to this day. 'The giant Degas late pastel-drawings of the Rouart children really got me thinking to do pastel seriously and I began to buy the very expensive Roché pastels still made in the Marais by two old ladies whose grandfather made pastels for Degas.' Hockney, too, suffering at the time from something of a painting block, was giving himself to a period of drawing solidly from life. Together the two artists began to question what was lacking in late Modernism and to seek the possibility of tracing back another route to the turn of the century. Kitaj took as his measure the great figure inventions achieved by Degas and Cézanne in their old age. His absorption in late nineteenth-century art, already evident in *The Autumn of Central Paris*, soon took on an overwhelming importance for him, to the extent that in 1980 he could maintain that 'I, for one, *feel* like a Post-Impressionist.'[58]

The excitement that Kitaj shared with Hockney about drawing the human figure and about pondering the lessons of nineteenth-century art led them both to become embroiled in a heated polemic, which was to fill the pages of the British art press in the late seventies.[59] Kitaj, who had always managed to maintain a low profile, was suddenly in the public eye to an extent that he began to find uncomfortable. In addition he held two exhibitions of his work at the Marlborough Gallery in London (1977 and 1980) and a third at the Marlborough Gallery in New York in 1979. A major retrospective followed at the Hirshhorn Museum, Washington, in 1981, travelling afterwards to the Cleveland Museum of Art and the Städtische Kunsthalle Düsseldorf. Also, Kitaj was asked by the Arts Council of Great Britain to purchase pictures on their behalf for a period of a year and to use these as a centrepiece for an exhibition – which Kitaj titled *The Human Clay*, after a line in a poem by W.H. Auden – held at the Hayward Gallery, London, in 1976 and then taken around the country. It was in this group exhibition and in the fervent text for the catalogue which accompanied it that Kitaj made public his impassioned interest in an art deeply rooted in human concerns.

Linked in Kitaj's mind to these reversions to drawing and to the late nineteenth century were his 'reversionist instincts toward a Jewishness'. Gradually he had come to recognize that even a non-practising, agnostic Jew himself was conditioned and defined by the fate of other Jews in the past and in our own time. In a lecture delivered to a small congregation at the synagogue in Oxford in 1983, Kitaj explained that 'It is the case, for now anyway, that Jews and what happens to them fascinate me more than Judaism does; *We*, more than the God of the Jews; the phenomenal history of anti-semitism tantalizes me more than a faith I never knew.'[60] The origins of his art, Kitaj felt more strongly than ever, were indissolubly connected to the origins and terms of his life:

It strikes me that these crucial reversions of mine are *three* and that the three epiphanies were not sudden but evolved slowly over the same period, picking up around 1970 or so and are today still gathering toward unknown futures – Degas the draftsman, Cézanne the (late) painter, and Kafka the Jewish artist are the indwelling choir of this very uncertain church of mine. I say church because these three large tendencies seem to gather in one quiet place – at least I hope they will ultimately gather in an (old age?) synthesis. Around 1900, Kafka began to turn toward his own very original and fearful Jewishness (as did many fascinating others); Degas was bringing to a

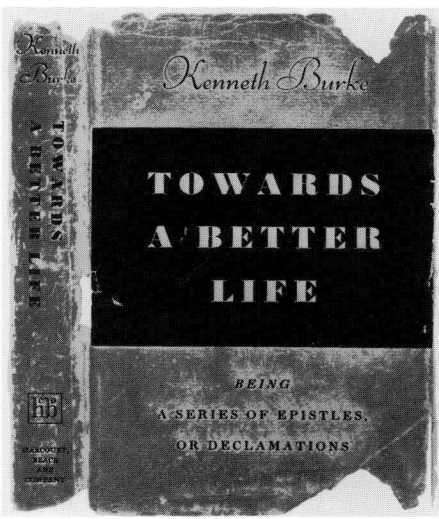

Fig. 6. Towards a Better Life, 1969, from *In Our Time*. Screenprint, 31 x 22½ in (78.7 x 57.2 cm.).

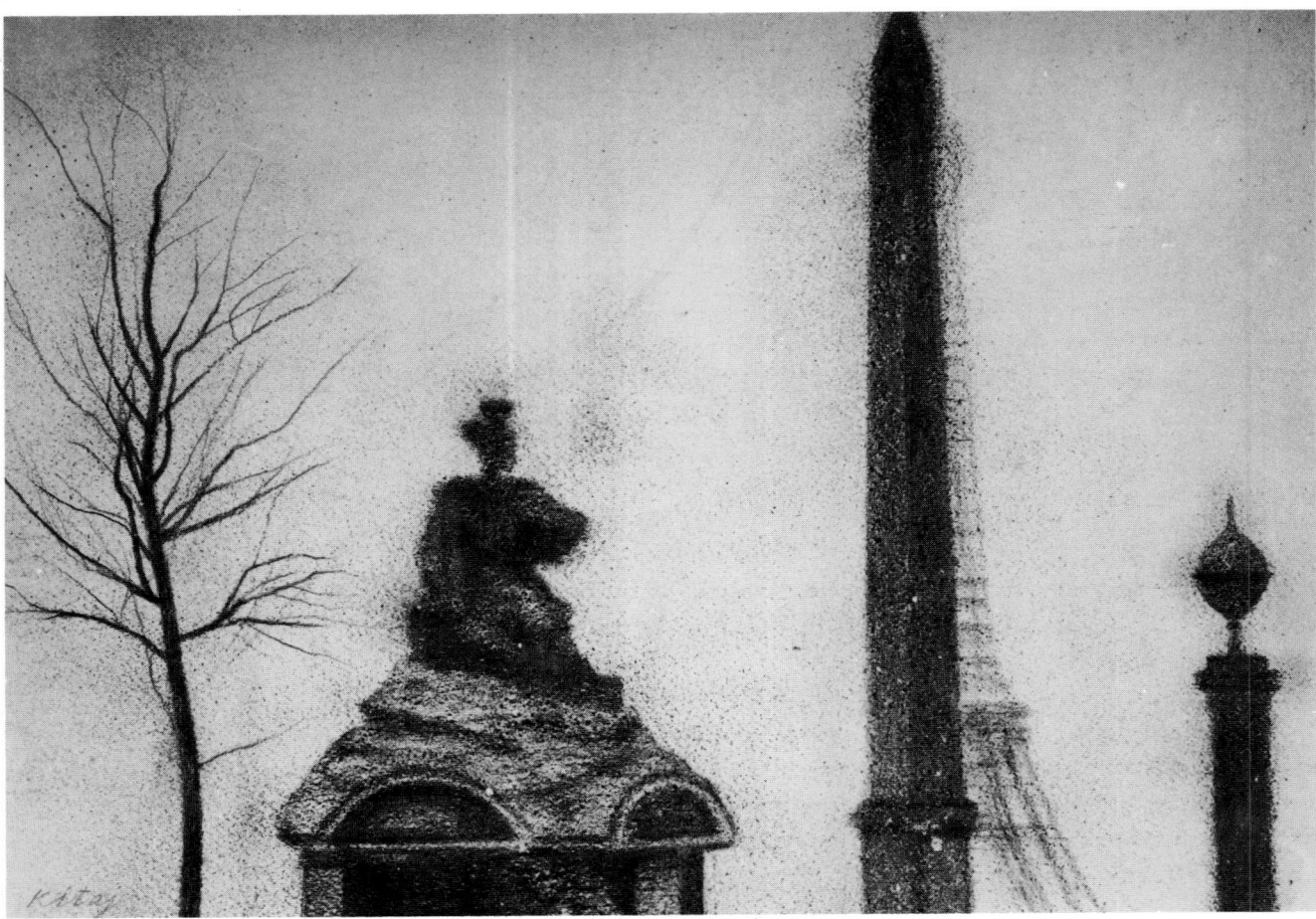

Fig. 7. Place de la Concorde, 1983. *Cat. no. 351.*

(near-blind) head the greatest drawing performance since the Renaissance, and Cézanne was *instigating* what, for Picasso, Matisse and Bonnard would become the light which would illuminate *their* way, and what, for *me*, suggests a depictive mystery-play which somehow agitates my own powers, whatever they prove to be.

I just don't accept what 78% of our art people take for granted – that one acts upon the art of one's immediate past. In 1947 and in 1952, Bonnard and Matisse were *still* absorbing lessons from Cézanne!

Kitaj remarks facetiously that he qualifies as a Post-Impressionist by virtue of the fact that he was born six years after the death of Monet, and adds: '1880-1920 was the last time the depictive blood ran *so* strong (*and* innovating), so why not go to school where the real stuff left off? It's funny that the new young guys are getting off on Picabia, Nolde and Kirchner etc. I guess it suits them.'

Having allayed his homesickness for America with a few months as artist-in-residence at Dartmouth College in 1978, followed by a year in New York City – where he produced, among other things, keenly-observed drawings such as *Ninth Street under Snow* (1979, pl. 110) – Kitaj decided in the spring of 1982 to move with Sandra Fisher to Paris for a year. It was a way for both of them to consummate their long romance with the city and its artistic heritage, and turned out to be a memorable and, in their view, an unrepeatable, year. Kitaj did a substantial amount of life drawing during this period, using both professional models and friends. With the encouragement and assistance of one of his closest friends in Paris, Aldo Crommelynck – the master printer best known for his work with Picasso but who in the mid-seventies also worked with Hockney on the remarkable *Blue Guitar* series – Kitaj made a group of soft-ground etchings, most of them self-portraits but including a highly atmospheric view of the *Place de la Concorde*. As far as painting was concerned, there were too many unusual distractions for it to be a very productive year for Kitaj. He and Sandra saw not only the Crommelyncks but also artist/scholar Avigdor Arikha and his wife, the American poet Anne Atik. 'We met or talked together almost every day and I felt hidden away from my usual habits and entered into a Paris I had never known, partly through the flowering of this friendship and partly inventing a Paris of my own.'

On 15 December 1983 Kitaj and Sandra Fisher were married in London's oldest and most beautiful synagogue, the congregation of Spanish and Portuguese Jews in Bevis Marks. With David Hockney as best man and with a *minyan* (ten Jewish men) which included some of their closest painter friends – Frank Auerbach (who gave away the bride), Lucian Freud and Leon Kossoff – Kitaj and his wife could have found no better means of declaring a future together both as Jews and as artists.

The World's Body

'Images with a meaning peculiar to their own time and place, once created,' wrote Fritz Saxl in 1947, 'have a magnetic power to attract other ideas into their sphere; … they can suddenly be forgotten and remembered again after centuries of oblivion.'[61] The conviction that the entire history of art was available as potential source material had been held by Kitaj as early as his student days, when he was immersed in the writings of Saxl, Wind, Warburg, Panofsky, Wittkower and other scholars intent on unravelling the meanings of the great art of the past. In his early work, however, Kitaj had approached the art of the masters in a tangential fashion, plucking images from the past and inserting them into his paintings along with obscure images from iconographic studies, literary quotations, personal references and details borrowed from more popular sources such as photography and film. The treasuring of images and their translation into a modern idiom were the primary goals; the original intentions and singularity of vision of the art thus referred to were somehow sidetracked and transformed along lines established by Modernism in the twentieth century.

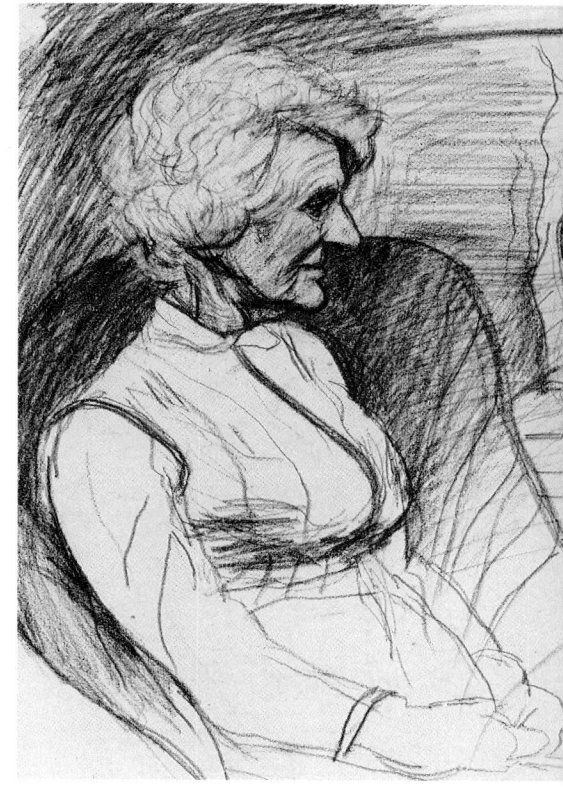

Fig. 8. Hockney's Mother, 1981. *Cat. no. 310*

In the mid-seventies Kitaj began to deal with the past art about which he cared passionately as far as possible on its own terms. The change in attitude was a fundamental one, as he reflected in a letter early in 1980:

I did love the grand masters when I was young but I did not know what to do with them … They were like roots deep in the earth (Giotto, Michelangelo, Rembrandt, Goya, Degas, Van Gogh, Cézanne) … and like so many young people, I was attracted by the pretty, frail wisps growing on the surface – the dandelion weeds (Duchampism, collagism, montage, Surrealism, the chimerical 'freedoms' young artists cherish so). These dandelions are so easy to pluck, so much easier to get at than the deep roots … They seem now like fool's gold in my own practice. I must leave their distinct potential to others.

In a period when many artists have been tempted to take as their model the work of their immediate predecessors or even of their contemporaries as a way of ensuring their modernity, it has been left to some of the most ambitious artists – artists, that is, who wish to ensure a lasting substance for their work rather than instant success – to look for guidance, as self-demanding artists have always done, to the work of the great masters. Kitaj is not alone of his generation in doing so, but even among like-minded colleagues he is unusual in aligning himself so openly and unreservedly with the artists whom he regards as his real mentors. In the second half of the seventies this meant, in particular, precedents in late nineteenth-century French art: Van Gogh's monumental single figure drawings, Cézanne's bathers, the brothel scenes of Toulouse-Lautrec, the distracted women of Degas and the Tahitian nudes by Gauguin, scenes of café life by Manet, Degas

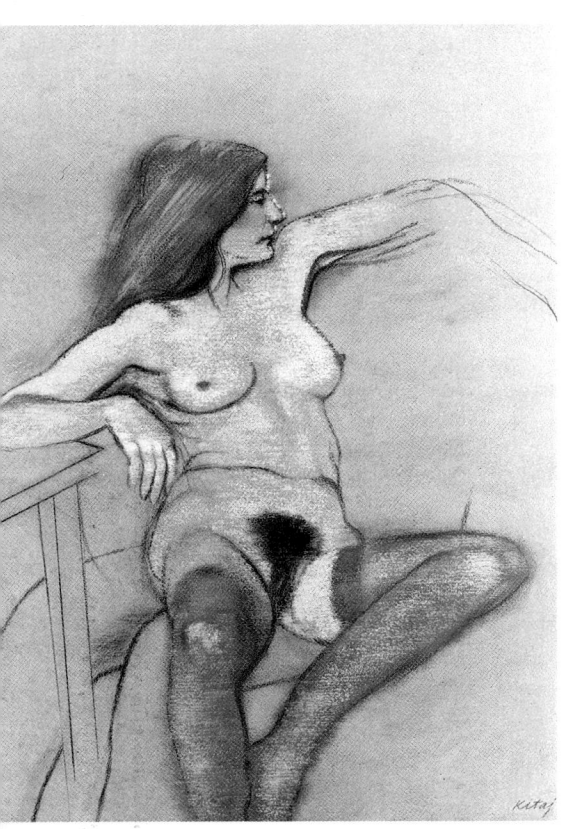

Fig. 9. Femme du Peuple 1, 1974. *Cat. no. 164*

and others, Seurat's atmospheric conté drawings, and pastels and drawings by Degas, Redon and Rodin are among the specific sources to which he has made reference. Kitaj, however, is no mere pasticheur. Rather he has taken this body of work – which thrills him for its wealth of inventions and for its omnivorous delight in making contact with everyday life in all its richness – as a set of premises on which to build a strong and *contemporary* art filtered through his own sensibility.

The aura of the turn-of-the-century art which Kitaj had decided now to take as his prime model, allied to his experience of Modernism and to direct study from life, is particularly evident in the pastel drawings which he began to produce in 1974. *Femme du Peuple 1* (1974) heralds a series of female nudes drawn from life and sets the tone for these with its frank eroticism and in its liberties with the human form both for the sake of expressive distortion – note the almost violent manner in which the left leg is flattened and joined to the thigh – and as a means of asserting the physical gestures made in establishing the marks, in the way, for instance, that the left arm trails out into nothing. In illusionistic and spatially convincing drawings such as *Marynka Smoking* (1980, pl. 112) one senses still a Modernist attention to the surface – for instance, in the pools of colour deposited by dragging the pastel across the rough texture of the handmade paper – which firmly establishes these drawings as of their own time. Many of the most touching and psychologically penetrating drawings are of the artist's own children, of poet and artist friends, of people well-known to him, so that the act of drawing is itself a symbolic recognition of the nature of that relationship. Who but a friend, for instance, could convey so perceptively the sadness and introspection beneath the brittle and witty surface of Quentin Crisp (pl. 88), former life model and self-styled 'Naked Civil Servant'? Conscious of the years lost when he did no drawing on paper, Kitaj seems to have taken a cue, in intention, if not in style, from the specificity of his own life drawings of the late fifties and early sixties:[62]

I was always a particularist and more so now than ever I like to think that universal values will prosper and reside in the most particular, subjective origins … that is to say that those origins are precious to me and I don't want to neglect them. This is the most emphatic 'lesson' I ever have to give a young painter – first, to try and register what you think you can see in that person posing there and, in one's more conceptual practice, to be true to what *you* are, to try to find out what you are, as opposed, for instance, to what much modern practice dictates. That's really harder to achieve than it sounds. Many many artists spend their lives the other way round – universalist, internationalist ambition drives away what may have been very special in the person.

Kitaj's convictions about drawing from the model have repercussions that go far beyond the confines of the life class. The artist points, for instance, to *Communist and Socialist (Second Version)* (1979, pl. 107) as an example of the way in which dealing head-on with the people who sit for him could act as a bridge in his work for conveying his views about contemporary events. Drawn from life in two separate poses, the picture depicts a Communist and a Socialist – both Catalans and one of them José Vicente Roma, a friend of the artist of nearly thirty years' standing – 'arguing in a café at a moment in Southern Europe, a few years ago, when nervous alliance between such people was in the balance'.[63] We don't, of course, know what they are saying, but we are reminded through this very direct image that in politics it is the interaction between people who hold strong convictions that is as important as the theoretical views to which they are so committed.

In *Study for Miss Brooke* (1974, pl. 90) Kitaj developed another function for life drawing which had remained of continuing importance to him: that of using an actual person as a starting-point for the creation of a fictional character, which then takes on a life of its own. As the title suggests, this is an imaginary portrait of a character in George Eliot's novel, *Middlemarch*. 'George Eliot had said (about Miss Brooke) that St Teresas are born every hour but that circumstance does not permit these wonderful people to become as extraordinary as St Teresa, or words to that effect; so I had just drawn this unremarkable girl and I just gave her the name from the novel I was reading.'

The portrait of Miss Brooke remains a rare and isolated instance in Kitaj's work of a figure invention directly related to a literary source, but it pointed the way to the sustained series of single figure paintings of the mid to late seventies, which remain some of the artist's greatest achievements: *The Arabist* (1975-6, pl. 96), *The Orientalist* (1975-6, pl. 98), *Smyrna Greek (Nikos)* (1976-7, pl. 122), *The Jew Etc.* (1976-9, pl. 97), *The Mother* (1977, pl. 119) and *The Hispanist (Nissa Torrents)* (1977, pls. 77 and 79). In creating this cast of characters Kitaj had at the back of his mind the example not only of Daumier's figure inventions, Ratapoil and Macaire, but of the characters which he himself had created a few years earlier in *Superman* (pls. 66 and 68), *Batman* (pl. 67) and *Bill at Sunset* (pl. 65). There are two crucial differences, however, between those precedents in his own work and the emblematic portraits that he now began to create. Rather than working purely from the imagination or from other representations, Kitaj now worked directly from life: this was the case with *The Mother* (not, incidentally, a portrait of his own mother); with *Smyrna Greek*, an imaginary portrait inspired by the poet Constantin Cavafy for which the artist's friend Nikos Stangos, himself Greek and a poet, posed; and with *The Hispanist*, a portrait of a Catalan friend resident in London. Secondly Kitaj was now taking as his subjects not ready-made characters but figure types of his own invention, each of whom represents a particular condition or role in life. Kitaj explained:

I want to distinguish between *prototype* which bores me and a *type* one tries to coin, which I believe succeeds to the extent I can make him memorable. That doesn't mean I *will* succeed, but I can try. So far, many of my fictive representations seem *underwritten* to me, to borrow a term from a sister art. When I can solve *that* I will have taken a giant step toward depictions which might lodge in the Social Memory.[64]

The literary tag so often flung at Kitaj as an accusation is triumphantly flaunted in these canvases, in which the painter's role is redefined as that of a novelist whose raw material is the image rather than the word. Though the pictures have their subtexts – *The Orientalist*, for example, in Hugh Trevor-Roper's biography of Backhouse; *The Arabist*, previously known as *Moresque*, in the life and work of a number of scholars in the field – the thrust of the portraits is a wholly visual one.[65] Of relevance to these pictures also is the devotion manifested in Kitaj's earlier work to iconography. Although he is now inclined to play this down, it is precisely because of his awareness of the richness of meaning achieved through transmutation of context that he is now able to quote from the repertory of his own images, creating a personal iconography from which to draw.

In *The Jew Etc.* we witness the first appearance of a character whom Kitaj was to name Joe Singer, after a friend of his mother's whom he remembered vaguely from his childhood, and who was to be spied again in later works such as *Bad Faith (Riga) (Joe Singer Taking Leave of his Fiancee)* (1980, pl. 117), *Study for the Jewish School (Joe Singer as a Boy)* (1980), *The Jewish School (Drawing a Golem)* (1980, pl. 114), *The Listener (Joe Singer in Hiding)* (1980, pl. 113) and, more recently, *Cecil Court, London WC2 (The Refugees)* (1983-4, pl. 143), *The Caféist* (1980-7, pl. 165) and *Germania (Joe Singer's Last Room)* (1987). In each episode we learn a little more about the figure, his past and his present predicament. Singer is for Kitaj what K. was to Kafka in *The Trial* and *The Castle*: an archetype representing a condition of man, and more specifically of the Jew, in the twentieth century, the anxious uncertainty of his fate made all the more urgent through the artist's identification with him.[66] It was several years after applying the name Singer to his invention that Kitaj learned just how appropriate a model he had found:

In the late thirties, my mother was dating a guy named Joe Singer. He was a lawyer and they were part of a circle of anti-fascist, bookish people typical of that period, which included refugees from

Nazism. (…) I remembered his name and began to use it. Then my mother told me she had expected him to ask her to marry him but meanwhile she fell in love with a handsome young refugee chemist from Vienna named Kitaj in their group of friends, and married him instead. I thought: how piquant, I happened to chance upon a dimly remembered name from childhood to give to a character I would draw and paint and imagine, a figure who would offer a certain secular impression of Jewishness, a representation as it were of a Jewish presence in painted pictures which, it could be argued, was kind of taboo (…) and, behold, the guy almost became my dad and I almost became R.B. Singer!

The fate of the Jews has become one of Kitaj's main preoccupations in recent years and a theme central to such paintings as *If Not, Not* (1975-6, pl. 92), *The Jewish School* (1980, pl. 114), *Rock Garden (The Nation)* (1981, pl. 129), *The Jewish Rider* (1984-5, pl. 164), the group of pictures initiated in 1985 under the collective title *Passion* (1940-5, see pl. 161) and another group, *Germania* (pls. 169, 174, 175 and 179), begun in the same year. Echoing Cézanne's ambition to do Poussin again after nature, Kitaj explained in the lecture on Jewish art which he delivered in 1983 that 'I took it into my cosmopolitan head that I should attempt to do Cézanne and Degas and Kafka over again, after Auschwitz. *That* may be the synthesis of my undoing, or, it'll make a mensch of me because artists tend to *create* their precursors.'

A single gatehouse at Auschwitz actually figures in *If Not, Not* (pl. 92) as one of a number of sinister intrusions into an otherwise idyllic landscape inspired by Giorgione's mysterious masterpiece, *La Tempesta*.[67] At the back of the artist's mind was a report, by someone who travelled to Auschwitz many years after the War, which remarked on the loveliness of the scenery en route. The presence of death and disaster within a scene of seductive exoticism and beauty thus becomes a metaphor for the shock and incomprehension with which Jews must have met their fate. Several critics have detected in this painting an allusion to Matisse's *Bonheur de vivre* (1905-6), in which a number of figures loll in innocent nudity within a tranquil and paradisical landscape.[68] Two world wars later, that idyll no longer seems possible, even as a fantasy; Kitaj's figures are shown not resting, but crawling fearfully away from imminent danger or even lying dead and abandoned. The tone of the painting and the kinds of imagery it employs have their basis largely in Eliot's *The Waste Land*, written in the aftermath of the traumatic carnage of the first World War. It is a measure of Kitaj's growth as an artist that nearly two decades after first using the poem as the inspiration for one of his pictures, *Tarot Variations* (pl. 4), he should create such a compelling reply to its harrowing content with its dark premonitions of the wholesale destruction of human life.

Land of Lakes (1975-7, pl. 100), conceived as a pendant to *If Not, Not*, represents an optimistic response to the despair of the other picture. In the essay that the artist had hung next to it when it was shown at the Hayward Annual in 1977, he described it as 'much more of an impersonal meditation than its bleaker companion' and as 'a token of better times to come'.[69] The pictures concerning Jewishness and particularly anti-semitism – 'a daily grind with me' – tend, however, to be among the most sombre and harsh in tone of all Kitaj's works. There might, at first, appear to be an almost light-hearted side to *Marrano (The Secret Jew)* (1976, pl. 83) in the hints of transvestism that form part of the picture's theme of dissimulation; the man is trying so hard, moreover, to be what he is not that even his head is not his own but a copy from a Giotto fresco.[70] Yet when one considers the identity of the figure in the light of the enforced conversion of Spanish and Portuguese Jews to Christianity in the late Middle Ages, the image takes on a much more sinister aspect. There is a confessional sense, too, in the implicit understanding that this is an image of the artist himself openly avowing his Jewish origins. Non-Jews may find it difficult to understand why this should be such an issue, but in a century that has seen the wholesale murder of Jews and continuing and insidious anti-semitism, it would, in the artist's view, be an abdication of responsibility and a betrayal of his forebears for even a non-practising Jew like himself not to stand up and be counted with the others.

'I believe that you can "invent" yourself,' explains Kitaj in particular relation to his fabricated Jewish characters:

I can, at least, attest to the profound fun, sometimes exhilaration, and more rarely revelation and insight caused by this game of remaking and making oneself … especially through one's art practice. By inventing characters, I can say, I think, that I go some way toward deciding what kind of character I may be myself. For instance, one's life, and thus one's art-life, has been a preparation for becoming a *kind* of Jew, etc., *what* kind, I have to try and invent!

Kitaj's most recent paintings on Jewish themes, such as *The Jewish School* (pl. 114), *Rock Garden* (pl. 129) and *Cecil Court* (pl. 143), all owe a debt, he says, 'to the rediscovery of the world and teaching and destruction (murder) of the Hassidic Zaddikim (magical holy men)'. Each of these pictures contains a narrative about the fate of the Jews, their exile and dispersal.[71] *The Jewish School*, closely modelled on a part of a nineteenth-century German anti-semitic engraving, transforms what in the original source was merely a swipe at the alleged anarchy of Jewish behaviour into a metaphor for the Jews' inability to defend themselves adequately against their persecutors. The meaning hinges on a single but crucial transformation from the source: the boy at the far right, who in the engraving is simply shown writing on the blackboard, in Kitaj's picture is drawing a golem, who in Jewish legend is an artificially created human being brought to life by supernatural means. The golem, however, is incomplete; he will not come to life in time to save them. *Rock Garden*, one of the cruellest and most anguished images which Kitaj has yet created, represents 'our Ghost-Nation, called by a Hebrew poet the great empty Kingdom of Death'.[72] Only *Cecil Court*, which treats those whose lives were set off-course, but not destroyed, by anti-semitic persecution, gives much cause for hope.

In the late seventies Kitaj spent an intense and concentrated period drawing, the subjects covering a wide range from straightforward life studies to imaginative compositions and allegories such as *The Rise of Fascism* (1979-80, pl. 94) and *Sighs from Hell* (1979, pl. 75). The group of *Bather* pastels (see pls. 76, 78 and 84), which constitute some of the most affecting works of this period, take their inspiration from Cézanne's paintings on a similar theme, which Kitaj admires not only for the usual formalist reasons, which have guaranteed their place in twentieth-century art, but also for their expressive awkwardness and sense of mystery.[73] Having decided to work for a couple of years solely on paper, in using pastels and in working sometimes on a large scale Kitaj was able to give these pictures the range and density of paintings. In the sixties, by contrast, he had worked for a long period exclusively on canvas, but had produced small-scale works on that support, which he himself regarded as drawings. It is as if the decision to concentrate more or less exclusively on one medium made it necessary for him subconsciously to find the means of making that medium do the job of both painting and drawing.

When Kitaj began painting again in 1980, he made a conscious decision to effect a radical change in his technique, 'disturbing' the paint to a far greater extent than he had been accustomed to. Not since the early sixties, in fact, had he used paint in a manner at all akin to this. Underdrawing has remained important, but as a working tool rather than as an end in itself to be protected and preserved at all costs. The initial drawing is readjusted until a satisfactory integration of the parts has been achieved, bringing with it a density of surface through the addition of successive deposits of paint and increasingly variable brushing.

There are, of course, evergreen precedents, techniques from the past which painters often like to use and, among those, I'll be found happily playing and daubing … for instance: Monet's interesting technique of piling layer upon layer of dried, rough stroking, allowing the previous colors to show through the brushmarks in a kind of opaque dazzle, led me to try something like that in

Fig. 10. Detail of G.E. Opitz, *Die Judenschule*, as reproduced in The Judensau by Isaiah Schacher, Warburg Institute Surveys, V, 1974

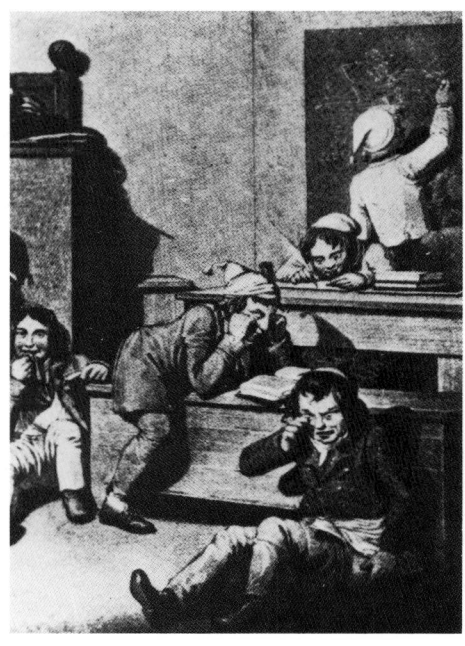

The Sailor (pl. 144), *Jewish School* (pl. 114), *Rock Garden* (pl. 129) et al. At the same time, I'd been moving away from the, what shall I call them – perfectionist, closely-ordered techniques of painting, culminating in *The Orientalist* (pl. 98) and *If Not, Not* (pl. 92) etc. ... and my brushing was to become more painterly, gestural, but no less careful... The large Cézanne *Bathers* in the National Gallery was constantly on my mind and, also, before my eyes, and literally in my hands, during that very crucial moment, those many months doing the *Artist's Eye* ... I go there every week, still, drawn mysteriously to that picture – my favorite in the collection.

Kitaj remarks that if there is an expressionist aspect to his recent painting, its roots lie above all in Cézanne.

Kitaj's abiding concern in recent years with the human figure has found one essential outlet in portraiture, primarily in the form of drawings from life but culminating, too, in a pair of double portraits conceived, perhaps, in a spirit of friendly rivalry to those painted in earlier years by Hockney. The first of these, *From London (James Joll and John Golding)* (1975-6, pl. 72), depicts John Golding – an intellectual with a cosmopolitan background and wide cultural interests, an abstract painter of considerable refinement and one of the great historians of Cubism – with his companion James Joll, the historian of anarchism. The picture is strewn with attributes of their interests (the books of Gramsci, Wollheim and Léger and the Mondrian exhibition poster), to the domestic tranquillity of their relationship and to their work; the very structure of the portrait, subdivided into three bands of unequal width, refers to the characteristic format of Golding's paintings of that period. The picture is both a private record of the friendship of the two men with each other and with the artist, and a synthesis of the various stands of modern European art and thought of which they are a part.[74] In the depiction of Joll in strict profile, the contours of his head 'crumbled away' as if they were part of an early Renaissance fresco, one gains a sense, too, of the uncovering of history that men such as these represent for Kitaj.

Kitaj's friendships with American poets of his generation have continued to make their mark on his paintings, as is evident from the second of the double portraits produced by him in the mid-seventies, *A Visit to London (Robert Creeley and Robert Duncan)* (1977, pl. 99), a straightforward memento of the mutual respect binding these men together. In the previous year Kitaj had painted *Houseboat Days (for John Ashbery)* (pl. 104) with a view to it being used as the cover illustration for a new volume of poetry with that title. Shortly after receiving the manuscript, he had remarked:

Ashbery explained to me that the title 'Houseboat Days' (of the book and of the title poem) had *no* real meaning for the poem ... it was just a chance treasure found in an old *National Geographic*. But that grand and sweet title will live on with the poem and in the social memory. Sometimes I think a title is remembered, like you remember a human face, a visage, which stands in the mind for a whole person.[75]

Though the image created by Kitaj in this painting recalls that of one of the book covers, *The Pursuit of the House-Boat*, used in the *In Our Time* series, it was, in fact, based on a film still of Simone Simon in *Lac aux Dames*, directed by Marc Allégret in 1933. Even without knowing the specific source, one can detect in the tonal greys of this painting a photographic or cinematic origin. Films continue to provide imagery for other pictures as well, such as *His New Freedom* (1978, pl. 93), which conflates a beautiful Rubens portrait of his first wife with a leering mouth from Carl Dreyer's film, *Vampyr*, to create a gruesome but memorable image of moral and physical decay.[76]

A more ambivalent attitude towards corruption can be detected in another drawing derived from a film still, *His Hour* (1975, pl. 109). The seated voyeur in the foreground of this picture was taken from Meyerhold's 1915 film adaptation of Oscar Wilde's *The Picture of Dorian Gray*,[77] but Kitaj maintains that he did not have the fictional character in mind when he made his pastel drawing. Moreover, he admits, 'I might've liked to have been in that chair in my picture myself, or in the place of the other man.' In the back-ground – drawn in outline only, as if they were partaking of another level of reality, another area of experience, to which the watching figure is not privy – a naked couple are shown in the blatant act of making love.

The dual themes of eroticism and prostitution have long featured in Kitaj's art, at least as far back as *Where the Railroad Leaves the Sea* (1964, pl. 36), *Walter Lippmann* (1966, pl. 40), *Erie Shore* (1966, pl. 43) and *Juan de la Cruz* (1967, pl. 61), and openly treated as the central subject by the time of *Casting* (1967-9, pl. 38) – conceived in the spirit of broad-sheets advertising the wares of American brothels – and *Shangai Gestures* (1968). In a series of drawings begun in the mid-seventies, however, Kitaj started to make images that themselves were erotic in intention, rather than merely about eroticism: images verging on the pornographic, such as *Communist and Socialist* (1975, pl. 89), others, such as *The Street (A Life)* (1975, pl. 136), taking up the image of the street and of the romance of prostitution and chance encounters earlier proposed in *Little Romance I* (1969, pl. 54). The attraction to brothel life is both personally rooted – as the artist confesses in incor-porating his self-portrait in the background of *Smyrna Greek (Nikos)* (1976-7, pl. 122) – and linked to a historical romance with fellow 'sleepwalkers': 'Degas, Baudelaire, Flaubert, Lautrec, Benjamin, Giacometti, Picasso, Kafka, Morandi and many others who seem to have known such places well, prowling those districts at night.'[78] Kitaj lists as one of his 'great literary influences' in this respect the anonymous and encyclopedic two volumes of sexual confessions first published in the Victorian era with the title *My Secret Life*.[79] The precedents in the visual arts, however, are equally important, as is attested by the evident relationship of a painting such as *Frankfurt Brothel* (1978) – which the artist now regards as one of his failed pictures – to the brothel pictures of Lautrec or Degas.

Kitaj has deliberately set out to explore the fine and explosive line between eroticism and so-called hard-core pornography, which he has used on occasion for details and poses. At a time when pornography itself has been under the close scrutiny of feminists as a measure of male violence against women, the mere use of such material, as Kitaj well knows, is problematic and dangerous. He remains, however, challenged by the possibil-ities of such subject matter.

Although I must admit I'm now rethinking this sort of sexual art in a spirit of something verging on contrition, ... I just don't want to be told what I can and can't do in art. Doesn't that confirm my pre-eminent modernism, as against those who think I'm reactionary, old-fashioned, retro-gressive, anti-modern etc., etc.? In fact, most of the places I try to take my art are condemned by many of those who think *they* themselves represent modernist freedom! – So my pictures are pornographic, or they're obscurantist, or they're literary, or autobiographical, or they hark back before last year's art, or they're (badly) political, or my drawing is academic and worse etc. Now, I've even heard that my Jewish pictures won't fly; that they're sentimental and nostalgic, *naturally*. I just don't think the last word has been said about so many of these taboos in art and I feel down-right incorrigible ... I don't really know what pornography is or what art is. I'm a strong feminist but feminism, like socialism and modernism and humanism, has many differing faces.

The task that Kitaj has set himself is a formidable one: that of producing an art which not only gives pleasure to the senses and stimulation to the intellect and to the emotions, but which also touches on his own life, and on that of his contemporaries, directly and without recourse to irony. If at times his meaning is still not clear, or if, in the pursuit of the depictive tradition as an anchor for his own inventions, Kitaj sometimes depends heavily on the aura of his sources, one should not be too harsh, for these are only signs of a vulnerability that other artists would seek to conceal. There is very little in the art of our century that is both challenging *and* self-evident: think, for instance, of Surrealism, with its private and inward-looking imagery, or of the highly-specialized body of theory that is taken for granted by the practitioners of abstraction, of conceptual art and of other

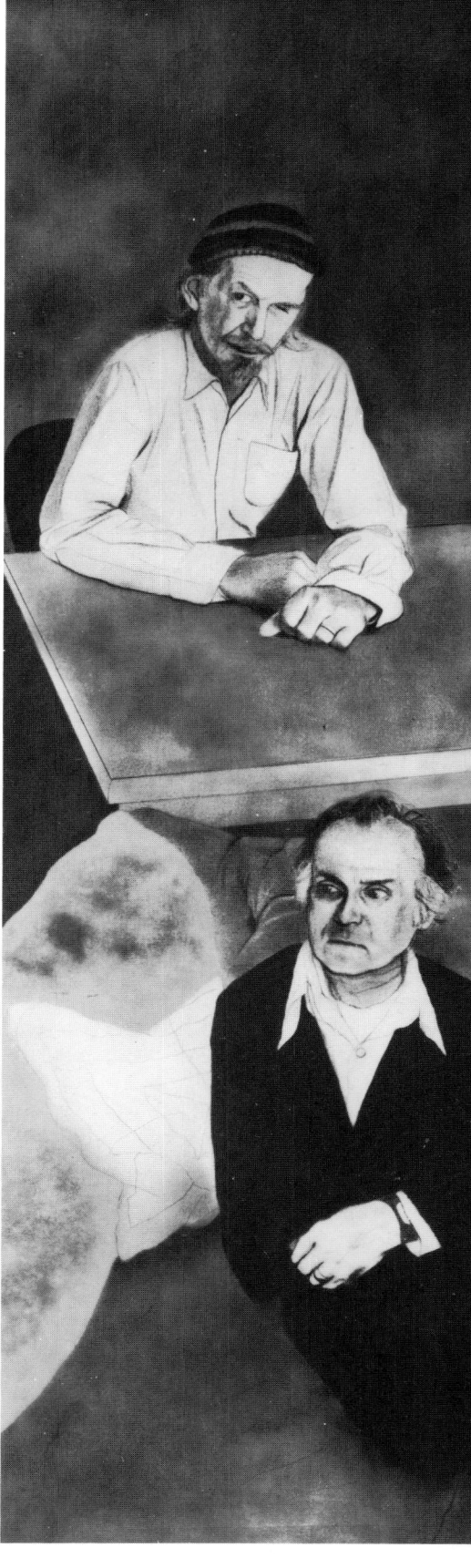

Fig. 11. A Visit to London (Robert Creeley and Robert Duncan), 1977-9. *Cat. no. 206*

forms of late modernism. This is not to excuse Kitaj the difficulties that his own work creates, but one should at least give him credit for admitting that they exist and for doing what he can, both in his pictures and by means of his explanations, to reduce the barriers between his audience and himself. His intentions – flawed, on his own admission, as they may be – remain honourable ones.

A Confessional Art

'I happen now to be in the grip of what I suppose to be great changes in my thinking and, I hope, in my practice,' Kitaj wrote at the beginning of 1983, 'which are related to what may be called autobiographical or confessional directions in my art.' These tendencies are intimately related, for him, to his growing concern over the past few years with his identity as a Jew, but they go beyond that to a desire for his pictures to be 'enshrouded' by a 'confessional aura'. As he remarks:

A great deal of poetry *and* art is 'confessional' anyway, in the sense that it is a personal, subjective record of one's state of mind and feeling but now I like to explore a deal more into the autobiographical realm where one's own history and interests get more of a hearing within the complex of (my) confounding pictures, especially because our modern art has discouraged that practice so much – not only abstractionism, but most of the artists I am close to would, I think, wish to refuse confession, as they do explanation. I've heard that getting something off your chest (and into your pictures??) is good for you; so, we'll see.

The roots of this confessional art in the circumstances of Kitaj's life are implicit at least as far back as *The Man of the Woods and the Cat of the Mountains* (1973, pl. 53), which I have interpreted as an image of the painter's relationship with Sandra Fisher, but the personal terms in that instance are concealed by secrecy and conveyed by metaphor. A more recent drawing such as *The Green Blanket* (1978, pl. 80), on the other hand, openly depicts the supportive friendship sustaining the couple; the source of the image in a self-portrait by Goya, rather than complicating the issue, helps to clarify its significance.[80]

Confession takes many forms in Kitaj's current work. The matter can be as straightforward as recording the memory of a prostitute's bedroom, as in *The Room (rue St Denis)* (1982-3, pl. 137), an eloquently simple image painted in Paris in a matter of days; though the theme is one that Kitaj has treated on many occasions over the years, never before has he dealt with it so directly. *The Garden* (1981, pl. 125), too, speaks for itself, as a loving refabrication of the garden that he had designed for his home in the previous year and which had now been planted according to his instructions.[81]

Cecil Court, London WC2 (The Refugees) (pl. 143), painted over the winter of 1983/4, was the first major canvas completed by Kitaj upon his return to London from Paris. Conceived in a spirit of competition with Balthus's paintings of *The Street*, on view at that time in Paris as part of the large Balthus retrospective,[82] Kitaj regards it as his most ambitious painting in recent years.[83] A reverie on the way in which his own life has been touched by that of refugees from the holocaust, the picture is a compendium of images rich in personal significance: the setting, an alley of specialist and antiquarian bookshops running between Charing Cross Road and St Martin's Lane, which has been one of the artist's constant London haunts; at the far left, Seligmann, one of the refugees who ran an art bookshop there for many years; at the far right, Kitaj's recently deceased stepfather; behind him, a shop inscribed with the name 'Joe S', for Joe Singer, the man who almost became Kitaj's stepfather and who as a fictional character has peopled many of his recent pictures; and in the foreground, a self-portrait based on the cover illustration of a pulp novel, the artist dressed in the clothes which he had worn at his recent wedding and seated on a famous chair designed by Le Corbusier.[84]

Two canvases on which the artist completed work during 1983-4 – *Amerika (John Ford on His Deathbed)* (pl. 148), based on his own sketches and snaphots of his favourite film director, and *Amerika (Baseball)* (pl. 152), a large painting loosely based on a landscape by Velázquez and the fruit of a longstanding ambition to produce a big baseball picture with elements of fantasy and reality[85] – suggested the beginnings of a major group of new pictures on the theme of his home country. Kitaj explained at the time that he used the spelling from Kafka's novel 'because I want to register my American self from afar and in exilic fantasy, to which (fantasy) I feel drawn. Kafka never went to America and *my* Amerika will allow me all the craziness I may need, upon his inspiration.'

Over the following six or seven years, however, Kitaj made only a few imaginative returns to his native country, such as *Foul Tip* (1986), a charming if modest reinterpretation of the baseball imagery that had long fuelled his romance with his own childhood. If the promised synthetic statements about his country of origin did not immediately materialize, one can only speculate that the change of heart was linked to events in his life. The United States was much on his mind during the latter part of the decade, to the extent that he even packed up his belongings in 1987 with the intention of moving to Los Angeles with his wife and young son Max, born in November 1985; there he would be near his friend Hockney, his mother, who had recently settled there after her retirement and bereavement, and his son Lem, who was already establishing himself as a highly successful Hollywood screenwriter working under the pseudonym Lem Dobbs.[86] Having rented a house not far from Hockney in the Hollywood Hills, Kitaj decided almost at once that the plan had been a mistake, and he and his family once again returned to London.

Jewish rather than American themes proved the most influential on Kitaj's thinking during the mid to late 1980s, giving rise to *The Jewish Rider* (1984-5, pl. 164) and a related group of pictures incorporating images of smoking chimneys as a symbol of Jewish suffering, bearing comparison with the Christian cross, and leading also to a number of ambitious reveries on the Holocaust steeped in tragedy, to which he gave the generic title *Germania* (pls. 169, 174, 175 and 179). Joe Singer, too, has further adventures, for example in the painting *Germania (Joe Singer's Last Room)* (1987), in which he imagines his protagonist in hiding in a house in Darmstadt – a city where Kitaj himself was stationed for four months while in the army – his life saved by a German so that he can reappear in other pictures. Joe is the protagonist also of *The Caféist* (1980-7, pl. 165), a painting which in its subject matter contains echoes of earlier works such as *The Autumn of Central Paris (After Walter Benjamin)* (1972-3, pl. 57), or of an even earlier café picture in a very different format, *Specimen Musings of a Democrat* (1961, pl. 12). The subtext in this case, however, is linked not so much to Jewishness as to a love of street life, dispassionately observed from the sidelines.[87]

The Jewish Rider harks back to an earlier painting, *The Jew Etc.* (1976-9, pl. 97), in which Kitaj had first created the image of a lone figure in a railway carriage as one appropriate to the accursed Wandering Jew in his twentieth-century form. The horse on which he might have travelled in an earlier age, borrowed, as the title hints, from Rembrandt's *Polish Rider* in the Frick Collection, remains a vestigial presence behind the figure. The identity of the man himself, a portrait of the philosopher Michael Podro, is deliberately left anonymous so that the figure can be taken as representative of all those Jews who have experienced the unsettling effects of sudden displacement from one culture into another. Through the window there is an inhospitable rocky landscape, its barren emptiness interrupted only by a cross, symbol of Christ's Passion, and an incinerator chimney spewing black smoke, Kitaj's cipher for the fate endured in our own century by six million Jews.

The compellingly simple image of the chimney became a central feature of a number of small pictures, together explicitly entitled *Passion (1940-5)*, as a moving, if barely endurable, memorial to the Holocaust. In *Passion (1940-5) Writing* (1985, pl. 161) the image of the chimney is multiplied on an ever larger scale, like visual equivalents to increasingly impassioned warnings of looming danger: the writer sits at his table, so engrossed in his thoughts that he fails to notice that he has become claustrophobically imprisoned within a chimney-like shape and that even his inkwell has become transformed into a miniaturized replica of the huge and ominous chimney just outside the walls of his study. In the pastel *The Painter (Cross and Chimney)* (1984-5), in which an artist is shown brushing in the finishing touches to a yellow cross, figures representing the Christian and Jewish Passion are shown slightly overlapping, one struggling under the weight of the cross and the other, in the foreground, dissolving in a plume of smoke within another chimney expressed simply as a silhouette in black outline. Chimney forms suddenly seem to appear everywhere as premonitory shapes, as in the scaffolding of lines housing three rather grotesque truncated heads in *The Divinity School Address* (1983-5, pl. 168). A chimney appears also in the background of *The Sniper* (1987), described by the artist as 'a picture-parable', which he did not base on a particular person or incident but conceived rather as a generic sniper and victim. The conjunction here of the smoking chimney with a church steeple surmounted by a cross proposes an unambiguous equation between the symbols of Jewish and Christian martyrdom that had featured in the preceding pictures.

Kitaj's archetypal Jew, as he appears in *The Corridor (After Sassetta)* (1988), can be taken as a representative not only of his race but of the old European intelligentsia under threat from the forces of barbarism. The torment suffered by this twentieth-century man, moreover, is explicitly compared through its source to the unmentionable punishments inflicted on the saints.[88] The animalistic thugs who attack the besuited gentleman are close relations, iconographically and in their style of execution, to the monstrous figures that Kitaj had introduced in early paintings such as *Pariah* (1960, pl. 21).[89] These descendants of the deformed and frightening races invented by the Greeks as personifications of their irrational fears can be taken, on first glance, as materializations of the paranoia and sense of persecution often ascribed to Jews; but as we well know that this persecution has been real and deadly in our century, and not just imagined, it may be more helpful to reflect instead on ways in which various evils have been ascribed to or projected onto the Jews, or for that matter any other misunderstood minority, as a way of giving form to anxieties that can then more easily be destroyed through verbal abuse or even physical violence. The onlookers in the background, shown frozen in terror or in the act of fleeing from the scene, allude to all those who have contributed to the persecution of others through their inaction and quiet compliance. Within this nightmare scene we are, in a sense, all implicated either as victims, oppressors or accomplices. Conversely in another painting, *4 A.M.* (1985, pl. 170), in which a family in hiding huddles together in terror from the world outside, of necessity we identify wholly with the predicament of the innocents and thus with their barely repressed hysteria.

Having spent some years deliberating on the Jewish predicament and on its repercussions both on his painting and on the lives of all those who have been displaced from one culture into another, in 1989 Kitaj published a book-length text on the subject under the title *First Diasporist Manifesto*.[90] Although his involvement with Jewish themes, and particularly with the notion of the Diaspora, remained undiminished in the years that followed the appearance of this text, Kitaj was almost immediately sorry that he had made his words public. 'It is true that I'm not happy with the *First Diasporist Manifesto*,' admitted Kitaj at the end of 1991, adding: 'The Jewish Question, as it is called, interests me greatly and I would hope its complexities will continue to feed into my pictures. Whether this complex is a by-way or a destiny in my art I can't know for sure.' Wishing to clarify his ideas on the subject and his misgivings about his first text, he began work in 1991 on a second, much shorter text called simply 'Diasporism':

I wrote a First Diasporist Manifesto during a bad period in my life. There's so much poor to middling writing and thinking in it that bothers me, I've come to regret its publication, the way I regret sending many paintings into the world unfinished, unrevised, undestroyed. As in those paintings, there are passages and ideas in the manifesto I still like. (…)

I imagined that I could paint a predicament, then (I'm still trying hard), like one paints a tree or an angel or a God. Diasporism became a painting predicament, a constant fantasy not wildly unlike Herzl's Judenstaat, only in *my* fantasy, the Jews would have a painting art *and* an exile as well as a state (which in my lifetime had not yet solved their predicament). I supposed that Jewishness could be a presence in art as it is in life. (…)

Some days I am still intoxicated by the unstable romance with which my little tract is saturated. Diasporism is not a painting style. It's a kind of life mode, the many by-ways of which lead me right *into* painting, as they have (I now realize) since I was young, and in that sense it may be said to be intrinsic to painting the way style is. At one of the pounding black hearts of the 'Jewish Question' has always been the problem of assimilation, chewed over in a thousand books, one of those enigmas Israel was to have resolved by returning Jews to a fabled normalcy. If I were to write down a second manifesto it would be very short and I think it would wish to address what I have called assimilationist aesthetics because I find I don't wish to escape the tremors of European host-art from Giotto to Matisse. I'm too old and I love those DWEMs too much. What I think may be new and radical, only suggested in the (unfinished) manifesto, are the energies I have found for my own painting at that crossroads, that very conjunction where pariah-art and host-art (terms I try to describe elsewhere) meet in passionate embrace. (…)

Kitaj's loss of confidence in the *First Diasporist Manifesto* may have had less to do with his feelings about it as a piece of writing than with his disappointment about the hostility – and, worse, indifference – with which a subject so close to his heart was received. The application of his thesis not just to Jews but to all people classed as outside the mainstream of power in their society, including women, foreigners, homosexuals and those of non-Caucasian racial origin, creates a potent image to anyone who feels both a part of that society and somehow also alienated from it. There are times when it seems that anyone who places a premium on culture and the artistic impulse – whether it be painting, music, literature or any other form of expression – willingly adopts the situation of the diasporist as he describes it, finding him or herself 'despised, disliked, mistrusted, sometimes tolerated' by much of the community at large. Opening out the definition of the diasporist, as he did, to encompass far more than just the question of Jewish experience, focused attention on the urgency of his words. In pressing for an understanding aimed at a much broader audience, and in so doing treating art as a real force for good rather than an élitist occupation, Kitaj was proposing a reassessment of attitude far more radical than has conventionally been permitted under the guise of artists' statements and aesthetic manifestos. With time, the importance of Kitaj's text and of its place in the development of his thinking is bound to take precedence over any reservations about its occasional lack of focus and its sometimes over-emotional and Messianic tone.

While Kitaj wrestled with the theme of Diasporism in his writing, he explored these issues also in his art, particularly in the group of paintings collectively entitled *Germania*, which he initiated in 1985 with *Germania (The Tunnel)* (1985, pl. 169), and followed with *Germania (Engine Room)* (1983-6), *Germania (Joe Singer's Last Room* (1987), *Germania (To the Brothel)* (1987, pl. 175), *Germania (Vienna)* (1987, pl. 174) and *Germania (The Audience)* (1989, pl. 179). They were not conceived as a series mapped out in advance, since the first simply led to the others, although most of them are in a similar format and all place the figures in a particular situation within an explicit setting. Although when seen together they could be thought of as a (subconscious) Jewish version of the Stations of the Cross, Kitaj stresses that these re-enactments of the drama of the Holocaust on

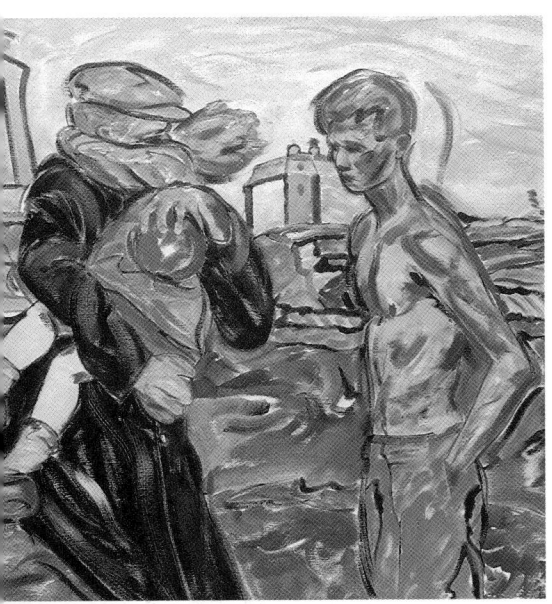

Fig. 12. The Heart Determines, 1989. *Cat. no. 461*

German soil were not conceived as narrative episodes in a particular sequence. On producing the first canvas, Kitaj recalls, 'I had no idea there would be others. They just found themselves linked by that title when I was in the most intense period of pondering the Jewish-German equation. I doubt if I will use the title again, so they are complete-incomplete-inadequate-uncomfortable-embarrassing etc. etc. and some of them may or may not be interesting art.'

Kitaj describes the *Germania* paintings as 'personal quirks, rather out of step, out of time', especially as each of them directs attention to a different aspect of the Jewish experience in Germany. '*The Audience* alludes directly to the to me fascinating and crucial issue of Germans who loved Nazism, Germans who hated it and all those Germans in-between.' By contrast, '*To the Brothel* is an altogether odd, oblique, personal member of these Germania pictures, not directly to do with the Holocaust at all.'[91] Perhaps even more cryptic is *Germania (Vienna)*, based on a still of a scene from *L'Histoire d'un crime* (1902) by Ferdinand Zecca, showing the imprisoned protagonist dreaming in his cell; while preserving the disjunction between the sphere of dreams and the earthly reality below, Kitaj has represented all six figures in the nude, turning two of them into women and the prisoner himself into a nude self-portrait in pensive pose.[92]

In *Germania (The Tunnel)* Kitaj portrays himself as a mis-shapen old man following his small son into an uncertain future. Paternal devotion mirrors a filial loyalty to two of the artists whom he regards as his mentors: the image of protective motherhood contains deliberate echoes of Matisse's sculptures of *The Back*, set into an enclosed and stifling corridor-like interior based on a view by Van Gogh of the hospital at Saint-Remy but suggestive, too, of concentration camps and the all too common torture chambers of our own time.[93] *Germania (Joe Singer's Last Room)* acknowledges the efforts made by some Germans to protect Jews from their fate. Although no allusion was intended to another work by Van Gogh, *The Night Café* (1888), in the use of the complementaries red and green to picture the interior as an airless and oppressive contained space, 'as a place where one can ruin oneself, go mad or commit crimes', it nevertheless conveys a comparable sense of estrangement and claustrophobia.[94]

The Jewish themes are linked in certain works to images of family life, with a strong autobiographical implication, as in *Arabs and Jews (Jerusalem)* (1985), an apparently straightforward portrayal of two infants in a nursery which is transformed, through the title, into a metaphor of hope in relation to the tensions still threatening world peace in the Middle East. A later painting, *The Heart Determines* (1989), in which Kitaj pictures himself with his two sons, mines the confessional vein of his recent work with particular poignancy. Coming close here to a very traditional form of genre painting, Kitaj nevertheless brings a new twist to an old subject, producing a picture on the theme of the father and child in part because it seemed to him that it was virtually unexplored territory by comparison with the prevalence of mother-and-child pictures. About a decade earlier Kitaj had first treated the subject in a charcoal drawing showing a well-built man striding forward with a baby tucked under his left arm; while the man's bulk, sheer size and muscular figure call attention to the frailty of the tiny child, the vulnerability of the man himself, displayed to us nude as he carries out his tender act, is also made manifest. The experience of starting a new family when he was in his fifties has lost none of its surprise for Kitaj; his imminent plans include another painting on the father-and-child theme, for which at the time of writing Max has begun to pose.[95]

The autobiographical strain in Kitaj's work became even more pronounced in the late 1980s. After suffering a mild heart attack in 1989 and later while undergoing withdrawal symptoms on giving up the sleeping pills that he had taken for years, Kitaj went through a period of intense depression. In several major canvases, such as *Melancholy* (pl. 180), *Melancholy after Dürer*, *Up All Night (Fulham Road)* (pl. 181) and *Burnt Out*, all painted in 1989, he sought to give form directly to this despairing state. The desperate and gloomy

Find more info.

wakefulness of the somnambulist staring vacantly into space in *Up All Night (Fulham Road)* conveys, however, not just the artist's own anxiety at the time but a general condition suffered by many denizens of big cities: this figure, in that sense, functions not just as a cipher for the artist but also as a representative of that whole rootless population in an urban society whose lives are carried on almost invisibly after hours. The two paintings of his melancholy frame of mind likewise have not only a highly personal purpose, but also a more general application, as Kitaj recalls in explaining the genesis of *Melancholy After Dürer*:

I have always considered myself a melancholic and assumed this temperament derived from my Russian grandparents. 1989 was a bad year and, after a heart attack, I fell into a slump. My friend Arikha told me to paint my depression and so I looked at the greatest image of this theme, Dürer's engraving, which I found in Panofsky's Dürer book which I have kept with me since teenage. Of course I have not done Dürer justice, but that is in keeping with what Panofsky says the print is about: 'the tragic unrest of human creation'.[96]

In the second painting on the subject, entitled simply *Melancholy*, Kitaj sets aside the Dürer source in order to imagine himself as a man bowed down by depression and besieged by his own daemons. The half-formed and threatening figures contribute to a foreboding atmosphere, the agitation of which is intensified by the neurotic flurries with which the paint itself has been applied.

The subject-matter of *Heart Attack* (1990) clearly relates to his recent brush with death, but the scene depicted, in which a young nude woman comes to the aid of an older man as he keels over backwards, bears no direct relationship to the details of the event in his own life. On the other hand two other paintings executed in that year, *The First Time (Havana, 1949)* (pl. 177) and *The Second Time (Vera Cruz)*, recalling his earliest sexual encounters, are among the most straightforward representations he has painted of his own experience. The idea of painting the first of the two, set in the Cuban brothel that he visited as a teenaged merchant seaman in the company of his school friend Jim Whiton, had been formulated as early as September 1983, when he and I spoke again of the description he had sent to me in March of his memory of the occasion:

Within an hour of stepping off our ship in steamy Havana, which was truly an American brothel before Castro, Jim and I were in a cathouse and our virginity was gone at the late age of 16. My first lady looked like Yvonne de Carlo and she had red underwear. All the years of groping those unyielding Catholic beauties in cars and couches and movies arrived in that cool, tiled Hispanic Heaven to be followed by all the other heavenly pastures in Mexico and points south. (…) That tragic and wondrous theme began there in Batista's Cuba and has run thru many of my failed pictures to this day (…).

That this painting had been on his mind for more than six years before he started work on it may be an extreme example of the slow gestation of his pictures, but it is by no means untypical. As he had explained in 1980, 'I carry themes in my mind for years before I will try to compose them. I've got themes that will last me now till I die.'[97] In *The Second Time (Vera Cruz, 1949)*, the Mayan heads that watch the action from the foreground, bringing us into collusion with them as voyeurs, were intended as references to the presumed racial origins of the Mexican girl with whom he made love on that occasion. Any iconographic resemblance between this compositional scheme and Gauguin's *The Vision after the Sermon* (1888), with the naked lovers taking the place of Jacob wrestling with the angel, is purely coincidental, as Kitaj asserts that the Synthetist masterpiece was not on his mind when he produced his own picture. Nevertheless the juxtaposition of the two images can be instructive, with the secularization of the religious subject hinting at ways in which we wrestle with our own consciences.

I Married an Angel would seem on the surface to be another remembered scene from his life, like the pictures about his first sexual encounters, which it recalls in its format and

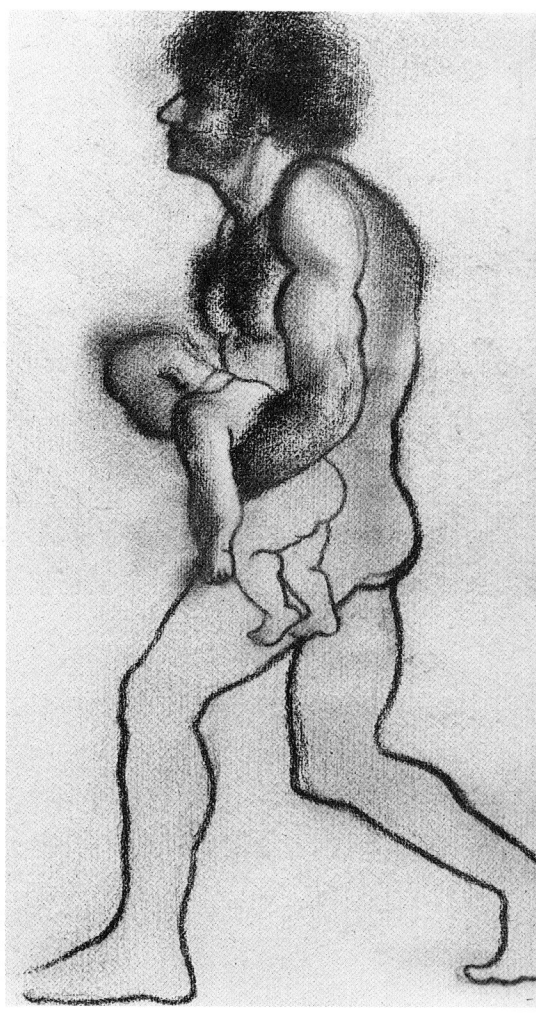

Fig. 13. Man and Child, 1978. *Cat. no. 209*

composition. However, in representing himself now not with a prostitute but with Sandra, pure in her nudity beneath a diaphanous white gown, there is an implicit if unintentional contrast with the carnality of those other pictures: an image of renewed sexuality through the fidelity of the marital bed. The title was taken from a Broadway musical by Rodgers and Hart, starring Vera Zorina and Walter Slezak, from which in 1942 MGM produced a cinematic version starring Jeanette McDonald and Nelson Eddy, described in *Halliwell's Film Guide* as the story of an attractive angel who lures a playboy from his earthly girlfriends. While this is not how Kitaj thought of his relationship with Sandra, he admits that 'I did intend the picture, in the spirit of comedy, to be mildly funny. I'd love to achieve a great Comic painting or two before I die – maybe something as memorable as one or another of the great New Yorker cartoons (my favorites are by George Price), but more solid and built to last, like Cézanne wanting to make something more solid out of ephemeral Impressionism – "for the museums", I think he said, didn't he?'

Kitaj's wife appears also in other recent paintings, such as *The Drivist* (1985-7), an allusion to her assumption of the role of family driver abdicated by the artist as a result, he says, 'of nameless fears and boredom with technology'. In *Unpacking My Library* (1990-1) Sandra looks on wide-eyed from the doorway at Kitaj, hunched over as an eccentric bibliophile neurotically attending to his cartons of books, as yet unpacked. Here again Kitaj has combined a found title and subject, this time from the 1931 essay by Walter Benjamin, with explicitly autobiographical features.[98] It does not represent a particular incident in his life, such as the abandoned plan to move to Los Angeles several years earlier, but a lifelong habit: 'I'm always unpacking my library like that. Always packing part of it up and unpacking sometimes years later, thrilled with forgotten treasures and surprises.'

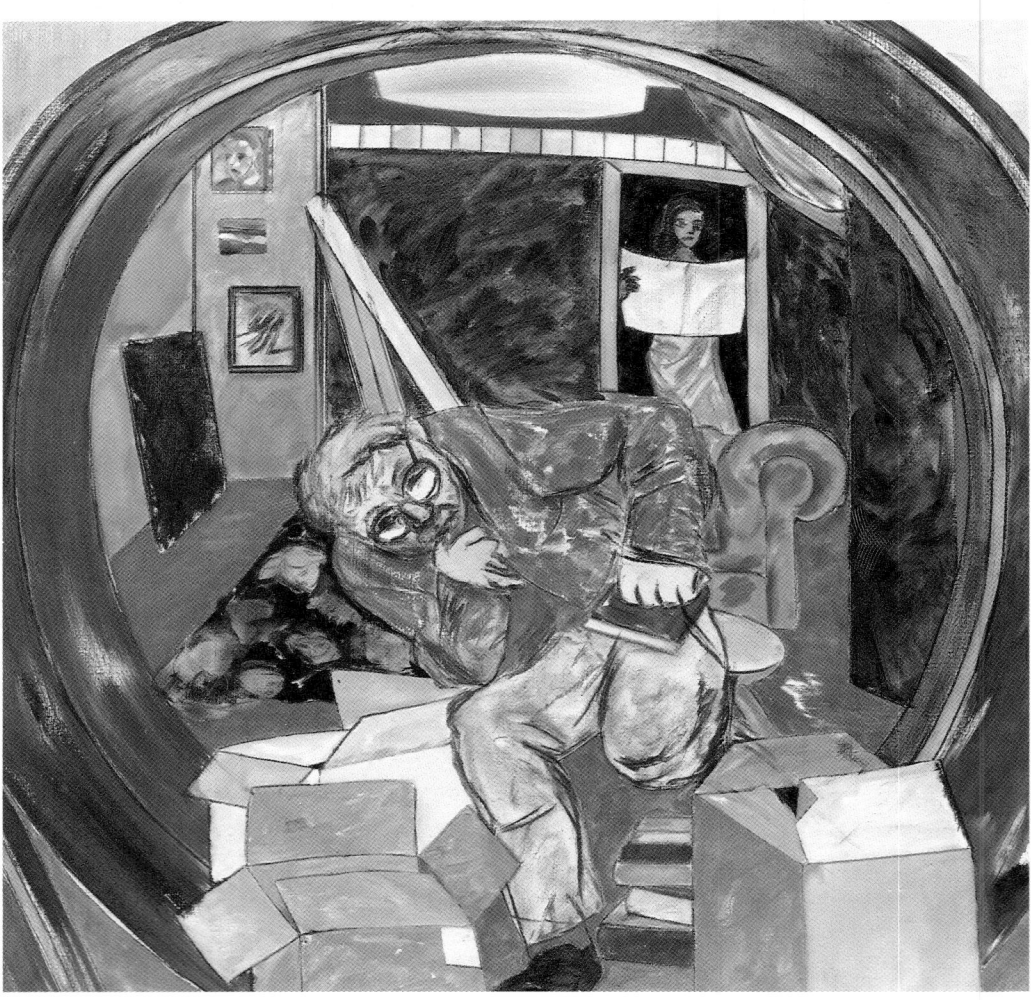

Fig. 14. Unpacking my Library, 1990-1.
Cat. no. 489

In 1988 Kitaj painted a picture featuring his local cinema, *Fulham Road Cinema Bathers*, and another in which he represented himself in the nearby restaurant that he visited every lunchtime, *The Fulham Road, SW10 (After Bruegel)*, thus establishing the principle of using his immediate environment as a fitting subject for his art. There was nothing revolutionary in this, since there is a long tradition for such subjects; within London itself, for example, there was the example earlier in the century of Sickert and the Camden Town painters. For Kitaj, however, the theme took on a new urgency after his heart attack, when he was advised by his doctor to take a daily walk for the sake of his health. He chose to take his exercise at the start of every day, around 6 am, when the streets were still and deserted. The routine introduced him to a new range of subjects drawn from the Chelsea and South Kensington districts of London, which he brought into the foreground of paintings such as *Hotel Rembrandt* (1989), *Sorbonne Hotel (SW7)* (1990) and *De Morgan's House* (1991, pl. 178). In November 1991 Kitaj listed some of the other local scenes already on his mind as potential subjects: his heart hospital; the church where Dickens was married; Whistler Tower; an Erich Mendelsohn house, his picture of which was then already half-finished; and another painting of De Morgan's House, within view of his own front door, with the possibility of others to come as a cycle in the sense of Monet's haystacks or Cézanne's views of Mont St Victoire.

Together with Kitaj's life drawings of the human figure, these are among his most refreshingly direct images, a fitting counterpoint in both mood and method to the more oblique strategies of his more characteristic synthetic formulations from existing images in league with the imagination. Unlike his friend Arikha, however, who has sought always to empty his consciousness of all knowledge in front of the motif, Kitaj even in these paintings of his neighbourhood has continued to allude to the interlocked origins of his pictures not only in direct observation but also in the stimulation offered by other art. On the most immediate level, for example, *The Oak Tree* (1991, pl. 173) is simply an image of his own garden, yet there is a Japanese quality to this picture in its flat arabesques traced against the sky. It is suggestive, moreover, of some of the pictures of trees painted by Mondrian shortly before World War I.[99] Kitaj readily admits to the possibility of their influence, at least on a subliminal level: 'I love those tree Mondrians and his pink-blue abstractions. He was surely on my mind.'

While these cityscapes represent something of a new departure for Kitaj, the figure and the dramas of human behaviour remained his most pressing subjects. In 1985 he began work on an entire sequence of paintings inspired by Shakespeare's *Hamlet* as a result of a commission from the Old Vic theatre in London for a permanent safety curtain. In the end his designs were not used, but they led him to further paintings inspired by the text.[100] He decided to represent Hamlet not only at different points in the unfolding of the drama, as in *Hamlet (Pretending Madness)* (1985) or in *Hamlet and his Father's Ghost (Study for the Old Vic)* (1986, pl. 166), one of the two paintings conceived specifically in the proportions of the drop curtain, but also in various guises: for example as *Yiddish Hamlet (Y. Löwy)* (1985), a largely invented figure, or as played by Raymond Massey (pl. 163), as found in a still from a book on the theatre.

In paintings such as *The Cézannist* (1980-5, pl. 159), *The Neo-Cubist* (1976-87, pl. 160), *The Drivist* (1985-7), *The Sniper* (1987), *The Caféist* (1980-7, pl. 165), *The Londonist* (1987) and *The Paintist* (1987) Kitaj added to the cast of characters that he had first proposed in the mid-1970s in single-figure paintings such as *The Arabist* (1975-6), *The Orientalist* (1975-6) and *The Sensualist* (1973-84) and even earlier in *Batman* (1973) and *Superman* (1973). In extending his single-figure inventions into new territory, sometimes as imaginary portraits and on other occasions as studies from life, Kitaj asserts that he had no plan but that 'They just evolved as characters in the stream of my painting life.' Nevertheless from *The Cézannist* onwards there are consistent allusions to the role of the painter, with references to some of the artists to whom Kitaj has been most devoted, that give these recent works a particular autobiographical thrust. This is true, too, of thematically related works such as *His Last Painting* (1987, pl. 172), in which the elderly Bonnard is viewed crouching over as he puts the finishing touches to his picture of a tree.[101] Another work, entitled simply *Painting* (1983–5, pl. 167), is an image of the artist as a kind of Neanderthal Man with subhuman intelligence, calling to mind the expression quoted by Duchamp in explaining his retirement from painting: 'bête comme un peintre'.

For *The Neo-Cubist* Kitaj reworked a more straightforwardly presented portrait of one of his most intimate artist friends, David Hockney, which he had commenced in 1976. The portrait as it stood was rare among his paintings in being charged with the directness of his drawings from life. Given his insistence at that time on the importance of life drawing of the human figure, and the closeness that he felt in this regard with his old friend Hockney, it is particularly striking that he decided to alter the image in this way rather than simply redrawing the figure as the basis for a new work. He agrees that he deemed it necessary to the meaning of the painting to bring together the two spheres to which he and Hockney alike were most devoted: that of direct observation and that of the imagination. Kitaj explains that there were other reasons, too, for the particular nature of the alterations: 'I wished to indicate his neo-cubism by a kind of disjunction arranged in the classic cubist oval device. There are other aspects: the recent death of Isherwood (can you see a bent superimposed head bowed in death?) and a general tragic sense (AIDS) as countertheme in that exotic California, which was weighing on him – disjunction again.'

Kitaj has been referred to by some writers in recent years as a post-modernist. If the term has any application in his case, it would be not on the grounds that he has turned his back on modernism, to which he is still in many ways devoted, but on the basis of his anachronistic interweavings of reference for symbolic purposes. As Kitaj explains:

The term [post-modernism] means very little to me. But, … it would depend on complex issues and definitions. For instance, if Cézanne in 1906, Degas in 1917, Kafka, Joyce, Eliot in 1925, Matisse in 1953, Picasso in 1971, Auerbach in 1991 etc., etc. are modernists then so am I. If not, not. If post-modernism means that the stranglehold of Greenberg/Duchamp/Warhol/Beuys et al on post-war art and theory is now balanced by other bloodlines, well, maybe there's an interesting case for the term post-modernism. If, as I suspect, a modernist impetus has become institutionalized, if the interesting legacies of the great formalist and dadaist years have created a new *Pompier* Art then I would hope and pray to be post-*that*.[102]

Whatever usefulness the term post-modernist may have in describing Kitaj's outlook, it makes only as much sense in relation to his recent work as it does to the whole of his production since his student days in Oxford and London thirty years earlier. One of his most ambitious recent paintings, for example, *Against Slander* (1990-1, pl. 171), provides evidence above all of his growing mastery as a draughtsman and his emphatic conviction about the central role of drawing in his paintings.[103] Nevertheless there is no doubt that its deft mixture of idioms is very much of a piece conceptually with the strategies he had employed in a much earlier picture such as *The Red Banquet* (1960), in which a spartan architecture had likewise provided a coherent setting for figures in a variety of techniques bordering at times on caricature.[104] The grotesque visages spouting their slanderous bile at each other, Kitaj's admonition to himself and to others not to speak evil of anyone, including oneself, are like the vivid ghosts that populate all our lives.[105] Here, as in other pictures, Kitaj's own past as an artist – for which he himself has often had such harsh words – seems to have crept up on him unawares, reminding him and his audience alike of the threads of continuity tying together one of the most diverse and wide-ranging bodies of work produced by any painter in the latter half of the twentieth century.

The Last of England

In the summer of 1994 Kitaj's first full-scale retrospective in Britain opened at the Tate Gallery in London. He had been approached about doing such a show in the early 1990s by the director, Nicholas Serota, a longstanding admirer who more than a decade before had been disappointed in his wish to bring the 1981 Hirshhorn retrospective to the Whitechapel Art Gallery in London. The invitation and the challenge it represented inspired Kitaj, who until then had been known for his slow and painstaking methods, to begin working more quickly. The period from 1990 to 1994 was extraordinarily productive for him in terms of paintings: there were 35 canvases from this period in the Tate show alone, and another 64 recent paintings and drawings in the solo show at Marlborough Fine Art in London that opened at the same time.

With this drastically increased rate of production came a corresponding change in style to a much looser, more spontaneous manner corresponding to his notion of 'painting-drawing'.[106] He had been fond of quoting Degas's description of himself as 'the least spontaneous of men' and had also remarked in 1980 that he had enough ideas for paintings to last him the rest of his life. Yet suddenly he had a torrent of new ideas which he was able to unleash in a more rapid style of execution, an extension of the expressionistic manner that he had introduced in the early 1980s. Some works take up earlier themes, as in the case of *The Third Time (Savannah, Georgia)* (1992, pl. 183), another episode in his retelling of his youthful sexual experiences.

Glance (1991-2, fig. 15) reworks the sexually-charged encounter between strangers seen in earlier pictures such as *The Street (A Life)* (1975, pl. 136) or *Smyrna Greek (Nikos)* (1976-7, pl. 122); he describes it in the following terms: 'A seated woman and a male

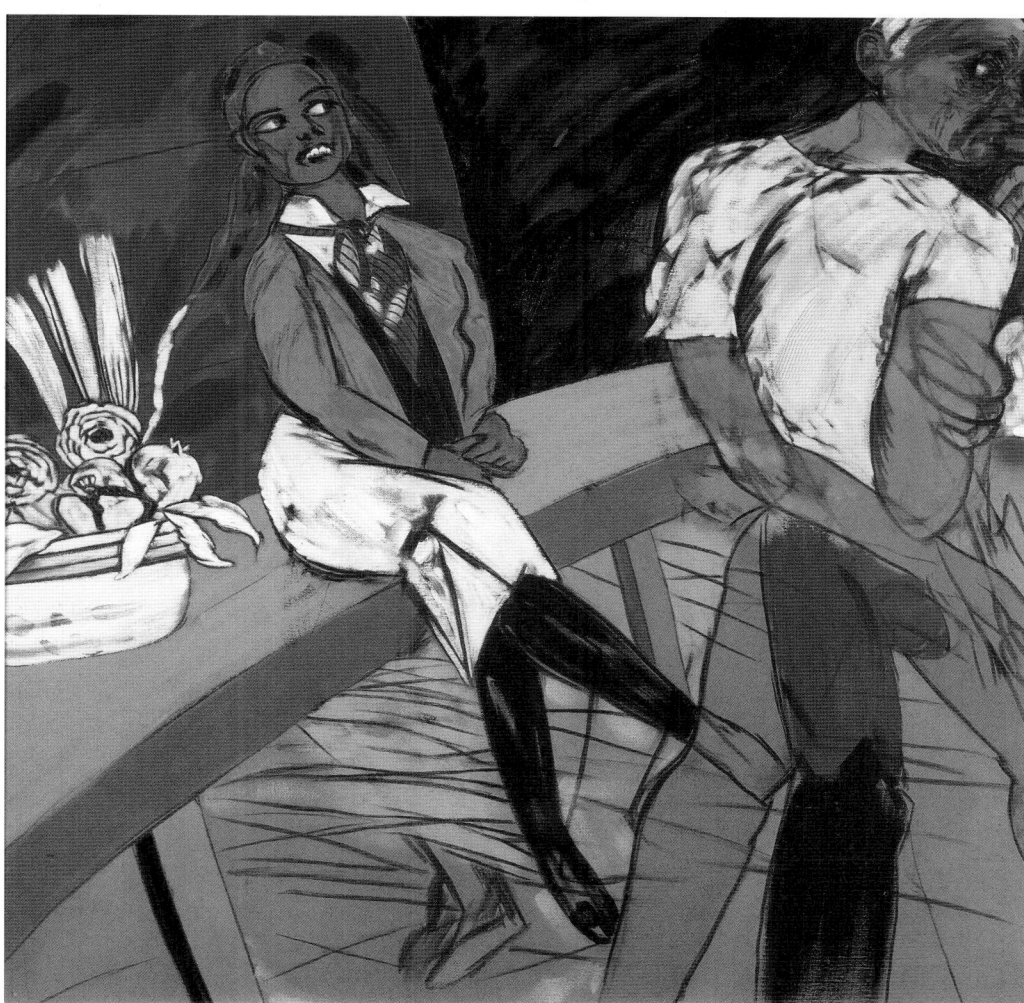

Fig. 15. *Glance*, 1991-2. *Cat. no. 519*

passerby are *glancing* at each other – That's all!' Others, such as the mysterious interior called simply *The Flat* (1993, pl. 190), suggest new directions as yet barely explored. Two of the most memorable paintings of this period were inspired in part by favourite works in London's National Gallery. The first of these, *Women and Men* (1991-3, pl. 186), his most blatant exposition to date of the timeless drama of the battle between the sexes, was prompted by an early work by Degas, *The Young Spartans*, which Kitaj referred to in his catalogue essay as 'my second favourite painting in London' (see below, pp. 196-7).[107] The second work, treated as an even more broadly comic but affectionate parody, is *Western Bathers* (1993-4, pl. 187), a brilliant conflation of two artistic forms that have long inspired him: Cézanne's late paintings of Bathers, including above all the National Gallery's *Large Bathers* of 1894-1905,[108] and the Hollywood Western.

The shift in Kitaj's style must in part have been attributable to the urgency he felt about the impending Tate show, but may have been affected also by a feeling that as he was getting older time was running out and he needed to paint more quickly and therefore in a more impetuous way. When he was barely in his mid-forties, he had already begun dreaming of moving on to his 'old-age' style. There is a degree perhaps to which he willed himself to make a strong visible shift in his work away from the characteristic style that he had by then made his own. His consciousness of making the most of the time left to him, as he reflected on the adventures of his life, even became the subject of paintings, as in *My Cities (An Experimental Drama)* (1990-3, pl. 188), in which he depicts himself with humorous self-awareness at three different stages of his life – as a robust young man, in somewhat infirm middle age and finally as an old man unable to remain standing – walking a kind of gangplank over a baseball dugout sheltering some of his demons.[109]

Fig. 16. *Bad Sinus*, 1990-2. *Cat. no. 517*

Fig. 17. *Bad Character*, 1990-3. *Cat. no. 537*

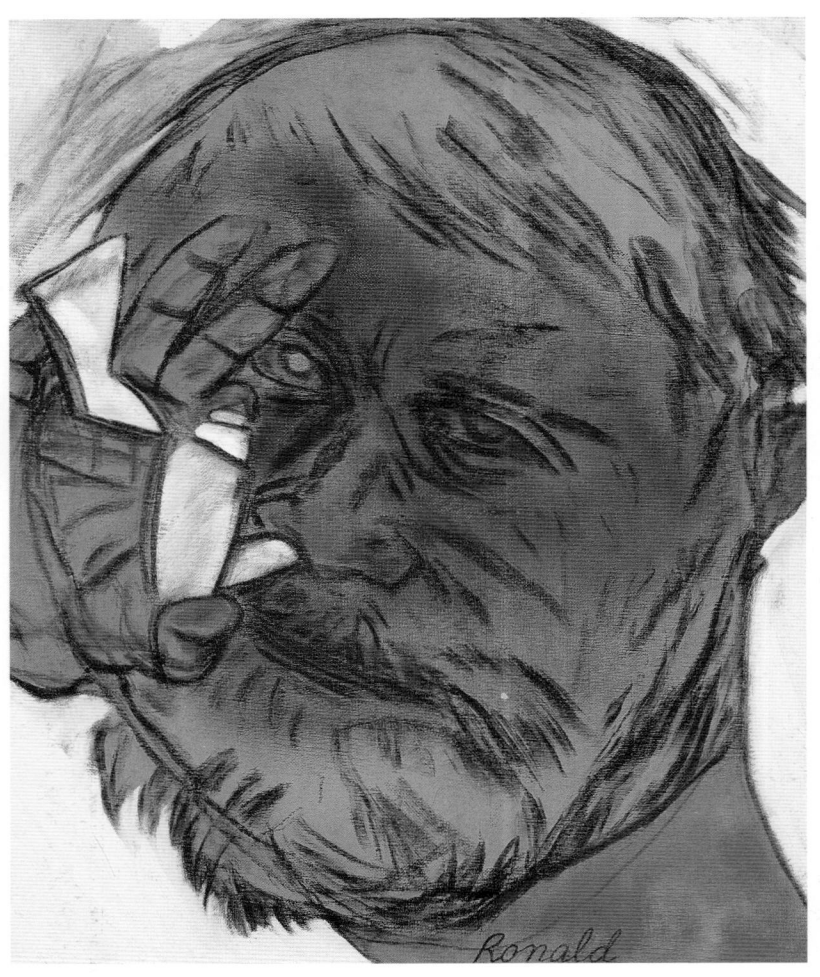

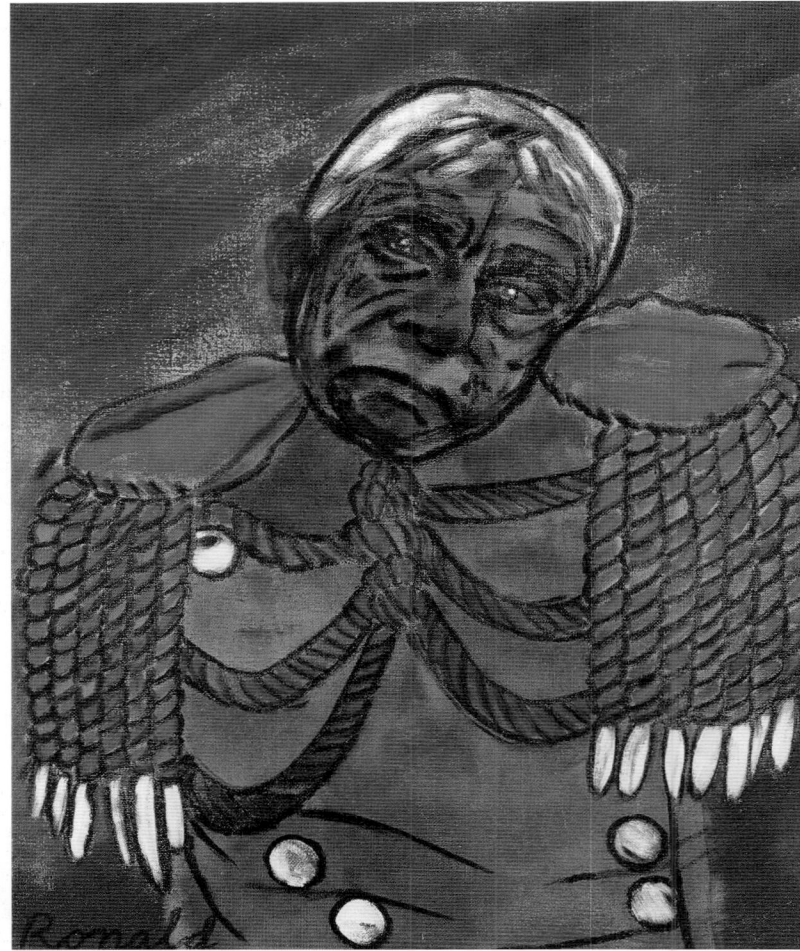

In 1990 Kitaj began work on a series of small canvases, each measuring about 24 x 20 inches, in which he represented himself in a self-deprecating way as a grumpy old man suffering from one affliction or another: *Bad Back, Bad Eyes, Bad Foot, Bad Thoughts, Bad Sinus* (fig. 16), *Bad Knee, Bad Heart, Bad Teeth, Bad Hearing* and (on his own admission) *Bad Character* (fig. 17). The titles, one long *kvetch* about his real and imaginary ailments, underline the comic overtones of a man whose dry sense of humour was not about to desert him just because his body was showing signs of deterioration.[110] However much he seemed to be dwelling on the prospect of his mortality, the paintings he produced during the early 1990s suggest that this was a happy and optimistic time for him and that he was in an unusually relaxed and buoyant mood. As he recalled in 1999:[111]

I think I had about 3 years to prepare for the Tate show. And, yes, I was jolted into action. I felt inspired, encouraged, and I worked harder – I think most artists do that; I've noticed that they do before important shows. Auerbach thought the last room was the best and I love to listen to his opinions.[…] And Sandra and I were more deeply in love than ever before, as if we had little time left together … Those years before the Tate War were a blessing, a doomed blessing.

Many artists get less tight as they grow older. No one knows why. An older artist's vision seems to loosen – Michelangelo, Titian, Rembrandt, Degas, Goya, Cézanne, Turner, Monet and so on. I'm not in that league, but neither are Duchamp, Warhol and Beuys. I think many good painters don't wish to repeat the exactitude of their youth. Freud and Hockney and I are examples. But you're right, I did have a torrent of new ideas – history will judge me.

The 'Tate War' to which Kitaj refers, and about which he has written a long essay which is yet to be published, was by any standards one of the most disgraceful episodes in the recent history of controversies surrounding contemporary art.[112] Although the show proved popular with the general public during its London run and was well received when it travelled to the Los Angeles County Museum of Art and the Metropolitan Museum of Art in New York, a small number of London critics attacked it with a vehement destructiveness that was shocking and distasteful even to those who were not known to be particular supporters of Kitaj's work. The unusually personal tone of the worst of these mean-spirited articles – which not only failed to find a single virtue in his art but also seemed tainted with antisemitism, xenophobia and envy of his success and status in the British art world – made it evident that their aim was nothing less than to destroy him and his career.

Though he had longstanding enemies in England and had been attacked by them before, Kitaj was of course much affected by the relentless hatred displayed in reviews that appeared in some of the national papers. The worst was yet to come: only a couple of weeks after the Tate show closed, on 19 September 1994, his wife Sandra died suddenly and unexpectedly of an aneurysm on the brain at the age of only 47. Since she, too, had clearly suffered greatly from such vitriol, Kitaj not unreasonably came to the conclusion that she had died from the stress caused by these critics, whom he came to regard as her murderers. What should have been the crowning glory of his life as an artist in England became, instead, the occasion for tragic events from which he will never fully recover.

Some of the most important paintings produced in the build-up to the Tate exhibition, such as *Against Slander* (1990-1, pl. 171), proved unnervingly prophetic of Kitaj's life during and after the Tate War. This is true even of the most tender in mood, such as *The Wedding* (1989-93, pl. 185), a composite memory image of his marriage to Sandra in 1983. In *I and Thou* (1990-2, pl. 182) the artist depicts himself in quasi-rabbinical mode as his young son's companion and educator, while in *Father Reading Tom Sawyer to his Son* (1994, pl. 191), chosen as the cover illustration for the Marlborough show that coincided

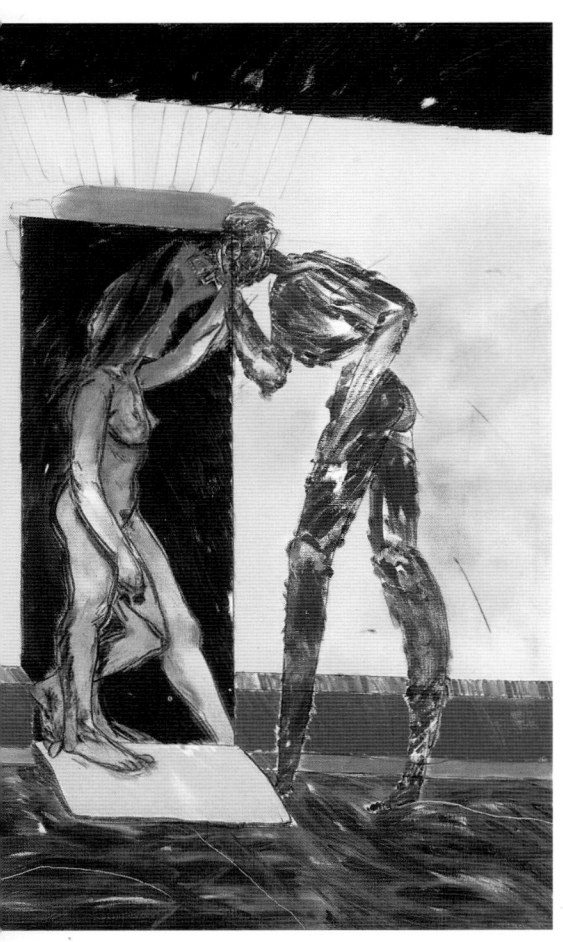

Fig. 18. *She and He (La Vie)*, 1994. *Cat. no. 585*

with the Tate retrospective, he seeks to pass on his enthusiasm for literature; although both these pictures were painted when Max was looked after more by his mother, after Sandra's death it is impossible not to respond to them as images of father and son brought closer by their mutual loss. Nor is this the only instance of a sad confirmation of Kitaj's longstanding belief that interpretations of earlier works inevitably will be subject to constant revision. *The Sculptor* (1992, pl. 184) is even more haunting as a kind of premonition of the gloom and solitude to come. Here the deceased wife of the fictional artist, eerily echoing the position in which Fisher was shown only a year earlier in *Unpacking My Library* (fig. 14), appears in the doorway as a mirage, in Kitaj's own words 'calling to him [...] just like she used to call him to put his tools down, wash up and get ready for the evening movie they would watch on television.' As described in Kitaj's text for the Tate catalogue (see below, p. 196), written when there was no reason to suspect that his vibrant young wife would not outlive him, his identification with the artist depicted is clear.

In the immediate aftermath of Sandra's death, Kitaj was understandably too depressed to make any new work. But when he did return to the studio, it was to do what many of his friends felt he was particularly well-equipped to do given the intimate self-exposure of his recent work: to pay homage to the woman whose beauty, joie de vivre and affectionate nature had sustained him for more than twenty years. In the first of these he memorialized her in paintings he had started while she was alive. *He and She (The Sickness unto Death)* (pl. 196) and *She and He (La Vie)*,[113] both of 1994, remain among his most poignant memorials to her: in the former they sit, face to face, his arms reaching out to grasp the naked flesh still so fresh in his memory; in the latter (fig. 18) the woman's face appears already to have left her body as she reaches forward to give her husband one last kiss.[114] The confessional strain in Kitaj's recent art also took an unexpected new twist with the thinly disguised transformation of the artist into the central character of the novel *Sabbath's Theater* by his old friend Philip Roth.[115]

Having vowed after the Tate débâcle not to show his work again in London, Kitaj came to see the Royal Academy's annual Summer Exhibition as a forum through which to present occasional glimpses of his work to a large and decidedly unspecialized audience.[116] In fact, the contempt habitually expressed by British art critics for this show (as an indigestible mixture of the old-fashioned, the mediocre and the occasional good work) almost certainly added to its attractions as a venue as far as he was concerned. In the 1996 Summer Exhibition he presented a painting with collage on which he wrote the phrase 'THE CRITIC KILLS' and which he co-signed 'Ron and Sandra', conceiving it as the first issue of a magazine bearing Sandra's name that would continue to take many forms: not just as printed publications, as in the case of the second[117] and fourth issues,[118] but also as paintings and temporary installations.

Soon after returning to work, Kitaj had become engrossed in the subject of 'Revenge Tragedies' as fuel for new pictures in which he could vent some of his anger at the people who ruined his life:

Revenge Tragedy is a well-known tradition or genre in literature, drama and movies. Of course it attracted me because I want to Fight Back. The term is often associated with the Elizabethan dramatists – Shakespeare and the lesser ones, Kyd, Marlowe, Tourneur and Chapman ... but it goes back to Greece and Rome ... all blood and guts which suited my mood toward my enemies. But those plays were not only deadly; they bored me – I couldn't use the language. However, the concept of Revenge plus Tragedy has entered into my ideas for the art of easel painting, like a heretofore neglected genre in the painting art. All the while, Revenge is a great ongoing noir and Western movie device, convention etc. which I draw upon. The Revenger takes matters into his own hands, because, as in my case, one can't fight a Yellow Press on equal terms. Someone said that the defectiveness of the status quo is virtually a precondition of the Revenge drama ...

Hamlet to Clint Eastwood! In any case, Revenge drama appeals to my various senses of what easel-painting can do now. As to having ruined my life – We'll see – the War ain't over till it's over, to paraphrase Yogi Berra.

The most obvious outcome of this obsession with revenge was the *Sandra Three* installation at the Royal Academy Summer Exhibition in 1997 (fig. 19), and in particular the painting *The Killer-Critic Assassinated by His Widower, Even* (1997, pl. 193). Here the artist, fortified in his righteous battle by the presence of Manet in his final illness (after the amputation of his gangrenous leg), takes aim at the monstrous critics whose bilious prose has threatened his very existence. Kitaj clearly took great pleasure in throwing back at his critics all the aspects of his art to which they had expressed such violent objection. Pretentious allusions to great works from the history of art? Then why not base the entire composition on Manet's *The Execution of Maximilian* (1868), itself a paraphrase of Goya's *The Executions of the 3rd of May* (1814) and add further references to modern masterpieces, such as the phrase *'Ma Jolie'* (from Picasso's Cubist portraits) and the allusion to Duchamp's *The Bride Stripped Bare by her Bachelors, Even* (1915-23) in the very title? Too literary, too full of quotations, too self-serving in his self-alignment with great writers and artists? That is just an invitation to write some favourite quotes directly onto the canvas surface, or better yet revise them to his own ends – as in his brazen correction of 'from' to 'to' in T.S. Eliot's aphorism 'Art is the escape from personality – and append to that already sated surface provocatively titled book covers as collage elements. Too crude, sexual and violent? So he displays himself as a rapacious old man with dripping prostate. Too obsessed with his Jewishness? Well, then, he will substitute the Hebrew initial for his surname in place of his head. What could the final outrage be? Oh, yes, a success unwarranted in the eyes of his enemies. In that case, he will make public an outrageously high price of £1 million for the work.[119] Of course, some of the same critics took the bait and failed to see the humour interlaced with the demented rage and lust for revenge. The book spine pasted at an angle from the artist's body, like a second phallus, reads: 'Nice Guys Finish Last.' But Kitaj had the last laugh, quickly finding buyers for both the *Killer-Critic* (sold to one of the museums that have shown him such support) and

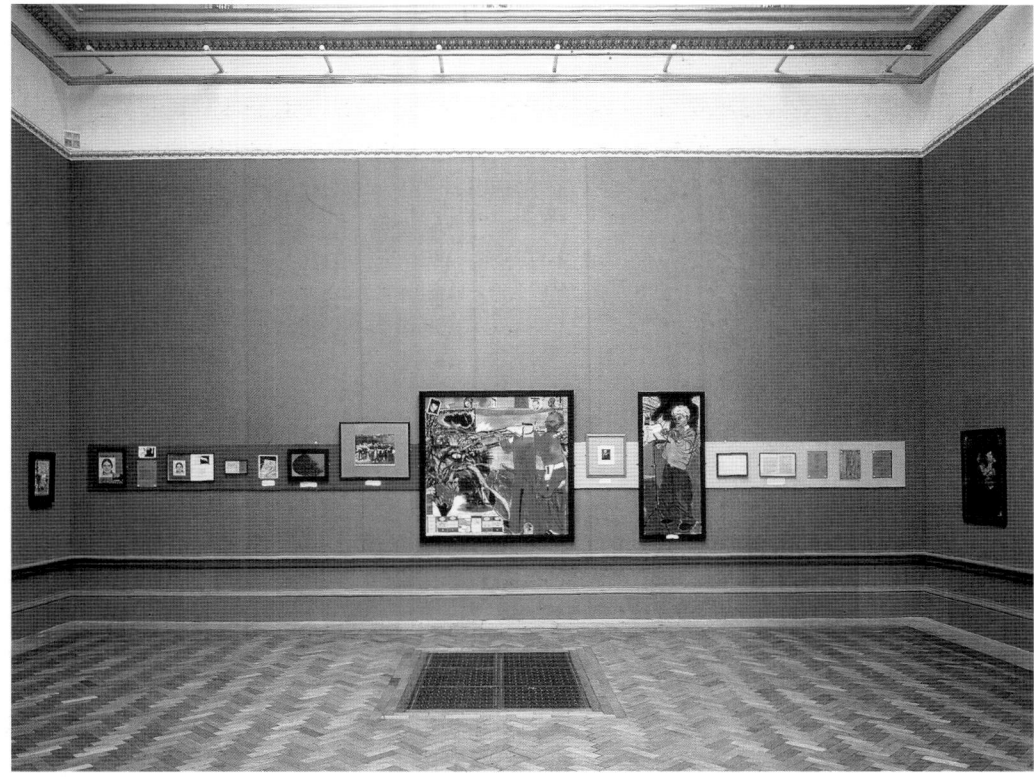

Fig. 19. *Sandra Three,* installation at the Royal Academy, London, 1997

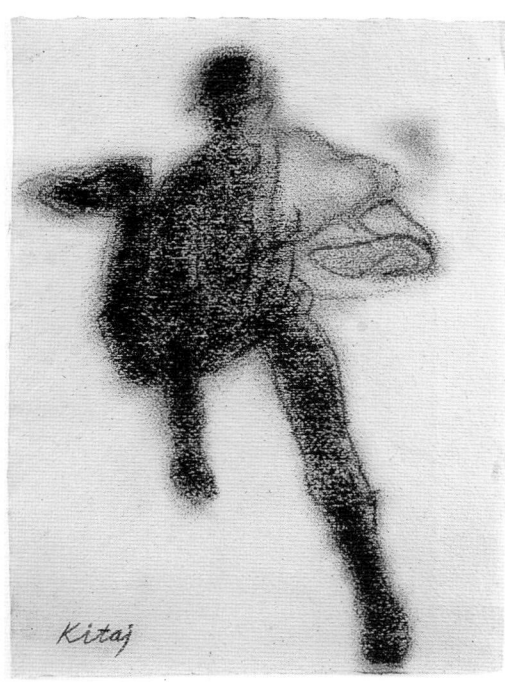

Fig. 20. *Death Pitches a Curve (My First American Picture)*, 1997. *Cat. no. 635*

the other major painted element, the gentle portrait of Max as *The Violinist with the Spirit of his Mother* (1997, pl. 192).

In July 1997, just after *Sandra Three* went on display and almost forty years after he had first settled in England, Kitaj and his young son Max left London for good, moving to Los Angeles to be near relatives and friends including the artist's elder son Lem and his new family. The very first picture he made after his arrival was a tiny sketch, *Death Pitches a Curve (My First American Picture)*, (1997, fig. 20) which combines baseball imagery and the confrontations with mortality that have increasingly preoccupied him since his heart attack and especially since Sandra's death. Much of his first year in southern California was spent acclimatizing himself, organizing his life, refurbishing the Spanish Colonial style house he had purchased in Westwood Village and converting the garage into a studio. Then he was ready to put his art back on course.

Kitaj began painting and drawing again as soon as he could, and though little of his work was seen in England a retrospective of paintings and drawings that toured Europe throughout 1998 gave him a strong presence in countries that had been particularly important to him either for personal reasons or because of the themes of his work: Spain, Austria and Germany. The exhibition, for which I served as curator at Kitaj's suggestion, was initiated by the Astrup Fearnley Museum of Modern Art in Oslo, whose impressive collection of postwar art was formed by the most passionately committed private collector of Kitaj's works, Hans Rasmus Astrup. It was Astrup himself, in fact, who proposed the exhibition to the artist in the immediate aftermath of the Tate show, wishing to lend his moral and practical support in this way. Once out of the poisonous atmosphere by which he had been surrounded in London because of the 'Tate War', Kitaj was able to return to a calmer mood in his work. The first sign of change visible to a British audience was his relatively modest contribution to the Royal Academy's 1998 Summer Exhibition, in the form of an old self-portrait lithograph reworked with pastel and collage, entitled *The Enemy Within* (1990-8): the angry distorted face looming inside the contours of his features in more reflective mood acknowledge here, for the first time, that the troubles he suffers are at least partly the product of his own combative nature.

Second Diasporist Manifesto (Marx Brothers) (1997-8, pl. 195)[120] was the first major painting on which Kitaj began work after moving to Los Angeles and getting his new studio in order. This picture of the Marx Brothers and Margaret Dumont[121] cavorting by the side of a swimming pool and Spanish Colonial house combines two important aspects of what the city, and specifically Hollywood, represented to him: the home of the film industry, of course, and of the Jews and European exiles who contributed so much to it;[122] and the city so memorably documented in the paintings of his friend Hockney. Los Angeles has many detractors (New Yorkers in particular) who tend to say that it is a place devoid of culture, but Kitaj points out – through these references to the cinema and painting – the ways in which it most certainly has contributed in important ways to the aesthetic life of the twentieth century.[123] 'Hollywood is fun,' Kitaj remarks, 'and of course it begins to re-invent my pictures.' The Spanish Colonial arcade in *Second Diasporist Manifesto*, together with the swimming pool and palm tree, are not invented but studied from his own house in Westwood Village: in that sense they are a celebration of the environment in which he and his son began creating their new life.

Since settling in Los Angeles, Kitaj has wasted no time in reaffirming his devotion to the human figure. Three of the most memorable paintings created during his first two years in Los Angeles – *The Cleveland Indian* (1995-8, pl. 194)[124] *Circumcision Chair* (1998, pl. 197) and *The Archaeologist* (1997-8, pl. 199)[125] – all make use of the elongated vertical format with which Kitaj had framed many of his single figure inventions since the mid-1970s. Kitaj chose the format for *Circumcision Chair* because it suited the elongated dimensions of the chair, but also because he saw the object as in some way a personage in itself, an inanimate but explicitly Jewish stand-in for the figure.[126] The continuing centrality of the human figure is evident also in *Moonlightist* (1998, pl. 198), a portrait of the nineteenth-century American painter Albert Pynkham Ryder,[127] and *Koufax* (1999, pl. 201), Kitaj's homage to the great baseball player whom he sees now as part of his pantheon of Jewish heroes.[128] From the collaged French revolutionary slogan of 'LIBERTÉ, EGALITÉ, FRATERNITÉ', one may conclude that the figure of *The Parist* (1997-8, pl. 200) derives from the name of the French capital. 'I took the figure from a really *tiny* man in a photo of Paris said to be the FIRST human ever photographed! Around 1839.'[129] Contrary to appearances, he is not striding forward but holding a pose: 'He must have had to stand *very* still in those early days. I'm very surprised that this photo is not better known given its claim to be the FIRST one. I did the painting and I'm also doing a drawing of the guy I call PARIST.'

At the Royal Academy Summer Exhibition that opened its doors to the public in June 1999, Kitaj presented *Sandra 5*: a large multipartite work again named in homage to his late wife and conceived as the latest 'issue' of the theoretical and polemical magazine that he had started in her memory. This installation consisted of three paintings hung with their frames edge to edge: at the left, *Mendelsohn House* (1988-9, pl. 189); in the centre, *Bed and Sofa (After Abram Room)* (1998, pl. 202); and at the right, *Sandra 5* (1999). The blocks of colour that surround Sandra Fisher's collaged image in the separate canvas entitled *Sandra 5* read as a comment on Constructivist abstraction. But the painting is also conceived as the cover of a magazine, explicitly identified as such by the presence of the title 'Sandra 5' along the top edge, 'special issue' along the diagonal line of the triangle in the lower right, and 'Jewish art and xenophobia' as the theme. Suddenly, through the use of language here, the subtexts of the adjoining two paintings are brought to the fore: both the architect Erich Mendelsohn (1887-1953) and the film-maker Abram Room were Jews whose creativity somehow triumphed against the odds and in spite of the barriers erected for them. Mendelsohn left Germany on Hitler's rise to power in 1933 and came to England via Holland, having already established a considerable reputation with his Expressionist experiment the Einstein Tower (1919-24) in Potsdam and striking department stores and office buildings in an elegant and refined modernist style. His De La Warr Pavilion of 1933-4 in Bexhill, one of the buildings he designed in collaboration with the Ukrainian Serge Chermayeff (1889-1951), is one of the acknowledged masterpieces of 1930s architecture in England. But like Mondrian and so many other European modernists who temporarily settled in England but quickly moved on to the United States when they found themselves neglected and unappreciated, Mendelsohn was able to produce little in the way of actual buildings during his short time in Britain. In the late 1920s he had run one of the largest and most successful architectural firms in Europe, yet his three-year partnership with Chermayeff, from 1933 to 1936, resulted in the construction of only three buildings. The last of them, the subject of Kitaj's painting, was built as the Cohen House on Old Church Street in Chelsea, near the junction with Elm Park Road, where Kitaj had bought his house in 1972. Mendelsohn's sleek, low-lying concrete, steel and glass building, a very rare example in British residential architecture of such uncompromising modernism, later became the home of the publisher Paul Hamlyn, brother of Kitaj's friend the poet Michael Hamburger. Kitaj passed the house often on his walks – it faces the rather grand house once occupied by the Arts and Crafts potter William De Morgan, the subject of Kitaj's 1991 painting *De Morgan's House* (pl. 178) – but never managed to see it inside.

In many ways, and not just in its spontaneously brushed surfaces, *Mendelsohn House*, like *Sandra 5* itself, is a play on the language of geometric abstraction and on abstract paintings based on colour relationships. Using the International Style architecture of the 1930s house to support an affectionate play on the language of Constructivism, he restates his affiliation to modernism in defiance of those who would accuse him of reactionary tendencies. Although started many years before he knew he would be leaving England, the fact that he was able to finish this painting after moving to Los Angeles reveals that there is at least a trace of feeling for the home life he enjoyed in Chelsea for more than 25 years.

Kitaj took his inspiration for *Bed and Sofa*, which in the *Sandra 5* installation served as the central element linking the other two paintings, from a highly regarded early Soviet film of the same title by a Jewish Director called Abram Room.[130] 'It is said to be his masterpiece before the Soviet crackdown. I'm told *Bed + Sofa* is still taught in film schools. The images I saw were in my full set of *Close Up*, the very rare and maybe best movie magazine, published in London in the twenties. I made up the forms of the bed and sofa in my picture.' In spite of its acknowledged source, it is impossible to avoid reading the motif – with both bed and sofa portrayed as empty – as anything other than a reflection on the loss of his wife, his solitude as a widower, and the weary sadness of absence. Temporarily viewed together as a single work, the three elements of *Sandra 5* constitute a persuasive restatement of Kitaj's affiliations and identity. His triumvirate of isms – modernism, Judaism and diasporism – are once again seen as closely interrelated, presided over by the loneliness of aesthetic singlemindedness and personal exile.

Kitaj has said many times that 'London died for me when Sandra died.' It is perfectly understandable why he no longer wanted to live in the city he had made his home for nearly forty years, in spite of having such close artist friends integrated into his life there. But he had always looked to Europe, even before going there as a student, and had seen himself as part of a lineage of expatriate Americans whose cultural allegiances were to the Old World and who put down their roots there. In spirit, there must be part of him still in Europe.[131] Now that he can be described as an expatriate repatriated to his homeland, he may have to reconsider his whole identity as a person and more particularly as an artist.

'I *still* have a lot of ideas back home in California. And, yes, I feel that life is too short. I'm an old man now […] I do revisit Europe in imagination and dreams, but not much – I'm too busy getting on with my Third Act.'

THE PLATES

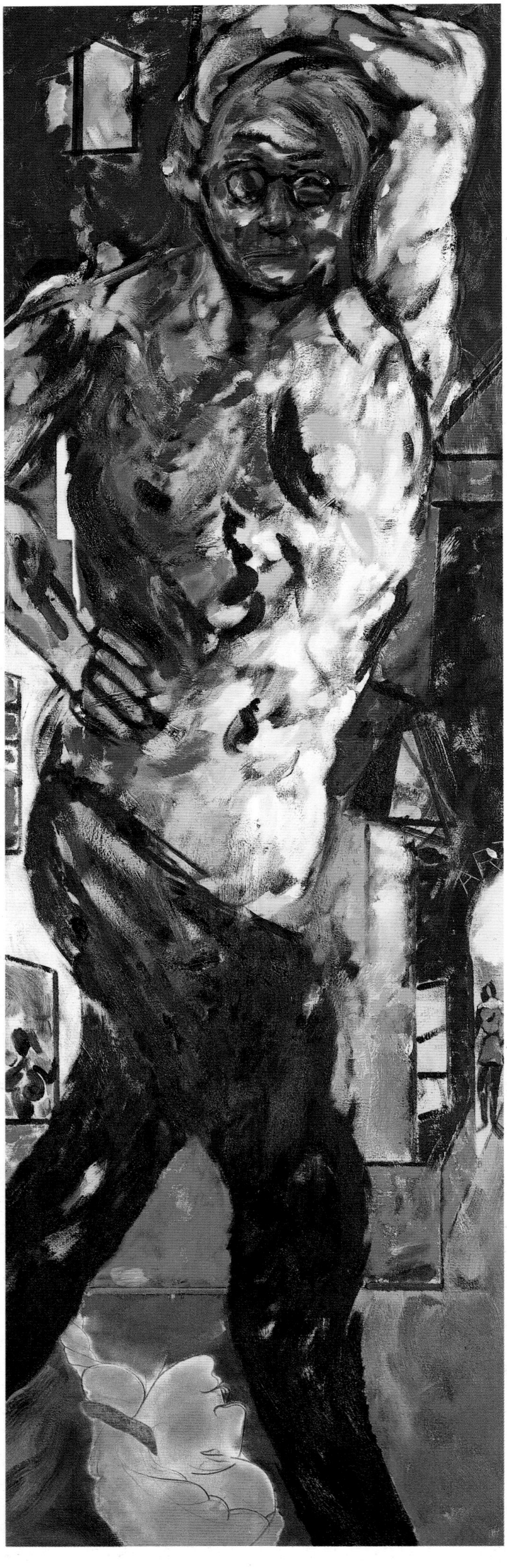

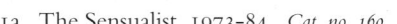

1a. The Sensualist, 1973–84. *Cat. no. 160.*

1. Erasmus Variations, 1958. *Cat. no. 3.*

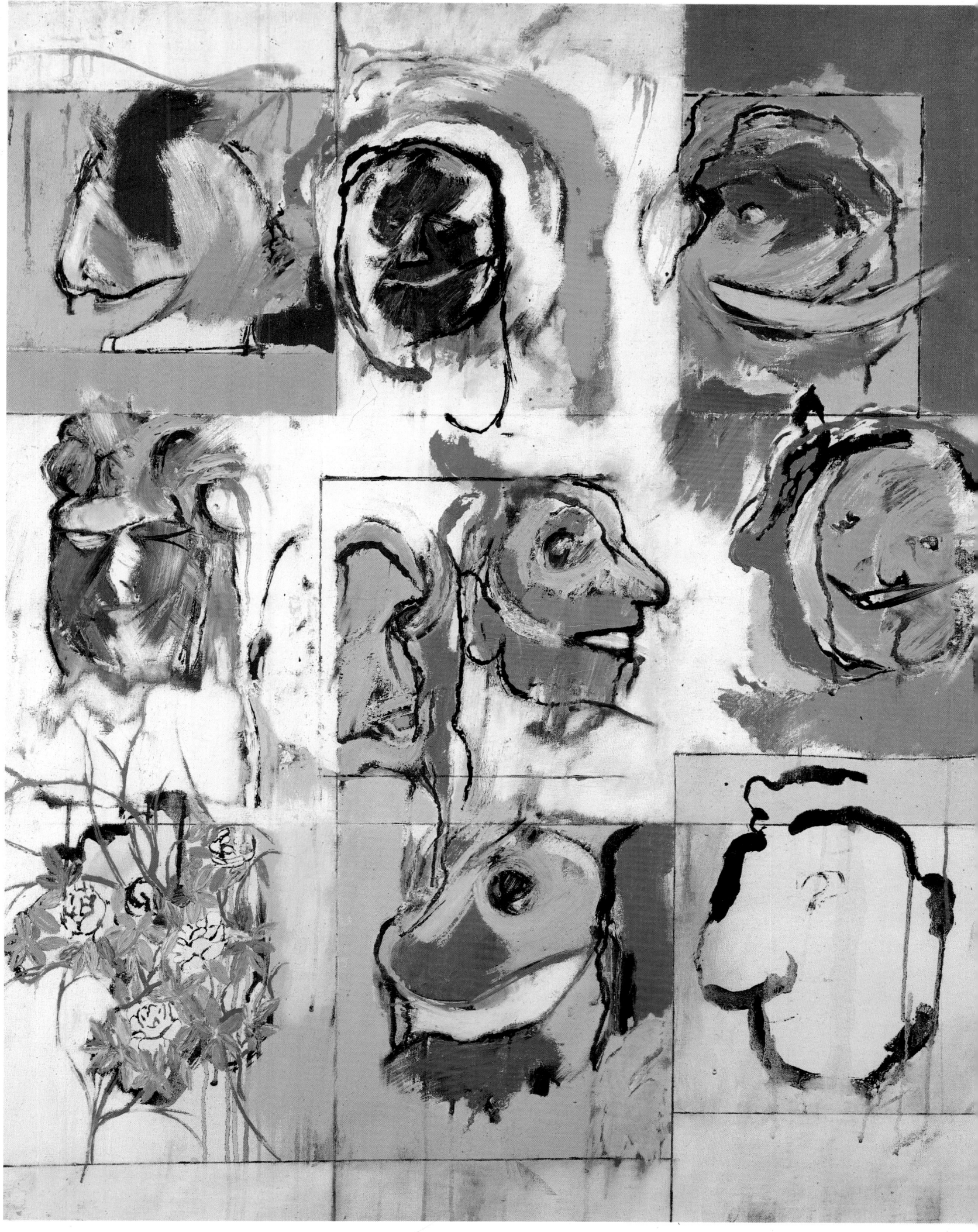

2. Miss Ivy Cavendish (Oxford), 1958. *Cat. no. 4.*

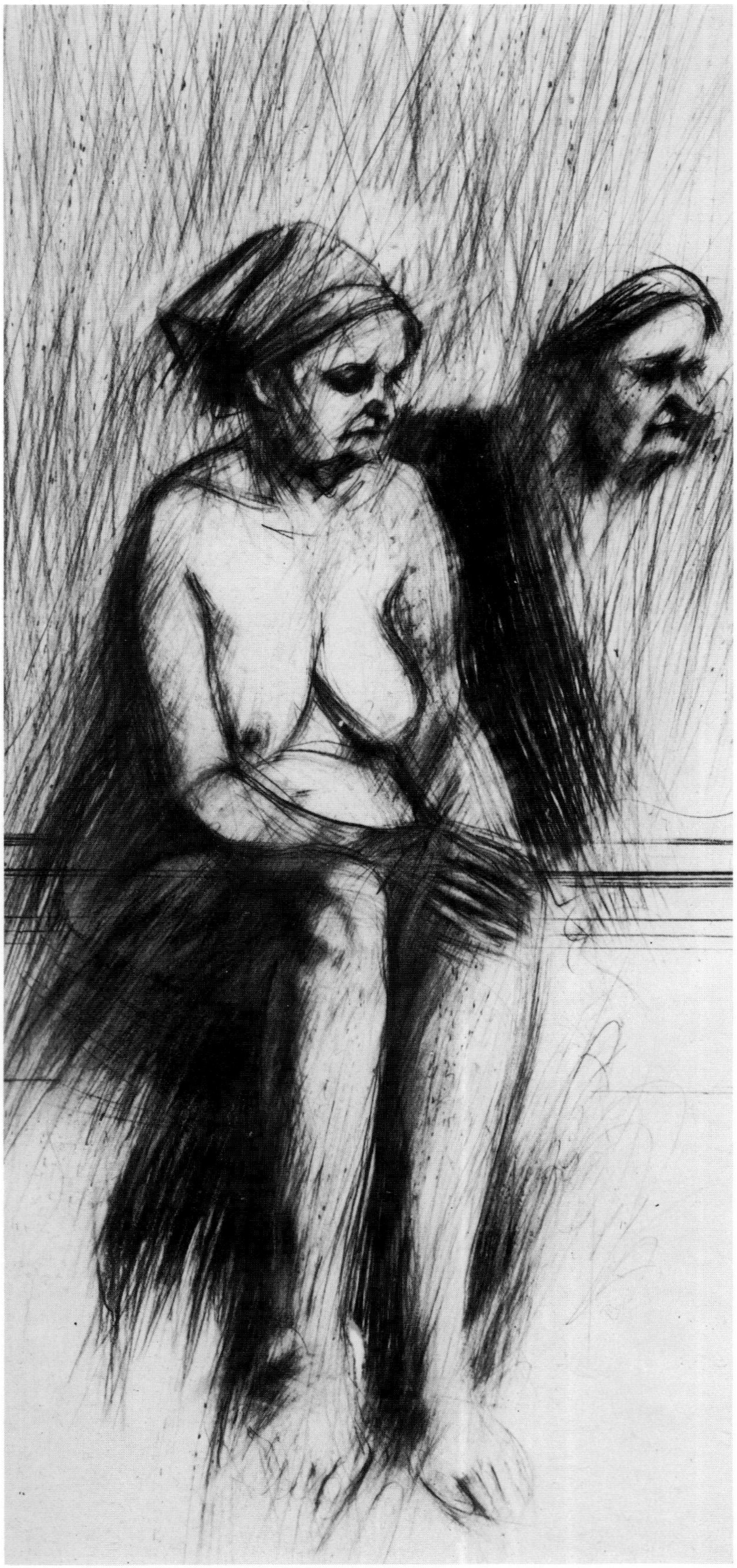

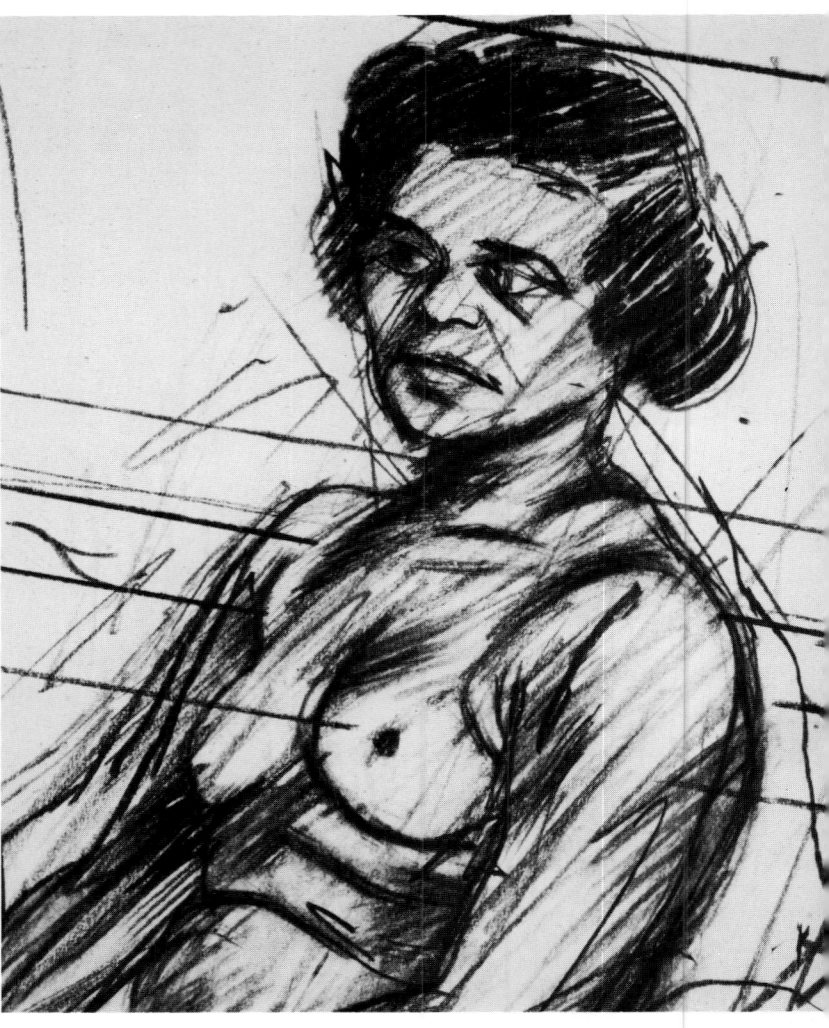

3. Oxford Woman, c.1958. *Cat. no. 500.*

4. Tarot Variations, 1958. *Cat. no. 2.*

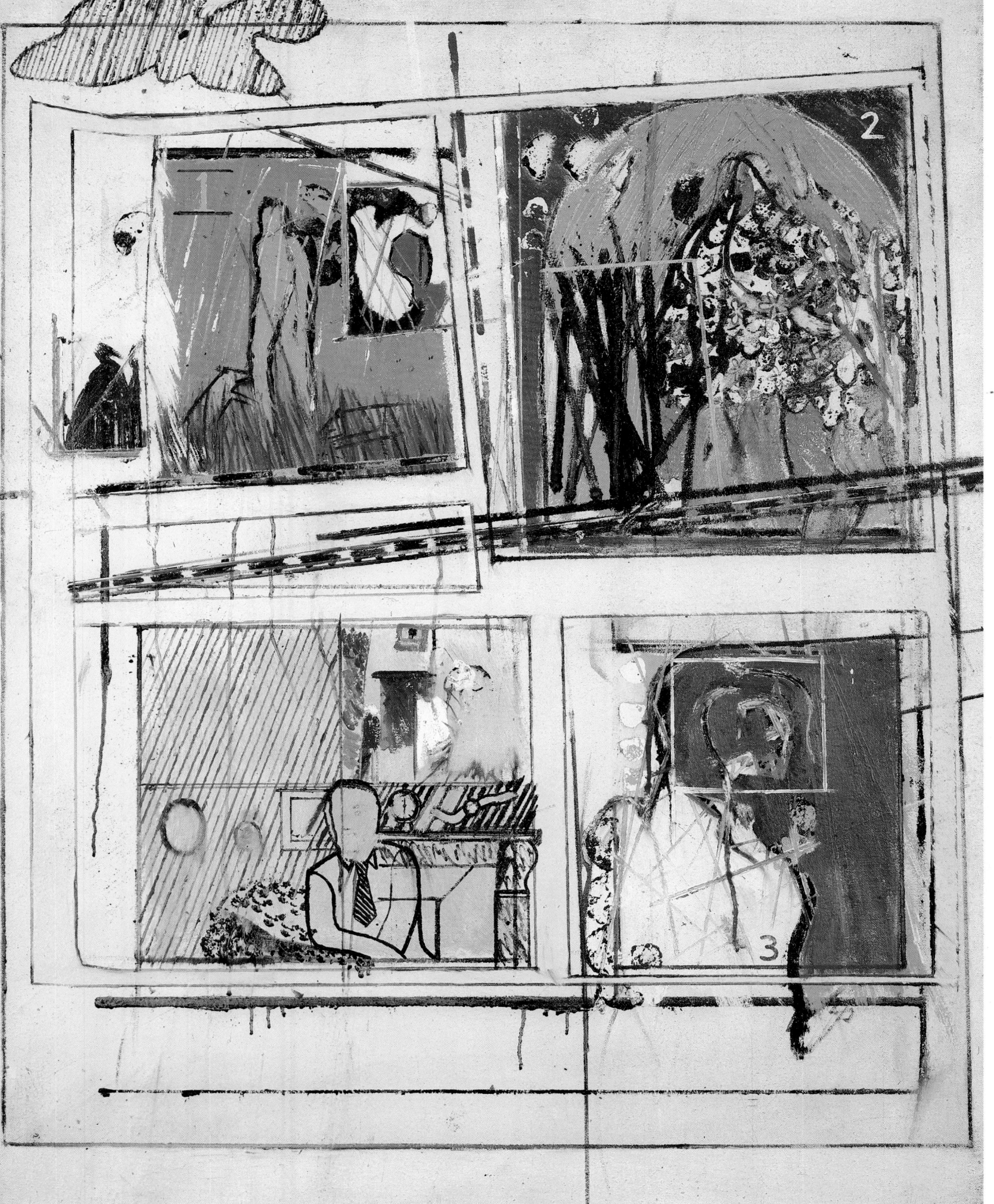

7. Words, 1959. *Cat. no. 8.*

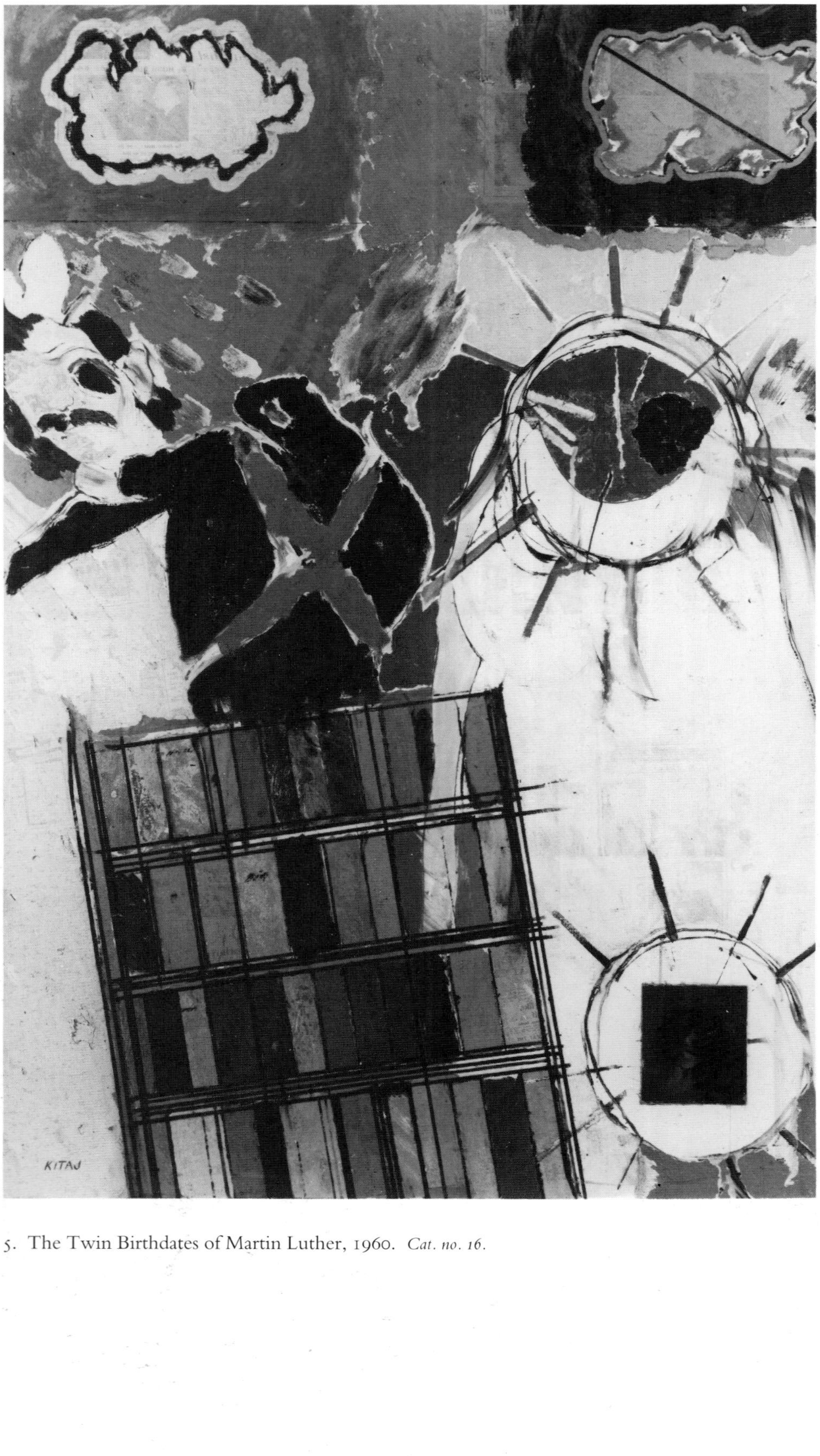

5. The Twin Birthdates of Martin Luther, 1960. *Cat. no. 16.*

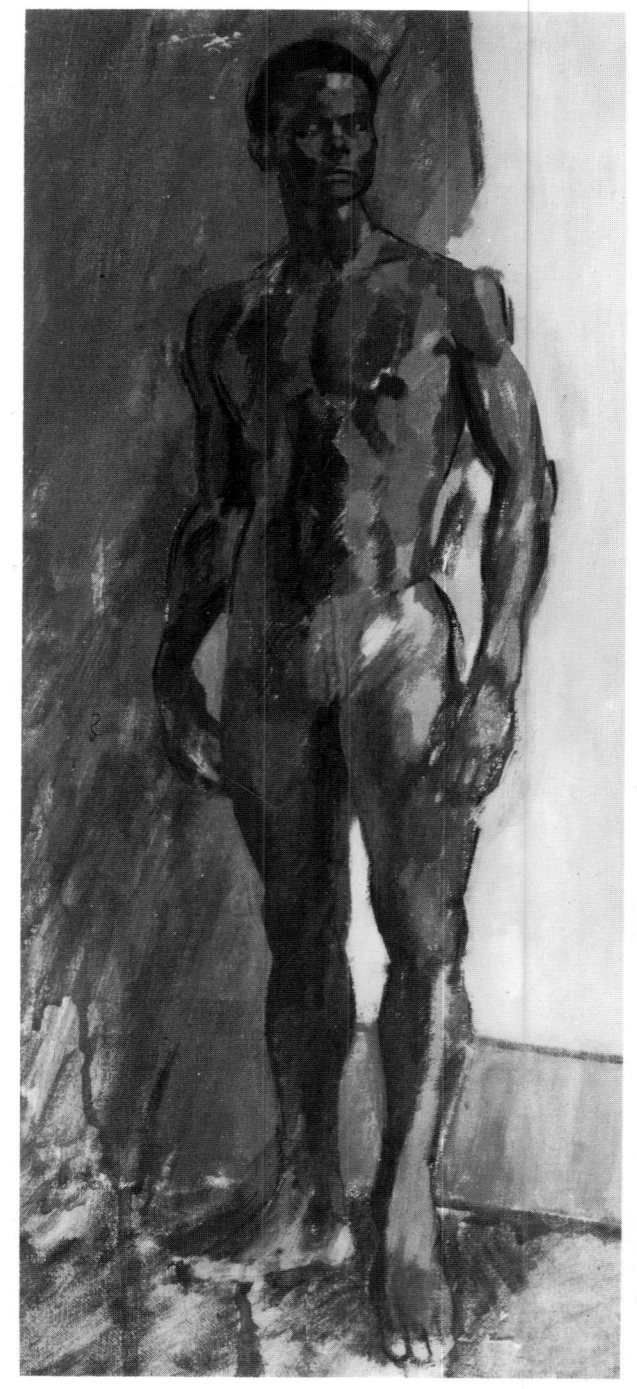

6. Oxford Man, c.1958. *Cat. no. 501.*

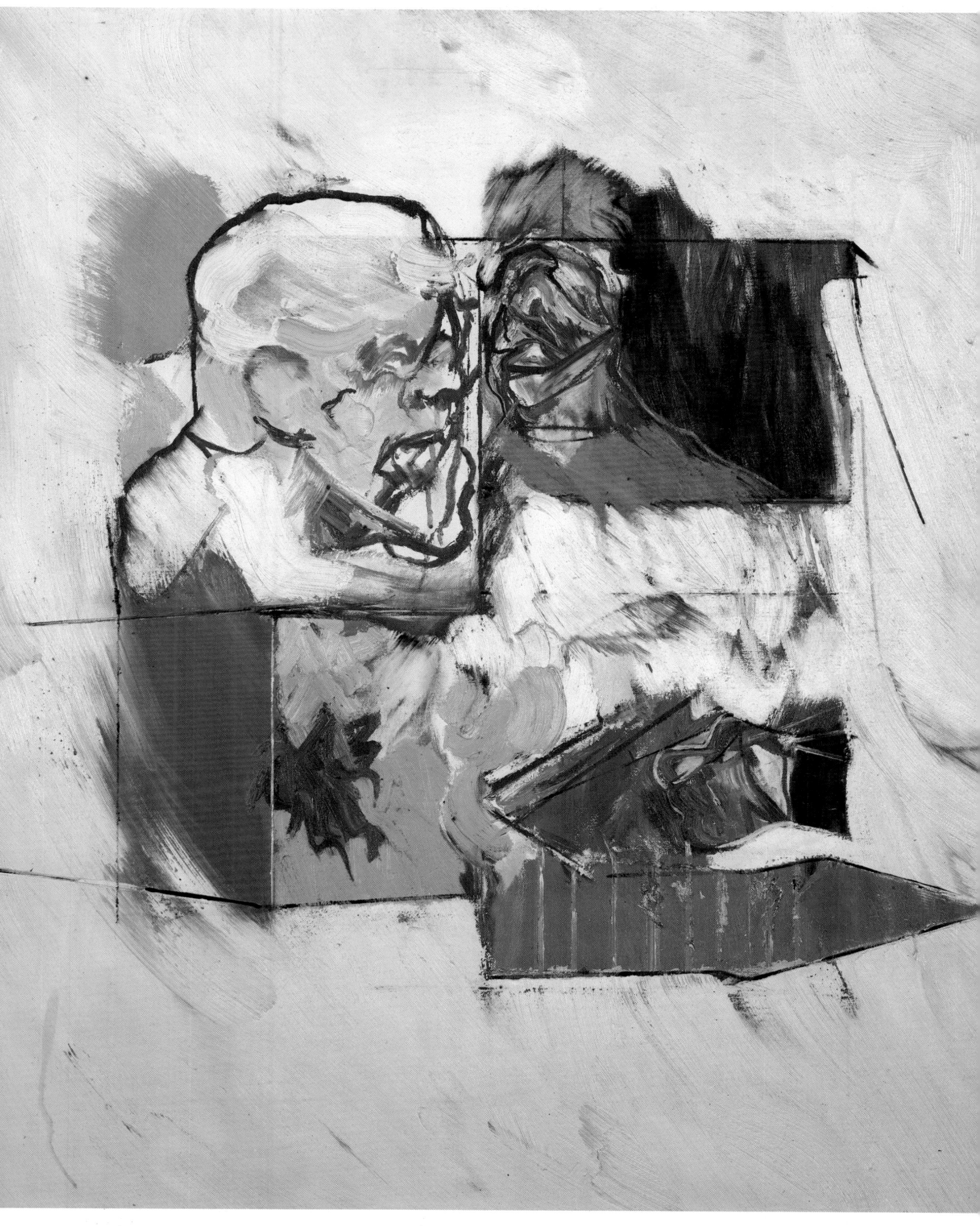

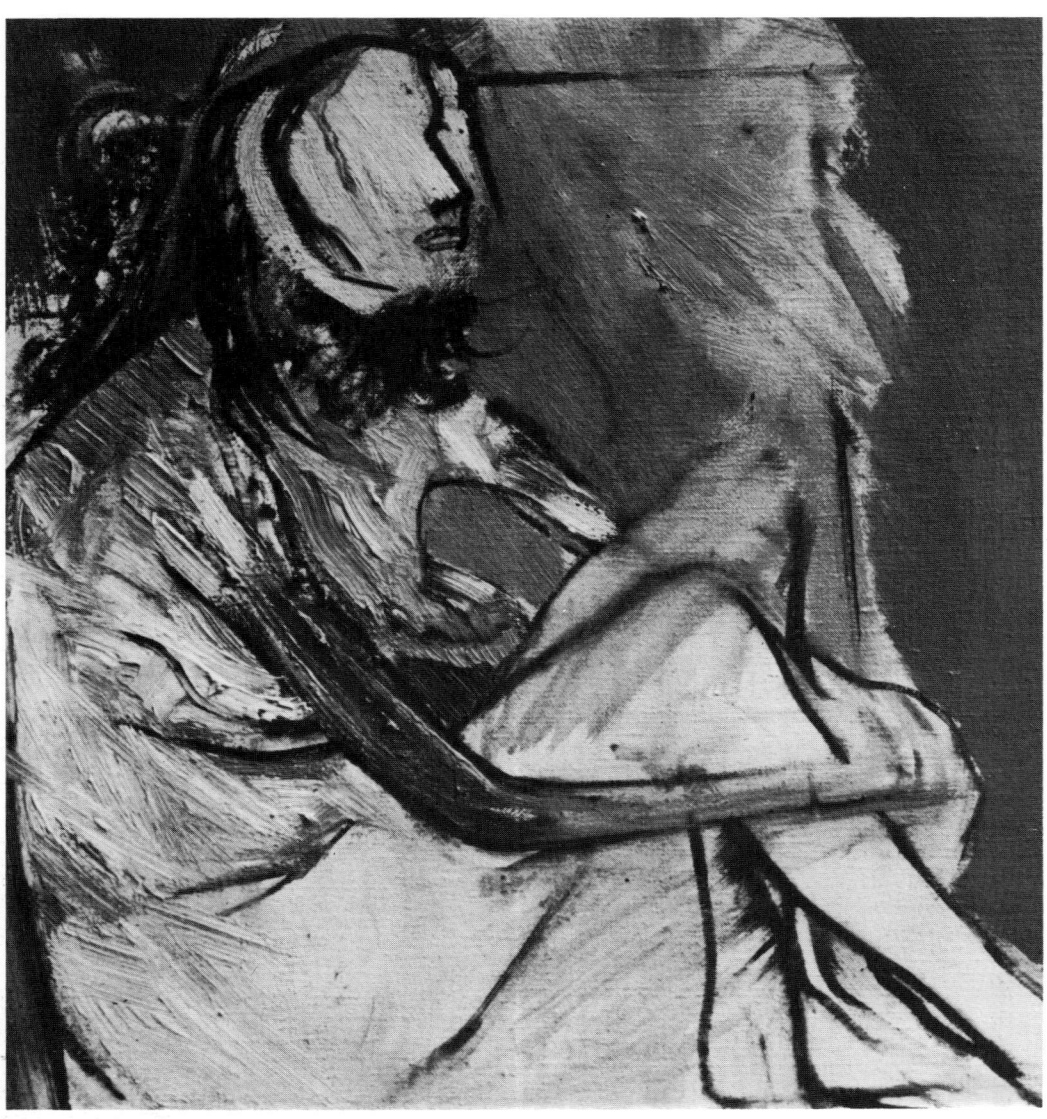

8. Red Nude, c.1960. *Cat. no. 502.*

9. *(below left)* The Red Banquet, 1960. *Cat. no. 10.*

10. Homage to H. Melville *(detail)*, 1962. *Cat. no. 31.*

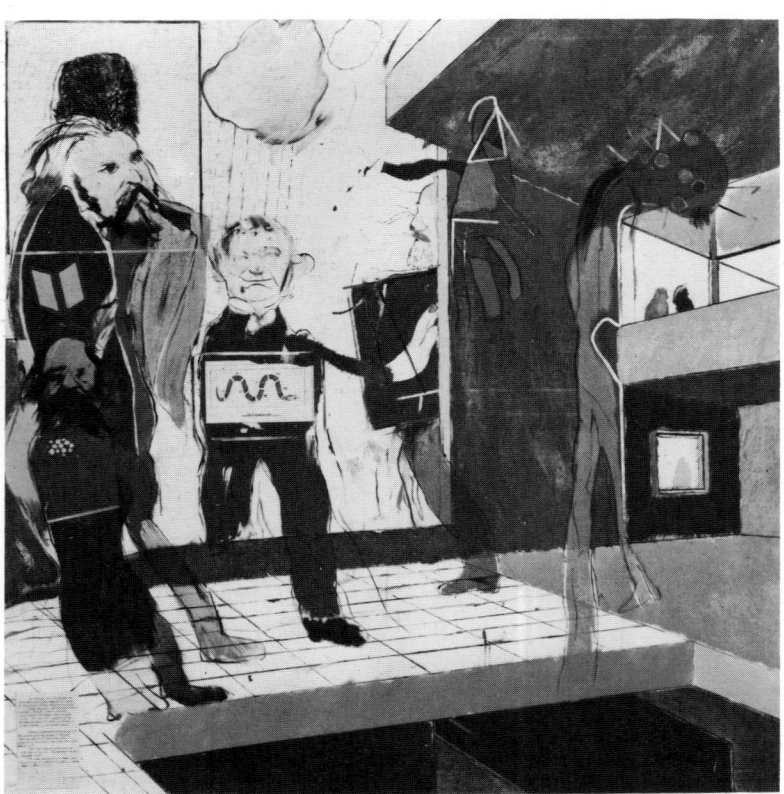

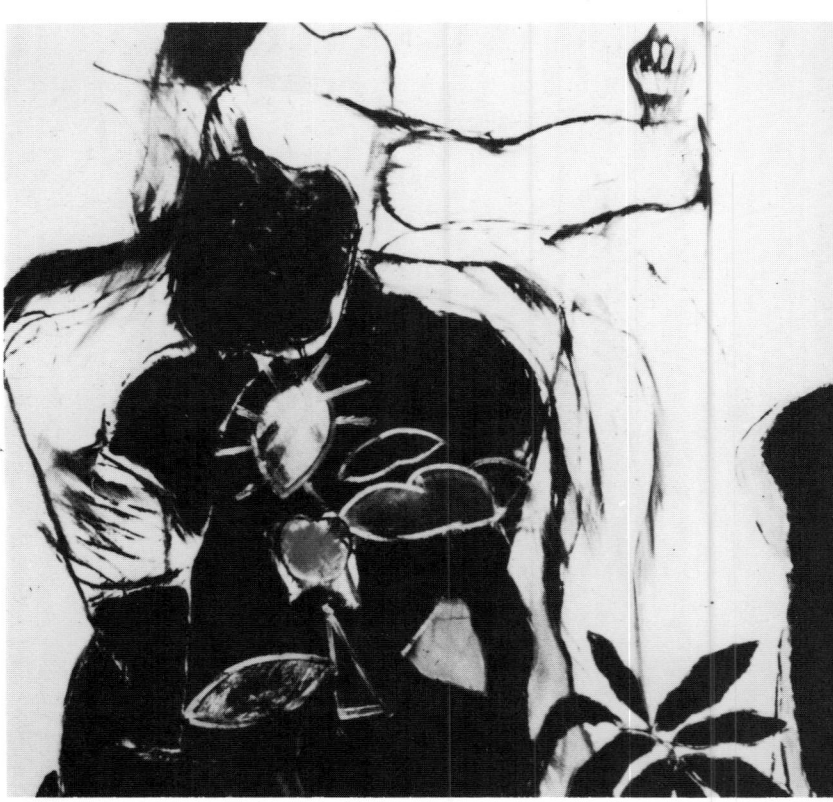

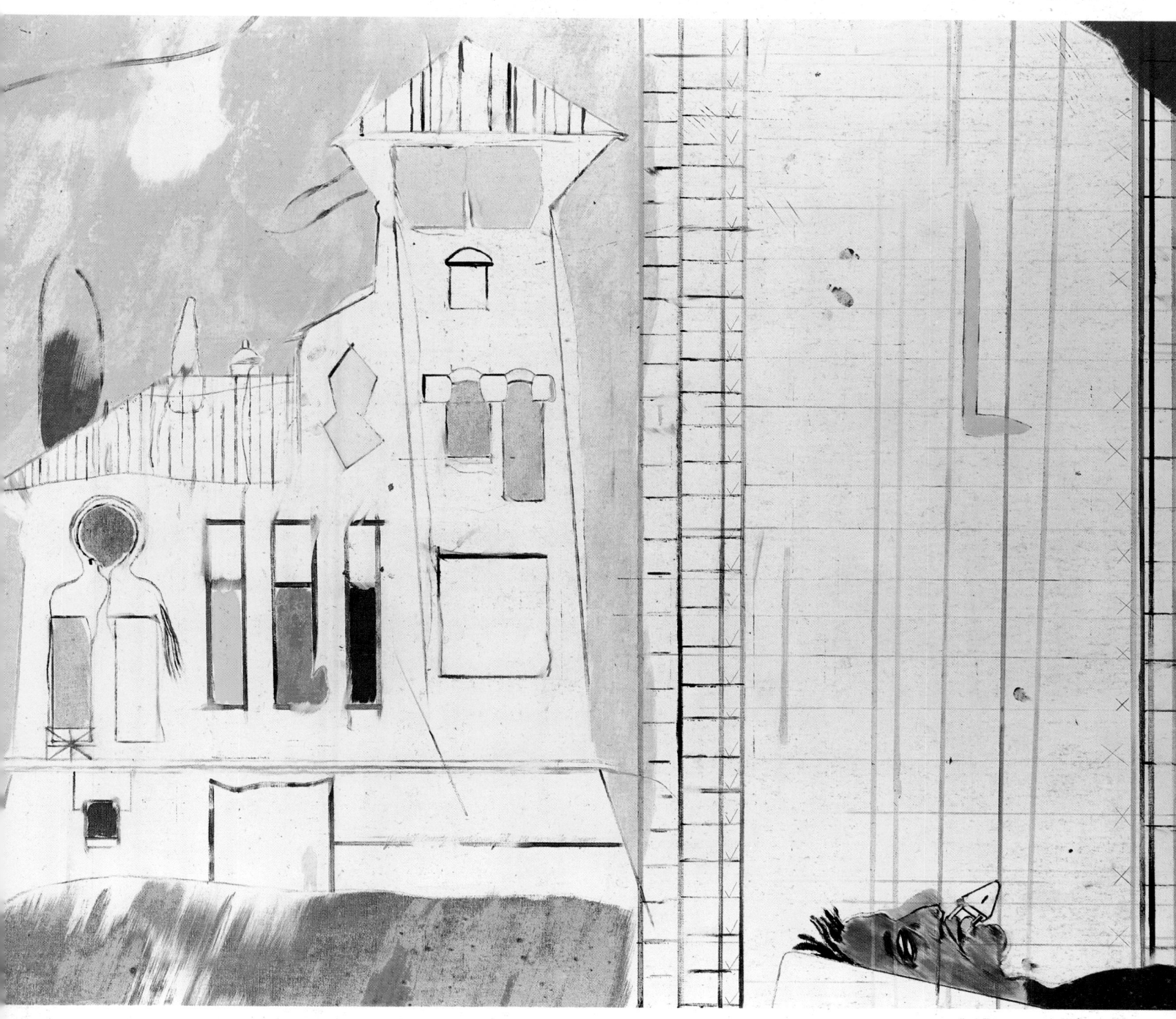

11. Yamhill, 1961. *Cat. no. 20.*

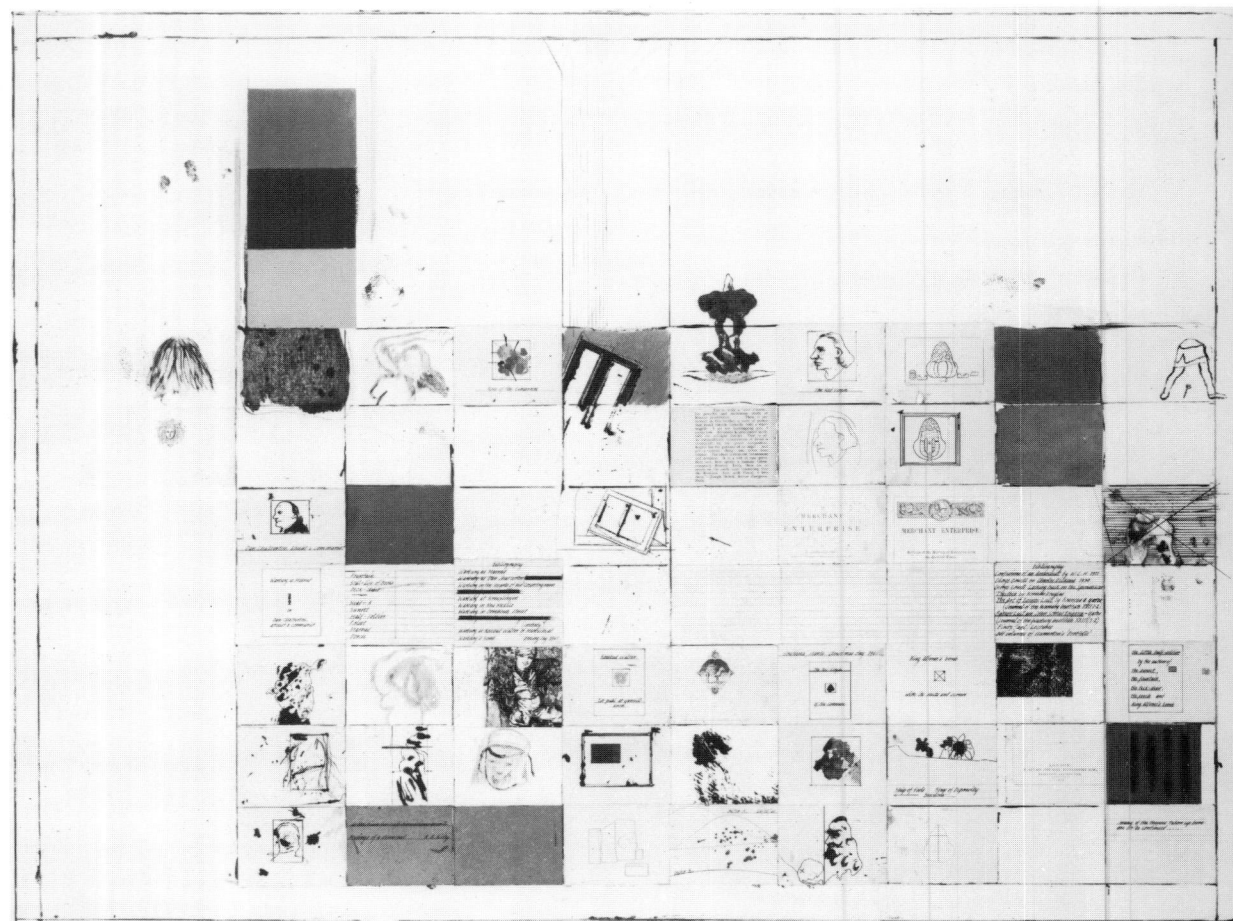

12. Specimen Musings of a Democrat,
1961. *Cat. no. 23.*

13. Girl on a Scooter *(detail)*, 1970.
Cat. no. 141.

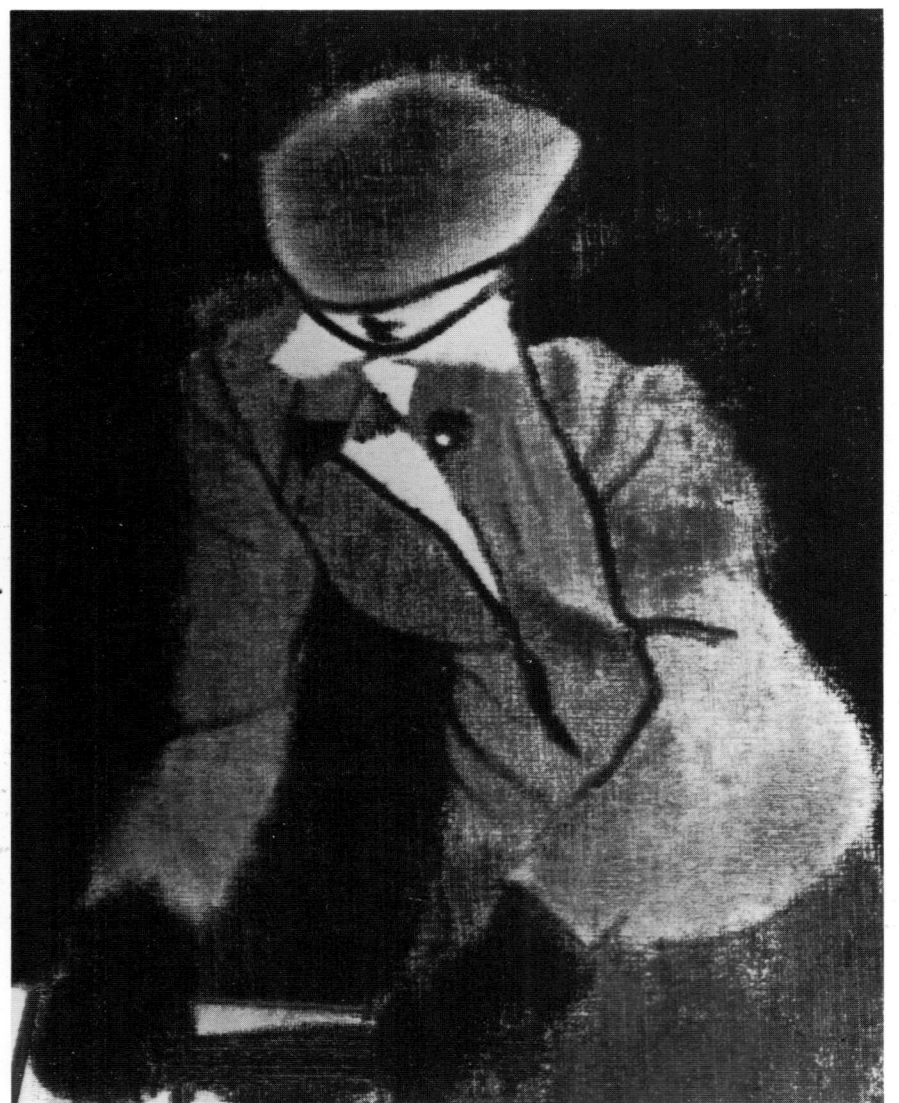

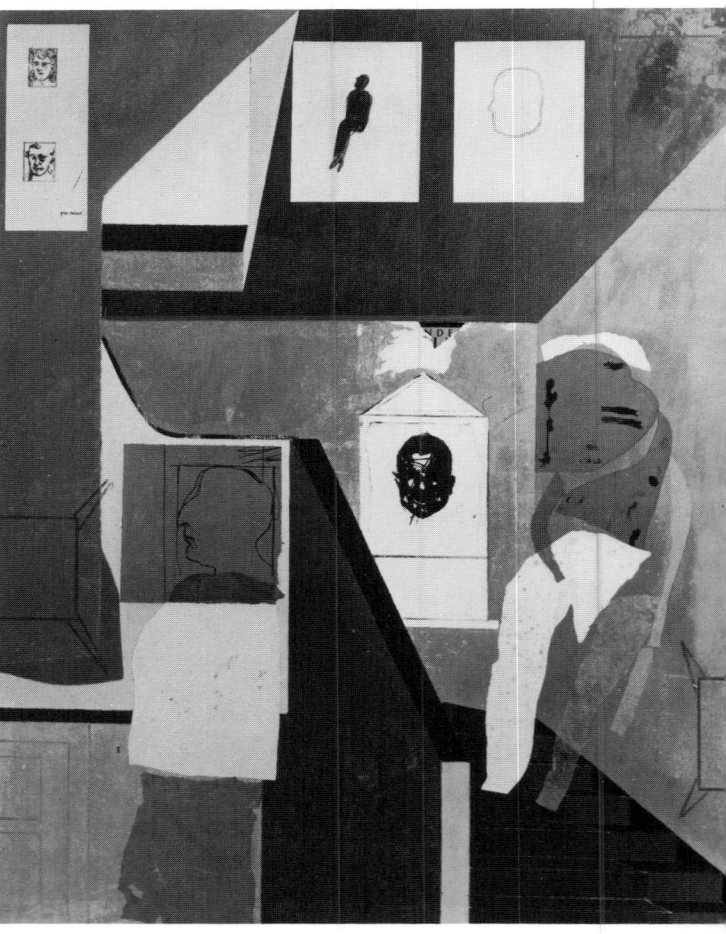

14. Interior / Dan Chatterton's Town House, 1962. *Cat. no. 39.*

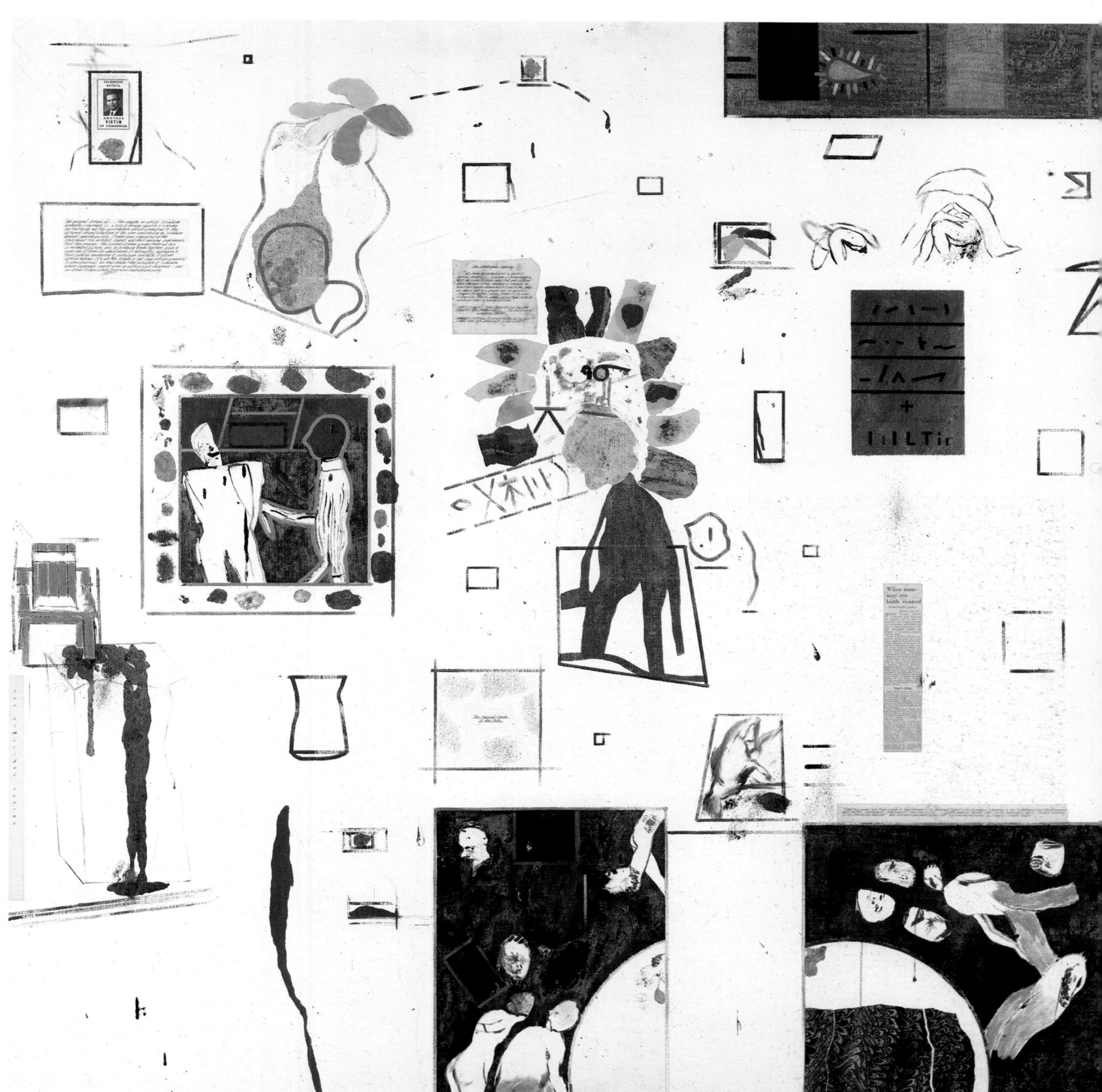

15. Reflections on Violence, 1962. *Cat. no. 34.*

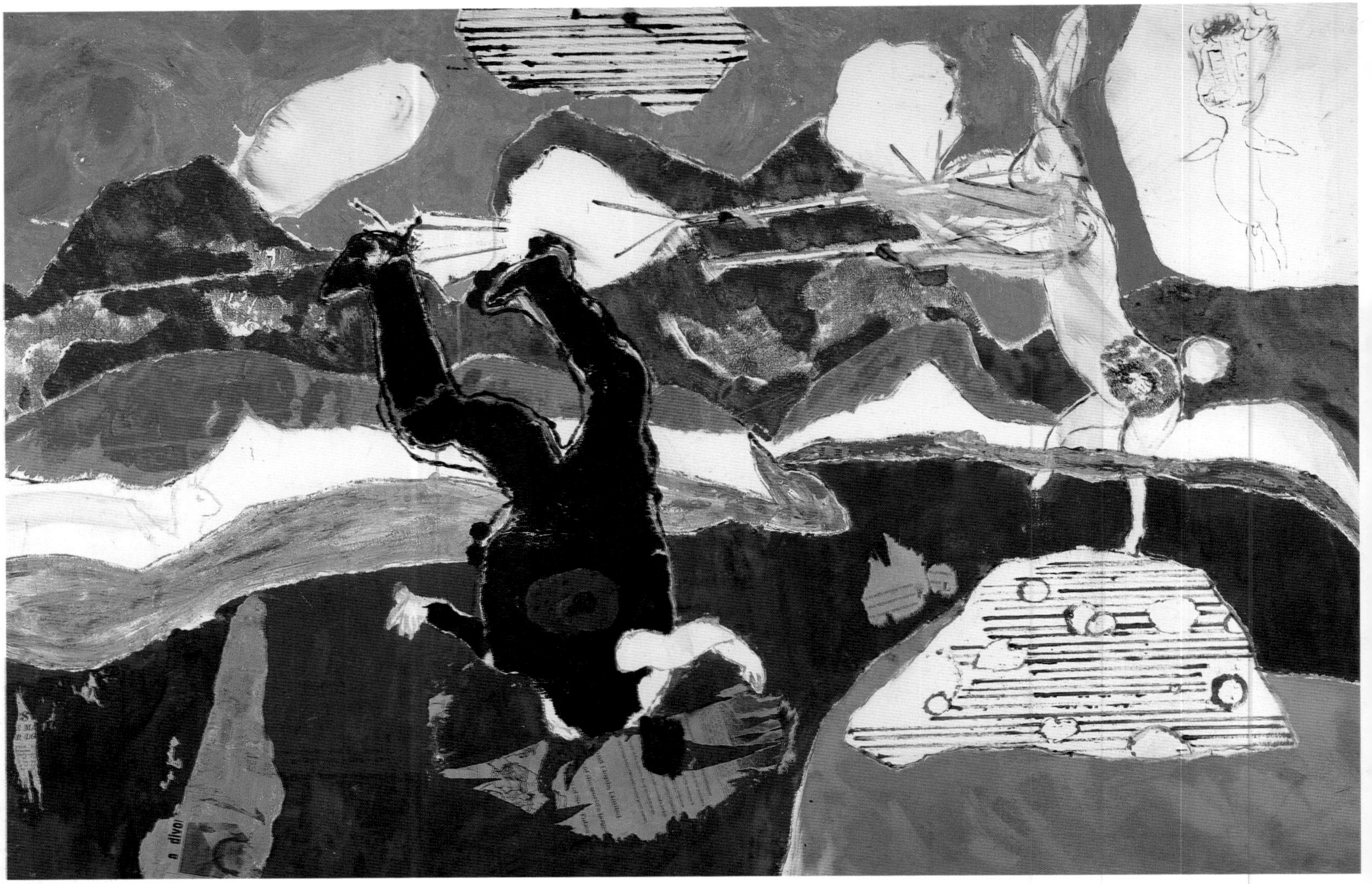

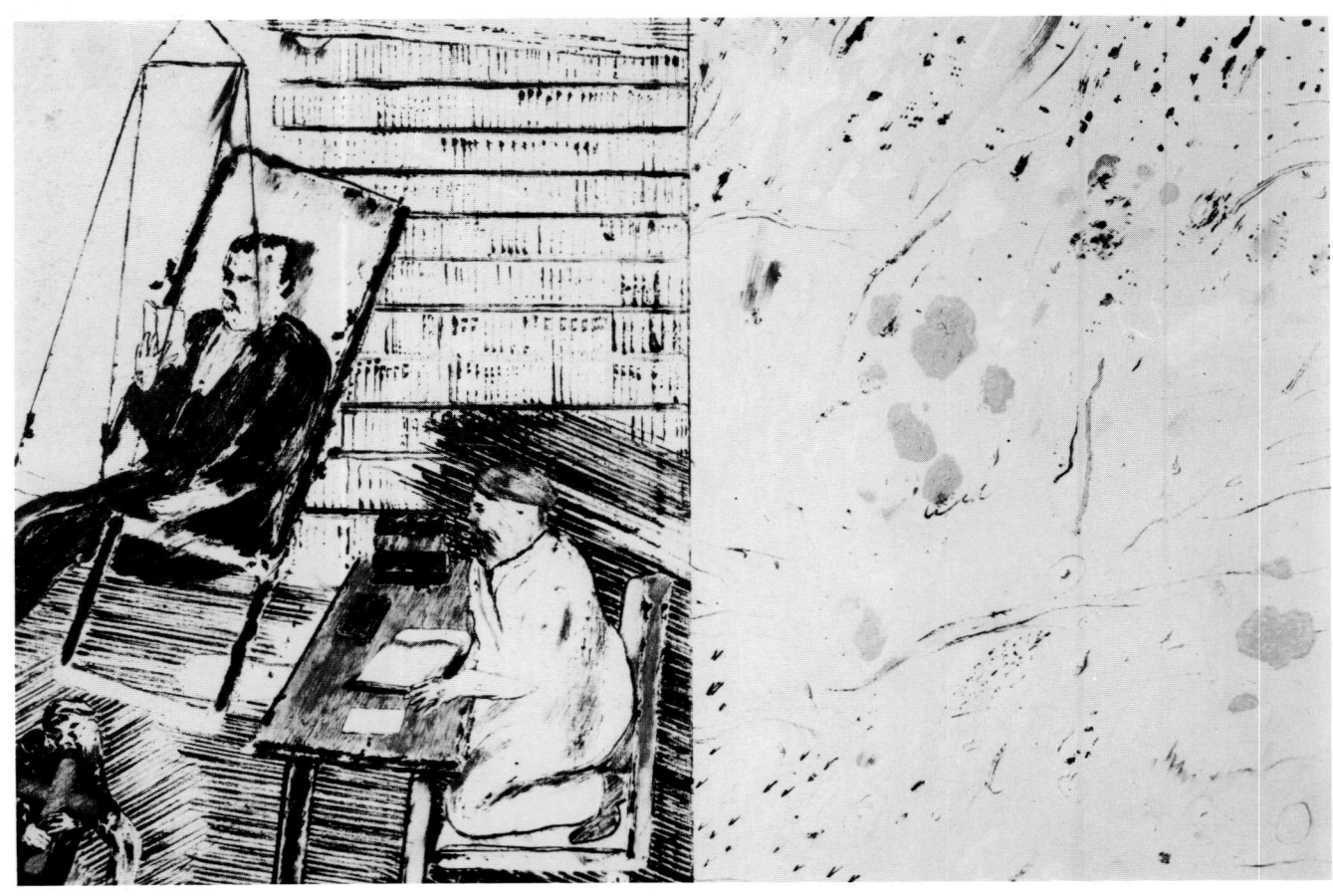

16. Oh, Lemuel, 1960. *Cat. no. 15.*

17. Certain Forms of Association Neglected Before, 1961. *Cat. no. 19.*

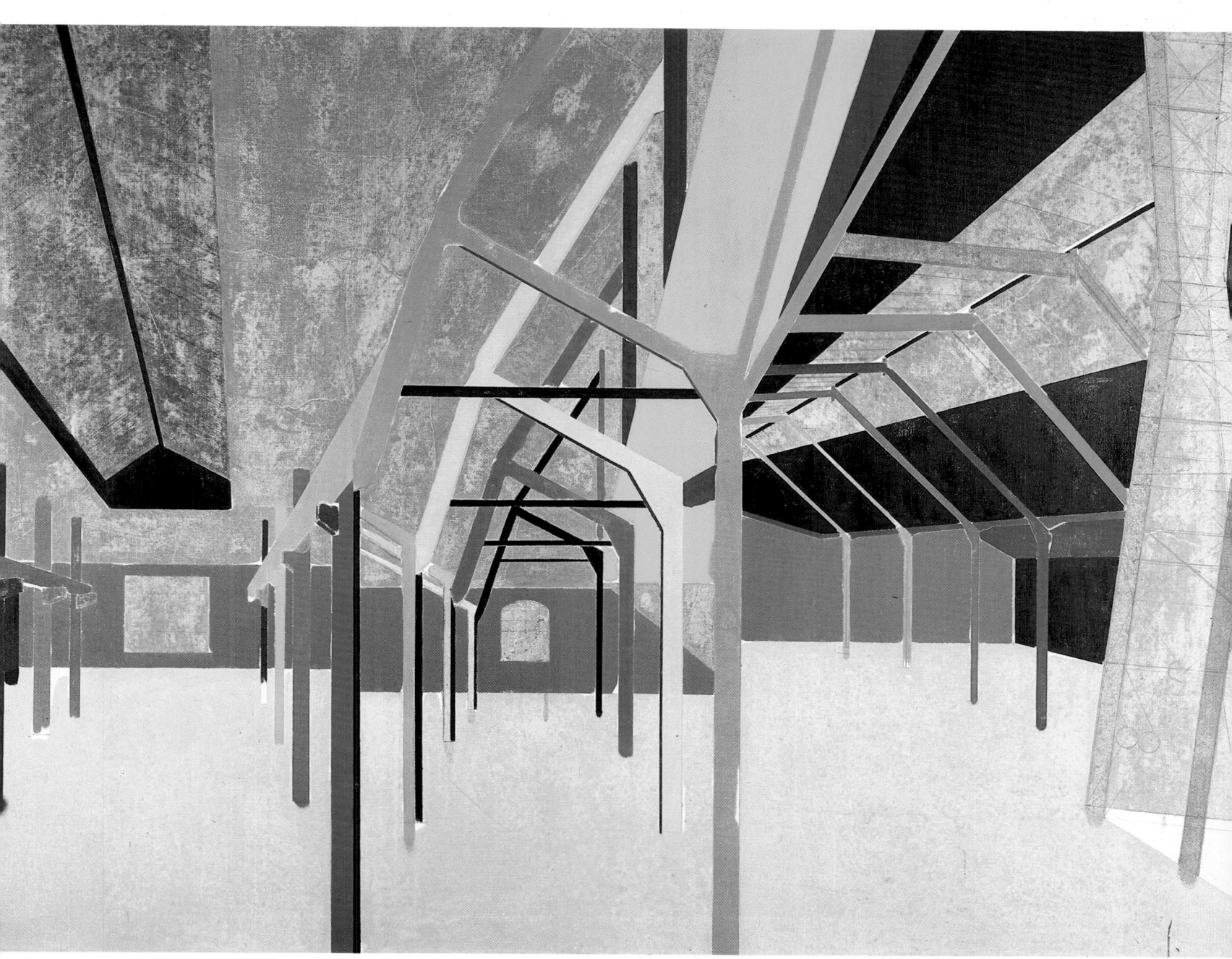

18. Apotheosis of Groundlessness, 1964. *Cat. no. 52.*

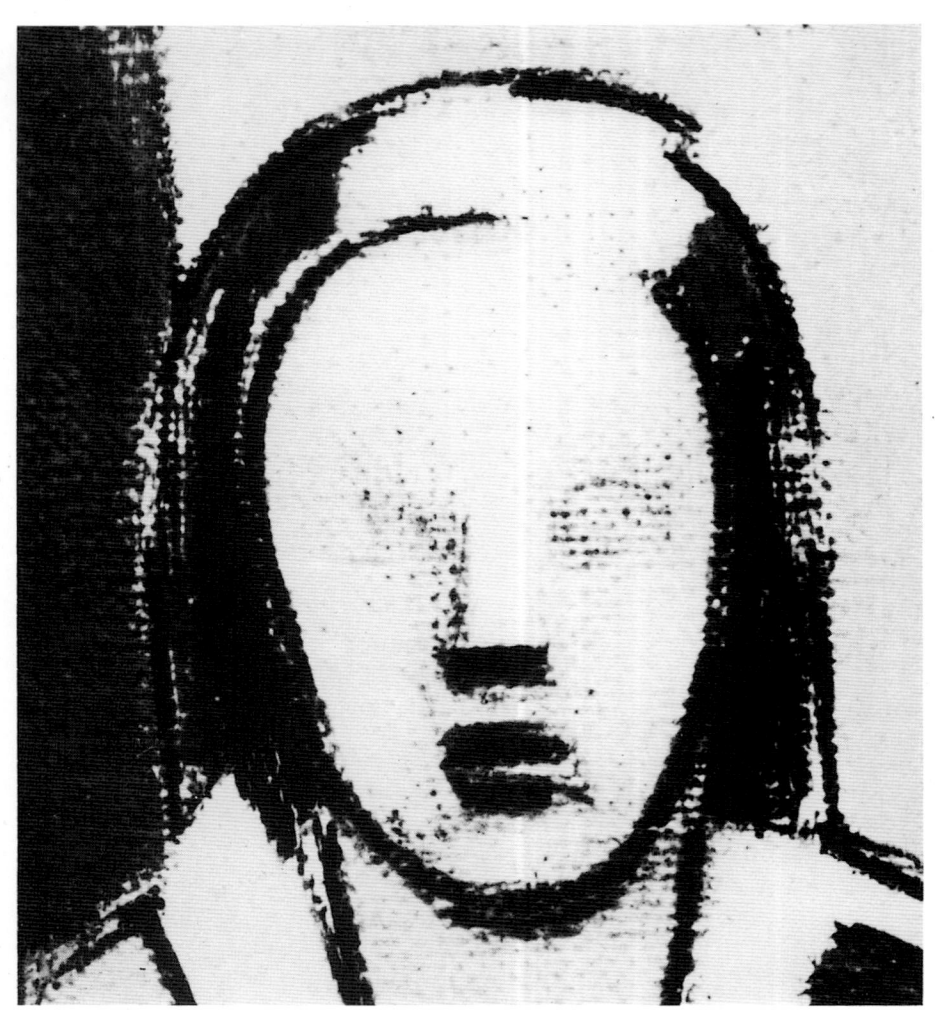

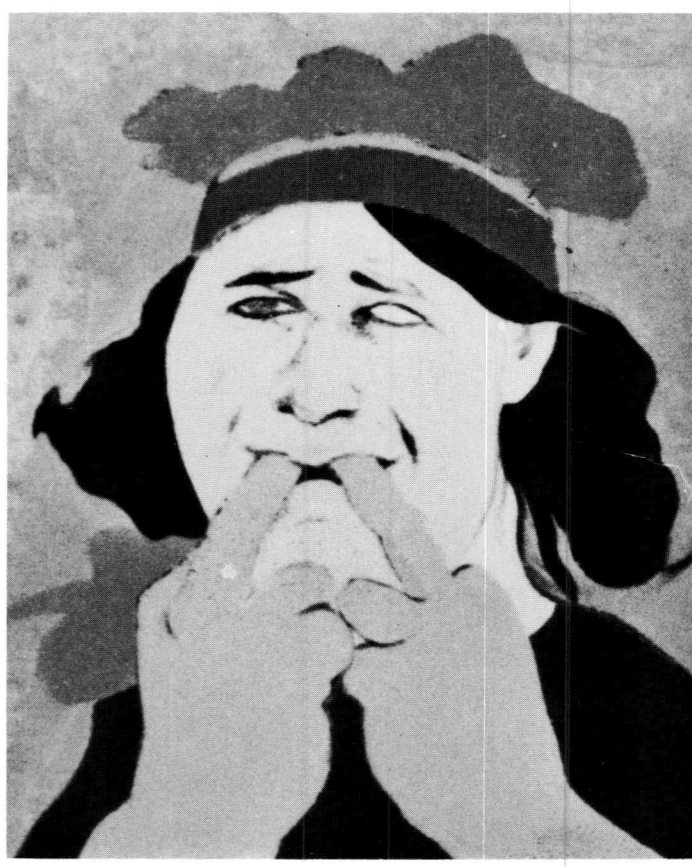

19. *(above left)* The First Terrorist, 1957.
Cat. no. 1.

20. *(above)* Value, Price and Profit *(detail)*,
1963. *Cat. no. 47.*

21. Pariah *(detail)*, 1960. *Cat. no. 14.*

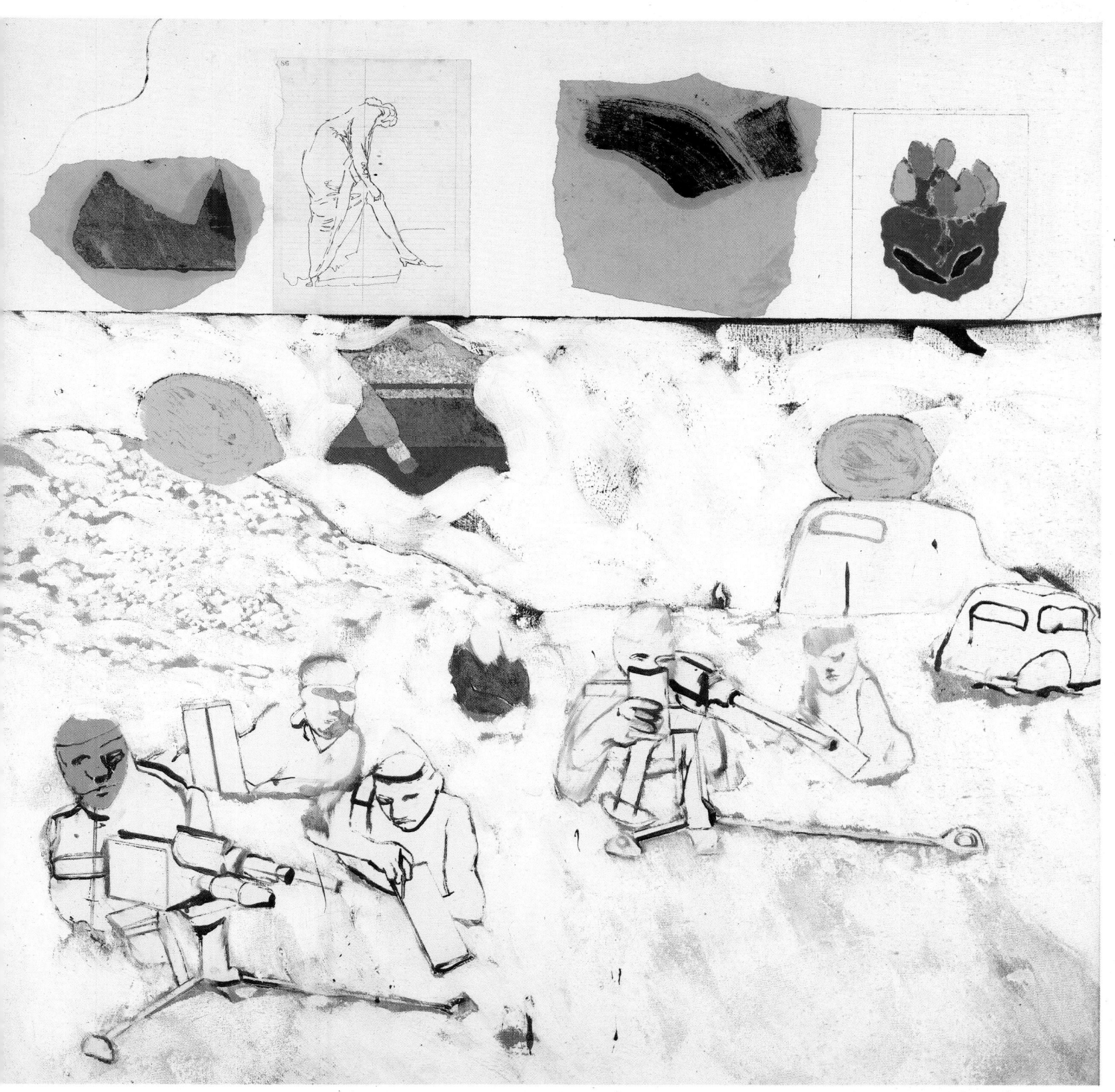

22. Kennst du das Land?, 1962. *Cat. no. 32.*

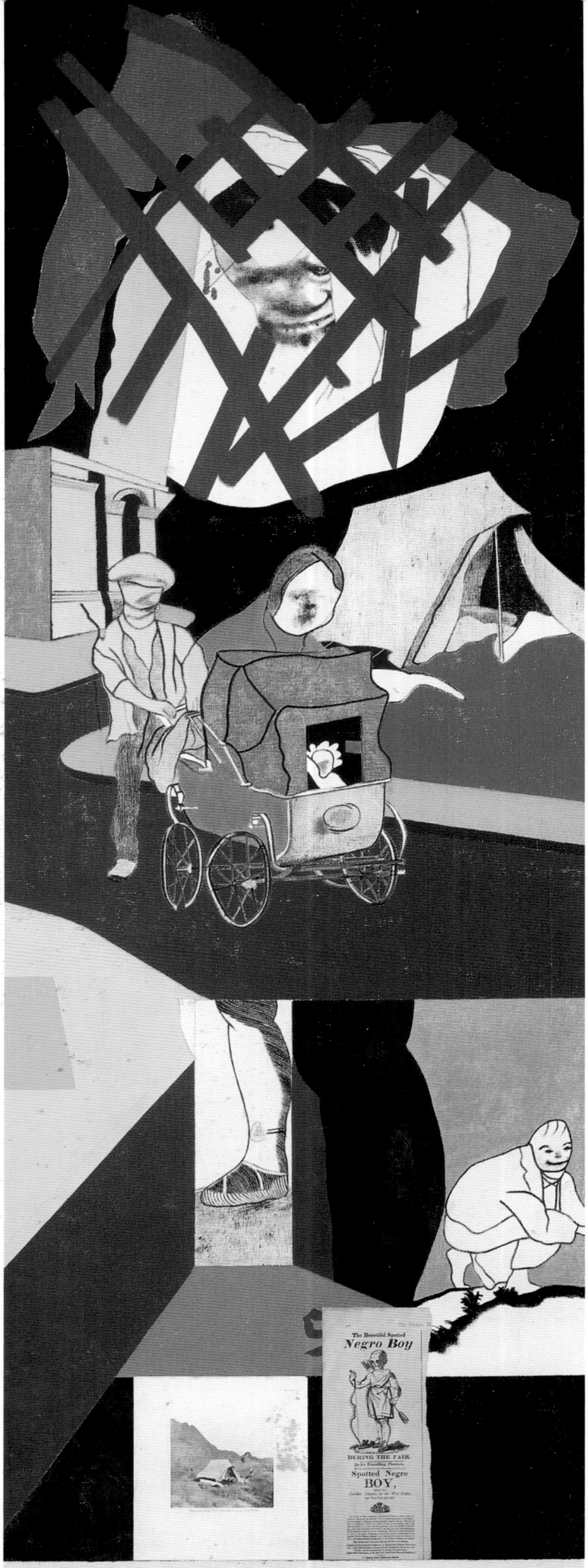

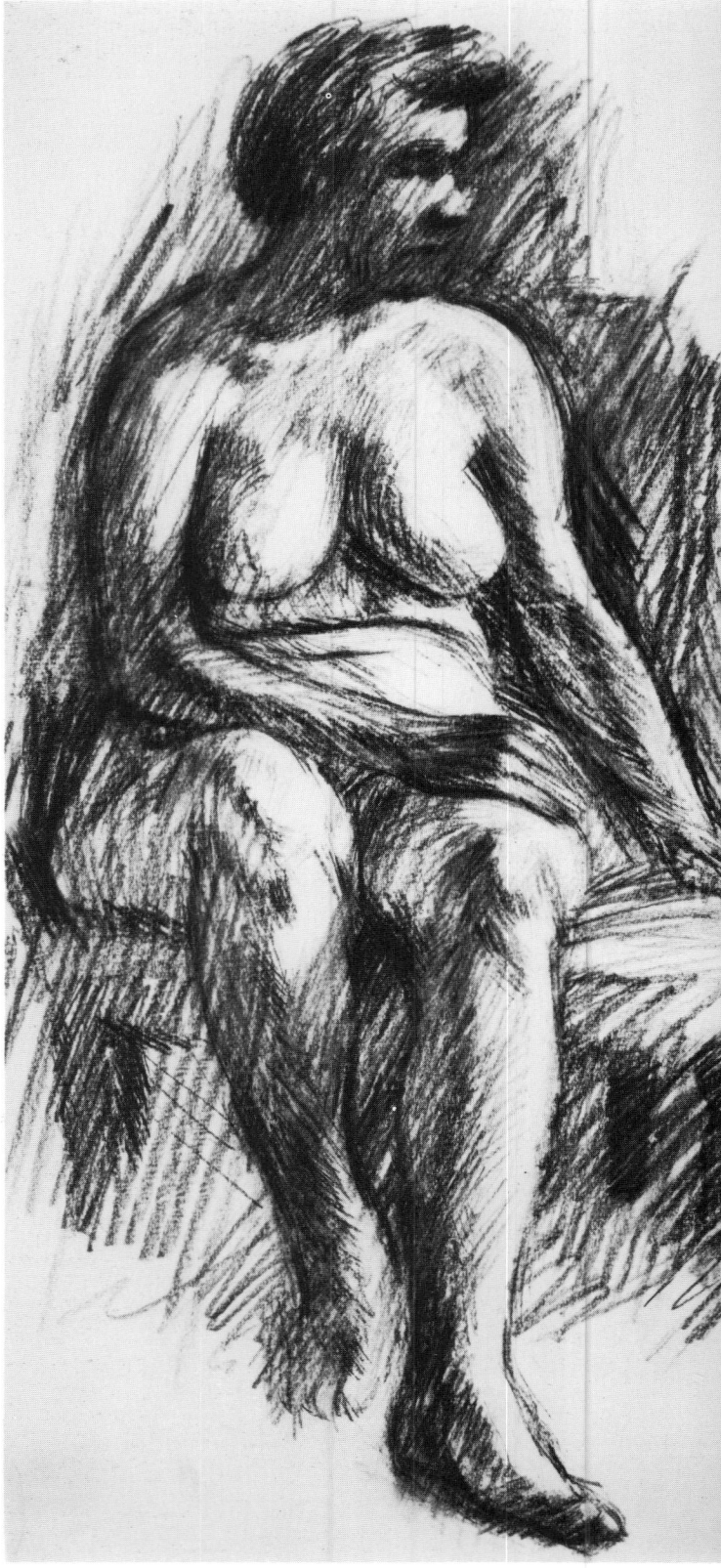

24. Life Study, c.1958. *Cat. no. 503.*

23. *(left)* The Baby Tramp, 1963/4. *Cat. no. 51.*

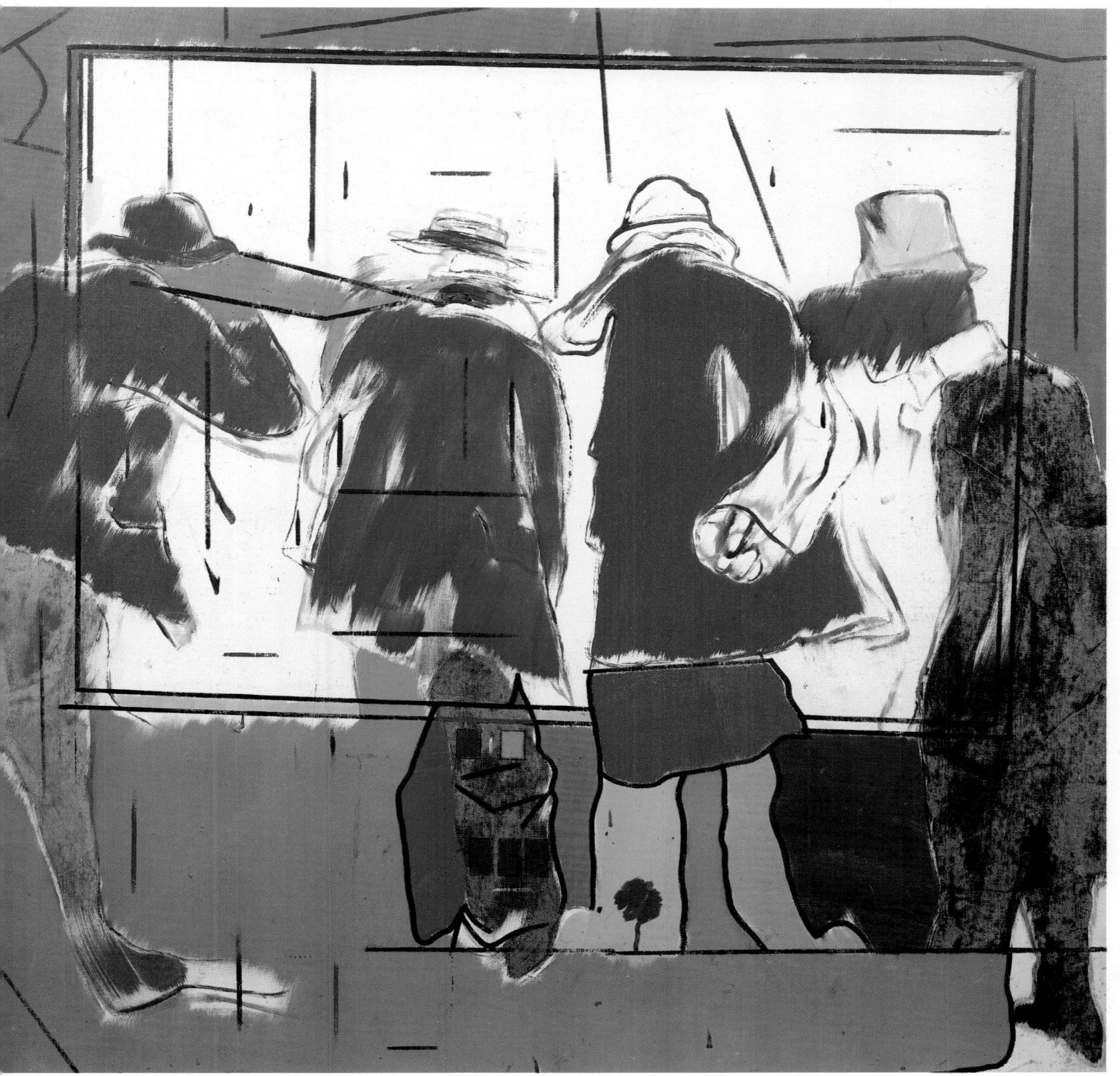

25. Nietzsche's Moustache, 1962. *Cat. no. 29.*

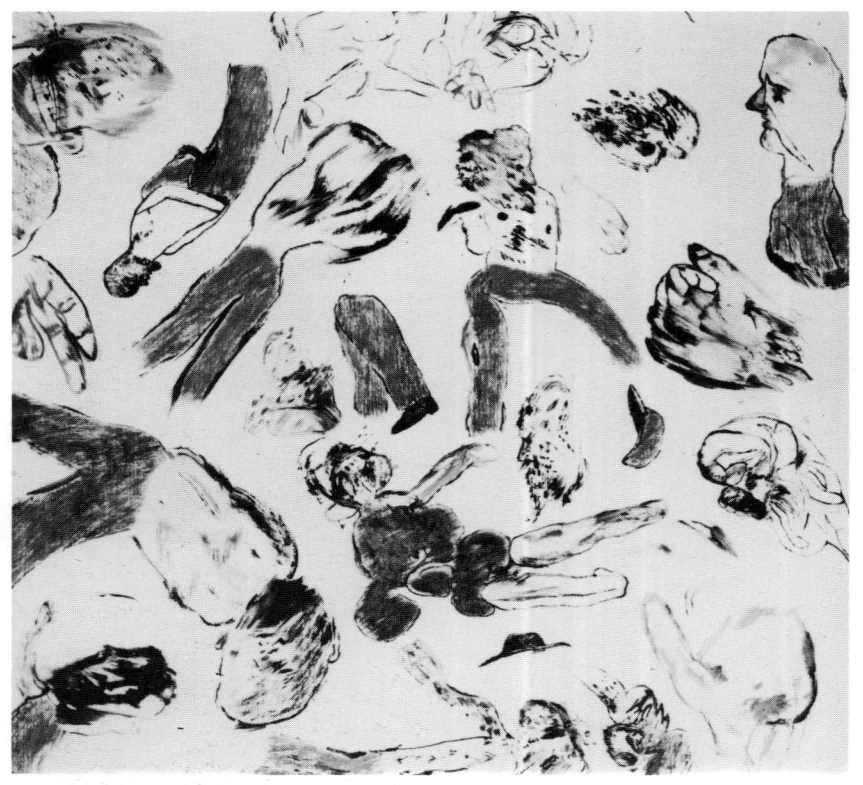

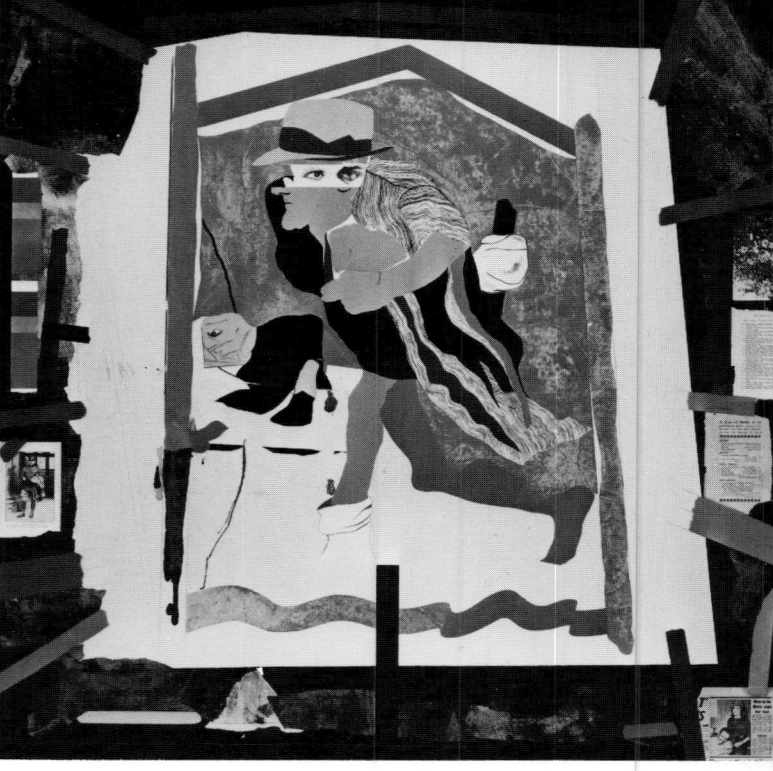

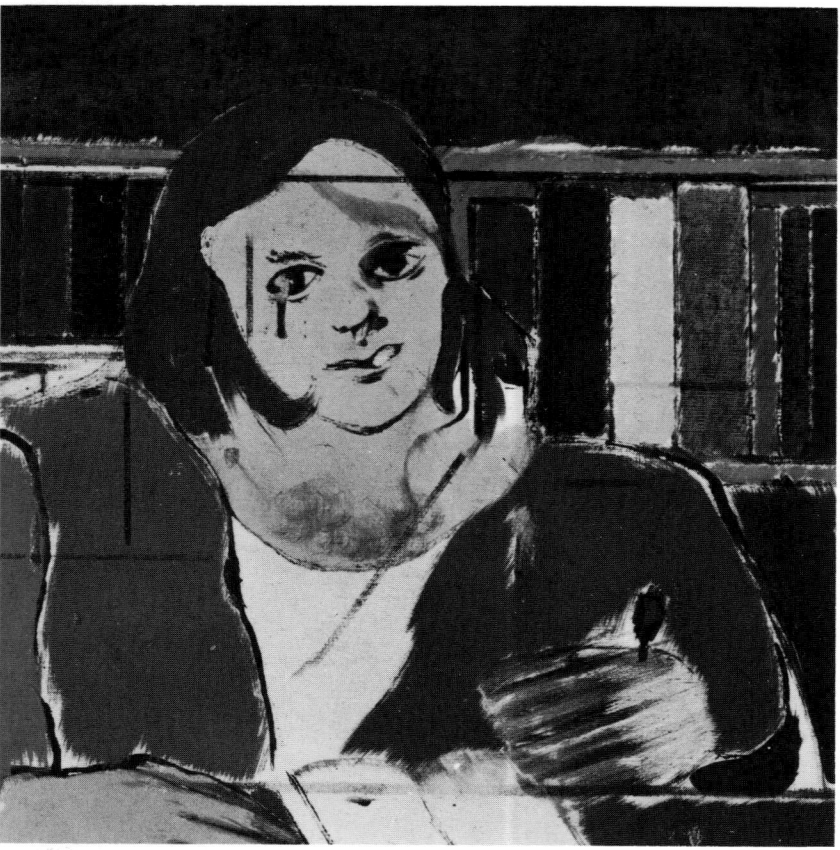

26. *(above left)* The Bells of Hell *(detail)*, 1960. *Cat. no. 12.*

27. *(above)* Randolph Bourne in Irving Place, 1963. *Cat. no. 50.*

28. A Student of Vienna *(detail)*, 1961-2. *Cat. no. 26.*

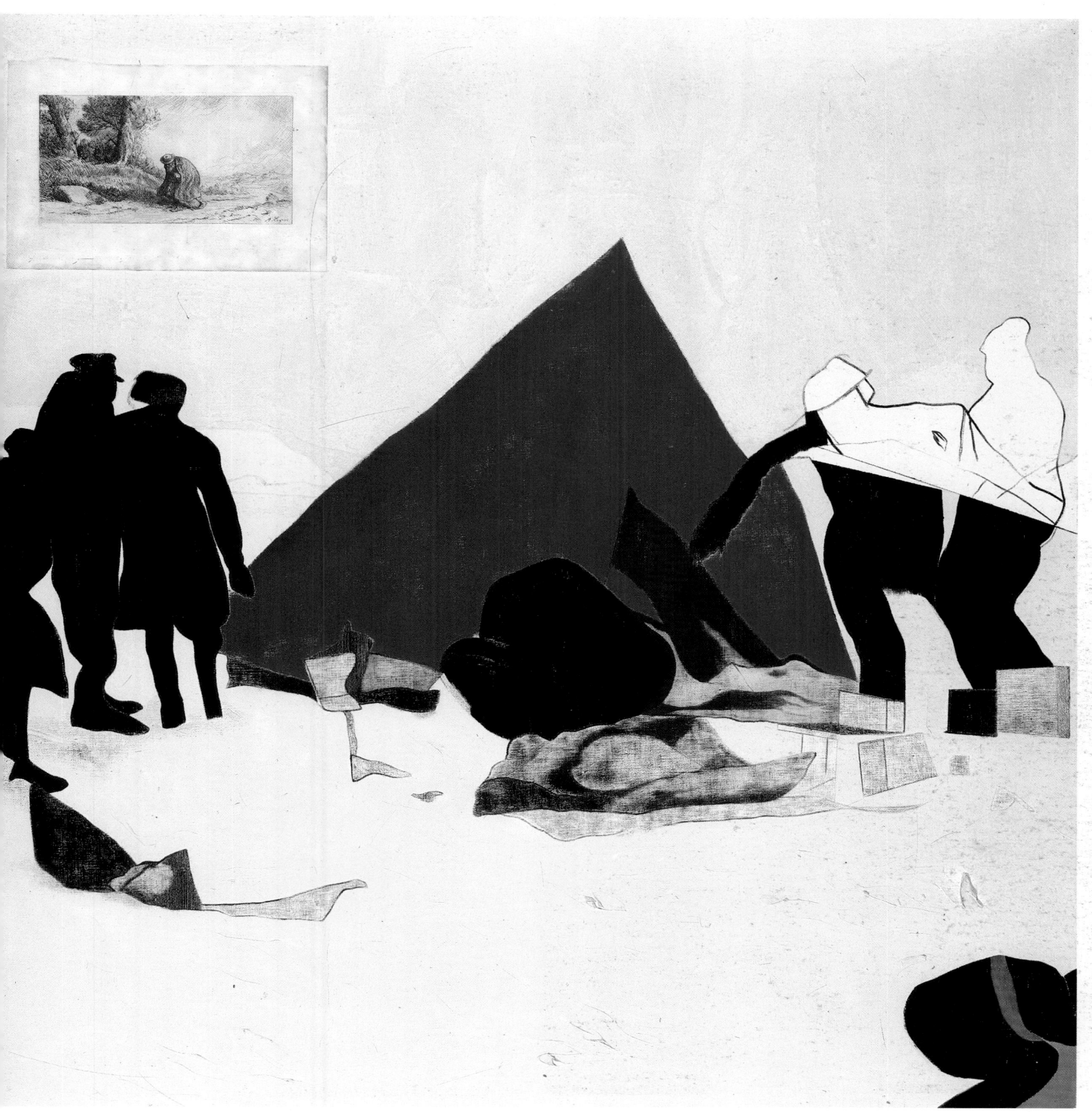

29. Dismantling the Red Tent, 1964. *Cat. no. 75.*

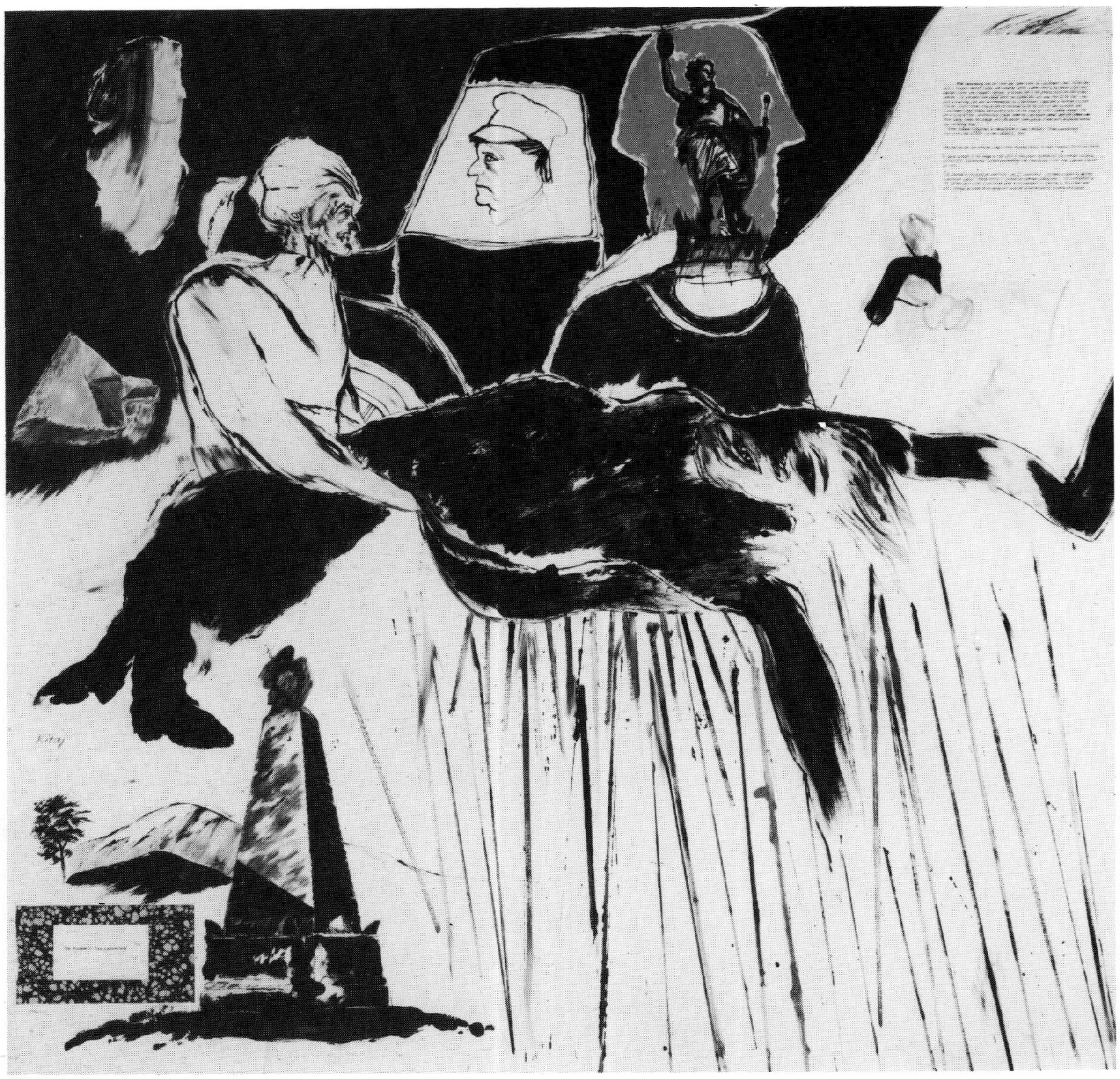

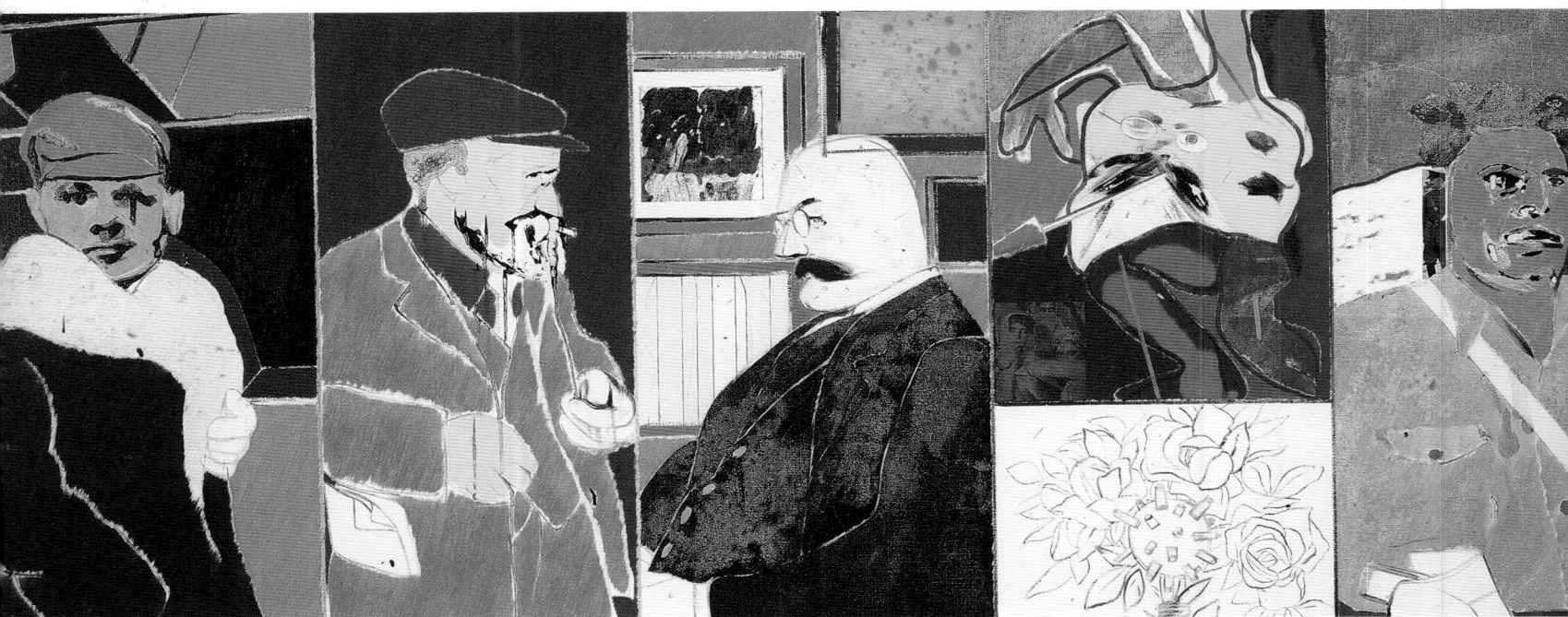

30. The Murder of Rosa Luxemburg, 1960. *Cat. no. 13.*

31. Junta, 1962. *Cat. no. 30.*

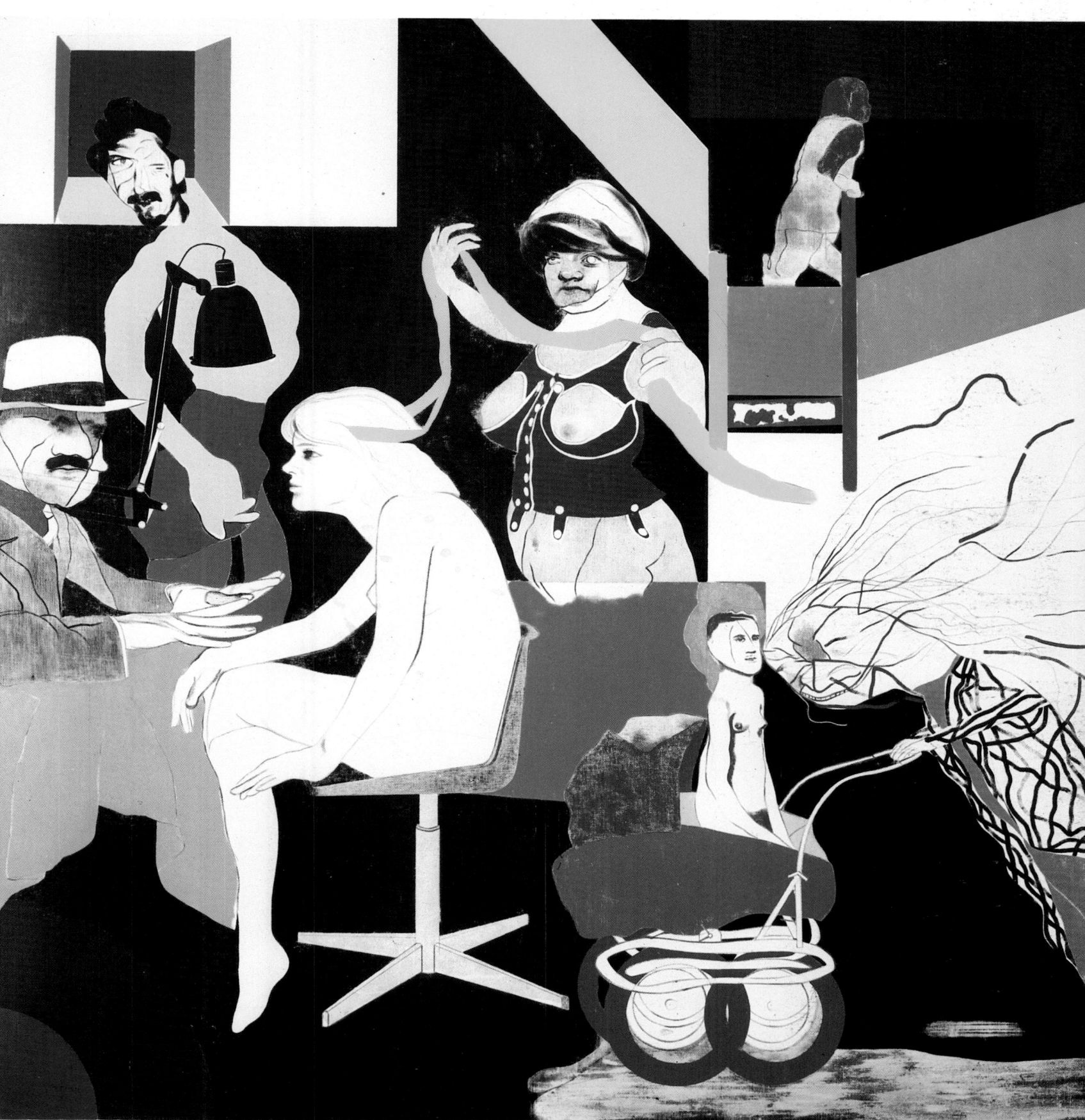

32. The Ohio Gang, 1964. *Cat. no. 53.*

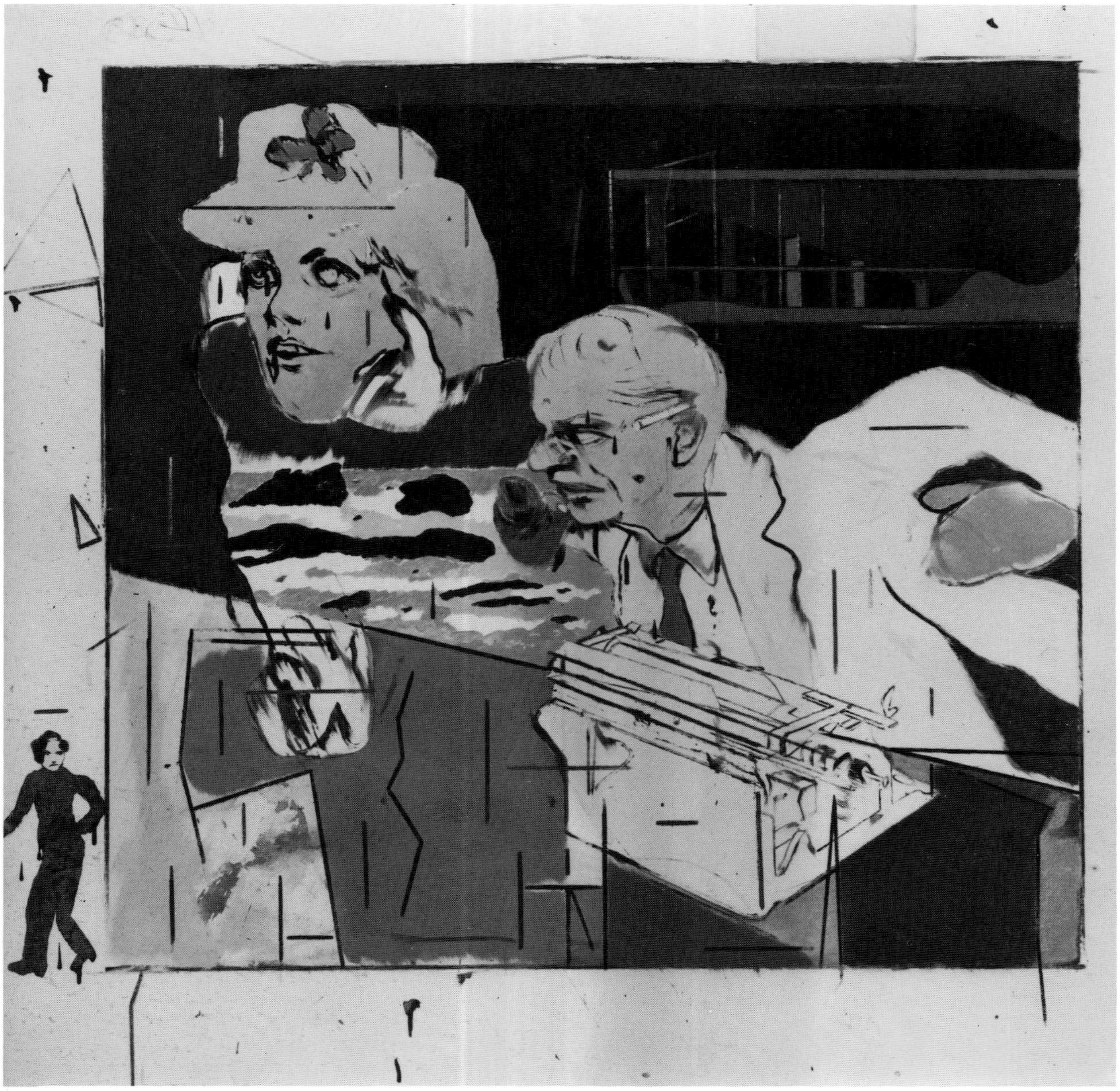

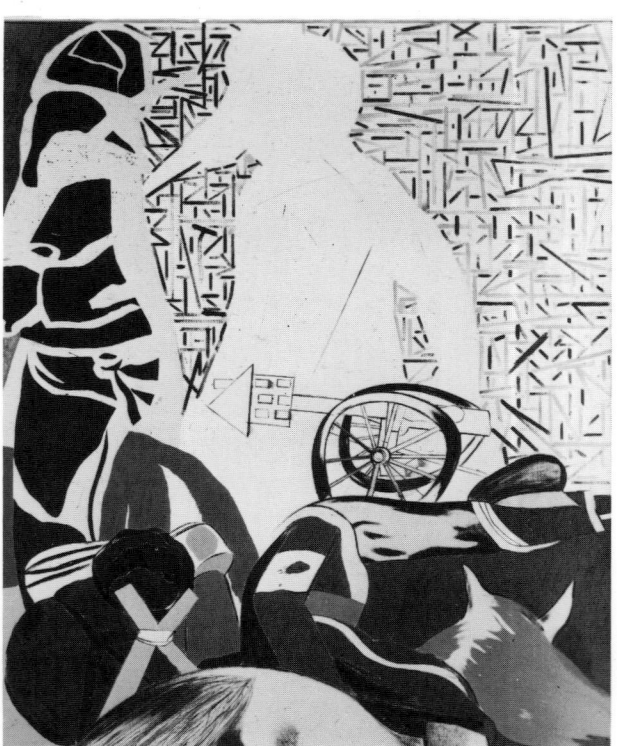

33. Good News for Incunabulists, 1962. *Cat. no. 33.*

34. *(far left)* Isaac Babel Riding with Budyonny *(detail),* 1962. *Cat no.35.*

35. *(left)* Priest, Etc., 1961. *Cat. no. 25.*

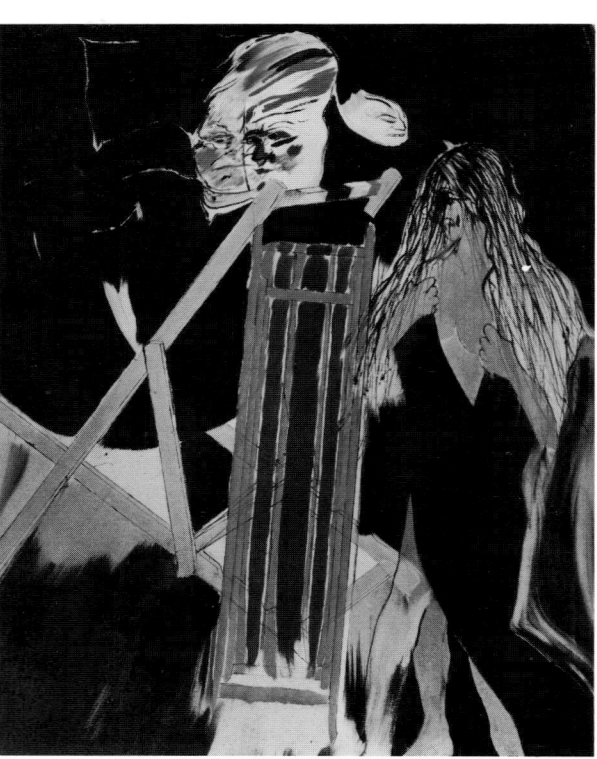

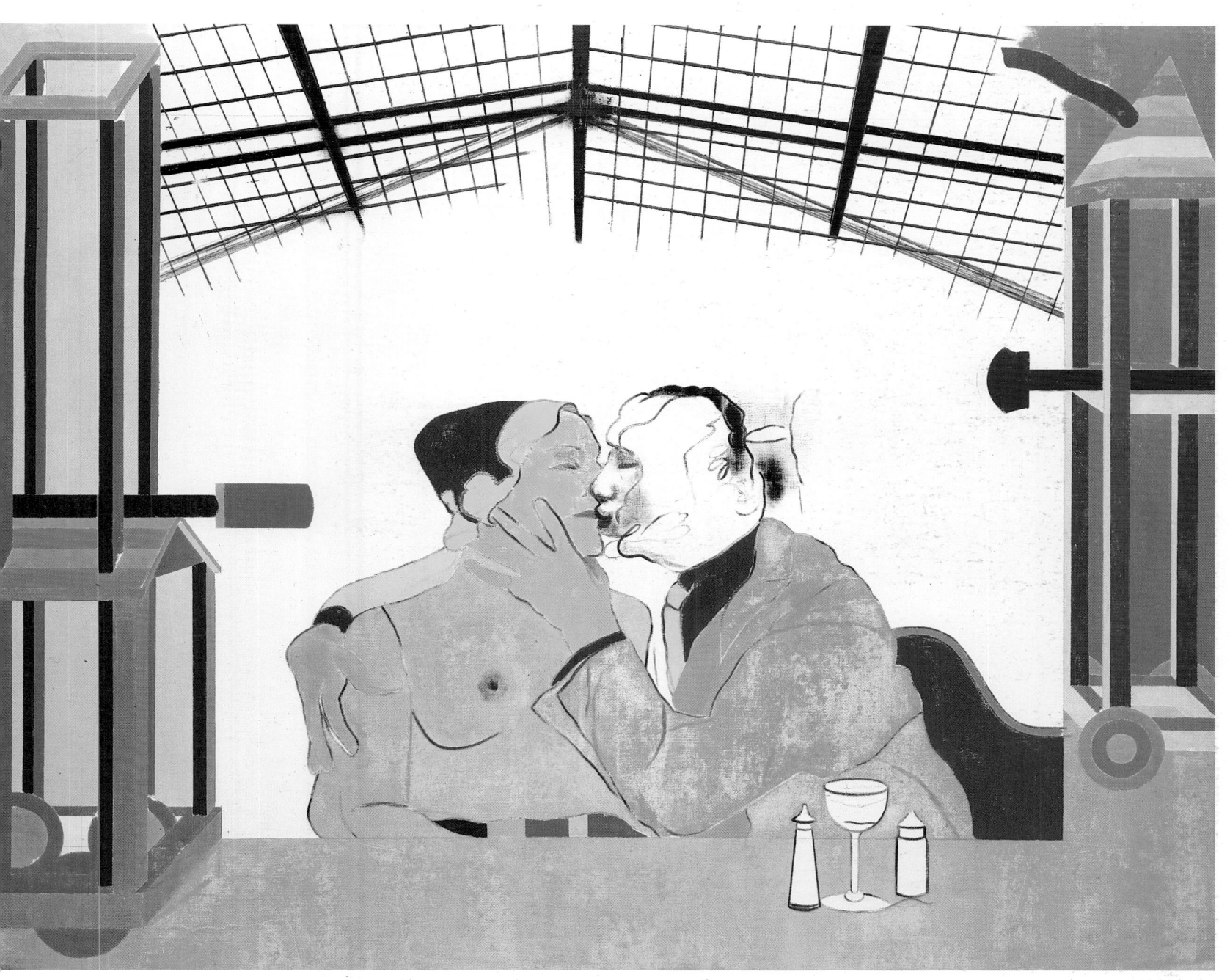

36. Where the Railroad Leaves the Sea, 1964. *Cat. no. 57.*

37. Maria Prophetissa, 1964.
Cat. no. 66.

38. *(far right)* Casting *(detail)*,
1967-9. *Cat. no. 104.*

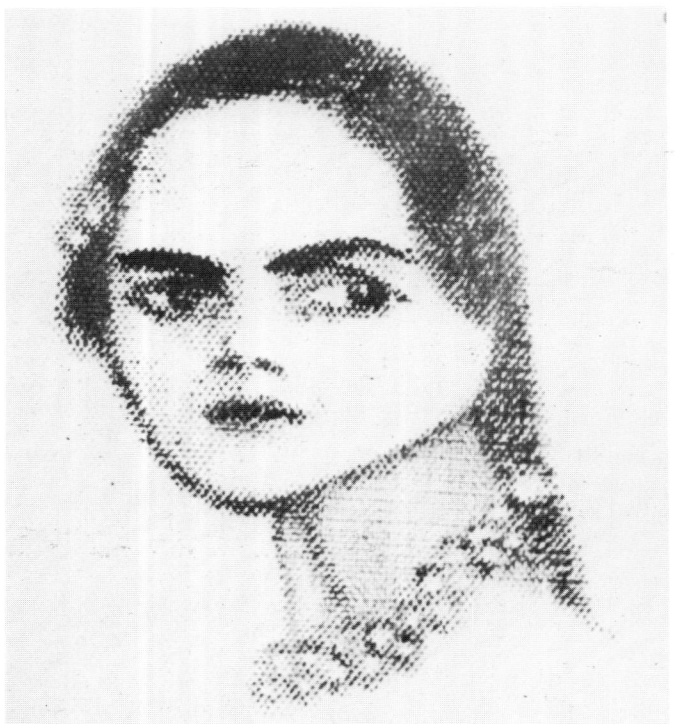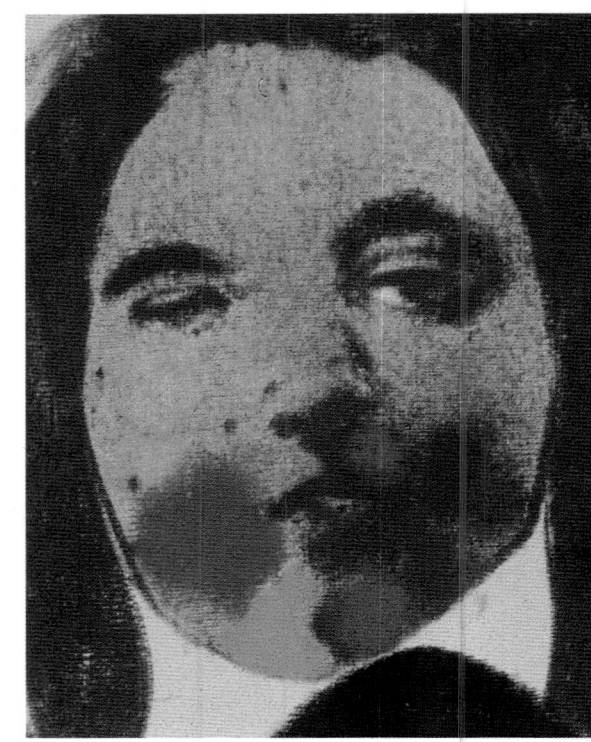

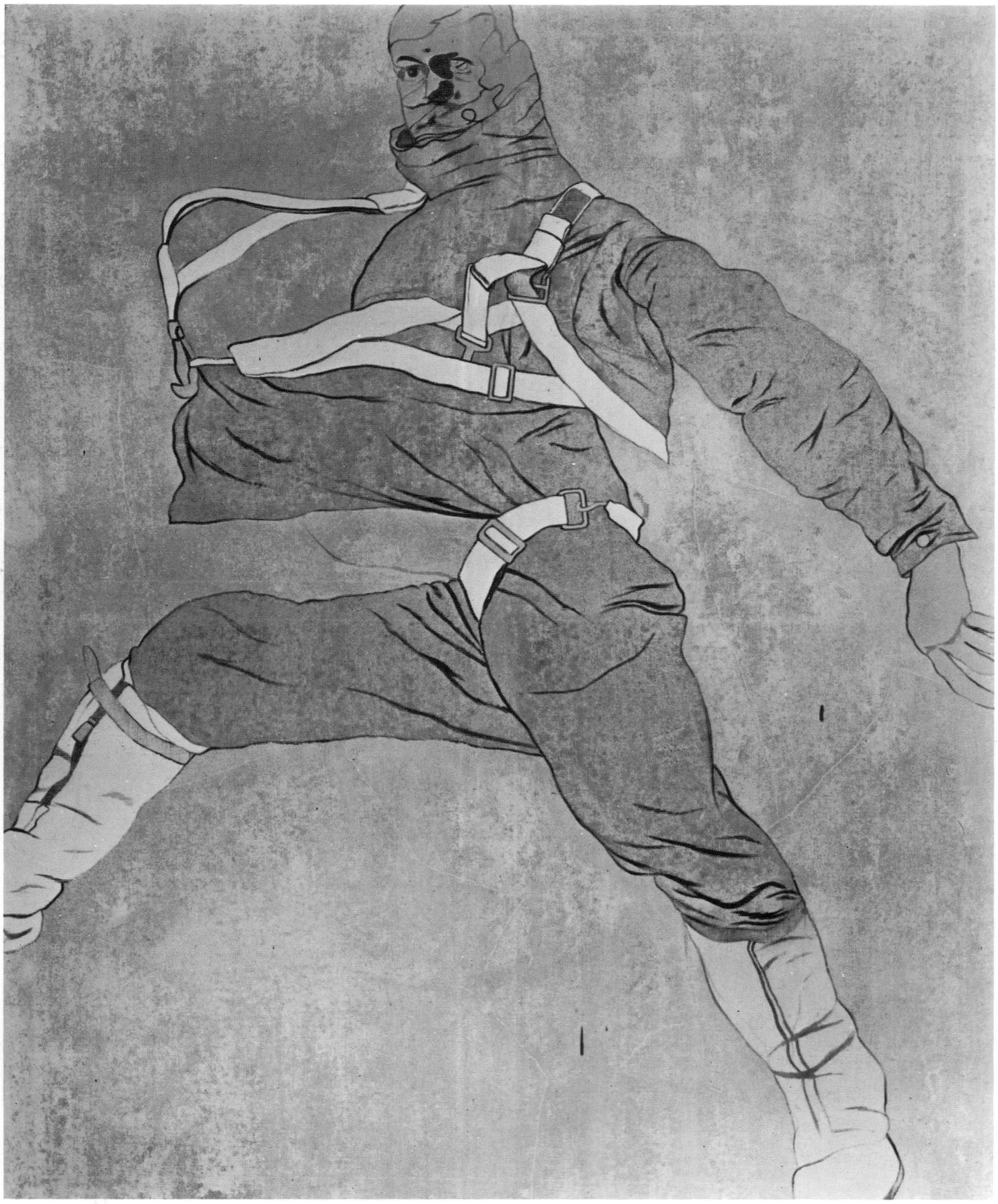

39. Aureolin, 1964. *Cat. no. 76.*

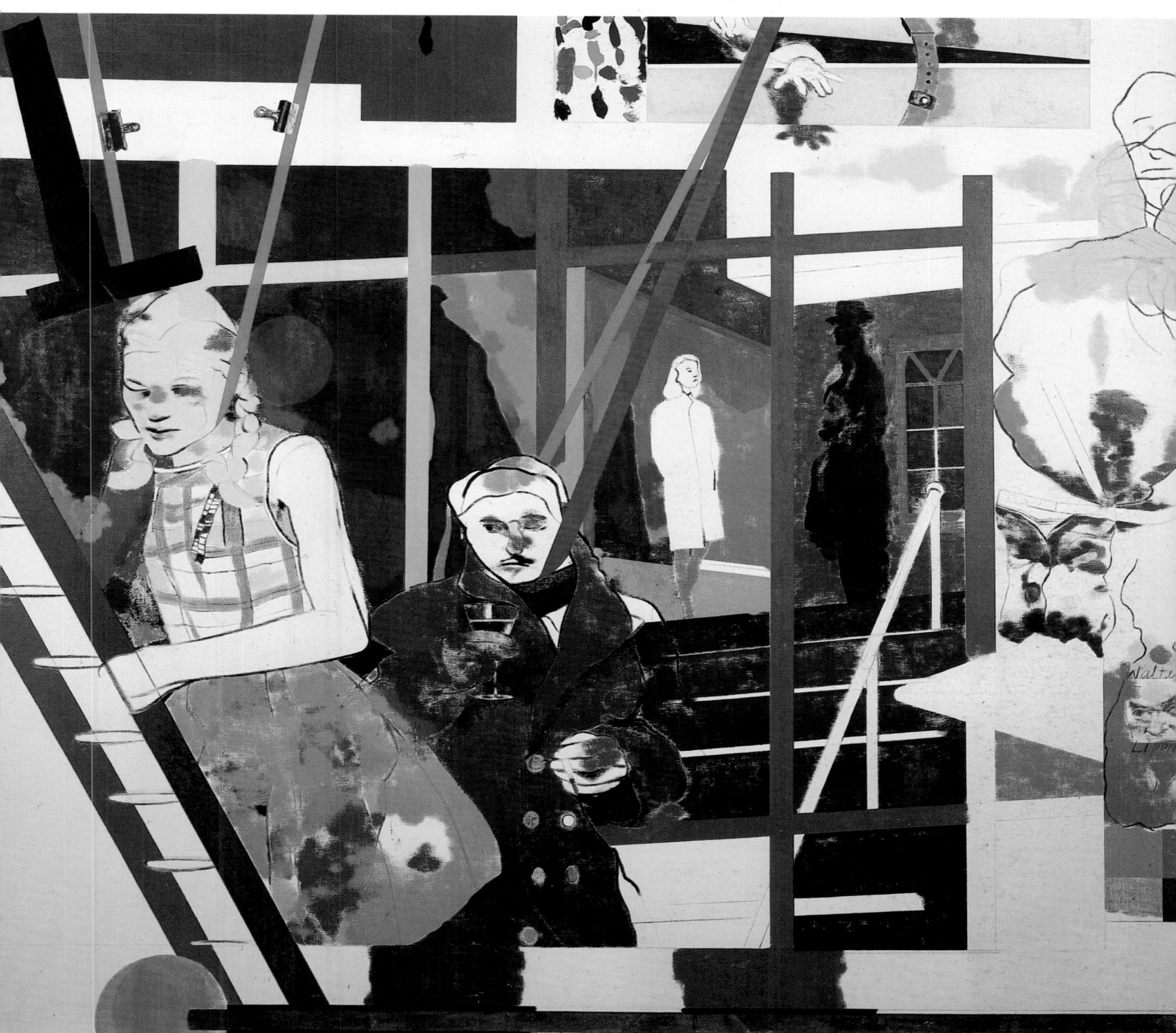

40. Walter Lippmann, 1966. *Cat. no. 88.*

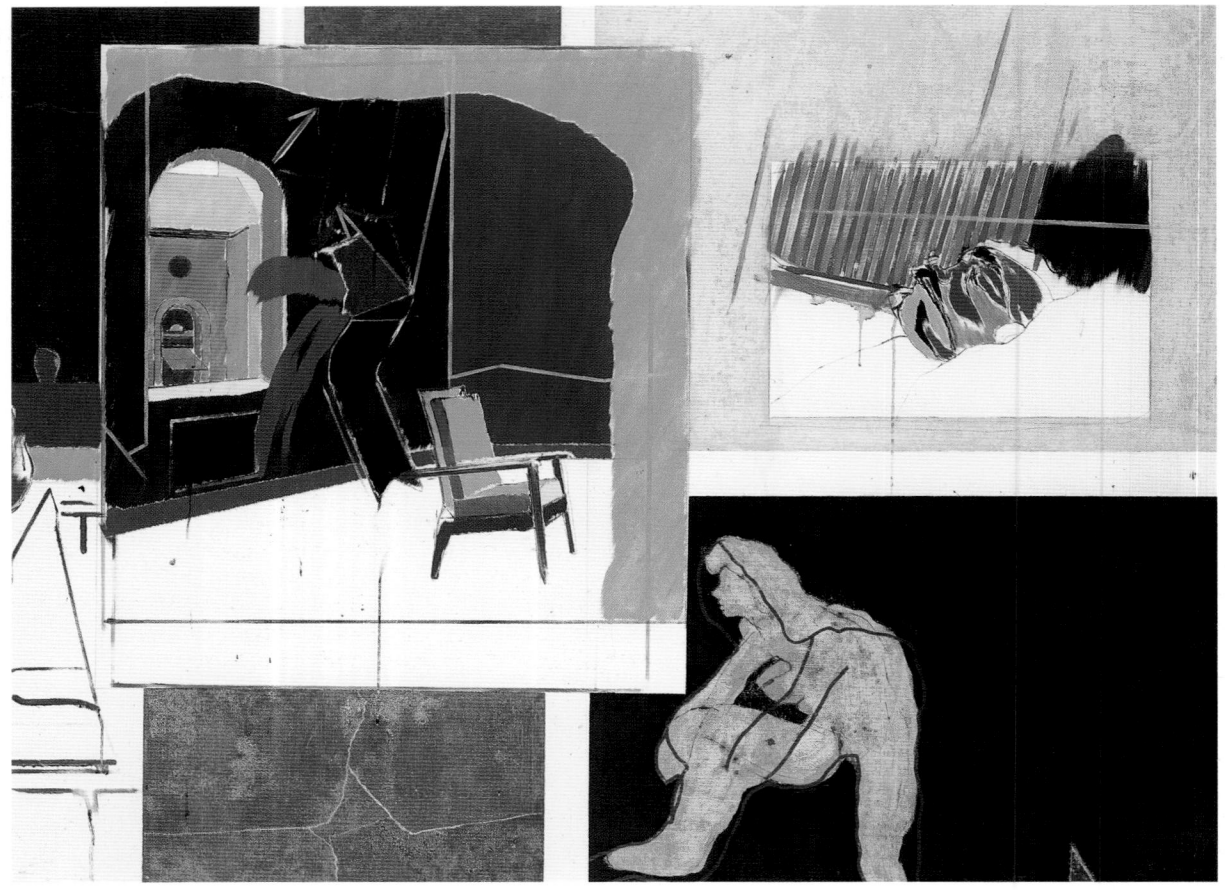

41. Notes Towards a Definition of Nobody *(detail)*, 1961. *Cat. no. 22.*

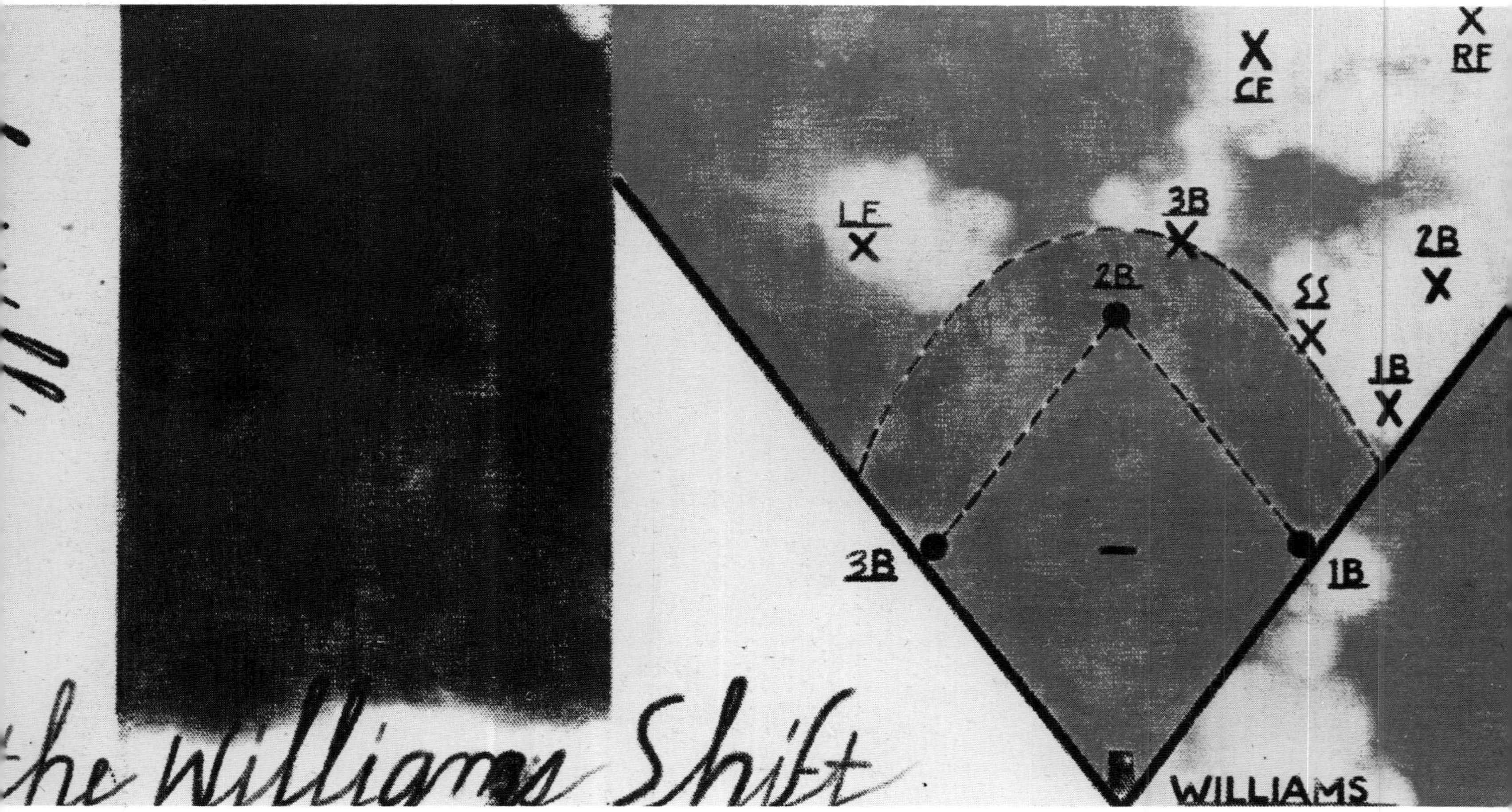

42. The Williams Shift (for Lou Boudreau), 1967. *Cat. no. 94.*

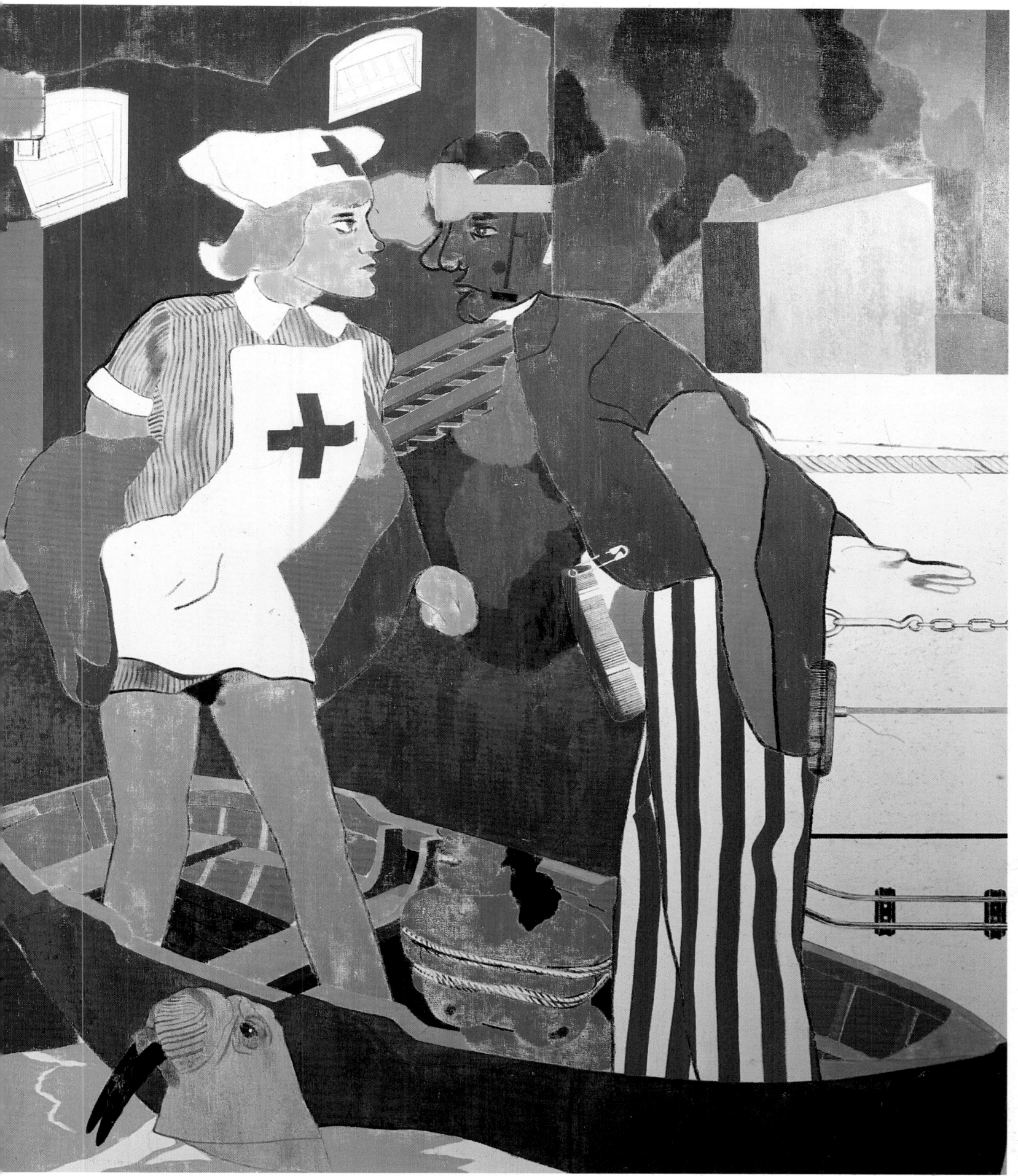

43. Erie Shore *(detail)*, 1966. *Cat. no. 89.*

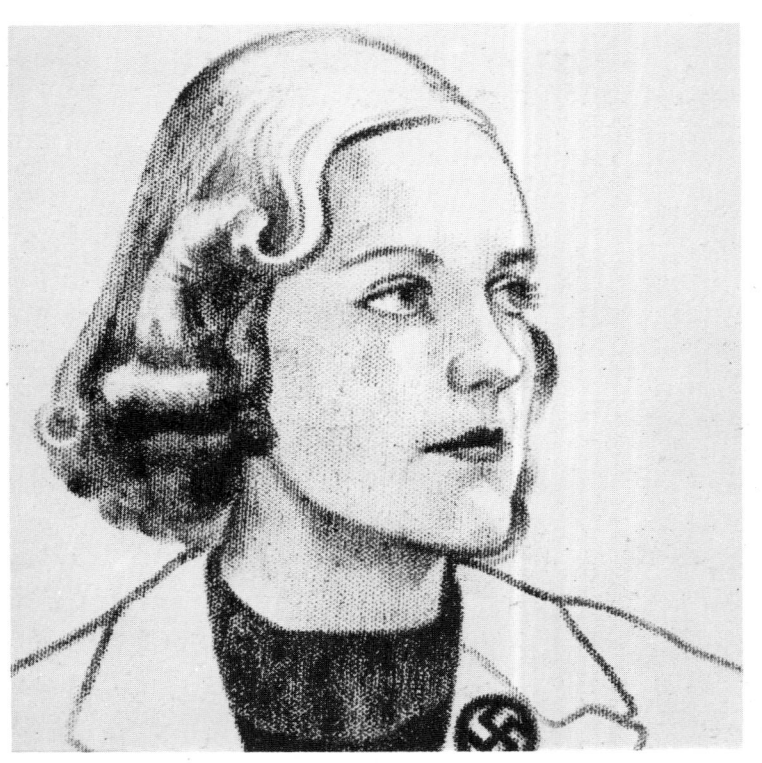

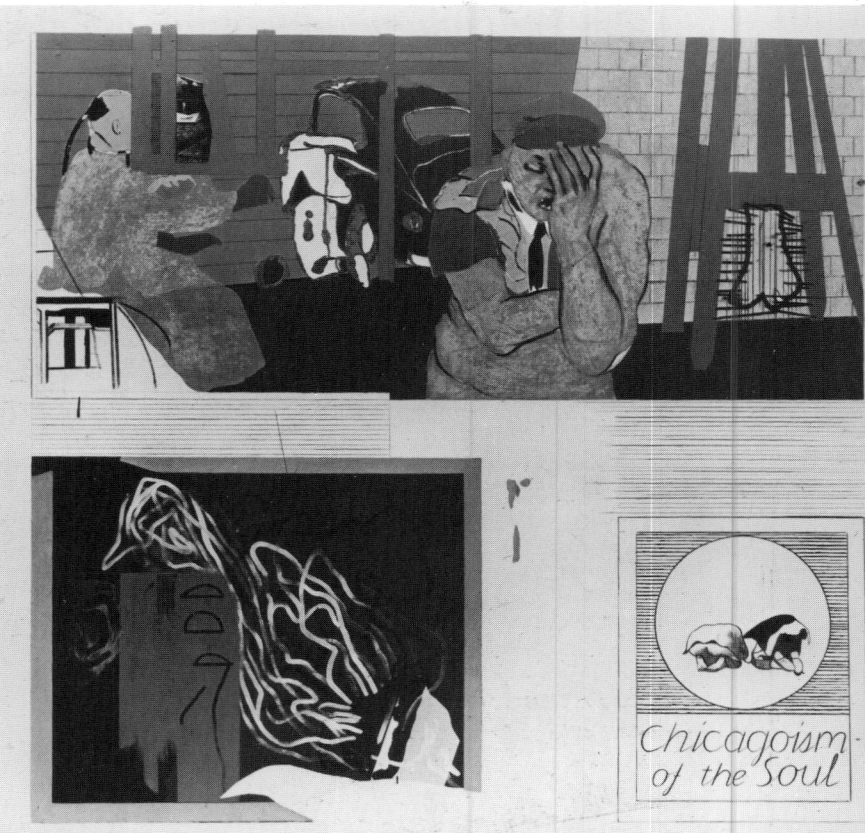

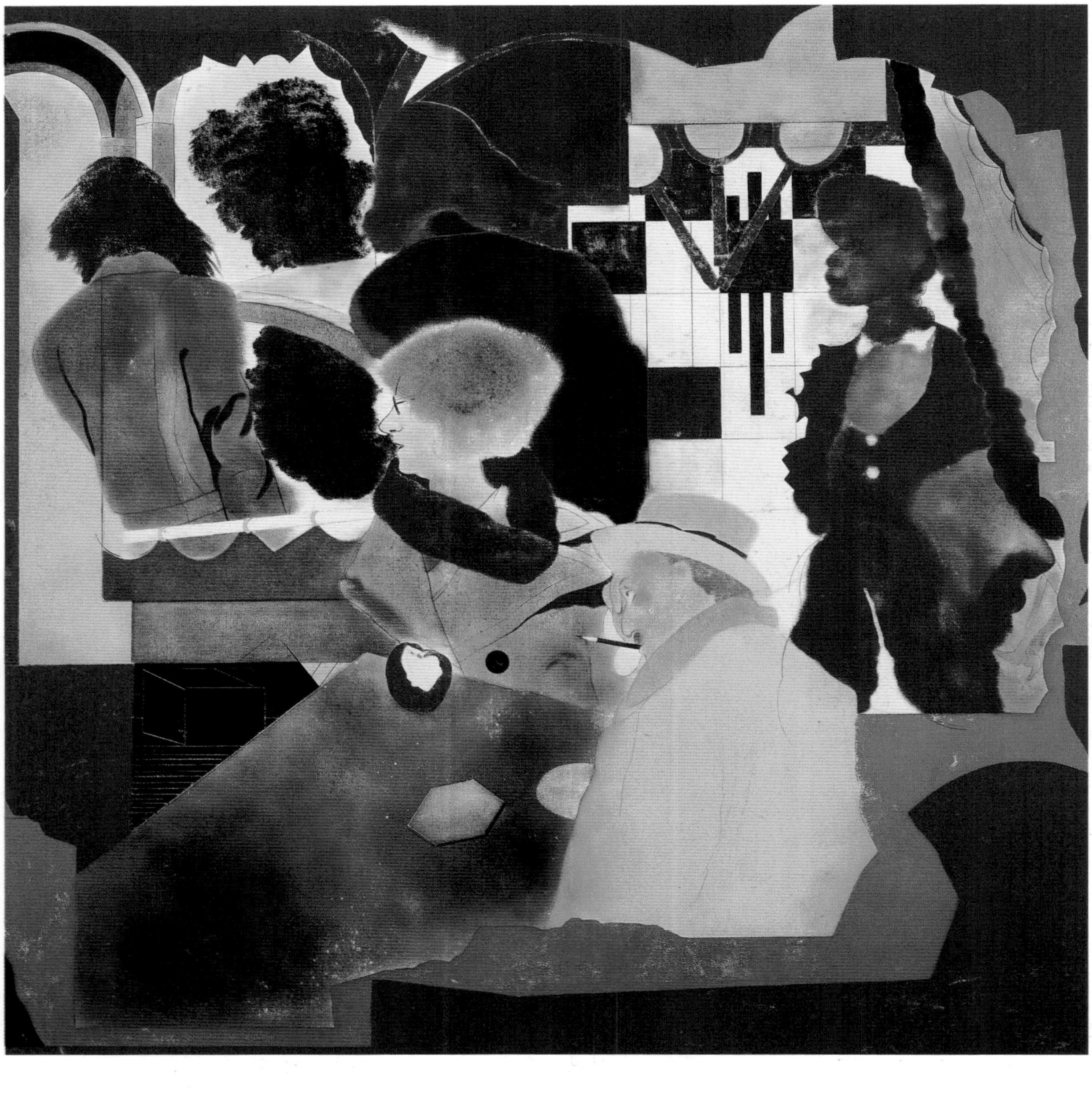

44. *(above left)* Unity Mitford, 1968.
Cat. no. 107.

45. *(above right)* The Perils of
Revisionism, 1963. *Cat. no. 49.*

46. Arcades (after Walter Benjamin),
1972–4. *Cat. no. 150.*

47. *(opposite)* Synchromy with F.B. –
General of Hot Desire *(detail)*, 1968–9.
Cat. no. 113.

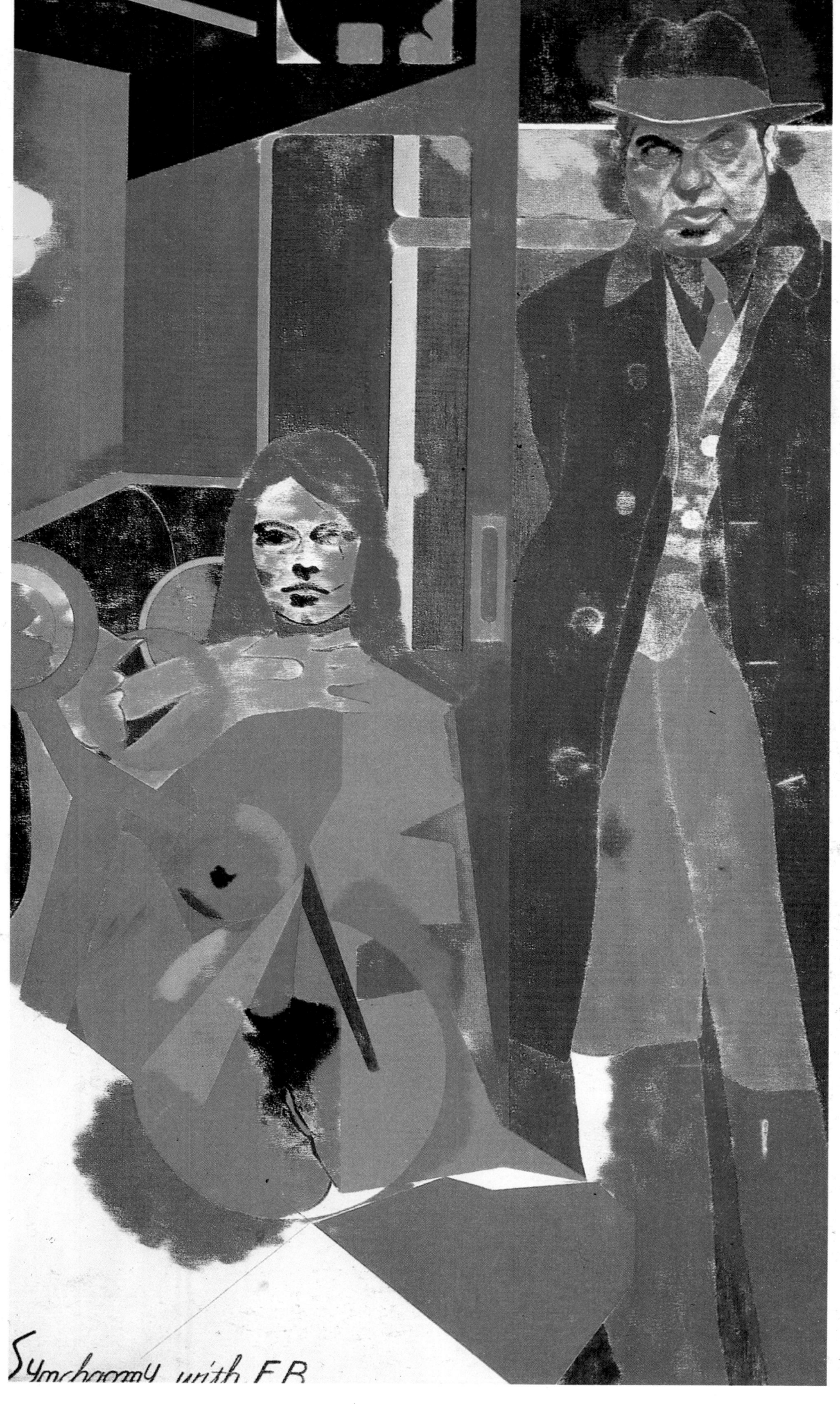

Symphony with F.B.

little slum pid

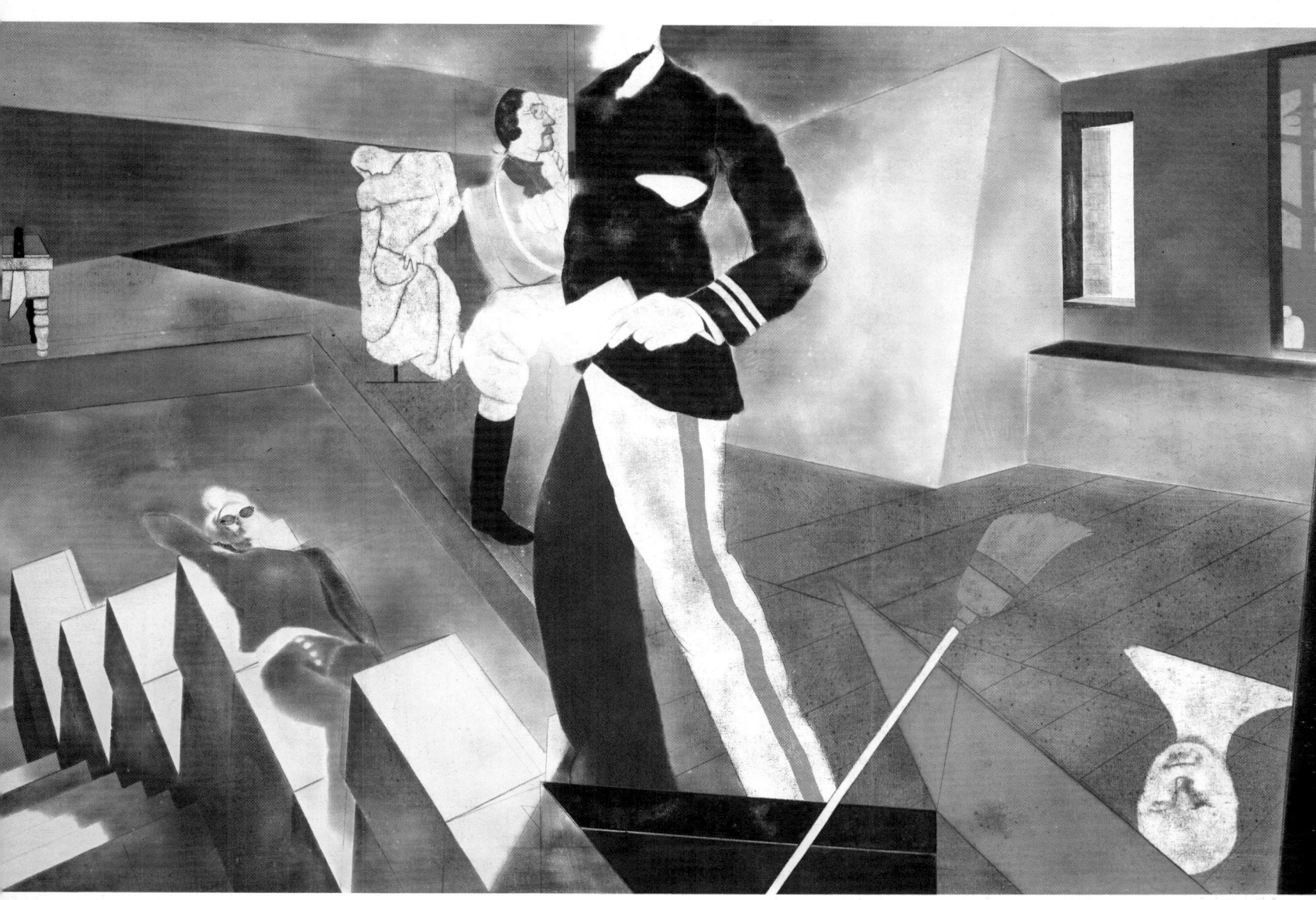

49. Malta (for Chris and Rose), 1974. *Cat. no. 162.*

48. Little Slum Picture, 1968. *Cat. no. 106.*

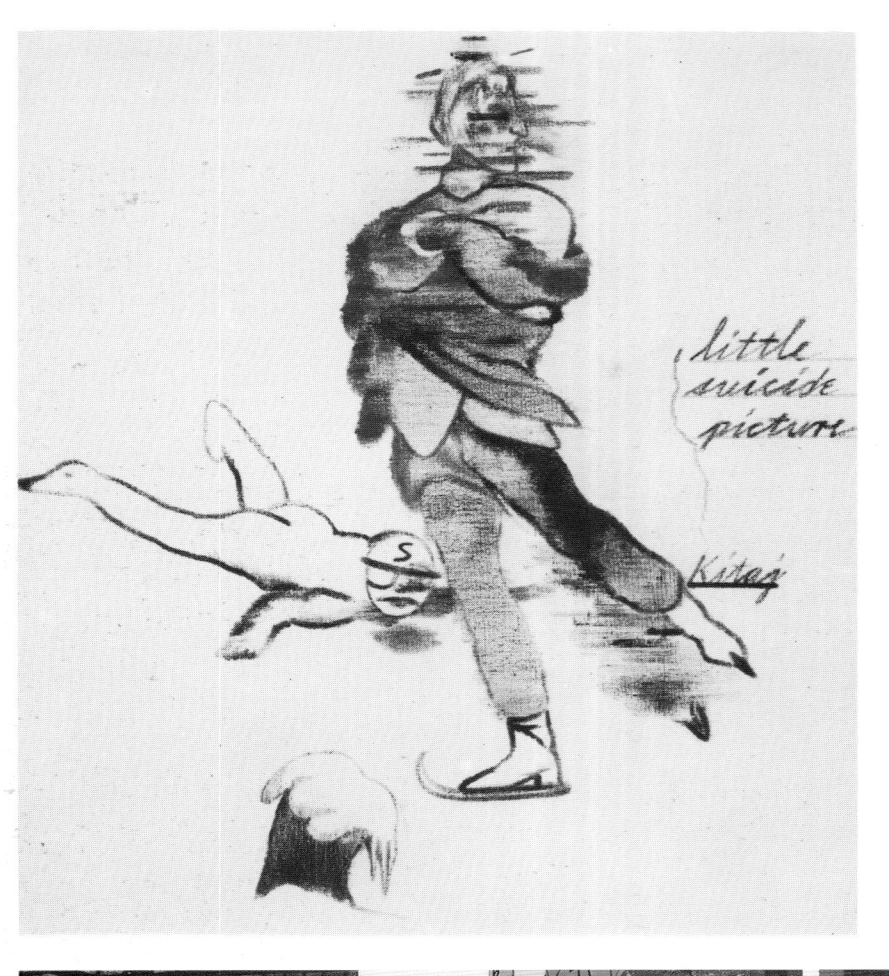

little
suicide
picture

Kitaj

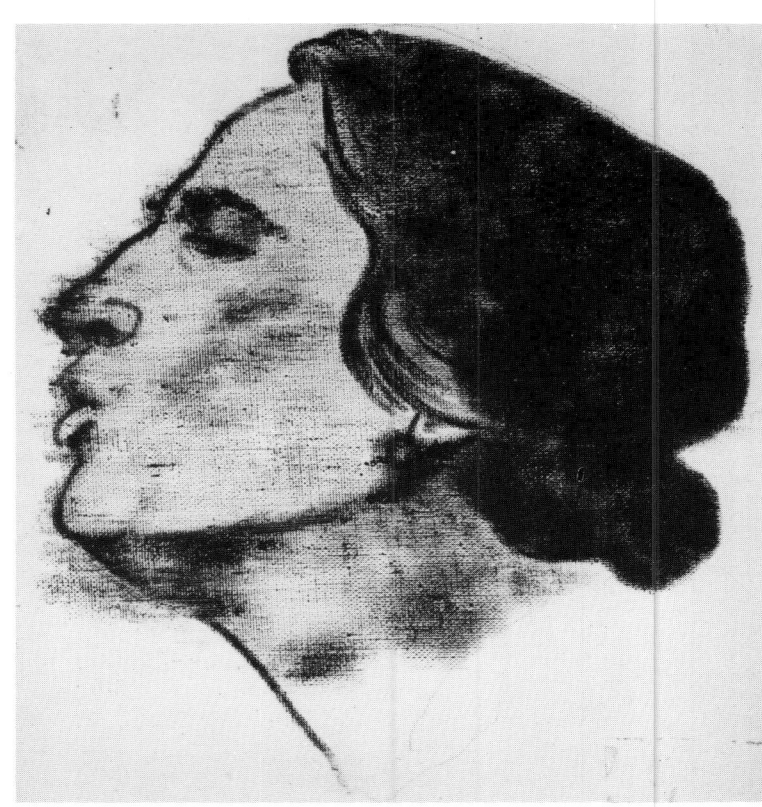

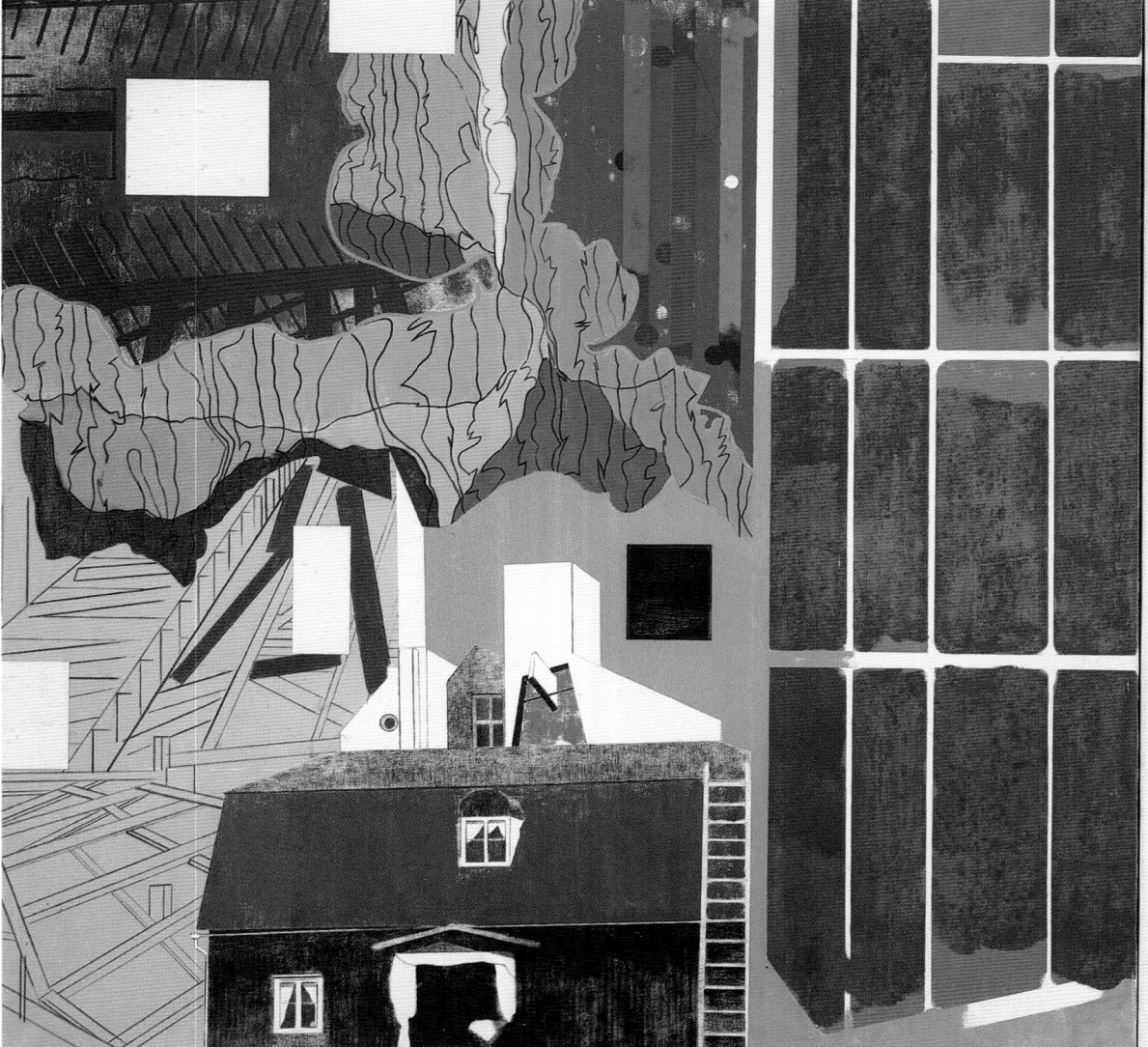

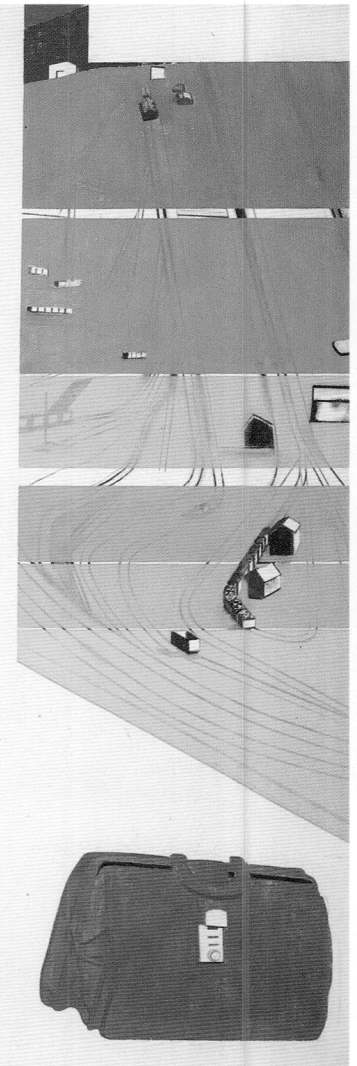

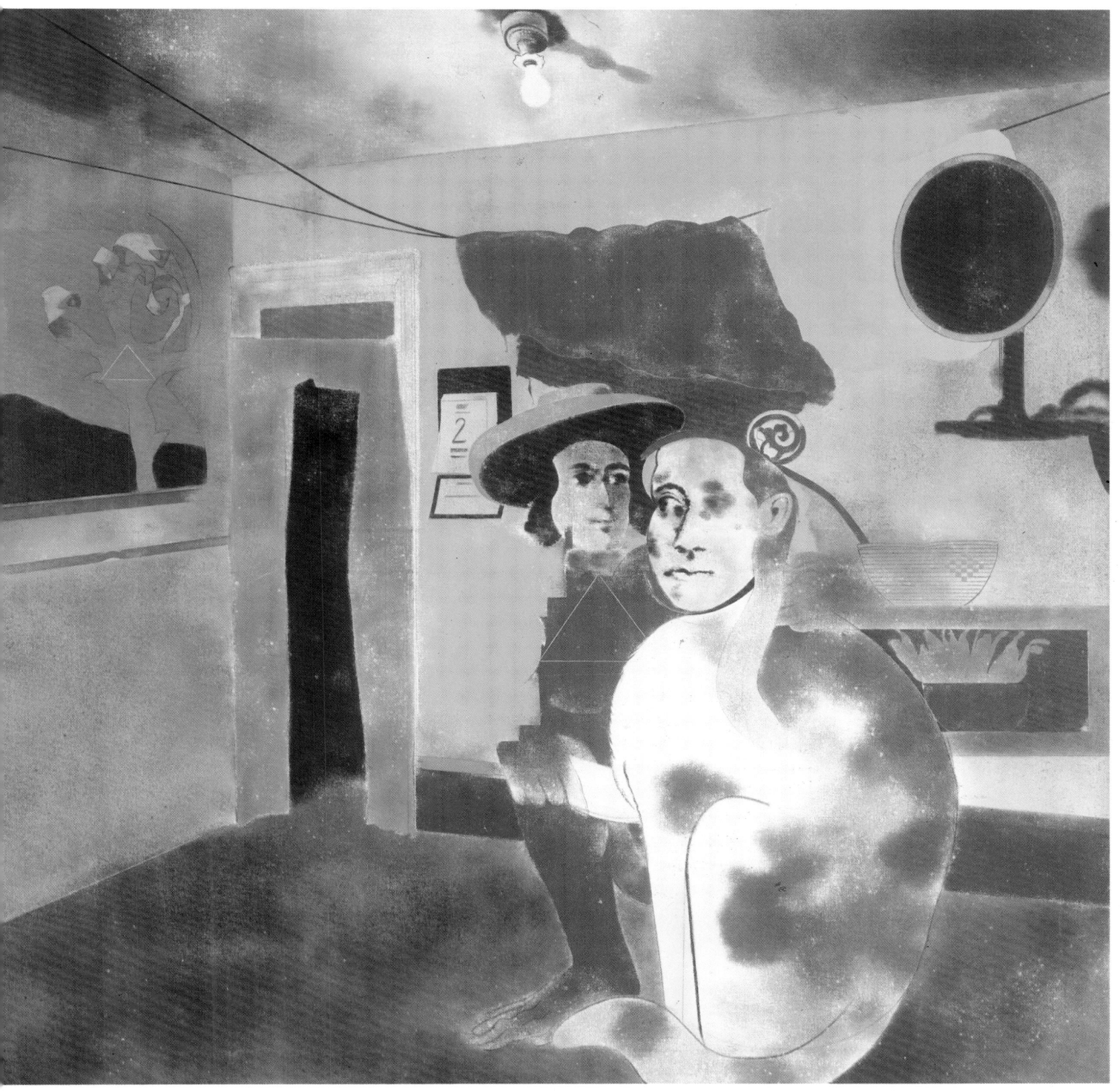

53. The Man of the Woods and the Cat of the Mountains, 1973. *Cat. no. 158.*

50. *(opposite, top left)* Little Suicide Picture, 1969. *Cat. no. 125.*

51. *(opposite, top right)* La Pasionaria, 1969. *Cat. no. 120.*

52. *(left)* Trout for Factitious Bait, 1965. *Cat. no. 84.*

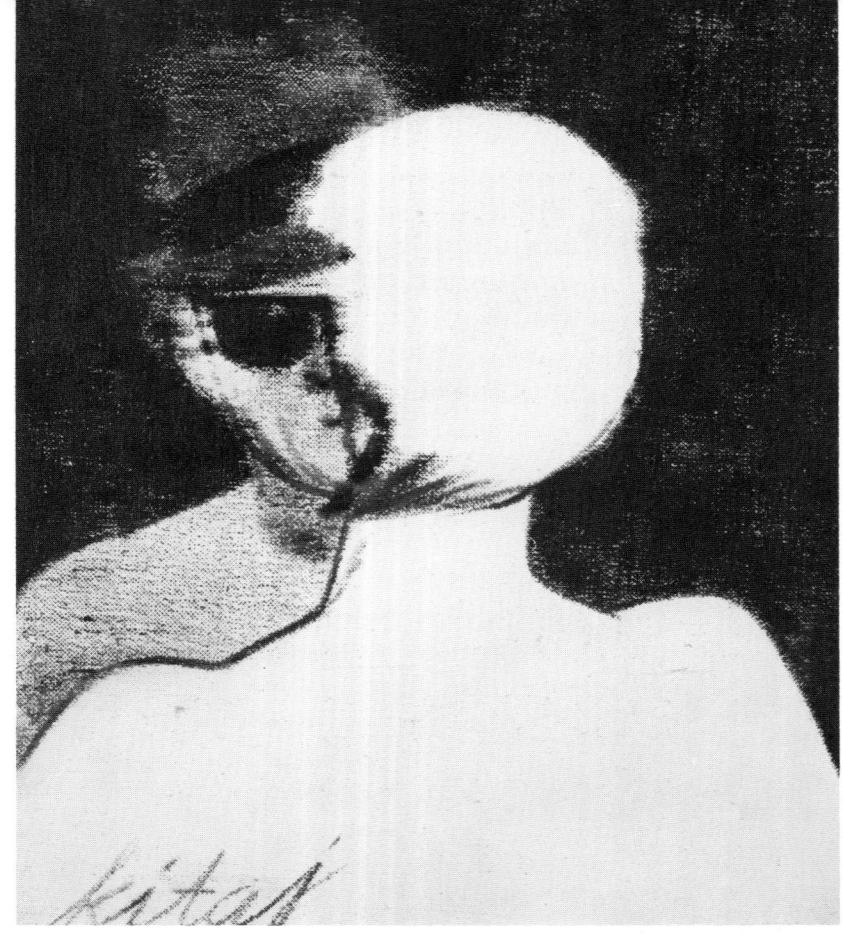

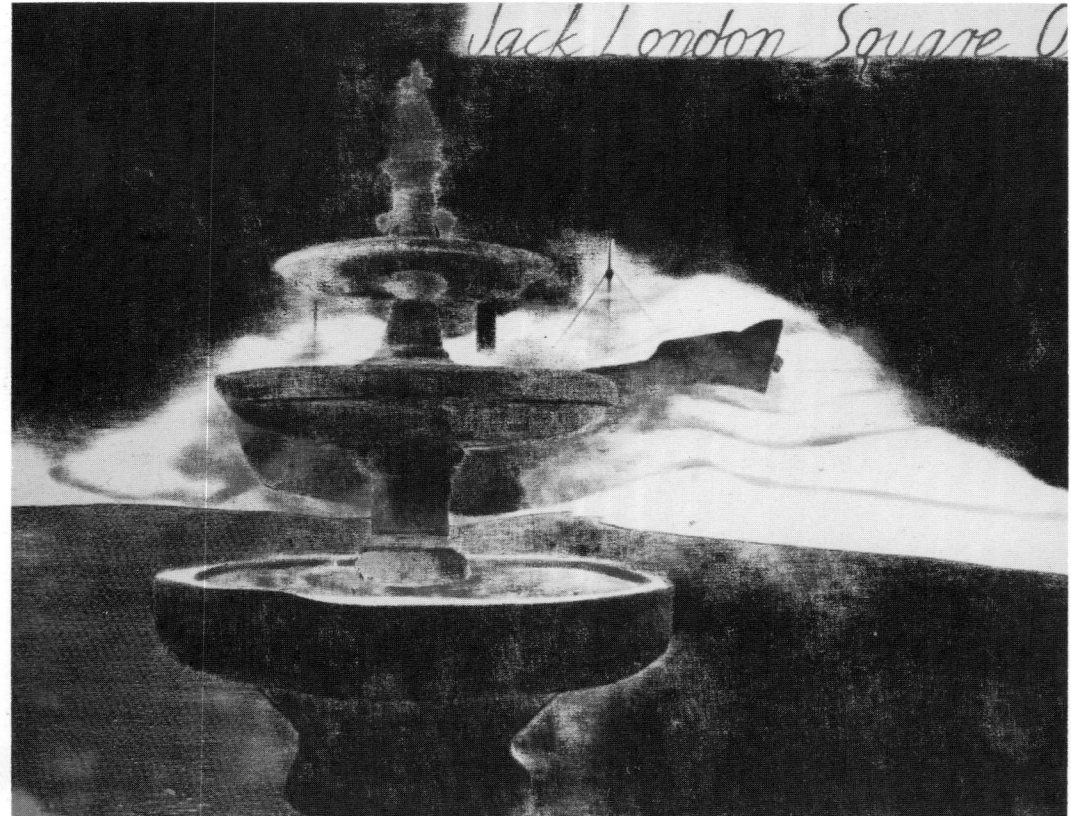

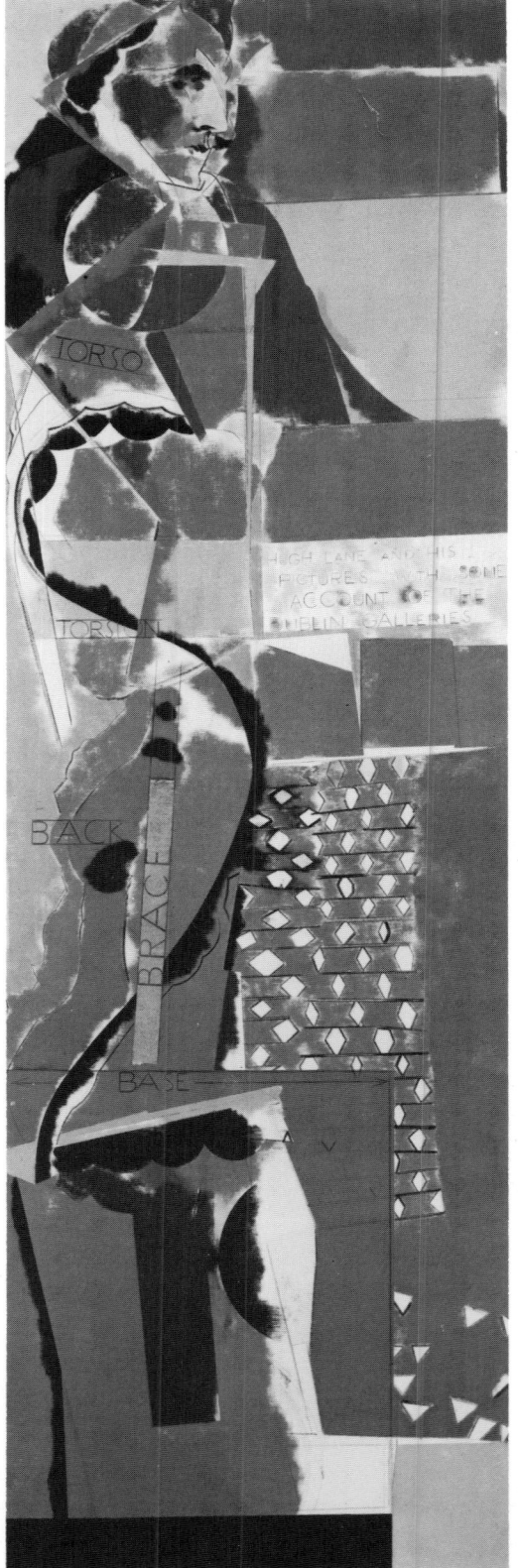

54. *(top)* Little Romance I, 1969. *Cat. no. 116.*

55. *(above)* Jack London Square, Oakland, 1969. *Cat. no. 114.*

56. *(above right)* Hugh Lane, 1972. *Cat. no. 148.*

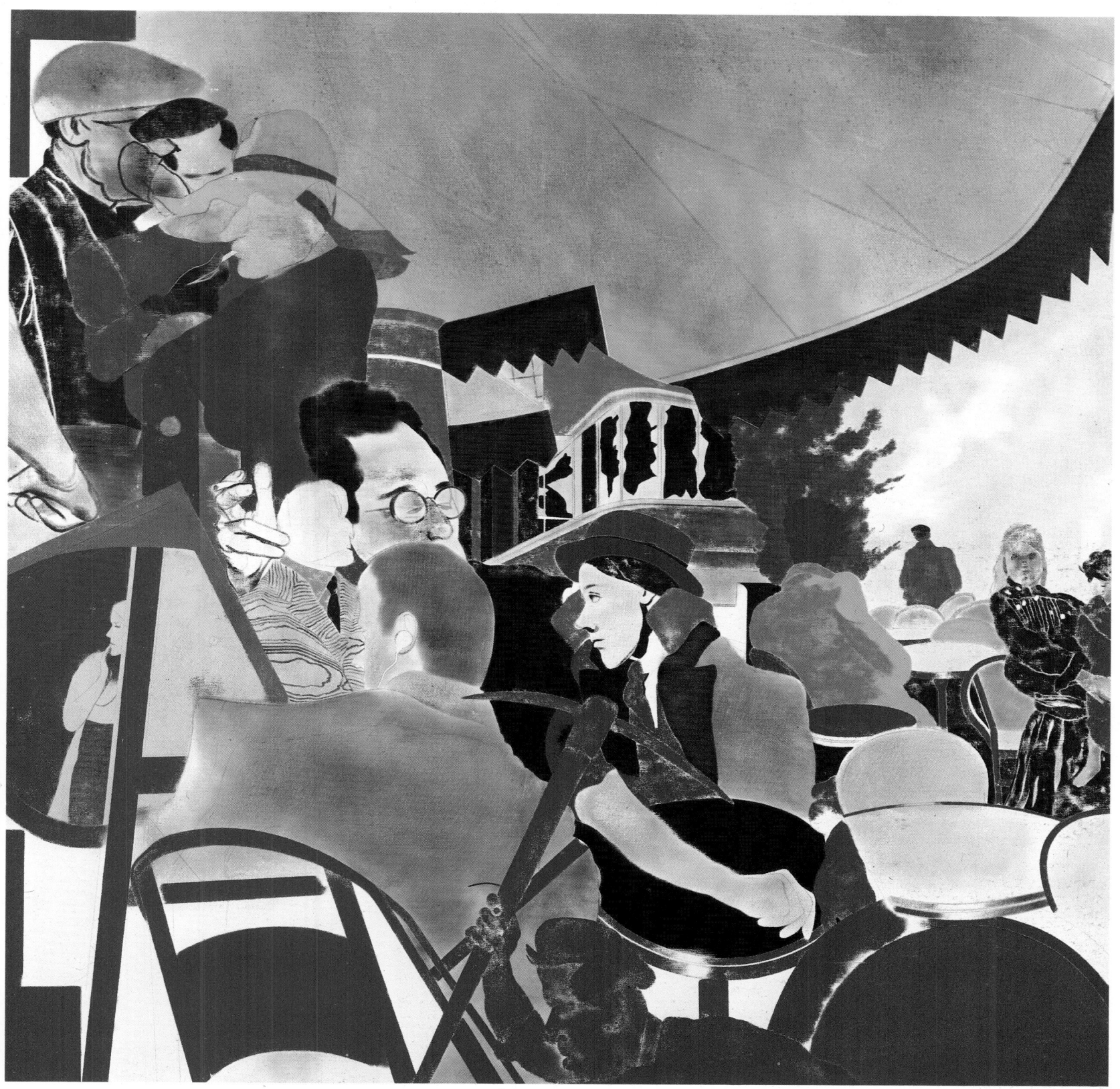

57. The Autumn of Central Paris (after Walter Benjamin), 1972–3. *Cat. no. 149.*

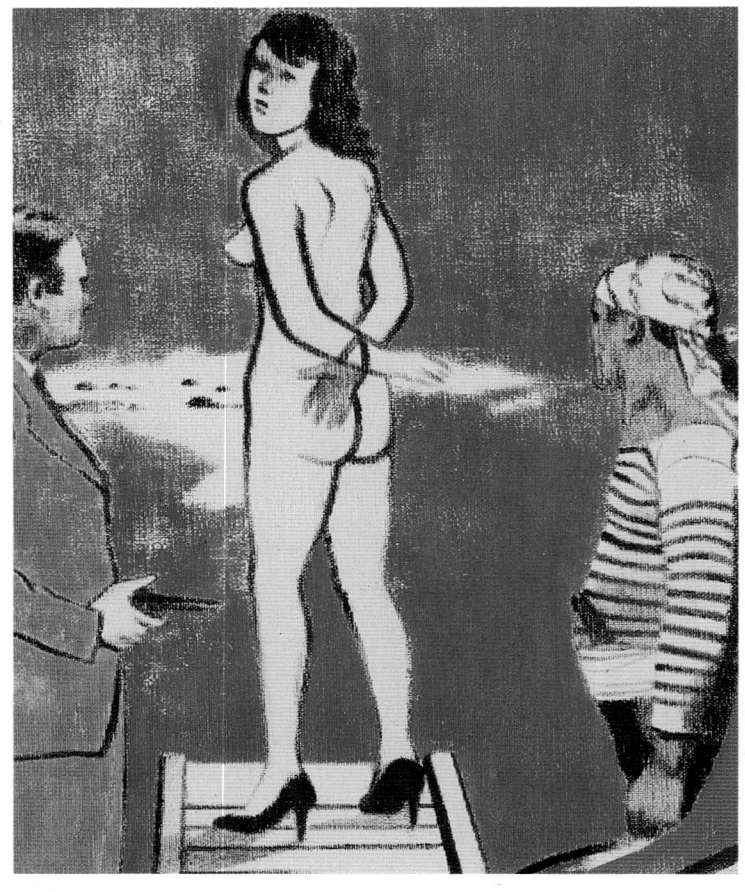

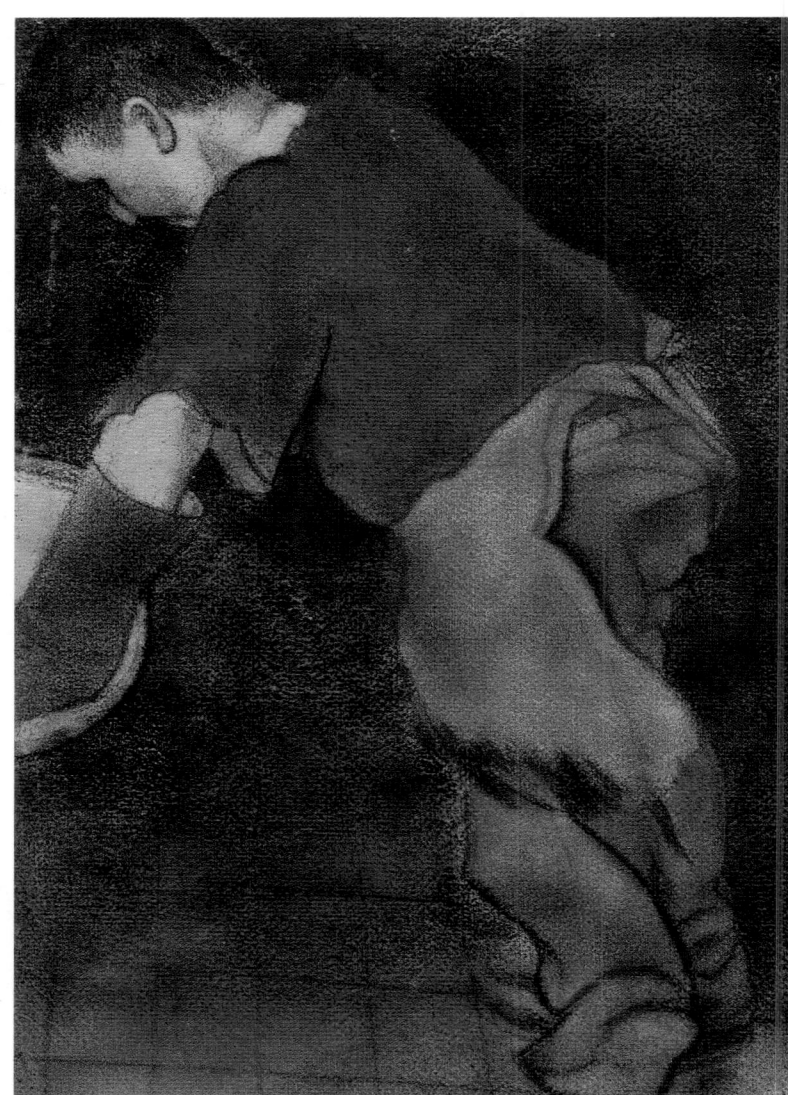

58. *(above)* St Teresa
(detail of Plate 61).

59. *(above right)* Washing Cork
(Ramón), 1978. *Cat. no. 234.*

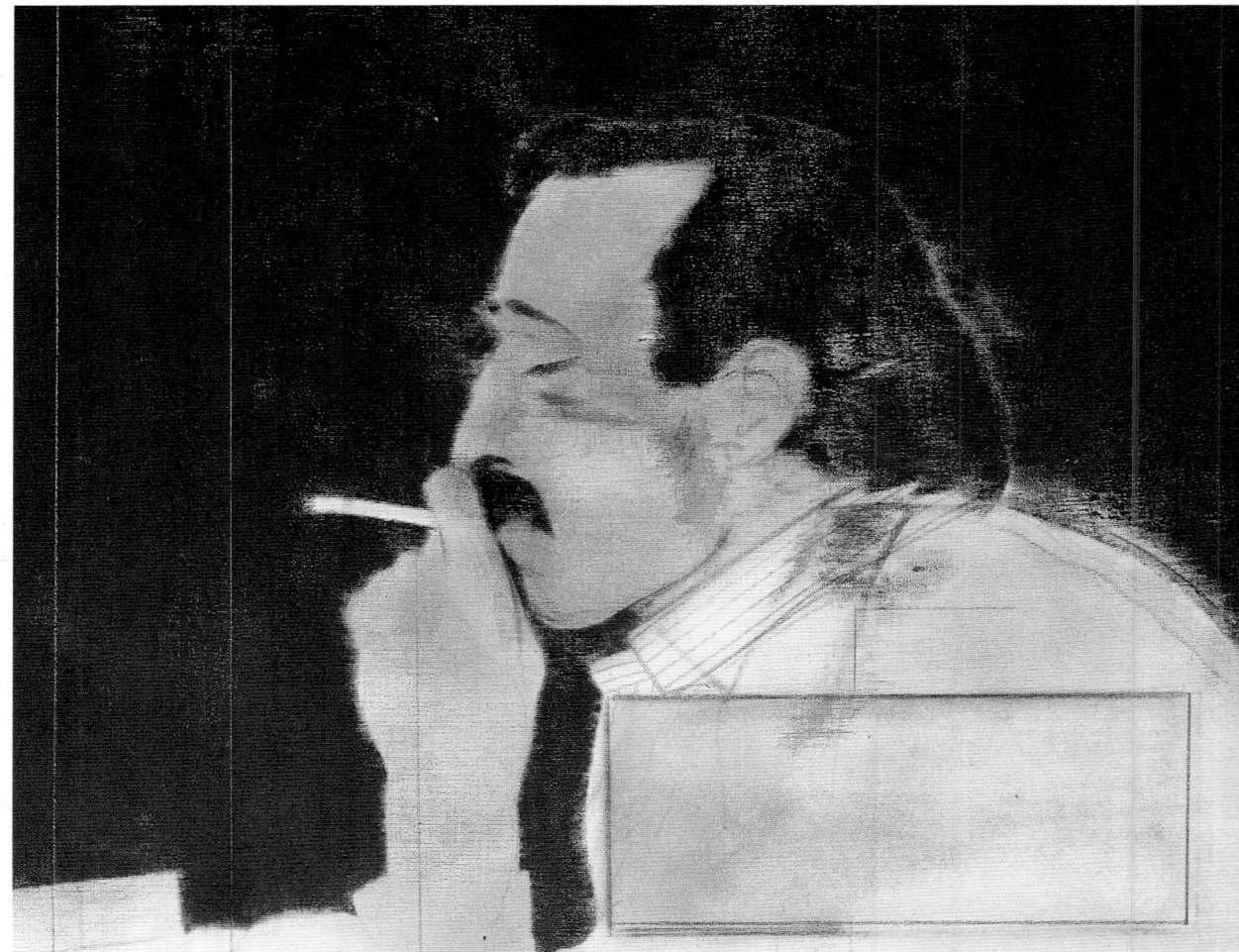

60. José Vicente (unfinished
study for The Singers), 1972-4.
Cat. no. 151.

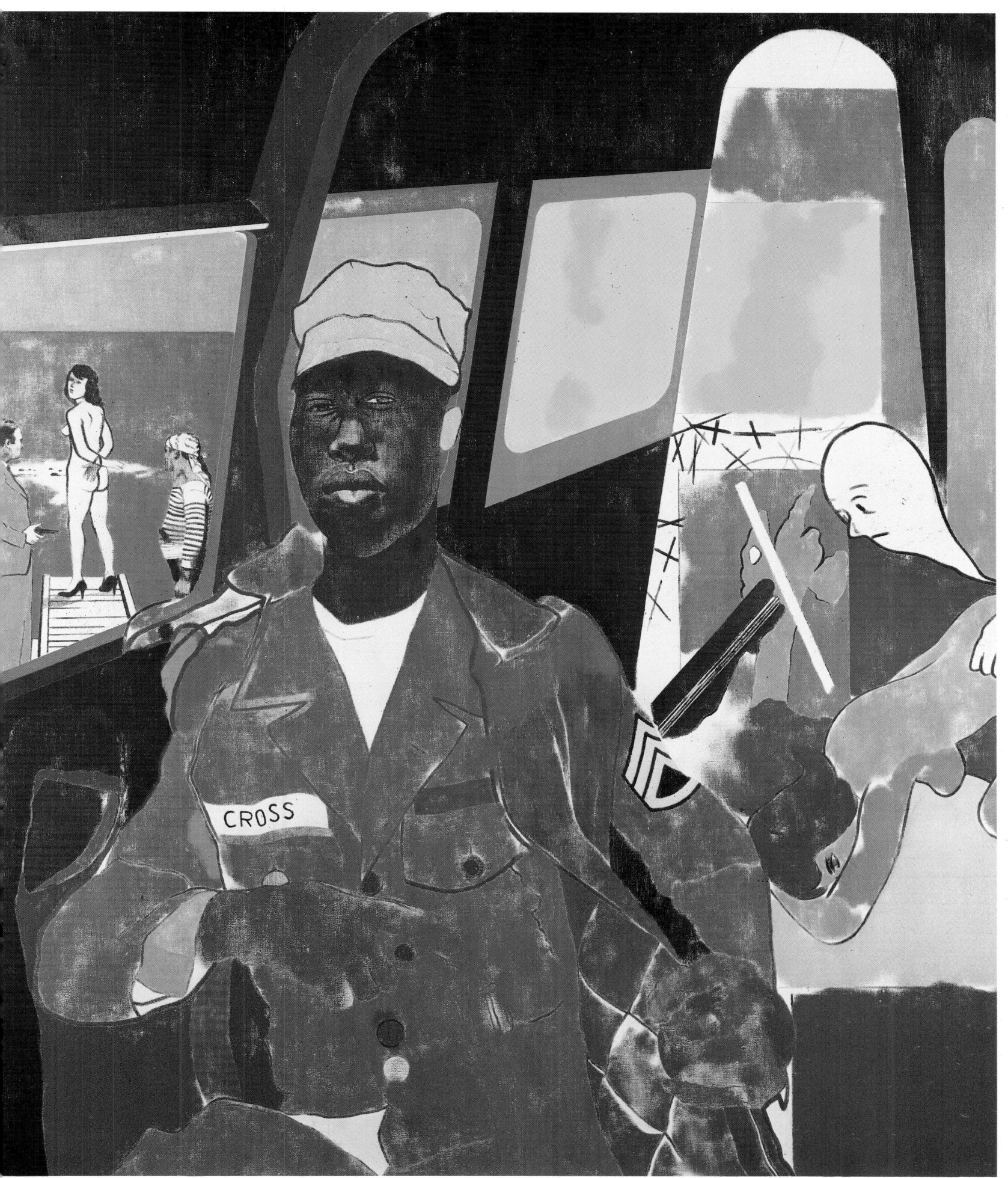

61. Juan de la Cruz, 1967. *Cat. no. 93.*

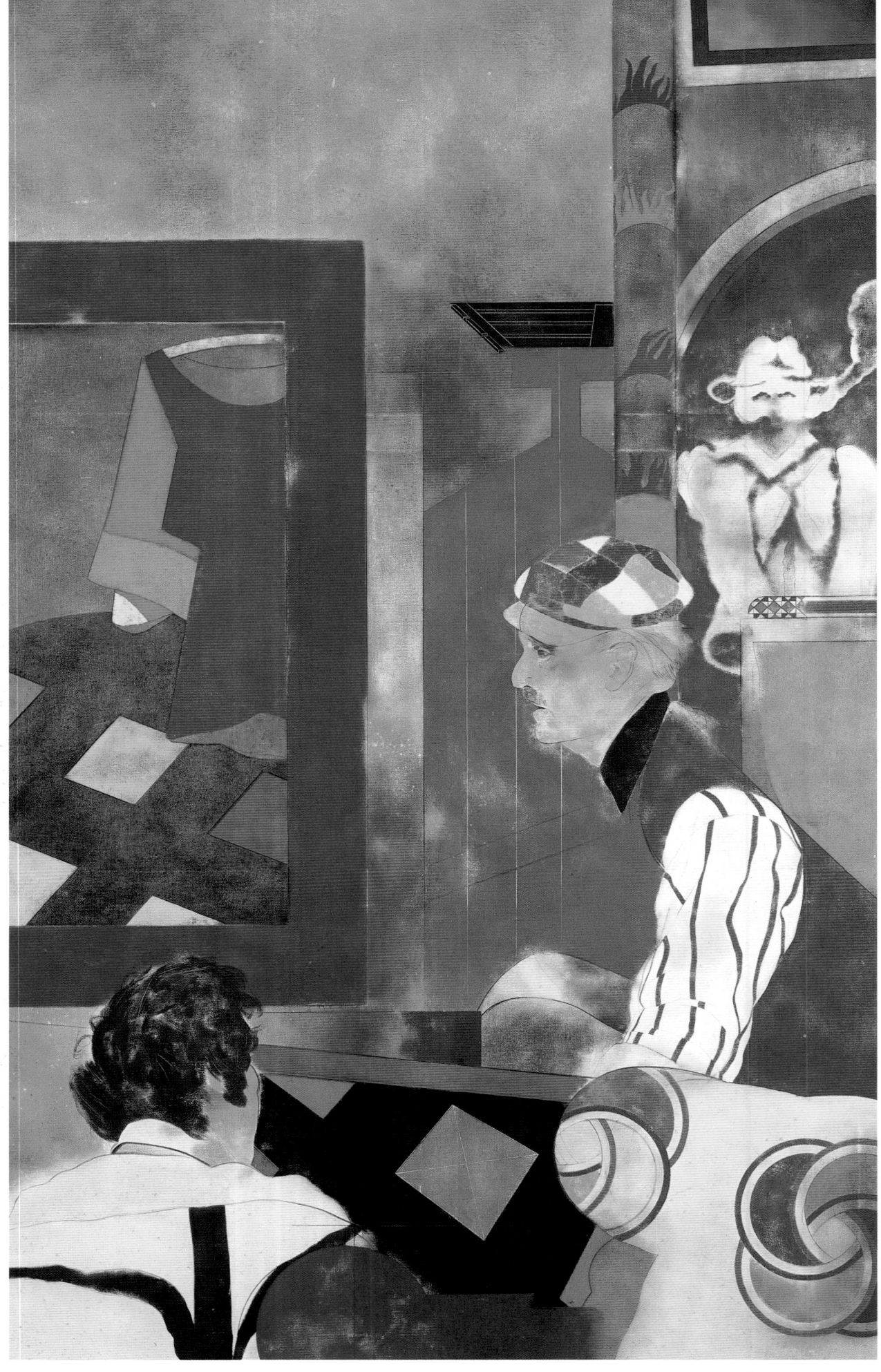

62. Kenneth Anger and Michael Powell, 1973. *Cat. no. 155*.

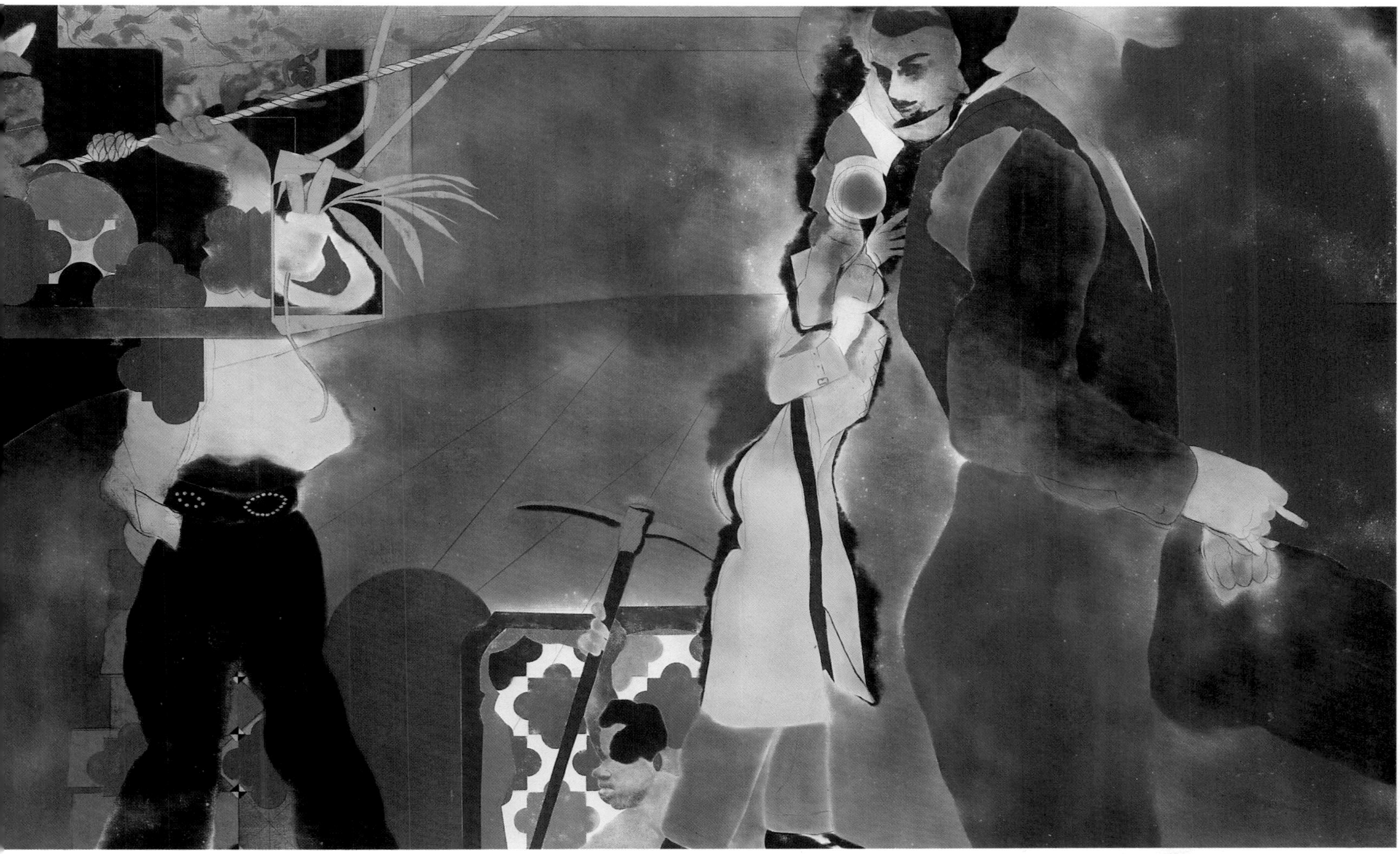

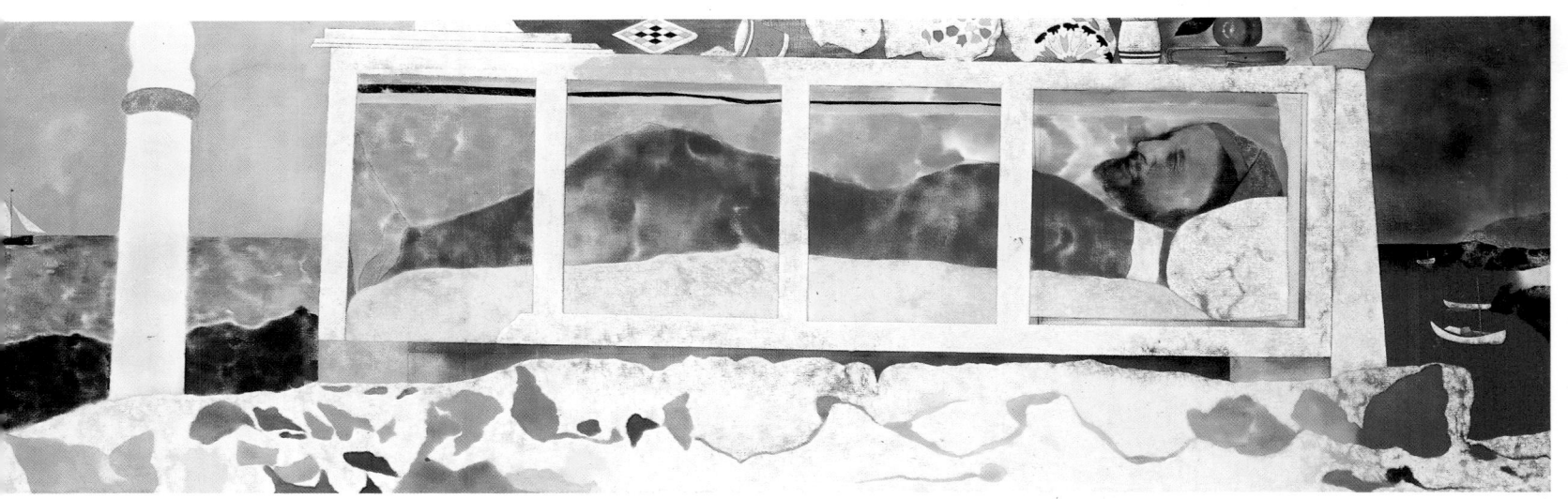

63. Pacific Coast Highway (Across the Pacific), 1973. *Cat. no. 154.*

64. Catalan Christ (Pretending to be Dead), 1976. *Cat. no. 190.*

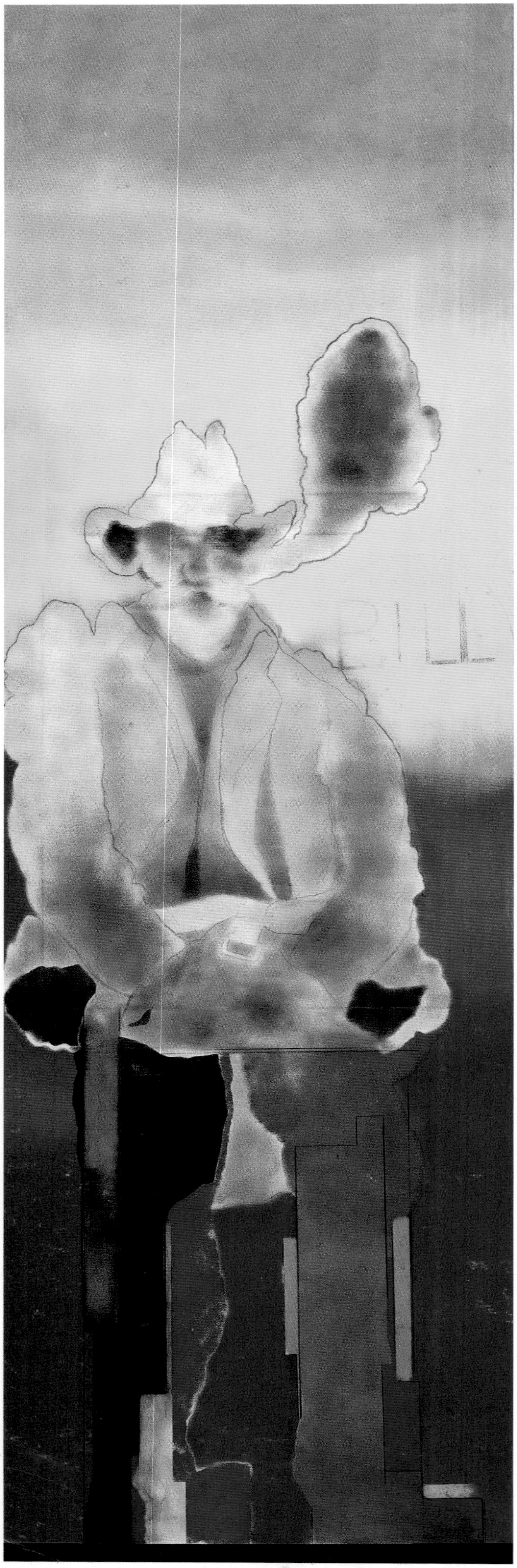

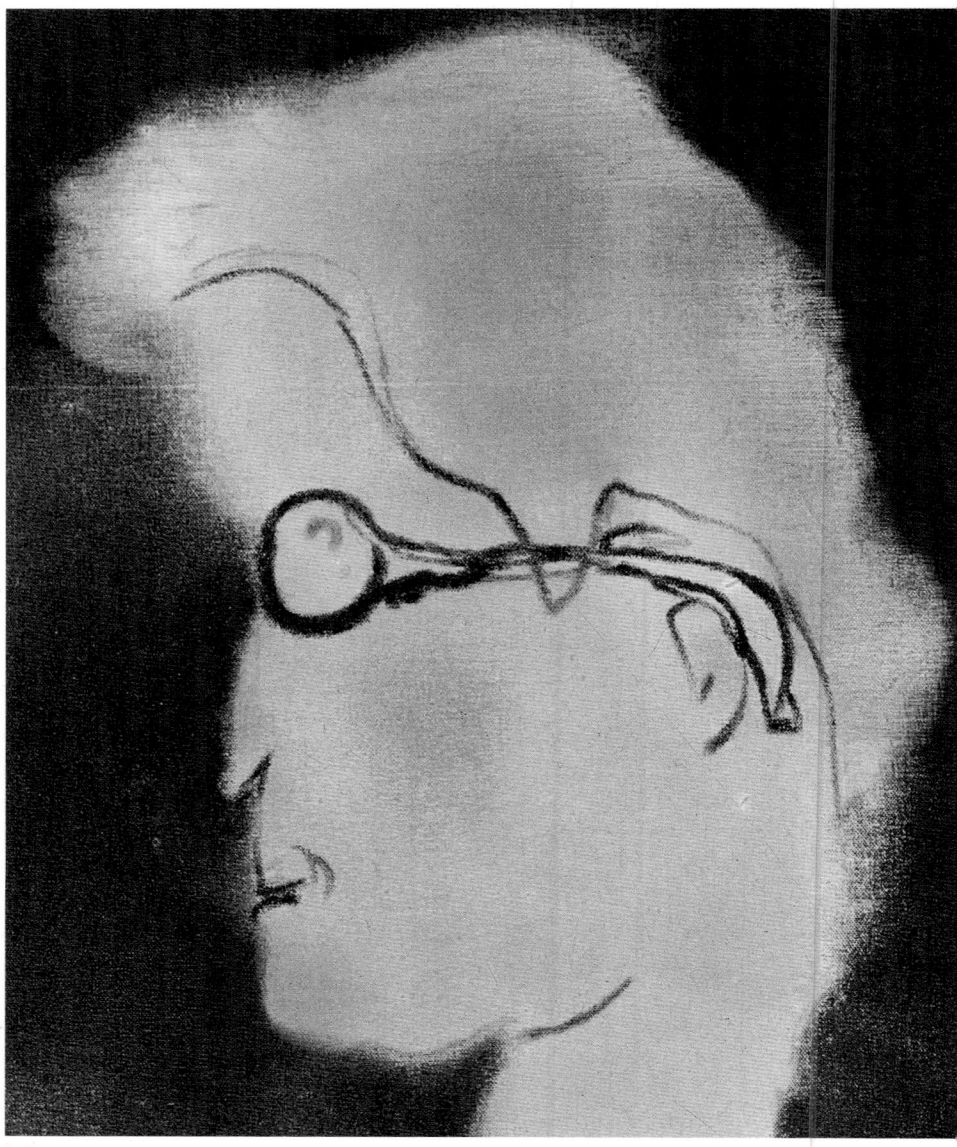

66. *(above)* Superman *(detail of Plate 68).*

65. *(left)* Bill at Sunset, 1973. *Cat. no. 156.*

67. *(opposite, left)* Batman, 1973. *Cat. no. 152.*

68. *(opposite, right)* Superman, 1973. *Cat. no. 153.*

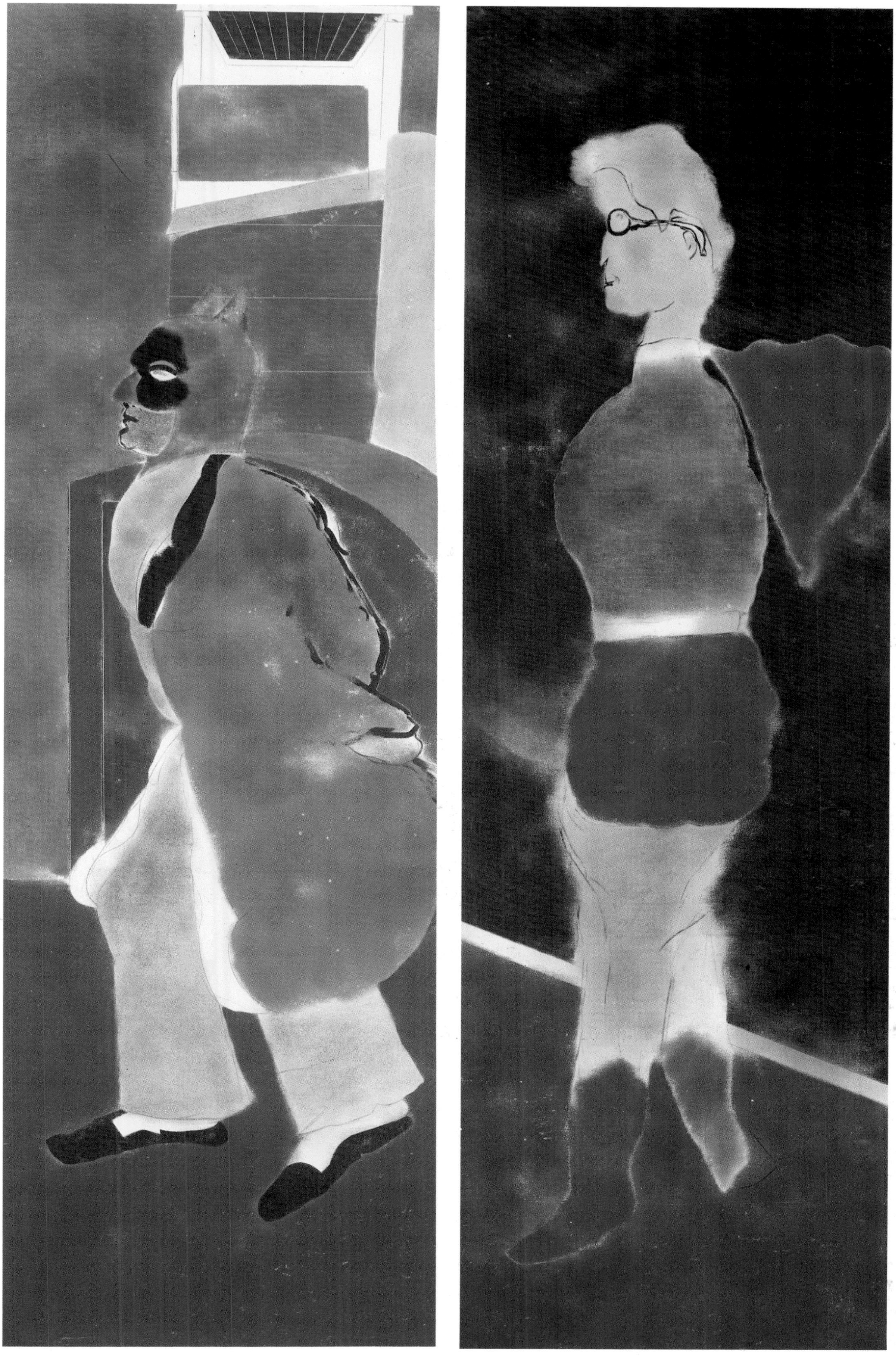

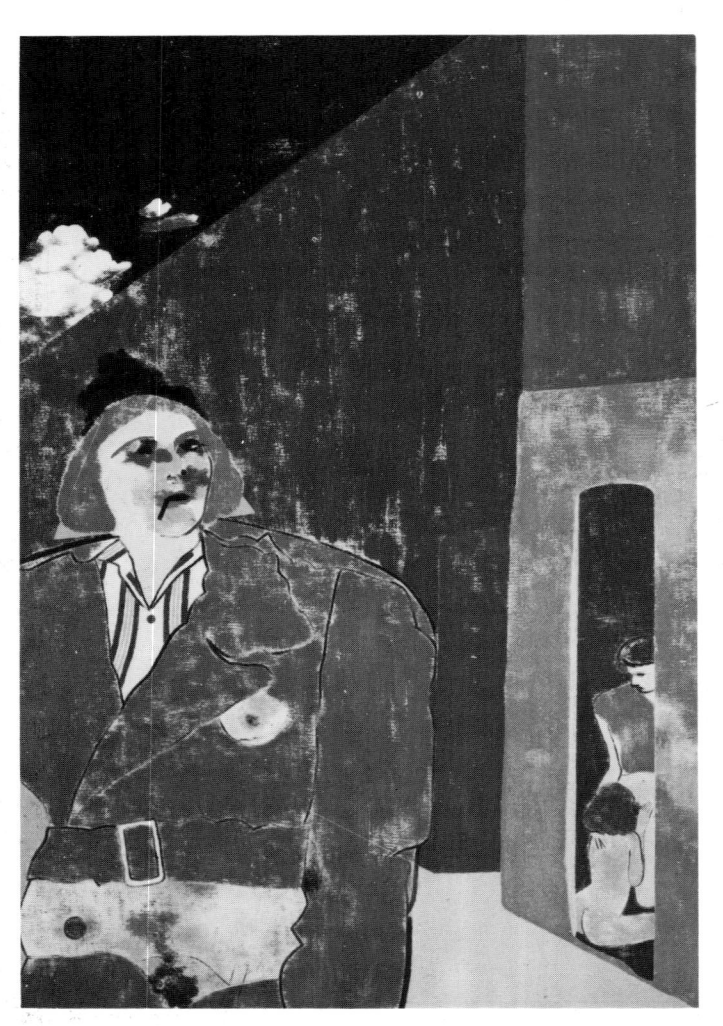
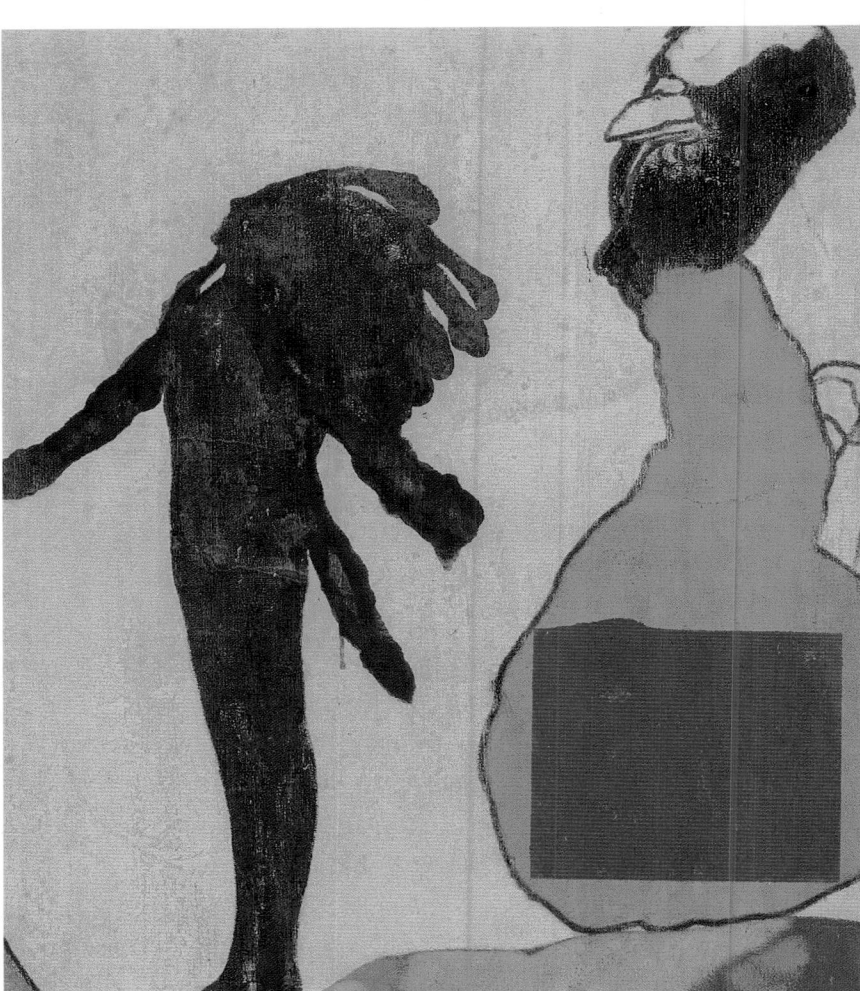

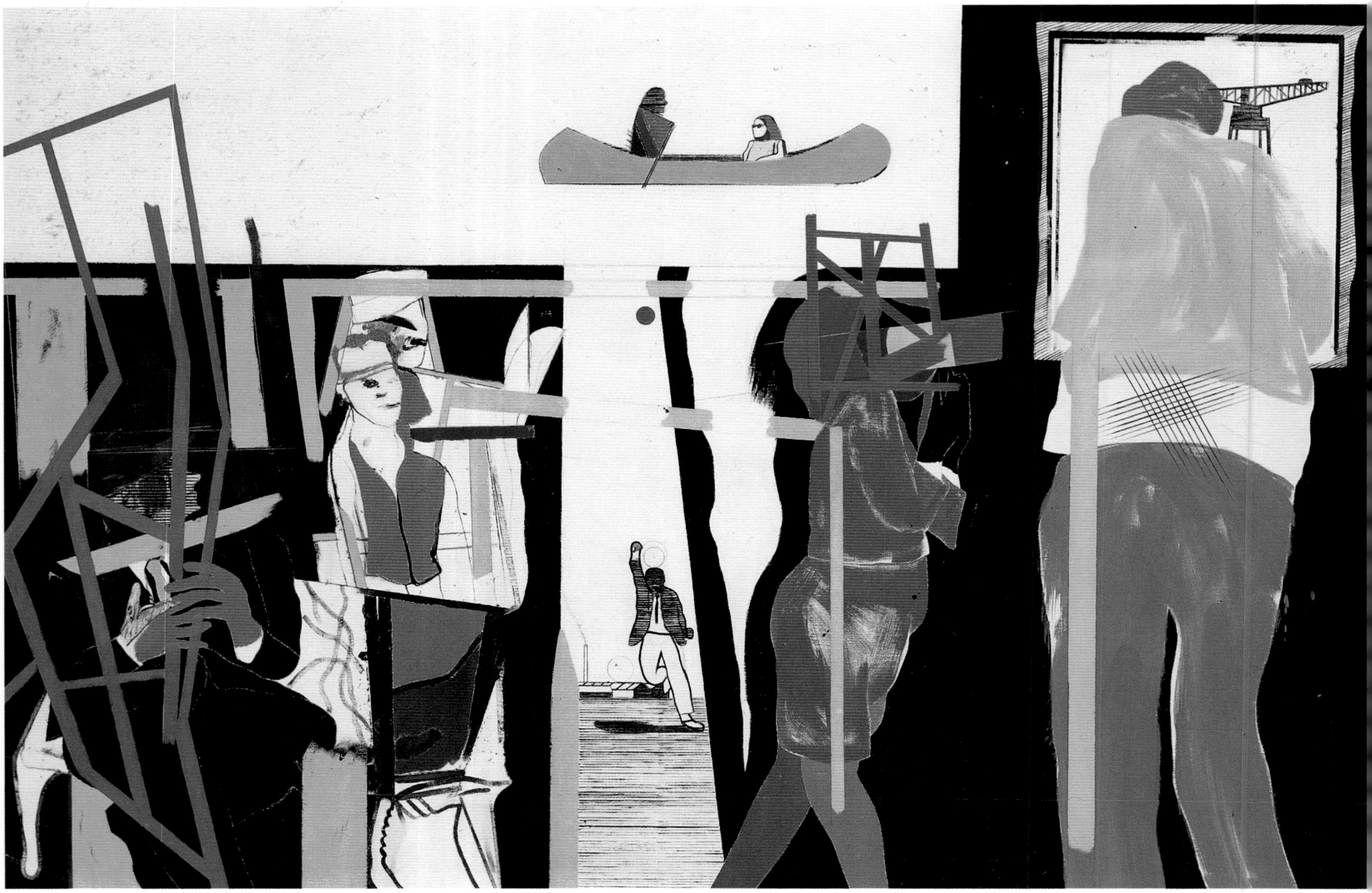

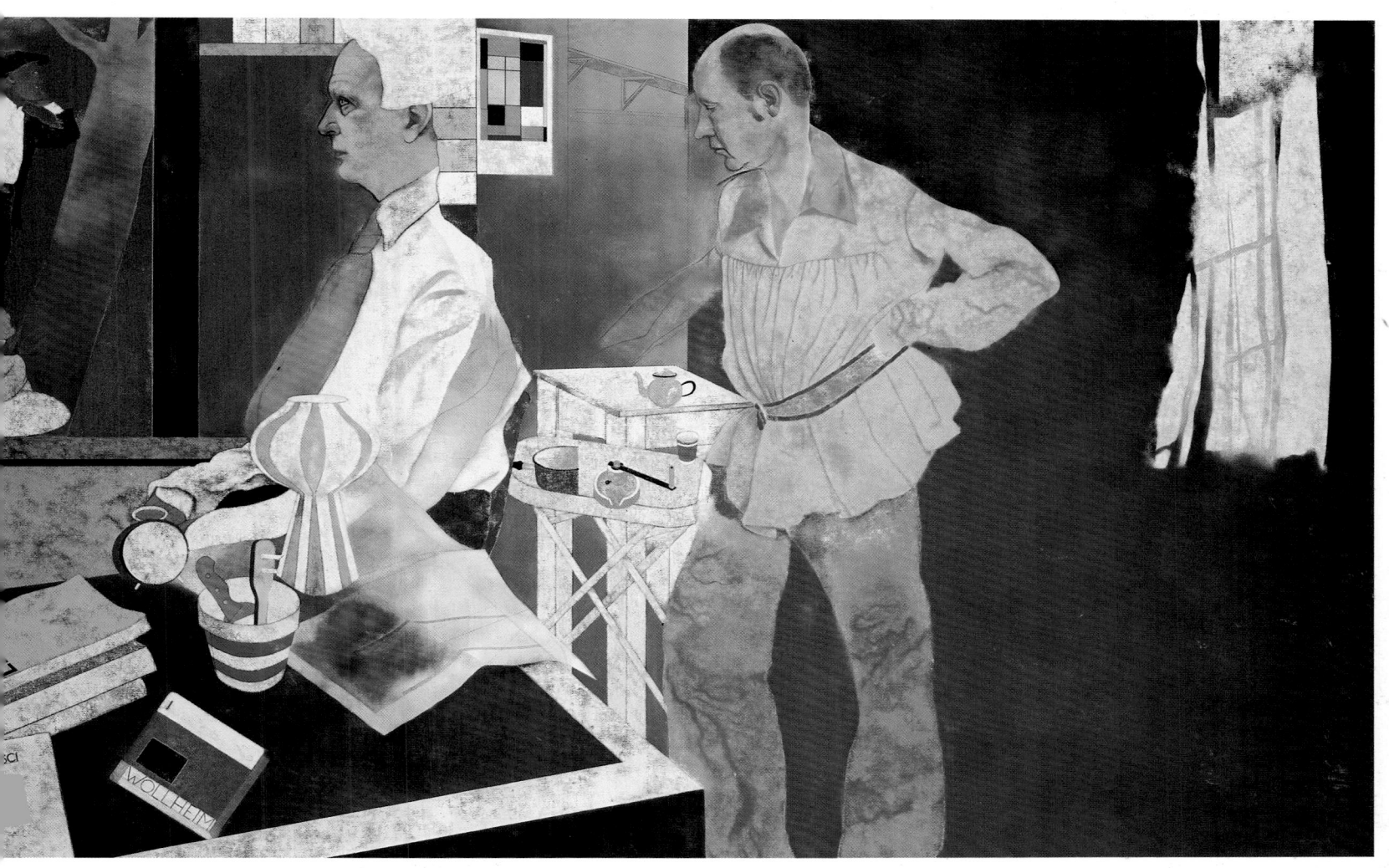

72. From London (James Joll and John Golding), 1975–6. *Cat. no. 185.*

69. *(opposite, top left)* Outlying London Districts (in Camberwell) *(detail)*, 1969. *Cat. no. 122.*

70. *(opposite, top right)* Thanksgiving *(detail)*, 1966–7. *Cat. no. 92.*

71. *(left)* Tedeum, 1963. *Cat. no. 45.*

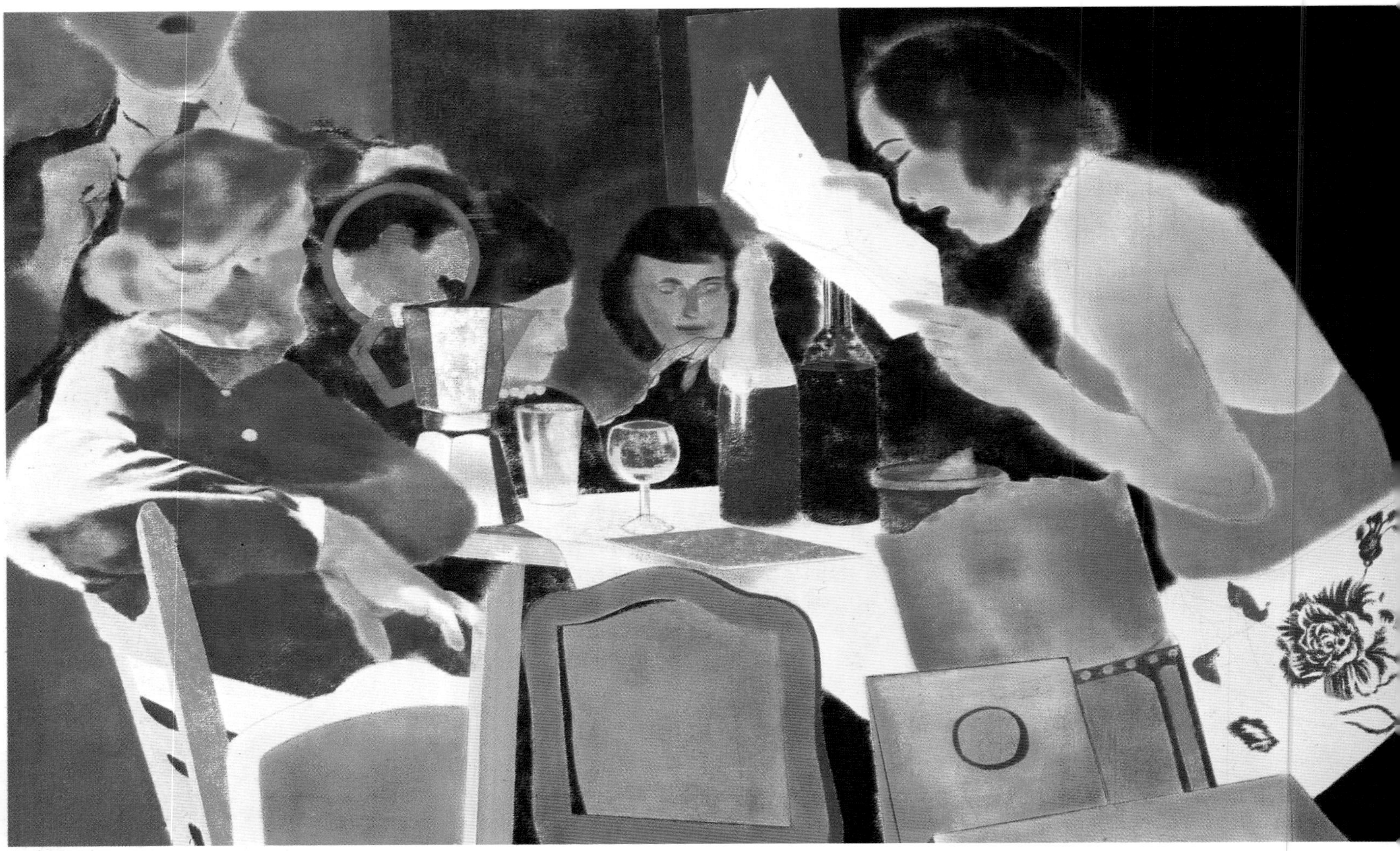

73. To Live in Peace (The Singers), 1973-4. *Cat. no. 159.*

74. My Cat and her Husband, 1977. *Cat. no. 201.*

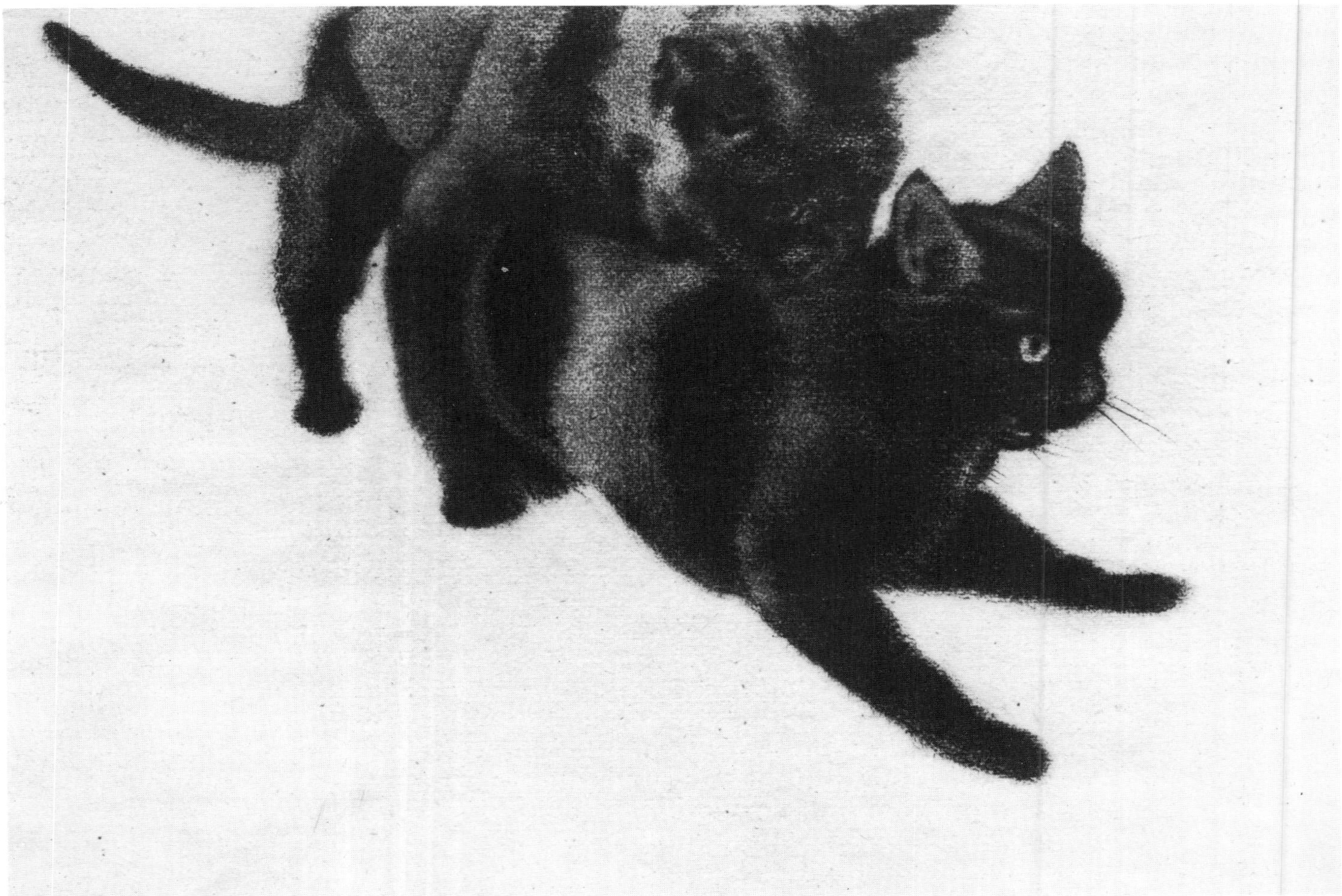

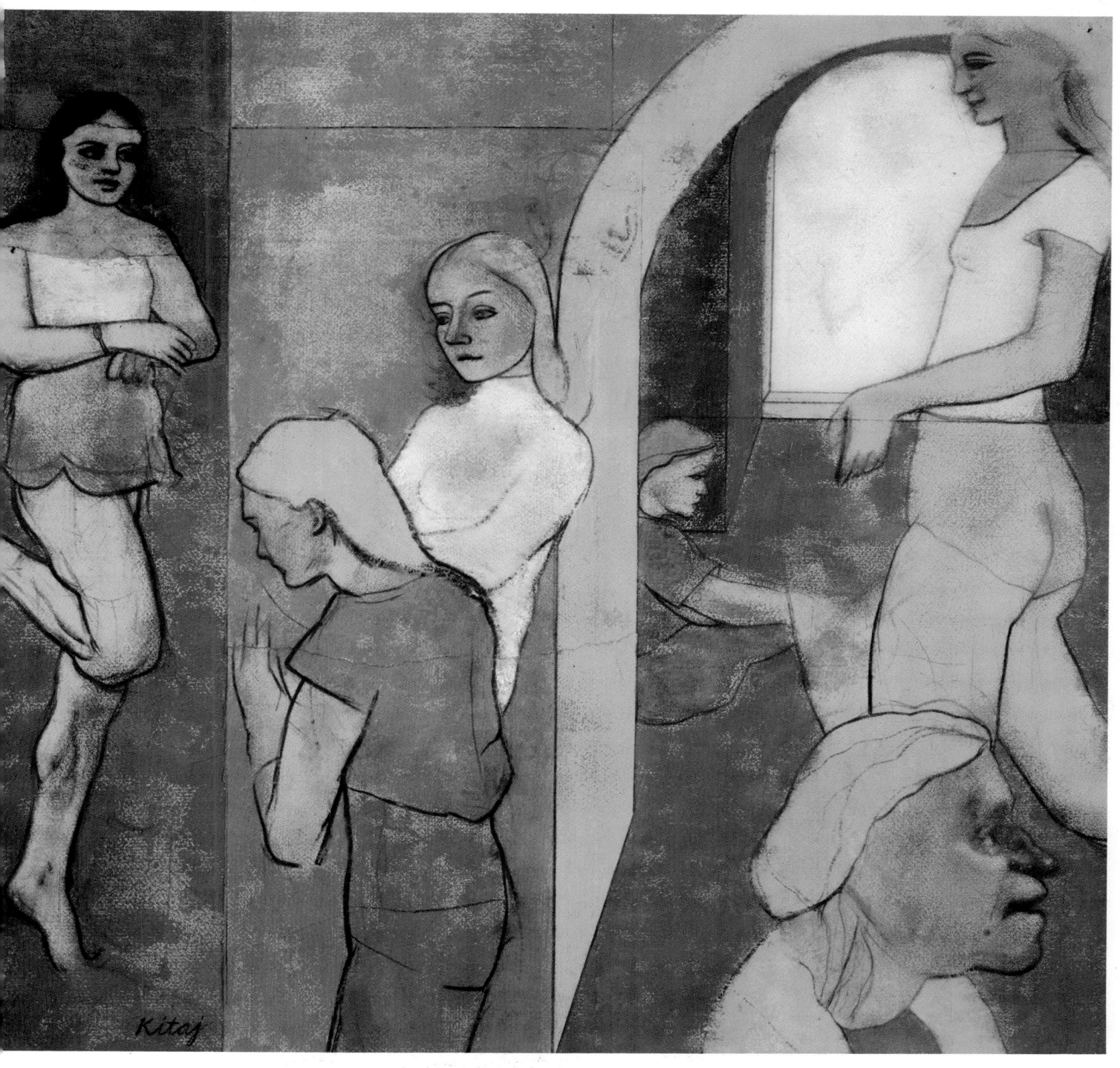

75. Sighs from Hell, 1979. *Cat. no. 241.*

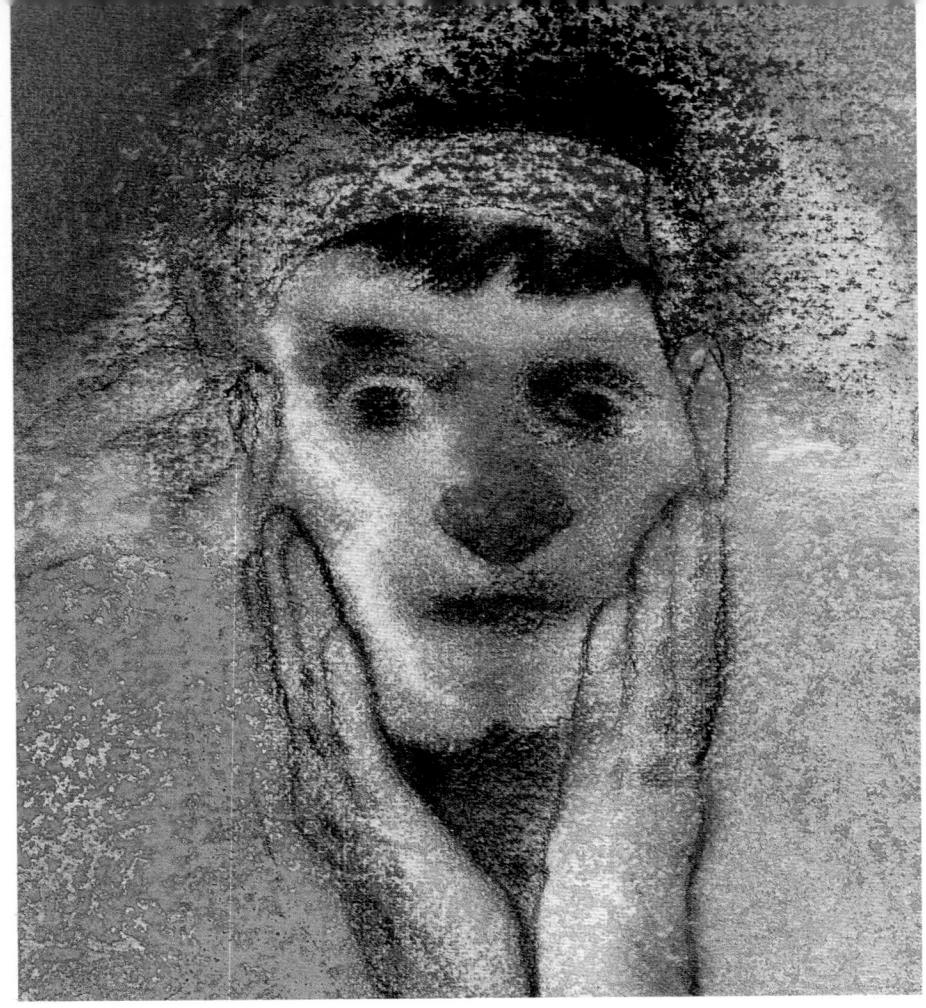

76. Bather (Torsion) *(detail)*, 1978. *Cat. no. 228.*

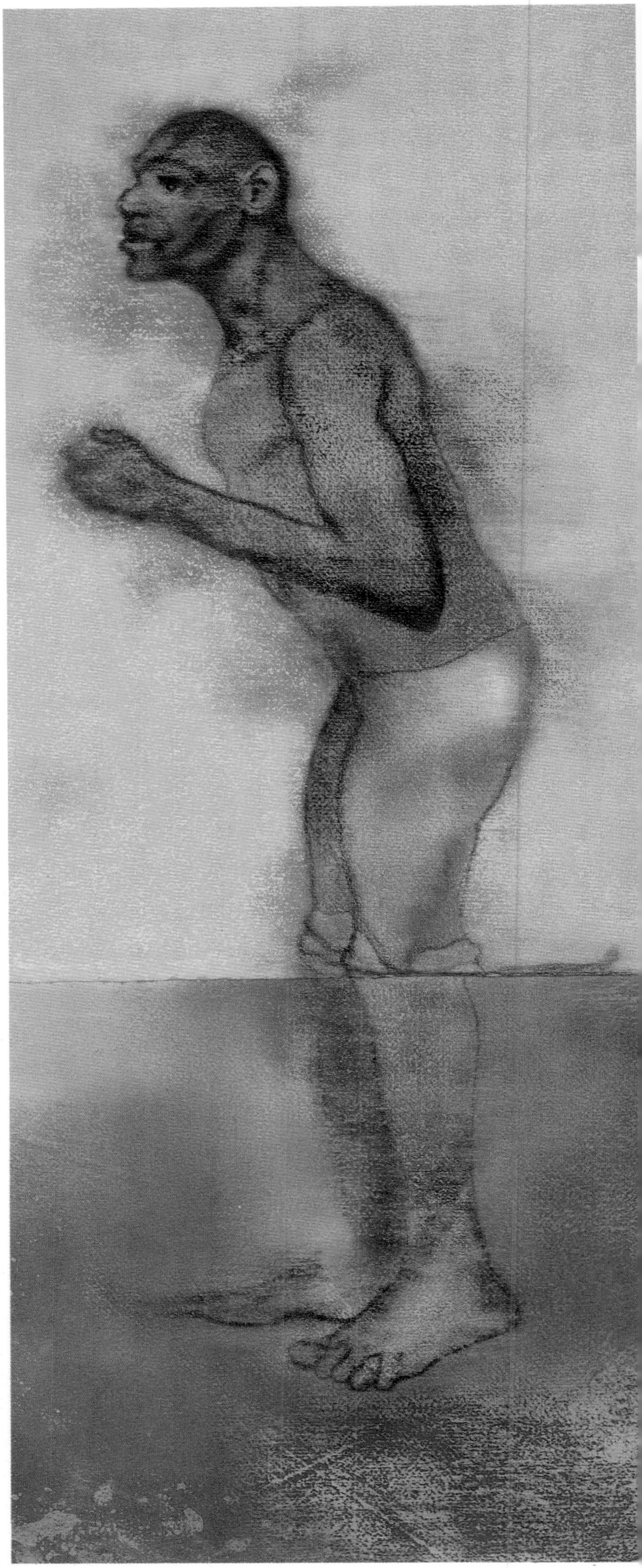

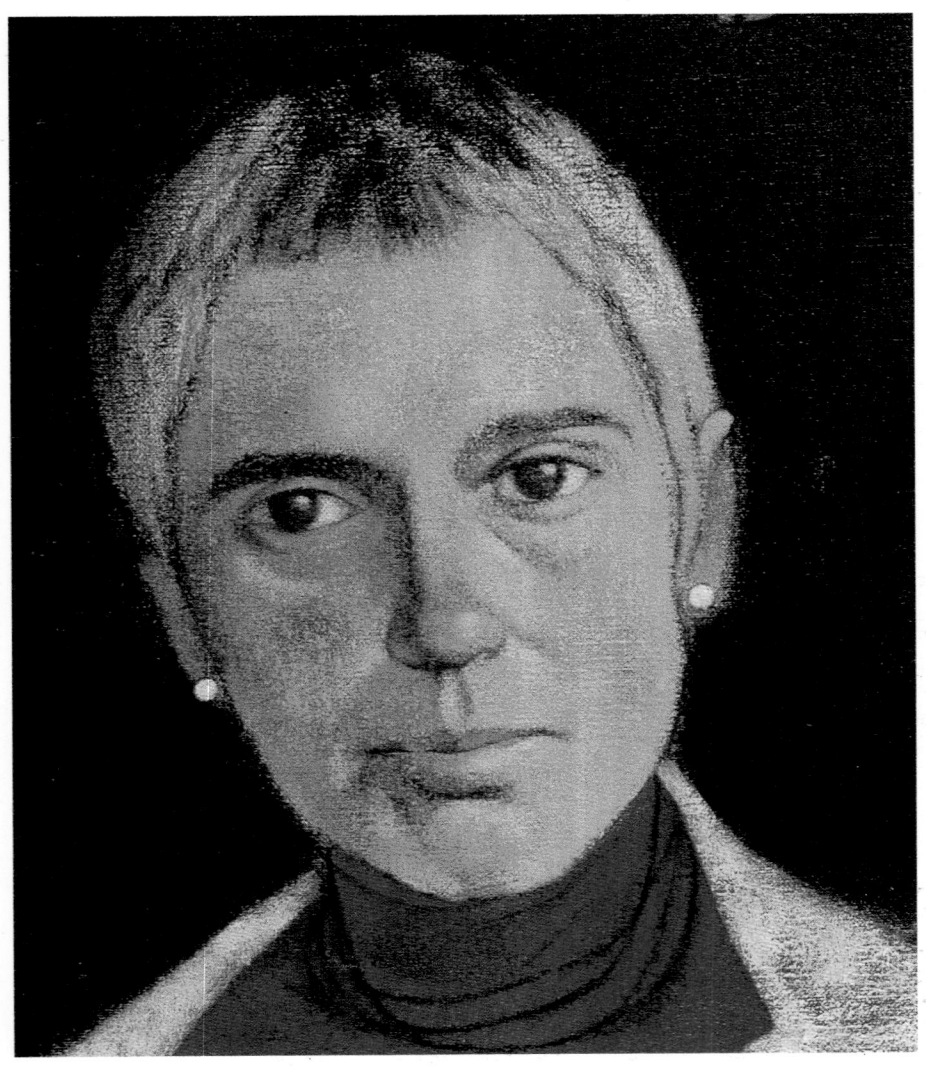

78. Bather (Wading), 1978. *Cat. no. 224.*

77. Nissa Torrents *(detail of Plate 79)*

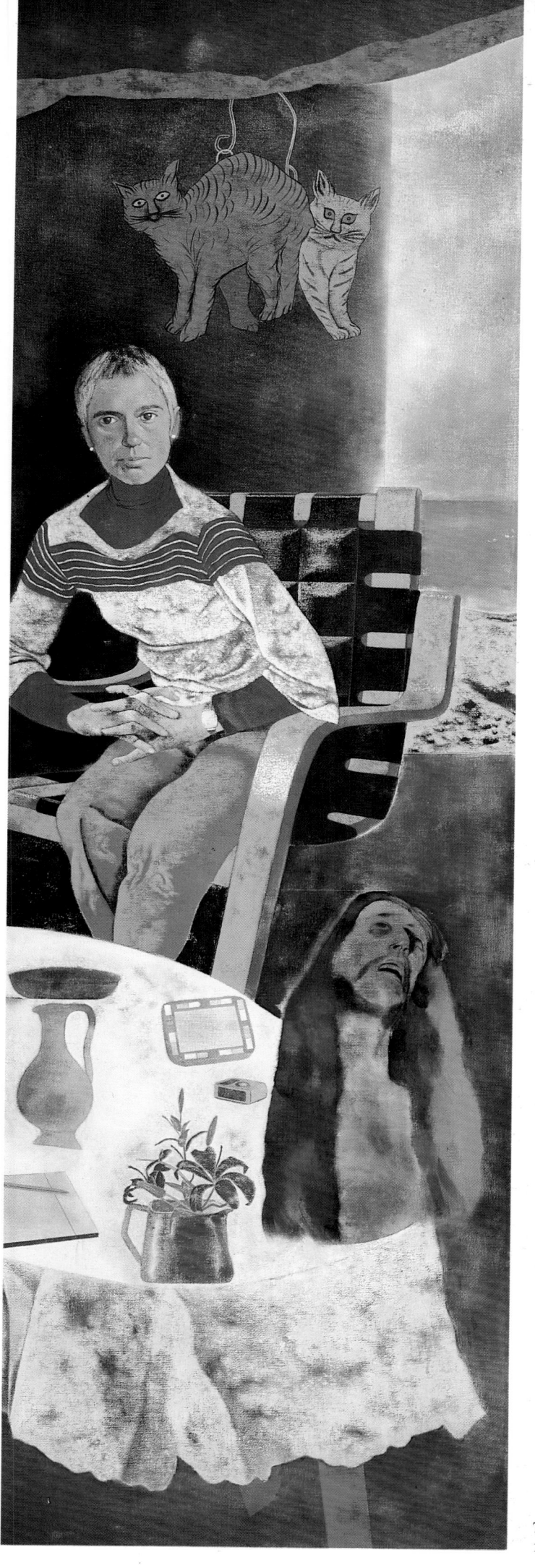

79. The Hispanist (Nissa Torrents),
1977-8. *Cat. no. 205.*

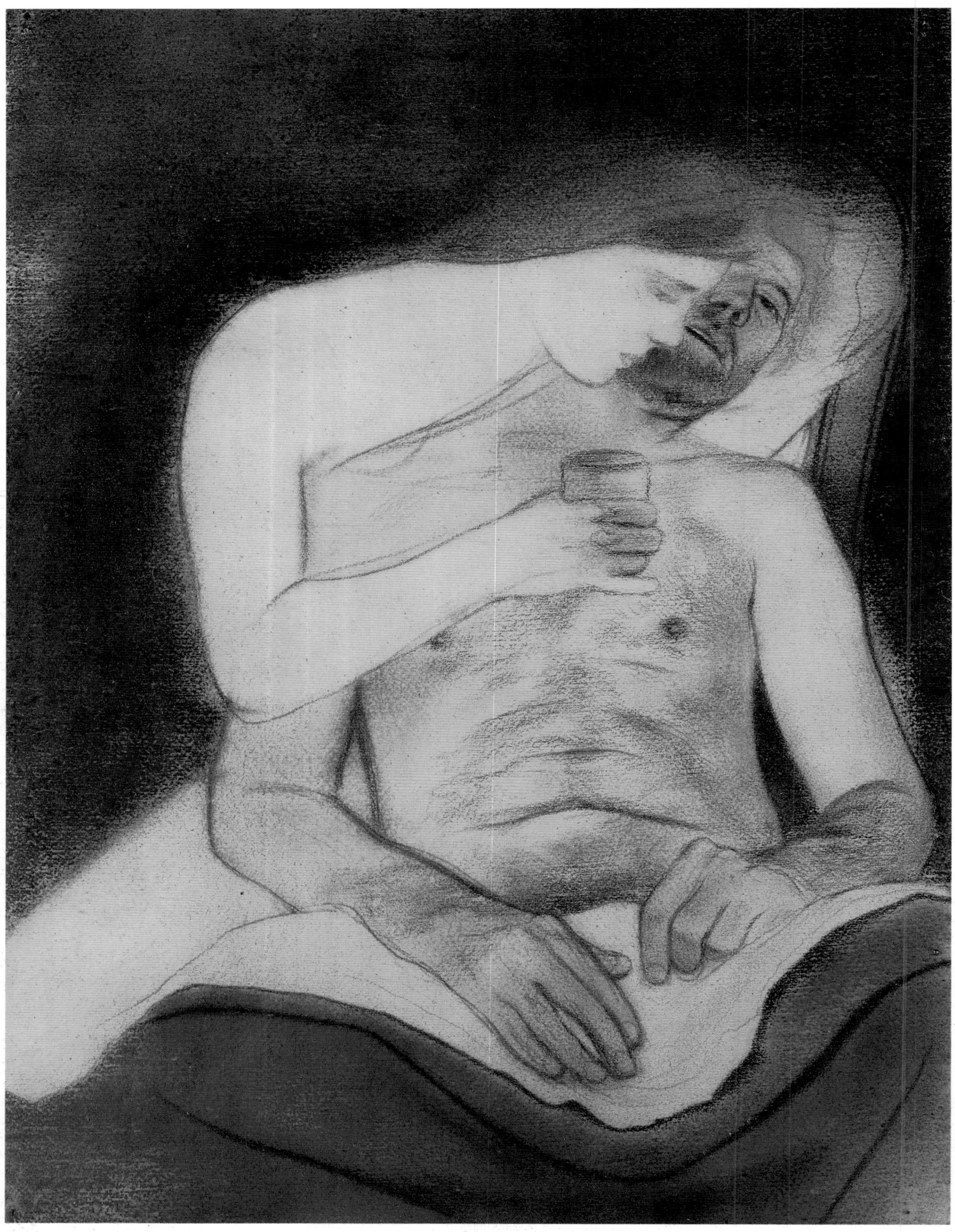

80. The Green Blanket, 1978. *Cat. no. 231.*

81. The Philosopher-Queen, 1978-9. *Cat. no. 239.*

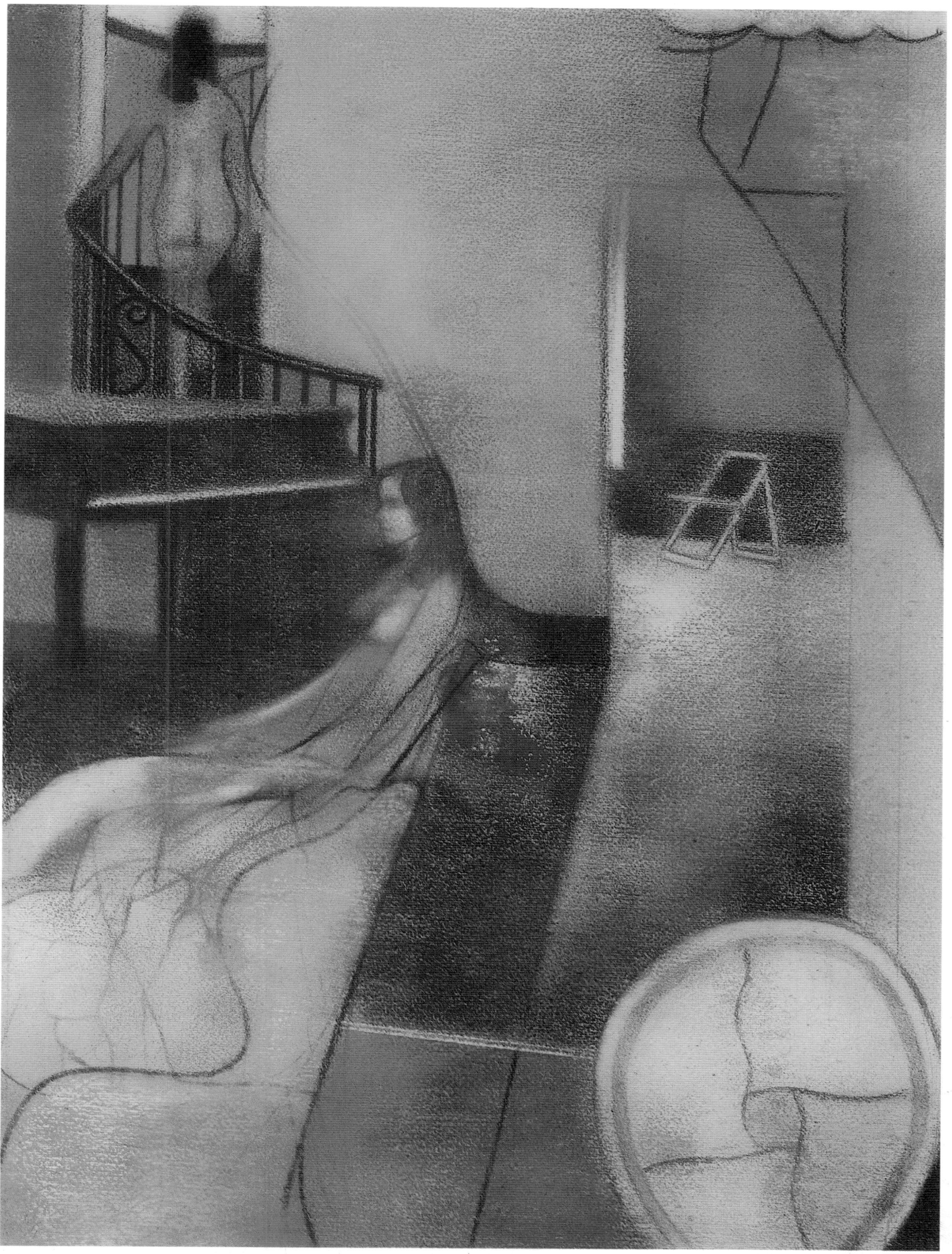

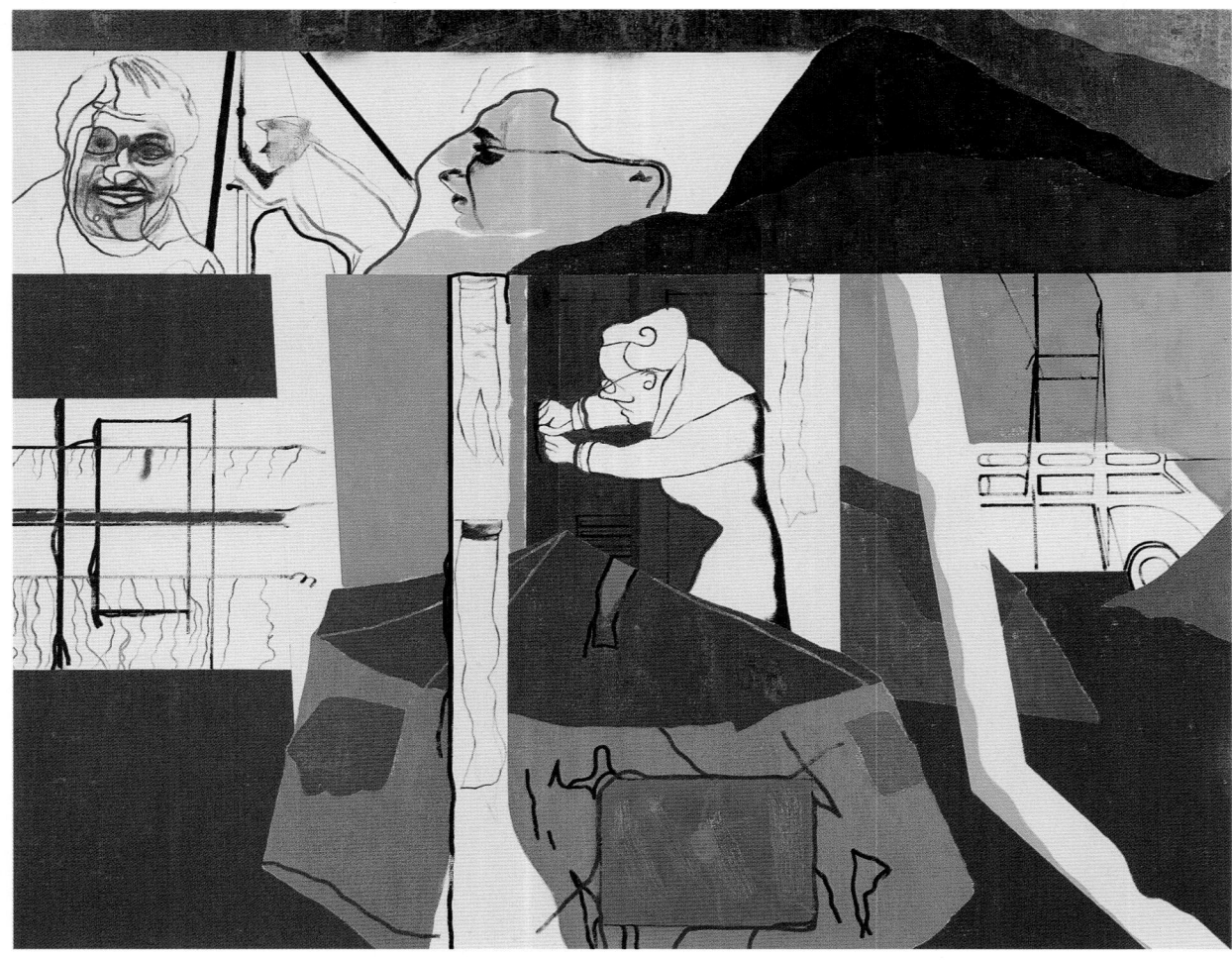

82. Primer of Motives II (Intuitions of Irregularity)
(detail), 1965. *Cat. no. 81.*

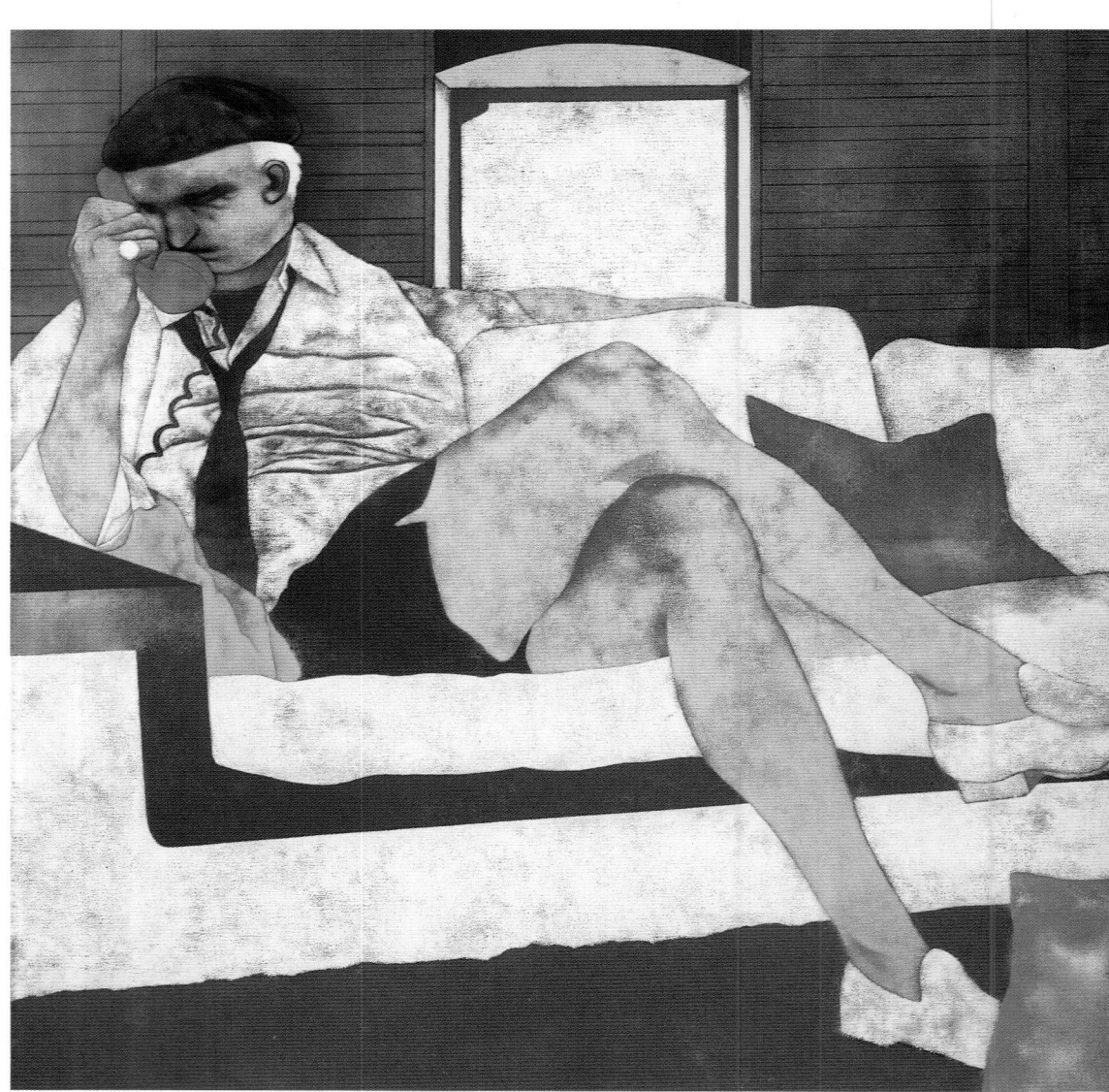

83. Marrano (The Secret Jew), 1976. *Cat. no. 195.*

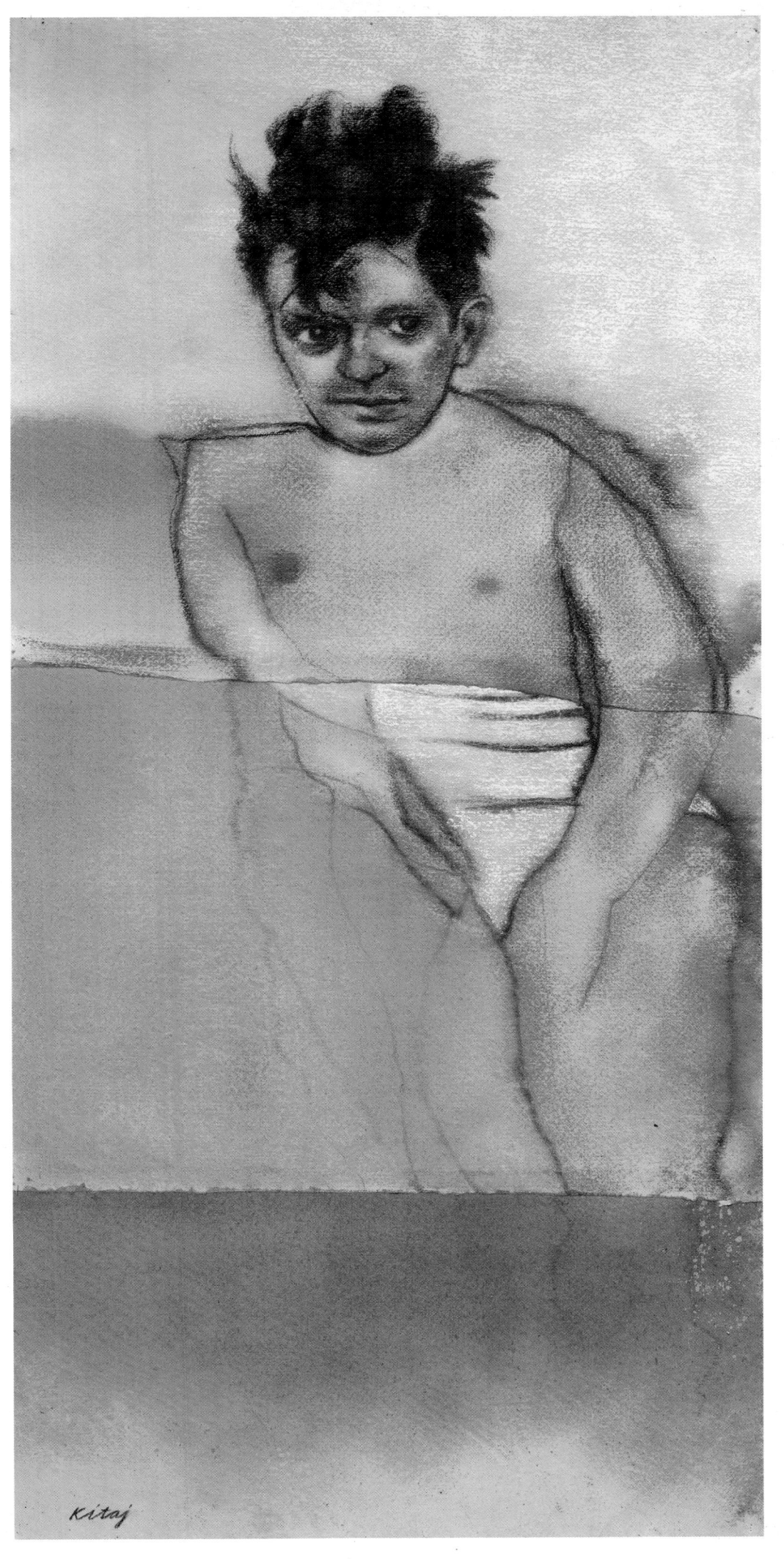

Kitaj

84. Bather (Tousled Hair),
1978. *Cat. no. 223.*

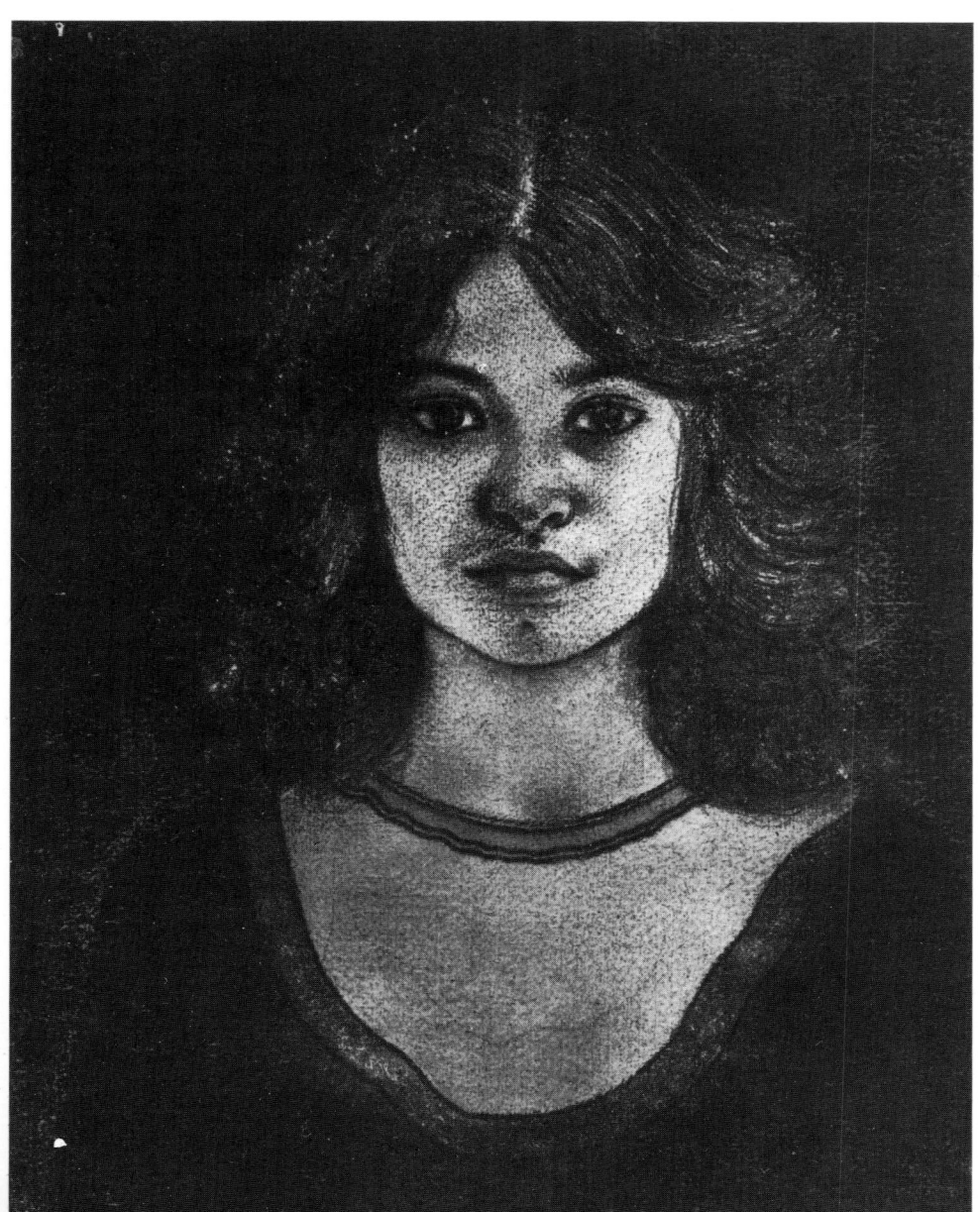

85. Dominie (San Felíu), 1978. *Cat. no. 219.*

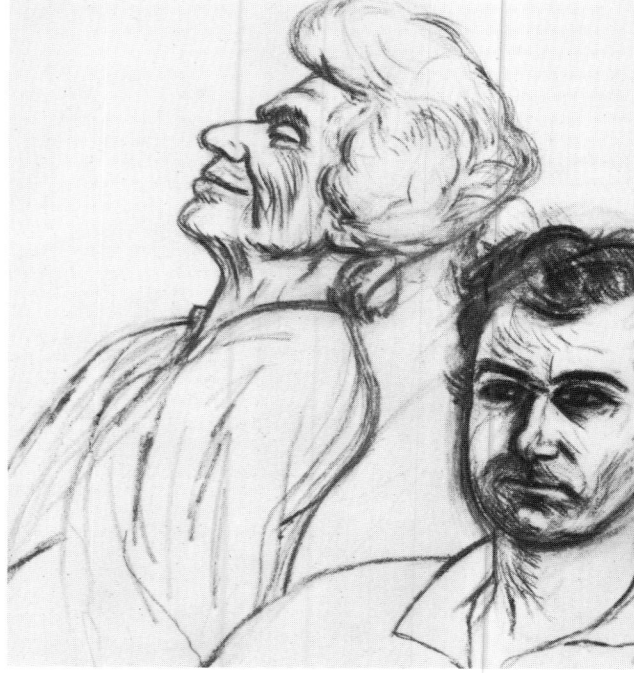

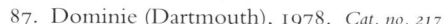

86. Sacha and Gabriel, 1981. *Cat. no. 300.*

87. Dominie (Dartmouth), 1978. *Cat. no. 217.*

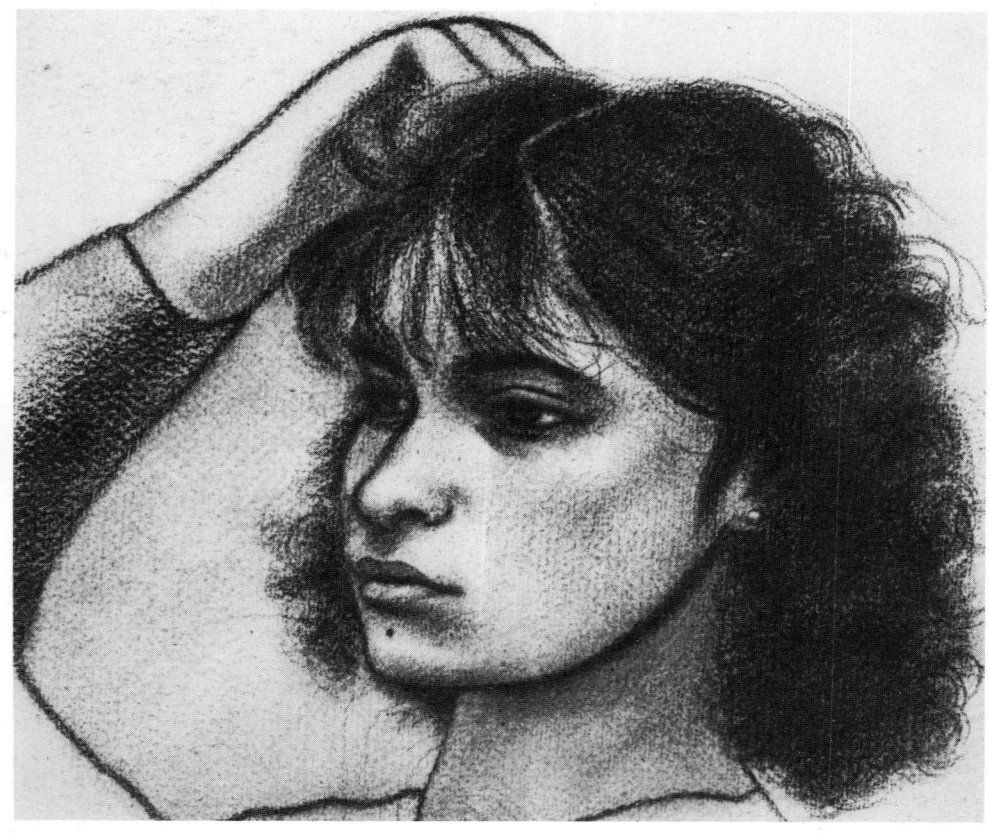

88. Quentin, 1979. *Cat. no. 254.*

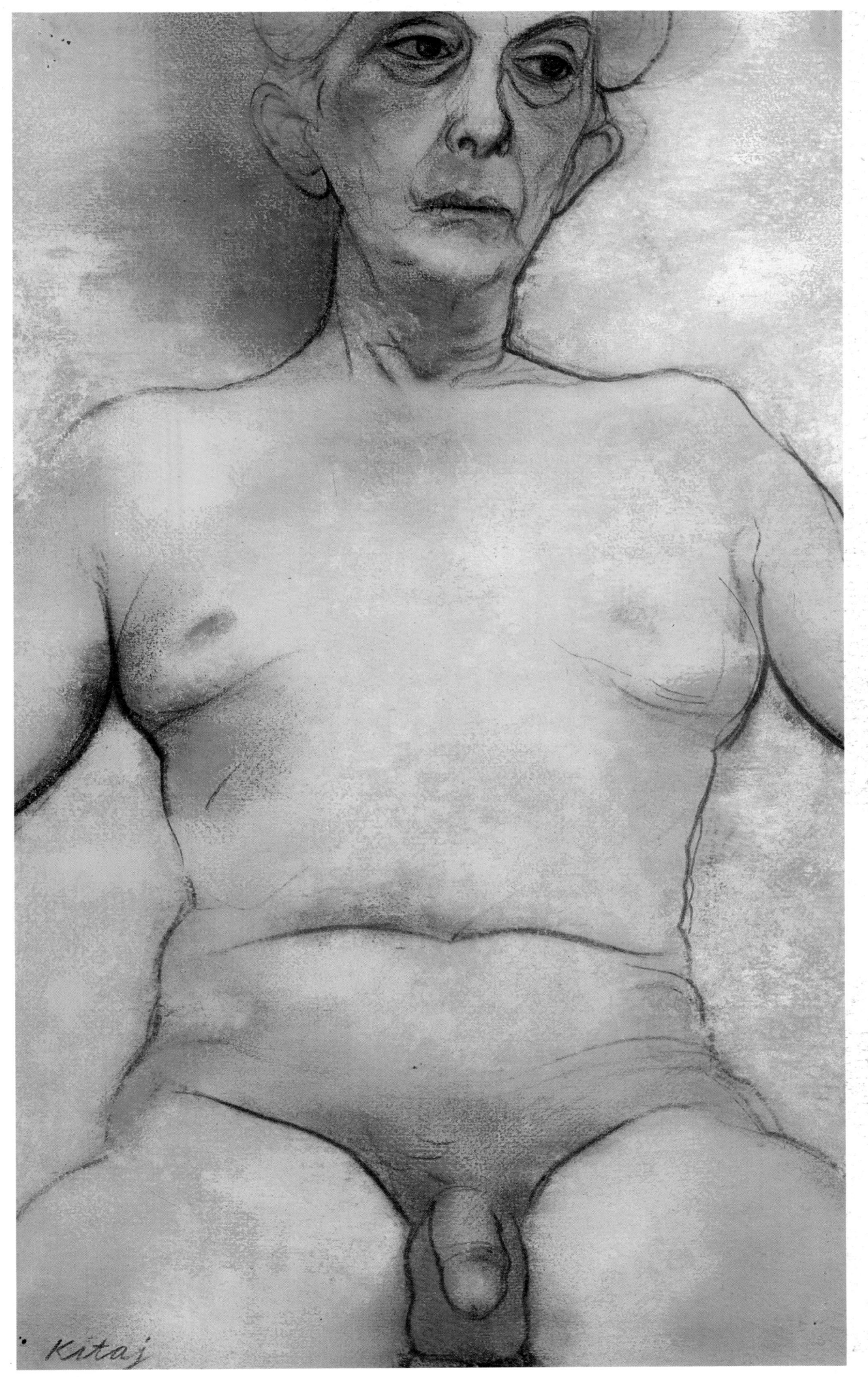

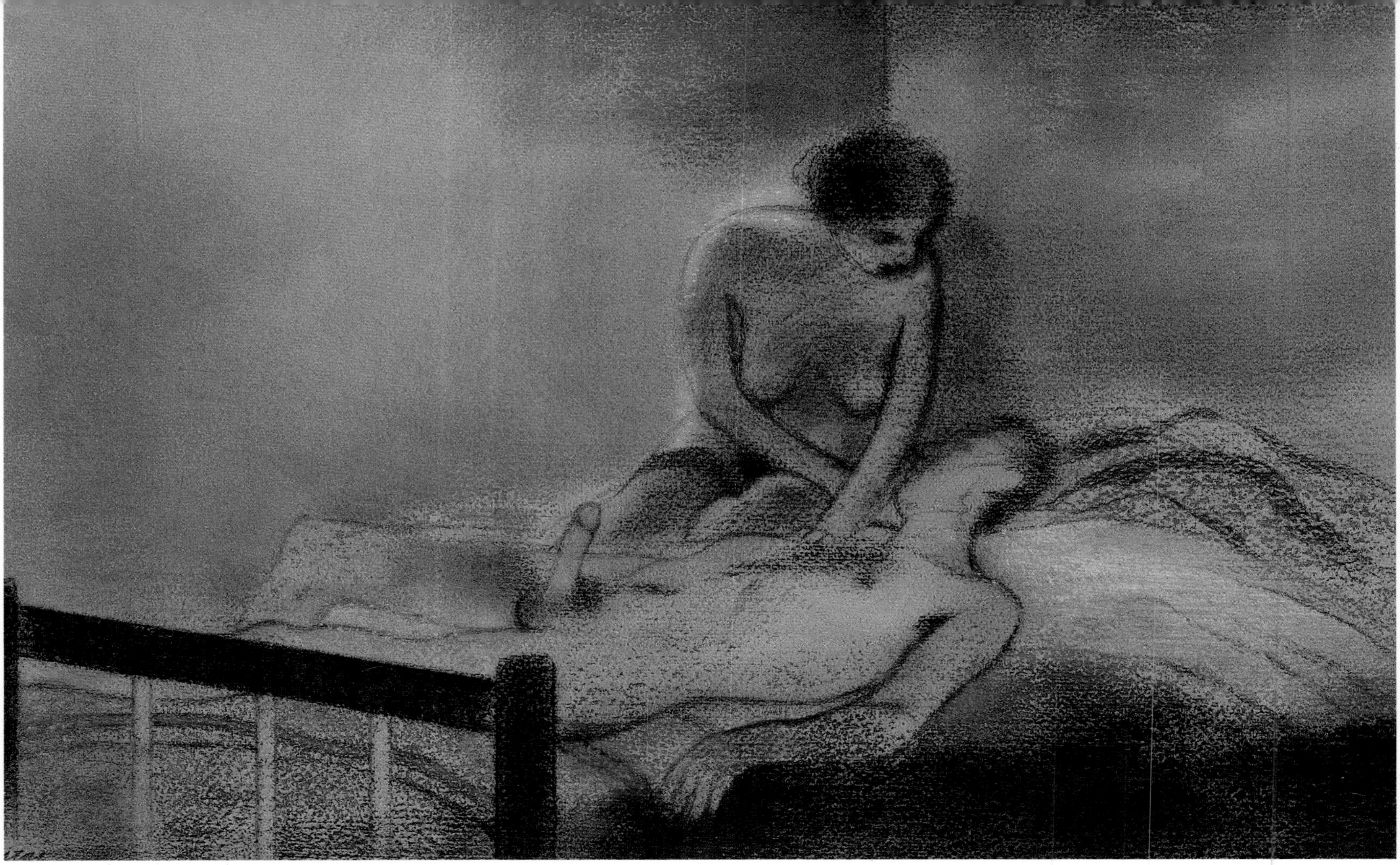

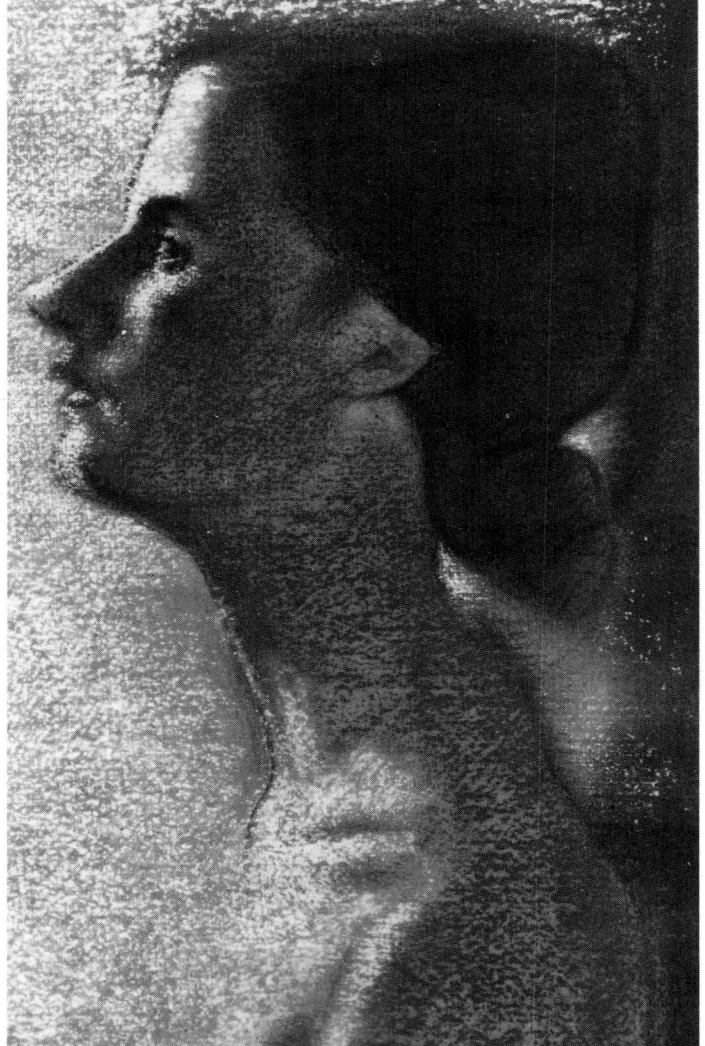

89. Communist and
Socialist, 1975. *Cat. no. 173.*

90. Study for Miss Brooke,
1974. *Cat. no. 166.*

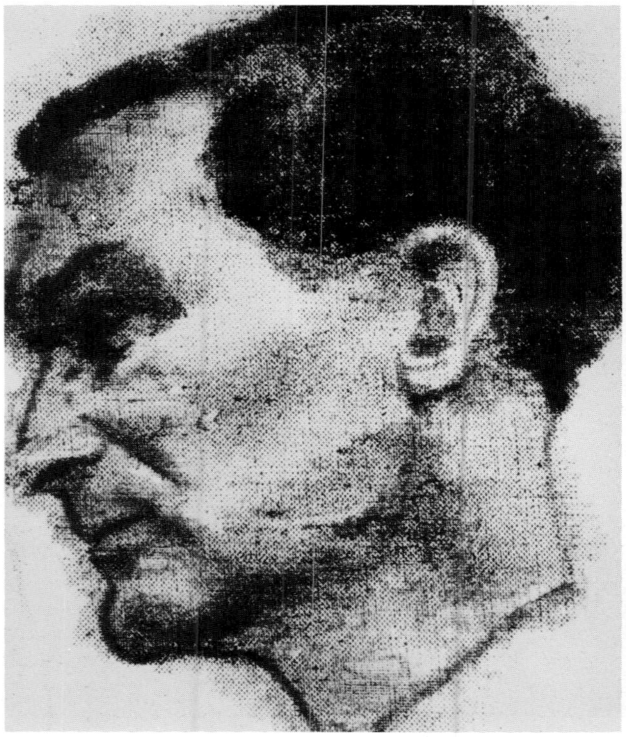

91. Study (Michael Hamburger), 1969. *Cat. no. 115.*

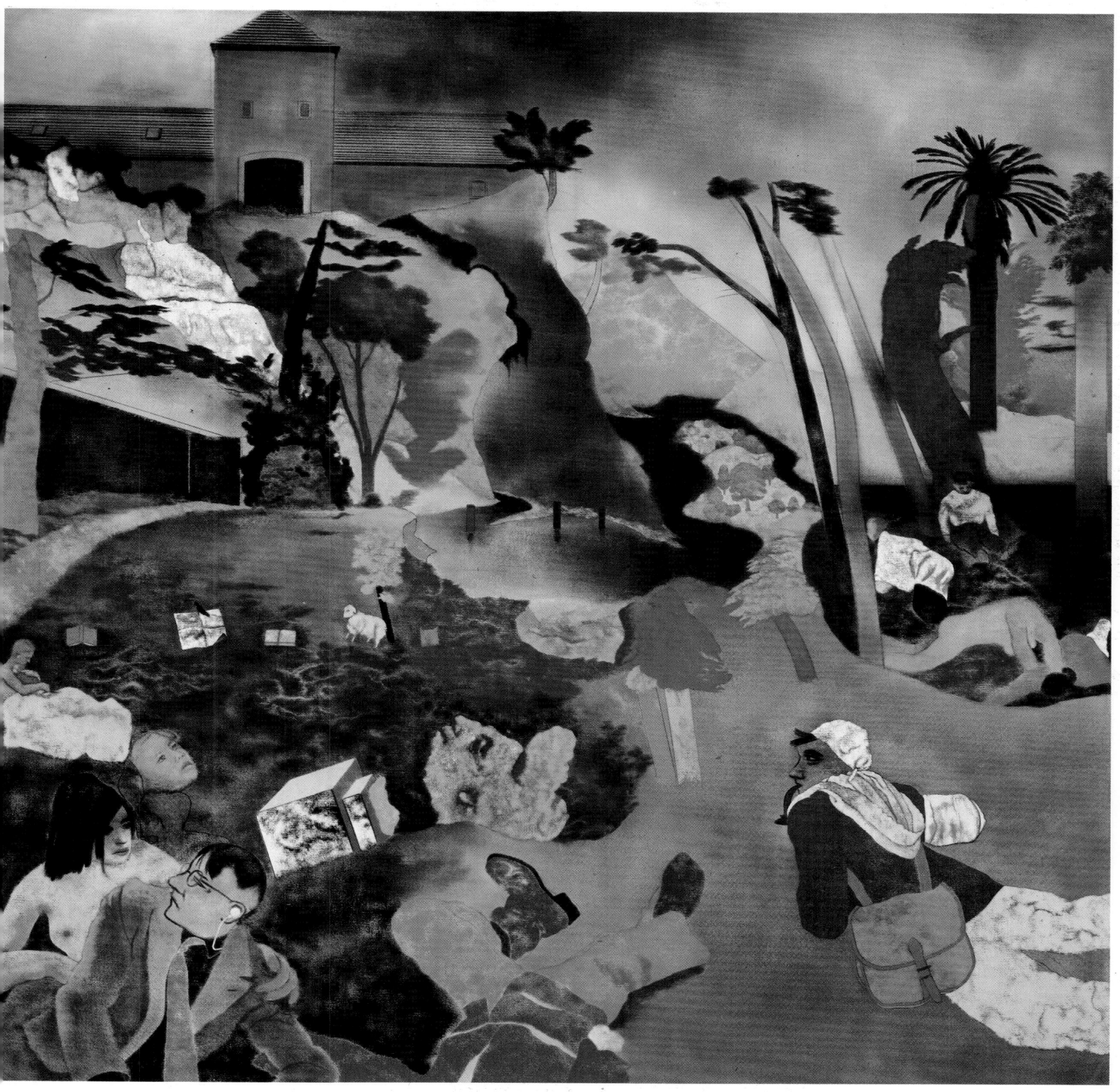

92. If Not, Not, 1975–6. *Cat. no. 186.*

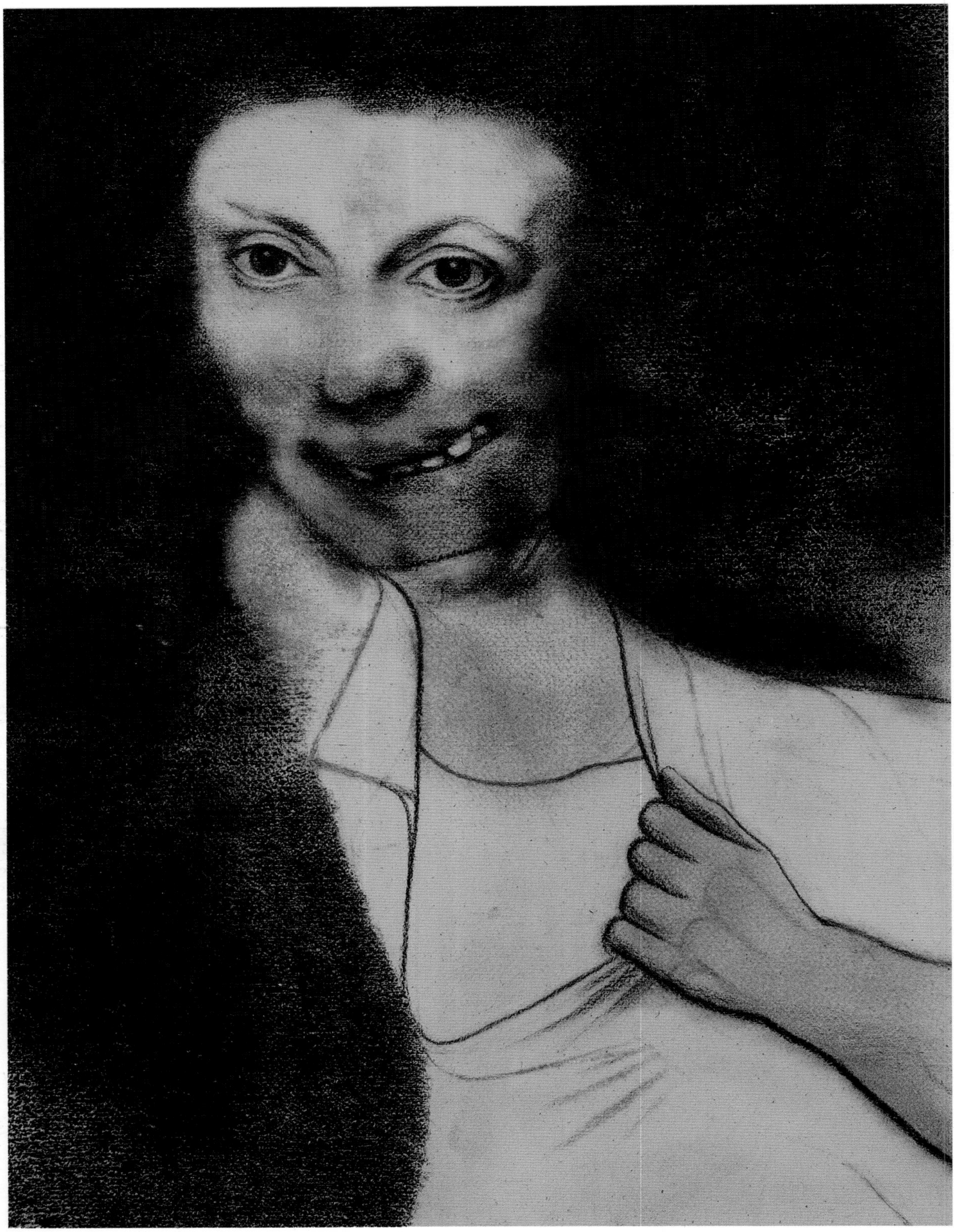

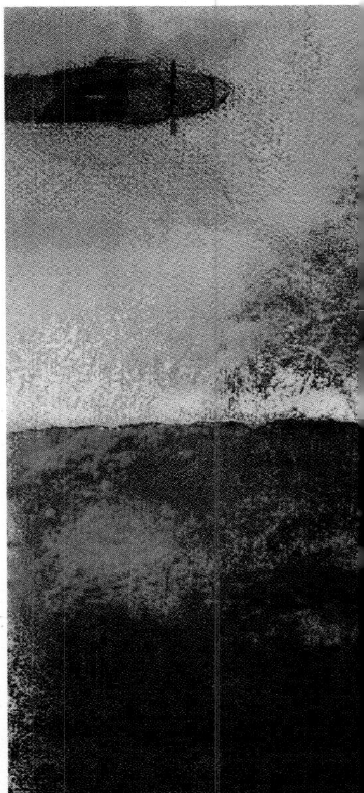

93. His New Freedom, 1978. *Cat. no. 236.*

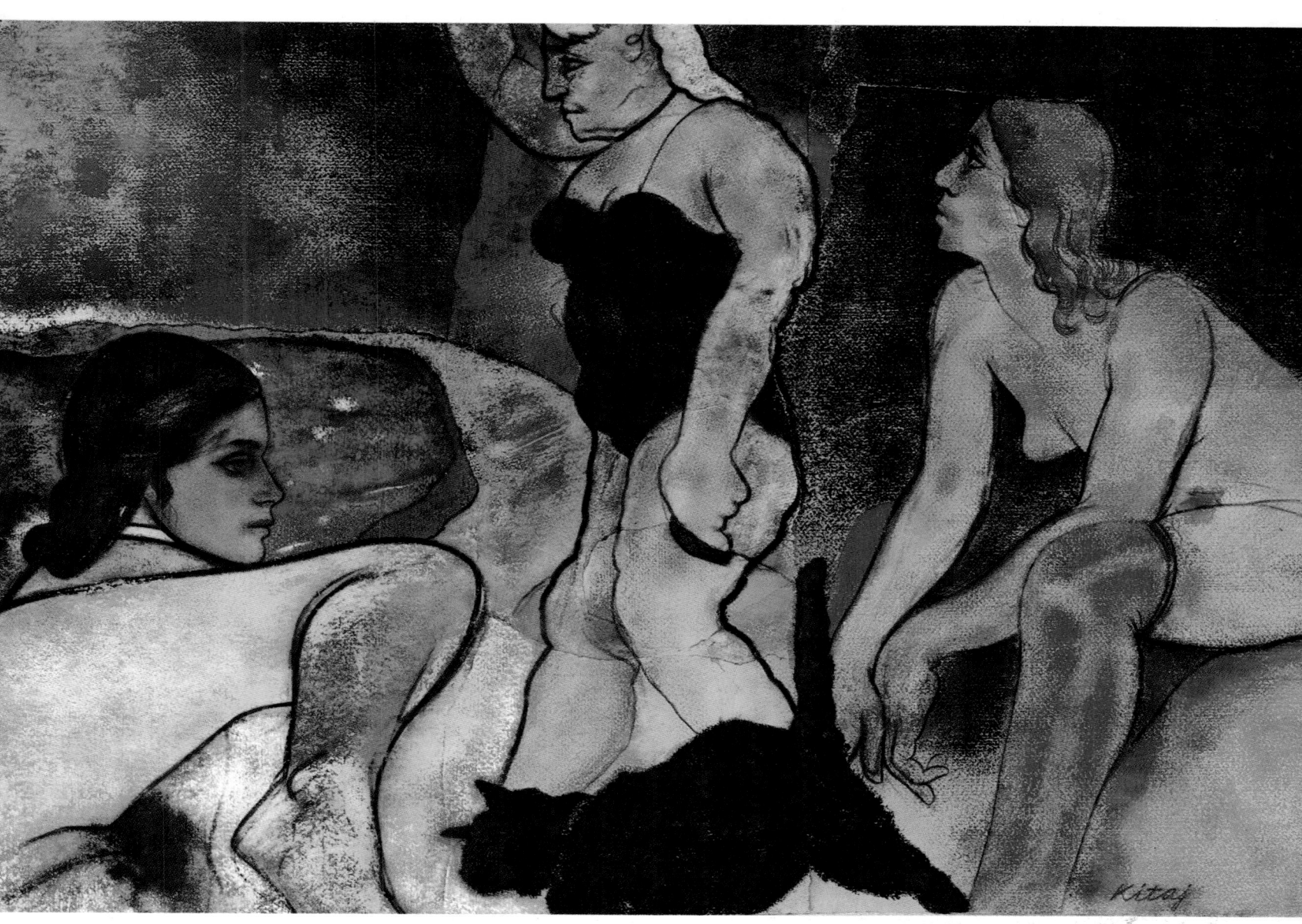

94. The Rise of Fascism, 1979–80. *Cat. no. 260.*

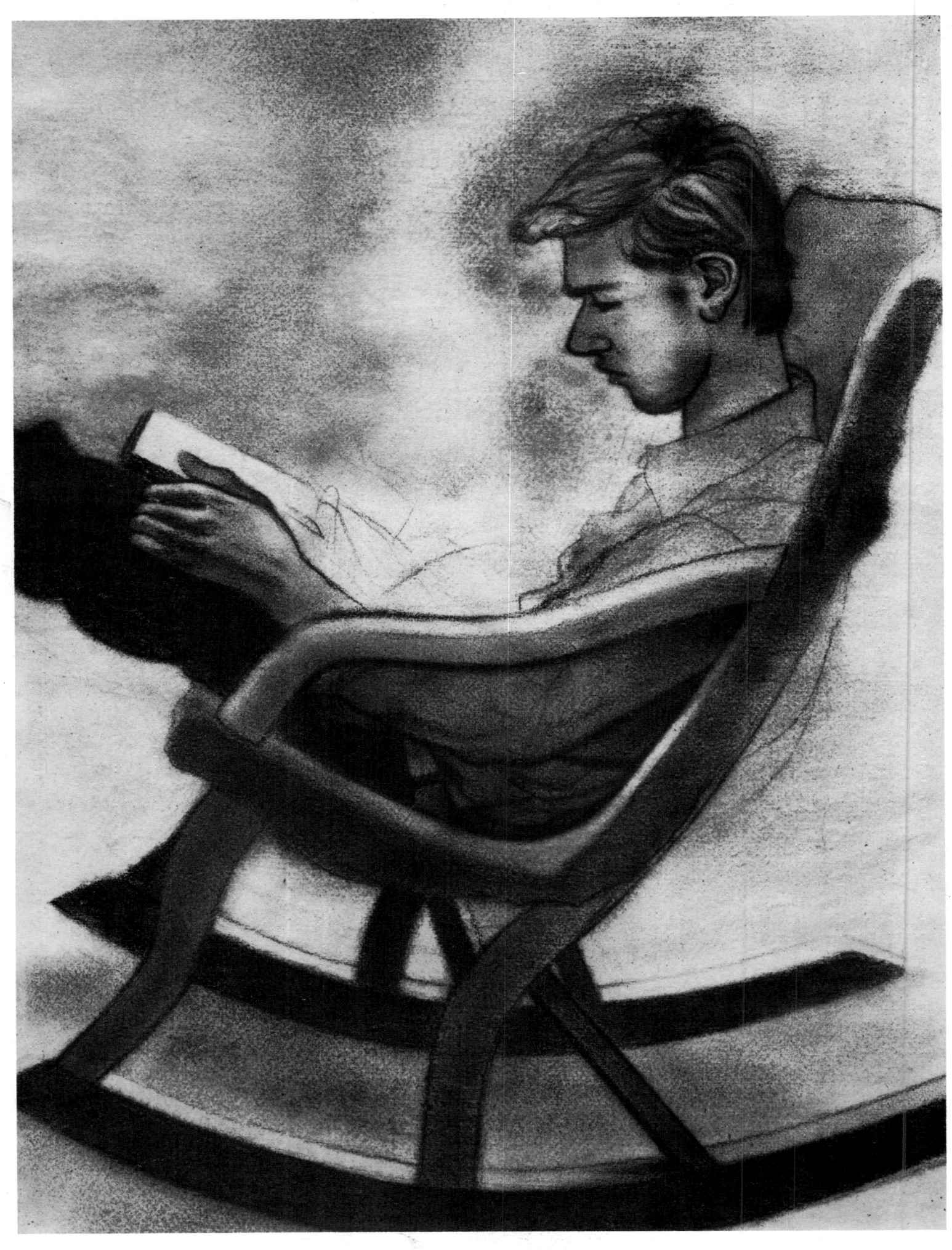

95. Lem (San Felíu), 1978. *Cat. no. 220.*

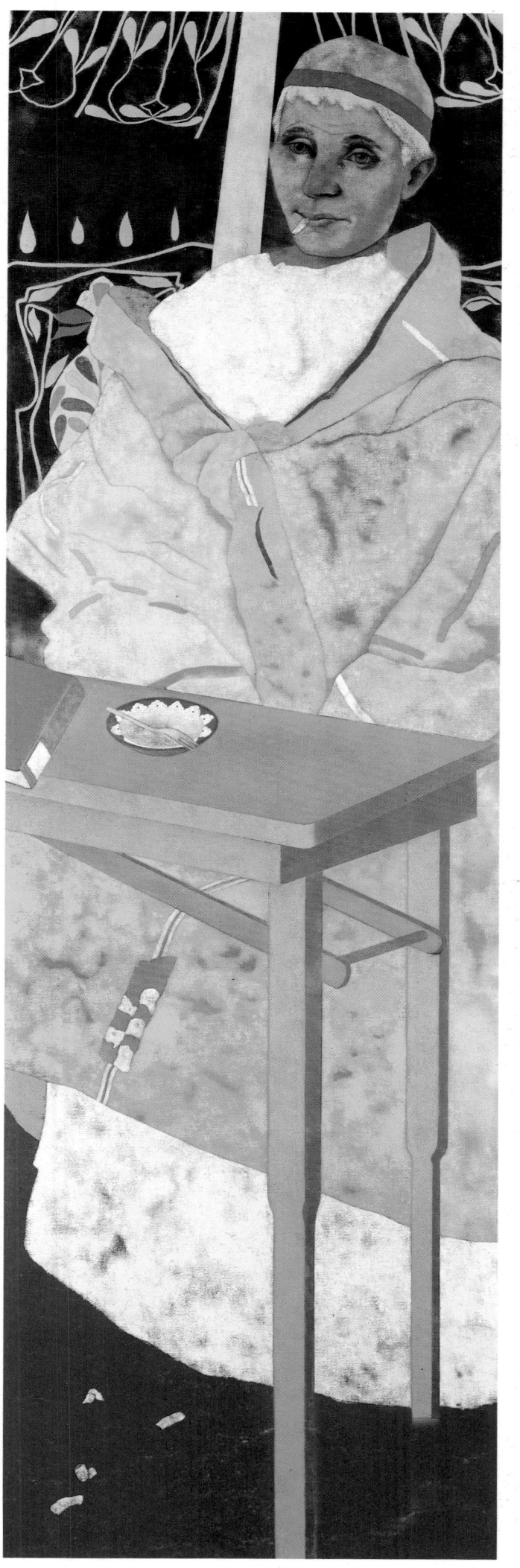

96. The Arabist (formerly Moresque), 1975–6. *Cat. no. 187.*

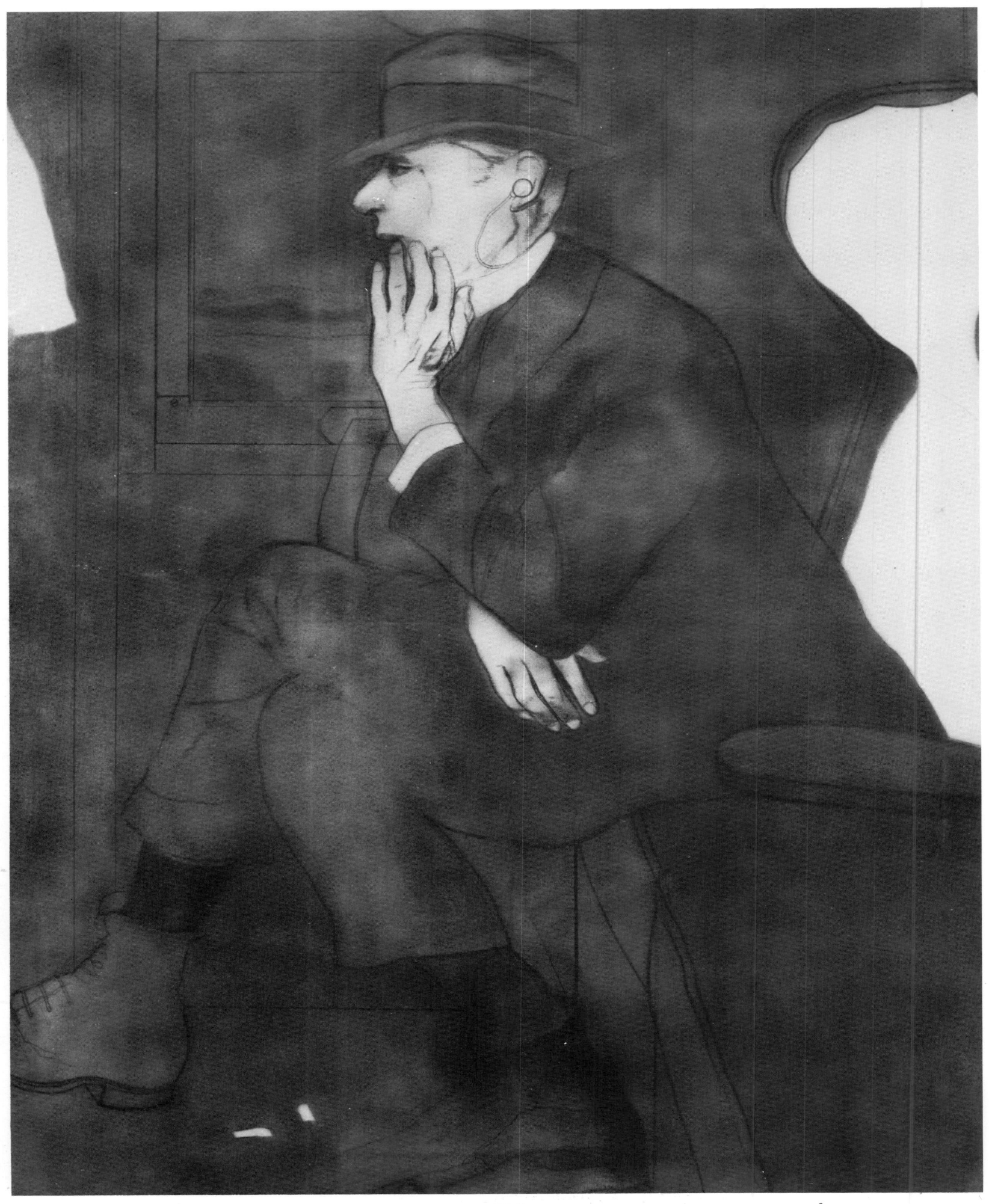

97. The Jew Etc., 1976-9. *Cat. no. 199.*

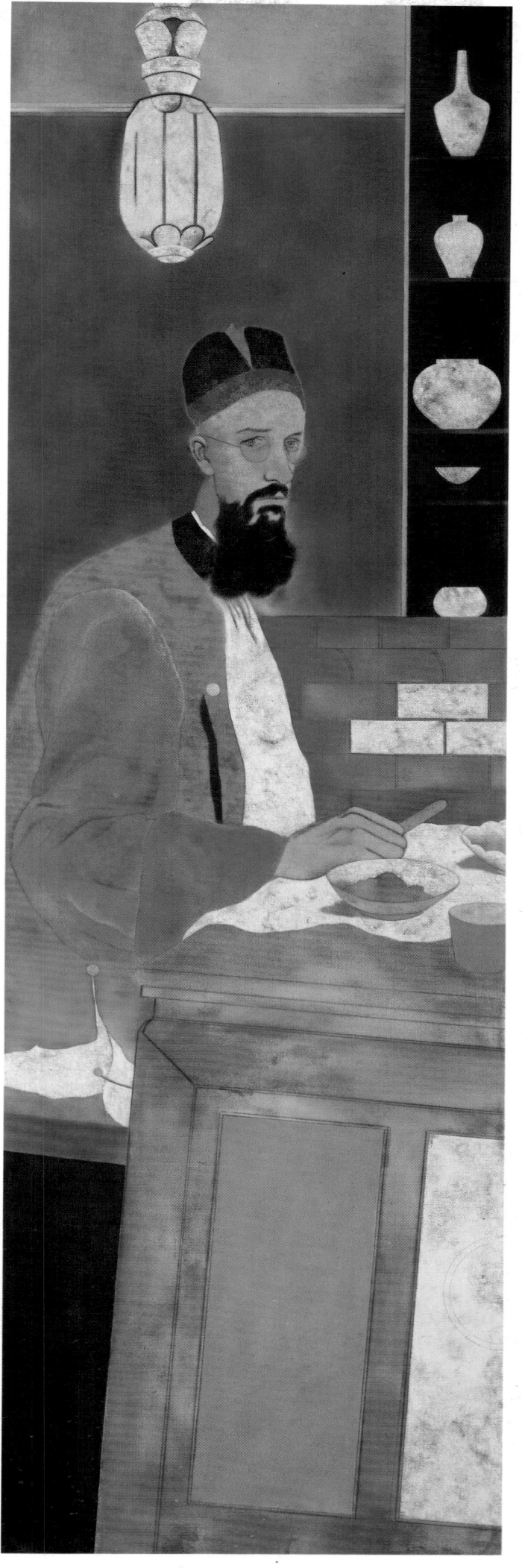

98. The Orientalist, 1975-6. *Cat. no. 188.*

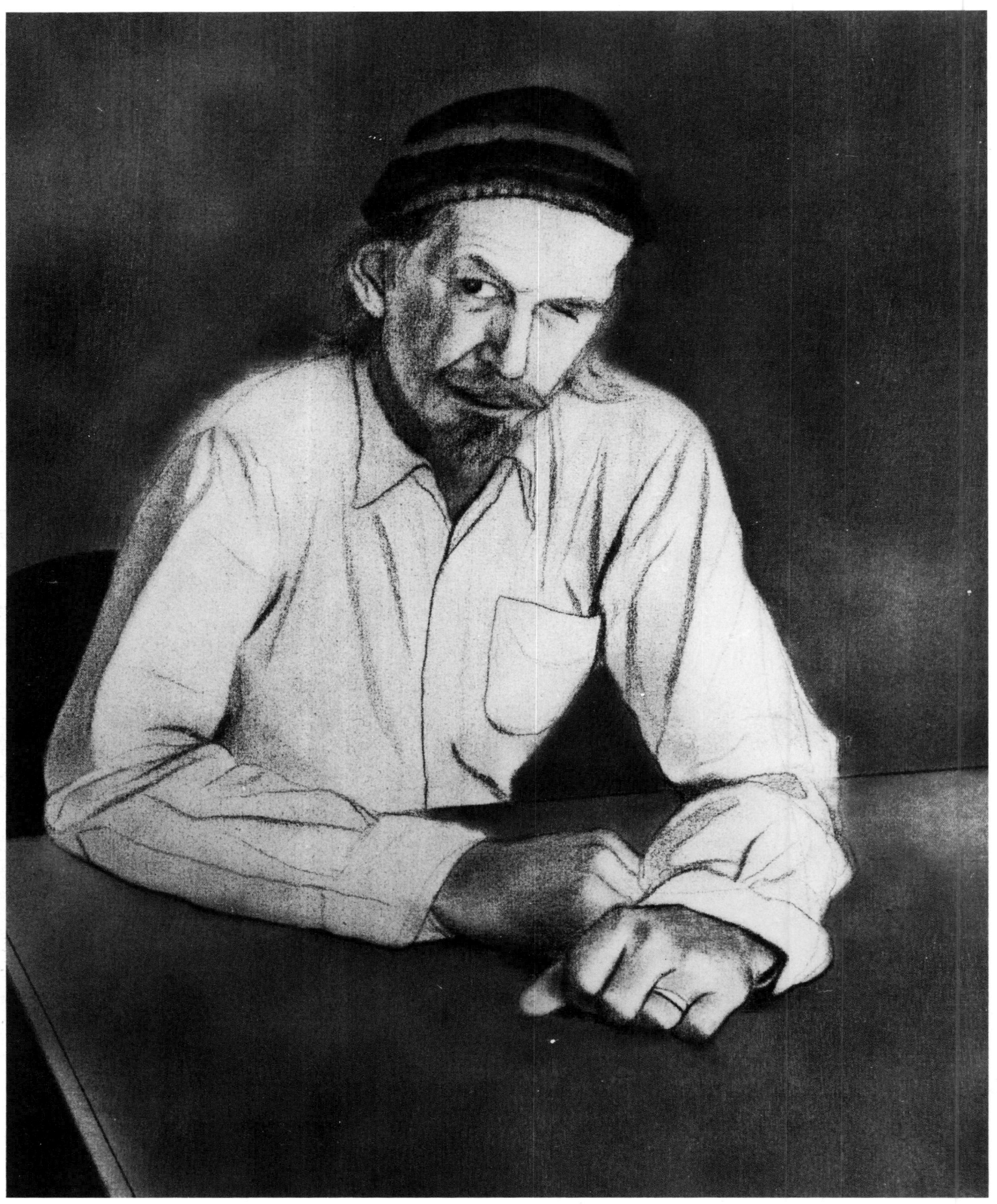

99. A Visit to London (Robert Creeley and Robert Duncan) *(detail)*, 1977–9. *Cat. no. 206.*

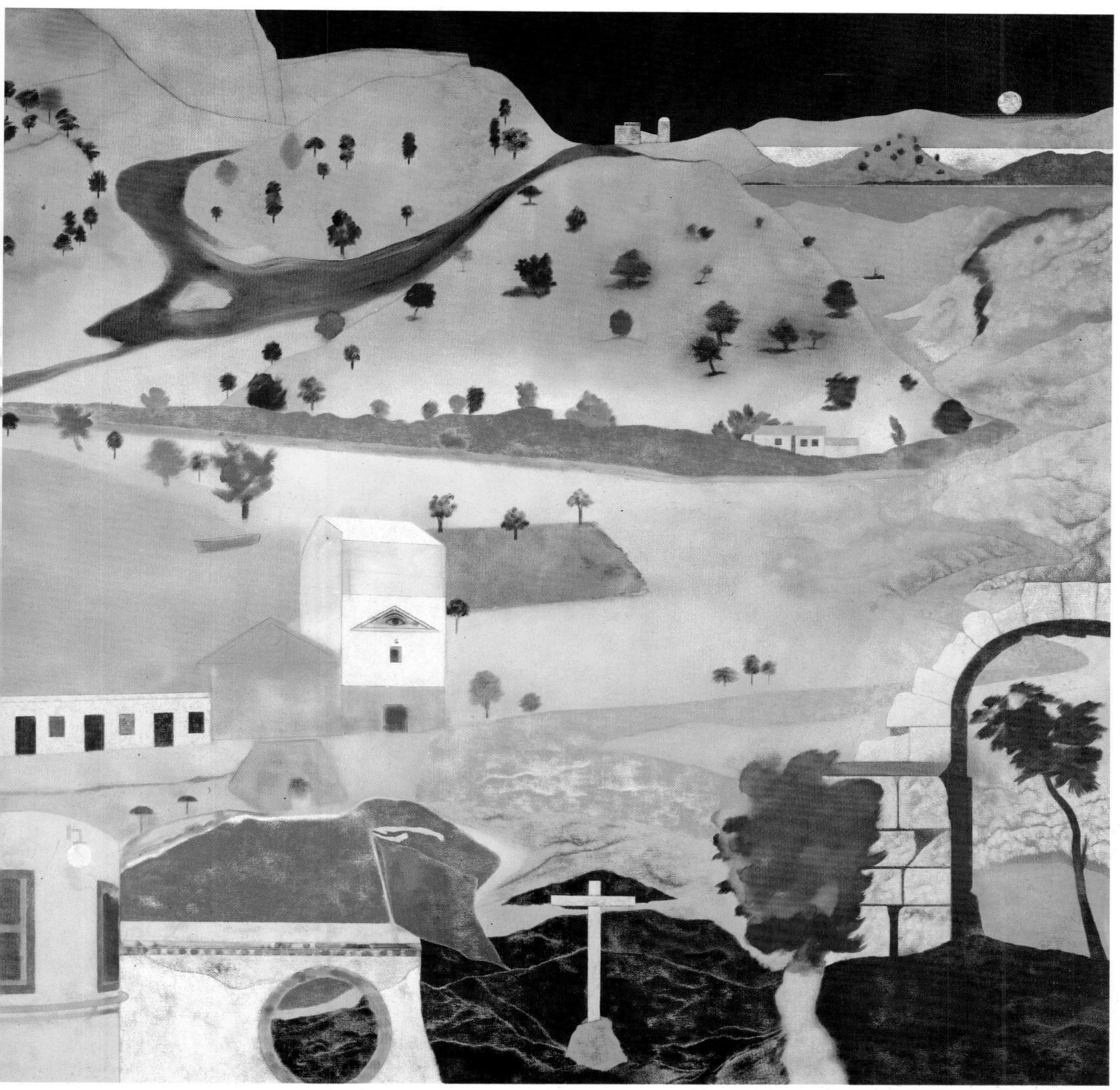

100. Land of Lakes, 1975-7. *Cat. no. 189.*

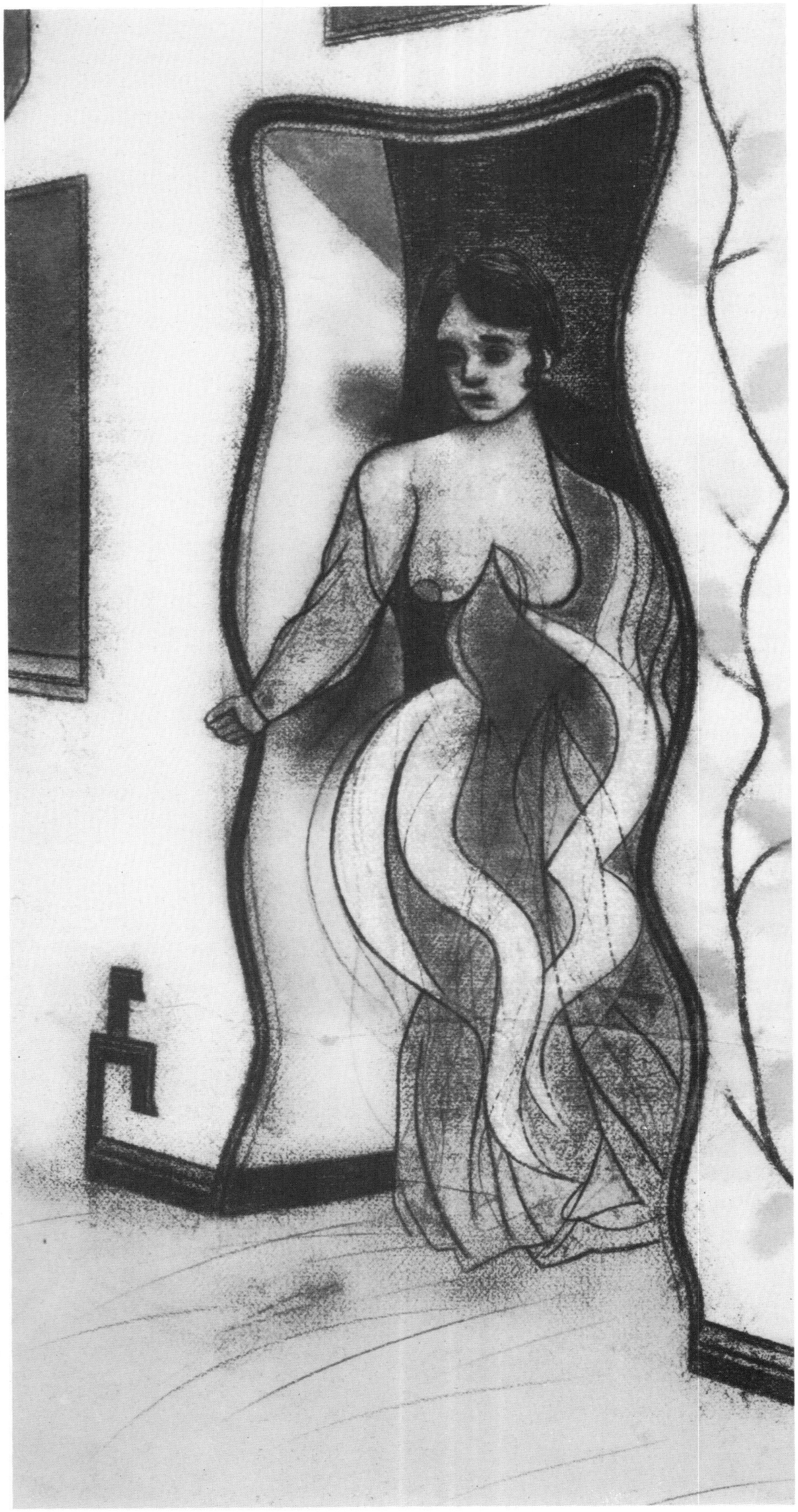

101. Manchu Decadence, 1979. *Cat. no. 245.*

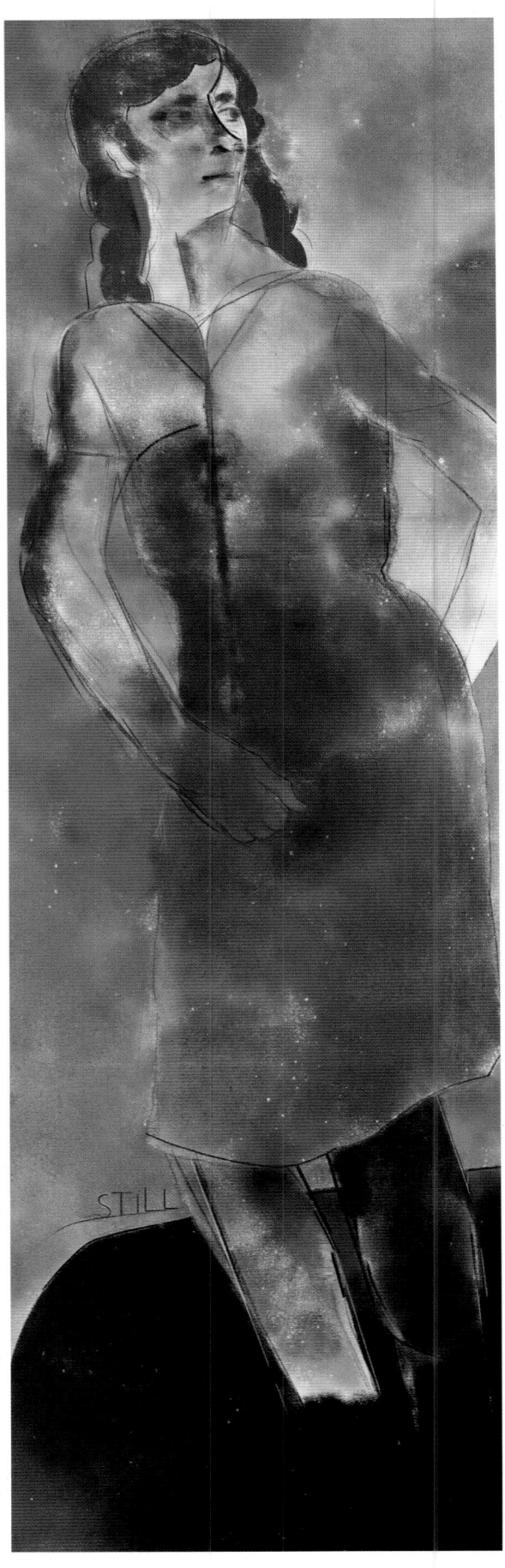

102. Still (The Other Woman), 1973. *Cat. no. 157.*

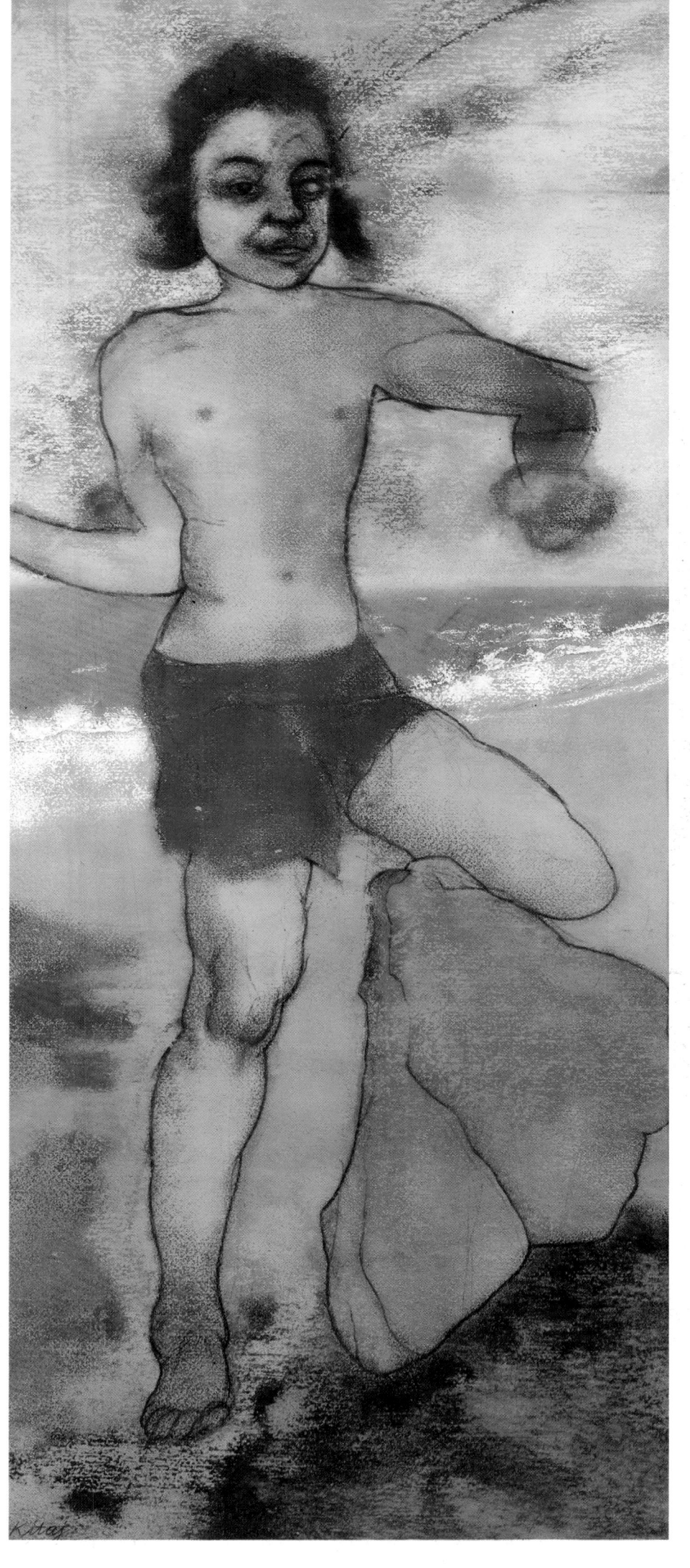

103. Bather (Psychotic Boy),
1980. *Cat. no. 281.*

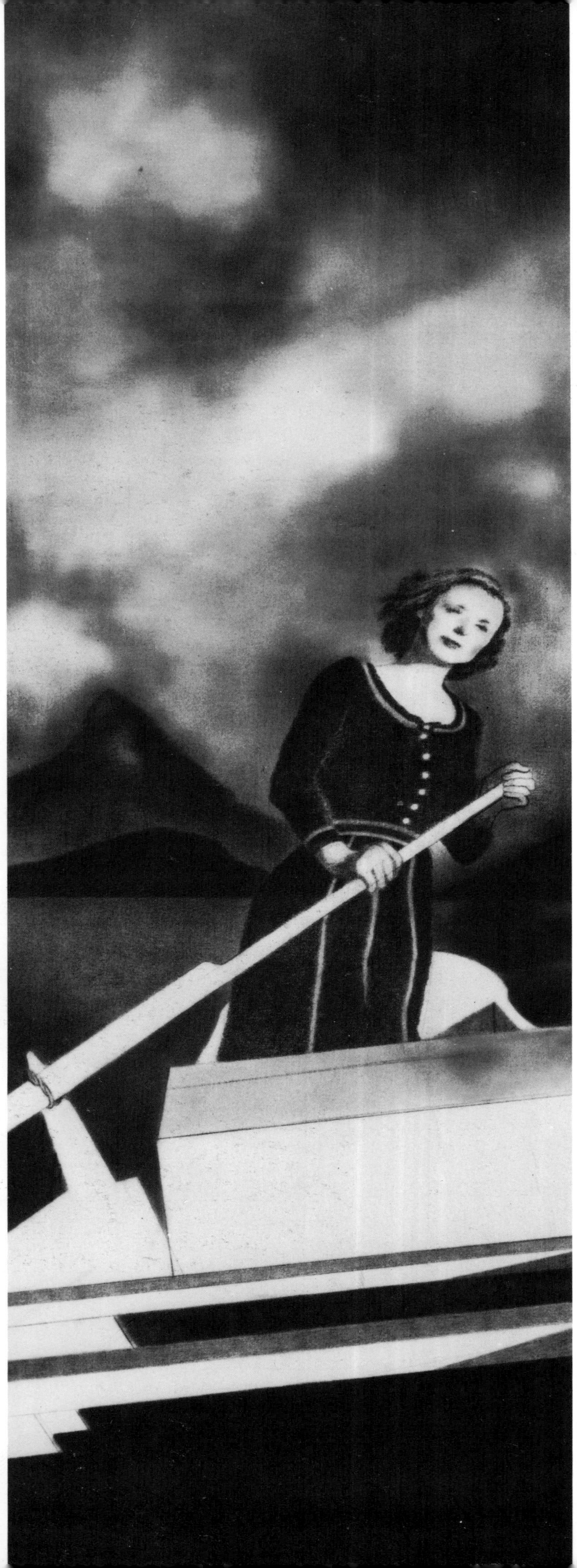

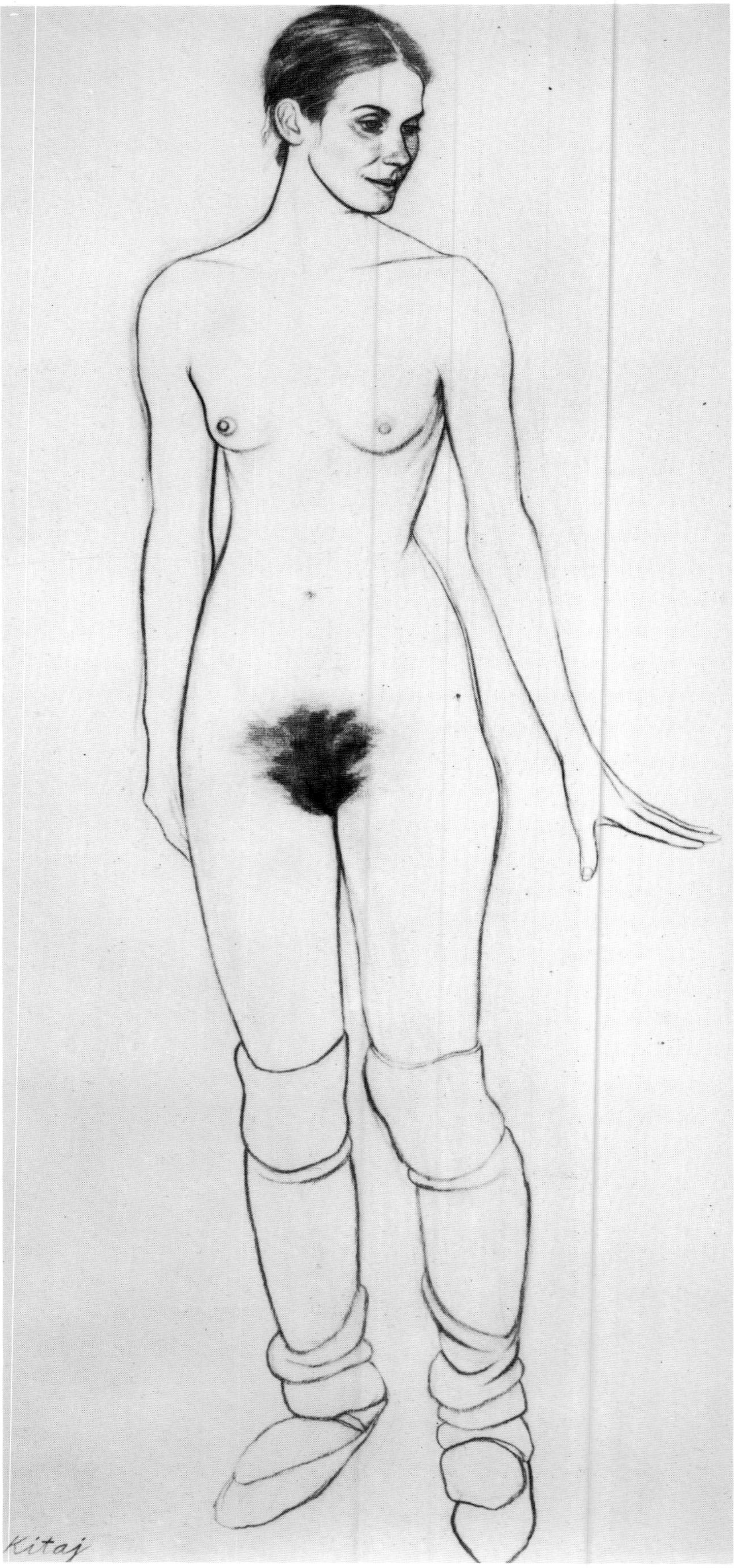

104. Houseboat Days (for John Ashbery), 1976. *Cat. no. 191.*

105. The Dancer (Margaret), 1978. *Cat. no. 212.*

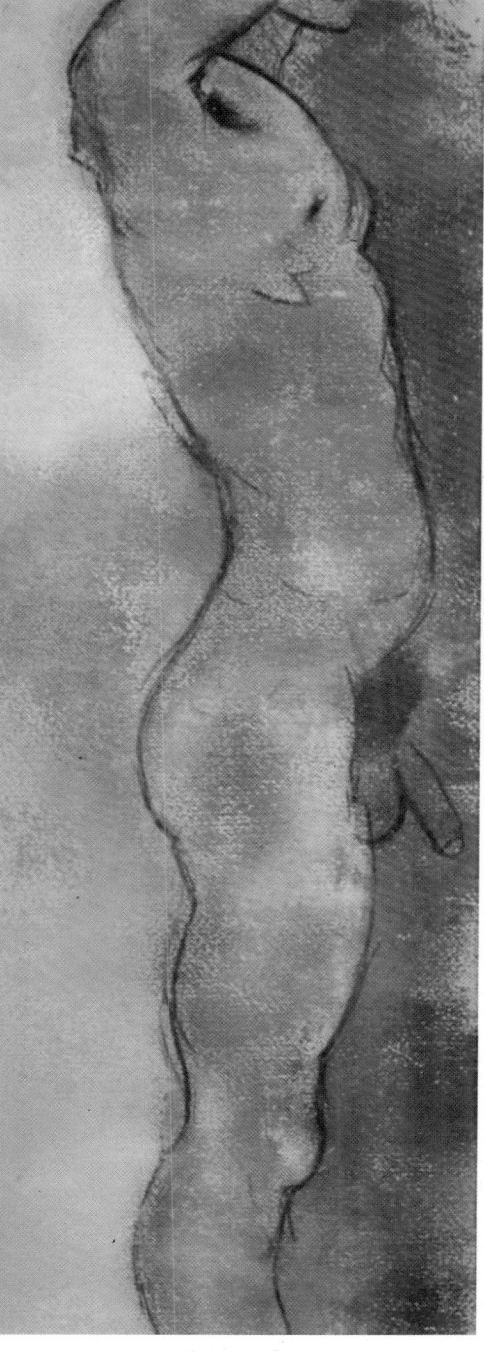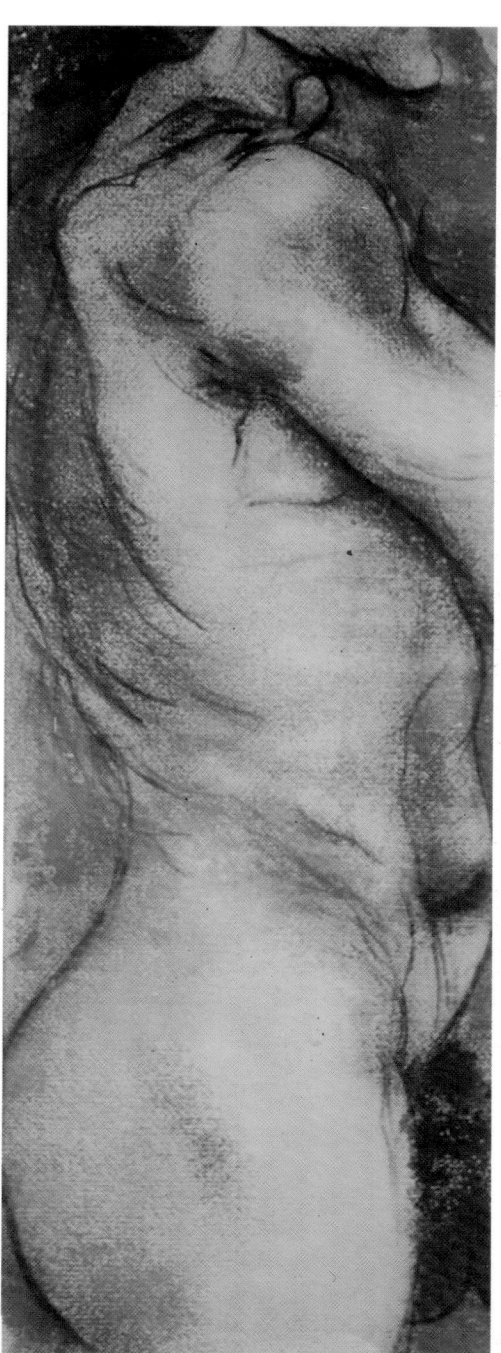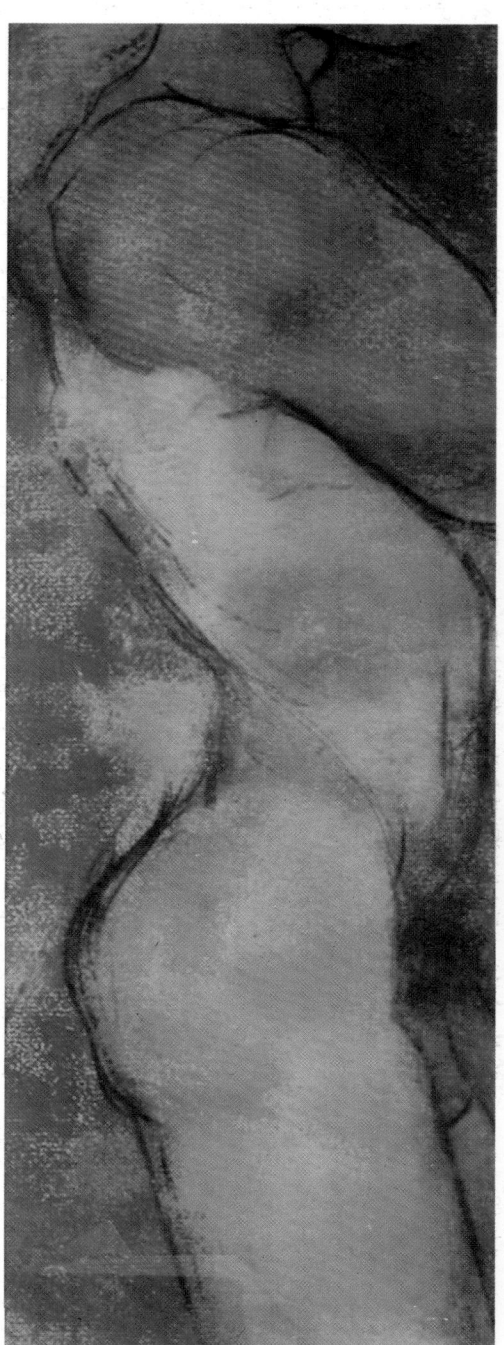

106. Sides, 1979. *Cat. no. 248.*

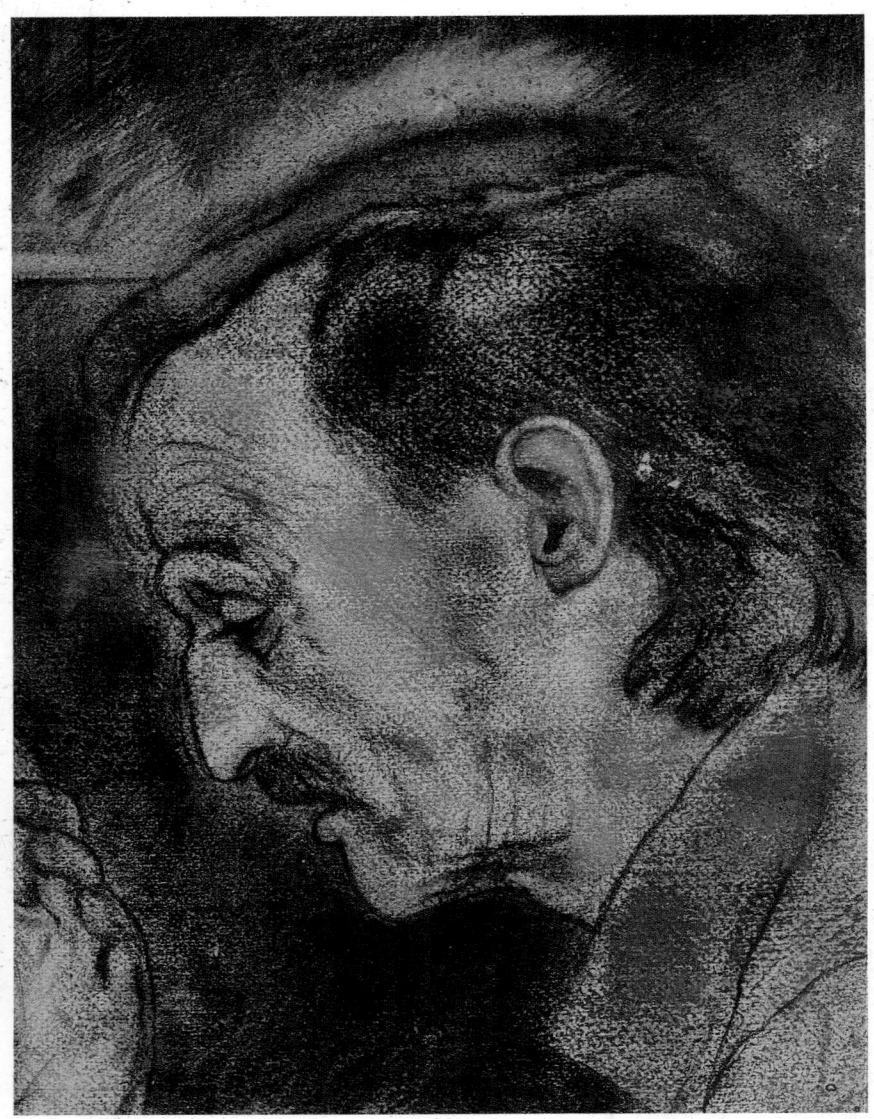

107. Alcalde, *detail from* Communist and Socialist (second version), 1979. *Cat. no. 247.*

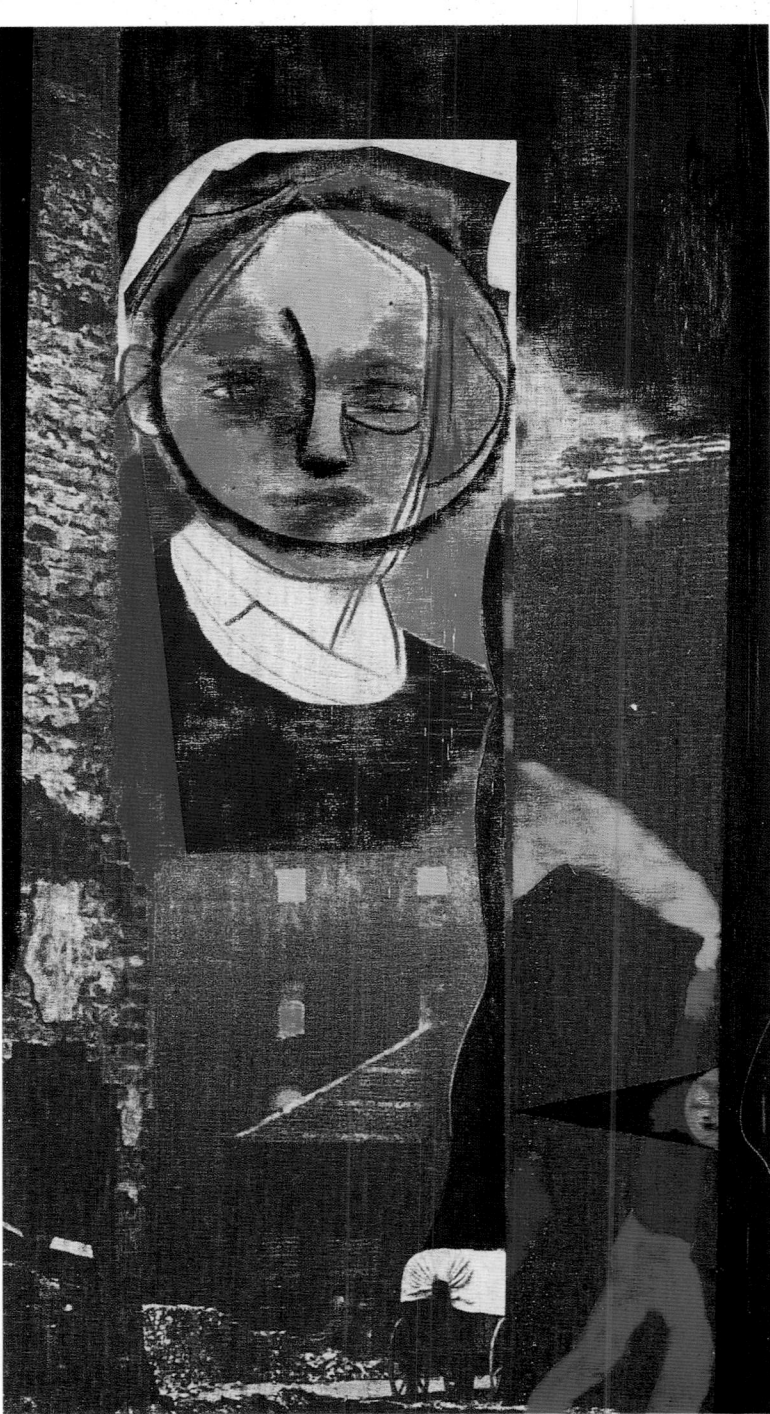

108. On a Regicide Peace, 1970. *Cat. no. 139.*

109. His Hour, 1975. *Cat. no. 171.*

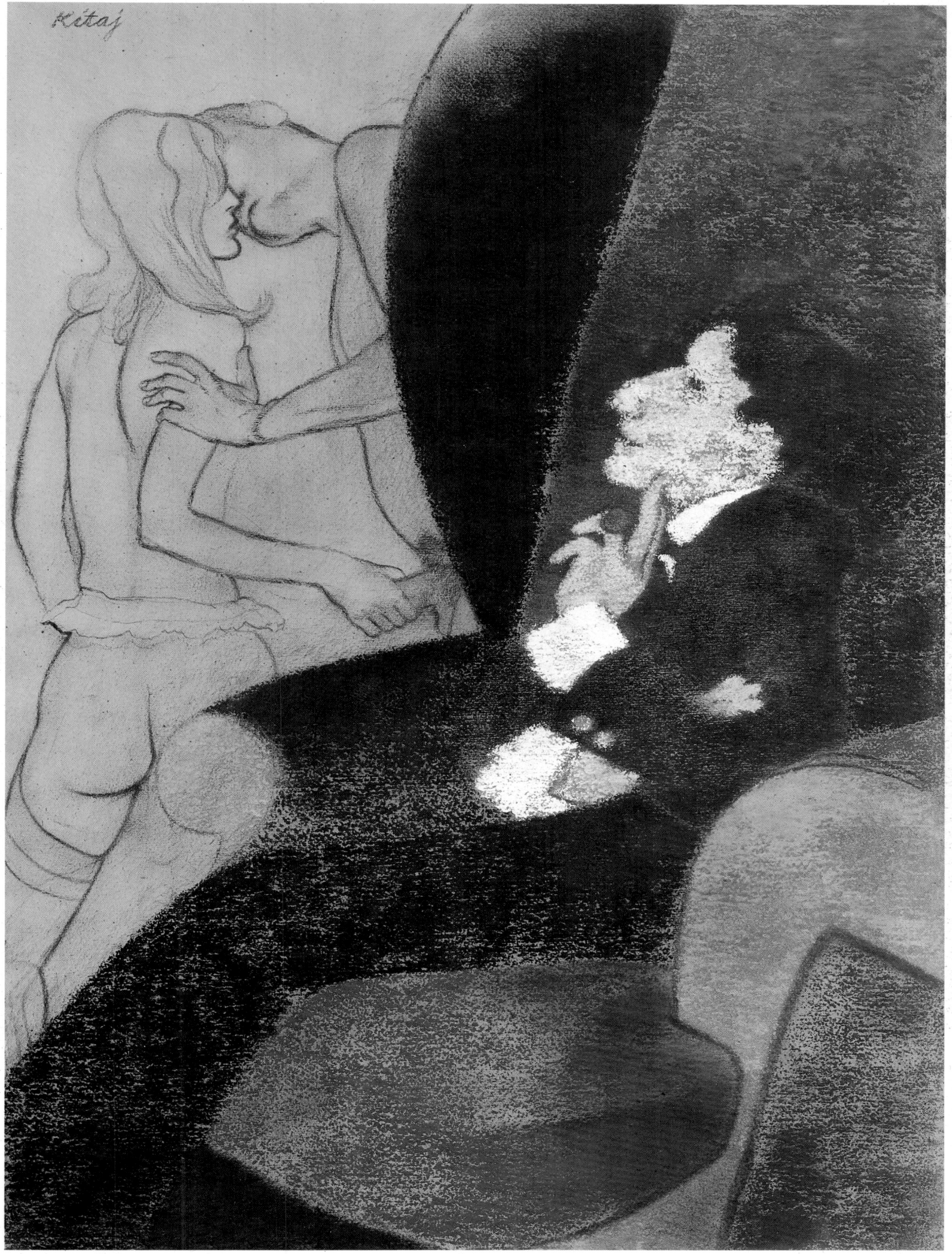

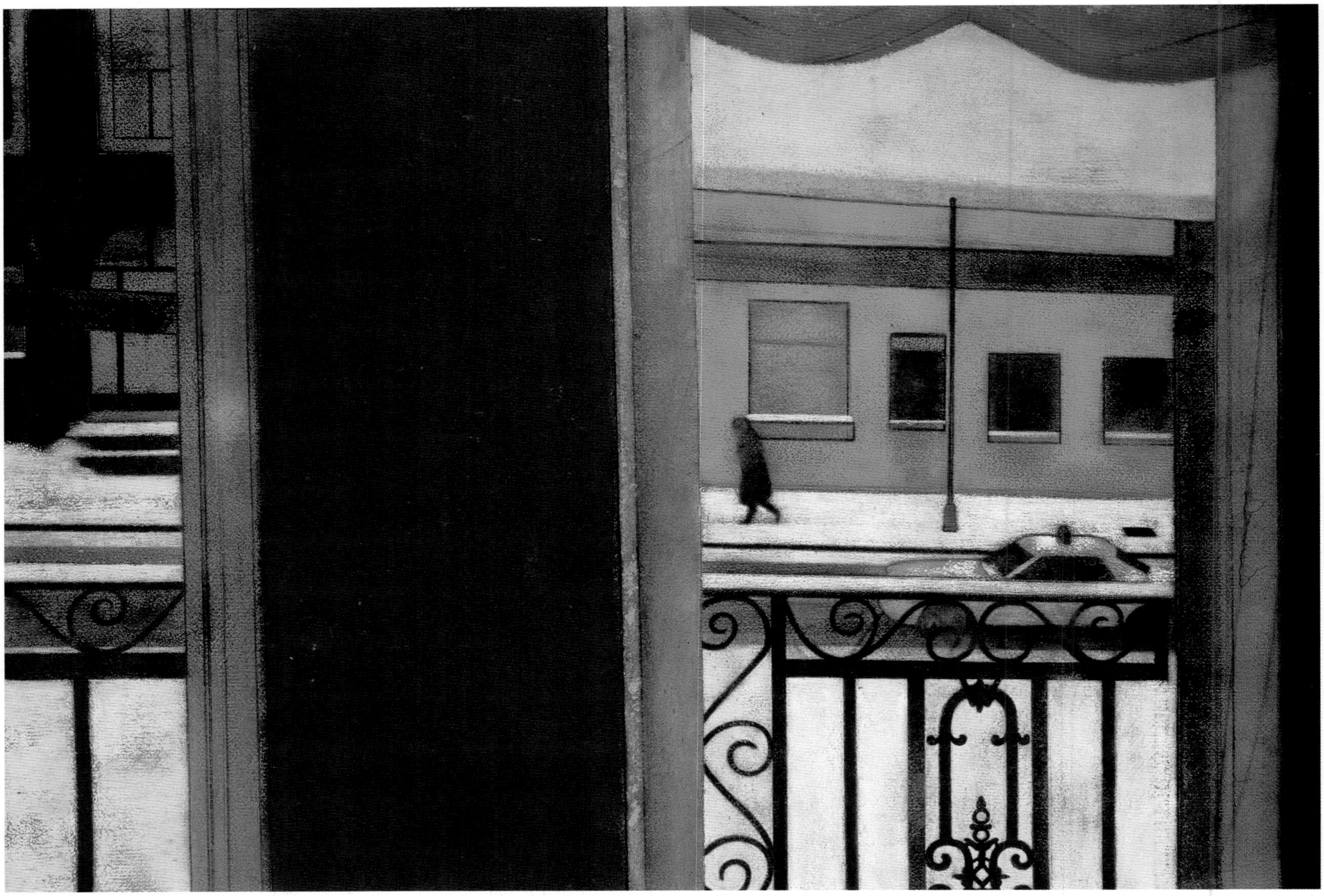

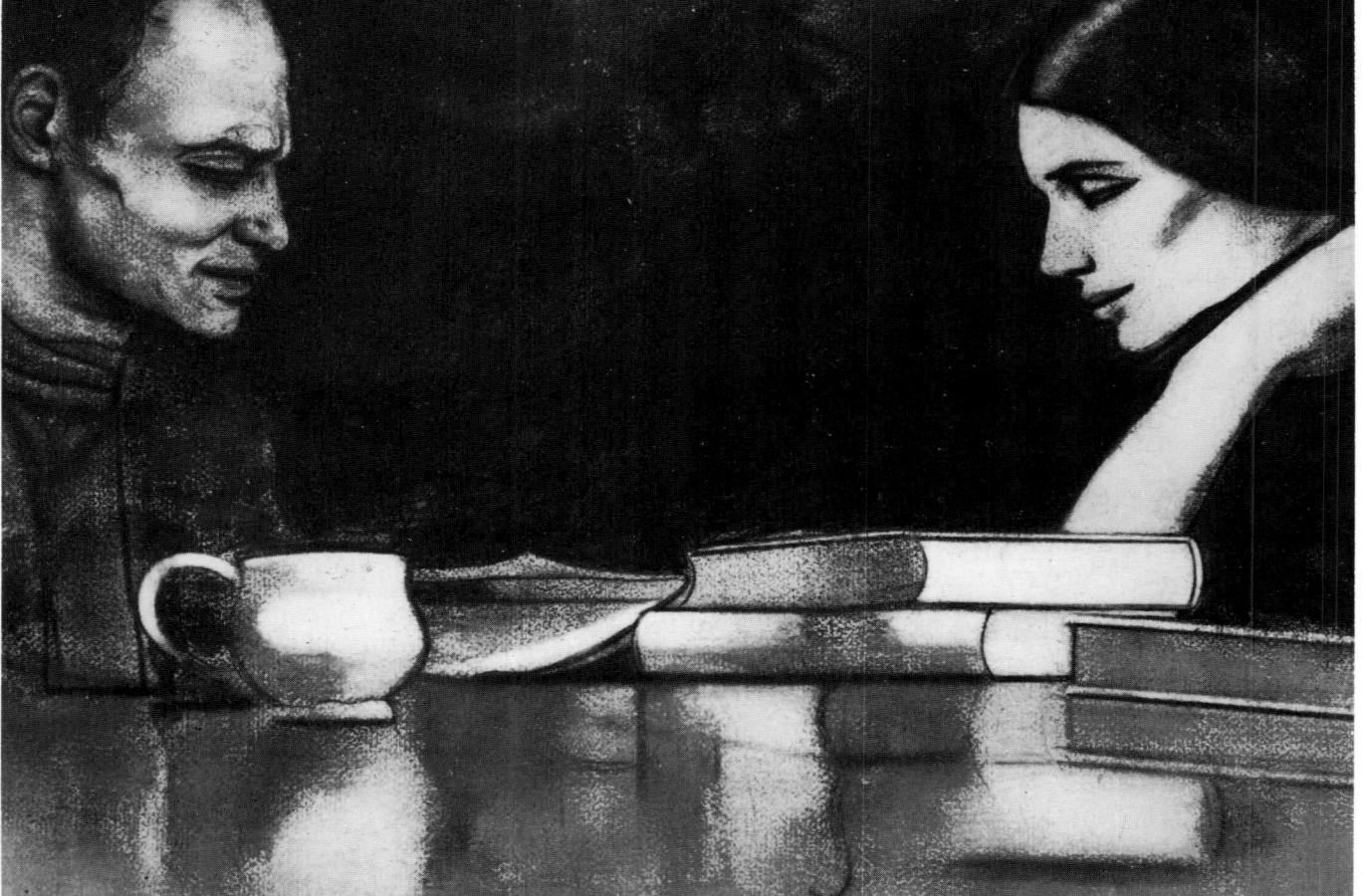

110. Ninth Street under
Snow, 1979. *Cat. no. 244.*

111. Two London Painters
(Frank Auerbach and
Sandra Fisher), 1979.
Cat. no. 246.

112. Marynka Smoking,
1980. *Cat. no. 269.*

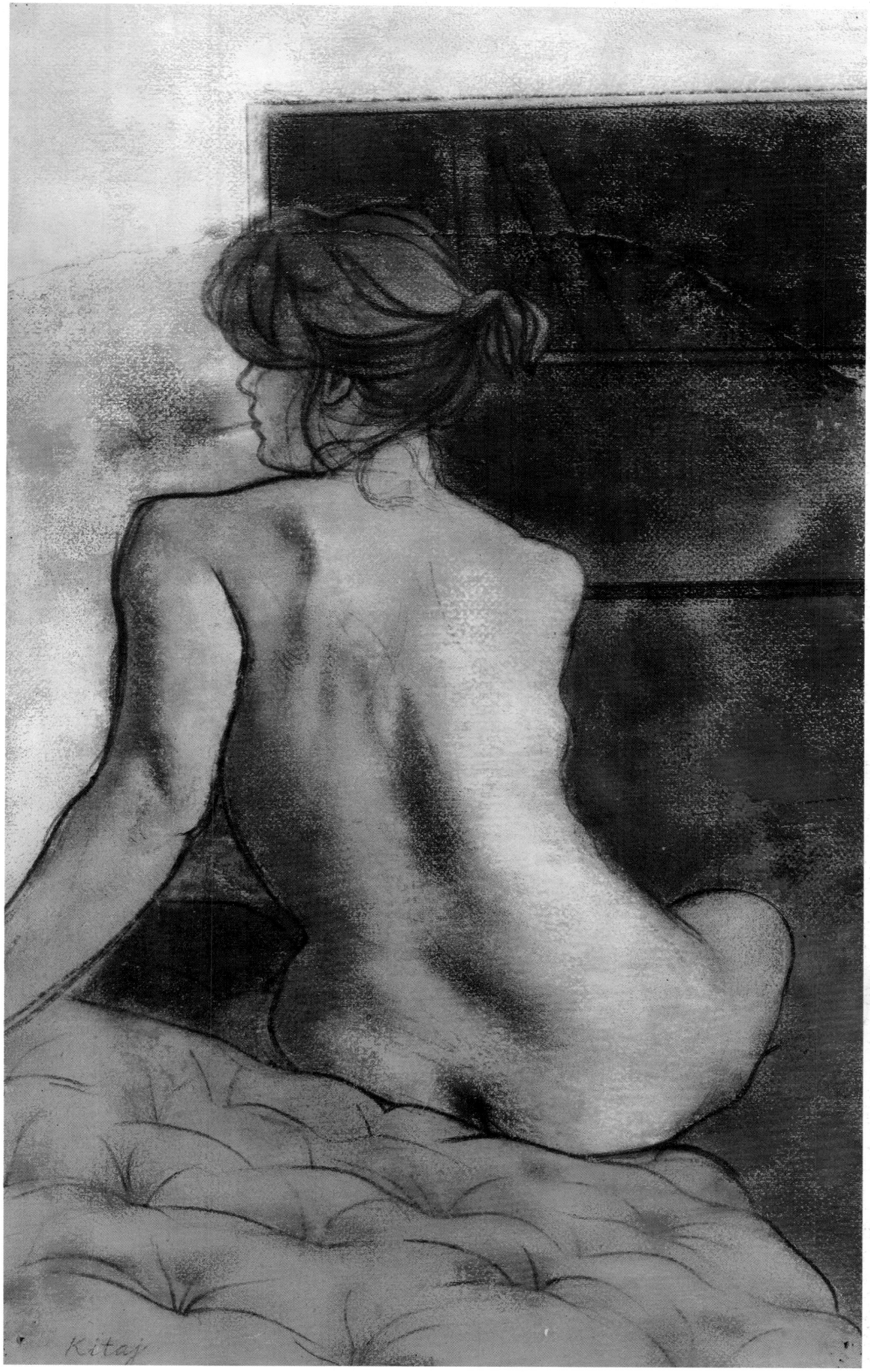
Kitaj

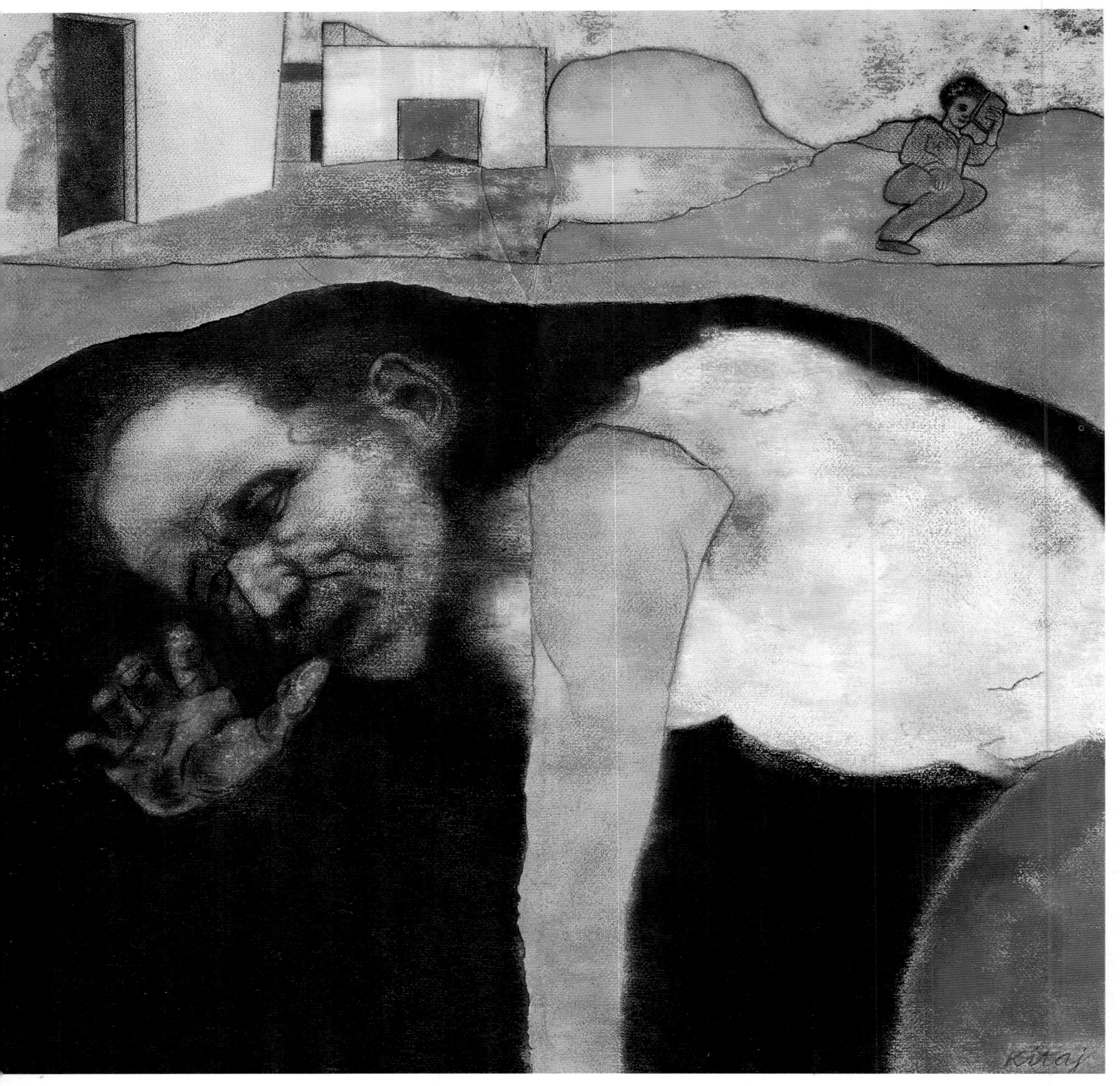

113. The Listener (Joe Singer in Hiding), 1980. *Cat. no. 280.*

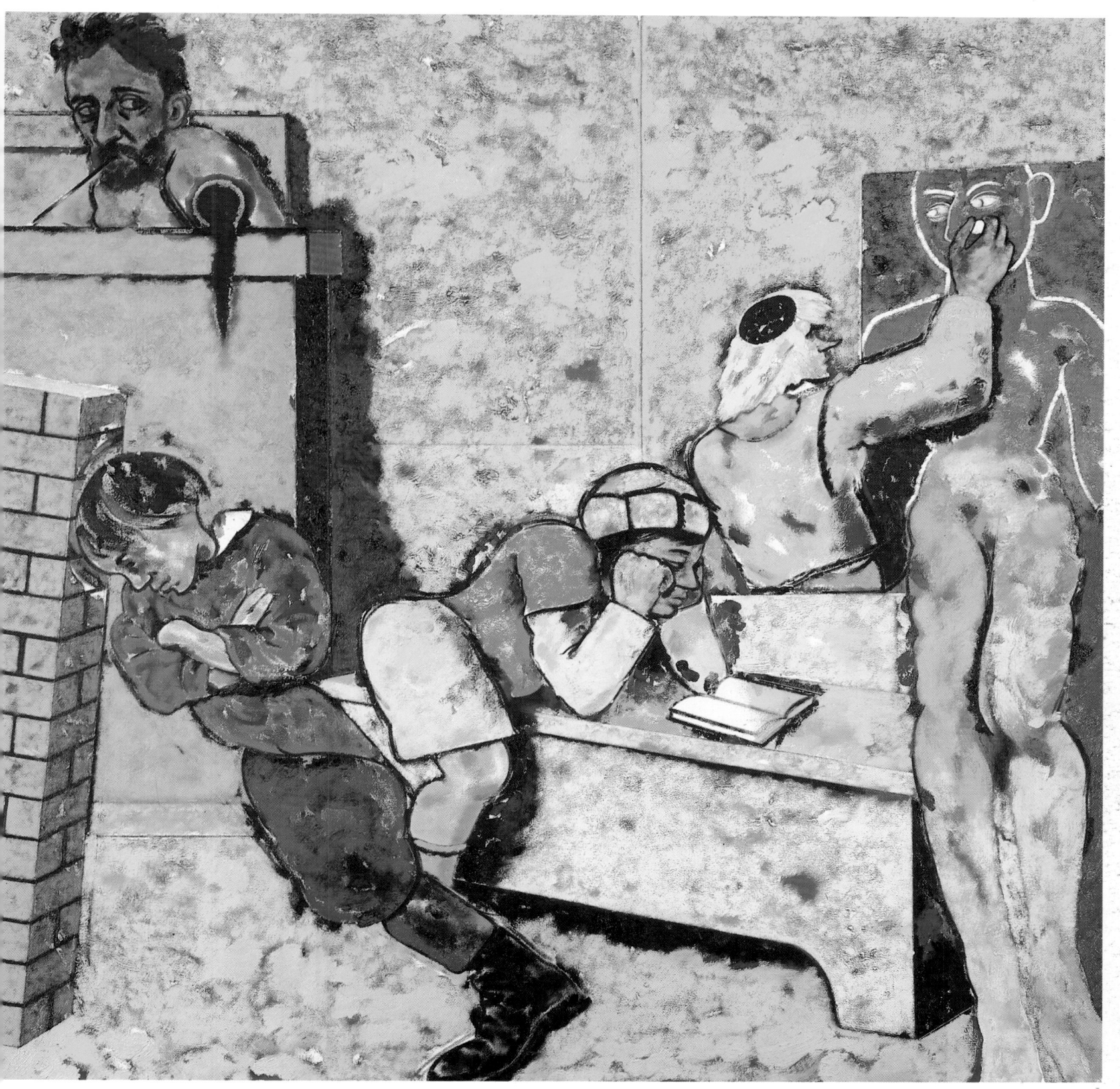

114. The Jewish School (Drawing a Golem), 1980. *Cat. no. 290.*

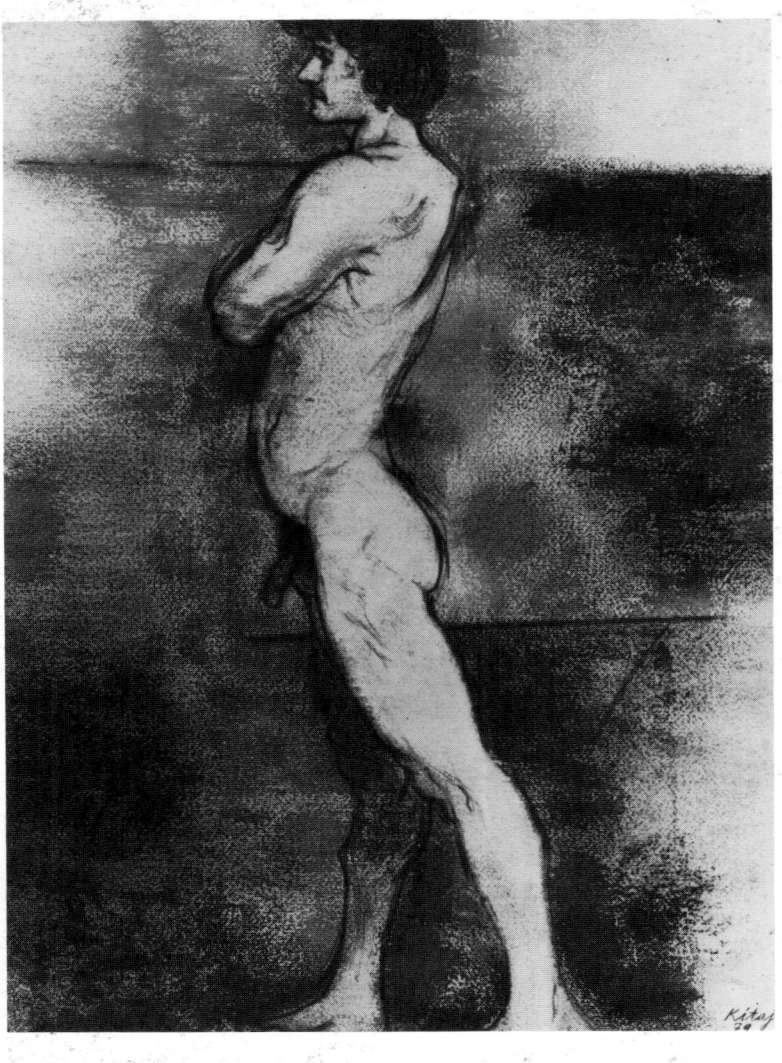

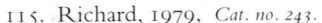
115. Richard, 1979, *Cat. no. 243.*

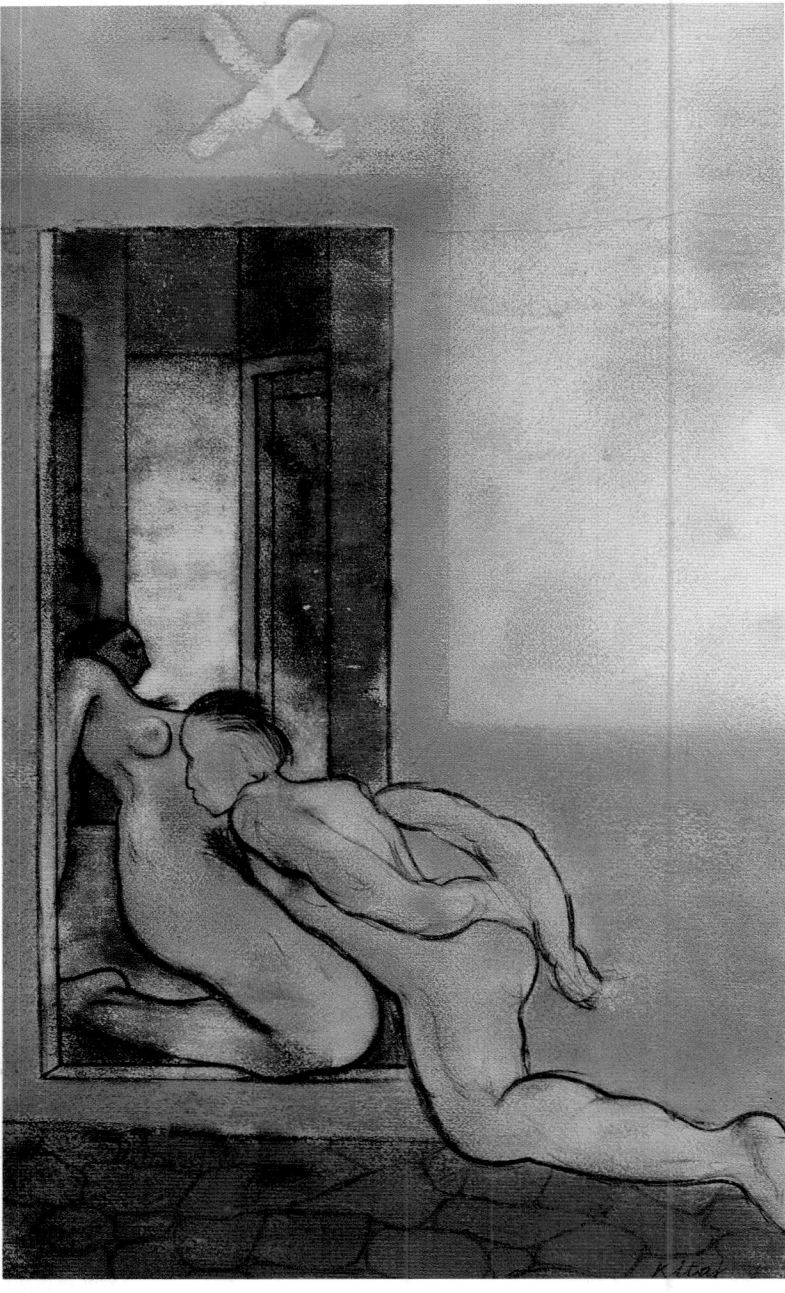

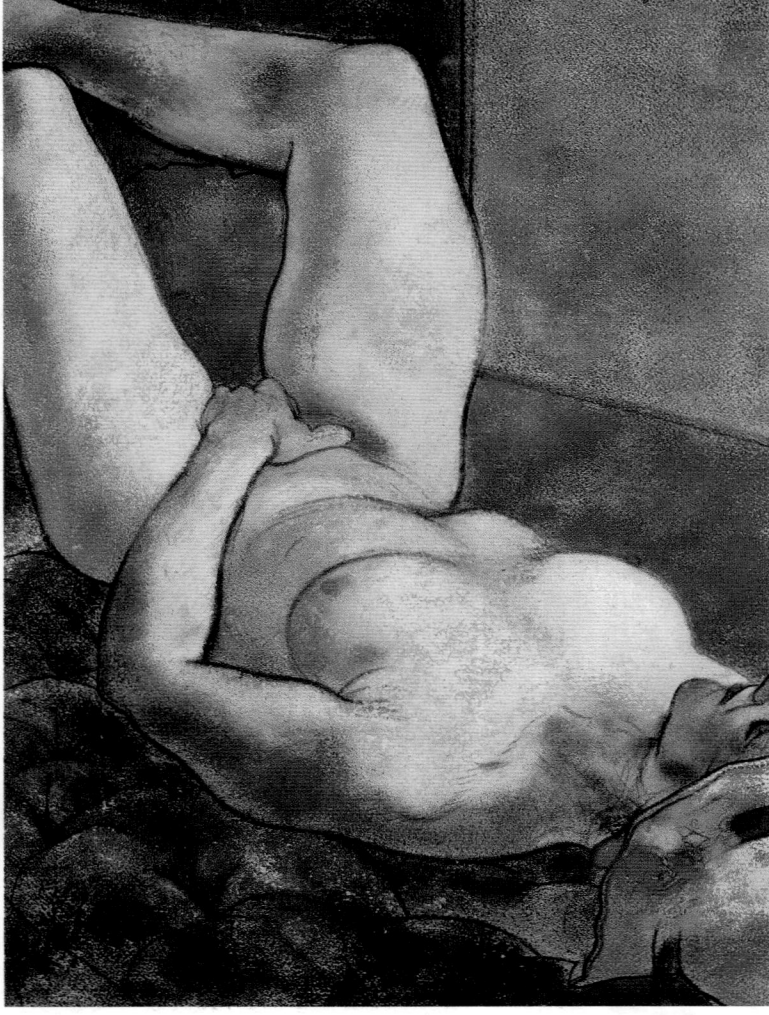

117. *(above)* Bad Faith (Riga) (Joe Singer Taking Leave of his Fiancée), 1980. *Cat. no. 285.*

116. *(left)* The Yellow Hat, 1980. *Cat. no. 284.*

118. Degas, 1980. *Cat. no. 266.*

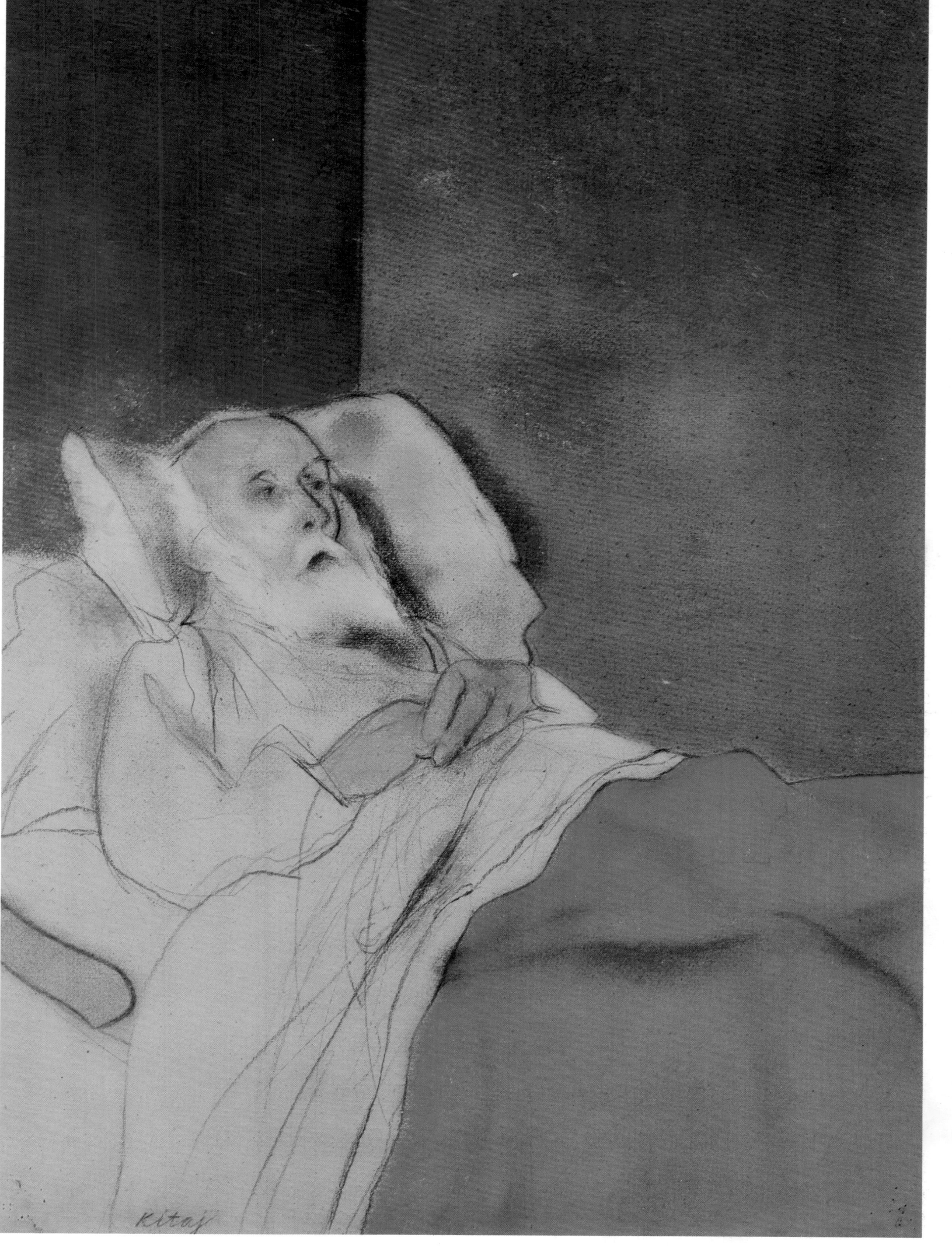

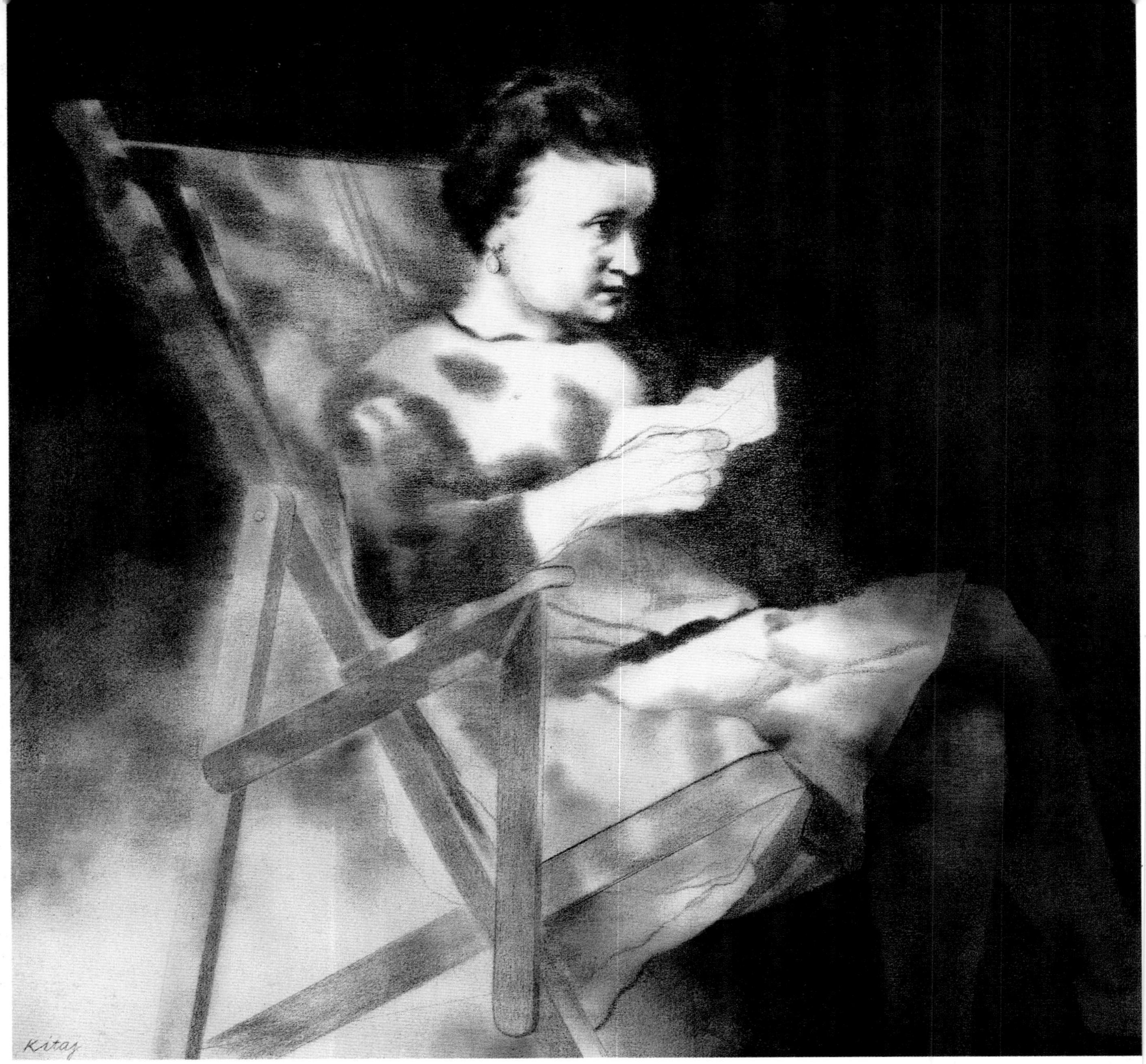

119. The Mother, 1977. *Cat. no. 203.*

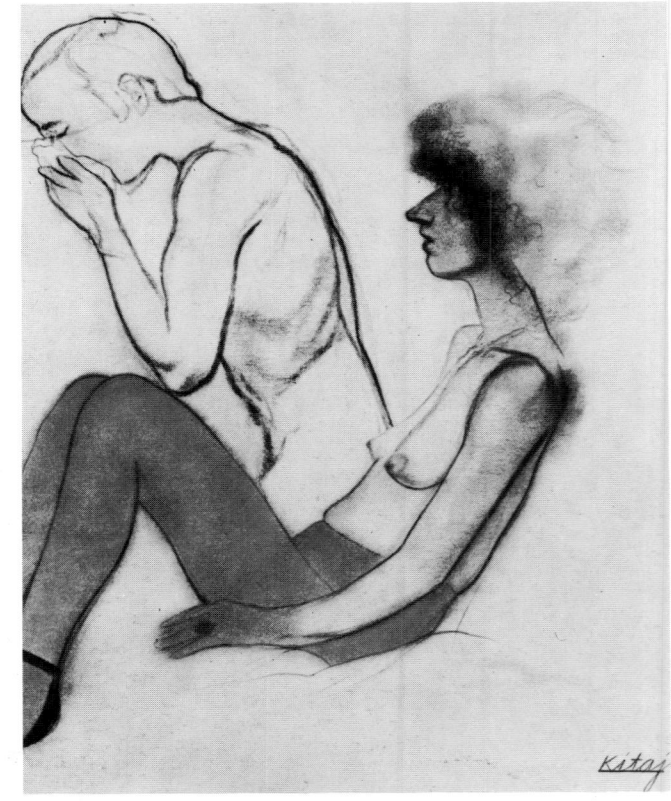

120. The Sneeze, 1975. *Cat. no. 179.*

121. *(opposite)* Mary-Ann, 1980. *Cat. no. 270.*

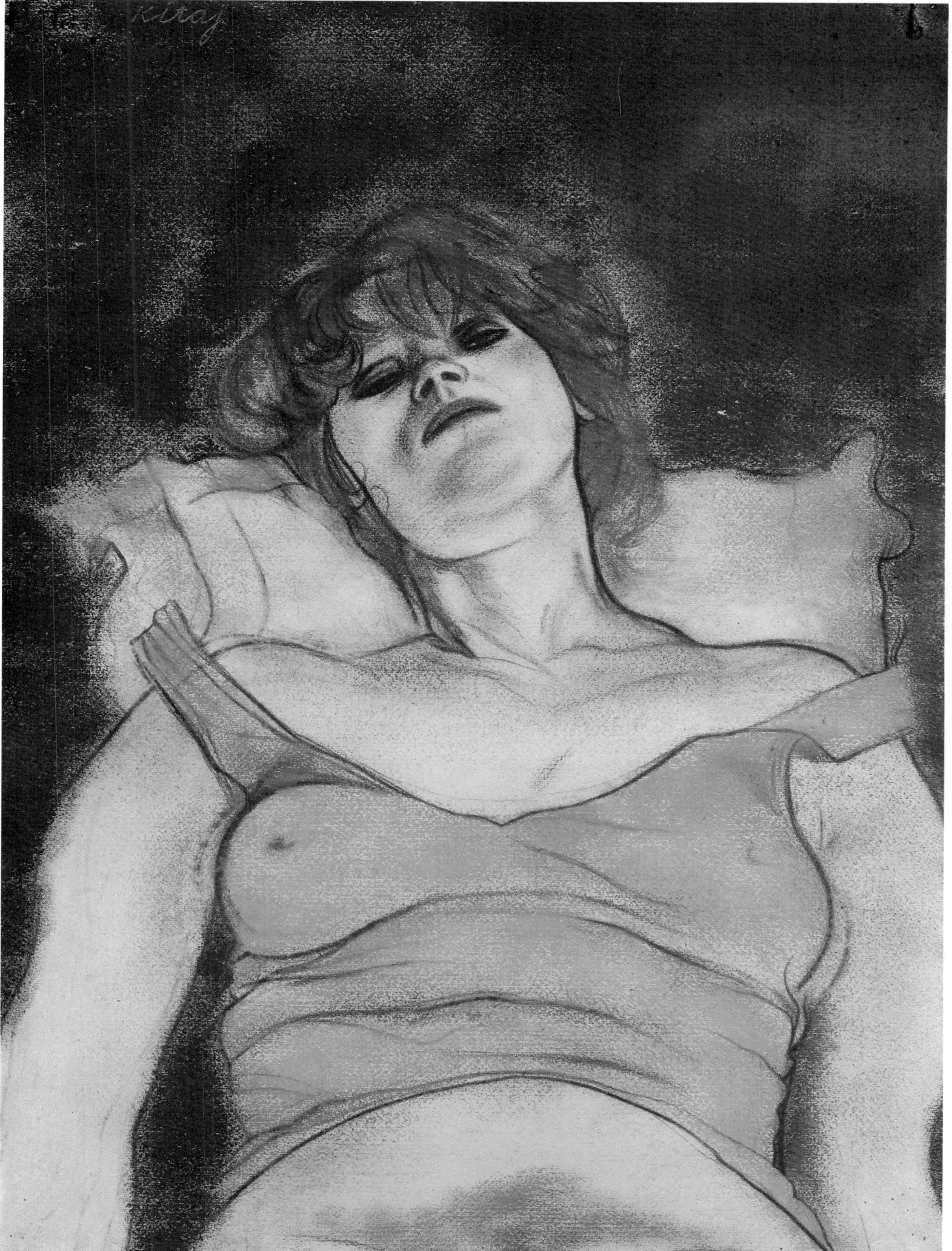

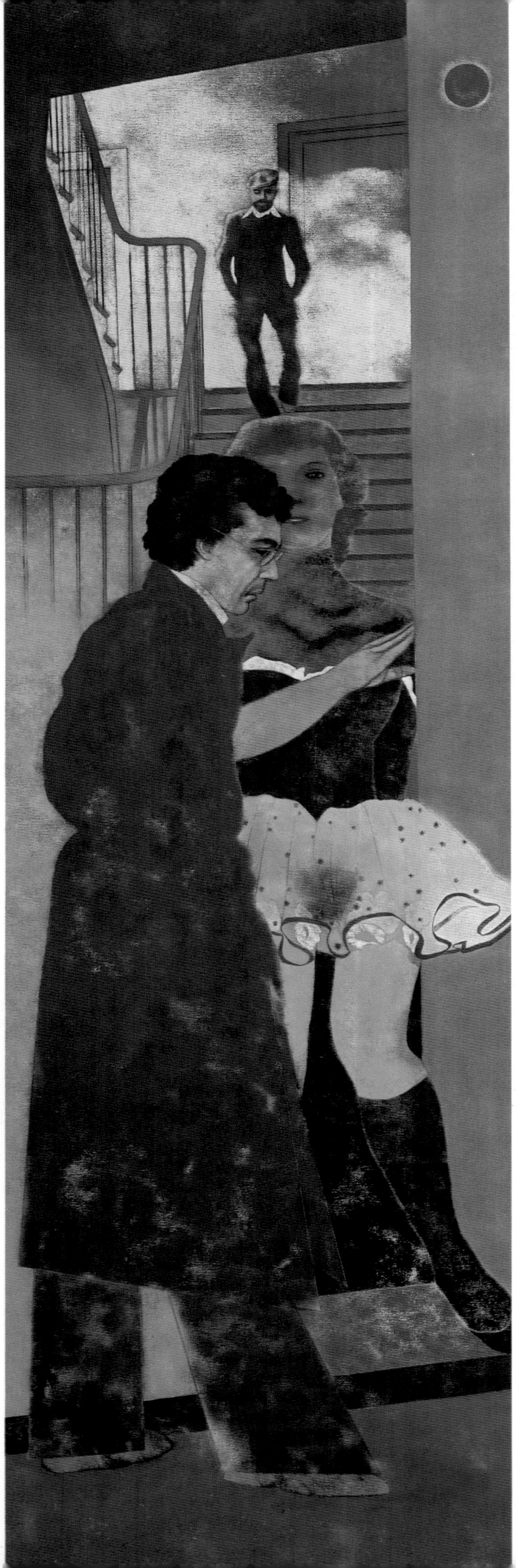

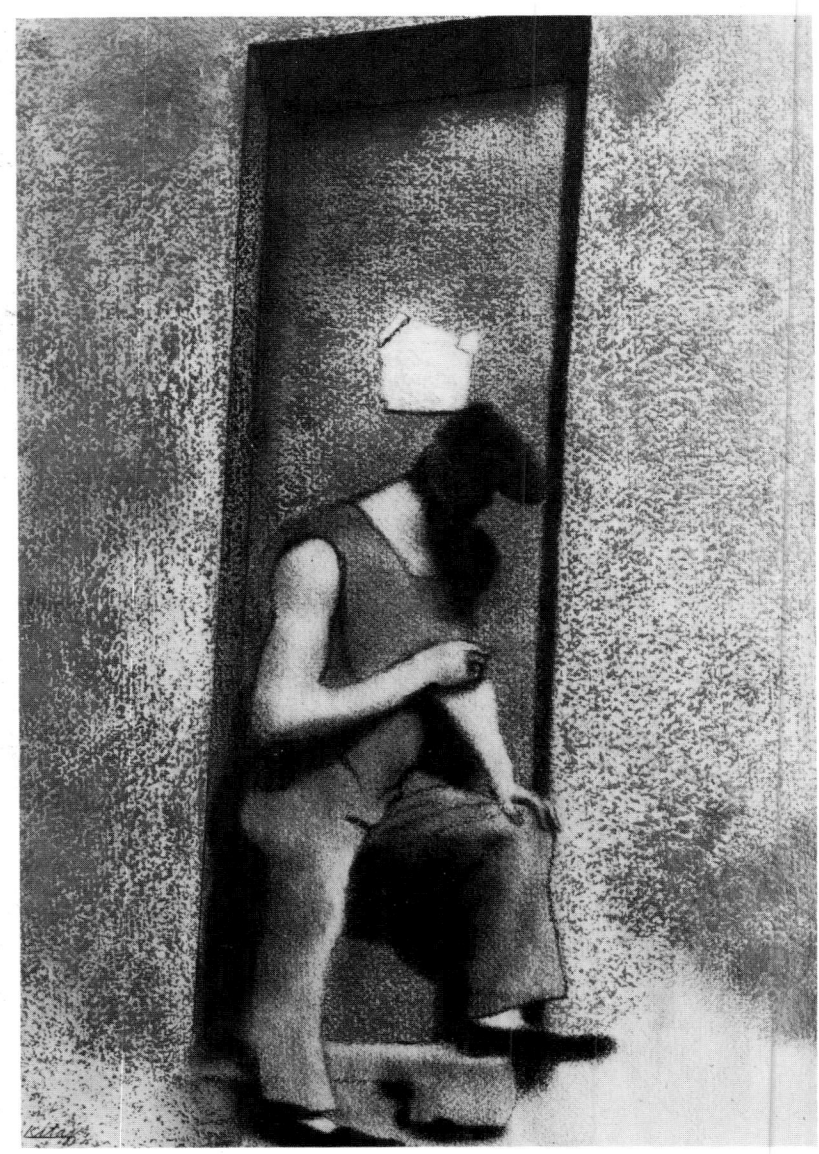
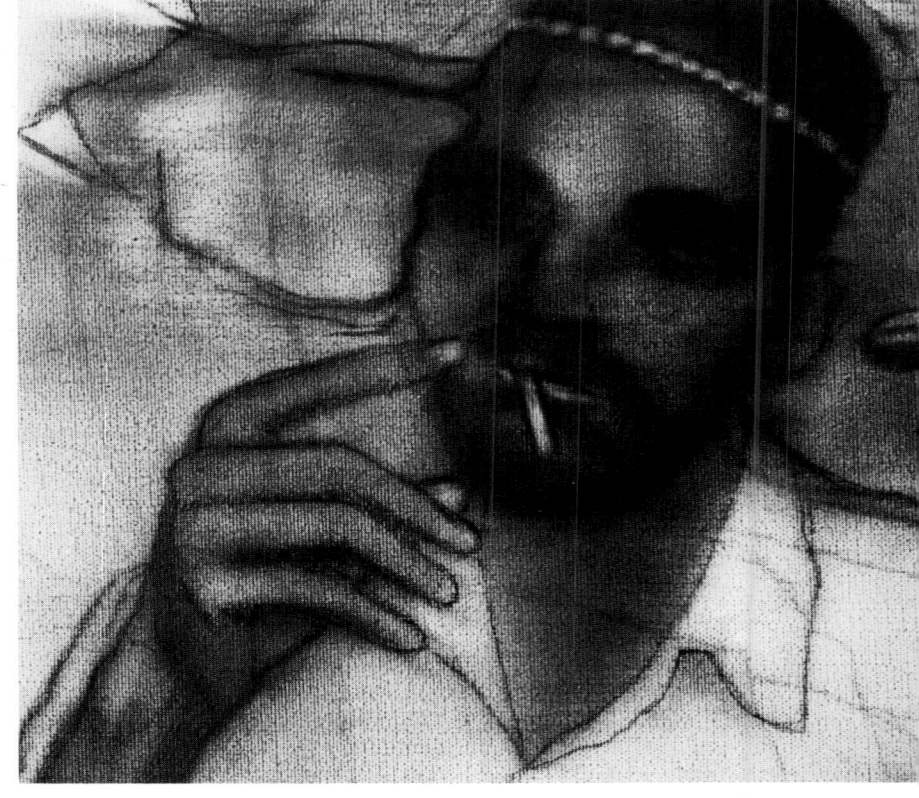

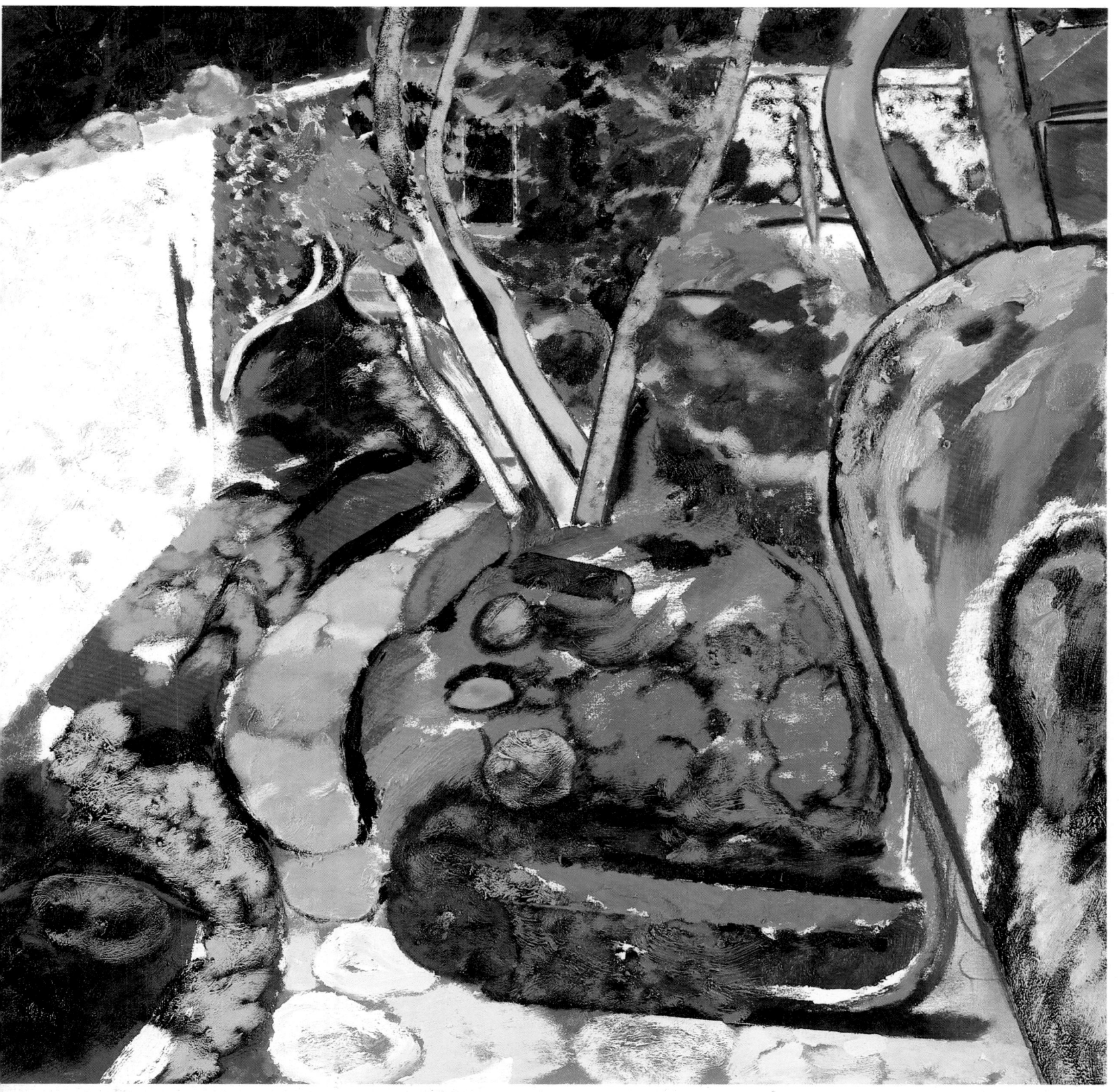

125. The Garden, 1981. *Cat. no. 296.*

122. *(opposite, far left)* Smyrna Greek (Nikos), 1976–7. *Cat. no. 198.*

123. *(opposite, top)* In Catalonia, 1975. *Cat. no. 175.*

124. *(left)* After Giotto *(detail)*, 1976–9. *Cat. no. 200.*

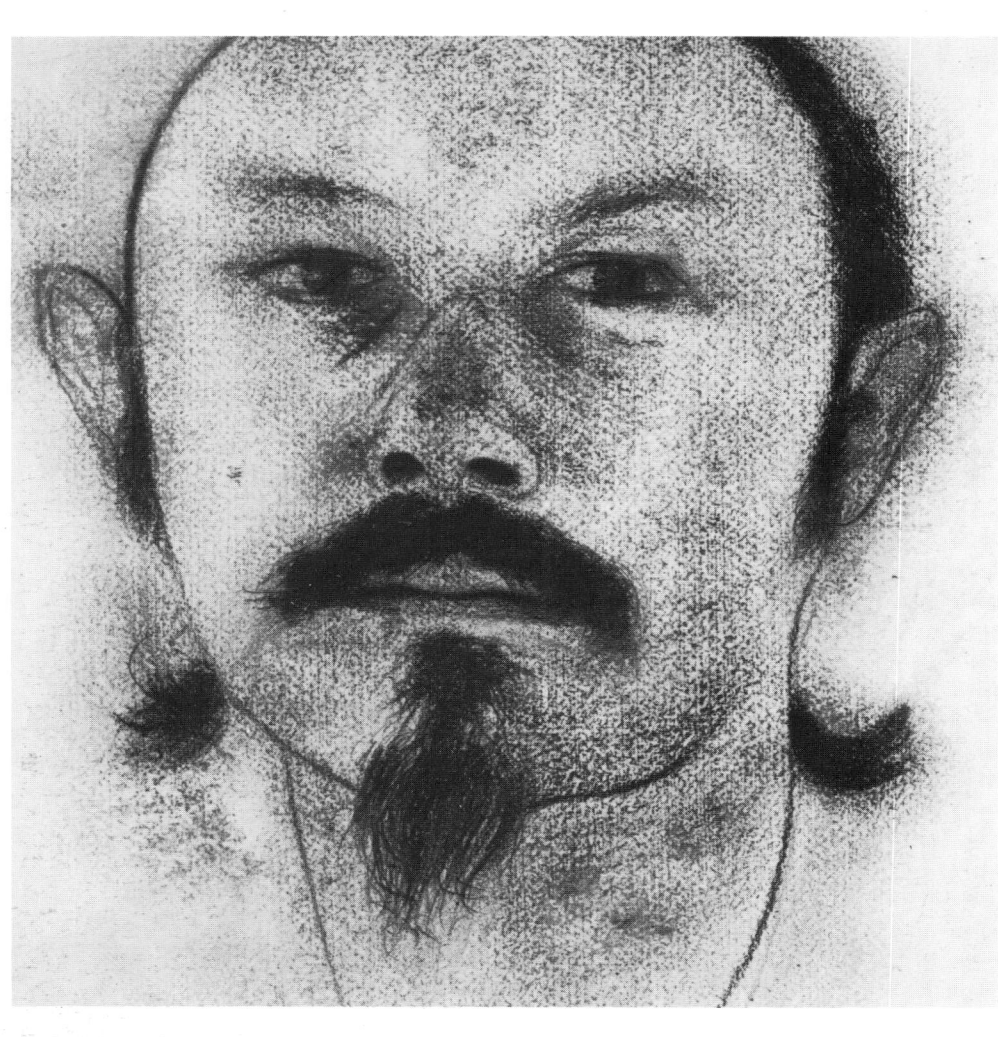

126. Paul Blackburn, 1980. *Cat. no. 268.*

127. *(below left)* The Poet and Notre Dame (Robert Duncan), 198.
Cat. no. 320.

128. *(below)* Chimera, 1980-1. *Cat. no. 294.*

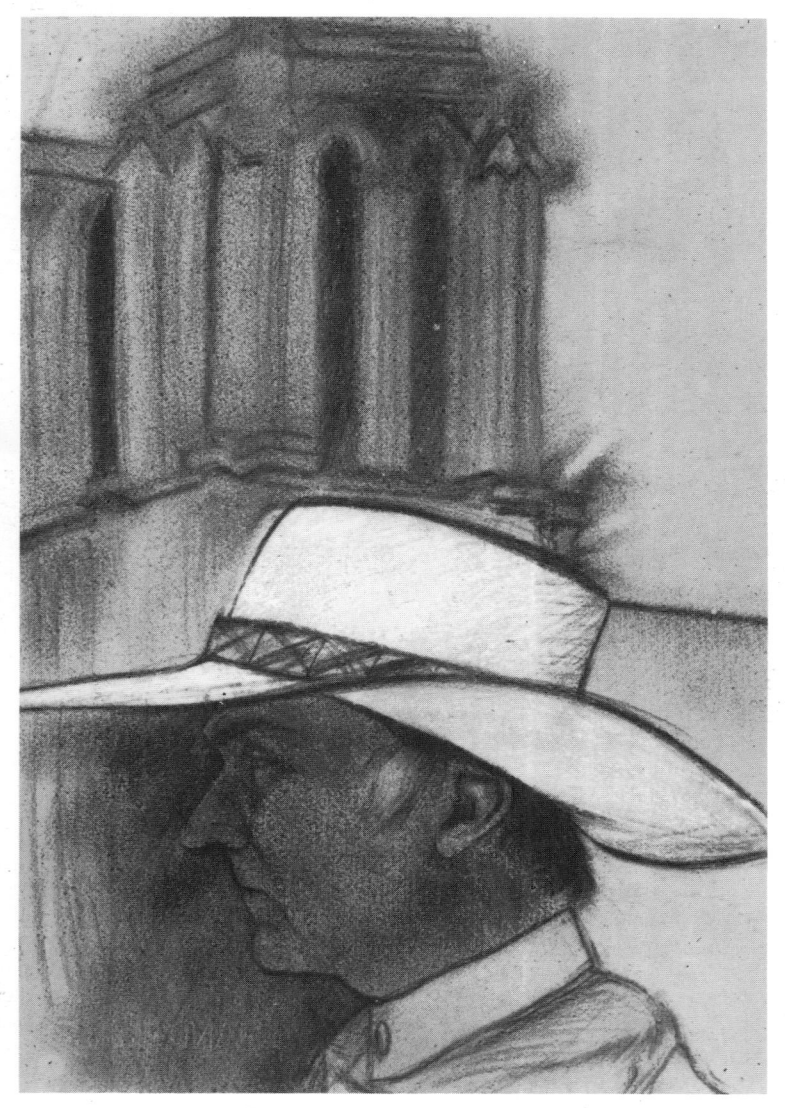

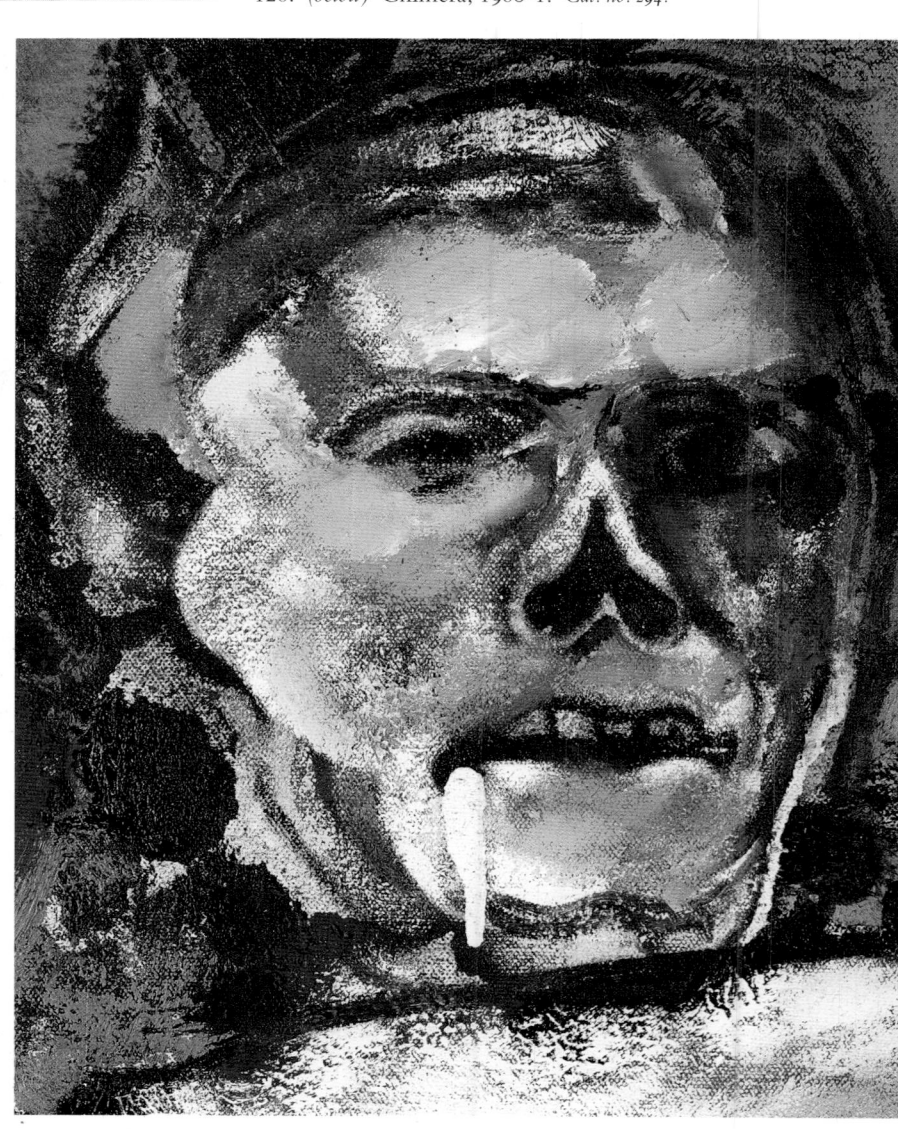

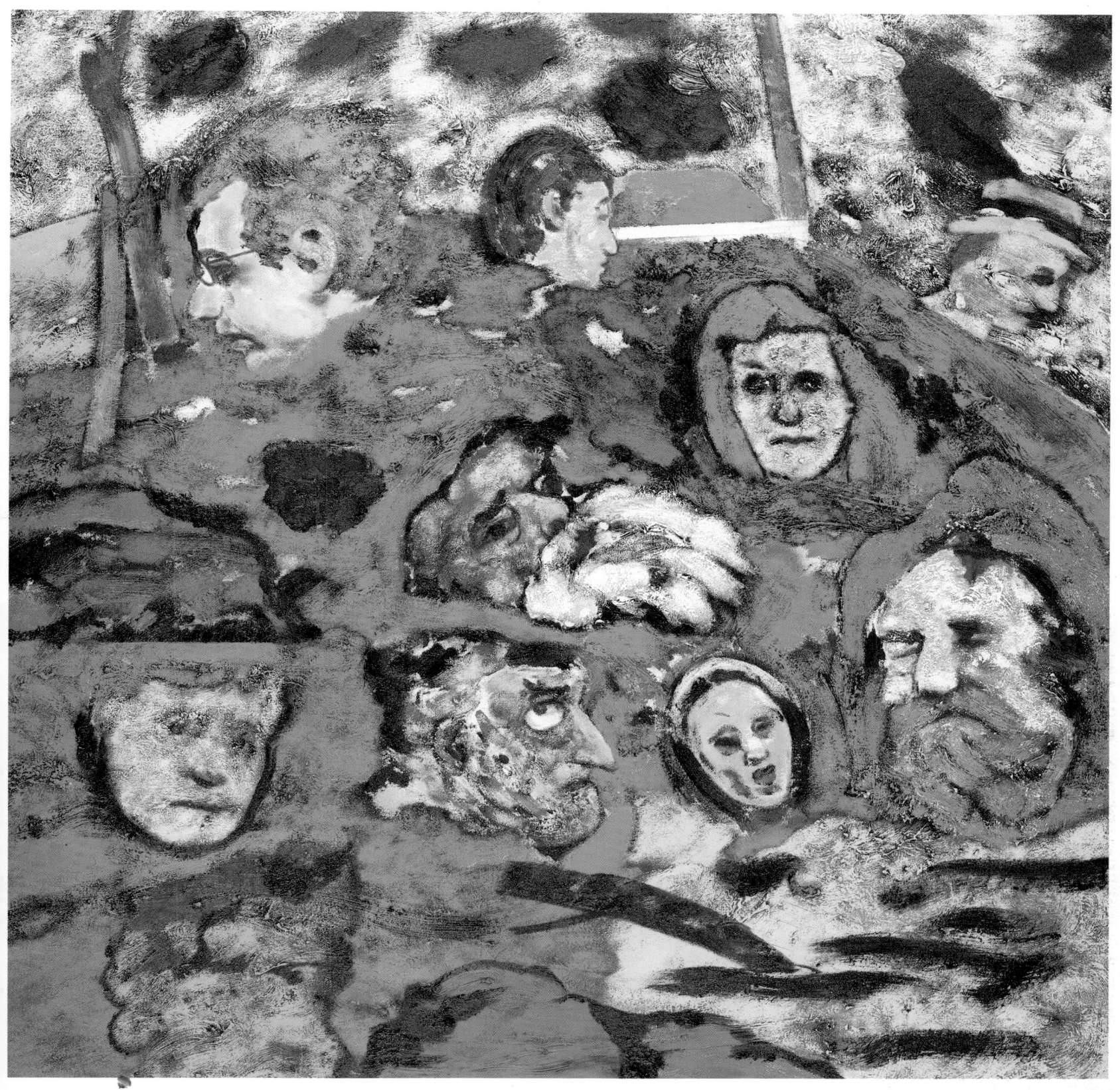

129. Rock Garden (The Nation), 1981. *Cat. no. 299.*

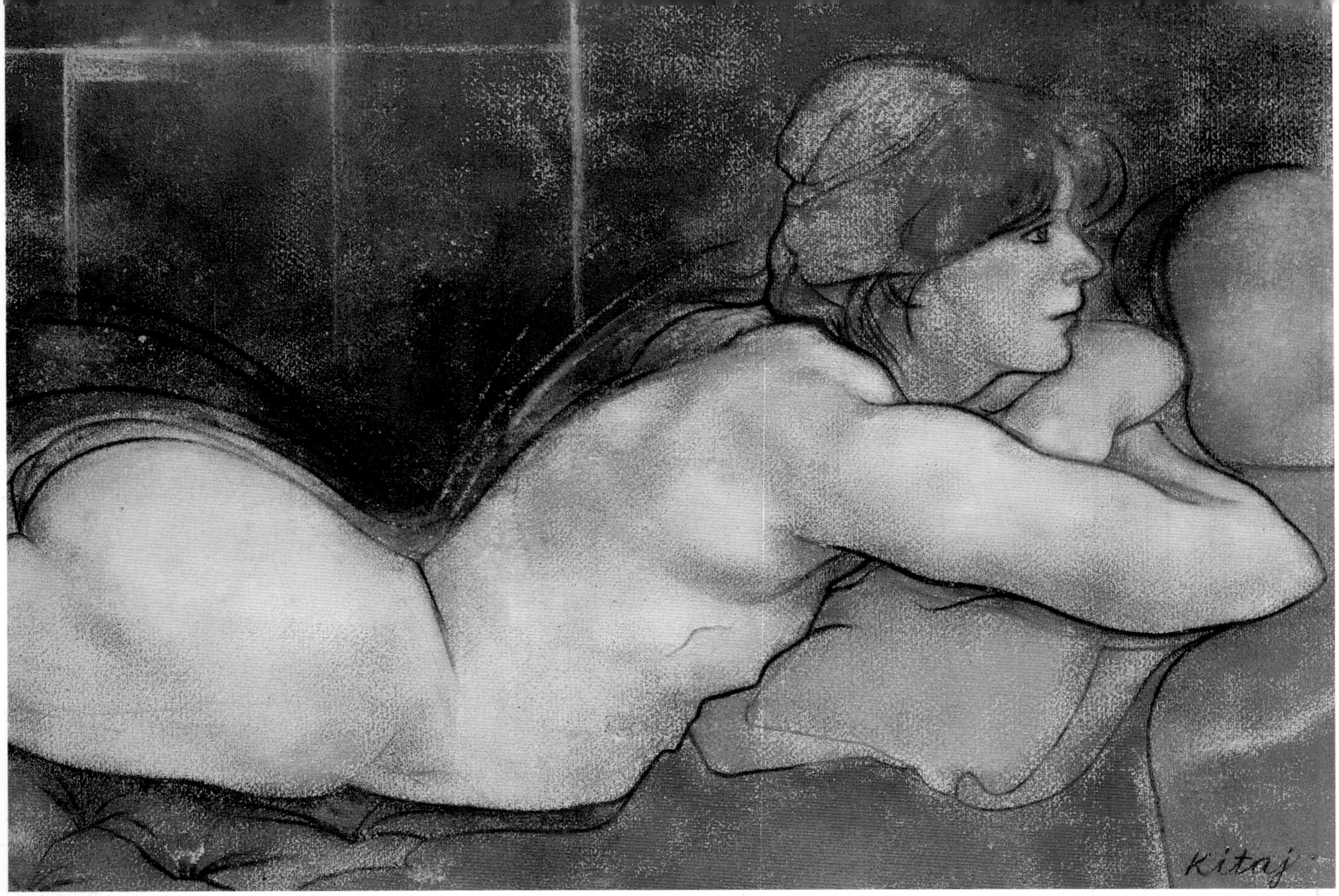

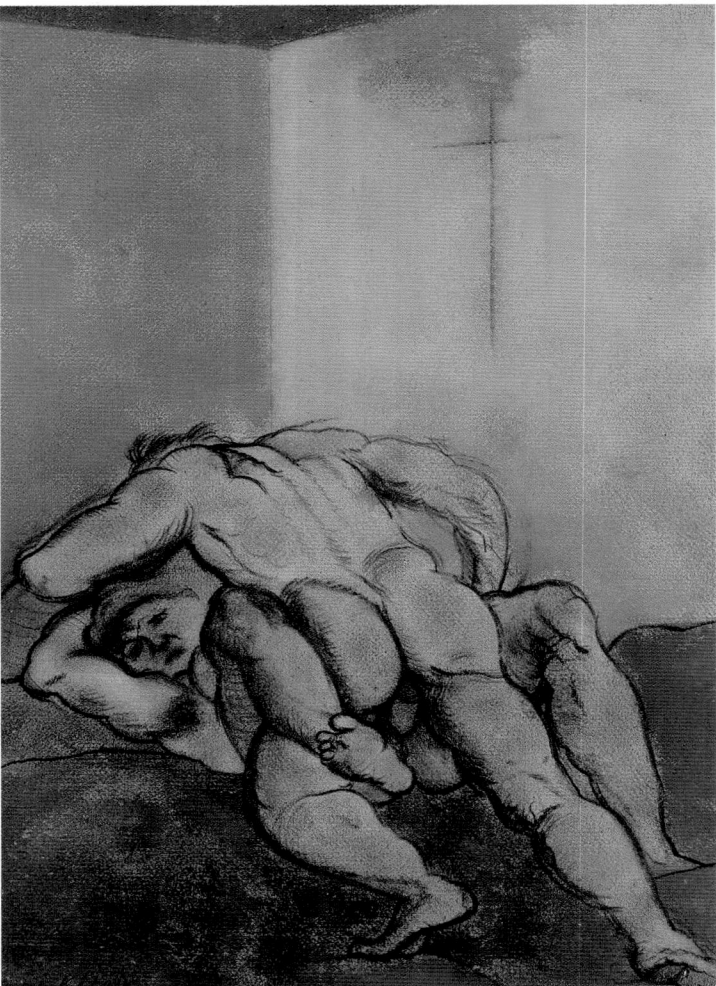

130. Mary-Ann on her
Stomach (face right), 1980.
Cat. no. 271.

131. Form and Content
(after Giulio Romano),
1979. *Cat. no. 255.*

132. Self-portrait in
Saragossa, 1980. *Cat. no. 288.*

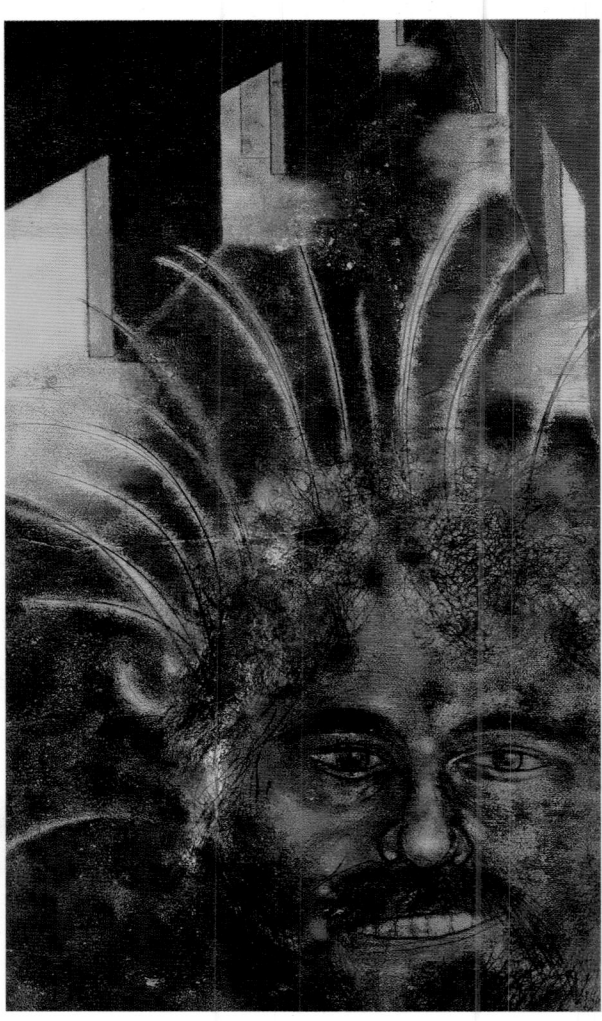

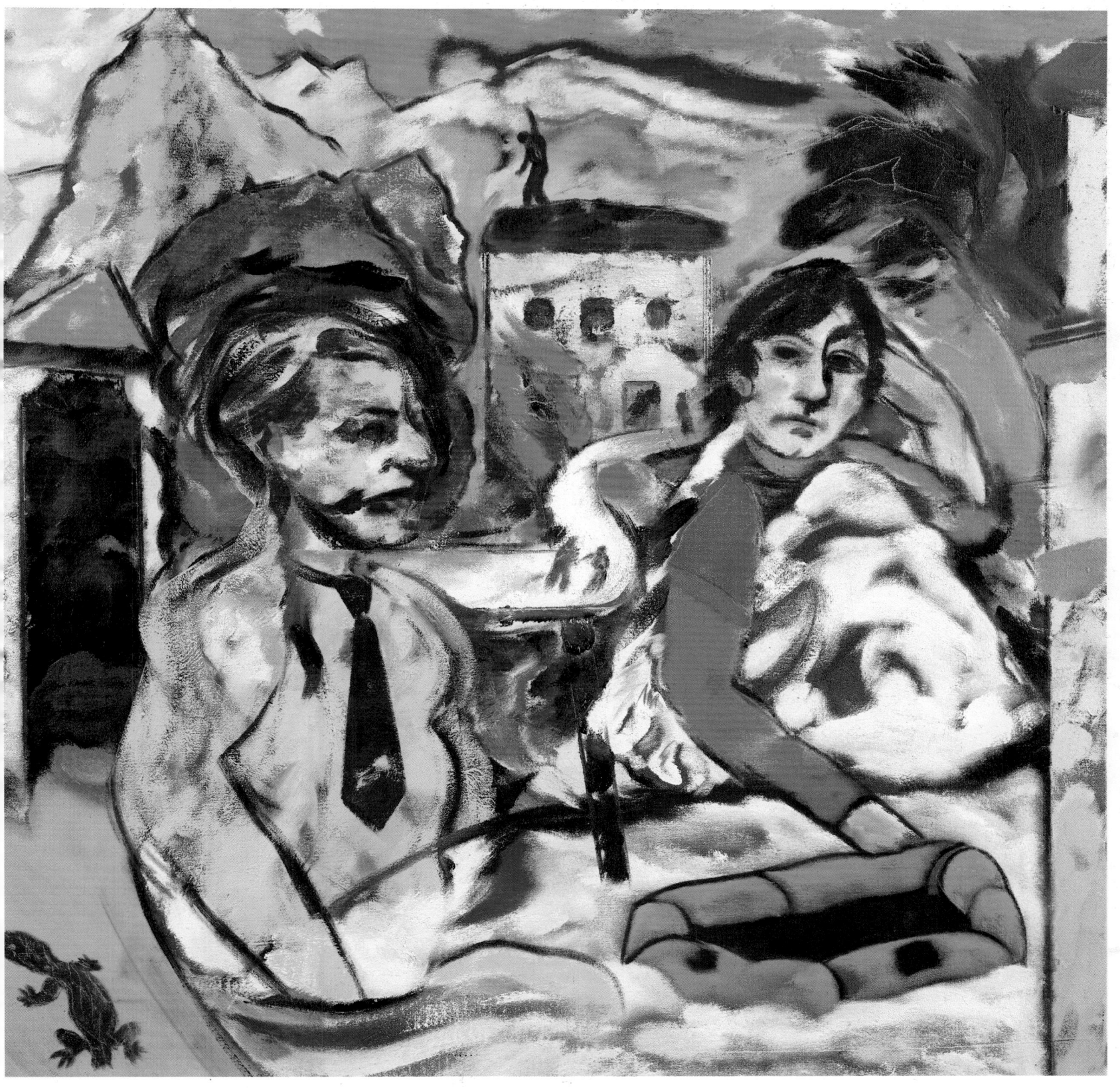

133. The Cure, 1982. *Cat. no. 332.*

134. Wollheim and
Angela, 1980. *Cat. no. 267.*

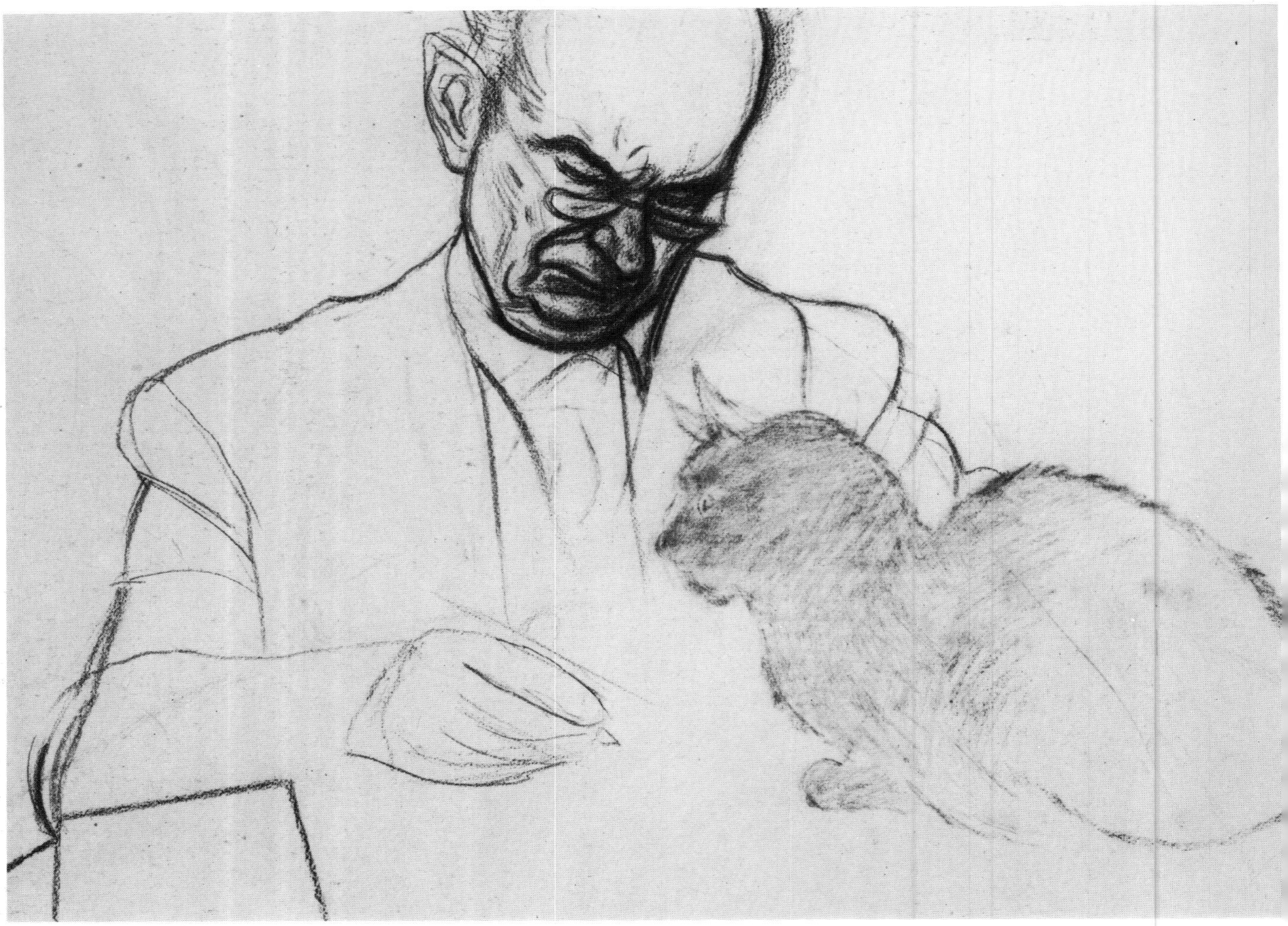

135. Courbet's Sister,
1981. *Cat. no. 306.*

136. The Street (A Life),
1975. *Cat. no. 181.*

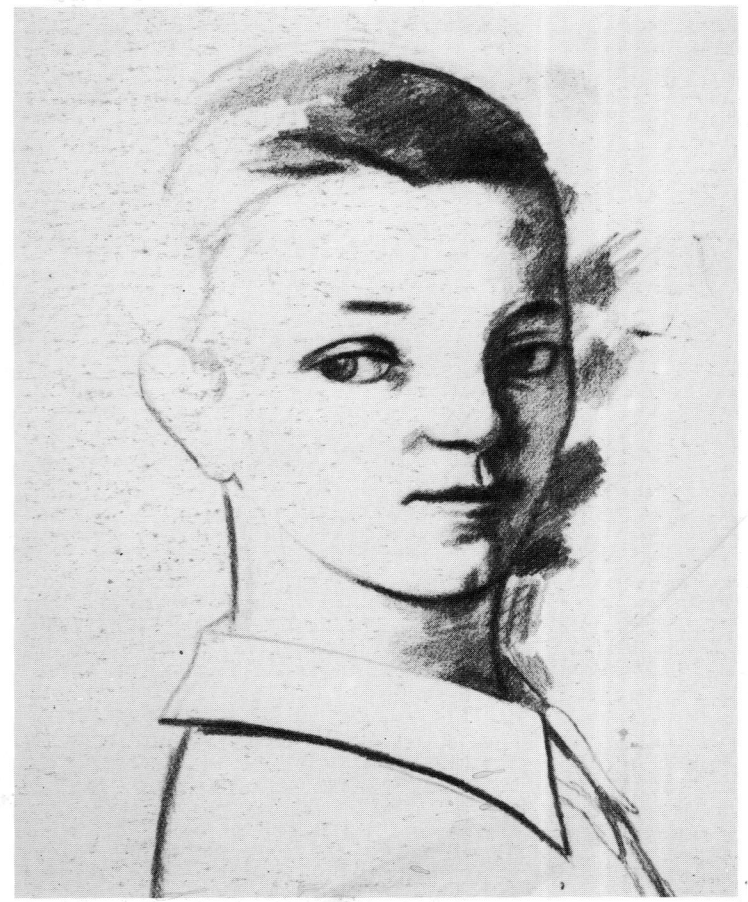

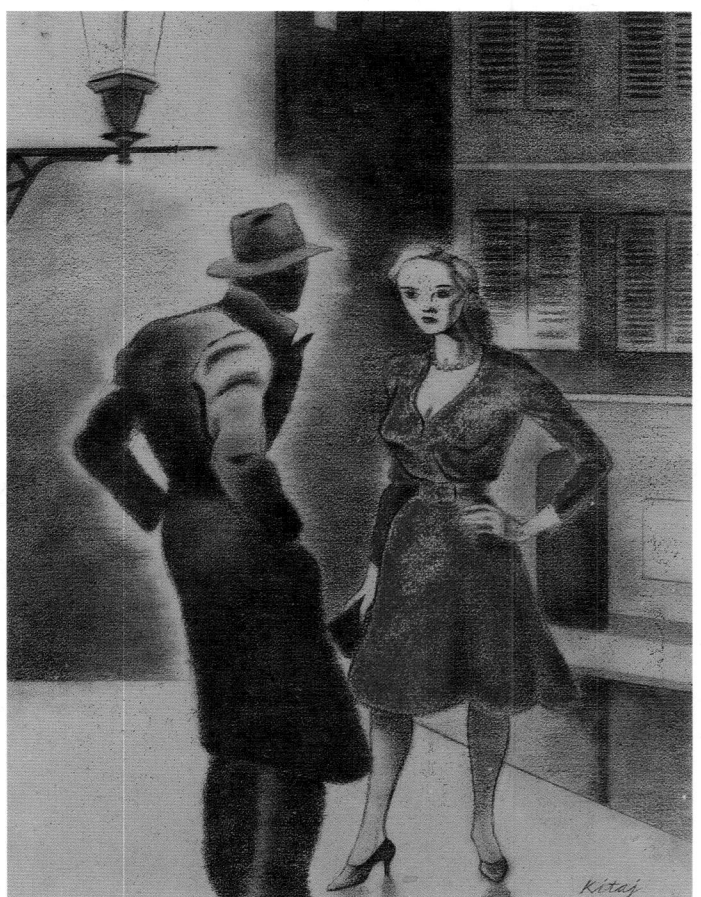

137. The Room (rue St Denis), 1982-3. *Cat. no. 334.*

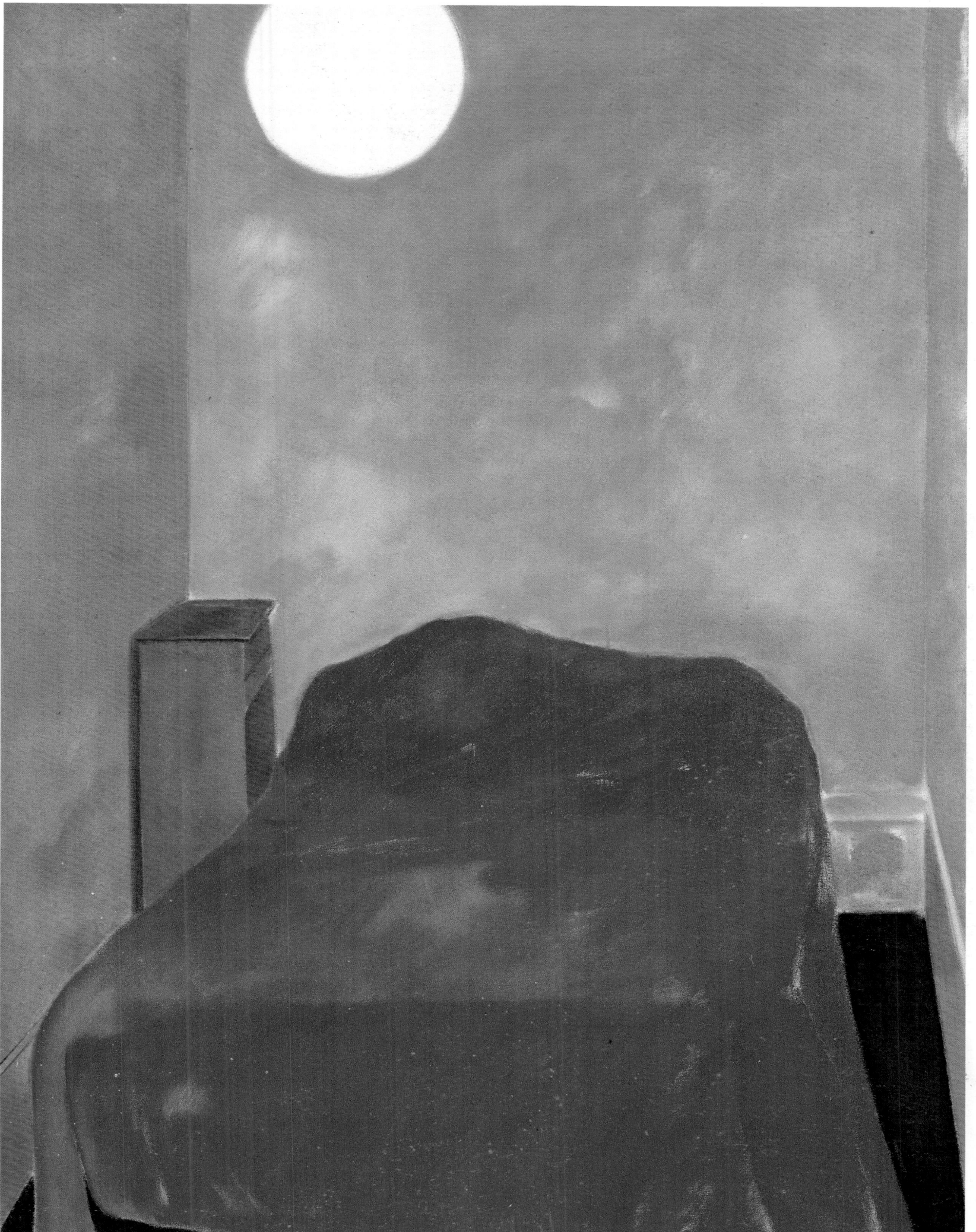

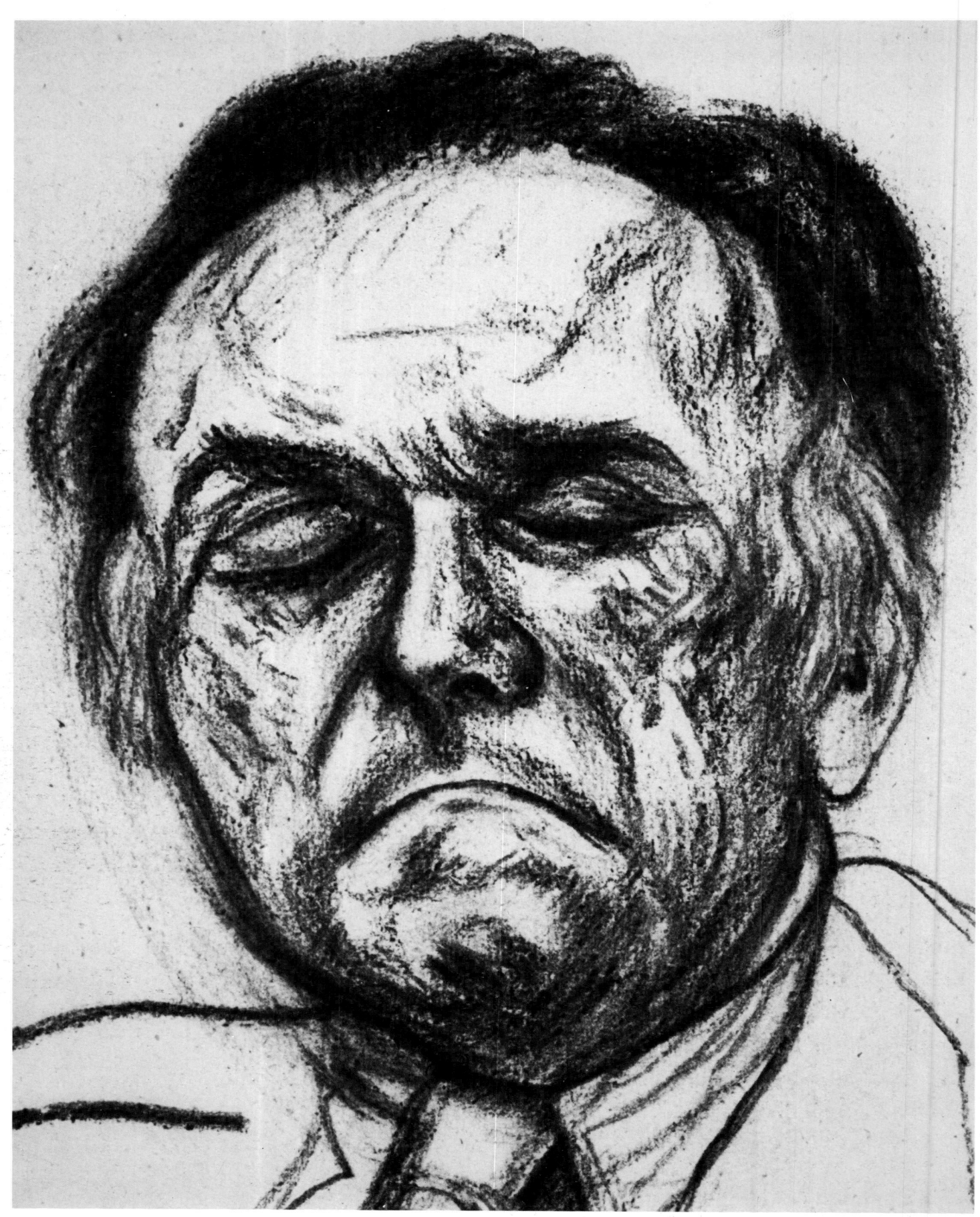

138. The Poet, Eyes Closed (Robert Duncan), 1982. *Cat. no. 319.*

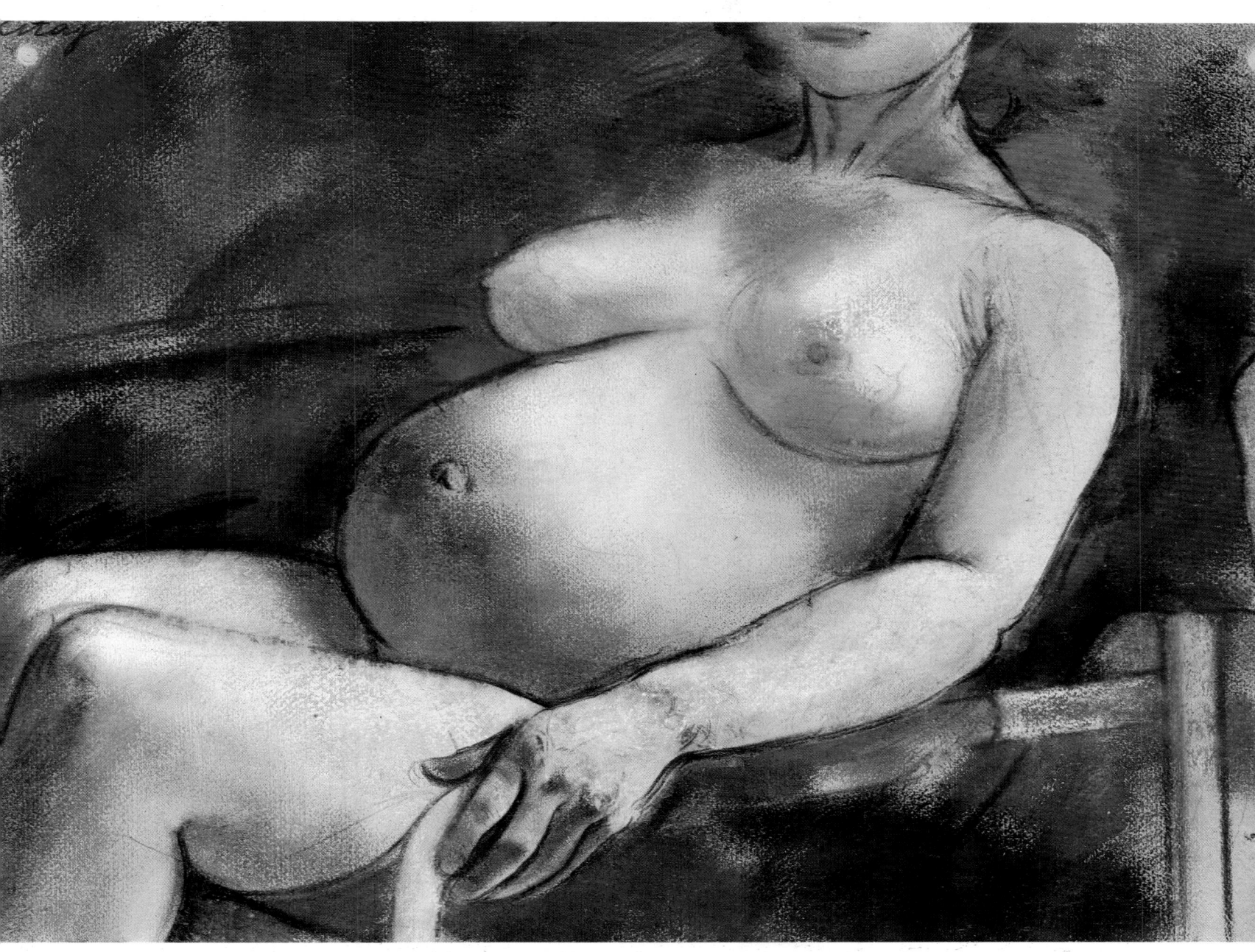

139. Marynka Pregnant II, 1981. *Cat. no. 301.*

140. Ellen and Shofar, 1983-4. *Cat. no. 356.*

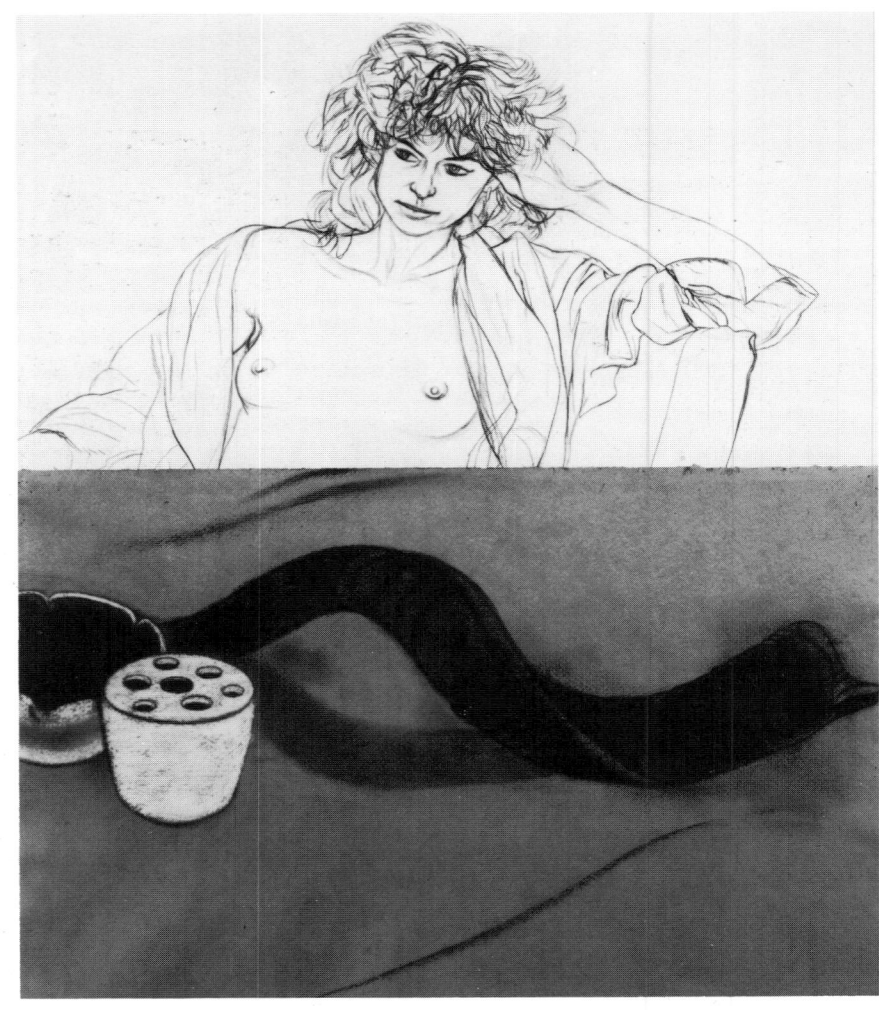

141. *(below)* Doctor Kohn, 1978. *Cat. no. 221.*

142. *(below right)* Garth, 1981. *Cat. no. 303.*

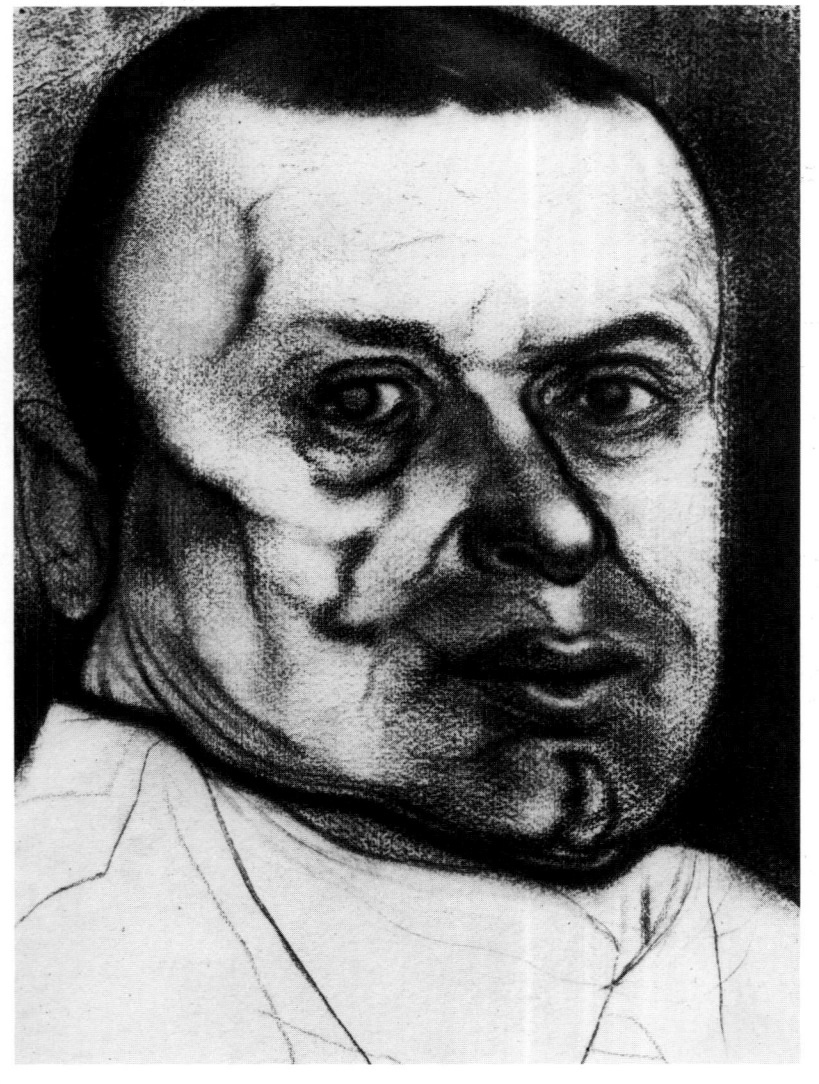

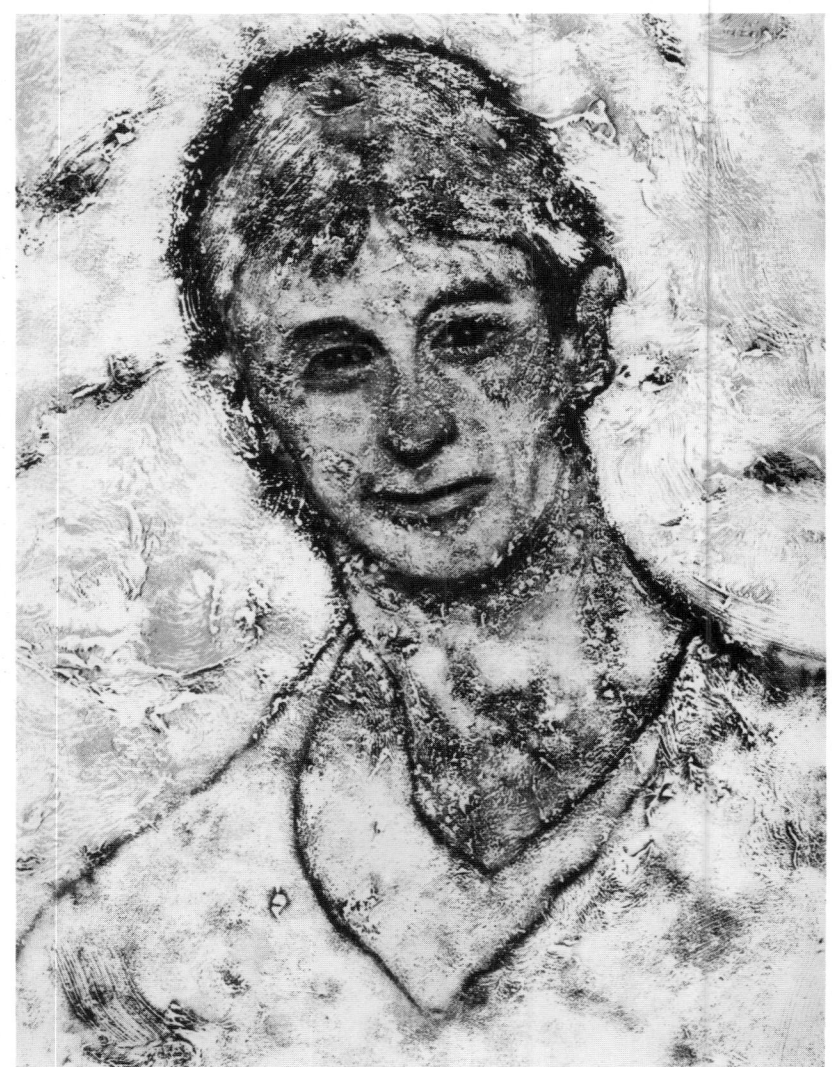

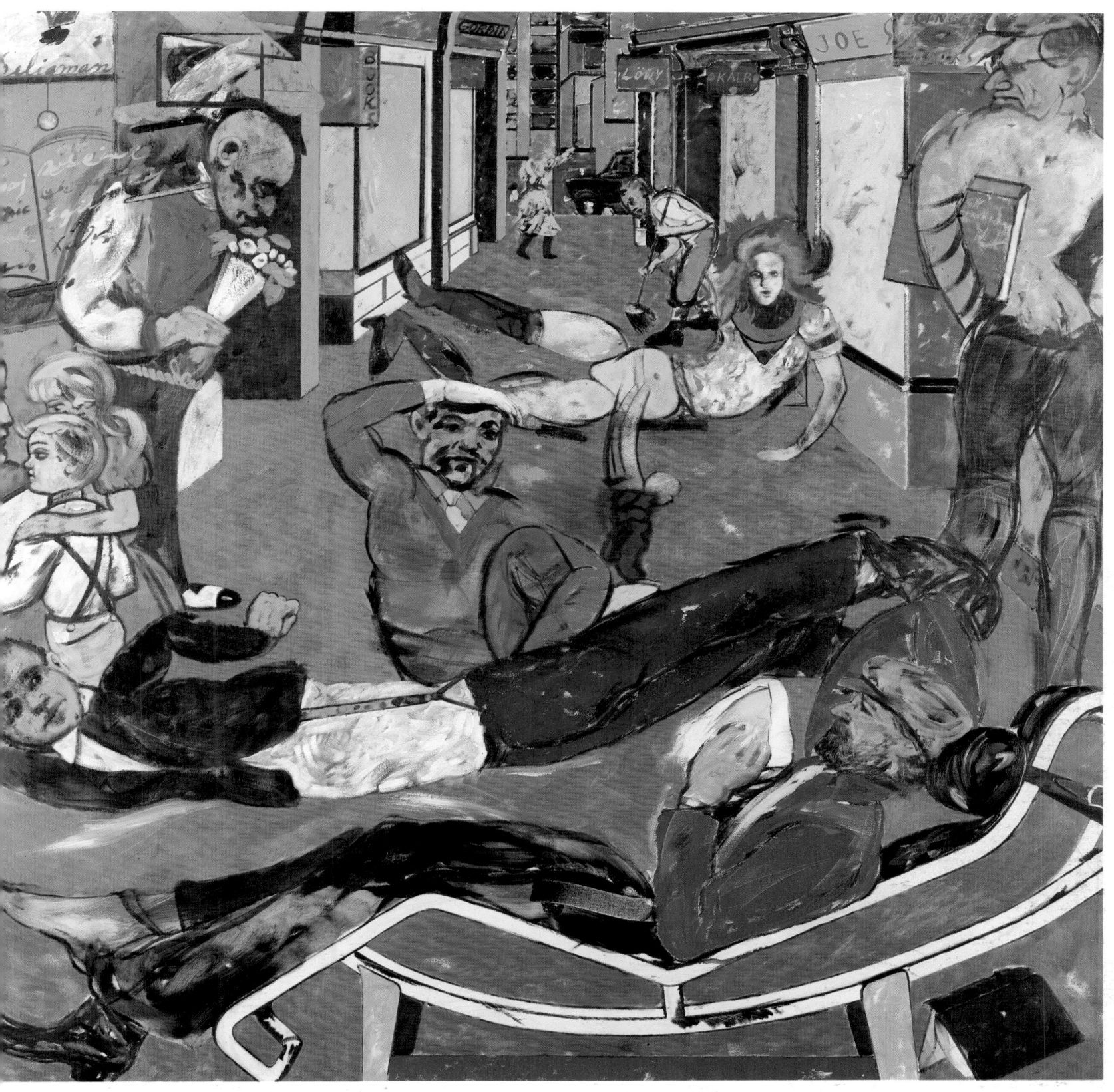

143. Cecil Court, London WC2 (The Refugees), 1983-4. *Cat. no. 357.*

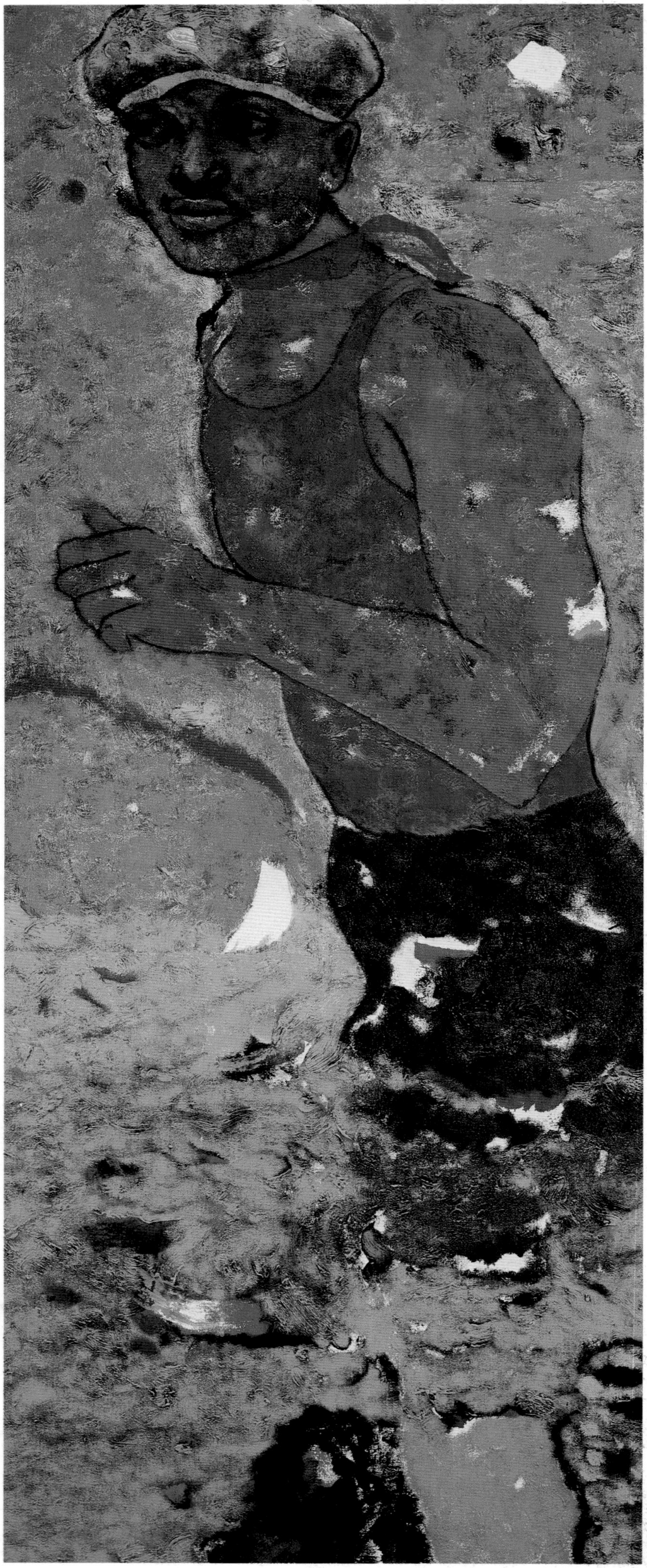

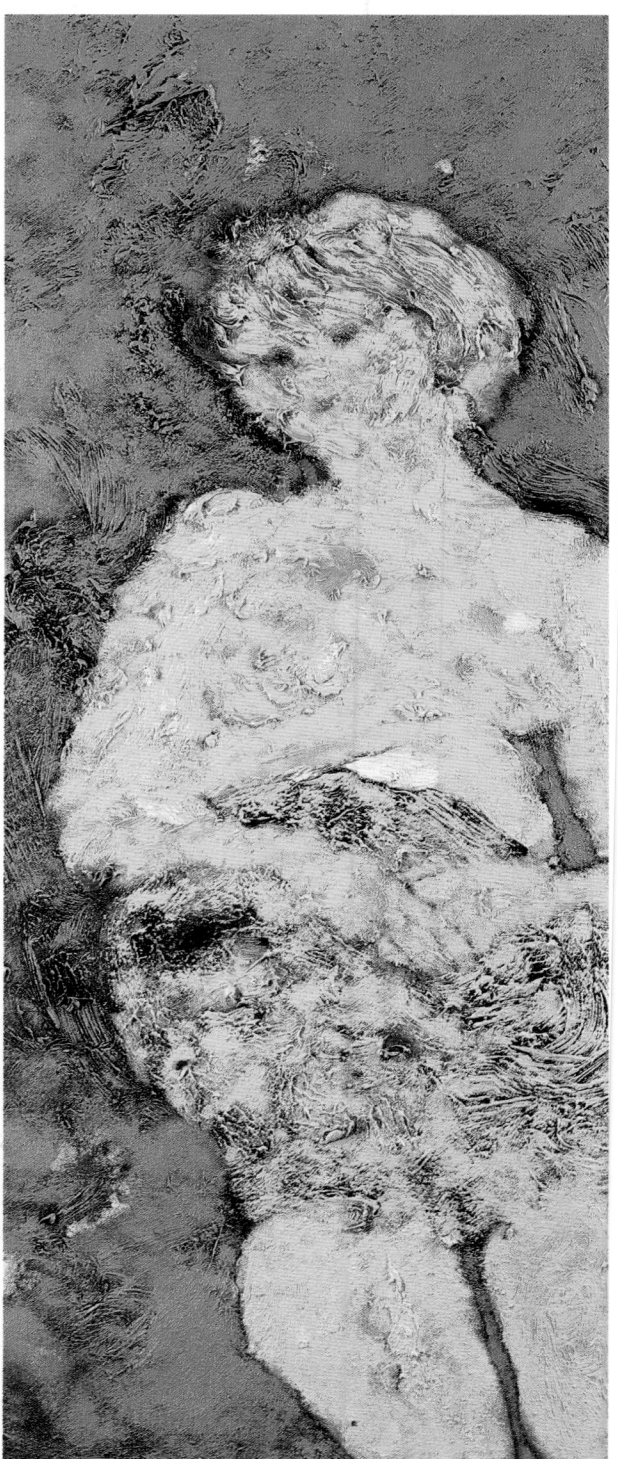

145. Grey Girl, 1981. *Cat. no. 297.*

144. The Sailor (David Ward), 1979–80. *Cat. no. 261.*

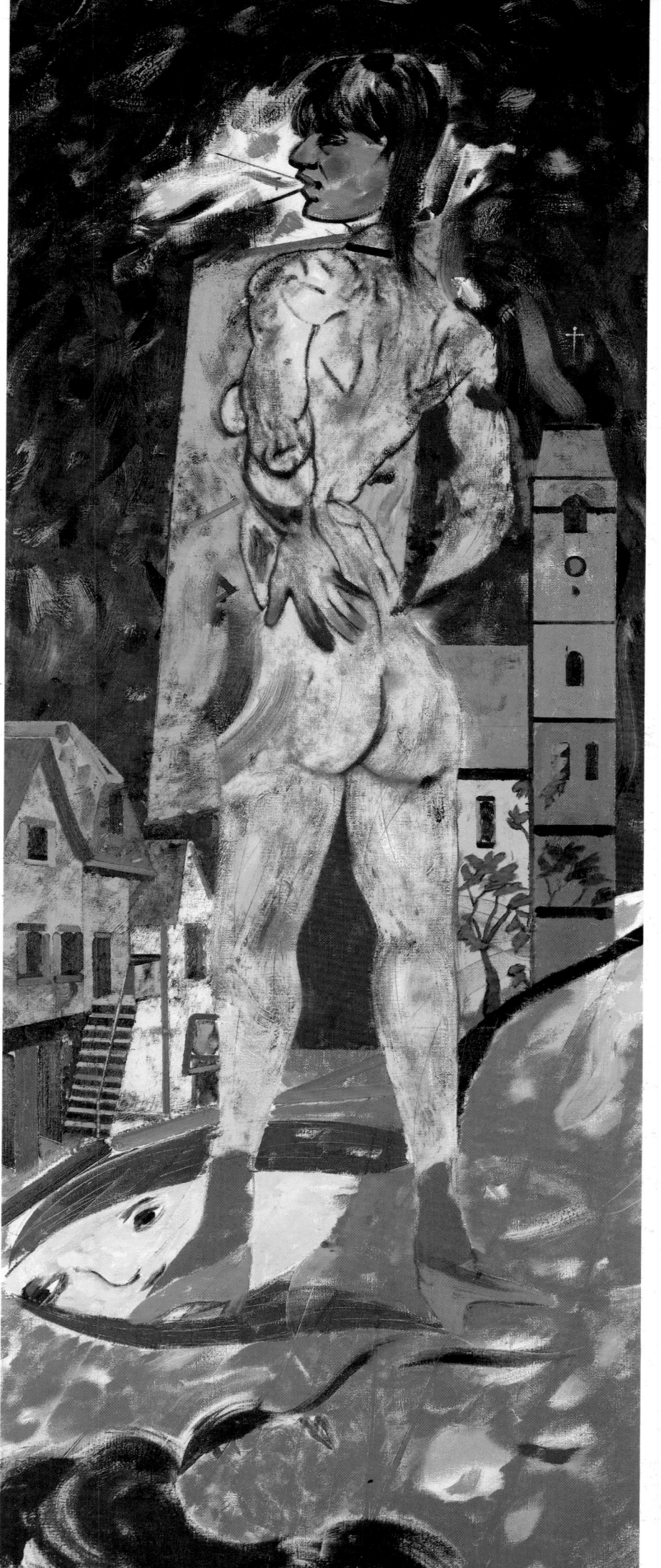

146. Self-portrait as a Woman,
1984. *Cat. no. 361*.

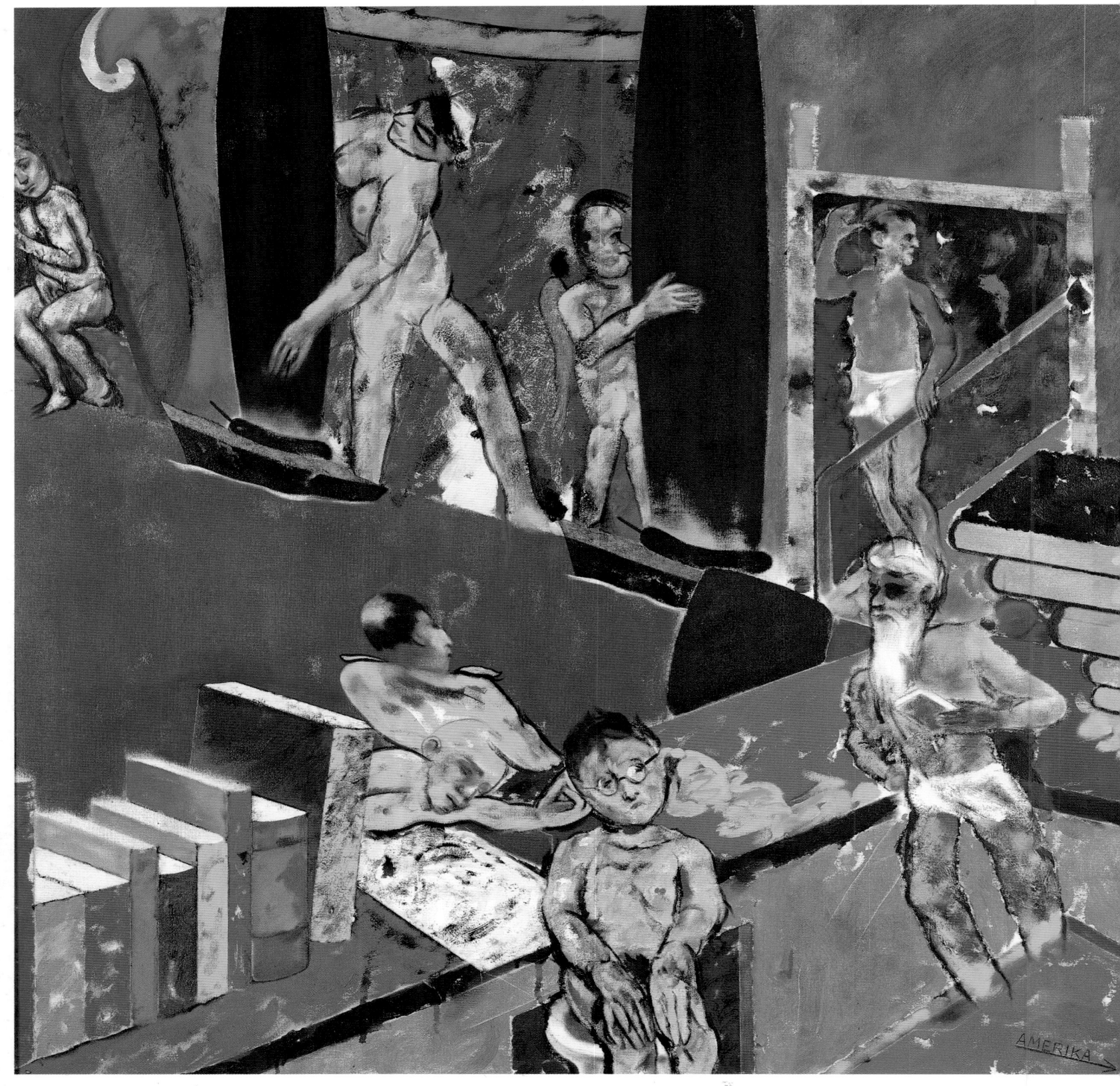

147. London, England (Bathers), 1982. *Cat. no. 323.*

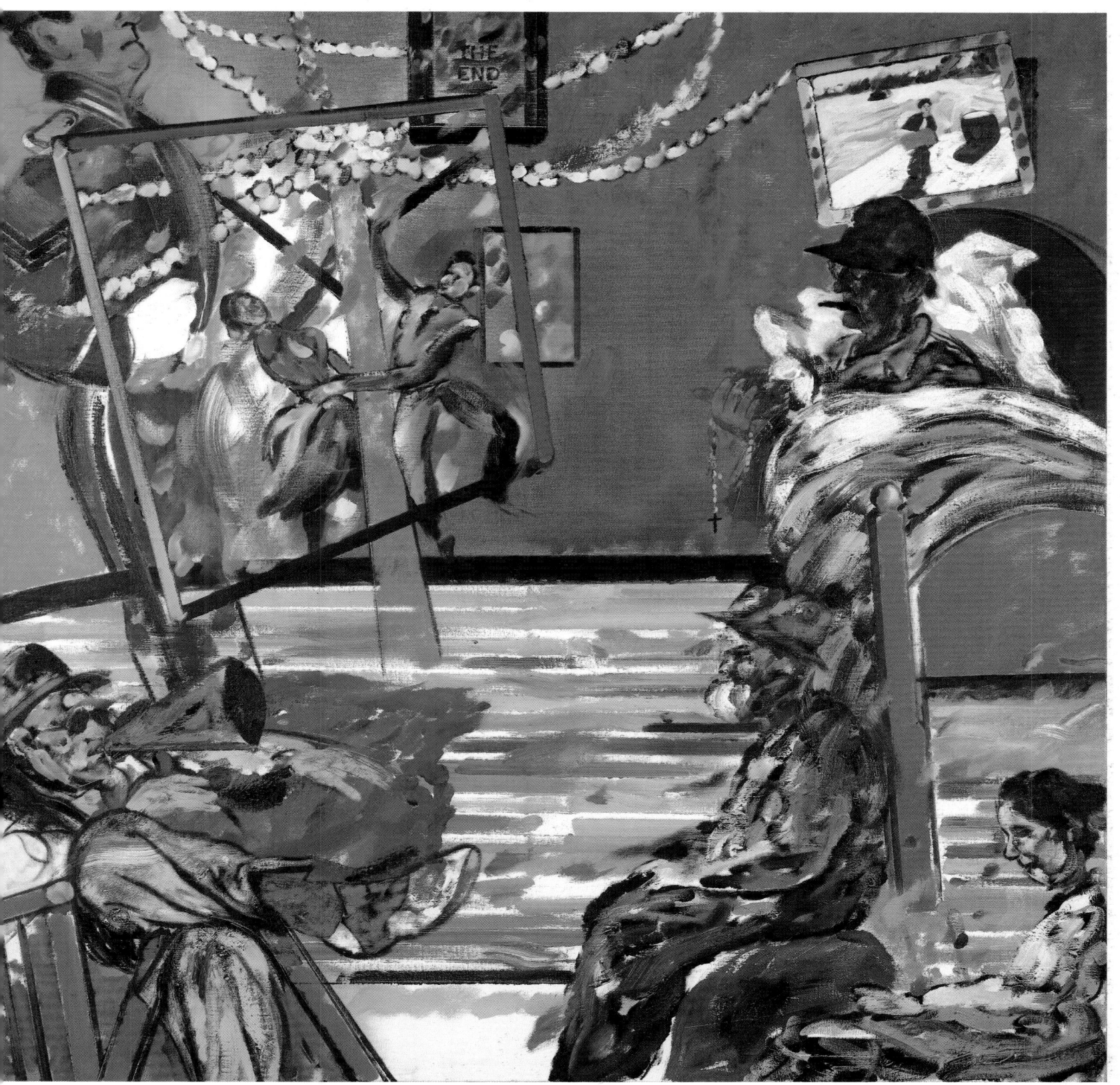

148. Amerika (John Ford on his Death Bed), 1983-4. *Cat. no. 362.*

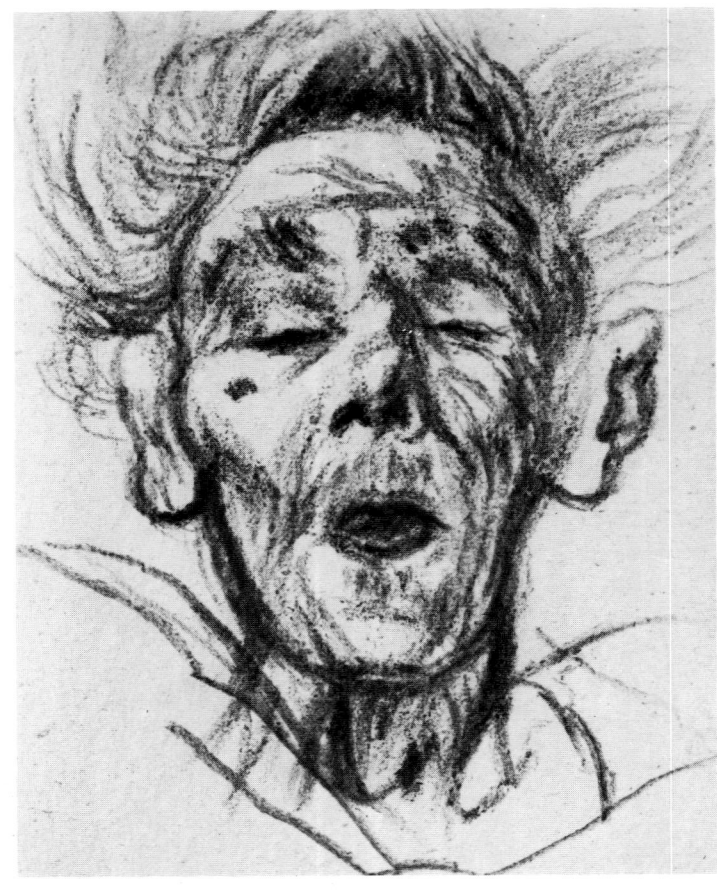

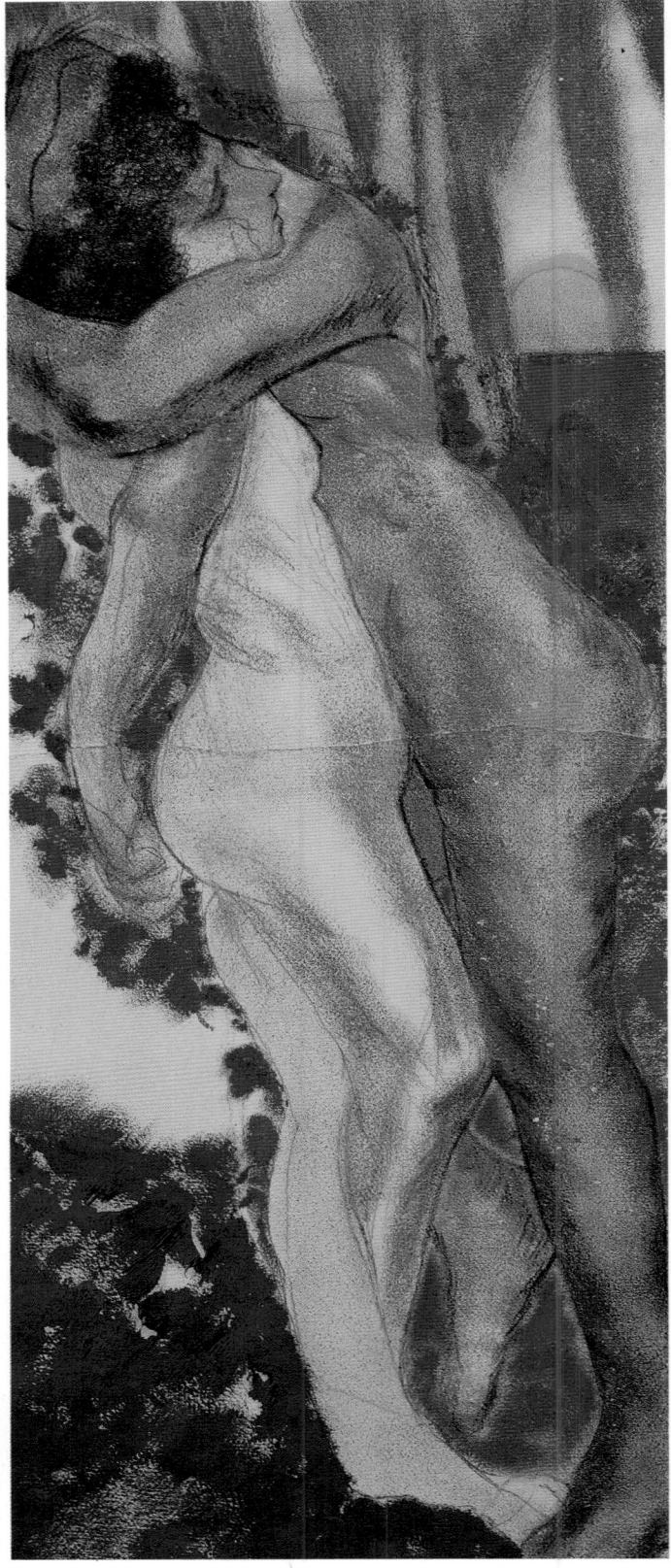

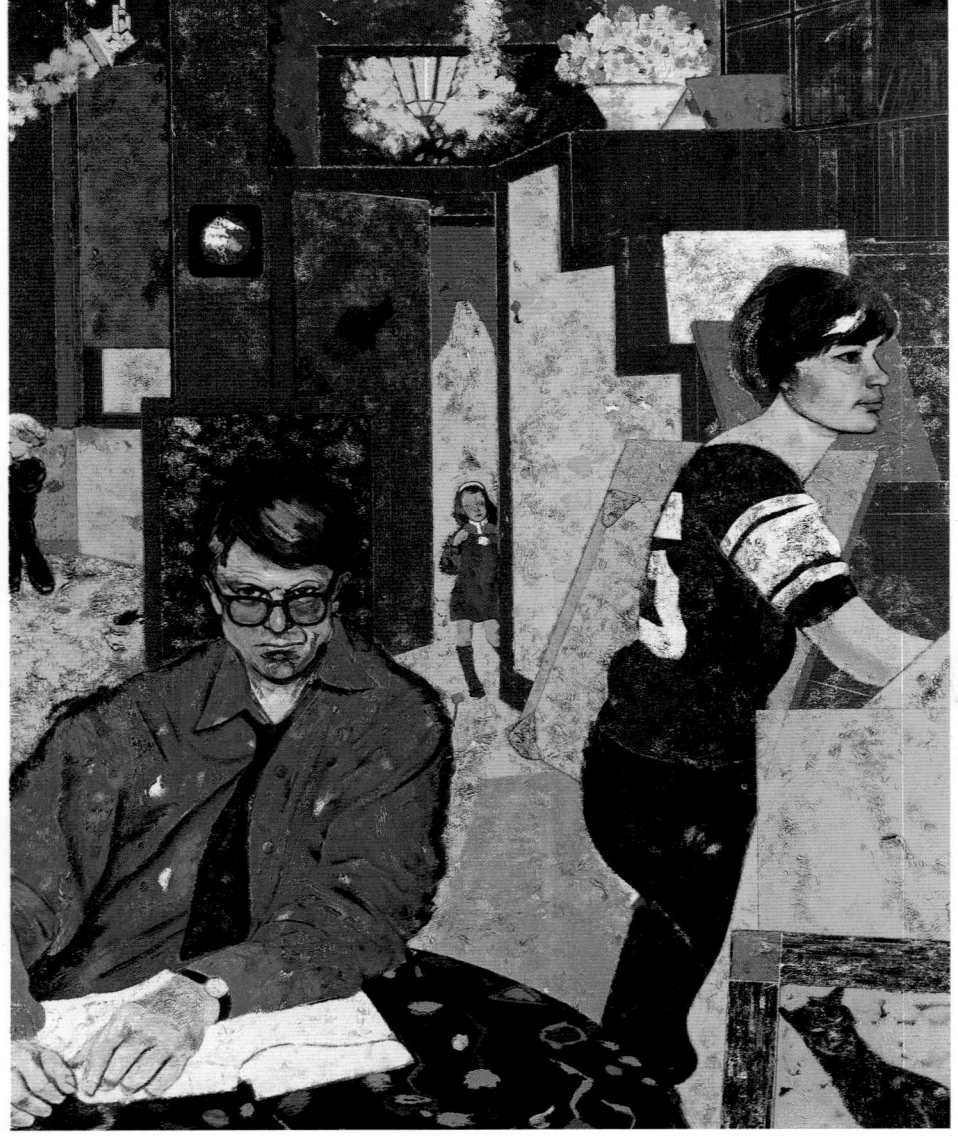

151. *(above)* The Red Embrace, 1980–1. *Cat. no. 292.*

149. *(above left)* Grandmother Kitaj, aged 102, 1983. *Cat. no. 369.*

150. The Architects, 1980–4. *Cat. no. 504.*

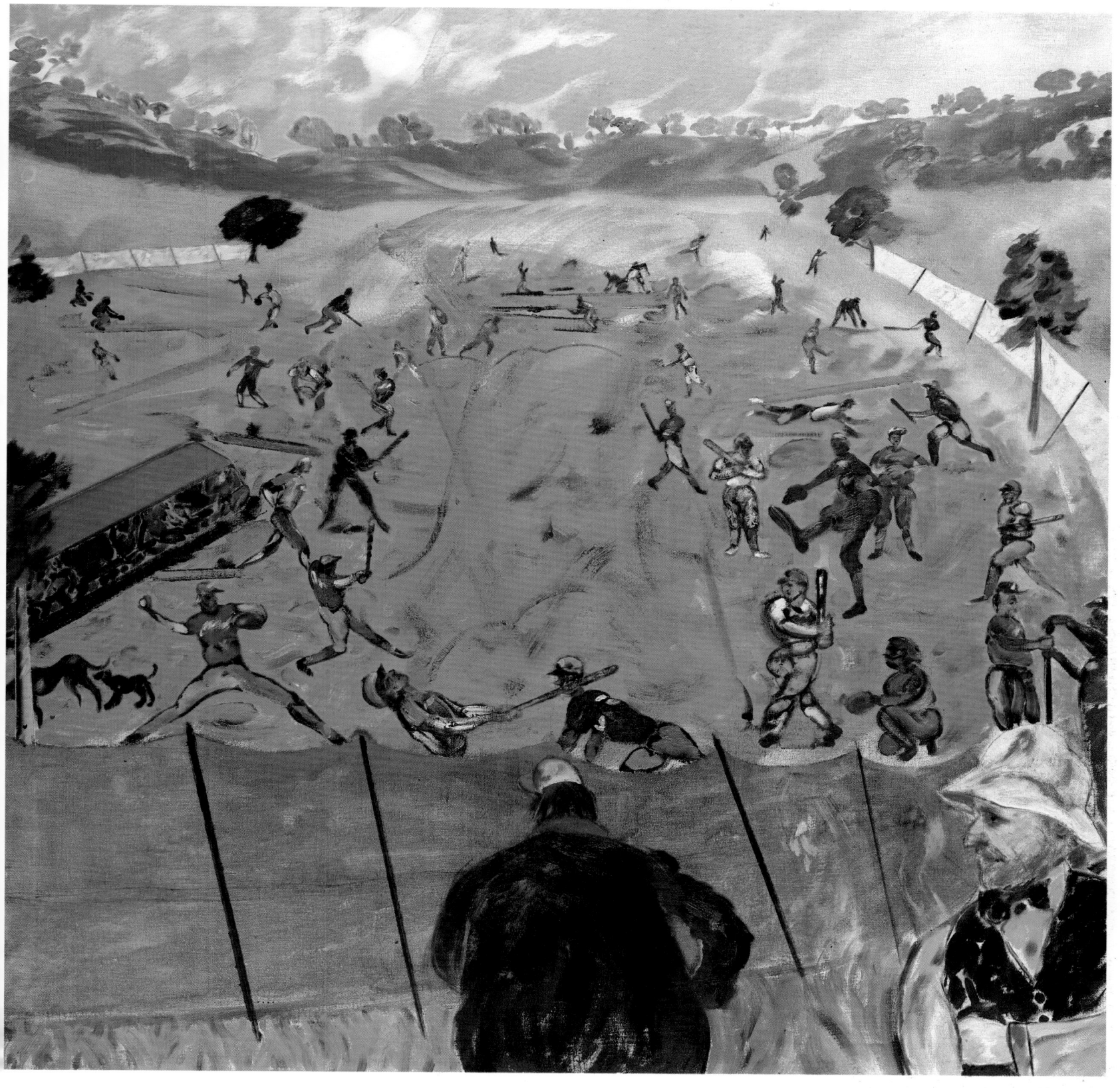

152. Amerika (Baseball), 1983-4. *Cat. no. 363.*

153. Starting a War *(detail)*, 1980–1. *Cat. no. 291.*

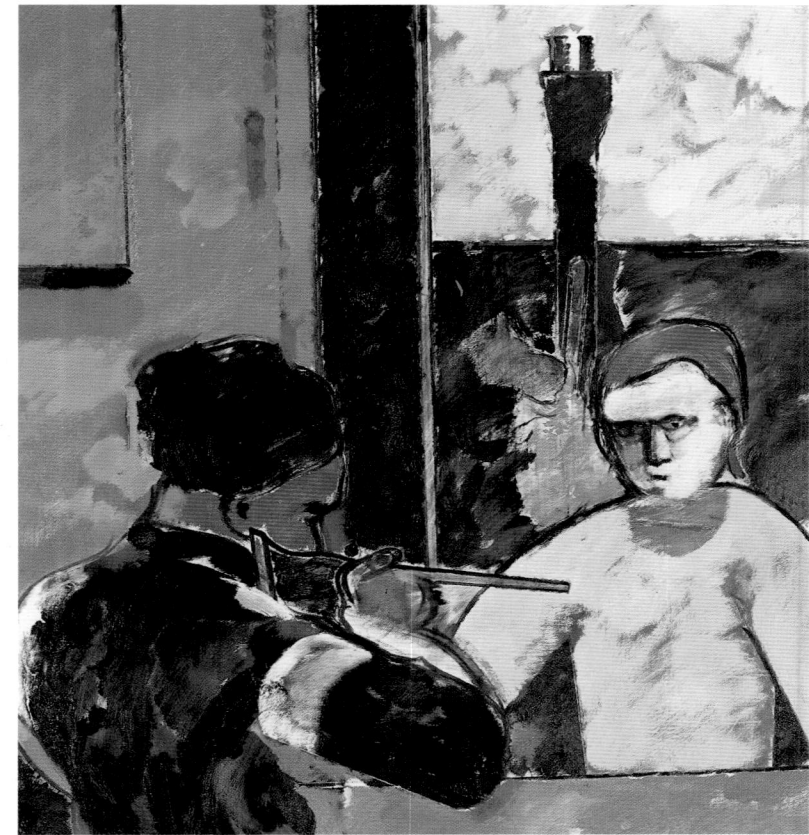

154. The Red Brassière, 1983. *Cat. no. 353.*

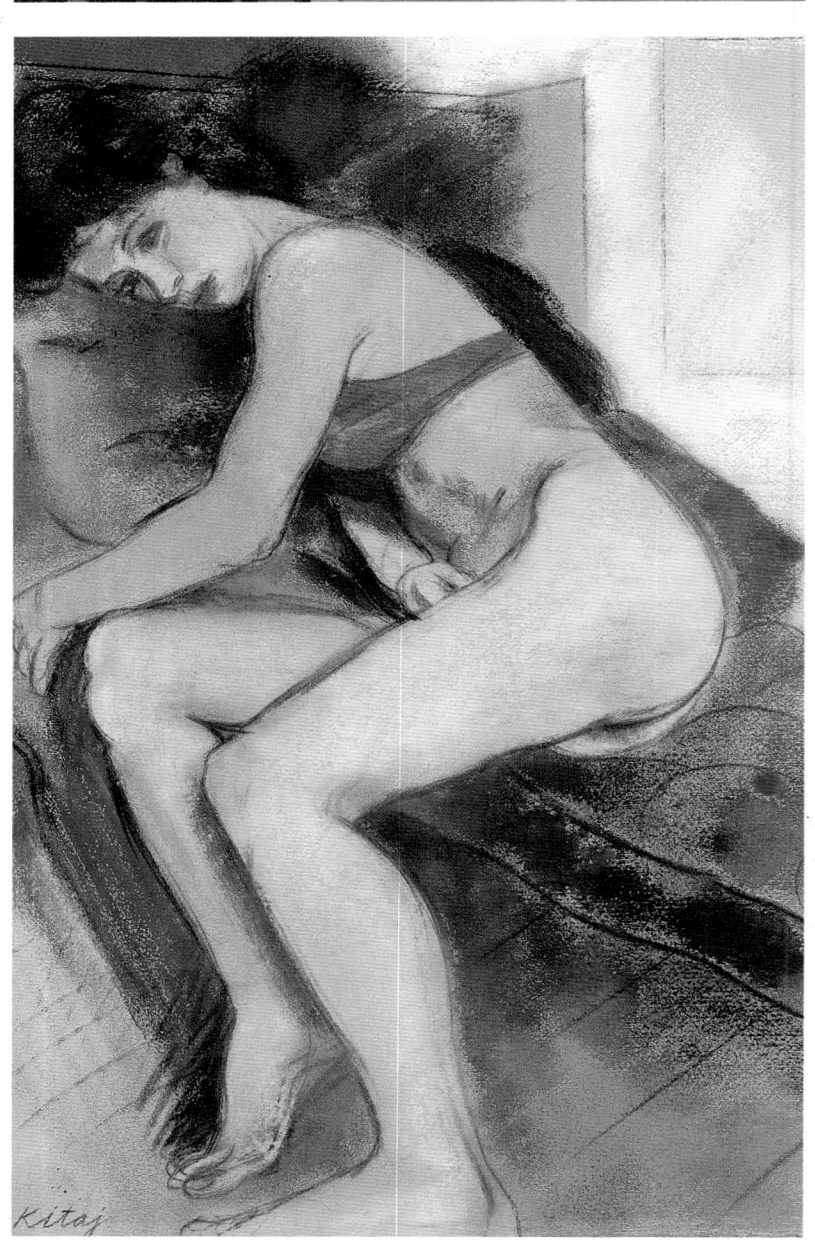

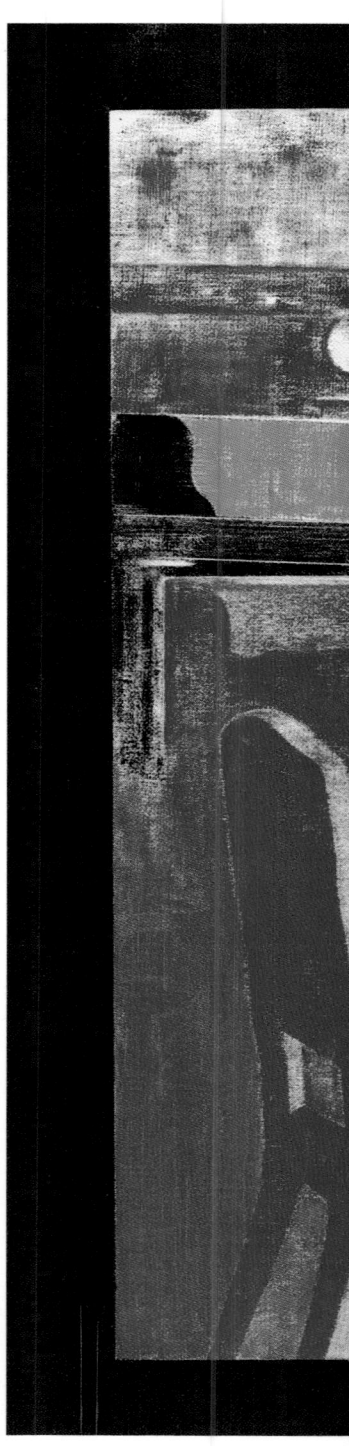

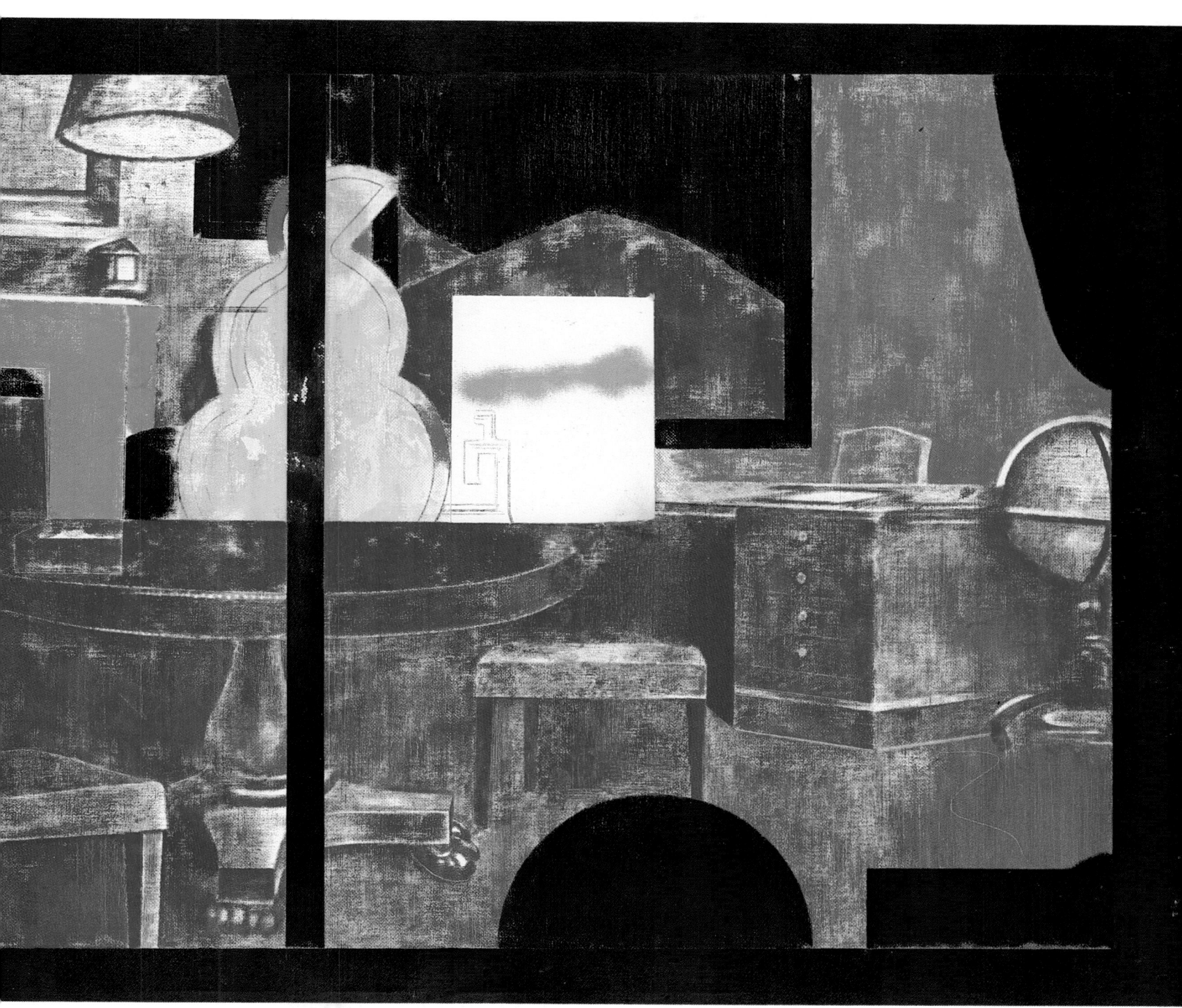

155. Desk-Murder (formerly The Third Department (A Teste Study)), 1970–84. *Cat. no. 142.*

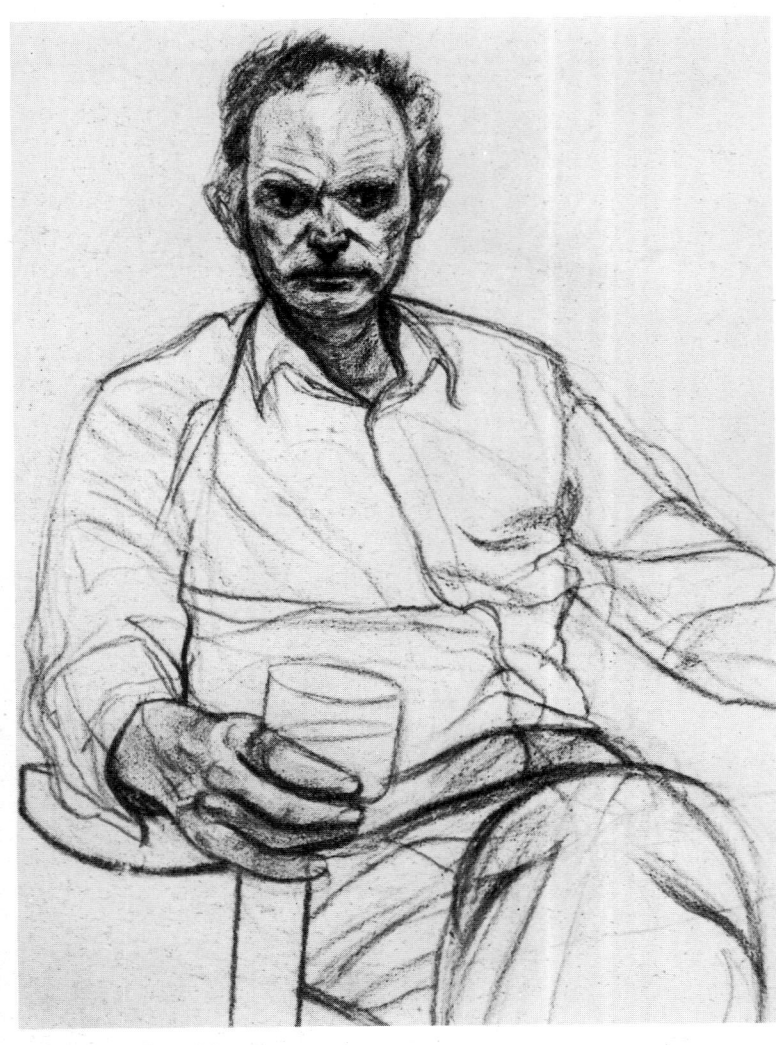

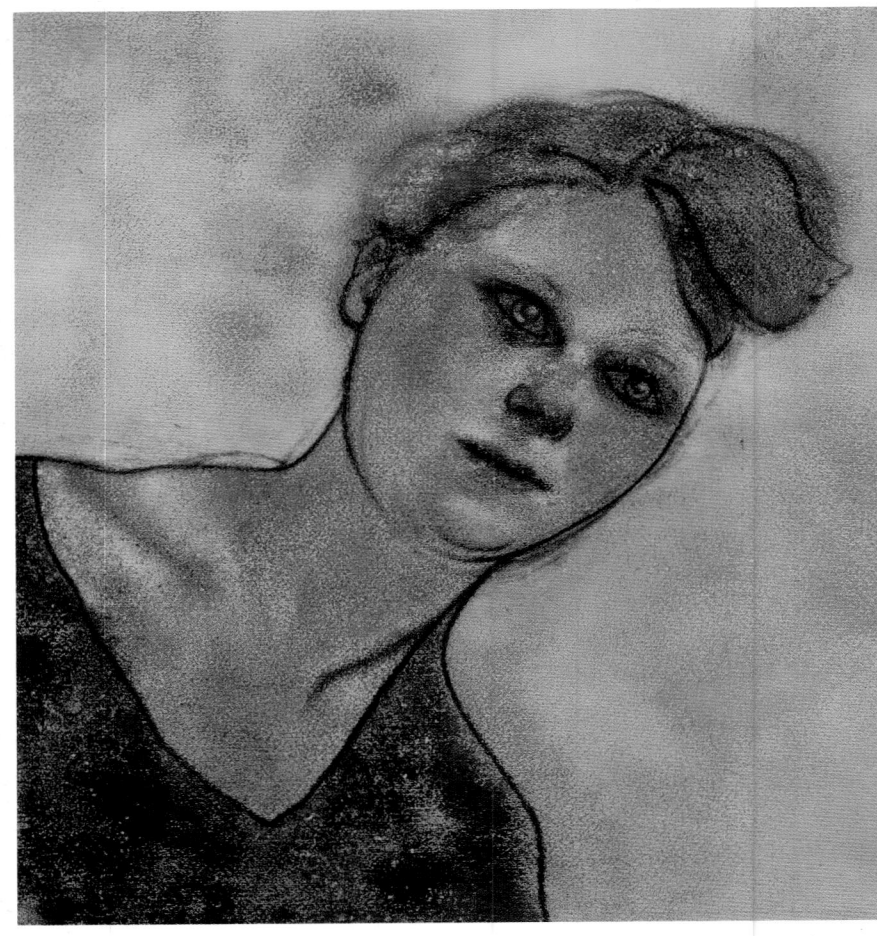

156. *(above)* Yona in Paris, 1982. *Cat. no. 328.*

157. *(above right)* Red Eyes, 1980. *Cat. no. 275.*

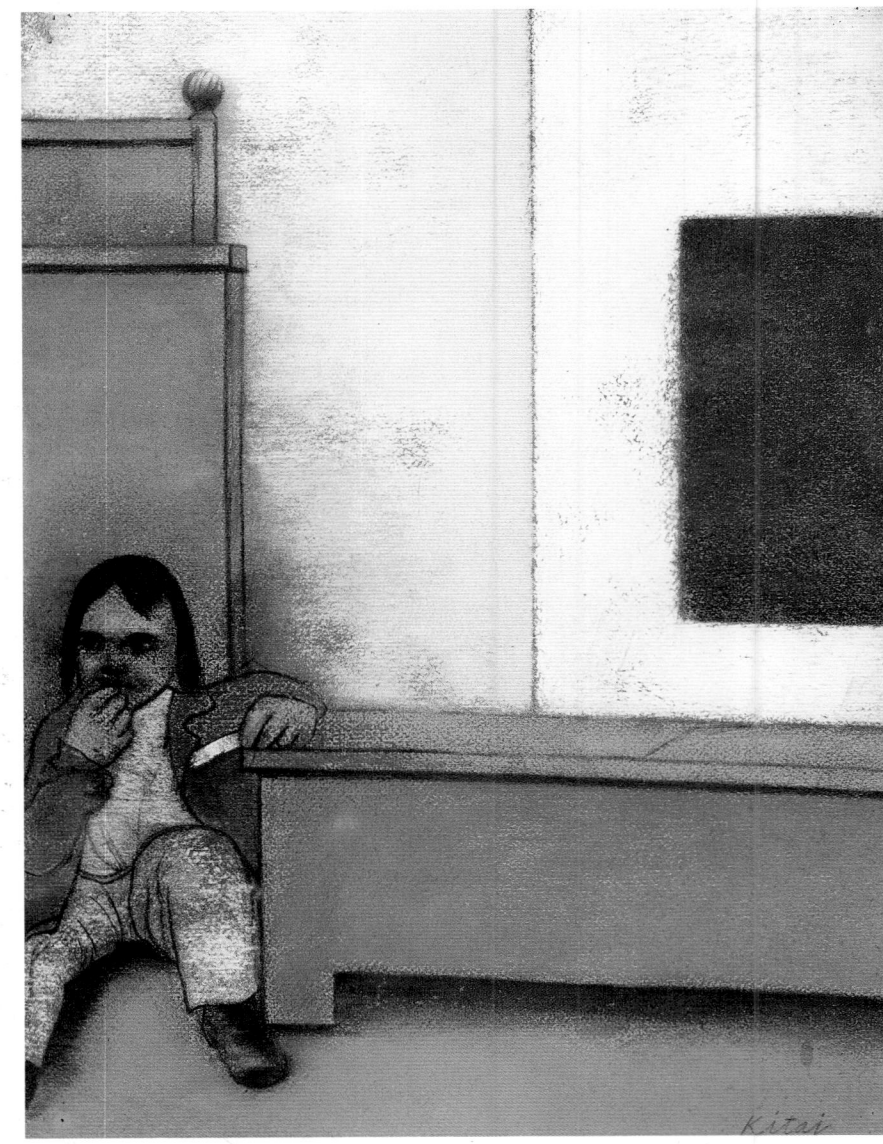

158. Study for the Jewish School (The Last Day), 1981. *Cat. no. 307.*

159. The Cézannist, 1980–5. *Cat. no. 372.*

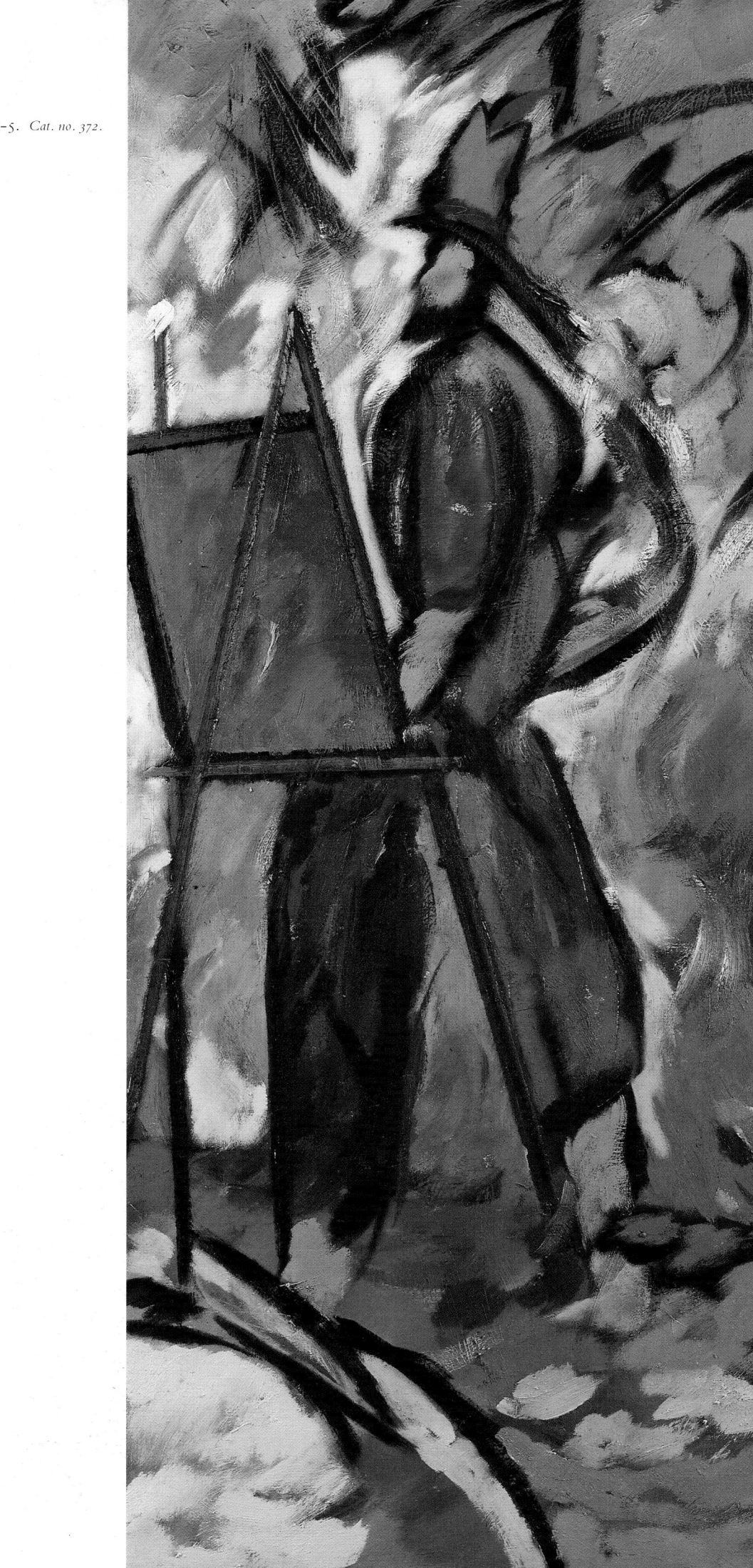

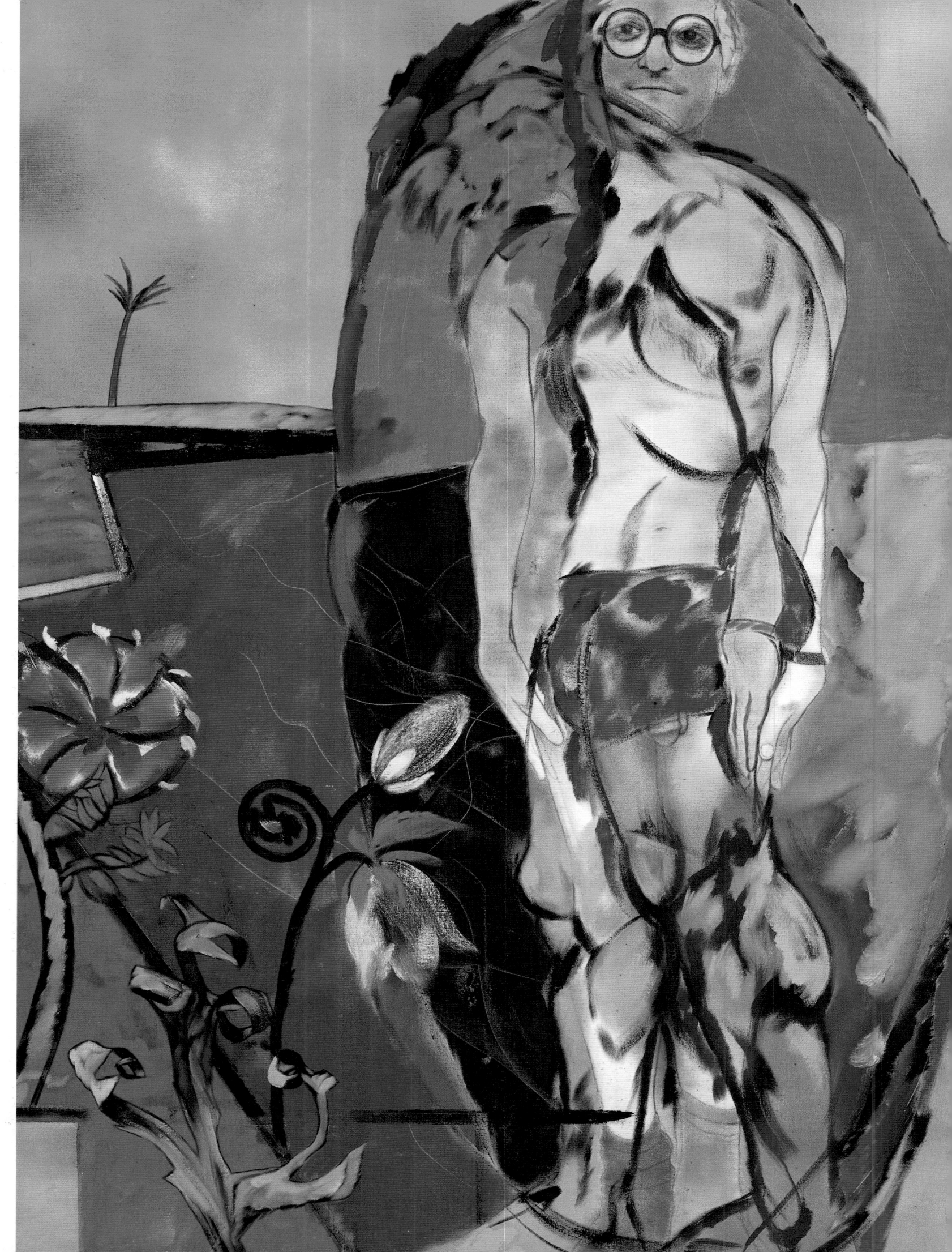

160. (*opposite*) The Neo-Cubist,
1976–87. *Cat. no. 422.*

161. Passion (1940–45) Writing, 1985.
Cat. no. 394.

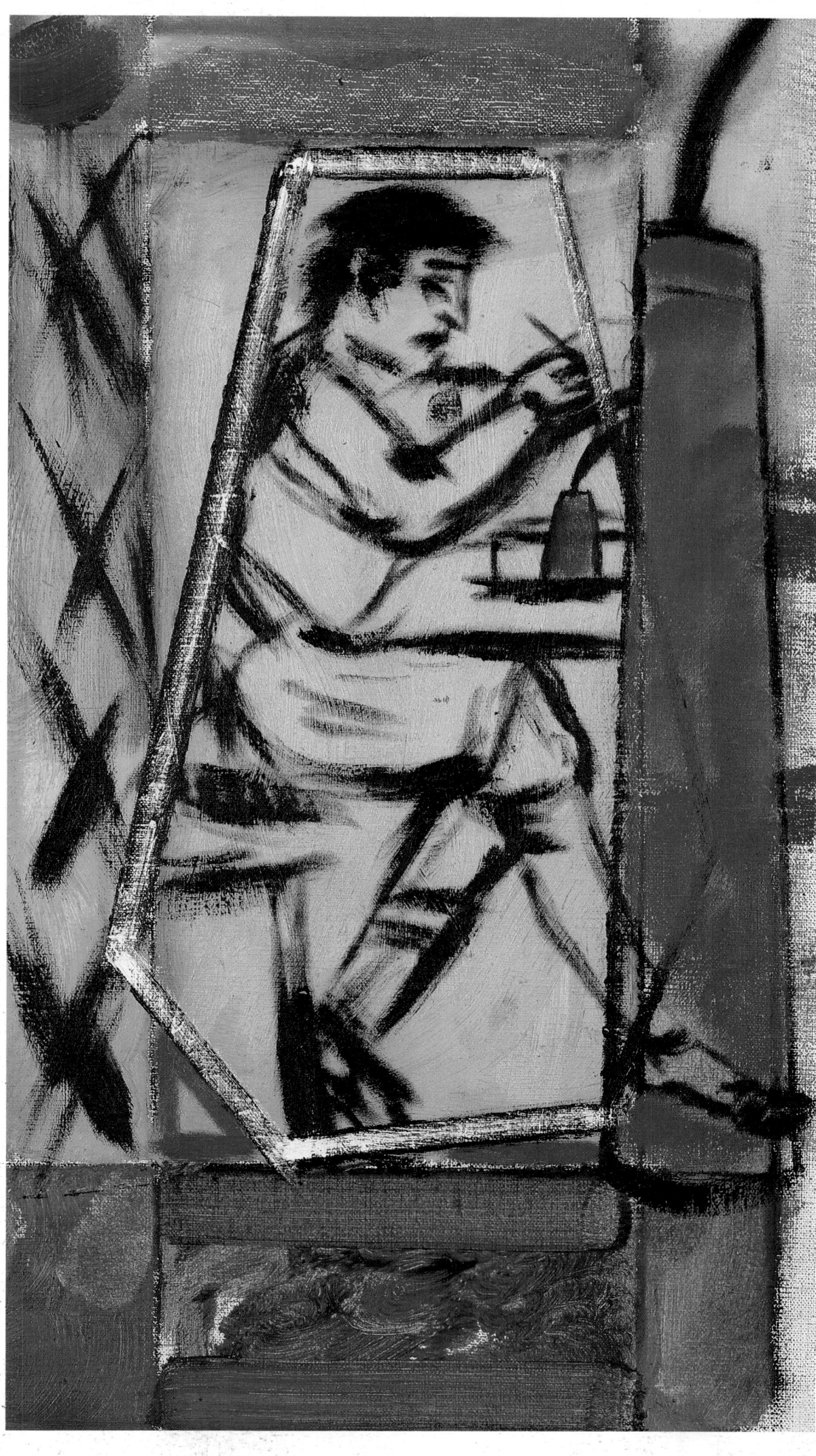

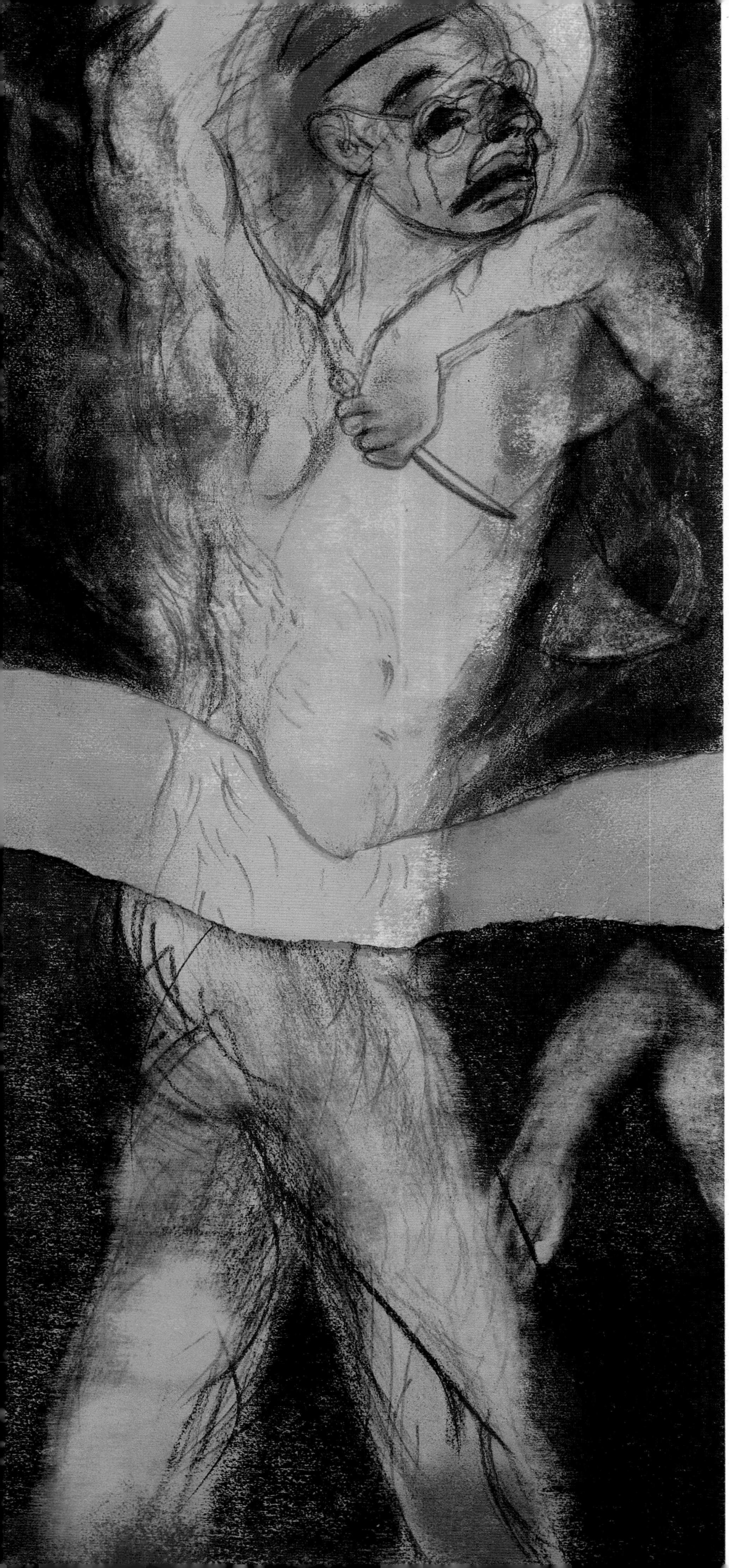

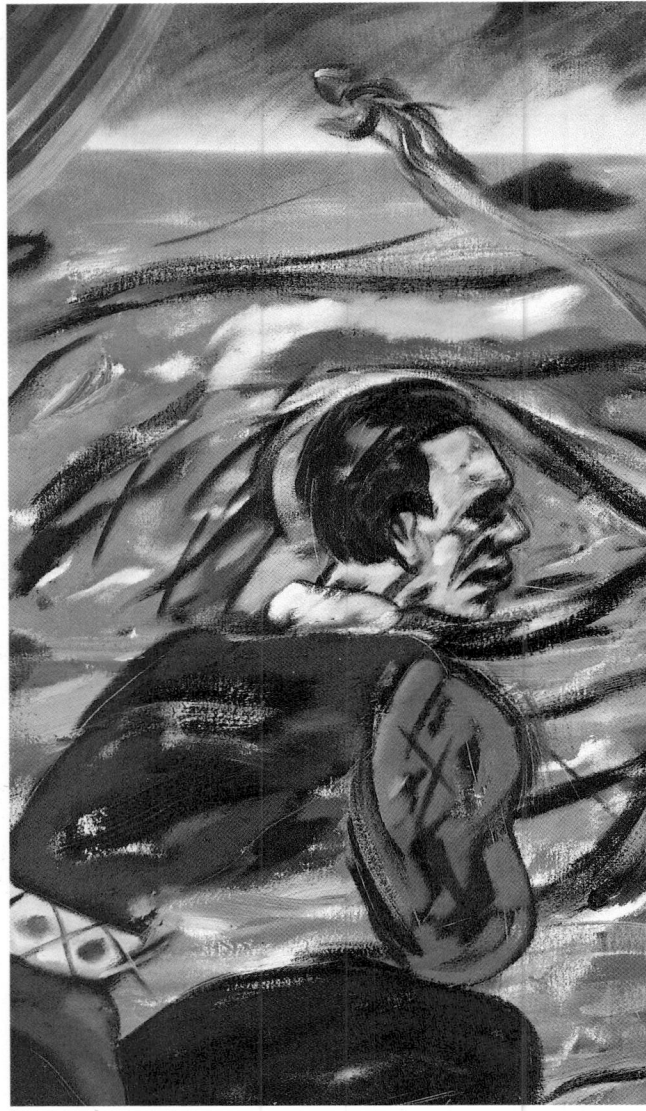

163. Raymond Massey as Hamlet (Study for The Old Vic), 1985.
Cat. no. 378.

162. Bather (Frankfurt), 1985. *Cat. no. 392.*

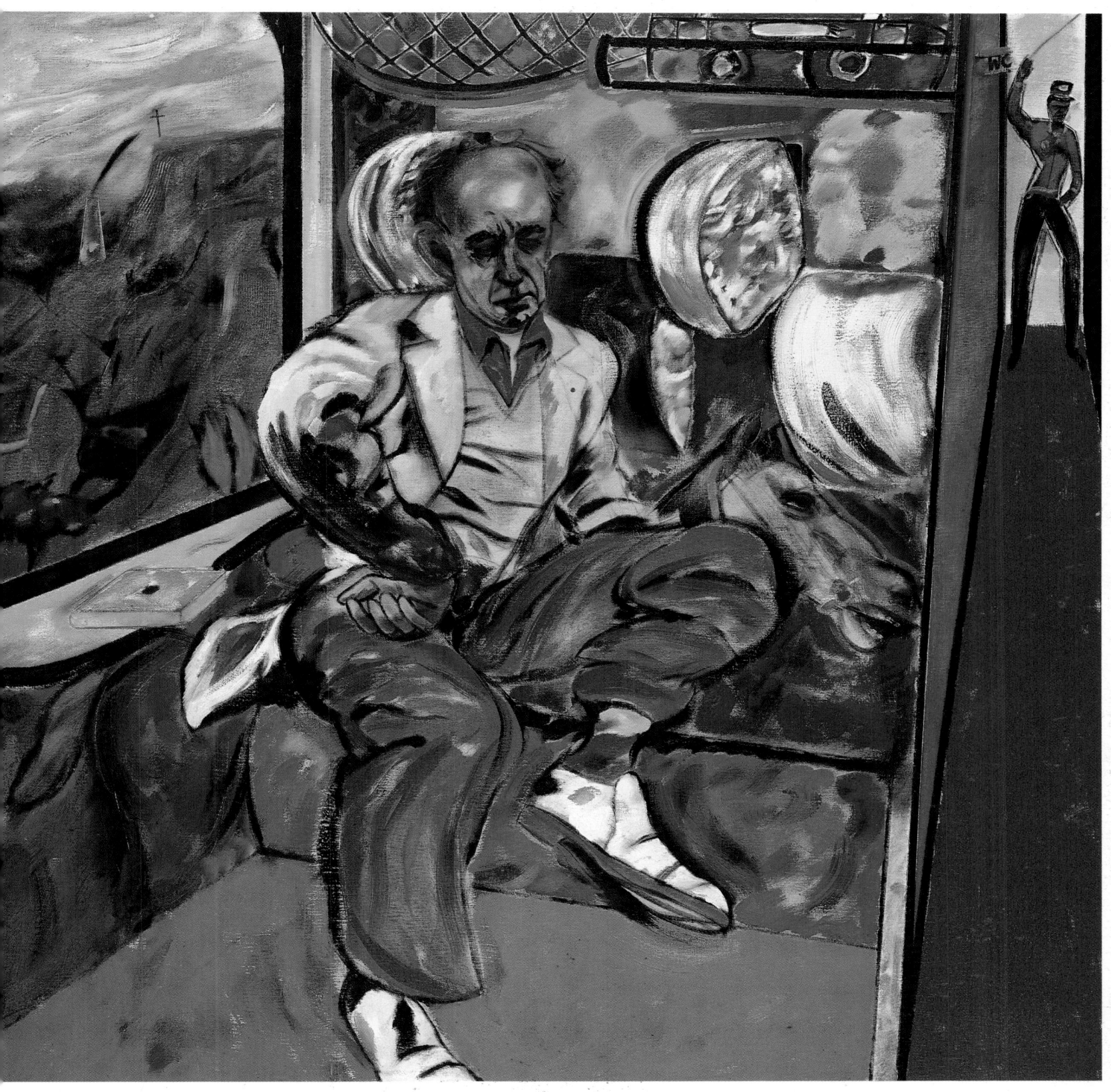

164. The Jewish Rider, 1984–5. *Cat. no. 375.*

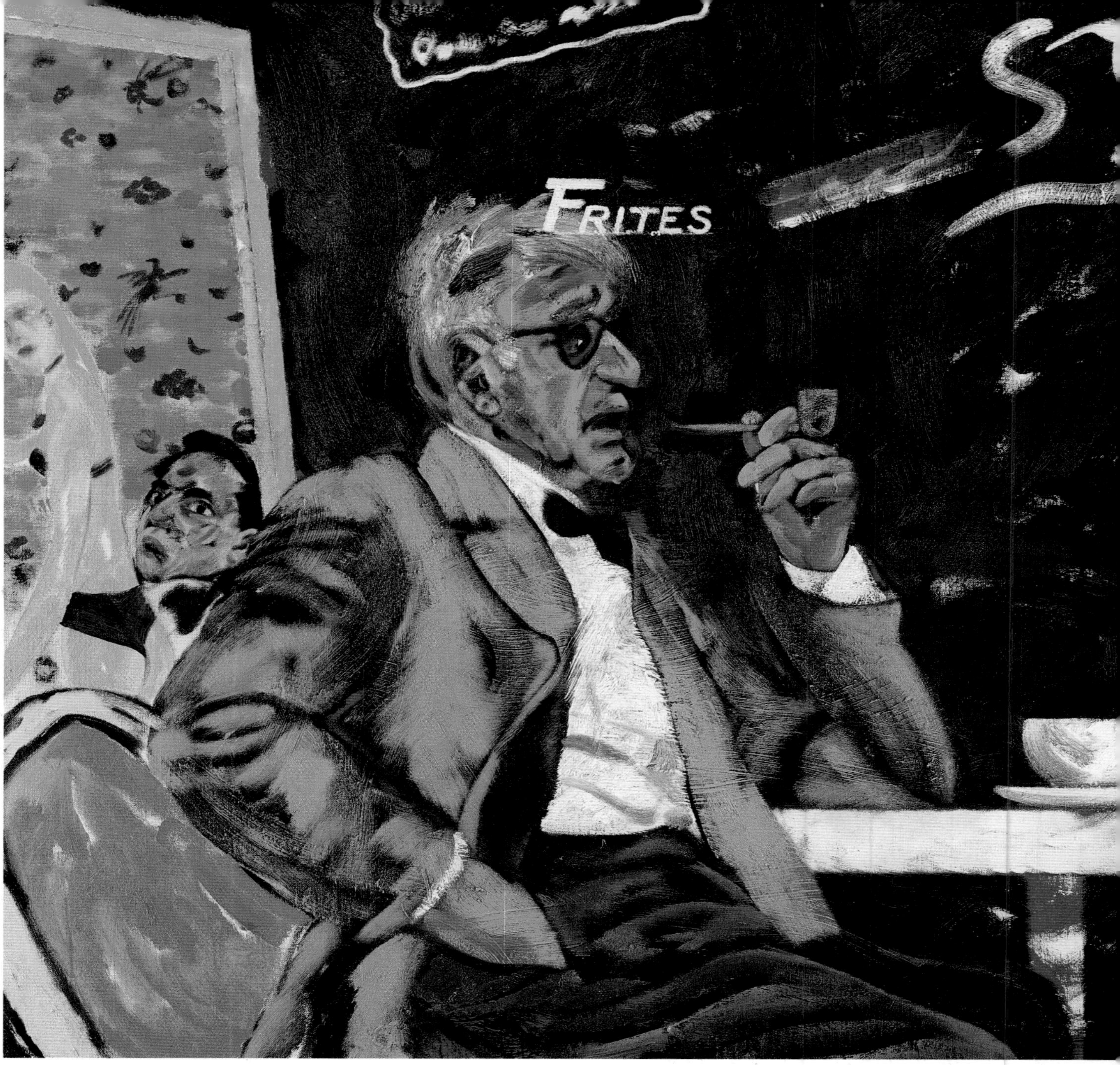

FRITES

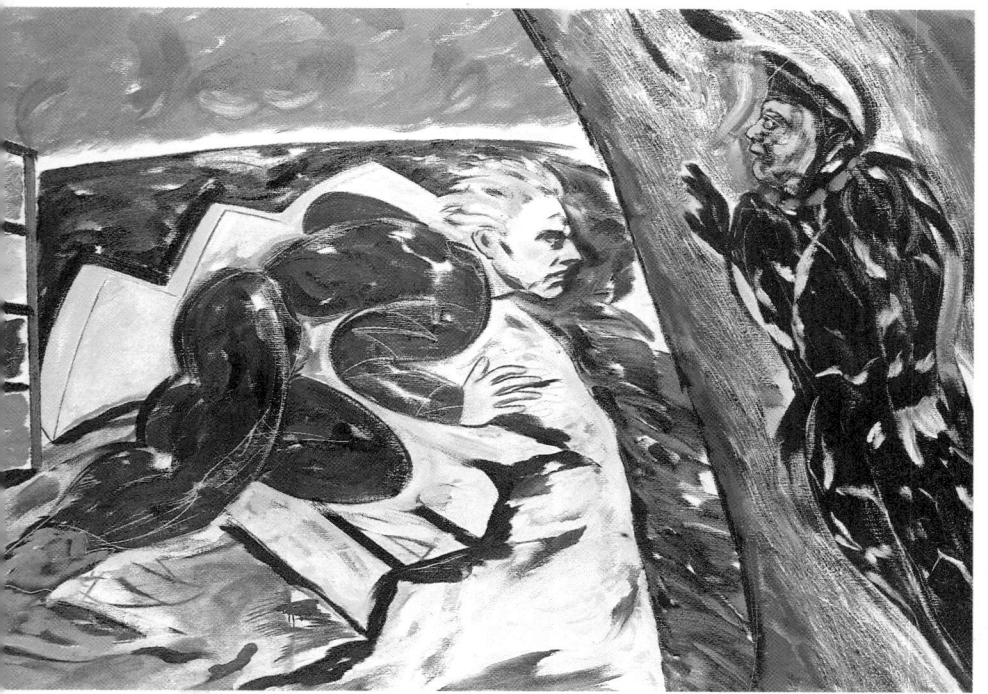

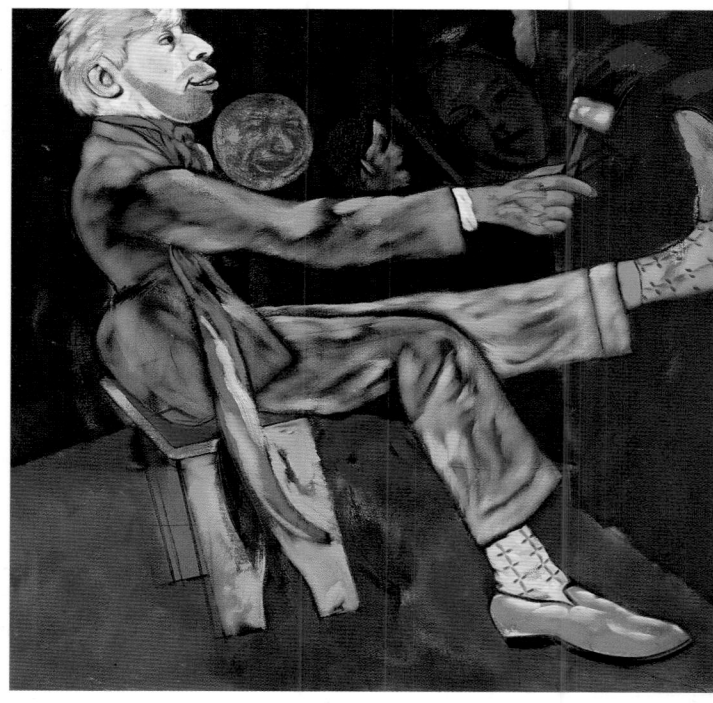

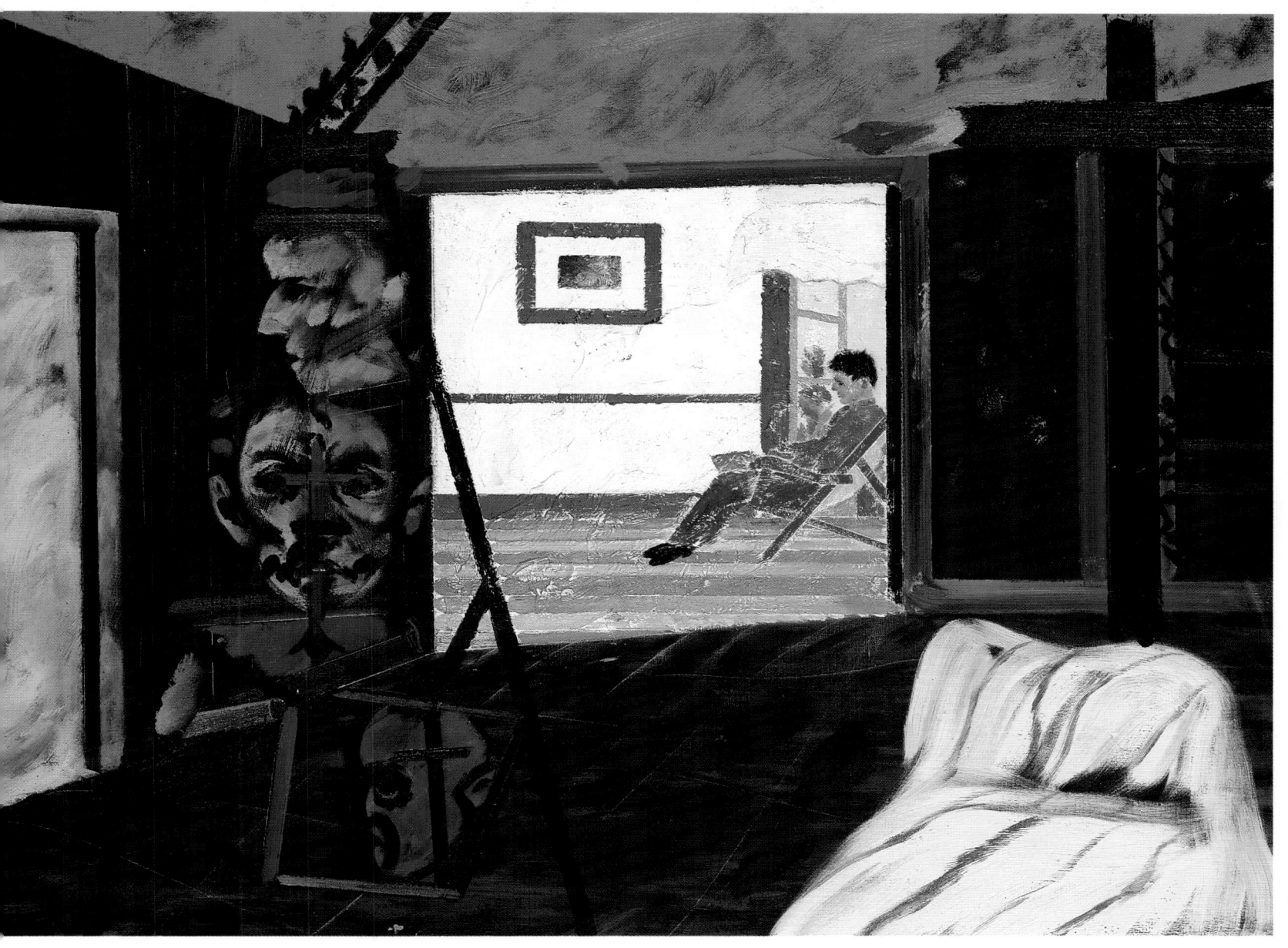

58. The Divinity School Address, 1983–5. *Cat. no. 374.*

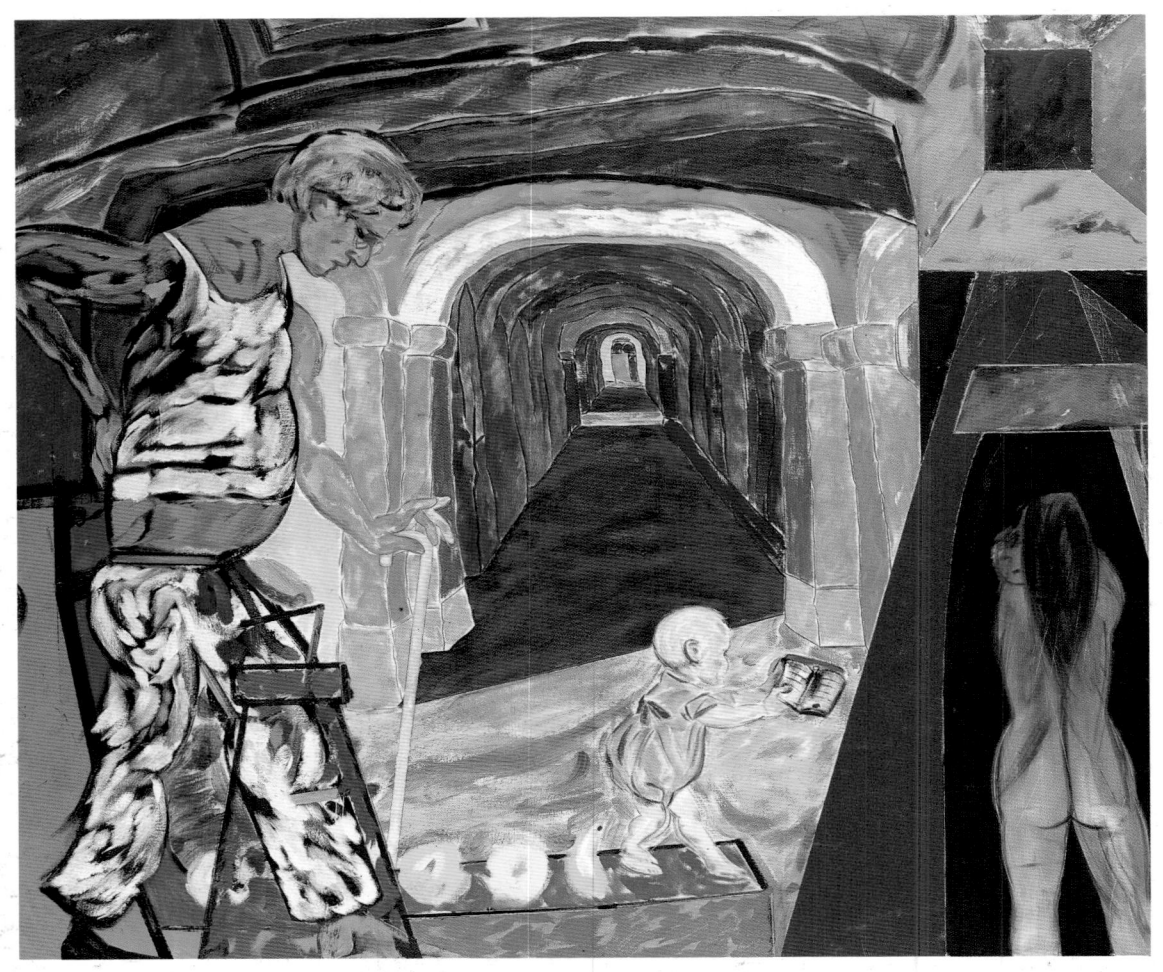

169. Germania (The Tunnel), 1985. *Cat. no. 382.*

170. 4 A.M., 1985. *Cat. no. 388.*

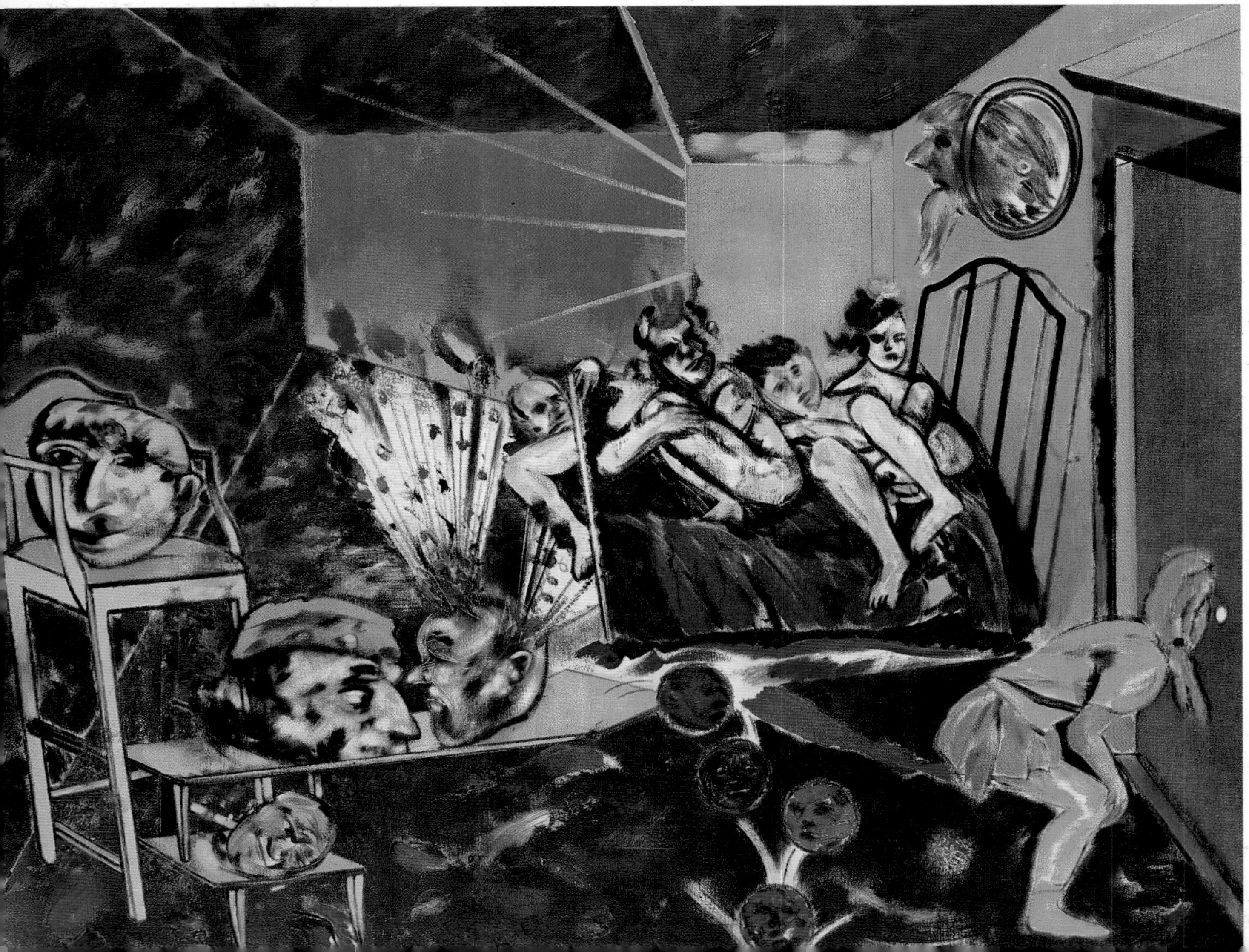

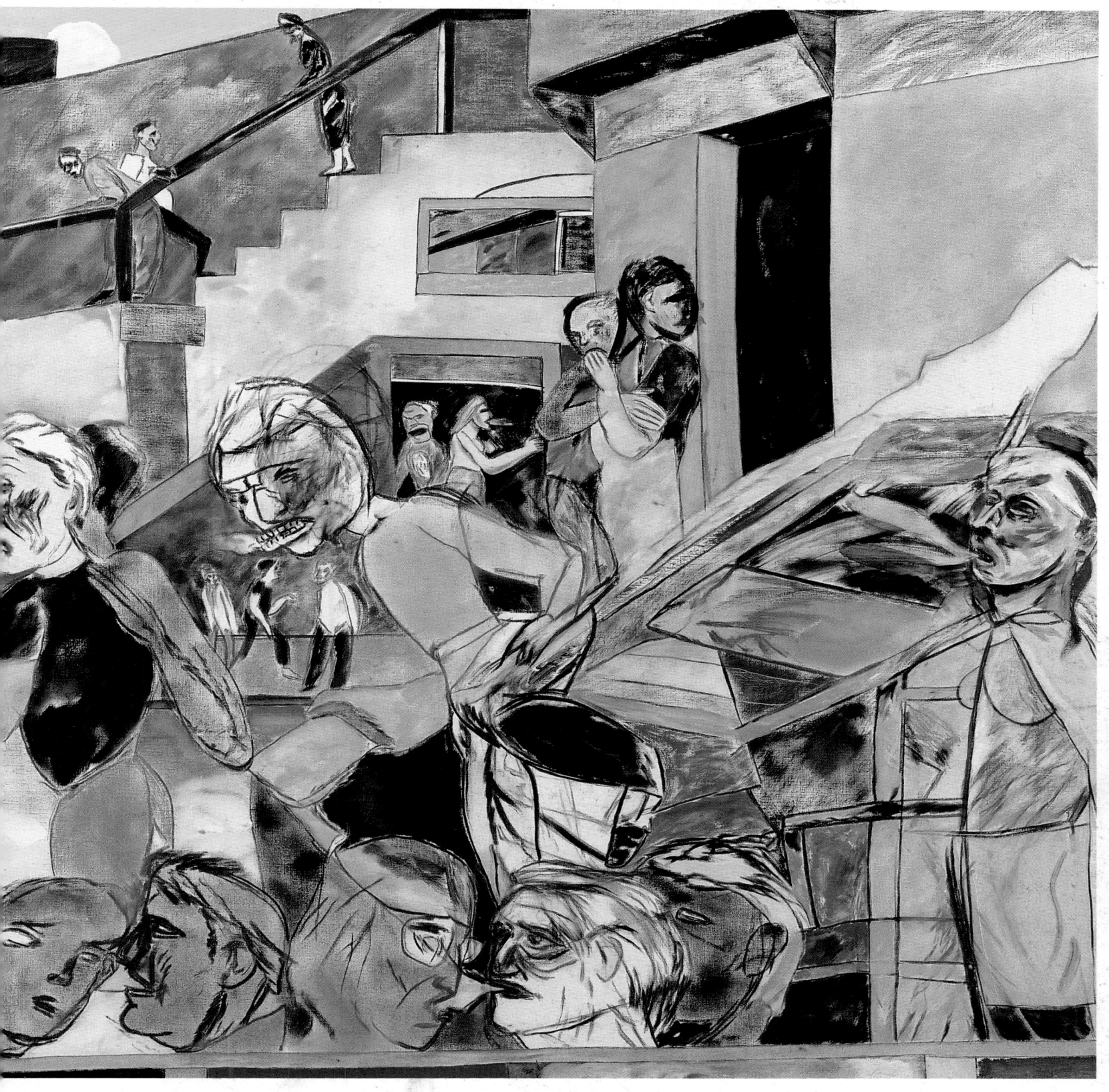

171. Against Slander, 1990–1. *Cat. no. 490.*

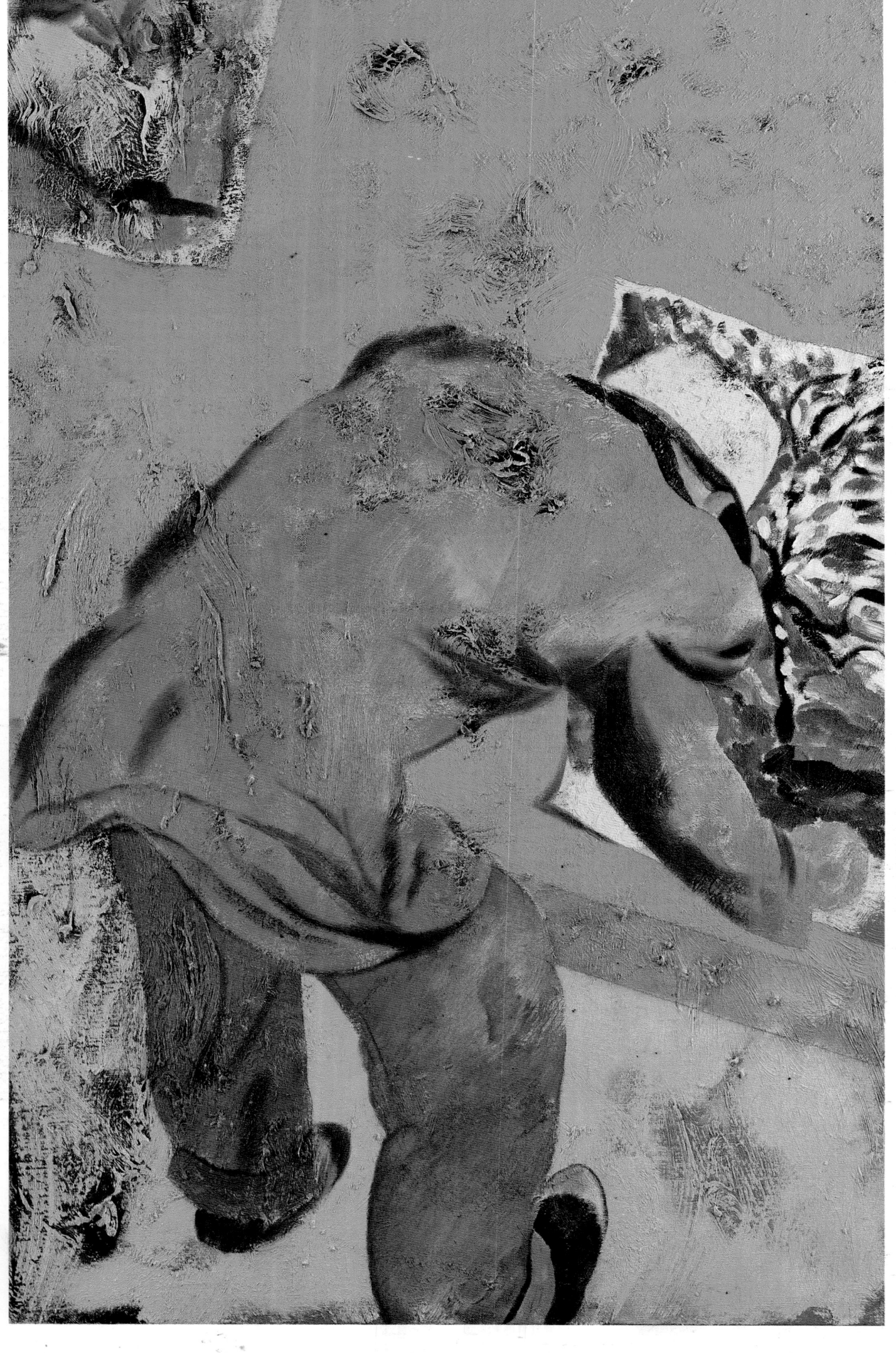

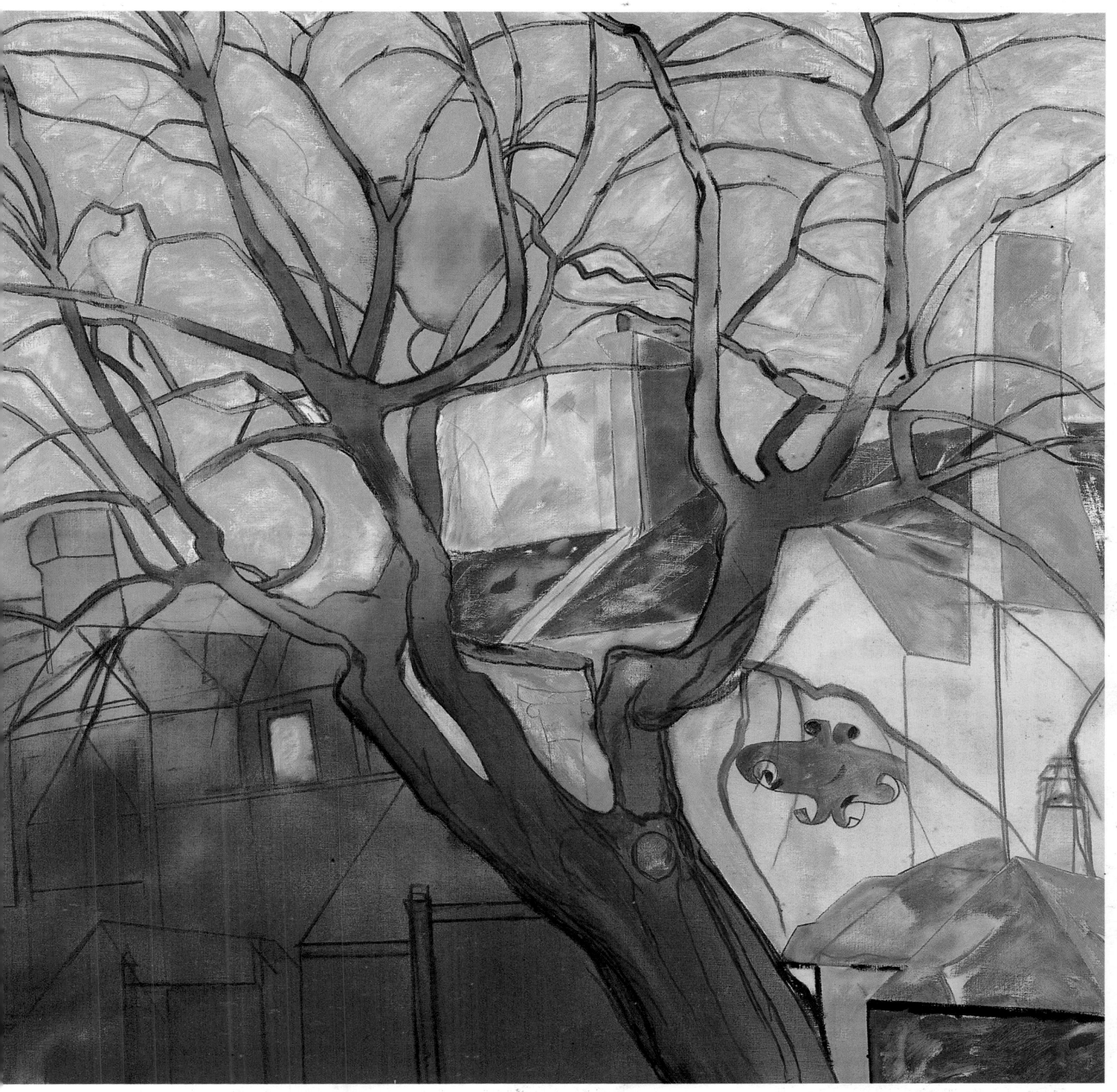

173. The Oak Tree, 1991. *Cat. no. 492.*

172. *(opposite)* His Last Painting, 1987. *Cat. no. 429.*

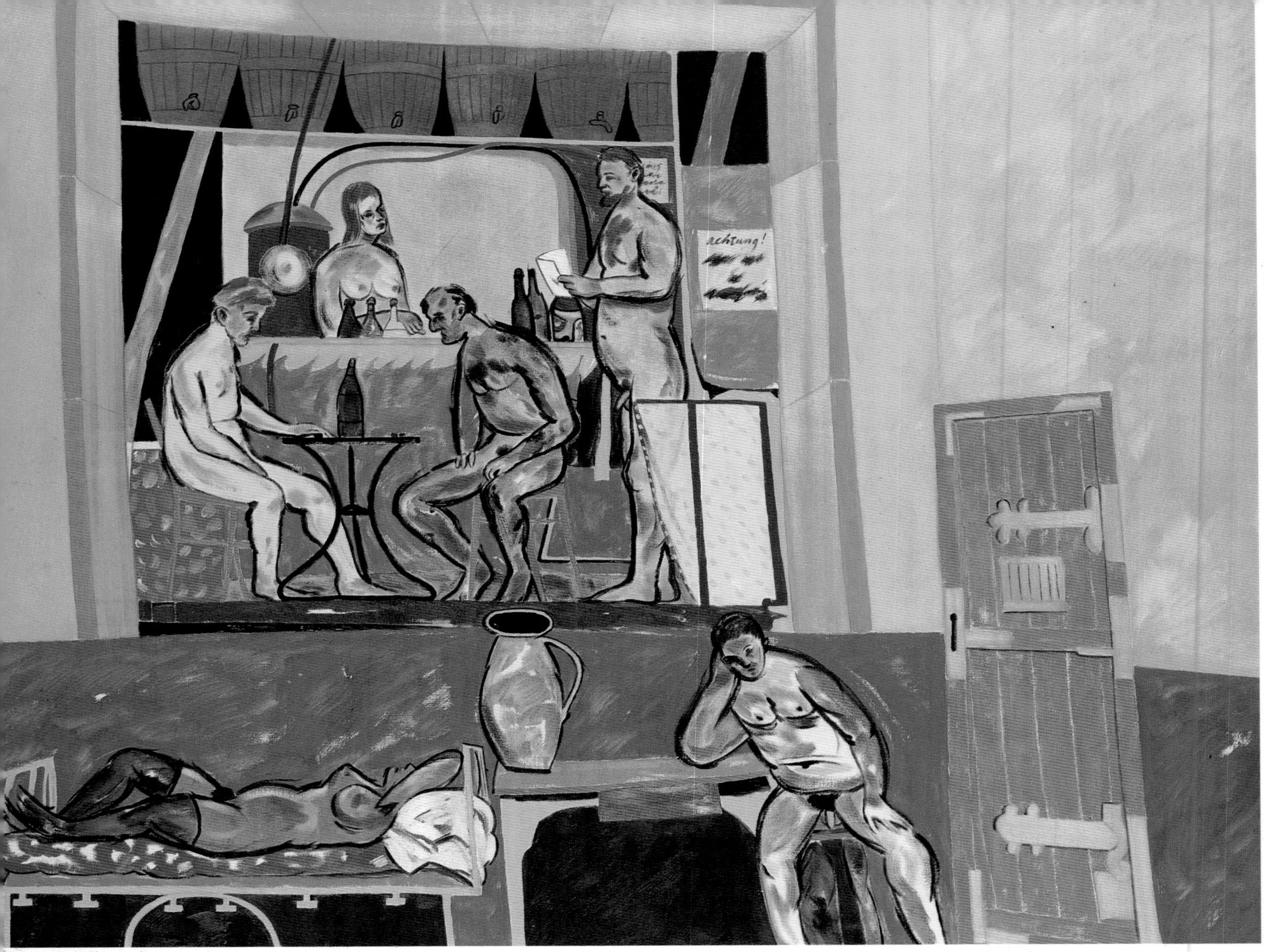

174. Germania (Vienna), 1987. *Cat. no. 436.*

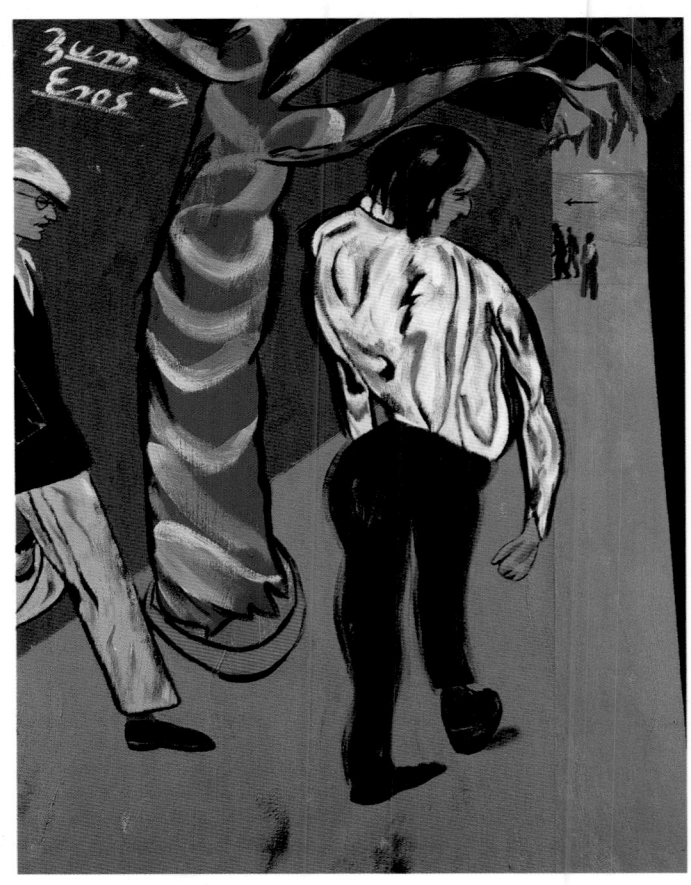

175. Germania (To the Brothel), 1987. *Cat. no. 428.*

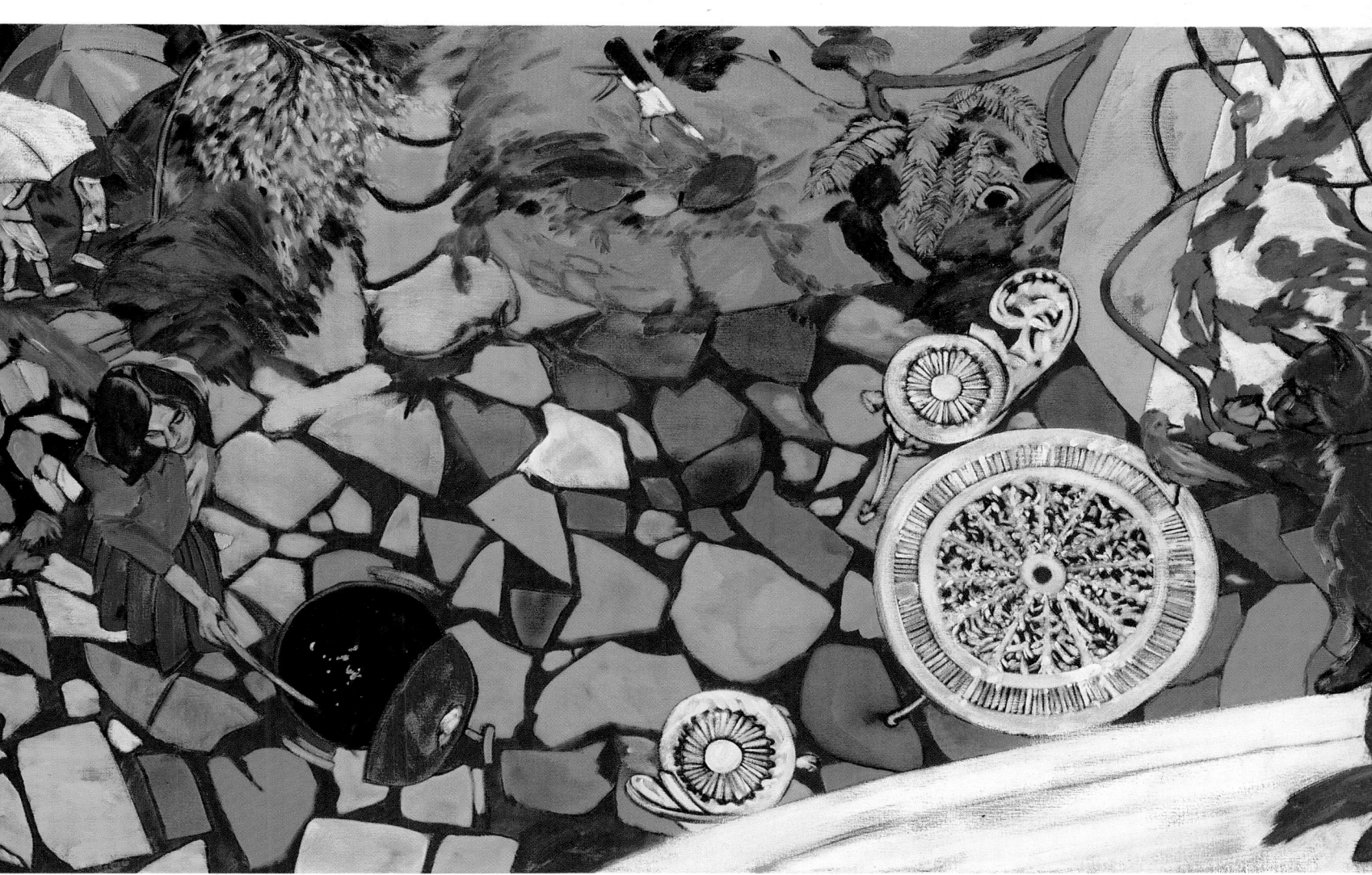

176. Sunday, 1991. *Cat. no. 497.*

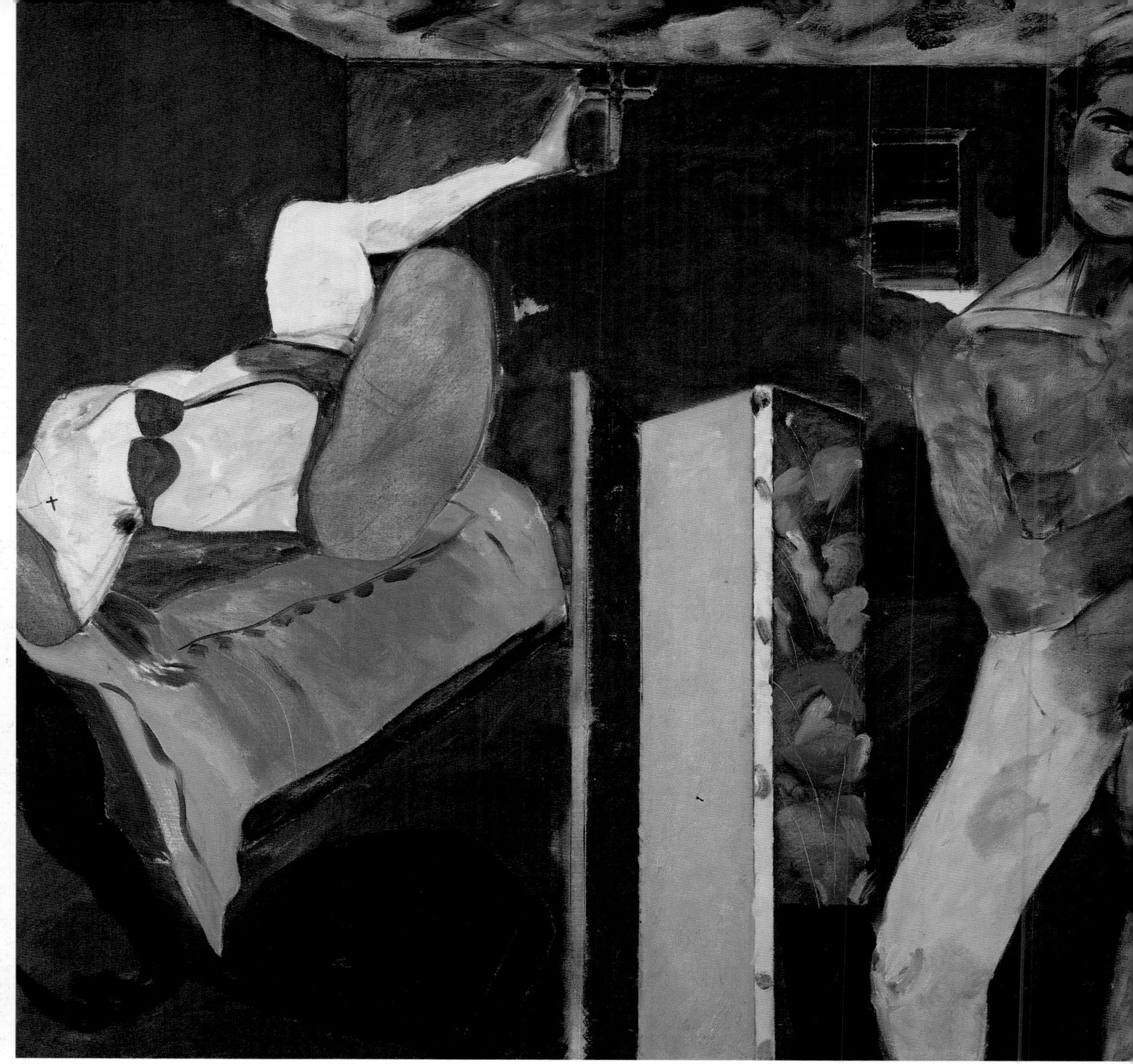

177. The First Time (Havana, 1949), 1990. *Cat. no. 475.*

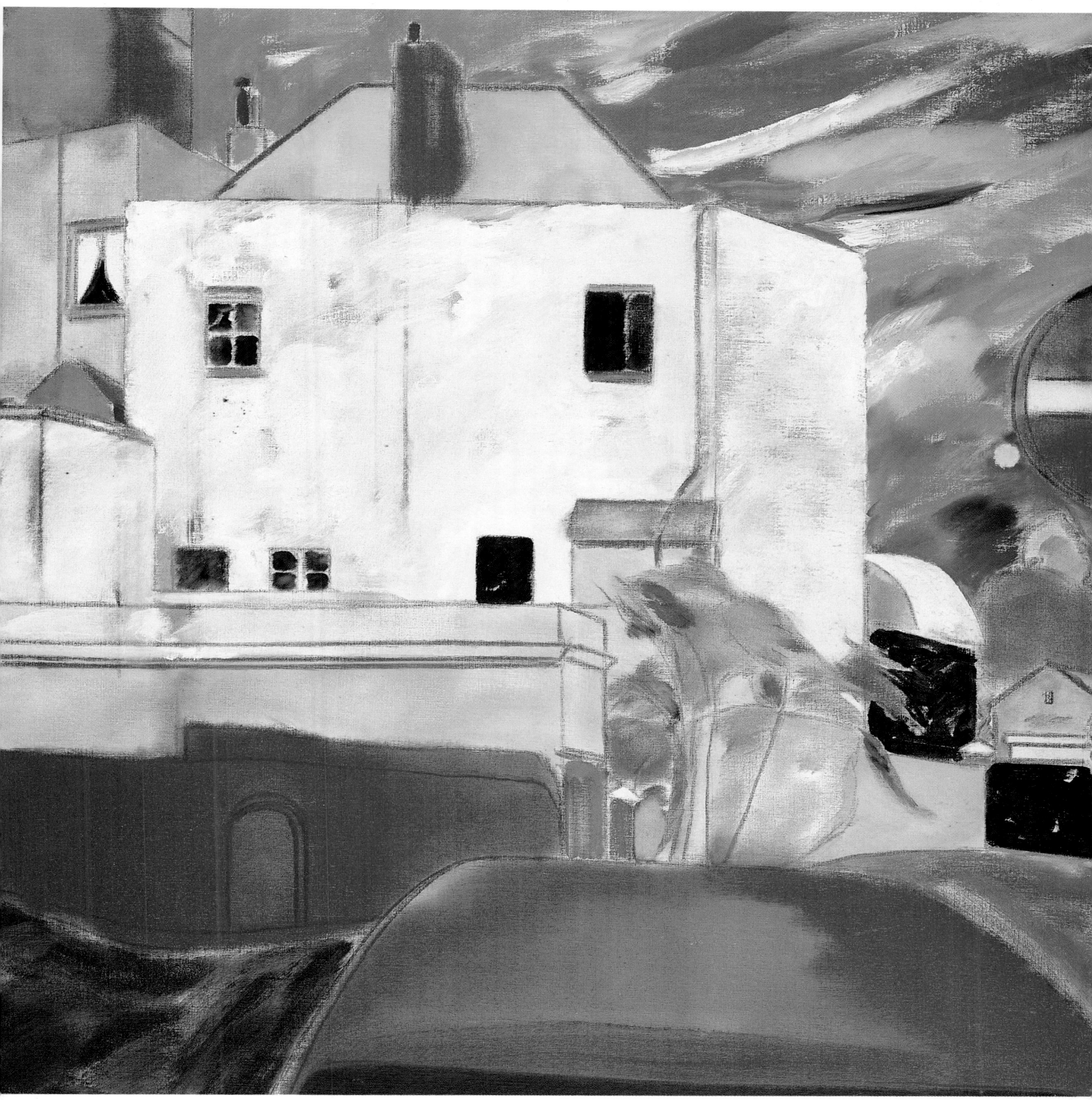

178. De Morgan's House, 1991. *Cat. no. 494.*

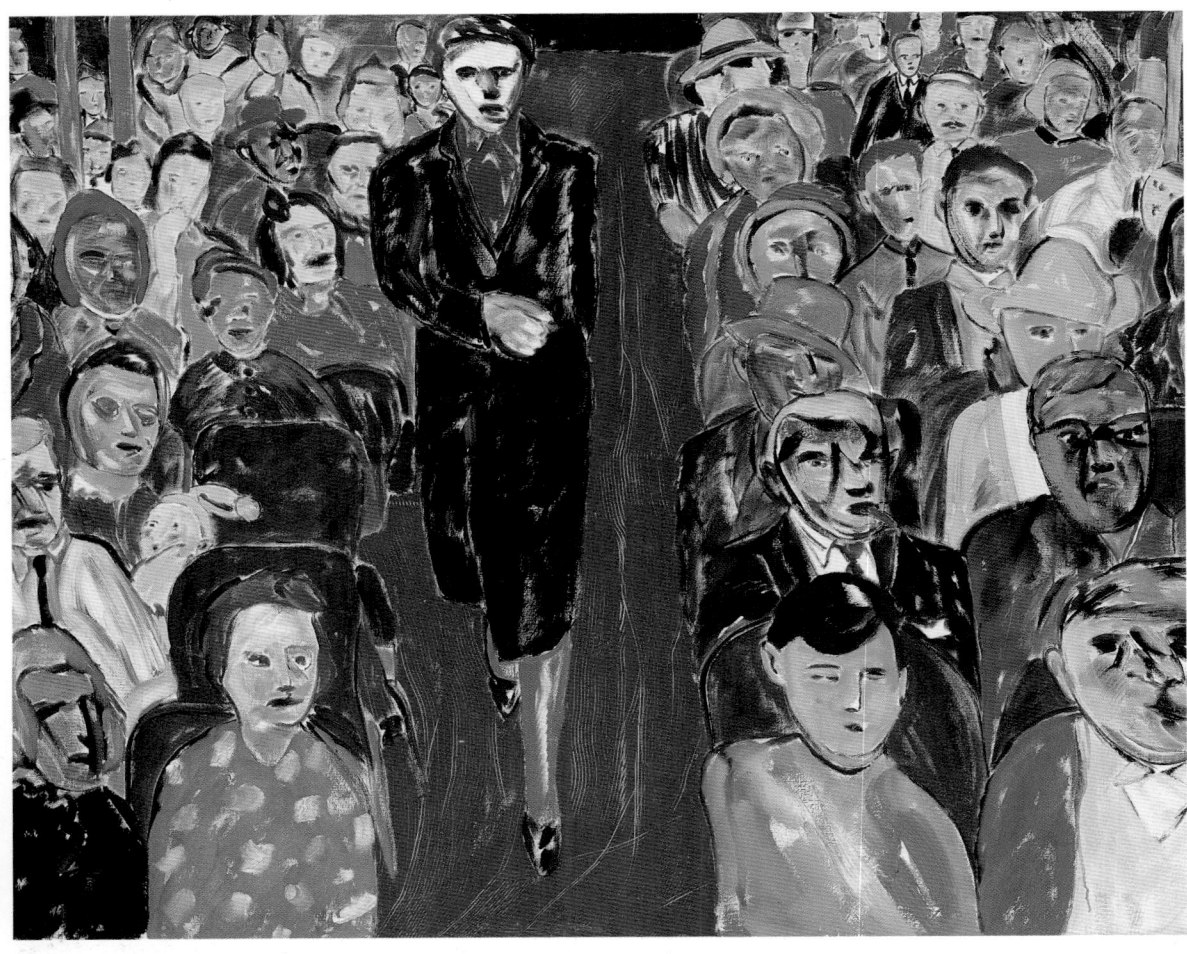

179. Germania (The Audience), 1989.
Cat. no. 459.

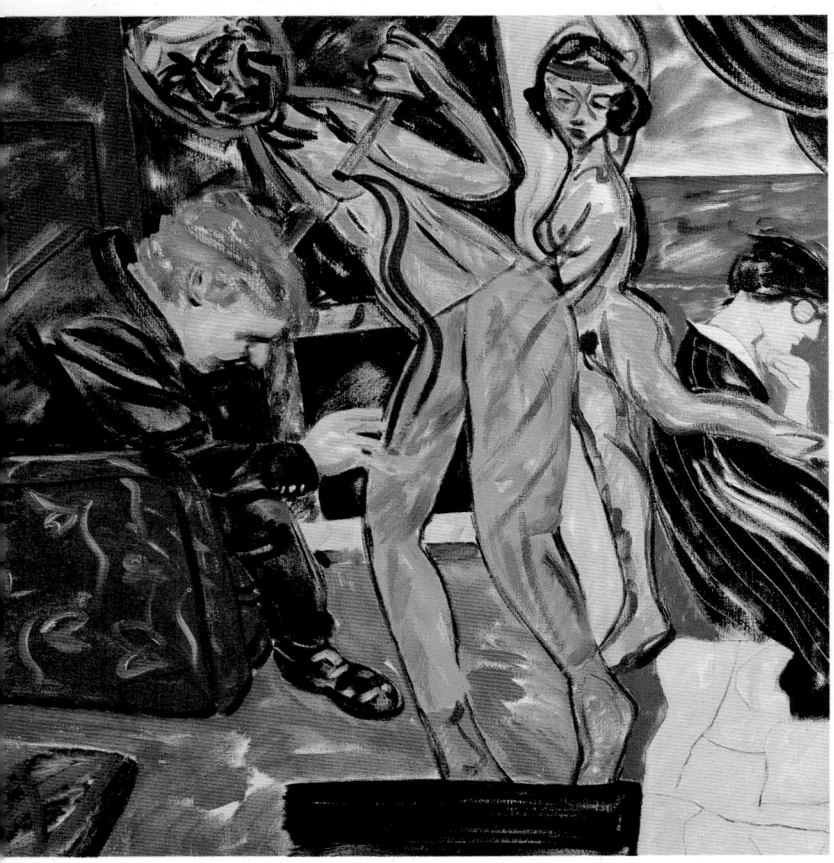

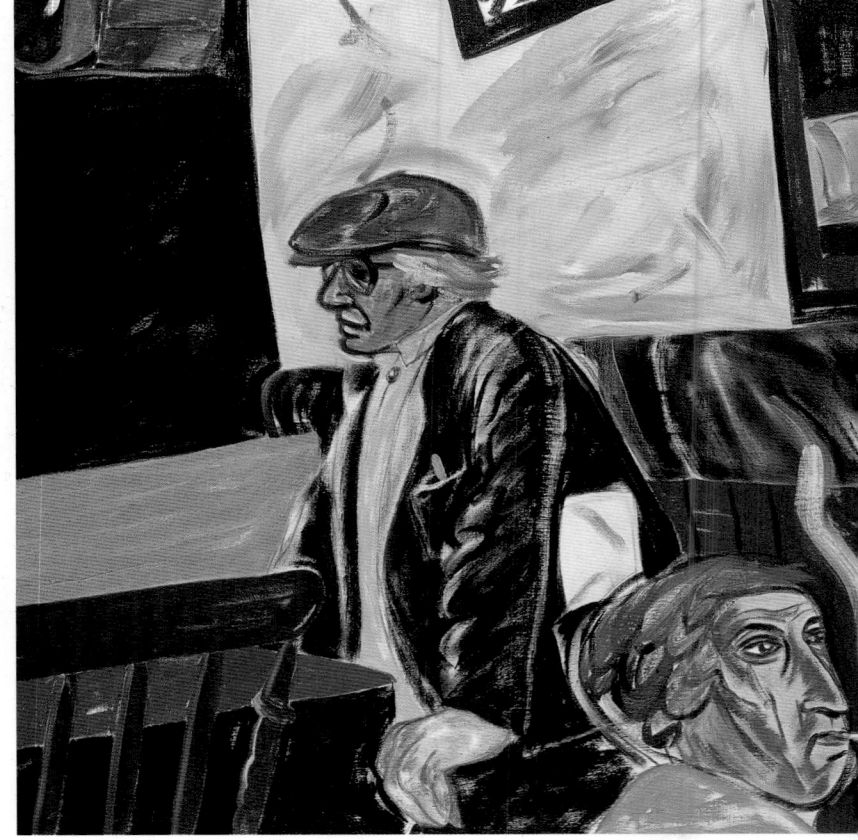

180. (below, left) Melancholy, 1989. Cat. no. 4

181. (below) Up All Night (Fulham Road), 1
Cat. no. 469.

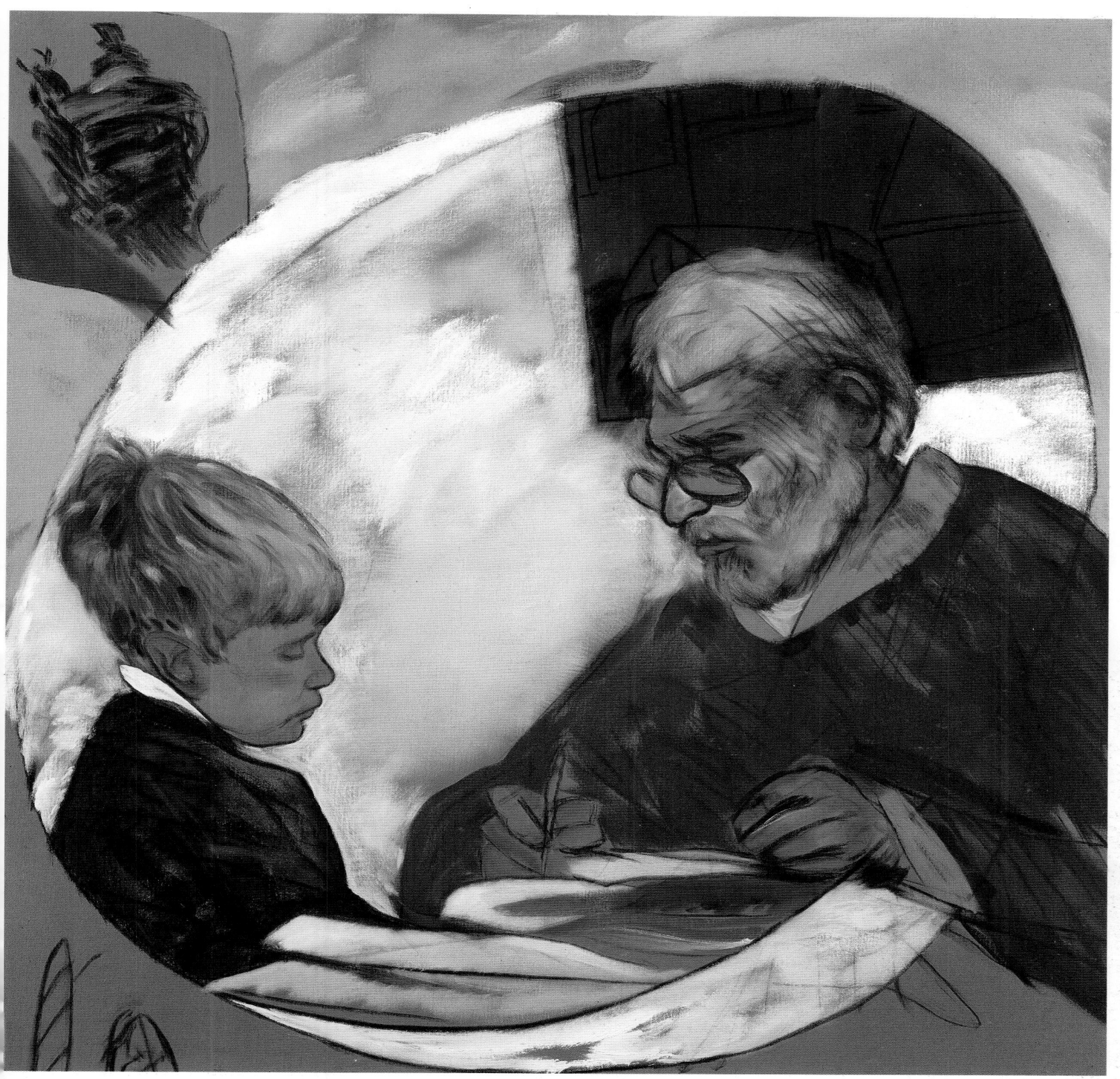

182. I and Thou, 1990–2. *Cat. no.* 511.

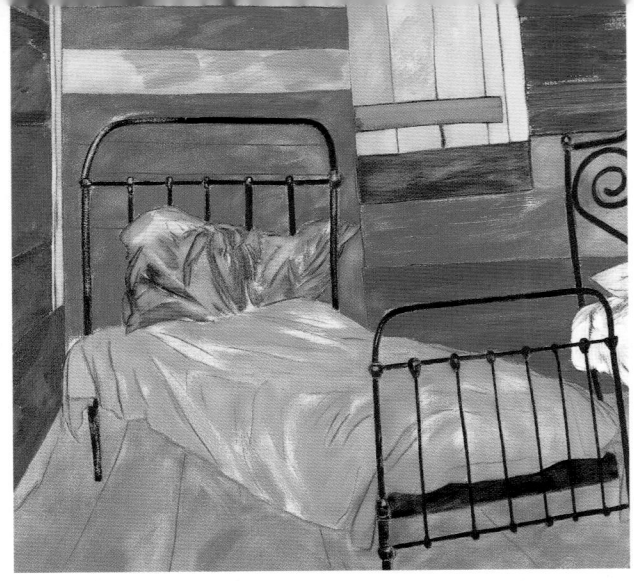

183. The Third Time (Savannah, Georgia), 1992. *Cat. no. 527.*

184. *(below)* The Sculptor, 1992. *Cat. no. 528.*

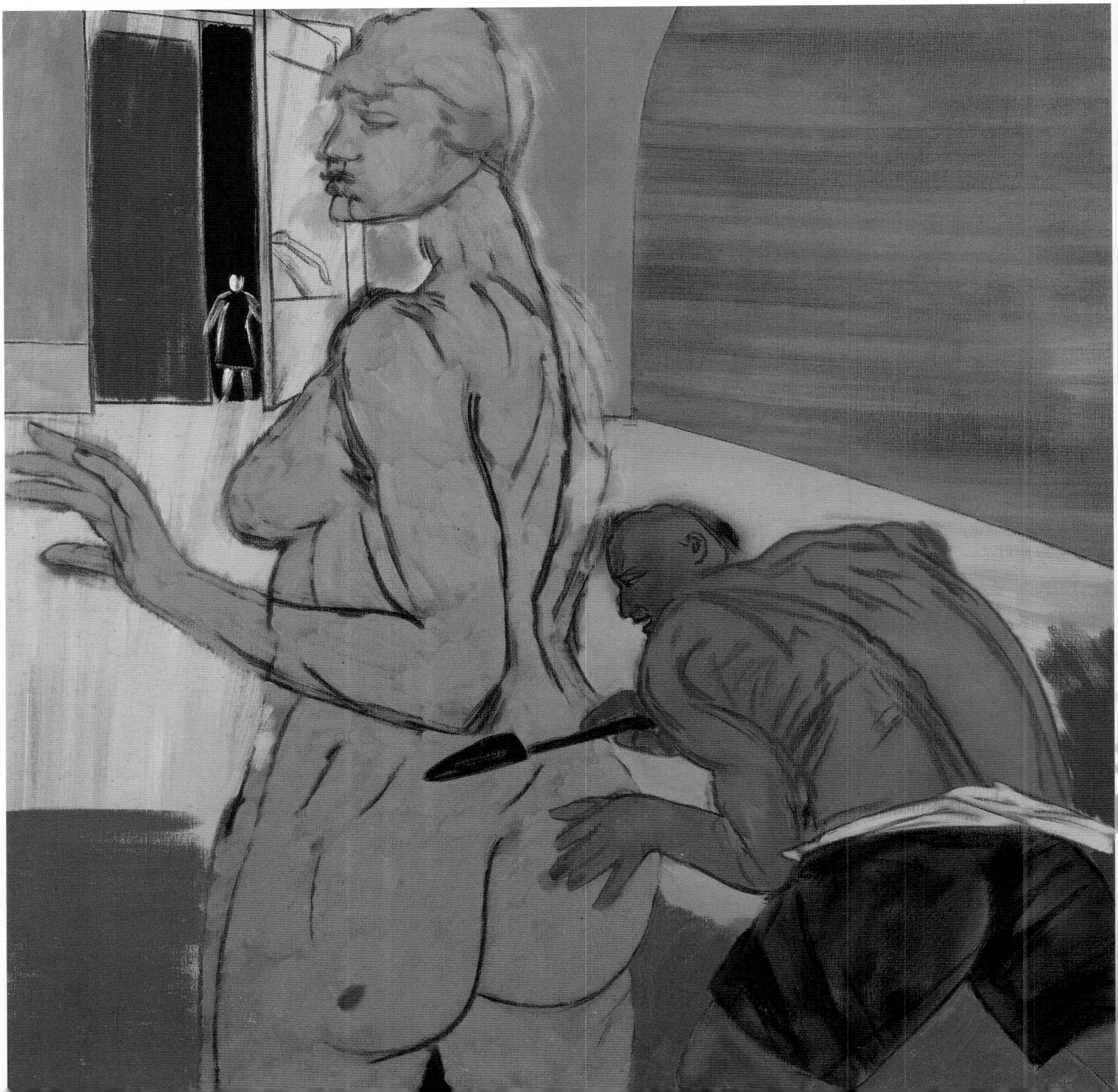

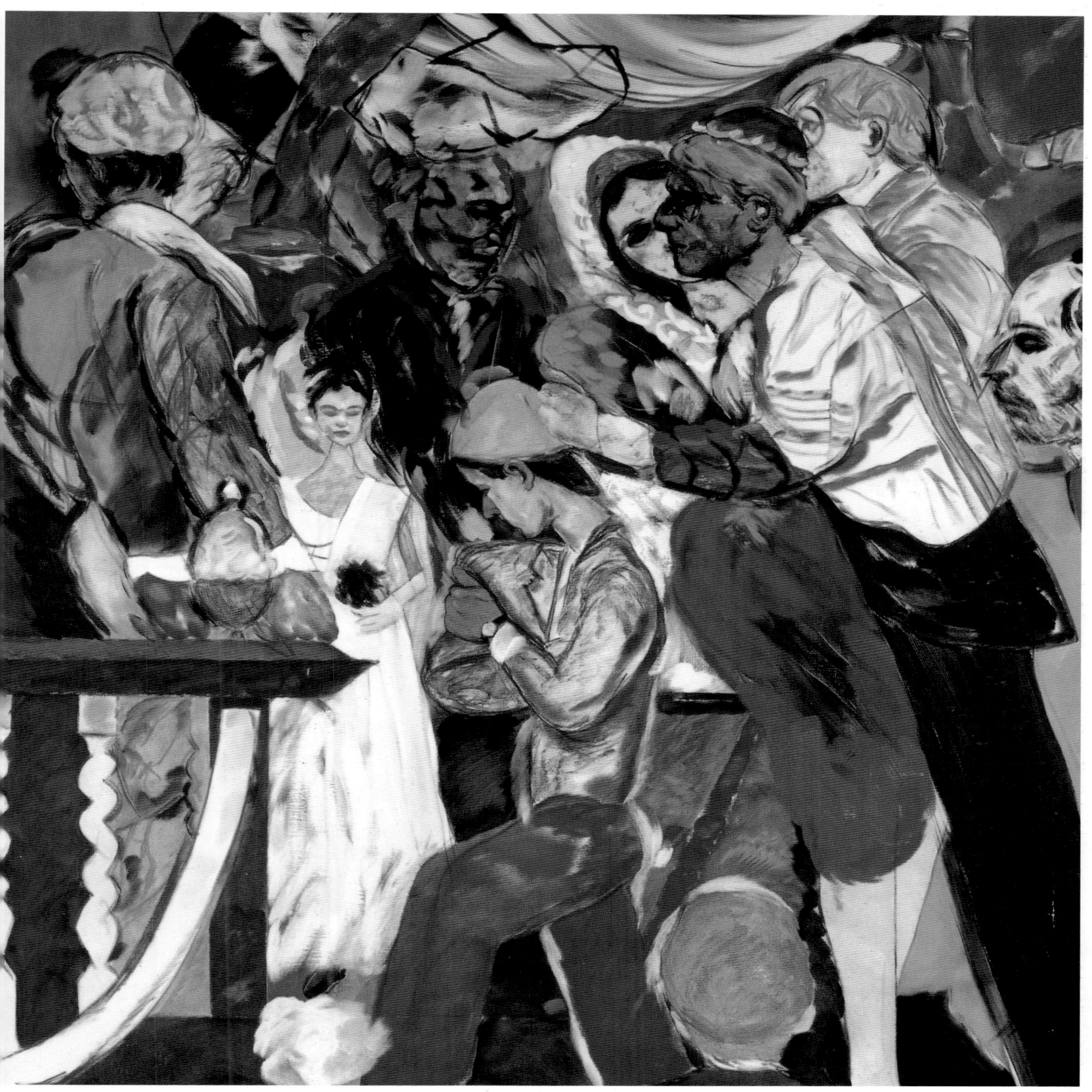

185. The Wedding *(detail)*, 1989-93. *Cat. no. 534.*

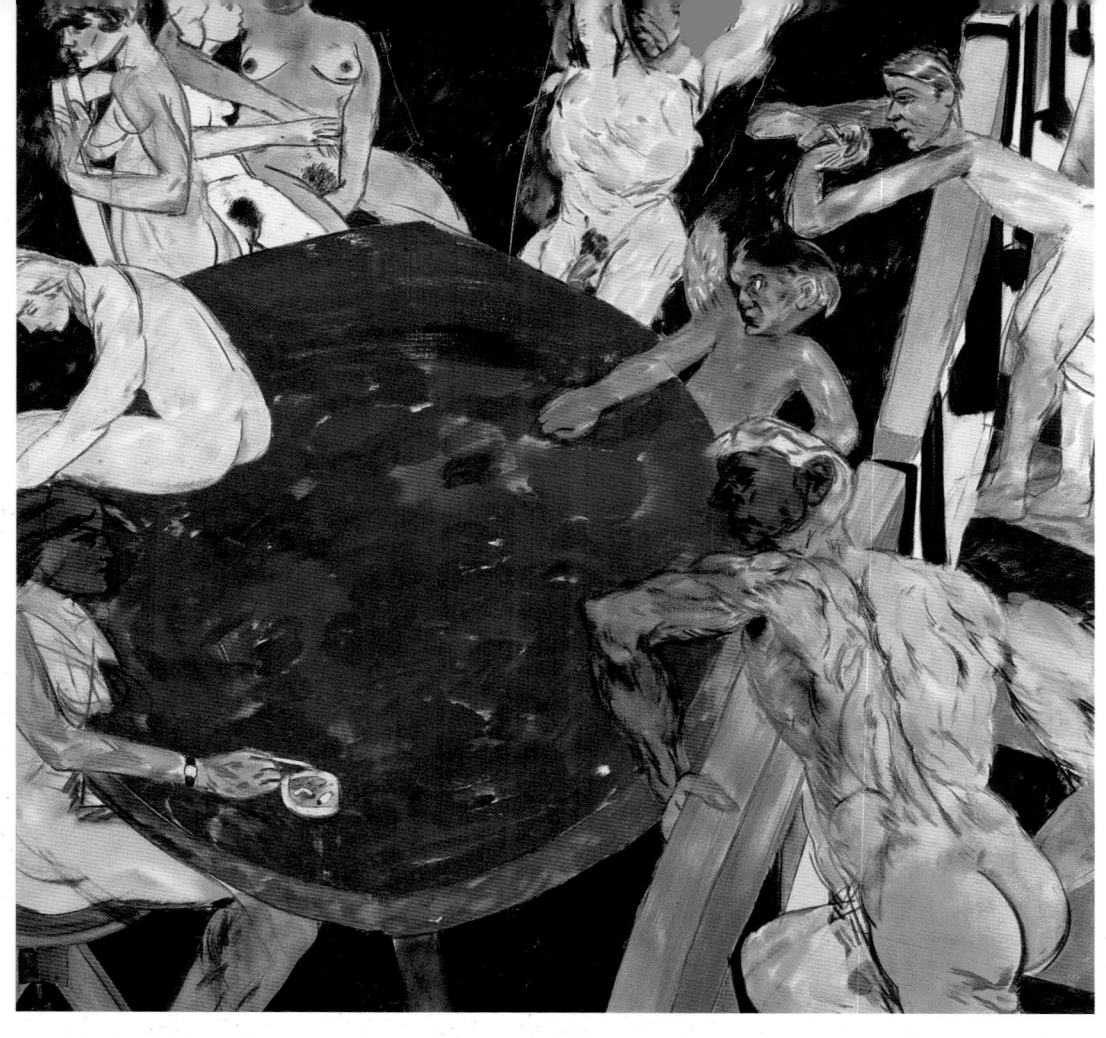

186. Women and Men, 1991–3. *Cat. no. 542.*

187. *(below)* Western Bathers, 1993–4. *Cat. no. 566.*

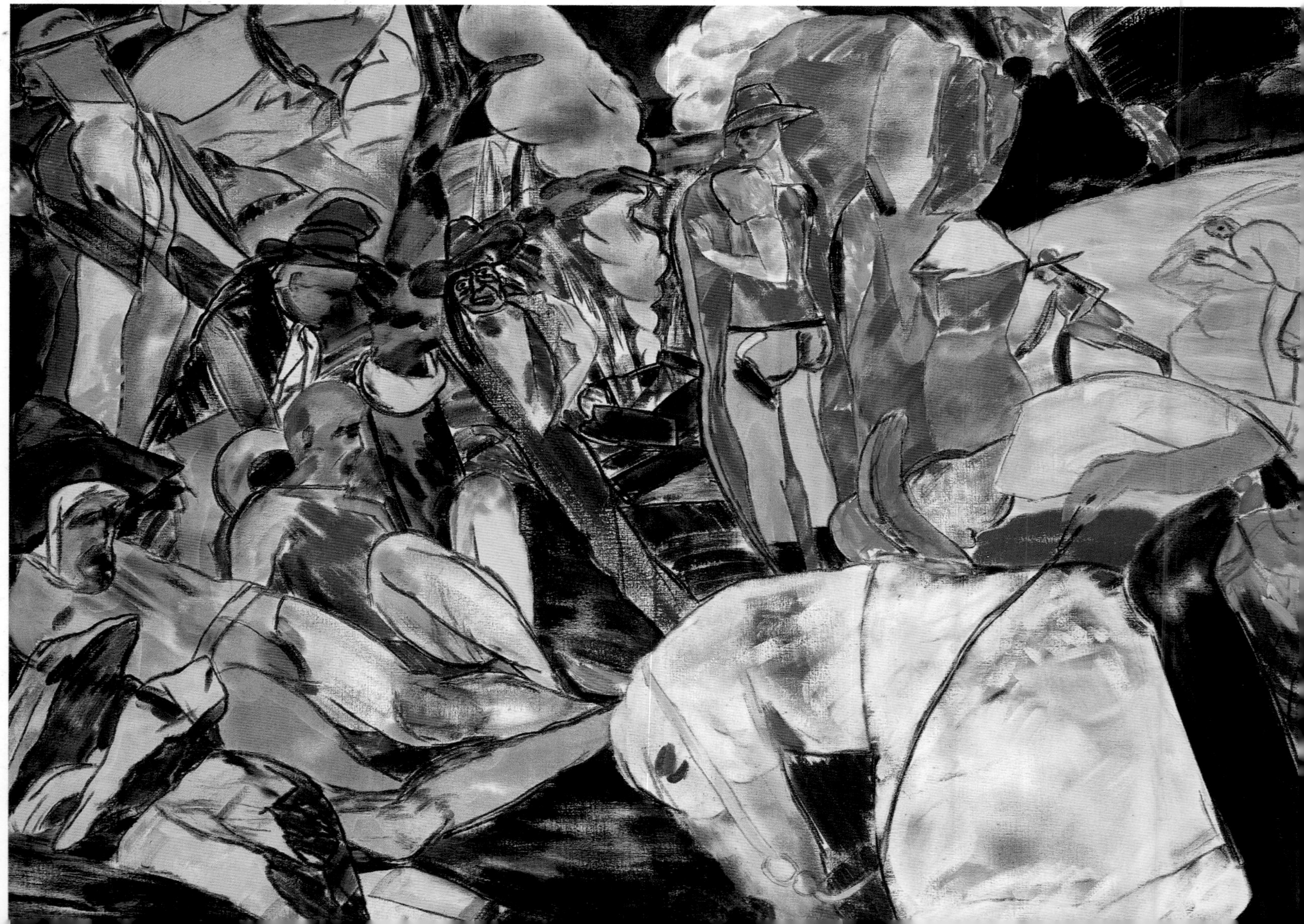

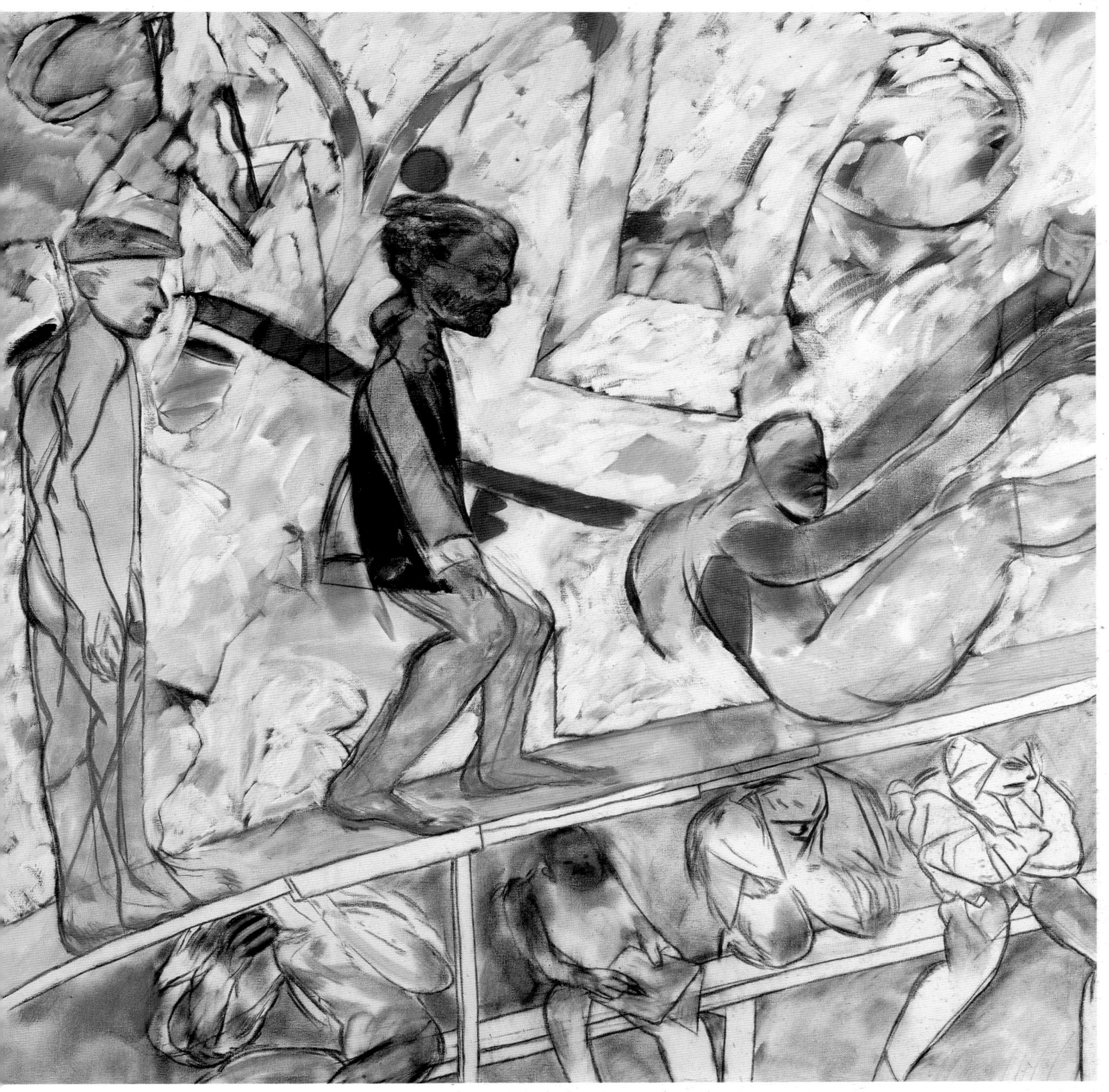

188. My Cities (An Experimental Drama), 1990–3. *Cat. no. 539.*

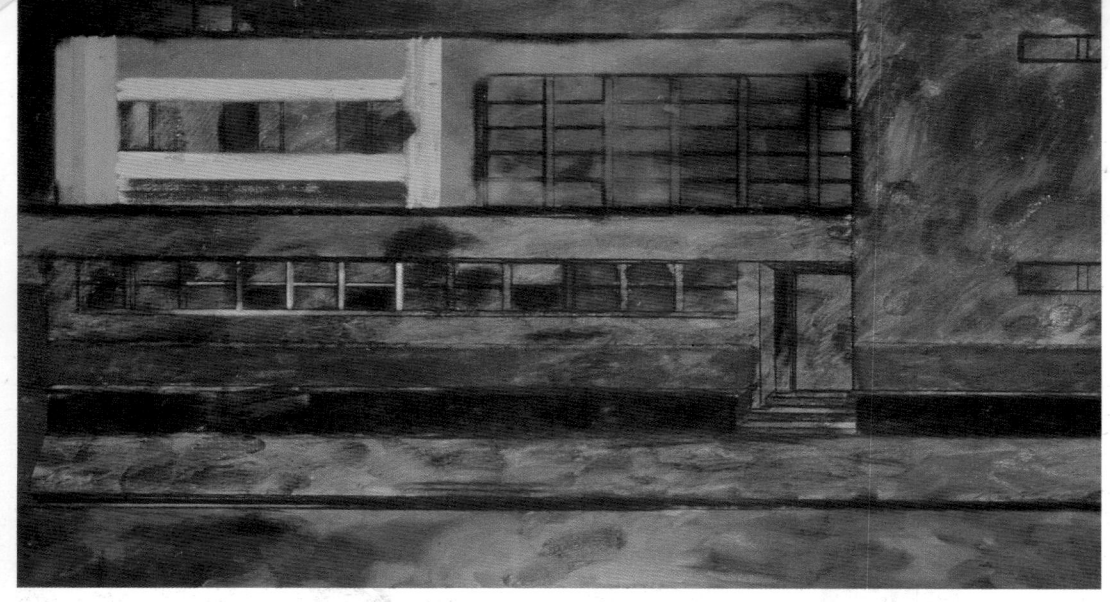

189. Mendelsohn House, 1988–98. *Cat. no. 636.*

190. *(below)* The Flat, 1993. *Cat. no. 556.*

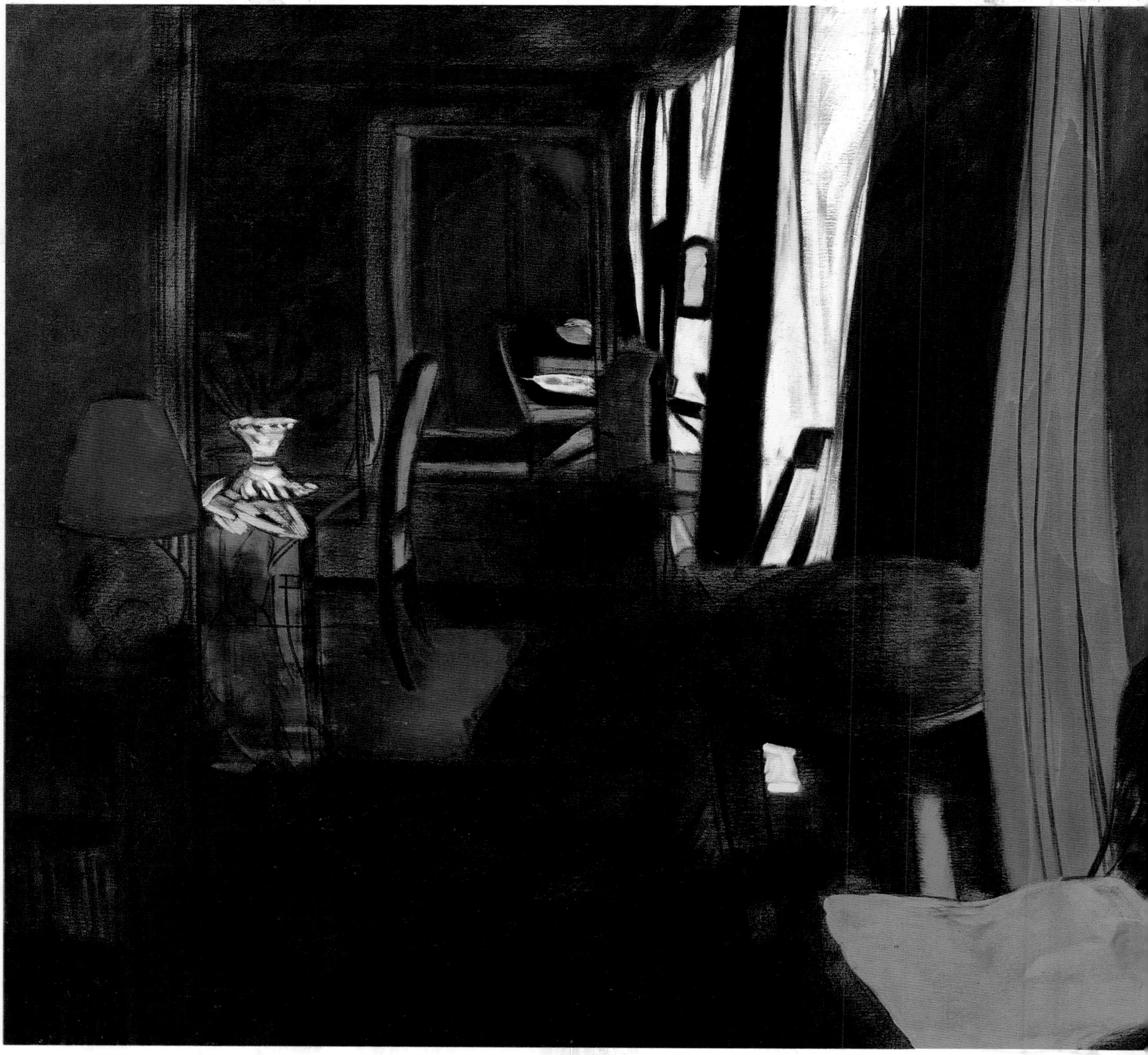

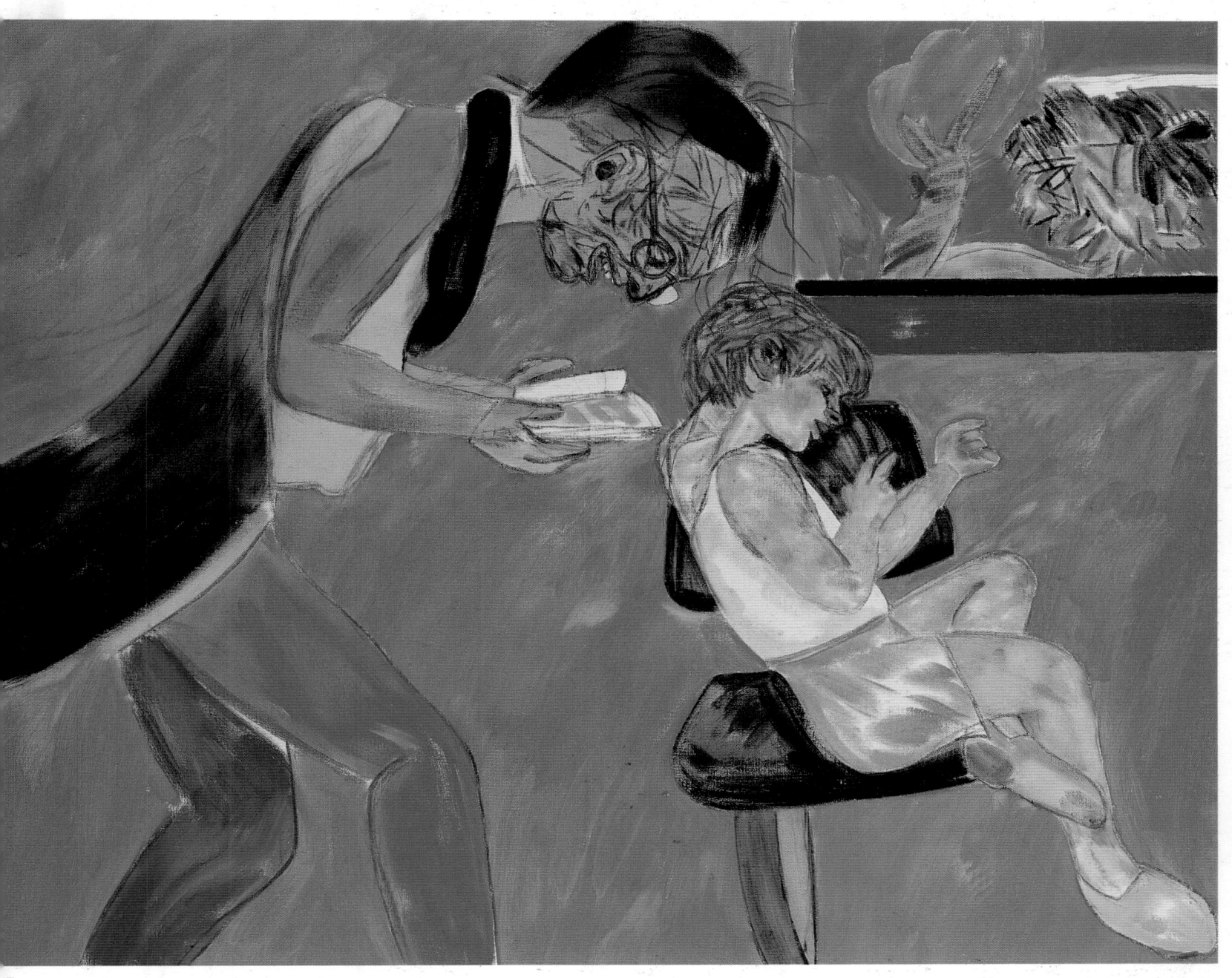

191. Father Reading Tom Sawyer to his Son, 1994. *Cat. no. 572.*

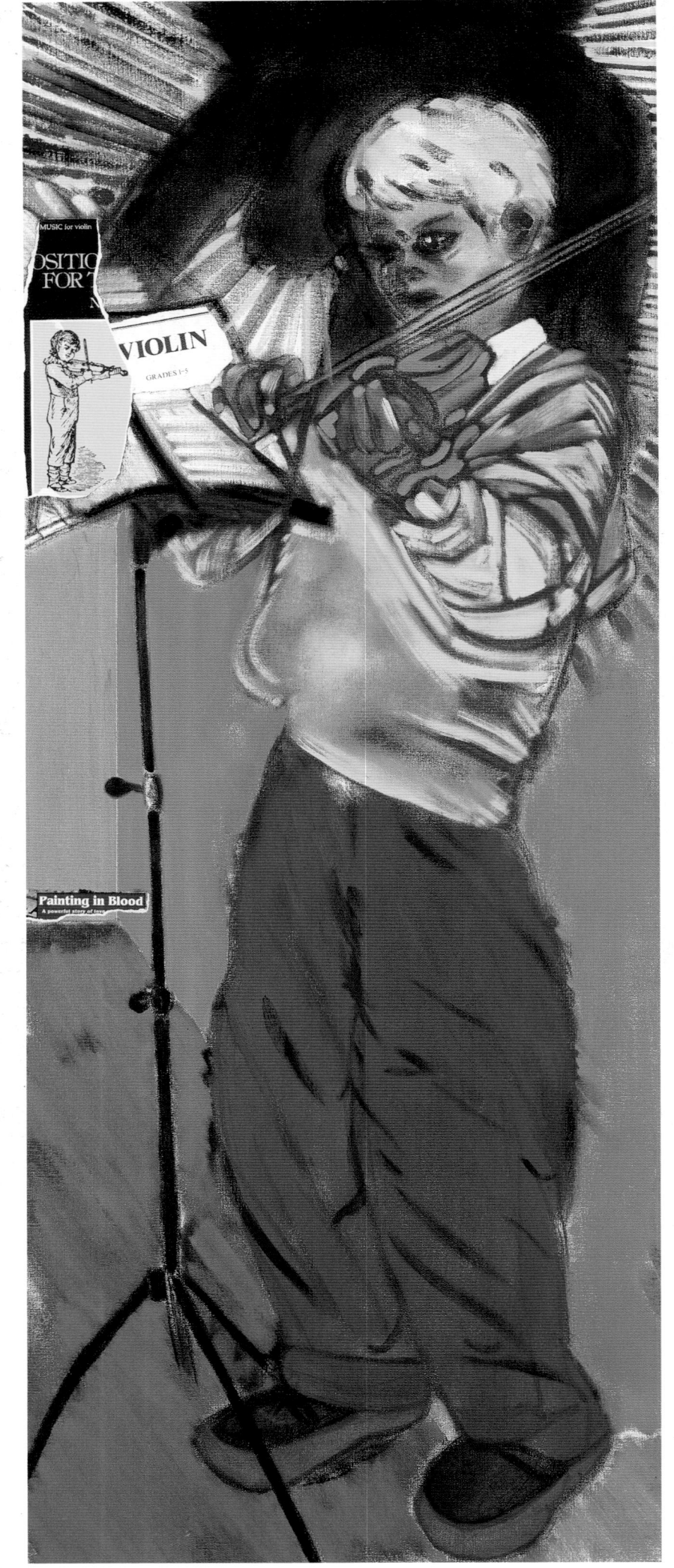

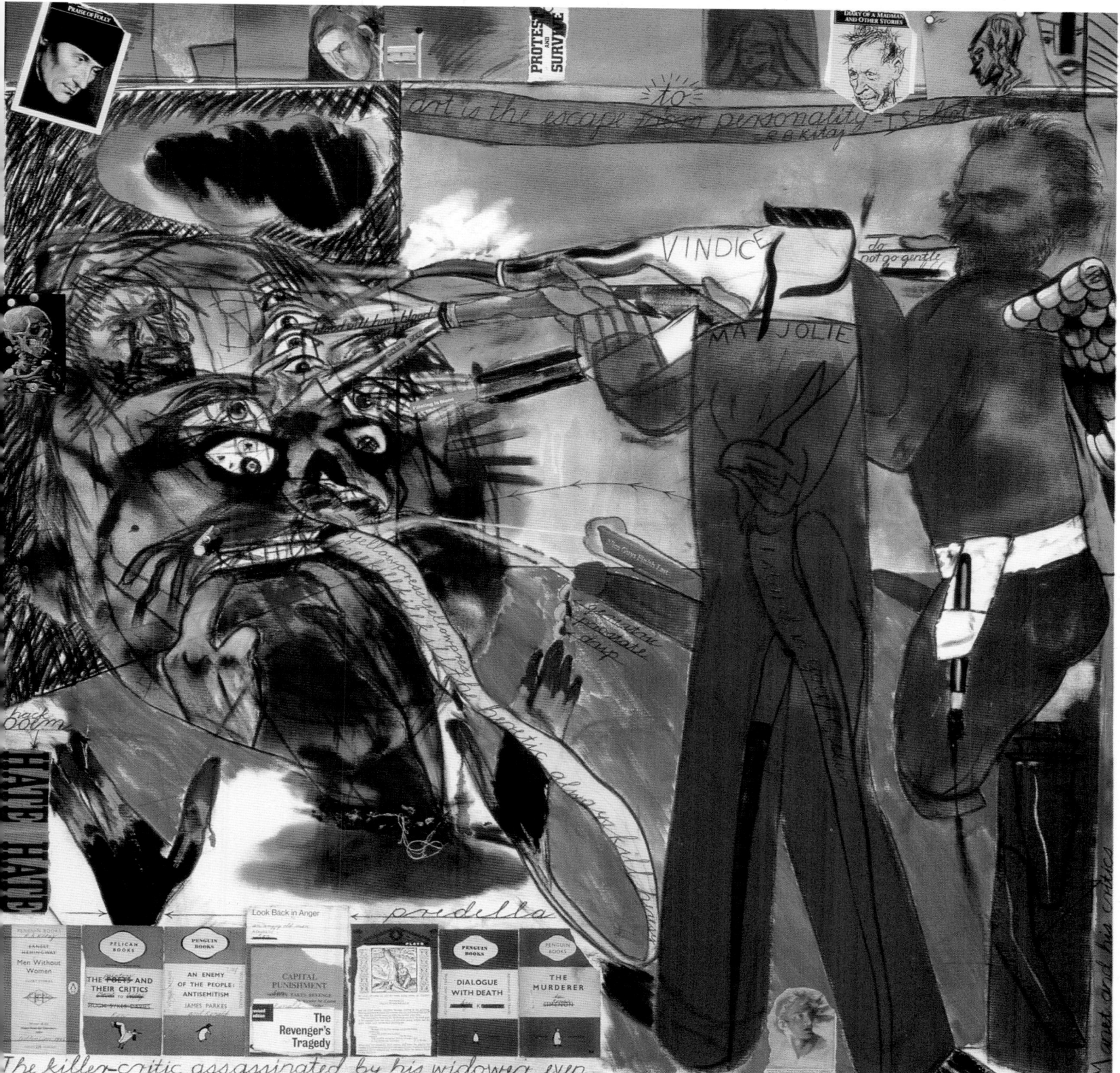

193. The Killer-Critic Assassinated by his Widower, Even, 1997. *Cat. no. 633.*

192. *(left)* The Violinist with the Spirit of his Mother, 1997. *Cat. no. 634.*

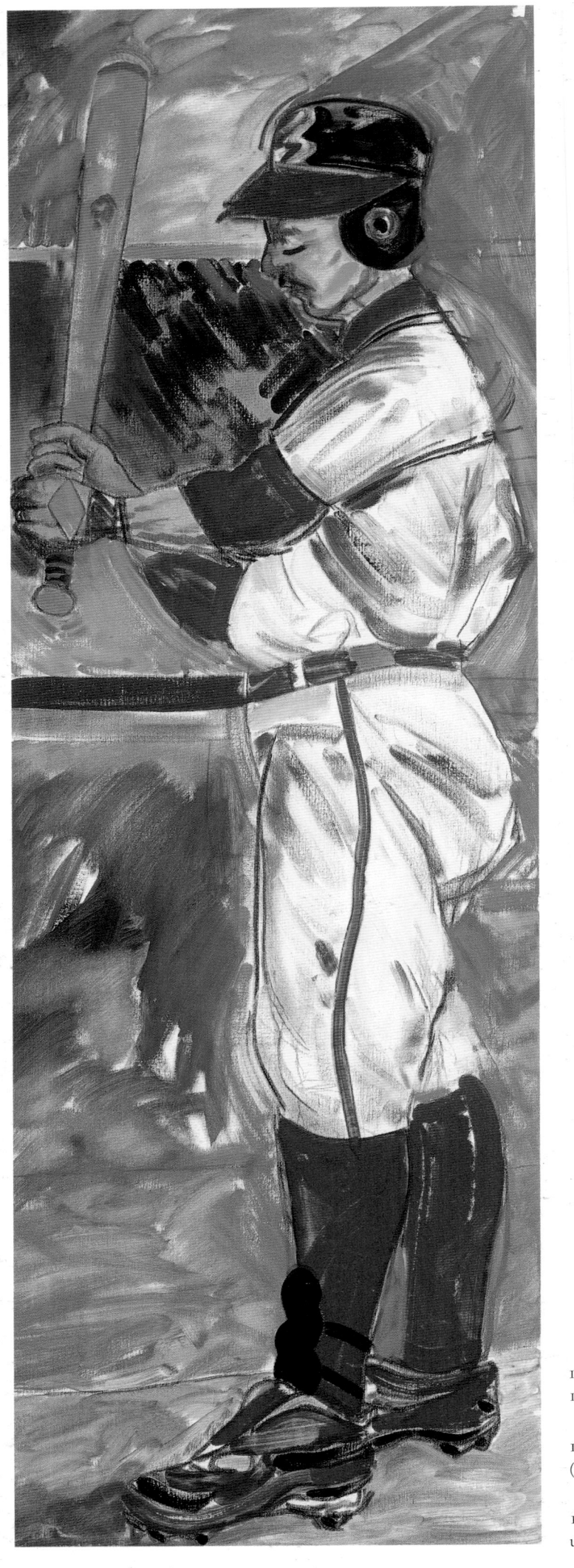

194. *(left)* The Cleveland Indian, 1995–8. *Cat. no. 638.*

195. *(above right)* Second Diasporist Manifest (Marx Brothers), 1997–8. *Cat. no. 643.*

196. *(right)* He and She (The Sickness unto Death), 1994. *Cat. no. 586.*

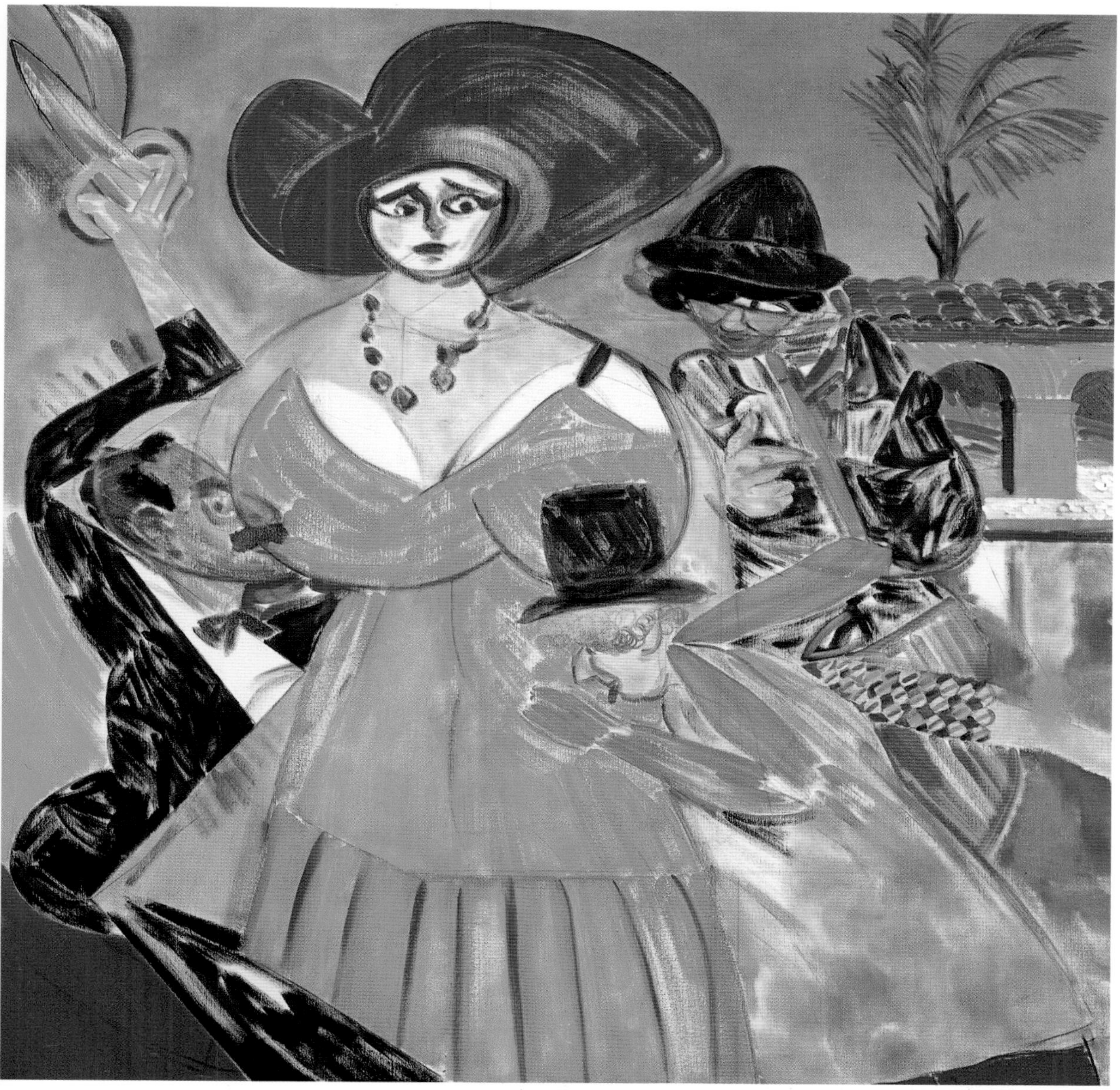

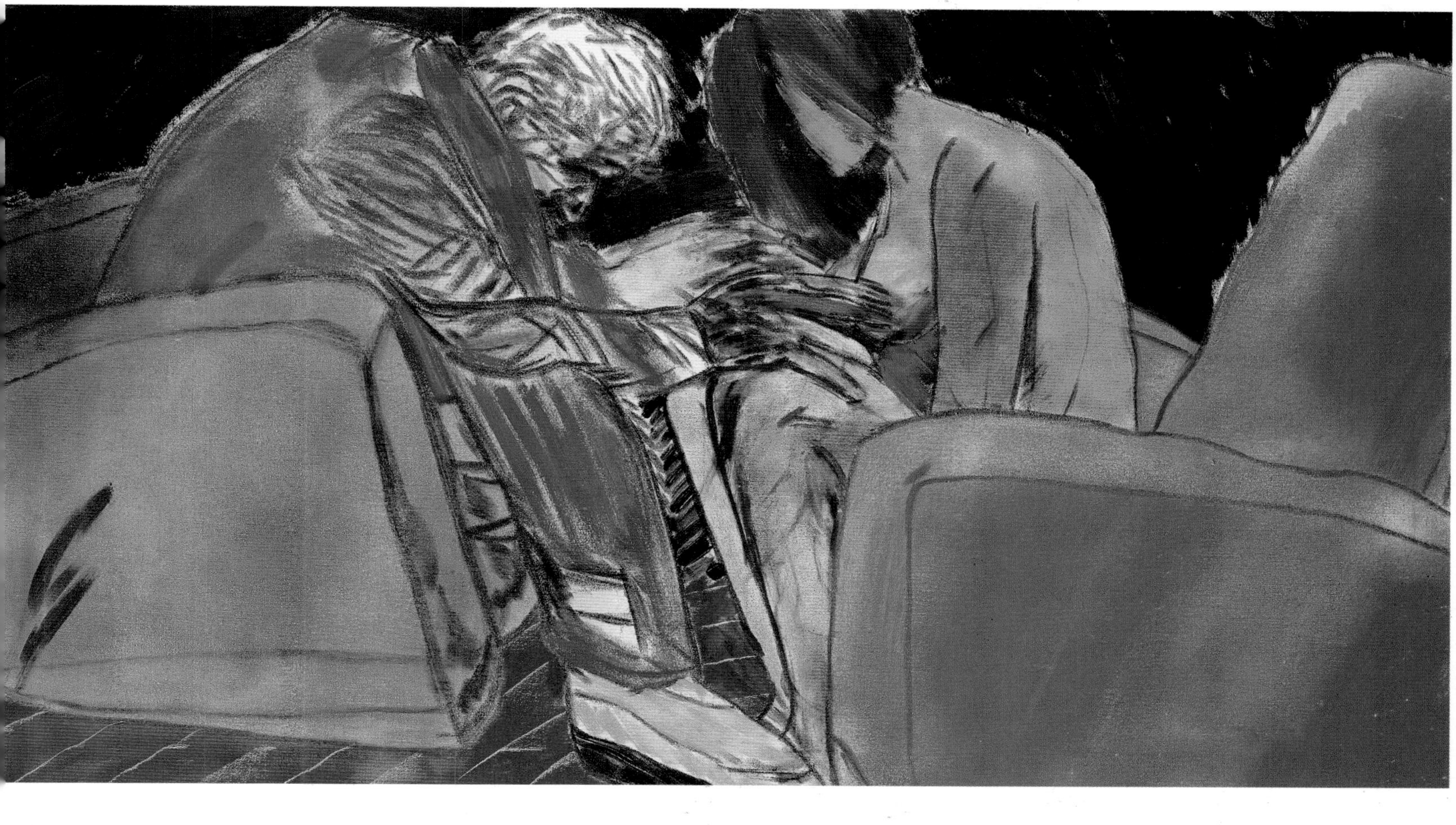

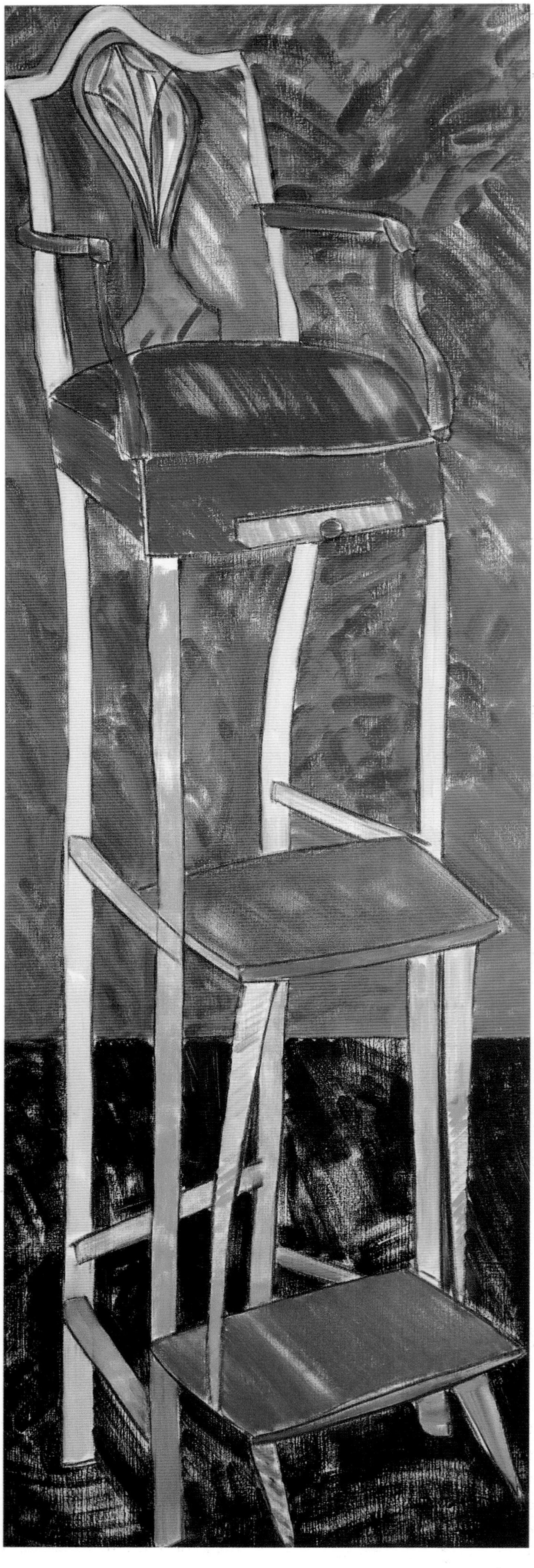

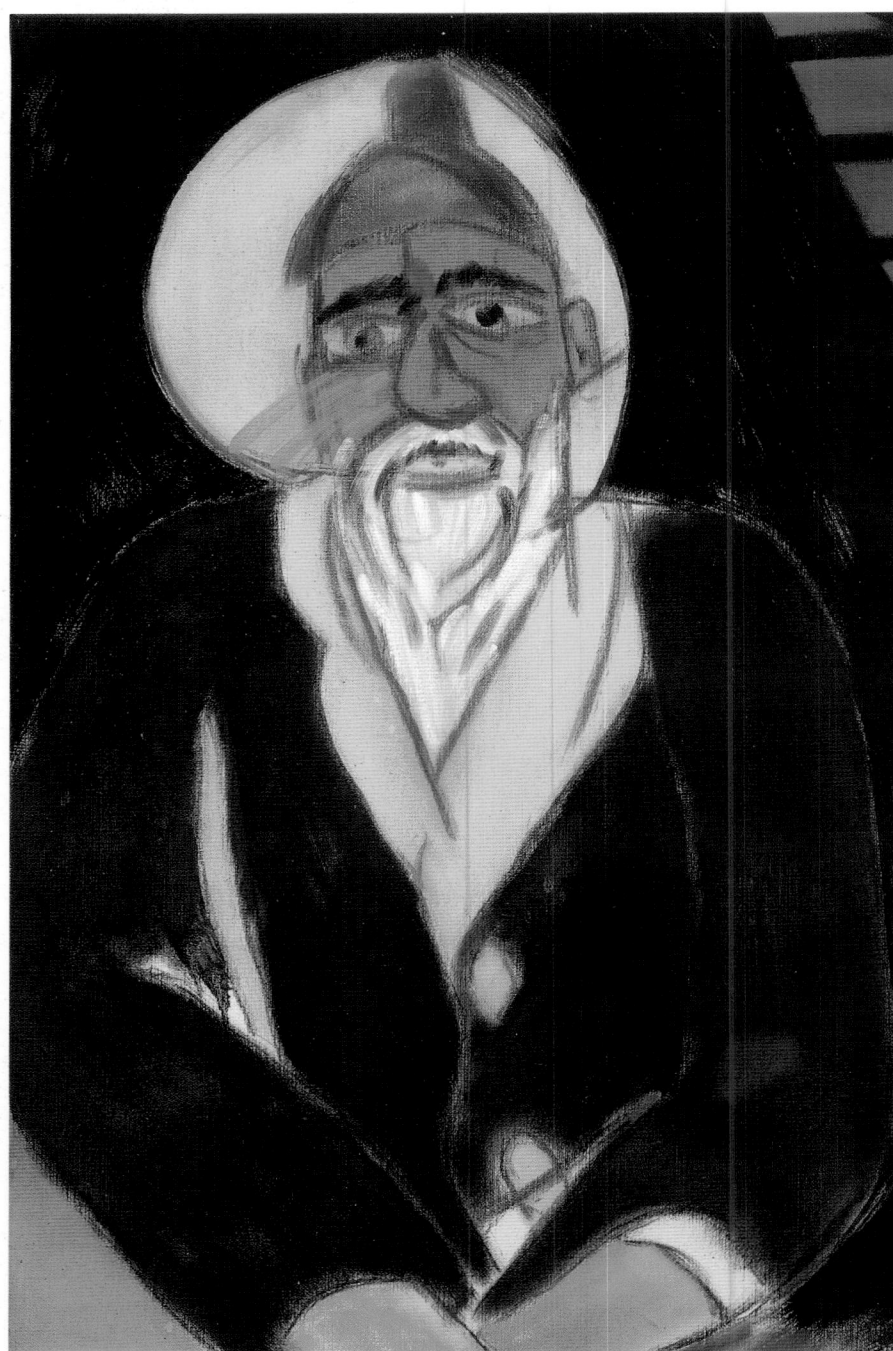

198. Moonlightist, 1998. *Cat. no. 644.*

197. *(left)* Circumcision Chair, 1998. *Cat. no. 645.*

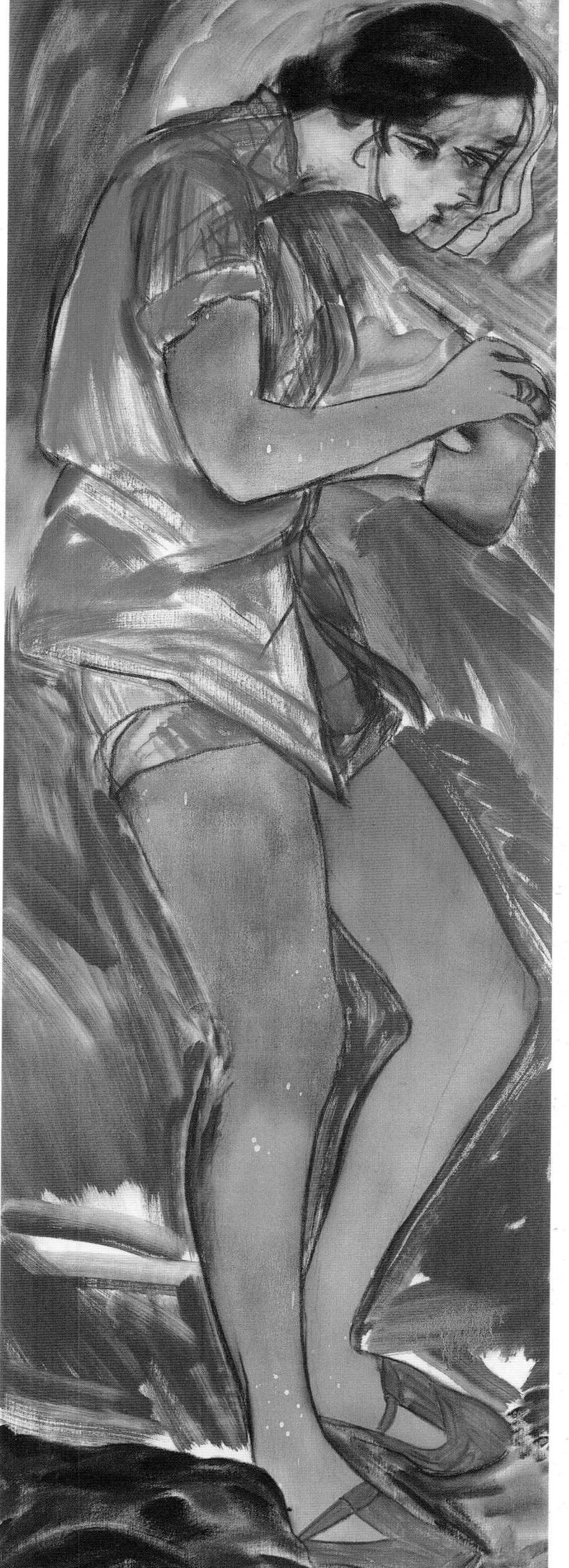

199. The Archaeologist, 1997-8. *Cat. no. 642.*

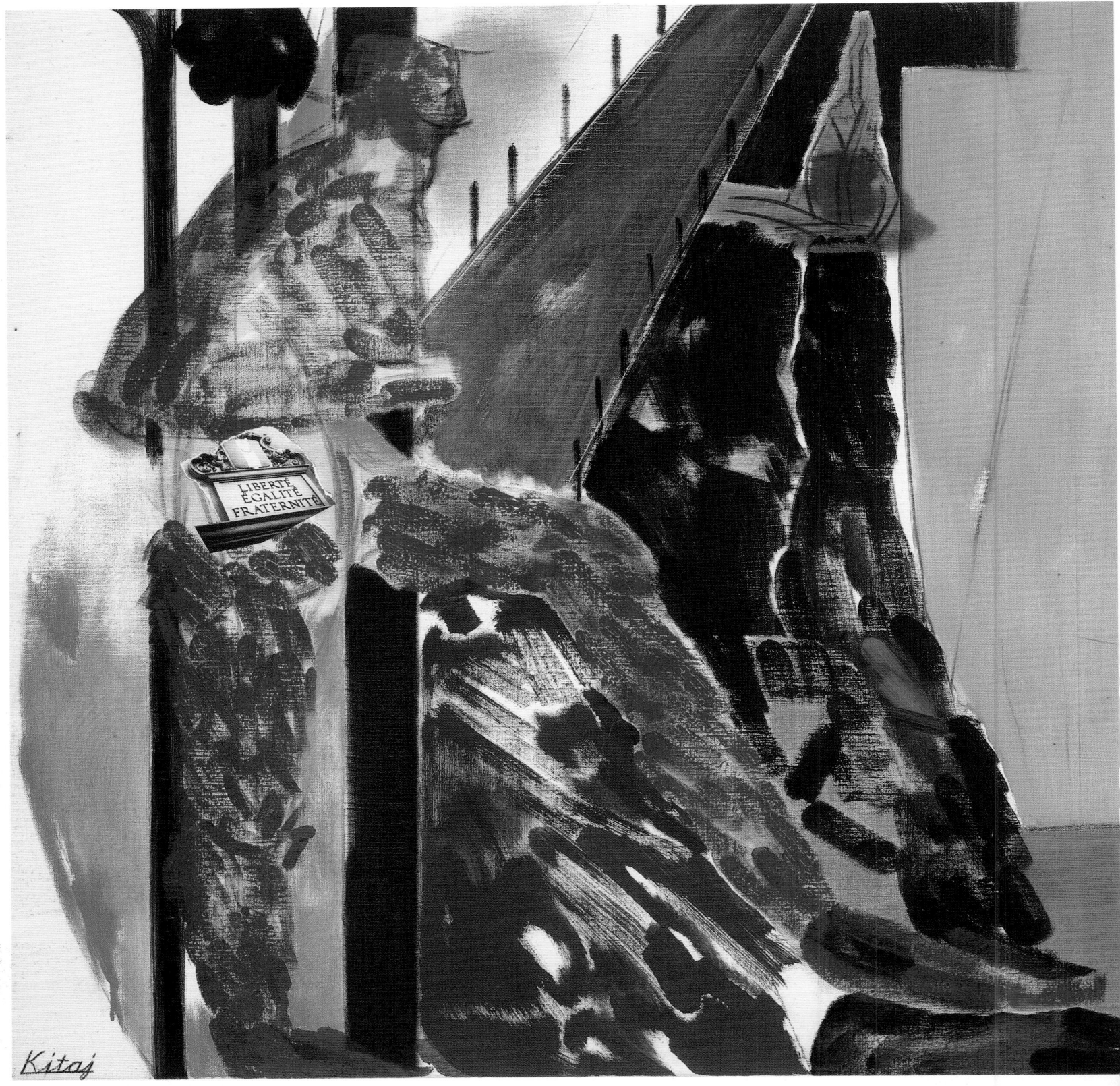

200. *(above)* The Parist, 1997–8. *Cat. no. 641.*

201. *(above right)* Koufax, 1998. *Cat. no. 647.*

202. *(right)* Bed and Sofa (After Abram Room), 1998. *Cat. no. 646.*

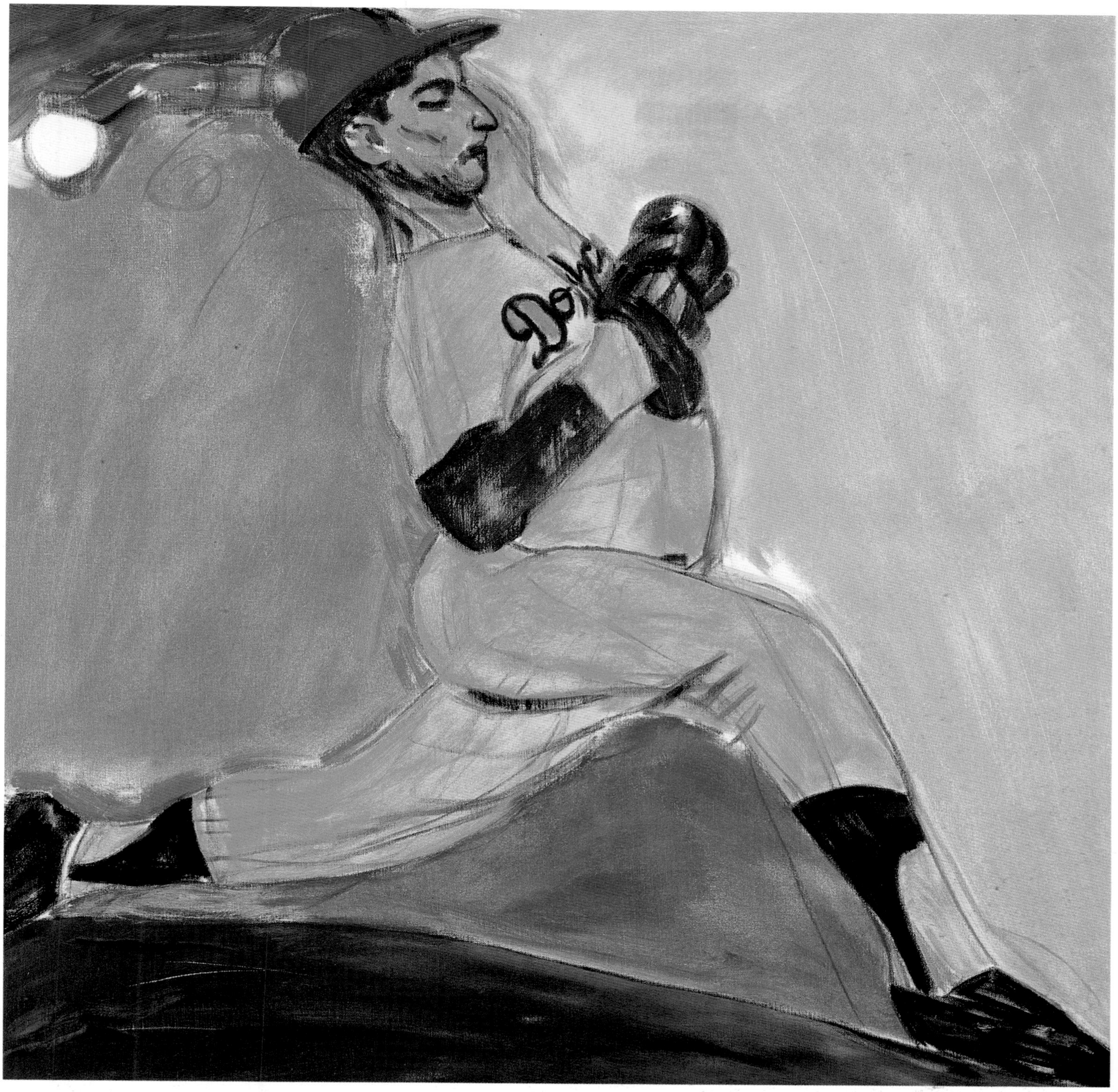

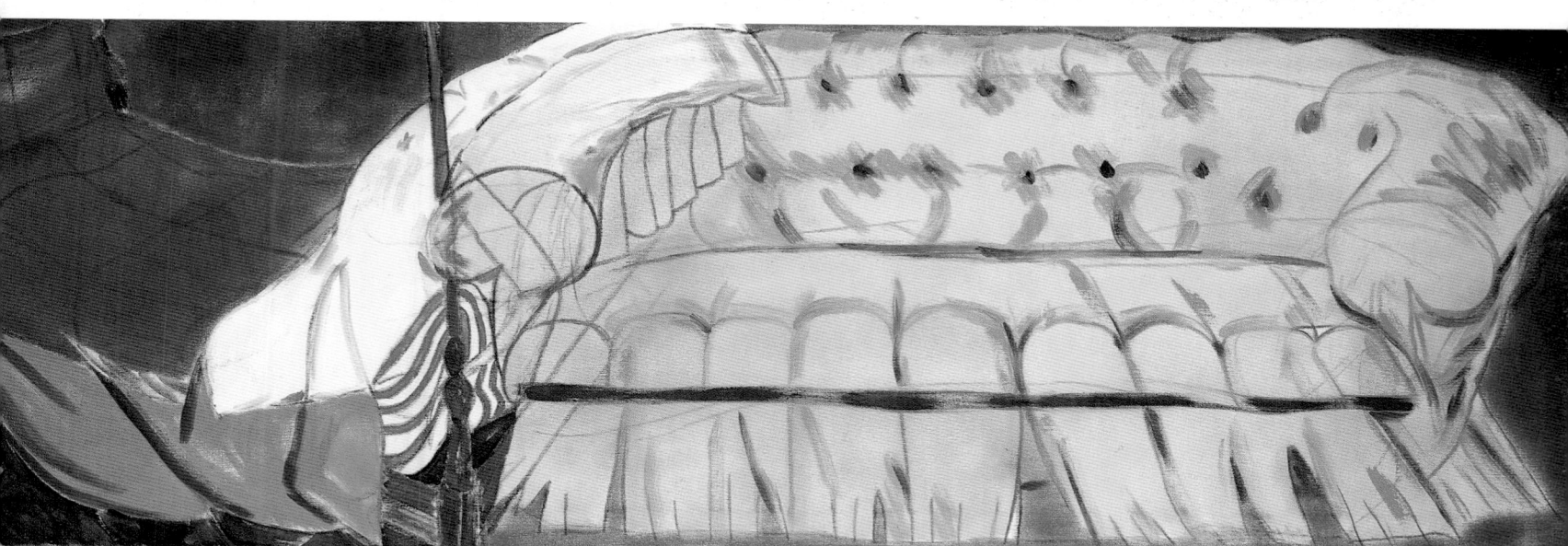

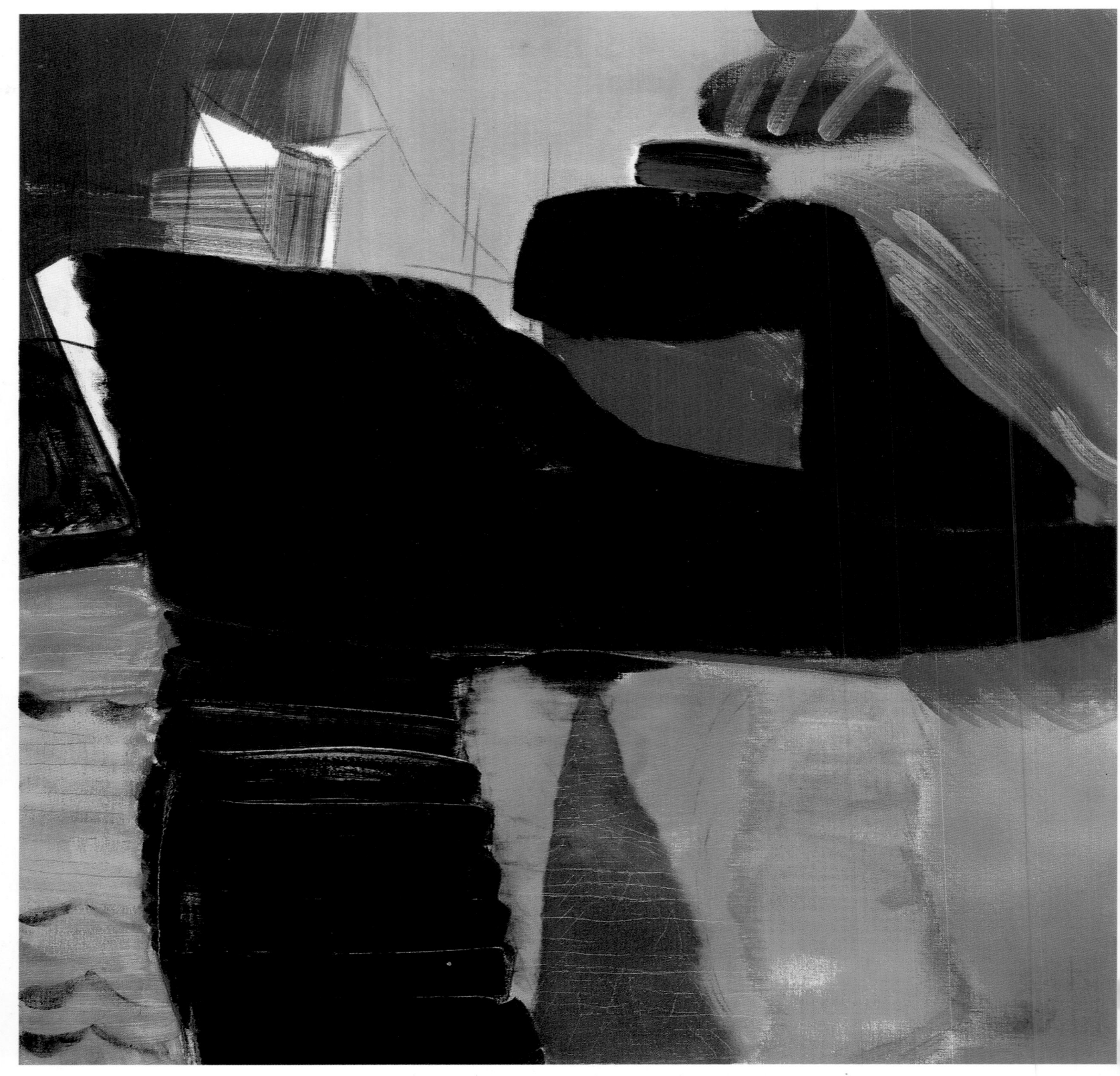

203. My First Ship, 1996–8. *Cat. no. 639.*

Gentlemen never explain
JOWETT

Thomas Hardy wrote to an unfriendly critic that 'there is no enlightened opinion sufficiently audible to tempt an artist.' I guess it was a sarcastic rejoinder, but as much as I like Hardy, I don't believe it. All artists in my time are tempted by the quarrelsome opinions enlightening our age, but being a herd of loners, few will own up. Some say that a good work of art *is* an end in itself (Cynthia Ozick calls that 'idolatrous' in her religious-covenant view). Others want to believe that art is an ally in their own version of the moral life (I've even heard said that art is the moral life). Opposite opinions like those do tempt me, but not every day, and only in uneven dosage. A third world of underdeveloped opinion, just as wobbly as the other aesthetics, may be called biographical heresy. Some of the lines of that heresy can be traced in what follows and in the uncertain prefaces to some of my certain paintings. If you have a weak stomach for such things, don't read on because I don't wish to offend. When I was a young painter, I wrote that some books have pictures and some pictures have books. As often as not, books (and pictures in books) happen to uncover many of the terms of my painting addiction, as landscape does for some painters. All histories and religions have both written and oral traditions which explicate each other because one or the other alone may not convey ultimate meanings. So may the painting-religion have these two traditions, its visual tradition fuelled by the other two, and its little sensations arising from ideas as they can from staring at mountains.

I'd like now to make an arguable general claim and a more easily defensible personal one: my experience of painting and painters tells me that the written and oral work opens a hell of a lot of doors into the painter's world of ideas ... and, speaking for myself, the spectres in books have attracted me all my life toward a dimly perceived crossway where even a false scholar (and not very retentive reader) like myself seems to arrive, by some natural (inherited – Jewish?) order of things, at painting by way of the word, which may come on some days before art and chance for a few of us, as it was said to in the beginning. A ratiocinative case is harder to make for straight drawing, upon one's sensations after life, but who's straight?

Harold Bloom has written, in a fearful essay about the survival of the Jews (as a Jewry) of their 'text-centeredness', their 'text-obsessiveness'. I believe that one of the most touching gifts this refractory people of mine has left to our painting art, to its cosmopolitan modernism, is justly described by Bloom's terms. Even Rothko, in his visual purity, has been called 'Yaweh's Stenographer', which is funny and great. It's a complex, untold story, brimfull of unspoken interest and taboo. I'm not learned enough to tell it but I do know that my own life in art has been illuminated by just talismanic centeredness ... to do with my own painting.

O.K., text-centeredness and biographical heresy; uncommon modern painting senses which don't replace good old ones like Make it New, truth to materials, and art for art's sake. I'd like to center the rest of this heretical text on Robert Lowell's line:

Yet why not say what happened?

All paintings tell what happened to the artist (not only depictive, narrative or naturalistic painting). In that sense they are all autobiographical and some of this may be confessional, which I take to be more of an intentional act like its counterparts in religion, therapy, poetry and friendship. The formalist churchmen and the biographical heretics both tell what happened (to them). As surely as intelligences are dispatched (or whispered), you know, just from seeing what you see in the painting, in its dispositions and touches and allegiances, a lot about who did it. Not everything, by a long shot, because of the separation of powers between painting and painter, which places the one over here and the other over there, thus blunting *real* frankness. That's one of the moments where words flourish as secret agents for painting, like these prefaces, or anything or anyone else who (so often) tries to tell what happened to the picture that tells about the life. Many, many painters claim to paint in a new language. Well and good, but even old languages have to suffer translation for most of us who want that, which brings me to these prefaces and to the last few things which I can only glance at here. They are among the first things that excite me now about my own art prospect.

Hemingway told Fitzgerald we're all bitched from the start and that we have to use that hurt; … I think the modern term is *identity*, and its art can be the examined life, which is not very heretical after all. There are even a very few strong voices around, such as that of I.B. Singer, who say that good art springs from one's tribe. He once wrote: 'Only dilettantes try to be universal; a real artist knows that he's connected with a certain people.' Singer knows he has a people; I seem to have almost three. The one which tantalizes me the most these days is the one the Koran calls the book people, and a few years ago I set about learning something of them (and me).

My idea of art is to make picture-studies, to act upon what can be learnt about the world (according to one's sensations) in these 'studies'. My idea of art is that even though you stay in your own room a lot, you still find out about the world; you *find*, like Picasso said, disguises of things learnt which become new and discrete (paintings) in a changeful history of subjectivity. My idea of art is that it conceals and reveals one's life and that what it confesses, is as Kafka called it 'a rumour of true things'.

I began all this by disagreeing with Hardy. Now I want to end by agreeing with the eternal art flame which burns away behind those angry words of his. My pictures and their evidences (as in these next prefaces) are not everyone's cup of tea; I know that. But our sainted Emerson spoke for me as I could never do when he said in his Divinity School Address: 'That is always best which gives me to myself. The sublime is excited in me by the great stoical doctrine, *obey thyself.*'

*for my son Max,
a few hours old,*

R.B. Kitaj, 1984

Junta, 1962 *Plate 31*

I meant to illustrate, to invent the (imaginary) members of a benign revolutionary government, so it's an early form of the idea I took up ten years later (Orientalist, Arabist, Marrano, etc.), that painters should be able to make up characters, like novelists always do in so many ways. A very few of those ways are: only slightly after the life (of someone known); composites taken from one's more general experience of people; figure-inventions (like Ratapoil and Macaire) meant to strike as lasting or glancing a blow as an artist can ever expect to commit against perceived wrong; disguised self-portraits, and so on.

Junta was painted partly in Catalonia and grew out of my friendship with Josep Vicente which began in 1953. He used to talk fondly of the grizzled old anarchists he would introduce me to and of how well they fought in what he still calls 'our war' and of their only very brief historical success, organizing some coastal villages before oblivion came down on them and Europe. The fifth, last panel in my painting was modelled after Durruti, the anarchist leader who fell, and the others are composite inventions. The bomb disguised by flowers was a favourite anarchist number and the doppelgänger above the bomb was meant to symbolize ideological compromise in such United Fronts; figures in tandem, often doomed to split apart or to murder each other in the name of some purity or other. Such fronts or their shadows are with us today, everywhere, even in England, so if my old picture seems like a backward glance, it was a student work, and everything else is past as well; even last week's dramas. Paintings may stop time in its tracks though, in homage, in reverie, in elegy, in remembrance, in fear and trembling … all more or less honorable things. My characters should have names maybe, to make them more real and memorable (the way I, for one, like to remember Greta Prozor, Eva Mudocci, Yvonne Landsberg, etc.), so I may give them names some day, which task will keep the old painting alive and unfinished in my mind at least.

Perils of Revisionism, 1963 *Plate 45*

The Chinese and the Russians had just begun their great split-off and they were accusing each other of Revisionism and its Perils. Schism, I think, is a good subject for painting; splitting, dissociation, free association are said to manifest self-awareness in psychoanalysis, and not a bad business at all. The question of a picture's integrity or not is very unresolved in my own interest and practice. Pictures can be split, as against the concern for a picture's unity and coherence prevailing in art theory during the first part of my life (which theory I also rather like) – thus, one of my primitive attempts here at dissociation. Like Splitting, Revisionism has good and not so good aspects in history and in art. Not too good are its reactionary, dogmatic, fanatical, fundamentalist impulses. What seems sweet to me is to revise art and politics for the sake of keeping good things alive, changed and renewed – like social democracy and depictive drawing for instance, and our various freedoms. To be sure, one must turn away from consensus of opinion; one must break ranks (especially the ranks of the faithful), but Revisionism still imperils as ever (Khomeinism, Jabotinskism, etc.).

I made this picture long before I saw Michelangelo's Last Judgement wall in the Sistine Chapel, I guess my favorite (big) painting of all time. When I came to do the imperilled Chinese figure clutching his face in horror, I only had a tattered reproduction of Michelangelo's great Sinner from *Life* magazine (kept since I was a kid). He suddenly realizes he's condemned to Hell forever, which somehow exercises me more and more as I grow older and realize that old age isn't so bad when you consider the alternative.

Dismantling the Red Tent 1964 *Plate 29*

'Mean something! You and I, mean something! Ah, that's a good one!' SAMUEL BECKETT

Kennedy had just been killed and I meant *Dismantling the Red Tent* to paraphrase the surprising longevity of an American democracy which works pretty well, which I rather like, and which belongs to a quite rare species: government by consent. I've been told by experts that democracy, about two centuries old and experienced by only a tiny minority of people, may have been an historical accident whose days look numbered. As often as that thought scares me, another, similar intelligence keeps sneaking up on me, about our art – that this art, with which you and I try to mean something, and about which so few of us agree, for all its modern attractiveness, seems (to me anyway) a frail exercise, like democracy itself, practised almost hopelessly at the far margins of a vast world bent on the destruction of democracy by Men Without Art.

The Red Tent was a beacon used by polar explorers in the wastes. Men could return to it in some hope. Around the time I painted the picture, I was becoming a very suspicious reader of the left certainties which swirled about my youth and I designed a nice Red Tent to come to, not from the God That Failed so many others but just out of the cold for a moment. Coming in to warm from the cold I take to be one of the meanings of art, and the political men in my picture (some hollow, some not) hover about the Red Tent for warmth after a regicide, a perpetual play of governance by consent in what Hannah Arendt called 'the public space'.

Twenty years later, I wish this little mystery-picture had been more profoundly painted because I like its terms even more deeply now than I understood then.

Walter Lippmann 1966 *Plate 40*

Every day since I was in high school I read political criticism of many stripes. In the beginning was the word, and a columnist I often read said that the picture was not far behind.

Although this painting is a little too oblique for my taste, it's one of my few favorites among my pictures because I'm so pleased with the configurational debt it expresses to this type of journalism I read each day, that I fancy some of the pleasure I've had from columnists, like the pleasure another painter may get from trees or ancient ornament, has translated into the painted correspondences I've collected here. Now, people like Lippmann, Aron, Izzy Stone, Conor Cruise O'Brien and George Will write clear prose for their millions of readers, but perhaps I can be forgiven the difficulty of the stream-of-consciousness into which the parts of my picture flow if only because the eventful world those editorialists try to explain doesn't really come to order very often either. So, in my own practice, some art is fairly straight and some need not be, just like news, and, like stale news and ancient art, some of the original meanings in this picture are lost.

W.L., at stage right, is the voyeur and explainer of complex events he was in my youth. I took the liberty of embroidering those serious events in terms of romance, intrigue, spies and alpine idyll, like movies did in those days, often made by refugees, themselves escaping from serious events. When movies were first shown, the form was so new and unusual that most people found it difficult to understand what was happening, so they were helped by a narrator who stood beside the piano.

Juan de la Cruz 1967 *Plate 61*

Interesting about Vietnam …. (and art) …. Heresies and orthodoxies are always changing places, just as the line between heresy and orthodoxy in St Juan's time was very fine indeed. Many people saw the Vietnam war as something clear-cut, evil against good. Now, only a few years later, many of those same intellectuals are not so sure. Communist Vietnam, ally of Communist Russia, at war in Communist Cambodia, ally of Communist China … Cambodia itself the scene of a Communist Genocide against its own people. How nutty can the world get? That one's a corker. So was the Inquisition and Juan's harassed 49 years in and out of its claws – born to an underclass, like my Sgt Cross, torn between devotion to his calling and tradition on the one hand and St Teresa's Reform on the other, like the American Black must have been in Vietnam. The subtitle of this picture is *Dark Night of the Soul*, after Juan's famous prose work. I was somewhat, but not overly curious about mysticism in those days. I loved the small body of poems written by St John of the Cross (mainly in prison) even though the Christian and Jewish mystics have always communicated something to me beyond any real understanding, which may be quite appropriate because mystical experience is said to be ineffable, a denial of any familiar experience, anyway. Mystics are said to discover a new world, very different from our familiar one. This is very much one of the things I like to think a painting might be – a discovered world, an unknown, made of assonances, surprise associations and this and that … his picture and other, better ones.

The Mystic enjoins a new kind of love, remote from hot sensual love, after a sort of death which purges (Vietnam?). My poor and maybe tasteless couple to the right of Juan celebrate a blasphemous mystical union. Bridgeroom and Bride are St John's own symbolic forms for this union. St Teresa, whose protégé was St John of the Cross, is made to walk the plank by Inquisitors … Juan's poems express Christian Mystery; the Vietnam wars are most awful expressions of political mystery, the mystery of Realpolitik; so the painting is a Mystery-picture. The very mysterious origins of St Teresa and her Juan intrigue me at a personal level – St Teresa was of proven Jewish origin; St Juan's possible Jewish descent is unproven. Teresa's grandfather was accused by the Inquisition of having relapsed into Judaism, and so on …. It's a long story, like art. I was just beginning, when I made this picture, to become fascinated with secret Judaizers and such mysteries.

The Autumn of Central Paris (after Walter Benjamin) 1972-3 *Plate 57*

Dear Benjamin is now a truly chewed-over cultural spectre, not least in art writing. I started to chew on him myself in the late sixties after having fallen upon him, before the deluge, in a publication of the Leo Baeck Institute. His wonderful and difficult montage, pressing together quickening tableaux from texts and from a disjunct world, were called *citations* by a disciple of his who also conceded that the *picture-puzzle* distinguished everything he wrote. His personality began to speak to the painter in me – the adventure of his addiction to fragment-life, the allusive and incomplete nature of his work (Gestapo at his heels) had slowly formed up into one of those heterodox legacies upon which I like to stake my own dubious art claims – against better judgements of how one is permitted to burden the crazy drama of painting. When I first showed this picture, a reviewer even began his attack by choking on the title, which he said I'd stolen from a sociological treatise having nothing to do with Benjamin. The critic was dead right. Benjamin thrills me in no small measure because he does not cohere, and beautifully. He was one of those lonely few who lived out Flaubert's instruction: 'Not to resemble one's neighbor; that is everything.' A lot of people, a whole lot of artists would wish for that, I think, but it eludes us more than we imagine it does. His angry neighbors drove him to kill himself in that very Autumn of 1940 which saw the Fall of France and in which I've set this picture, some of my working notes for which follow below. I feel I ought to apologise for this type of painting because it's such a rouged and puerile reflection upon such vivid personeity, but maybe I won't (apologise); maybe a painter who snips off a length of picture from the flawed scroll which is ever depicting the train of his interest, as Benjamin did, *may* put a daemon spirit like Benjamin in the picture.

Citations (sketchbook entries for Benjamin painting)

B's montage practice, which he called 'agitational usage'. See fractured *suggestion* in *trompe-l'oeil* example … (things covering up, overlapping other things, fooling the eye in painting depiction …).

THE DIORAMA ('for the last time, in these DIORAMAS, the worker appeared, away from his class, as a STAGE-EXTRA in an IDYLL'). Painting as *Diorama/Tableau* (ask Cleveland Museum if they still have those dioramas they showed in my childhood; also sculpture of workmen (by Max Kalish?) I must have seen those dioramas as B was about to die in 1940.)

Café-life as an AUTUMNAL REVERIE of bourgeois society; NATURE MORTE; café as OPEN-AIR INTERIOR (past which the LIFE OF THE CITY moves along).

Collage implication in B's treatment of THE BARRICADE; B cites barricade metaphors like: 'broken irregular outlines, profiles of strange constructions' – from *Les Misérables*.

PILE-UP (BARRICADE) of figures as in THE MOVIES POSTER.

THE SMOKERS; THE PASSERBY; MEN ABOUT TOWN; RUMOUR and IDLENESS; THE COCOTTE IN HER DISGUISES; OCCASIONAL CONSPIRATORS; THE SWIFT GLANCE; CROWD AS REFUGE; CHANCE (as a guide through city-life); PROSTITUTION (the life of the erotic person in the crowd); FETISHISM (as the 'vital nerve of fashion'); PROLETARIAT driven out of CENTRAL PARIS (title) leading to emergence of a RED BELT (margins of picture).
ANGEL OF HISTORY – IDLE STROLLER face turned 'toward the past', blown backwards into the future by the storm of progress while the pile of ruins before him grows skyward (PILE-UP of images).

MAN WITH HEARING-AID … THE POLICE-SPY/SECRET AGENT.

THE MAN WALKING AWAY … B's suicide? (the *flâneur's* last journey: death … 'to the depths of the unknown to find something new' – from *Flowers of Evil*).

The Street (A Life), 1975 *Plate 136*

Baudelaire said there is no exalted pleasure which cannot be related to prostitution. Now, that's the strong stuff of some very great poetry, but my own exalted pleasures are far less exclusive, while my most exalting sense of a modern art is, I think, an art of Renewal in which one's own changeful poetics, mind-sets, nerve systems, fired by the ups and downs and dreadful secrets of one's modern lives, seize up and become pictures. Of all modernist Sleep-walkers, Benjamin set a renewing pace (for a possible big-city art) quite familiar to me as he prowls those networks of streets he says prostitution opens up 'across the threshold of class'. Strangers are drawn (alone in crowds) into these districts of minor crime where one is allowed but does not belong (like some Diaspora), where danger, in its very excitement, has been known to feed the art of the quiet studio. Among those loveless alleys (where Baudelaire says he found both love and God), which are, like pictures, the same and different across the world, I have always been enchanted by an art-god plying there, as Benjamin, Picasso and Degas were. I don't mean to exalt this little pastel illustration of mine. It's just a memory-aid styled after the jacket of a pulp thriller. Each painter has his own minor deity who looks after the special art interests of his client. In this pastel, mine is talking to the woman in The Street. I think it's not the first time I'd drawn him but he is my own creature, who appears through the ether, like Daumier's Ratapoil, to agitate and excite the stuff of life into pictures recollected in tranquillity. He can act unspeakably but always in the name of my art.

If Not, Not, 1975-6 *Plate 92*

Two main strands come together in the picture. One is a certain allegiance to Eliot's *Waste Land* and its (largely unexplained) family of loose assemblage. Eliot used, in his turn, Conrad's *Heart of Darkness*, and the dying figures among the trees to the right of my canvas make similar use of Conrad's bodies strewn along the riverbank.

Eliot said of his poem, 'To me it was only the relief of a personal and wholly insignificant grouse against life; it is just a piece of rhythmical grumbling.' So is my picture … but the grouse here has to do with what Winston Churchill called 'the greatest and most horrible crime ever committed in the whole history of the world' … the murder of the European Jews. That is the second main theme, presided over by the Auschwitz gatehouse. This theme coincides with that view of *The Waste Land* as an antechamber to hell. There are (disputed) passages in the poem where drowning, 'Death by Water', is associated with either the death of someone close to the poet or the death of a Jew … like most of the poem, these passages are fraught with innuendo.

The man in the bed with a child is a self-portrait detail in the waste-like middle ground which also shows scattered fragments (such as the broken Matisse bust) being sucked up as if in a sea. This sense of strewn and abandoned things and people was suggested by a Bassano painting, of which I had a detail, showing a ground after a battle. Love survives broken life 'amid the craters' as someone said of the poem.

The general look of the picture was inspired by my first look at Giorgione's *Tempesta* on a visit to Venice, of which the little pool at the heart of my canvas is a reminder. However, water, which often symbolizes renewed life, is here stagnant in the shadow of a horror … also not unlike Eliot's treatment of water. My journal for this painting reports a train journey someone took from Budapest to Auschwitz to get a sense of what the doomed could see through the slats of their cattle cars ('beautiful, simply beautiful countryside') … I don't know who said it. Since then, I've read that Buchenwald was constructed on the very hill where Goethe often walked with Eckermann.

Land of Lakes, 1975-7 *Plate 100*

'Grub first, Art after.' BRECHT

I'm not an optimist, but the other night we were watching a television program about Lord Beveridge and his famous Plan to eradicate poverty in England, and the telly and I fairly glowed with warmth for the old man and his hopeful scheme for things to come. 'Good Government', I said to my wife. A minute later I thought: Bloody Hell, England owned one fifth of the world's body, against the will of those bodies, at the same time old Beveridge and his pals, like the Webbs, were designing 'beautiful eyes' for their island.

My pretty painting, *Land of Lakes* (with its beautiful eye), is an optimistic scenic view. It takes its first inspiration from a detail of Lorenzetti's *Effects of Good Government* fresco at Siena, said to be the first landscape of its kind to have survived, and its next influence from the 'Historic Compromise' I used to read about when this picture was being made, between the Christians and the Left (cross and red flag). There are no people in my landscape. They are holding their breath somewhere while a Polity is being determined from them in our own time. This impersonal meditation takes its name from the water which is the symbol of renewed life and which courses in the southern countryside from the north of the same land. If Good Government has been known to disguise Bad Government, then what can Picasso have meant when he said that art is a lie?

The Jew, Etc. 1976-9 *Plate 97*

I have long since resolved to be a Jew ... I regard that as more important than my art.' SCHÖNBERG

I've seen people wince at this title; sophisticated art people, who think it's better not to use the word Jew. Kafka, my greatest Jewish artist, never utters the word once in his work, so I thought I would. This name-sickness, which many Jews will recognize and understand in different ways, is so touching to me, that I've also given my Jew a secret name: Joe Singer. Now it's not secret anymore.

In this picture, I intend Joe, my emblematic Jew, to be the unfinished subject of an aesthetic of entrapment and escape, an endless, tainted Galut-Passage, wherein he acts out his own unfinish. All painters are familiar with the forces of destiny embedded in happy accident and other revelations and failures which inform one's painting days. In that way, I'd like to expose Joe, in his representation here, to a painted fate not unlike the unpredictable case of one's own dispersion in the everyday world. For instance, before long I may name Joe's fellow passengers, those you can't see unless I paint them in; even though there's not much room left. In fact, I've begun to people this train-compartment in my journal. One of Joe Singer's jobs relates to a tradition of our exile, which influences this picture, whereby living messengers are trained up, who take the place of books, in order to preserve a freshness of teaching, not endangered by date or dogma. Joe is the messenger-invention of my own peculiar dispersion (Galut), about which I learn more every day. His depiction on his expiatory pilgrimage, presides over what belongs to my sense of that changeful exilic condition and its uncertain art habits and futures, as in these beautiful lines about the Jews by the Catholic Péguy: '*Being elsewhere, the great vice of this race, the great secret virtue, the great vocation of this people.*'

The Orientalist 1975-6 *Plate 98*

I did not come to England as a refugee, nor did I emigrate here as so many did to America, but I stayed on, and it became a habit. Some people live out their lives in places they don't come from, assigning themselves to a strange race of men and an alien sense of land and city. Who is to say why they do what they do with their lives, or for that matter, why painters do what they do with their painting lives? This picture belongs to such questions. Getting dressed up in another culture is no more a mug's game, I guess, than dressing our pictures in the borrowings, trickery and deceit we all affect, which Degas likened to the perpetration of a crime. Speaking of tricksters, my Orientalist relates to Trevor-Roper's amazing book about Edmund Backhouse, the Hermit of Peking. The setting was inspired by Whistler's Peacock Room in Freer's Detroit house. The real subject here is un-at-homeness.

The Rise of Fascism, 1979-80 *Plate 94*

I used to mean these bathers to allude to the classic Fascist period only, but now I don't. The bather on the left is the beautiful victim, the figure of Fascism is in the middle and the seated bather is everyone else. The black cat is bad luck and the bomber coming over the water is hope.

The Sensualist, 1973-84 *Plate 1a*

'Cézanne! He was my one and only master!' PICASSO

I think Cézanne is my favorite painter too. This picture belongs some to one of my hobbies: trying to figure him, trying to figure his little and big sensations all over again. Pete Rose said: 'Nobody's got a book on me.' Cézanne could have said it. Maybe that's why he draws so many of us to him.

This (canvas) began life 11 years ago, the other way round, as a woman. You can still see her pink head upside down at the bottom. I don't remember who she was but I think she represents the real woman in the Sensualist's life in the repainted picture. This studio picture was not painted from life. First, I painted over the woman a kind of copy of the famous Cézanne male *Bather* of 1885 (itself painted after a photo). Then, the Titian *Marsyas* came to the Royal Academy and blew everyone's mind. I'd put a postcard of it upside down on my wall and meanwhile Kossoff, who'd been drawing from the Marsyas, gave us one of those drawings as a wedding present. The drawing was lying on the floor, again upside down, looking like a man walking, so I painted from that over my bather, which became the final version. All too artful, so I wrote ART over the mean street doorway, for Art's sake. In the end oneself is the making of it; not after life but about the life, I think Pound said. Titian came to exploit what has been called the victory of the subjective principle, then only recently prepared. The depiction of human proportions would always now turn on the mystery of subjective styles – never more so before or since Cézanne's bathers, bemused as they often are by a torsion like that in the dangling Marsyas, though not in the frontal magic of the great N.Y. Male Bather whose (implied) quadrifacial stance I grafted onto my tall canvas at first. I left his right hand on his hip as you can see, as an action between the crises of the torsion. In the end, the muscularity comprises frontal breast, three-quarter hips and profile legs, the transition or joining of which Titian seems to have beautifully fudged, for the sake of, I suppose, an animality.

Desk-Murder, 1970-84 *Plate 155*

The subject of this picture turns out to be hate. It was only upon reading the obituaries of Herr Walter Rauff that I knew my painting was finished. I hadn't touched it for many years, in its metaphysical desuetude, but the last stroke would be to give it this final title. Fourteen years before, I'd called it *Teste Study*, after Valéry's mindful Monsieur (based on Degas), who had so entranced my youth. Then, for a while, it was *The Third Department* … (political police; getting warmer). I think the new title is just right because the terms of the picture fit so well.

Herr Rauff, *Schreibtischtaeter* (Desk-Murderer), was dead, but I could now float this office picture out, with just a wee bit more confidence, into the same world in which his pals are still alive, including those who gave the Hitler-salute at his grave in Chile. Some people will laugh at my ignorance of the proper powers of the painting art (as if one *could* express an historical unhappiness), but I'll tell you, it makes *me* feel a little keener to get a painting to 'work' in my own way, and so there may be a very small art lesson in it. Let me go on:

Incredibly, there used to be a naval officer in my painting until I took him out years ago. Rauff, I just learned, had been a failed naval officer who turned to the SS after he was kicked out of the navy. At some point in the life of this picture, I stuck on a fragment of canvas and drew on it what looks like a contraption of some sort, emitting fume. Rauff was the guy who designed the mobile gas vans used by *Einsatzgruppen* in Eastern Europe before the German killing-centers became operational. At last I knew what my odd device was. I had even obliged fate by draping my composition in mourning black and sketching in an unlaid ghost. The murder office is empty and my banal picture of evil, like Rauff, is finished, its purpose, as Helen Gardner said of *The Waste Land*, altered in fulfilment.

Cecil Court, London WC2 (The Refugees), 1983-4 *Plate 143*

I have very little experience of water-lilies or ballet-dancers or jazz or long walks or wine or loneliness. Among some other things, I think I have a lot of experience of refugees from the Germans, and that's how this painting came about. My dad and grandmother Kitaj and quite a few people dear to me just barely escaped. One of the first friends to see this painting (a 75 year old refugee) said the people in it looked meshugge. They were largely cast from the beautiful craziness of Yiddish Theater, which I only knew at second hand from my maternal grandparents, but fell upon in Kafka, who gives over a hundred loving pages of his diaries to a grand passion for these shabby troupes, despised by aesthetes and Hebraists who were revolted by them. Painters are in the business of 'baking' (a plot device from Y.T.) pictures whose perpetration may be sparked by unlikely agents of conversion, which in Kafka's case really caused his art to turn when he met these players. Excited, according to my own habits, I began (in Paris, California, N.Y., Jerusalem and London), to collect scarce books and pictures about this shadow world, the trail of which has not quite grown cold in my own past life. I would stage some of the syntactical strategies and mysteries and lunacies of Yiddish Theater in a London Refuge, Cecil Court, the book alley I'd prowled all my life in England, which fed so much into my dubious pictures from its shops and their refugee booksellers, especially the late Mr Seligmann (holding flowers at left) who sold me many art books and prints. Another day I'll tell who the other people in the painting are supposed to be, whether aesthetes find such midrashic gloss and emendation revolting or not. For now, I must confess that I wish I could continue to paint the shopsigns in the spirit of a distinction made by my favorite antisemite, Pound, who said that symbols quickly exhaust their references, while signs renew theirs.

Amerika (Baseball), 1983–4 *Plate 152*

'The day Custer lost at the Little Big Horn, the Chicago White Sox beat the Cincinnati Red Legs, 3–2.' CHARLES O. FINLEY

About a year after I began this painting, a famous neo-Cubist friend took us to see a seventeenth-century Chinese handscroll by Wang Hui at the British Museum, which my friend said had changed his life. This very long (70 feet) Royal Inspection Tour down the Yangtse had confirmed for my friend his belief that one must (he must) set about representing the element of time in painted depiction, as Picasso had done to the end of his many days.

I thought the scroll was terrific but it didn't change my life. As you can guess, there were an awful lot of tiny people going about their business along that river, and what it tended to confirm for *me* was the unusual fun I was having at home, painting a whole lot of little baseball players on a vast metaphoric field, because painting is very rarely what I would call fun, in my own experience of doing it. The depiction of time, different kinds of time, had already deeply scored my baseball picture.

For most of my life I've lived thousands of miles away from real baseball and I've got to recollect such things past from an English setting which has warped time through these thirty years of mostly exile from the Summer Game; in fact, since my poor lost tribe of Cleveland Indians last won a pennant and began their three decades of decline by blowing four straight to Leo Durocher's Giants in the '54 Series. I sometimes fear my own decline began in that fall of 1954. Proust's sessions of sweet silent thought have deluded me into painted remembrance and I've not taken Satchel Paige's advice: 'Don't look back; something may be gaining on you.' Any baseball folk over the age of 50 who look hard will find that great man (Paige, not Proust) in my painting, as I remember him when Bill Veeck brought him up to Cleveland from the Negro League in old age.

This painting's title begins with *Amerika*, as will some others from time to time. Unlike Kafka, I've been there, know it well and get quite homesick for it, but Kafka's crazed, beautiful, unfinished book inspired me, years ago, to look at my exilic self in changeful ways. I would attempt to paint that selfhood, to reconstruct its homeland, as painters have always worked on machines, in the studio after sketches; only, my sketches would be sensory, invisible. One little sensation, for instance, arriving after I'd begun to dispose the players one sees from afar, was an unaccountable urge to open up the centre, either to show a clearing in the King's blue field or to endanger the players, to suck them toward a barren middle ground – I don't know which or why; not yet I don't …

I decided to paraphrase both Velázquez and Kafka, and so the great fieldscape of the Boar Hunt at London combined with a Cuckoo Nature-Theatre of Ohio and upstate New York; the Velázquez setting reminded me of the low hills of home which often framed the playing fields where we toiled at pick-up ball long after dusk blinded up. I was going to say how the little figures on that broad plain stand for the hundred ways that baseball lives mirror our own, teach me lessons – even *art* ones, but I think I'll leave that to the novelists for now and give these last words to Max Brod: 'In enigmatic language Kafka used to hint smilingly, that within this "almost limitless" theatre his young hero was going to find again a profession, a stand-by, his freedom, even his old home and his parents, as if by some celestial witchery.'

The Sculptor, 1992, *Plate 184*

This is a painting of a sculptor I know who is dying. When his wife died a few years ago, he fell into utter depression. Angry, he refused to contemplate that their life together had ended just like that, because their marriage had been so very good as marriages go – yes, happy even, in spite of what is considered to be his finest sculpture: *Who can be Happy and Free?* He borrowed that title from me, from a painting I'm still working on. His grief was so profound that I was shocked into delight when he began to work on a larger than life sculpture in order to recall, if not to relive, their marriage. It took me a while to see what he was up to … he wanted to keep the sculpture in a state of unfinish till the end of his own days. It is, perhaps, an original concept, to treat one's art as something which not only replaces the inertia of despair, which may be common enough, but to press art into a fiction which sustains an undying love. And then it was discovered he had a cancer, whereupon a transformation came upon him … he would continue to spend his days caressing his wife into art, as it were, but now he wanted to live long enough to finish his act, to climax one last time. He submitted to chemotherapy and other measures – that's why his hair is sparse and his skin looks flushed in my painting.

The sculptor is in a hurry now. His wife, impatient with her replica and eager for him to join her whether the damn thing is finished or not, appears at the enormous doorway to his studio, calling to him (so he tells me and as I've shown), just like she used to call him to put his tools down, wash up and get ready for the evening movie they would watch on television. Should he come to her in death as she insists? She is a spectre after all … or will he linger with her unfinished daemon, cleaving to what she was, or something like it in my painting?

Women and Men, 1991–3, *Plate 186*

This painting was inspired by my second favourite painting in London, *The Young Spartans* by Degas, which I had in my *Artist's Eye* exhibition at the National Gallery. I can't think of a sexier painting in my own experience of art and I can't think of another oil painting done before it which is so supremely drawing that it manages to suggest an exciting art form not tried out until then. Surely Matisse was encouraged by any number of Degas oil paintings in which drawing (as drawing) becomes at least as decisive as the thin painterly painting. For me, Matisse would bring this new kind of painting-drawing to an apotheosis of sorts in a picture like his *Violinist at the Window* of 1918, a painting I adore, which I try to visit every time I go to Paris.

I guess these are the two main themes in *Women and Men*, sexual drama and the idea of painting-drawing, both themes provoking each other, not unlike the provocation between the Spartan girls and boys. I prefer that each person makes up her/his own fantasy-story as to what's going on in my picture, if anyone's interested enough. But I will just say that as I enter my nightmare of sexual decline, I've noticed that I get a little less depressed as I take up sexual questions in my art with a new passion. I'm fascinated by all the furious sexual debates swirling around like crazy at the end of my century and I think that the hubbub maybe ought to take into account something I've noticed about our late modern art. It occurs to me that men and women are rarely seen together in paintings any more, at least they are not depicted together in heterosexual relationship in the work of the dozen or so very well-known painters I most admire. One must go back to late Picasso and early Balthus for this all too human stuff. Has our art been too exhausted by sophistication? Women and men will never be stale news in art. Women and men, as a subject in painting, can help bring beauty and good cheer and erotic pleasure back from wherever those things have gone. Amen and women.

Western Bathers, 1993–4, *Plate 187*

This is my first real Western. After sixty years of fumbling, I've become a fast gun, a regular shootist, and I did the damn thing within a one month shooting schedule. Western movies are among the happiest things in my life. In fact I own quite a few narrow escapes from boredom and desperation to their familiar intimacies, graces and subtexts, so I thought I'd better direct a Western picture or two before I ride into the sunset. My favourite painting in London is Cézanne's very late, absurd *Bathers* in the National Gallery. Sitting in front of it one day, the crazy figures looked like they were grouped around a campfire and so I got the idea for my first Western. I got a canvas the same size, in order to do my picture in the highest Western tradition and also the more specific genre which Matisse brought to a climax in his tremendous Chicago *Bathers by a River* and which Picasso pursued into the 1970s. I thought I'd try to get it up again, which is hard to do when you get to be sixty. Cézanne's *Bathers* are works of imagination, the opposite (in a sense) of his mode of observation, but I had to start somewhere, so I began to look at film-frames of Budd Boetticher's *Ride Lonesome* (1959) starring Randolph Scott and the heavenly Karen Steele. That got me going and then I adopted the techniques I love in Ford and Peckinpah of using a dependable stock-company to act the character roles. My own regulars are drawn mostly from figures and images in past art which tend to stay with me always – not unlike a habitual method of Cézanne and many painters from Michelangelo to Picasso. You want loyal friends around your campfire as a man grows older.

NOTES TO THE TEXT

1. All quotations from the artist, unless otherwise credited, are from my correspondence and interviews with him, dating back as far as April 1976 but primarily from August 1982, when I began research on this study, to July 1984. Although we remained in contact in later years, the correspondence for the final chapter of the revised edition took place essentially in October and November 1991. The artist has read through my complete text, and in doing so has made slight changes to his own writings for the sake of clarity. With regard to punctuation, ordinary ellipsis is the artist's own, but ellipsis in parentheses indicates that part of his text has been edited out by me.

2. 'I would get to encounter this viperish, cockeyed sort of genius in London in the late 60's just before he died, and I made a little painting of a ship gone on the rocks for a Dahlberg Festschrift.'

3. Another painting executed in 1961, *The Disinterested Play of Thought*, took its title from the same source. This picture is unpublished but a photograph of it is on file at Marlborough Fine Art, London.

4. On our first meeting Kitaj remarked that 'The great Surrealists, for me, are not the orthodox Surrealists, who are generally lesser artists, but people like Picasso, Bacon, Balthus, and so many others.' In a letter written several years later he expanded on his views of the movement: 'Surrealist ideas like bringing images together in unlikely and unfamiliar conjunction (in hope of producing magic), and other such ideas, attracted me when I was young. Now I can see that what may have seemed outrageous and valuable in that practice was often only an exaggerated form of what is substantial and even life-giving in *all* art ... I mean to say that so much of what I care about in art has to do with the unfamiliar, prodigious, surprising character of what a truly original artist does in his pictures anyway.'

5. 'Ernst certainly was, for me, the best of the orthodox Surrealists, but most of Ernst doesn't interest me. What did interest me were the great steel engraving collages: the *Semaine de Bonté*. I'm a bibliomaniac. I've been a bookman all my life. I remember when I was at the RCA I was chatting with a bookseller friend, and an old cockney man came in with a package under his arm and said, "This has been giving me nightmares for twenty years." It was the *Semaine de Bonté*, published in five parts in the 1930s. He sold it to my friend for two pounds and I bought it back for two pounds ten. I've still got it.'

Another artist whose work was grounded in Surrealist collage was the Scottish sculptor Eduardo Paolozzi, now regarded as one of the founders of Pop Art in Britain, whom Kitaj met on the occasion of a lecture by the other artist in Oxford. They formed a close but brief friendship after Kitaj's arrival in London in 1959 and went so far as to collaborate on two works: *Warburg's Visit to New Mexico* (1960-2) and *Work in Progress* (1962).

6. 'I saw Wind quite often. I went to all his lectures and classes and he invited me to his home a few times. Many years later, he surprised me by saying he had followed my progress as an artist after I left Oxford ... He was such an Olympian figure, I just never thought that he would make any time for new art.'

7. See *R.B. Kitaj*, exhibition catalogue, Kestner-Gesellschaft Hannover, 23 January-22 February 1970, cat. no. 122, for a reproduction of *Welcome Every Dread Delight*. In the exhibition catalogue *R.B. Kitaj: Pictures with Commentary/Pictures without Commentary*, Marlborough Gallery, London, February 1963, p. 9, cat.12, the artist himself provided the reference to Rudolf Wittkower, 'Marvels of the East: A Study in the History of Monsters', *Journal of the Warburg and Courtauld Institutes*, V (1942), pp.159-97.

8. In the 1963 catalogue, p. 5, cat.3, Kitaj referred to Gerta Calmann, 'The Picture of Nobody: An Iconographical Study', *Journal of the Warburg and Courtauld Institutes*, XXIII/1-2 (January-June 1960), pp. 60-104.

9. Mark Haworth-Booth, 'Kitaj / Brandt / Screen-play', *Creative Camera*, June 1982, p. 547.

10. Kitaj's new text about this picture was written after its purchase by the Tate Gallery, London, in 1980, in response to a request from one of the Gallery's curators to provide some information for the entry published in their *Illustrated Catalogue of Acquisitions 1980-82* (1984), pp.156-7.

11. Kitaj remarks that 'a feeling for Kafka touches, I believe, *Nietzsche's Moustache, Lemuel, Pariah* and other early things as well', and he reveals that, 'The central scene out of the window in the Toledo *Nobody* is taken from the Annagasse flat of my friend F.L. Sprague in Vienna – a distinctly Kafka-like place for a Kafka-connected picture (...).' *Notes towards a Definition of Nobody — A Reverie* (1961) is reproduced in the catalogue of the retrospective exhibition, *R.B. Kitaj*, Hirshhorn Museum and Sculpture Garden, Smithsonian Institution, Washington, D.C., 17 September-15 November 1981, cat. 6, republished in a slightly altered design by Thames and Hudson, London, 1983.

12. R.B. Kitaj, 'On Associating Texts with Paintings', *Cambridge Opinion*, 37 (undated: January 1964), pp. 52-3.

13. 'I was very very impressed with *The Wasteland* and I think I imagined it would be all right to append notes to and even *in* pictures. I thought maybe no one had done that before.'

14. 'On Associating Texts with Paintings', *op. cit.*

15. J. Huizinga, *Erasmus of Rotterdam* (London: Phaidon Press, Ltd., 1952), plate V. There were precedents in recent American painting for schemes by which the entire composition was based on a found source, e.g. *Washington Crossing the Delaware* (1953), a paraphrase by Larry Rivers of the famous picture by Emanuel Leutze, as well as the flag and target paintings of Jasper Johns, which achieved instant notoriety when they were shown in New York in 1958.

16. Garrick Mallery, 'Picture-Writing of the American Indians', *Tenth Annual Report of the Bureau of Ethnology, 1888-89* (Washington: Smithsonian Institution, 1893), pp.25ff. Kitaj refers to this study, unfortunately with an erroneous date, in the catalogue of the exhibition he held at the Marlborough-Gerson Gallery, New York, in February 1965, cat. 5, and on the surface of *Reflections on Violence* (1962).

17. Fritz Saxl, 'Warburg's Visit to New Mexico', *Lectures* (London: The Warburg Institute, 1957), vol.1, pp. 326ff. Kitaj quoted extensively from this chapter as an accompaniment to the painting *Warburg's Visit to New Mexico* (1960-2), on which he collaborated with Eduardo Paolozzi (1963 cat., pp. 7-9, cat.9). Closely related to this is another painting, *Warburg as Maenad* (1962), a detail of which is reproduced in the 1963 cat., p. 8. On p.15 of the same catalogue Kitaj reproduces a photograph of 'Warburg and a Pueblo Indian', from plate 231 of Saxl's *Lectures*, vol.II.

18. Saxl, 'Science and Art in the Italian Renaissance', *Lectures*, !, pp.117-24.

19. Saxl, *Lectures*, II, plates 62ff. For a further discussion of this picture see Richard Francis, 'The Red Banquet by R.B. Kitaj', Walker Art Gallery, Liverpool, *Annual Reports and Bulletin*, vols.II-IV (1971-4), pp. 84-7, and Walker Art Gallery, Liverpool, *Foreign Catalogue*, 1977, text volume, pp. 96-7

20. E.H. Carr, *The Romantic Exiles* (Harmondsworth, 1949).

21. Georges Sorel, *Reflections on Violence*, translated by T.E. Hulme and J. Roth, originally published in 1908. Kitaj refers to this book and identifies a number of the painting's themes and images in the 1963 cat., p. 9, cat.16, and in the 1965 cat., cat.14; the latter entry also includes a reproduction of the title page from the edition of Sorel's book which Kitaj owned.

22. Frances A. Yates, 'The Art of Ramon Lull: An Approach to it through Lull's Theory of the Elements', *Journal of the Warburg and Courtauld Institutes*, XXII, pp.115-73, and Yates, 'Ramon Lull and John Scotus Erigena', *Journal of the Warburg and Courtauld Institutes*, XXIII, 1960 (January-June), pp.1-44. These are listed by Kitaj in the 1963 cat., p. 5, cat.4. The reference is from p. 2 of the 1960 article.

23. The lines from Goethe's *Wilhelm Meister*, in Carlyle's translation, are quoted in the 1963 cat., p. 6, cat.8.

24. The drawing of a woman pulling on her stocking, collaged onto the surface in the upper register, is a copy after a study of a prostitute by Goya in preparation for plate 17 of the *Caprichos*. It is illustrated in André Malraux, *Goya: Drawings from the Prado* (London, 1947), pl.6. Kitaj has taken over the outline but not the style of Goya's drawing. The machine-gunners below, however, are drawn in thick smudged contours apparently achieved by dabbing the wet paint with a rag, in imitation of the effect of Goya's later sepia drawings (see, e.g., plates 68 & 72 in Malraux's book). For an analysis of the Goya image which Kitaj borrowed here, and of related themes in other prints from the *Caprichos*, see F. D. Klingender, *Goya in the Democratic Tradition* (London, 1948), pp. 87ff.

25. 1963 cat., p.3, and 'Painting: Literary Collage', *Time*, 19 February 1965, p.42.

26. Kitaj has produced two 'portraits' of Pound – a reproduction of the cover of his *How to Read*, in the *In Our Time* series (1969), and *Ezra Pound II* (1974), a screenprinted drawing of Pound upon a reproduction of a Matisse – as well as a third, *Yaller Bird* (1964), the title of which was taken from a Pound poem; the latter reproduces one of Kitaj's paintings of the same year, *Aureolin*. These, along with the pictures related to Eliot, are, says Kitaj, 'enough from a restless type like me, hungry for newer soul-food'. There was also a painting, *Cracks and Reform and Bursts in the Violet Air* (1962), the title of which – as Kitaj acknowledged in the entry on this painting in the 1963 cat., p.12, cat.20 was taken from line 372 of *The Waste Land*; the composition itself, with its collaged images laid out in horizontal rows, suggests the format of a poem.

27. See Kitaj's letter about this picture published in *R.B. Kitaj*, exh. cat., Kestner Gesellschaft, Hannover, 23 January-22 February 1970, n.p., and the note in the 1965 cat., cat.19.

28. Kitaj points to Lionel Trilling's introduction to the 1957 edition of Isaac Babel's *Collected Stories* (republished by Penguin Books, 1961) as an indication of his own, very similar, reactions to Babel's work. 'Trilling catches the complexity of the Babel conundrum. It was that complexity and ambiguity which determined my picture (and its failures). The discussions in Trilling about the place of Violence in the life of a thinking man, creative artist and much else is worth your attention. He also talks about *Benya Krik*. I had found an extremely

rare book in English by Babel called *Benya Krik*, which purported to be a film-novel (I think it was actually made into a (lost?) film). I used the cover unaltered in the *In Our Time* group (...).'

29. 'Rauschenberg', Kitaj recalled in 1976, 'had derived from De Kooning, Cornell, Duchamp and Surrealism and that context was very interesting in my youth.' More recently, he speculated that he must have seen the work of Rauschenberg and Johns in New York in the mid-fifties. 'I, too, had been fascinated by the collage and symbolising modes of the Breton circle as they (R. & J.) obviously were, but someone like Rauschenberg put his heart and soul into that practice; Johns too. I never did; I was too young and stubborn and confused to know where to row and I had no milieu to goad me (...).'

30. William Empson, *Seven Types of Ambiguity* (London, 1953), third edition (revised), p. 3. The book was first published in 1930.

31. See M. Livingstone, *David Hockney* (London, 1981), pp.18, 36 & 42, and M. Livingstone, *'Young Contemporaries' at the Royal College of Art, 1959-1962* (M.A. Report, Courtauld Institute of Art, London, May 1976), p. 7, for a further discussion of this influence.

32. Kitaj made periodic visits to San Felíu in the seventies but eventually sold his house there at the end of the decade, symbolically severing his relations with Spain with a final painting on the theme, *Goodbye to Catalonia* (1979-83). 'Something happened to me. I lost interest in a (Catalan) culture that was not my own. What the hell business did I have learning Catalan instead of Hebrew? My love affair with Mediterranean Romance from my youth had faded. I was approaching 50. The kids never used the house and Sandra and I hardly did. The Jewish interest, really close to the bone, was growing and so it was time to move on. I just sold the old house to a Catalan writer. So the place returns to its own. I feel heartsick about it.'

33. *The Times*, 7 February 1963. The reviewer was not named.

34. For instances of a figure reappearing from one work to another see, for example, the incorporation of the running figure from *Tedeum* (1963) into the screenprint *Go and Get Killed Comrade – We Need a Byron in the Movement* (1966), or the appearance of the same head in two prints made in 1967, *I've Balled Every Waitress in this Club* and *In his forthcoming Book on Relative Deprivation (Loneliness)*. The latter three prints are reproduced in the Hannover cat., *op. cit.*, cat. nos. 25f, 25j and 25k. The collage basis of Kitaj's screenprints facilitated such transferences and may have encouraged him in this new approach. In the mid-seventies Kitaj decided not to produce any more such prints, preferring to give himself to drawing or painting directly from the human figure; a decision which led him away from screenprinting in favour of etching and lithography. The experience of re-using elements from one screenprint to another, however, seems to have conditioned his attitude towards the recycling of images in his more recent work.

35. C.P. Cavafy, *Poems*, translated by John Mavrogordato (London, 1951), p.124.

36. The eight portraits, drawn in most cases from life on canvas and then transferred photographically to silkscreen, are of Robert Creeley, Hugh MacDiarmid, Ed Dorn, Robert Duncan, Morton Feldman, Charles Olson, Kenneth Rexroth and John Wieners. They are reproduced in the Hannover cat., *op. cit.*, cat. nos. 26a-h of the 'Complete Graphics' section. The Creeley print is titled *For Love* after the poem of the same name published in Robert Creeley, *Poems 1950-1965* (London, 1966), p.159.

37. Of this series, Kitaj remarks: 'The prints are very free collages, assembled in response to the Mahler Symphonies, not to Jonathan's

poems. Free Verse – like that. Jonathan loved Mahler and wrote his poems to the music. I came to Mahler then for the first time and did my visual poems to the music. They're kind of nutty but maybe not so bad as "citations" (in Benjamin's practice), aberrant quotations and pickings from the world. See also *The Tate Gallery 1968-70*, pp. 90-1, for further background and for the artist's comments.

38. See Van Deren Coke, *The Painter and the Photograph: from Delacroix to Warhol* (Albuquerque, New Mexico, 1972), pp.125 and 129 for a discussion of this painting and for Kitaj's reasoning in using the photograph as its source. The original film version of *The Front Page* was directed by Lewis Milestone in 1931; it was one of the first 'talkies'.

39. Benjamin wrote of 'the tremendous shattering of tradition' effected by films: 'Its social significance, particularly in its most positive form, is inconceivable without its destructive, cathartic aspect, that is the liquidation of the traditional value of the cultural heritage.' *Illuminations*, translated by Harry Zohn (Glasgow, 1973), pp.223; this translation was copyrighted in 1968 by Harcourt, Brace & World, Inc., and first published in Great Britain in 1970 by Jonathan Cape.

40. Kitaj says that although the painting has no direct connection with Josef von Sternberg's 1941 movie, *The Shanghai Gesture*, he 'used the title to suggest the same somnolent malaise of brothel life'.

41. See the letter by Kitaj written in July 1968 about this picture, quoted in *Contemporary Art 1942-72: Collection of the Albright-Knox Art Gallery* (New York in association with the Albright-Knox Art Gallery, Buffalo, New York, 1973), p.149, and the artist's new essay about this work published at the end of this book.

42. See Mark Haworth-Booth, *op. cit.*, pp. 546-9, for a fuller discussion of this picture.

43. *R.B. Kitaj: Paintings and Prints*, exhibition catalogue, Los Angeles County Museum of Art, 11 August-12 September 1965. On occasion Kitaj has produced studies for individual details, particularly in recent years, but it does not seem to be in his nature to build up the structure stage by stage in the form of compositional sketches or cartoons. He continued, instead, to improvise on the canvas itself, guided still by his instincts as a collagist. In contrast, though, to many of his contemporaries, Kitaj laid great stress on the role of under-drawing, which in his paintings of the mid-sixties to mid-seventies is generally allowed to remain visible right through to the finished painting, untampered, to the extent that the very weave of the canvas continues to be seen. The surface, in fact, often appears to have been rubbed down, so that one is left with a large scale drawing overlaid with a film of colour.

44. 'I wrote it because I was stimulated to collect my thoughts after a supper at my house with Clem Greenberg and Ken Noland which was so interesting, it sparked the polemicist in me.' For an account of the effect that this lecture had on the audience, see Timothy Hyman, 'R.B. Kitaj: Avatar of Ezra', *London Magazine,* August-September 1977, pp. 53ff.

45. The sculptures which Kitaj made for the Art and Technology project were collectively titled *The Lives of the Engineers*. Four of these pieces are reproduced in *R.B. Kitaj: Pictures from an Exhibition*, Marlborough Fine Art (London) Ltd,. April-May 1970.

46. The publication of Creeley's volume of poems, *A Day Book* (New York), followed in 1972.

47. See Pat Gilmour, introduction to *Kelpra Studio: The Rose and Chris Prater Gift*, exhibition catalogue, Tate Gallery, London, 9 July-

25 August 1980, pp. 32-4, and R.B. Kitaj, 'Chris – A Note Apropos', *Arts Review*, 5 August 1977.

48. See Kitaj's letter of 7 May 1974, quoted in the entry to *The Man of the Woods and the Cat of the Mountains* in the *Tate Gallery Biennial Report and Illustrated Catalogue of Acquisitions 1972-74*, pp.181-3, and his statement in 'Painters Reply ...', *Artforum*, November 1975, p.28.

49. 'R.B. Kitaj interviewed by James Faure Walker', *Artscribe* no. 5, February 1977, p. 5.

50. Robert-Macaire was the subject of one hundred lithographs published by Daumier between 1836 and 1838 and was based on the role of a swindler which had caught the public's imagination in a melodrama of 1823, *The Sign of the Turnip,* as played by a well-known actor of the time, Frédérick-Lemaître. Ratapoil was devised by Daumier during the Second Republic, in the wake of the Revolution of 1848, and was the subject both of sculpture and lithographs. 'This is the creature sent ahead when Louis-Napoleon travelled, to cheer him at railway stations, dispatched to the farms where peasants needed to be convinced and sent into alleys to club unlucky republicans.' Oliver W. Larkin, *Daumier: Man of his Time* (London, 1967), pp. 37ff and p.103.

51. George Heard Hamilton, *Manet and his Critics* (New Haven, 1954), p.152. For instances in Manet's work see, for example, the reappearance of the *Absinthe Drinker* (1858-9) as one of a larger group of figures in *The Old Musician* (1862), as well as the derivation from Old Master sources of such major paintings as *Le Déjeuner sur l'herbe* (1863), from an engraving by Marcantonio Raimondi after Raphael, and *Olympia* (1863), from precedents in Titian and Goya.

52. 'Michael Powell is a close friend and taught Lem a great deal; he even gave Lem a good part in his film *The Boy Who Turned Yellow*. They're still very close (...). Like he was to the young American directors (Coppola, Lucas, Scorsese et al) he was a legend to me and I've loved his films long before I met him (…). Anger, I only knew casually when he was camping out in a derelict house near me, here in London. I've only seen a few of his films. Yes, his life as a renegade is amazing. He's a Satanist, a follower of Aleister Crowley (...). No one ever knows where he is. He's always revising his strange book – *Hollywood Babylon*. Once in a blue moon he writes me from a blue moon. I brought Anger and Powell together because they admired each other. They're both quite mysterious and since I introduced them, I painted them together in their disjunction.'

53. This highly revealing essay, the first which Kitaj had written about any of his paintings for nearly a decade, was hung next to the picture when it was exhibited at the Hayward Annual, Hayward Gallery, London, 20 July-4 September 1977. It is printed in full in Michael Podro, 'Some Notes on Ron Kitaj', *Art International,* March 1979, pp.19-20. See also Podro's very pertinent discussion of this painting in the same article, pp.19-21.

54. See, in particular, 'The Task of the Translator' and 'On Some Motifs in Baudelaire', both published in *Illuminations*, *op. cit.*; see also the highly perceptive introduction to Benjamin in that volume by Hannah Arendt.

55. The small figure of a woman at the far left is from a photograph of British Troops, Londonderry, N. Ireland (1970), published without this title in *Is Anyone Taking Any Notice?: A book of photographs and comments by Donald McCullen. With phrases drawn from the 1970 Nobel lecture by Alexander Solzhenitsyn* (Cambridge, Mass., 1973), n.p. The bespectacled man holding a cigarette, whom one might assume to represent Benjamin, was, in fact, painted from a photograph of the American comedy playwright George S.

Kaufman, published in Kenneth Anger's *Hollywood Babylon* (New York, 1975), pp.196-7; Kitaj evidently used an earlier edition. I am very grateful to Frederick Leen for bringing these two sources to my attention. Among the films made from Kaufman's screenplays are *Once in a Lifetime* (1932), *You Can't Take it With You* (1938) and *The Man Who Came to Dinner* (1941).

56. See the entry on this painting in *The Tate Gallery Biennial Report and Illustrated Catalogue of Acquisitions, 1972-74*, pp.181-3.

57. Some of Kitaj's artistic friendships date back to his time at the Royal College, e.g. with Hockney, Adrian Berg and Peter Blake (who had left the College in 1956 but still had friends there), or to the period immediately after his departure, as with Francis Bacon (to whom he was introduced by Harry Fisher in 1962) and Richard Hamilton. Others, such as Lucian Freud, Howard Hodgkin and Frank Auerbach (whom he met while teaching at Camberwell in the early sixties), he has become close to only since 1970. The Israeli artist Avigdor Arikha, about whom he had heard much from Maurice Tuchman, he met in about 1971 and got to know particularly well in the year he spent in Paris in 1982-3. The one American artist included in *The Human Clay* (Arts Council of Great Britain, 1976) was Jim Dine, a fellow Ohian whom he had met in New York in January 1965 and with whom he shared an exhibition at the Cincinnati Art Museum in 1973. They were especially close in the mid-seventies, when Dine was making regular visits to London, usually staying with Kitaj, and when they were both drawing intensely from the human figure; Kitaj wrote a revealing introduction to the catalogue, *Jim Dine: Works on Paper 1975-76*, Waddington and Tooth Galleries II, London, 26 April-21 May 1977.

58. Catalogue to *The Artist's Eye, op. cit.* The sentiment echoed a half-jesting plea to be called a Post-Impressionist in the transcript, revised in December 1979, of the first interview we had held in April 1976. The mammoth *Post-Impressionism* exhibition shown at the Royal Academy, London, 17 November 1979-16 March 1980, was visited by Kitaj on numerous occasions. It made a great impression on him.

59. See especially the conversation between Kitaj and Hockney published in *The new review*, January/February 1977, pp. 75-7, and the interviews with Kitaj conducted by James Faure Walker, *Artscribe*, February 1977, pp. 4-5, and by George MacBeth, *Art Monthly*, April 1977, pp. 8-10.

60. Typescript of the lecture delivered by Kitaj at the synagogue in Oxford 25 November 1983, published in greatly reduced form as 'Jewish Art-Indictment and Defence: A personal testimony by R. B. Kitaj', *Jewish Chronicle Colour Magazine*, 30 November 1984, pp. 42-6.

61. Fritz Saxl, 'Continuity and Variation in the Meaning of Images', reprinted in *Lectures* (London: The Warburg Institute, 1957), vol.I, p.2, and in *A Heritage of Images* (Harmondsworth, 1970), p.14.

62. Two of these early life drawings were included by Kitaj in the opening pages of the catalogue of his April 1979 exhibition at Marlborough, New York, as if they were talismans of his current concerns.

63. Kitaj met José Vicente Roma during his first visit to San Felíu in 1953. 'Each day, at about noon, a young man leaned against the front of our house, in the winter sun, reading. His name is José (Josep in Catalan) Vicente and he became one of my closest comrades, like an older brother (10 years older), a guru, one of the handful of saintly creatures I've ever known. He was a clerk all his life in an ancient cork factory and a socialist idealist, always in danger under Franco.

He is a man of wide reading but hardly ever left San Felíu. *He* is the reason I returned over and over to San Felíu for many summers. Now he's the Mayor of San Felíu.'

64. See also the comment which Kitaj made in his interview with Tim Hyman, 'A Return to London', *London Magazine*, February 1980, p.24.

65. Hugh Trevor-Roper, *A Hidden Life: The Enigma of Sir Edmund Backhouse* (London, 1976).

66. Kafka represents to Kitaj 'Jewishness in danger'. He first read Kafka when he was at sea in about 1950, and then seriously in Vienna, 'where my life drew close to his own haunts and to his ghost'. Kitaj's renewed interest in recent years in his own identity as a Jew brought him back to Kafka 'in force', but he explains that 'I'm not interested in representations of *his* terms. I am interested in my own terms and how a work like *Amerika* helps toward what I sense to be an oncoming synthesis of those terms of mine.' In his 1983 Oxford lecture he said that 'To my way of thinking, Kafka was the greatest Jewish artist who ever lived; that is merely his measure in my own life-in-art, so you'll have to forgive me for invoking that strange man as much as I tend to do. You see, there has been, for me, no Jewish painter of that quality, that breathtaking invention.' See also Clement Greenberg's essay, 'Kafka's Jewishness', first published in 1956 and republished in his *Art and Culture* (Boston, 1961), pp.266-73, a highly stimulating interpretation of Kafka's work in terms of the Jewish condition. Kitaj regards this as one of the best things he has read about the writer.

67. Kitaj knew Edgar Wind's book, *Giorgione's 'Tempesta': with comments on Giorgione's poetic allegories* (Oxford, 1969), which speculates on the possible meaning of this picture as a 'pastoral allegory' rather than as 'free fantasy' or as an inexplicable story.

68. See Timothy Hyman, 'R.B. Kitaj: Avatar of Ezra', *op. cit.*, p. 55, and Michael Podro, *op. cit.*, p.21.

69. This essay has not been published, but includes background information incorporated into the new text printed in this monograph. Kitaj's painting is based on Ambrogio Lorenzetti's *Good Government in the Country*, one of four frescos on the theme of good and bad government in the city and country, painted in 1338-9 in the Palazzo Pubblico, Siena. In his monograph on *Ambrogio Lorenzetti* (Princton, 1958), George Rowley reproduces the four paintings, vol.2, plates 157-60, and discusses them in vol.1, pp. 99ff.

70. Kitaj worked from a reproduction in a magazine, but the image, a detail of Giotto's *The Funeral of Saint Francis* in the Bardi Chapel, Santa Croce, Florence is also reproduced in Cesare Gnudi, *Giotto* (London, 1959), colour plate LXIV. See also *After Giotto* (1976-9), which makes reference to *The Flagellation* in the Scrovegni Chapel, Padua (Gnudi, plate 111), without being a direct copy. Kitaj views the latter in the context of contemporary social and political issues: 'If you know the Giotto Christ being mocked, the transmutation into an American Black from the Giotto source is not so irrational.' Perhaps the closest of all Kitaj's borrowings from Giotto is the 1980 pastel *Red Eyes*, from a detail of *St Francis Appearing to the Bishop and Brother Agostino* in the Bardi Chapel (Gnudi, colour plate LXVII).

71. See the discussion of *The Jewish School* in Michael Peppiatt, 'R.B. Kitaj: pictures like novels', *Connaissance des arts*, September 1981, p. 33, and Frederic Tuten, 'Neither fool, nor naive, nor poseur-saint: Fragments on R.B. Kitaj', *Artforum*, January 1982, p. 66.

72. The head at the top centre of *Rock Garden* was derived from Jacopo Bassano's *Lazarus and the Rich Man*, which was one of the artist's favourite pictures in his childhood. For a reproduction of this

painting, see the *Handbook of the Cleveland Museum of Art*, 1978, p.114.

73. Kitaj says that his favourite painting in the National Gallery, London, is Cézanne's late, monumental *Bathers*, which he included in his *Artist's Eye* selection in 1980 and a detail from which he reproduced in the catalogue, *op. cit.*, cat.34. Another painting on this theme which he admires greatly is *Le Grand Baigneur* (1885-7, Museum of Modern Art, New York), of which he had a number of reproductions tacked on his wall while working on *Cecil Court* in 1983-4. Kitaj is fascinated by the derivation from a photograph of the painted figure, which is endowed with a convincing corporeal reality thanks to the functions of memory and experience. 'Cézanne transcended the photo because he was *Cézanne*, because his *moment* had come (1885), and it hardly mattered whether there was a model or a photo or just his imagination to work from. Even other wonderful things like the late Sickert paintings after photos are as nothing (to *me*) compared to *this* Cézanne. The reason lies in the greatness and mystery of Cézanne which I continue to ponder.'
     One of the series, *Bather (Torsion)*, is derived from Michelangelo's *Last Judgement*, which Kitaj calls his 'favorite painting of all time – a preposterous favorite'. Another figure from the same fresco had earlier acted as a source for *The Perils of Revisionism* (1963). The same reproduction from *Life* magazine was used by the artist in both cases.

74. The philosopher Richard Wollheim is, furthermore, a friend both of the two sitters and of the artist. The cover of his book on aesthetics, *Art and its Objects* (Harmondsworth, 1970), was designed by Golding. Wolheim himself was drawn by Kitaj in 1976 in preparation for a painting, *Three Philosophers*, which never materialized, and again in 1980.

75. Interview with George MacBeth, *op. cit.*, p. 8.

76. There are two versions of the Rubens *Portrait of Isabella Brant*, his first wife, both dating from *c.*1622: a painting acquired in 1947 by the Cleveland Museum of Art (reproduced in their 1978 *Handbook*, p.154) and a drawing owned by the British Museum, exhibited in the British Museum's 1977 survey, *Rubens: Drawings and Sketches*, and illustrated in the accompanying catalogue by John Rowlands both in colour (p.104) and black and white (p.115). Kitaj had thus had the opportunity to see both versions at first-hand. The Dreyer detail was taken from a book of frame enlargements from *Vampyr*, which Kitaj owns, and the cover of which he had used for one of the *In Our Time* prints in 1969.

77. Reproduced in Edward Braun, *Meyerhold on Theatre* (London, 1969), opposite p. 305.

78. See also Kitaj's comments in Hyman, 'A Return to London', *op. cit.*, pp.26-7.

79. In showing me his copy of *My Secret Life*, Kitaj remarked on the appeal of its Baudelairean flavour. 'It's about big city life and about the drama and fantasy which a person carries with him – and most people don't talk about it or admit to any of it. One wonders how many people *have* a secret life.'

80. Goya's *Self-Portrait with Dr Arrieta* (1820), reproduced in *European Paintings from the Minneapolis Institute of Arts* (New York, 1971), p. 504, is inscribed by the artist to his doctor, who 'saved his life during a painful and dangerous illness endured at the end of 1819 in the seventy-third year of his life'. The doctor is shown propping up his patient and offering him a glass of water, a scheme closely followed by Kitaj in his drawing.

81. The appropriation of the technique from Monet's late work is particularly apt in this instance, given the precedent of Monet's own

paintings depicting the garden which he had designed at Giverny as a peaceful retreat from the world.

82. The two versions of Balthus's *La Rue*, dated 1929 and 1933, had been known by Kitaj 'all my life', particularly as the later version was on display at the Museum of Modern Art, New York, during his youth. They are reproduced in *Balthus*, exhibition catalogue, Centre Georges Pompidou, Musée national d'art moderne, Paris, 5 November 1983-23 January 1984, cat. nos.2 and 8 respectively. Kitaj visited the exhibition with Sandra Fisher during their brief honeymoon in Paris just before Christmas 1983.

83. While working on *Cecil Court* Kitaj was looking closely at Venetian painting and made repeated visits to the exhibition *The Genius of Venice: 1500-1600*, which was on view during the winter of 1983-4 at the Royal Academy, London. Pinned to his wall were reproductions of two pictures from the exhibition, Titian's *The Flaying of Marsyas* (a major but little-seen late work from an eastern European collection), and *The Washing of Feet*, a huge painting from Newcastle-upon-Tyne's Cathedral only recently reattributed to Tintoretto; the figure at the far left of the latter supplied Kitaj with a suitable head for his portrait of Seligmann. The two paintings are reproduced in the catalogue of the exhibition (London, 1983), cat. nos. 132 and 101 respectively.

84. A photograph taken in 1929 of this chair in a setting also designed by Le Corbusier is reproduced in Henry-Russell Hitchcock and Philip Johnson, *The International Style* (New York, 1966), p.127. Another classic modernist chair, this time one designed by Alvar Aalto which Kitaj himself owns, appears in *The Hispanist (Nissa Torrents)* (1977-8).

85. The source for Kitaj's painting is Velázquez's *Philip IV Hunting Wild Boar* in the collection of the National Gallery, London.

86. Kitaj's son took his pseudonym from the character called Dobbs played by Humphrey Bogart in John Huston's *The Treasure of Sierra Madre*. By the end of 1991 he had worked on around ten films, of which four had been released: *Romancing the Stone*, on which he received no official credit, followed by *Hider in the House*, *The Hard Way* and *Kafka*, directed by Steven Soderbergh and starring Jeremy Irons. Disenchanted with the lack of control allowed to writers, he decided that the only way forward was to take things in his own hands by directing a film himself; at the time of writing he is preparing to direct his own screenplay, with David Lynch as producer. See Bernard Weinraub, 'The Writer vs. Hollywood, a Sequel', *International Herald Tribune*, 8 January 1992, p. 5.

87. As Kitaj explains in the following fragment of his unpublished preface to the painting: 'I am a Caféist. So is Joe Singer, who is at least ten or twelve years older than I am. Here is Joe in 1987 in the café called Le Central at the east end of the rue Blondel in Paris. A Caféist is one who prefers his own company, alone, in a café, with the life spinning around him, having nothing to do with him. The Caféist writes and sometimes furtively sketches in the café. He prefers cafés in districts like red-light areas – such as Le Central – where the Caféist rests his bones before taking to the streets yet again. (...) This painting began in the late seventies as a scene in a N.Y. brothel I used to like on 3rd Avenue which is now closed. When it shut down, I began this picture, leaving the lefthand side almost intact and overpainting the rest. Such places as Le Central have given me many ideas for painting and I owed it this picture.'

88. The painting by Sassetta used as Kitaj's source, *The Flagellation of St Anthony* (*c.*1423-32), is reproduced in John Pope-Hennessy, *Sassetta* (London, 1939), plate II. Pope-Hennessy remarks on p.10 that 'Sassetta … conceived the torturers of St. Anthony as half men,

half beasts, winged, clawed and horned and in one case with a face terminating in a snout,' adding that he might have been inspired to portray them in this manner by a literary account of the period. While working on *The Corridor (After Sassetta)*, Kitaj also produced *The Fulham Road, SW10 (After Bruegel)* (1988), in which he pictures himself seated at Tootsie's, his local restaurant on the Fulham Road, watching the passers-by; the striding couple is derived from two figures in the lower right-hand corner of Brueghel's heavily populated *The Numbering at Bethlehem* (1566) in the Musées Royaux des Beaux-Arts, reproduced in F. Grossman, *Peter Brueghel: Complete Edition of the Paintings* (first published 1955, revised London, 1973), plates 117 and 121 (detail).

89. See note 7.

90. R.B. Kitaj, *First Diasporist Manifesto* (London, 1989). The text had its origins, in the most general sense, in a lecture delivered by Kitaj in 1983 and in the article elaborated from it in the following year. See note 60.

91. Kitaj recounts the background to *Germania (To the Brothel)* in Julián Ríos, *Impresiones de Kitaj: La novela pintada* (Madrid, 1989), p.113. In the autumn of 1986 he travelled to Hamburg by private plane with Frank Auerbach, who was making his first visit to Germany in fifty years on the occasion of an exhibition of his work. After the show had been hung Kitaj went to the St Paul red-light district, where he saw a deformed young man dragging himself along towards a brothel; he was reminded of David Lynch's film *The Elephant Man* and wondered what kind of an encounter he could have with the prostitutes. Ríos's unconventional and illuminating study, much of it in the form of interviews with the artist, also contains other material relating to the *Germania* paintings, e.g. pp.195, 372 and 551-3.

92. The black and white photograph used as Kitaj's source is reproduced in Ríos, *ibid.*, p.554.

93. The Tate Gallery in London owns a set of the four bronzes by Matisse, *The Back I* to *The Back IV*, dating from *c.*1909 to 1930. Kitaj's interior adheres closely in composition to Van Gogh's gouache, *Corridor in the Asylum* (Collection Museum of Modern Art, New York), painted two weeks after his arrival in May 1889 at the asylum of Saint-Paul-de-Mausole, but the colour scheme is Kitaj's own. Both the gouache and a photograph taken by John Rewald of the hospital interior in *c.* 1935 are reproduced in Ronald Pickvance, *Van Gogh in Saint-Remy and Auvers*, Metropolitan Museum of Art, New York, 25 November 1986 – 22 March 1987, pp. 91 and 89.

94. Van Gogh's description of *The Night Café* is from one of his letters (number 534 in *Verzamelde brieven van Vincent Van Gogh*, 4 volumes, Amsterdam and Antwerp, 1973). The translation quoted here is from Evert van Uitert, Louis van Tilborgh and Sjraar van Heugten, *Vincent van Gogh: Paintings*, Rijksmuseum Vincent van Gogh, Amsterdam, 30 March – 29 July 1990, p.148.

95. Kitaj was surprised to hear through me in October 1991 that Richard Hamilton was planning a painting on the same theme, and for similar reasons: that he felt it had not really been done.

96. Kitaj's remarks are from an unpublished preface. The main discussion by Panofksy of the engraving *Melencolia I* (1514), which Kitaj credits as a source for his painting as important as the Dürer print itself, can be found in Erwin Panofsky, *The Life and Art of Albrecht Dürer* (fourth edition, Princeton, 1955), pp.156-71; the engraving is reproduced as fig. 209.

97. Interview with Tim Hyman, February 1980, *op. cit.*, p.22.

98. Reprinted in Walter Benjamin, *Illuminations, op. cit.*, pp. 59-67.

99. See, for example, *Blue Tree* (watercolour, 1909-10), *Grey Tree* (oil, 1912) and *Red Tree* (oil, 1908), all in the Gemeentemuseum, The Hague, reproduced in Maria Grazia Ottolenghi, *L'Opera completa di Mondrian* (Milan, 1971), plates XXVI, XXVII and XXVIII/XXIX respectively.

100. 'It was a blank thing that had never had a painting on it in all their history, I think,' recalls Kitaj of the Old Vic drop curtain, 'and they wanted to liven it up because it comes down a few times each night. I decided upon a Hamlet theme, re-read the play and painted a bunch of Hamlet pictures, one of which – *Hamlet and his Father's Ghost* – was painted to the correct proportion. Hockney told me which wonderful old firm to use to paint the picture up to the right scale. Jonathan Miller had just been appointed artistic director and he came to the studio to see my painting. He said he didn't want Hamlet and his bloody father coming down all during some other play like *Lady Windermere's Fan* or something. He was quite right and we both laughed. Then I painted *The Old Vic* to the right proportion. Silence from them. So I sold the two paintings and my career in the theatre came to an end some months after it began. Just as well because I never go to the theatre – it bores me. I'm a movie person.'

101. The painting considered to be Bonnard's last, *L'Amandier en fleur* (1947), is reproduced in *Bonnard*, exhibition catalogue, Centre Georges Pompidou, Musée national d'art moderne, Paris, 23 February – 21 May 1984, cat. no. 63.

102. See also the article by Avigdor Arikha, published under the title 'Painting and the end of communism: Brushes with Death,' *The New Republic* 16 December 1991, pp. 41-2, in which Kitaj's friend argues that both Communism and modernism eventually failed as utopian ideologies because they allowed no deviation from the strict credos they imposed.

103. 'I have been moving more and more toward a renewal of a tradition close to my heart,' explained Kitaj in October 1991, 'the tradition of extending the writ of *drawing* into the province of painting. My great precursors here are, of course, Degas, Lautrec, very late Cézanne and Matisse above all (lesser figures like Klee, Bonnard, Schiele are in this stream). (…) I am less and less inclined toward thick painting and more devoted to allowing my drawing to breathe throughout the whole life of the painting. Needless to say, painterly painting fascinates me as a tradition, in the practice of living painters I admire and also as a mode I don't wish to abandon altogether.'

104. In place of the modernist architecture that housed the figures of *The Red Banquet*, however, Kitaj devised the basic outlines of the staircase setting for *Against Slander*, and the positioning of the three figures on the stairs, from a reproduction of a detail of a small bronze relief by Donatello of *The Miracle of the Healing of the Irascible Son* (1445-8, Sant'Antonio, Padua). Kitaj recalls that the photograph from which he worked had been in his possession for more than thirty years. The entire relief is reproduced in Ludwig Goldscheider, *Donatello* (London, 1941), plate 101.

105. The subject of the picture had been suggested to Kitaj by books by and about the Hafetz Hayim (1837-1933), a man consistently referred to as a Jewish saint (his name means 'Who Desireth Life'). Kitaj was inspired particularly by the writer's first book, published anonymously, which he describes as 'a 300-page tract against slander (*lashon hara*), evil speech and defamation'; the fact that the book appeared around the time that Cézanne began to exhibit his paintings, and through them to suffer just such vilification, made the Hafetz Hayim's arguments seem doubly poignant.

106. In the unpublished typescript of a lecture about Van Gogh entitled 'My Vincent', which he delivered to a capacity audience at the Los Angeles County Museum of Art on 1 March 1999 in the context of the exhibition *Van Gogh's Van Goghs*, he remarked: 'I believe there is a stream of modernism other than the well known mainstreams, such as Abstract-Formalism and Dada-Surrealism-Duchampism and a Realism-Naturalism almost asleep during our time. The stream of art I want to identify, I will call *Painting-Drawing*, where the two methods are wed in a marriage perhaps neglected by critics and historians.'

107. See *R. B. Kitaj: A Retrospective*, exhibition catalogue, Tate Gallery, London, 16 June–4 September 1994, p. 180, for his discussion of this painting. Kitaj wrote a considerable number of new 'prefaces' for this publication; they were also printed on the wall labels hung next to the works. Three of them (including the one about *Women and Men*) are reproduced above, pp. 196–7.

108. Kitaj painted *Western Bathers* on a canvas with the exact dimensions of the National Gallery's Cézanne (his favourite painting in London). See his note about it in the 1994 Tate exhibition catalogue, *op. cit.*, p. 206, reprinted above, p. 197. Both the Cézanne and the Degas *Young Spartans* were among the works selected by Kitaj for his *Artist's Eye* exhibition at the National Gallery in 1980; they are reproduced as black-and-white details in the accompanying catalogue.

109. See Kitaj's note on the painting in the 1994 Tate exhibition catalogue, *op. cit.*, p. 221, cat. 104, in which he reveals that 'The idea for the painting comes from a page I've kept as long as I can remember, torn from a copy of the old American magazine Theater Arts, showing a scene from what is described as "an experimental drama", "A Happy Journey to Trenton and Camden" by Thornton Wilder.'

110. Tim Hyman, in his review of the Tate exhibition, 'The comic high priest of diaspora', *Times Literary Supplement*, 1 July 1994, pp. 16–17, underlined this new emphasis on humour in Kitaj's work and predicted it would emerge as a strong aspect of his later development. This might well have been the case had his life not taken a tragic turn.

111. Unless otherwise specified, all quotations from the artist are from correspondence and telephone conversations with the author between February and May 1999.

112. See 'The Gentle Art of Making Enemies One Hundred Years Later', Kitaj's interview with Susan Shaw, in *Sandra/Two*, exhibition catalogue, Marlborough Gallery, New York, and Marlborough Fine Art (London), at FIAC, Paris, 2–7 October 1996, pp. 5–12. The title refers to Whistler's famous book.

113. The subtitle and imagery alike recall Picasso's blue period masterpiece, *La Vie* 1903 (Cleveland Museum of Art), one of Kitaj's favourite works since childhood.

114. 'For about 1½ years after she died,' remarked Kitaj in a letter to the author postmarked 6 April 1999, 'I wanted to be dead. I talked to her each day. Isaiah Berlin told me she's not there! But I had our Max. Isaiah told me: "You are Job." Some of the last drawings in that show [at Marlborough, New York, in 1995] touched on our Great Love, such as the one called *The Last Time*. And I repainted the female head in *La Vie* late one night in rage and tears. Someone must have seen that pain because that painting was bought by the Fondation National d'Art Contemporain in France. London died for me when Sandra died and I laid plans to leave. Auerbach came every few weeks with Indian food for more than a year and Freud painted two small portraits of me because I couldn't work and he thought it would help.'

115. *Sabbath's Theater* grew directly out of Kitaj's experiences, specifically the loss of Sandra, and even incorporated almost verbatim transcripts of the conversations Roth and Kitaj held over the telephone. In his letter to the author postmarked 6 April 1999, Kitaj remarks: 'All characters in fiction and sometimes in my own art are complex *hybrids* from lots of sources in real life and imagination. Roth used *some* of me in Mickey Sabbath, mainly my conversations about my time at sea, and also Roth used some of what I was saying to him about Sandra's death. There is constant discussion among literary people over this business of fictional characters and real-life people all through the history of fiction … Fact and fiction weave in and out of novels like a shell game.' See also my essay in *R.B. Kitaj: An American in Europe*, exhibition catalogue, Astrup Fearnley Museum of Modern Art, Oslo, 10 January–22 March 1998, p. 124 and p. 125, note 16, for a more detailed discussion of the parallels between Mickey Sabbath (a former seaman and failed puppeteer grieving the loss of his mistress of thirty years) and Kitaj.

116. In 1985 Kitaj became the first American since John Singer Sargent (and before him Benjamin West) to be elected to the Royal Academy. As a Royal Academician he has the automatic right to exhibit up to six works in the annual Summer Exhibition.

117. See note 112.

118. 'Sandra Four', an interview with Werner Hanak concerning his years in Vienna, was printed as a chapter of *R.B. Kitaj: An American in Europe*, exhibition catalogue, *op. cit.*, pp. 131–4.

119. The price tag of £1m for *Sandra Three* was published in *Royal Academy of Arts Summer Exhibition 1997*, exhibition catalogue, Royal Academy of Arts, London, 1997, cat. no. 44.

120. Kitaj had already used the title *Second Diasporist Manifesto* for a screenprint and collage on canvas dated 1970-96 (reproduced in the Oslo exhibition catalogue, *op. cit.*, cat. no. 45), which he has since renamed *Study for Second Diasporist Manifesto*.

121. The figures were derived from numerous film frames in one of the books about the Marx Brothers owned by Kitaj.

122. Los Angeles, of course, has a tradition of sheltering European expatriates, many of them Jewish and many of them involved with the movie industry. Since Los Angeles was never home to Kitaj before, he admits that he felt some kinship with those earlier immigrants: 'Yes, in some ways I do feel like those settlers, but in my own land – like settlers in California in Westerns – Go West Young Man! (Horace Greeley?).' By his own admission, it was this sense of identification that prompted him to paint *The Second Diasporist Manifesto (Marx Brothers)* as one of his first major works after moving to California. 'It's about the most generous Diaspora the Jews have ever known.'

123. 'New Yorkers are wrong,' asserts Kitaj. '*Moses and Aron* (Schönberg) was written here. *Dr Faustus* (Mann) was written here. Brecht wrote here. etc., etc. … And the greatest Visual Art this century, the movies, were made here. Now I'm here!'

124. '*Not* a particular player. Just sketched onto canvas in Lond[on]. The pose is taken from a late 19th cent baseball player by Tom Eakins – in a Museum in Rhode Island I believe.'

125. 'In another book of mine I found a photo of a stunning Israeli girl Archaeologist at work with her little brush in the desert. I tried in this painting to possess her but now she's in a museum in Kansas City.'

126. 'I own a book about the artifacts owned by the Synagogue

where S + I were married (the Congregation of Spanish + Portuguese Jews) founded 1700 by Rembrandt's friend Menassah Ben Israel. This (18th cent?) chair is illustrated in the book and I just liked its unusual look and painted it.'

127. 'Moonlightist is not "Jewish",' Kitaj explained to me when I remarked on the sitter's rabbinical look. 'He is Albert P. Ryder as seen by Marsden Hartley in MH's great portrait of APR. I believe it may have been Hartley himself who called APR the Moonlightist because of APR's nocturnal life and nocturnal paintings. Hopper & Ryder are my 2 favorite American painters. And I love Hartley too.'

128. 'Sandy Koufax was one of the fastest and greatest pitchers in baseball history. He pitched for the Los Angeles Dodgers some years ago. He was a Jew who wouldn't pitch on the Jewish High Holy Days. I never saw him play but he is an American, Los Angeles, Jewish legend and legends are good for the painting art still, I believe and good for me anyway. KOUFAX is now in the LACMA collection.'

129. Kitaj worked from a photograph torn out from a mass-circulation magazine, the caption of which reads: 'Louis-Jacques-Mandé Daguerre's "Paris Boulevard" (daguerreotype, 1839) contains the first known photographic image of a human figure.' The ownership of the daguerreotype itself is credited to the International Museum of Photography at George Eastman House.

130. Robert Sklar, *Film: An International History of the Medium* (London: Thames and Hudson, 1993), pp. 164-5, remarks that 'The triumph of a performance oriented cinema was *Tret'ya Meshchanskaya* (*Bed and Sofa*, 1927), directed by Abram Room (1894-1976).' He describes it as a 'love-triangle story' in which a man's unhappy wife becomes the lover of their lodger, who had been sleeping on their sofa; on the husband's return from work outside Moscow, he is relegated from bed to sofa and all three end up sleeping alone.

131. When I put this to Kitaj, he replied: 'I've begun my Third (and Last?) Act. There's no London in it and hardly any Europe left … aside from books. I read more than ever now and some of that reading and some few pictures have something of Europe in them. When you saw me briefly in Oslo and Madrid, you saw me as a cat burglar in an old Feuillade movie – now you see me (in Europe), now you don't.'

SELECT BIBLIOGRAPHY

For the most comprehensive available bibliography (including writings by Kitaj) see the 1994 Tate Gallery catalogue.

Books by Kitaj

Erstes Manifest des Diasporismus. Zurich: Arche Verlag, 1988. German translation of text subsequently published in English as *First Diasporist Manifesto*. London and New York: Thames and Hudson, 1989. Hungarian translation published Budapest: Akadémiai Kiadó, 1994.

Monographs

DEPPNER, MARTIN ROMAN. *Zeichen und Bildwanderung: zum Ausdruck des 'Nich-Sesshaften' im Werk R.B. Kitajs*. PhD thesis, Universität Hamburg, 1988, published by Lit Verlag, Münster, 1992.

KINSMAN, JANE. *The Prints of R.B. Kitaj*. Aldershot: Scolar Press, in association with the National Gallery of Australia, 1994. Includes texts by the artist.

LIVINGSTONE, MARCO. *R.B. Kitaj*. Oxford: Phaidon, and New York: Rizzoli, 1985. Revised and expanded edition, retitled *Kitaj*, London: Phaidon, and New York: Thames and Hudson, 1992, reprinted with corrections 1994; third edition, revised and expanded, London: Phaidon, 1999. Includes texts by the artist.

RÍOS, JULIÁN. *Impresiones de Kitaj (La novela pintada)*. Madrid: Mondadori España, 1989. Published in English as *Kitaj: Pictures and Conversations*. London: Hamish Hamilton, 1994.

Retrospective exhibition catalogues [*listed chronologically*]

In the case of touring exhibitions, the details of the first venue only are given.

R.B. Kitaj. Hanover: Kestner-Gesellschaft, 23 January-22 February 1970. Introduction by Wieland Schmied and essays by Kitaj.

R.B. Kitaj. Washington: Smithsonian Institution Press, 1981, to accompany exhibition at the Hirshhorn Museum and Sculpture Garden, Washington, 17 September-15 November 1981. Foreword by Abram Lerner, texts by John Ashbery, Joe Shannon and Jane Livingston; interview with Kitaj by Timothy Hyman; chronology; list of exhibitions and bibliography compiled by Anna Brooke. Reprinted (without foreword or chronology) as *Kitaj: Paintings, Drawings, Pastels*. London: Thames and Hudson, 1983.

R.B. Kitaj: A Retrospective. London: Tate Gallery, 16 June-4 September 1994. Edited by Richard Morphet. Essays by Morphet and Richard Wollheim, interview with the artist by Morphet, chronology compiled by Joanne Northey, catalogue with notes by the artist and bibliography compiled by Krzysztof K. Cieszkowski.

R.B.Kitaj: An American in Europe. Oslo: Astrup Fearnley Museet for Moderne Kunst, 10 January-22 March 1998. Edited by Marco Livingstone. Essays by Livingstone, Francisco Javier San Martín and

Ulrich Krempel, interview with Kitaj by Werner Hanak, chronology and selective bibliography. English/Norwegian bilingual edition. A Spanish/English edition (for the Museo Nacional Centro de Arte Reina Sofia, Madrid) and a German/English edition (for the Jüdisches Museum, Vienna, and the Sprengel Museum, Hanover) were also produced.

Catalogues of other solo exhibitions [*listed chronologically*]

R.B. Kitaj: Pictures with Commentary, Pictures without Commentary. London: Marlborough Fine Art, February 1963. Notes and commentary by Kitaj.

R.B. Kitaj. New York: Marlborough-Gerson Gallery, February 1965.

R.B. Kitaj: Paintings and Prints. Los Angeles: Los Angeles County Museum of Art, 11 August-12 September 1965. Introduction and interview by Maurice Tuchman.

R.B. Kitaj. Berkeley: Worth Ryder Art Gallery, University of California at Berkeley, 7 October-12 November 1967. Text by Kitaj.

R.B. Kitaj: Complete Graphics 1963-69. Berlin: Galerie Mikro, 10 May-15 June 1969. Introduction by Werner Haftmann (German, with English translation) and essay by Kitaj (English only).

R.B. Kitaj: Pictures from an Exhibition Held at the Kestner-Gesellschaft, Hanover and the Boymans Museum, Rotterdam 1970. London: Marlborough Fine Art, April-May 1970.

R.B. Kitaj: Pictures. New York: Marlborough Gallery, 2-23 February 1974. Essay by Frederic Tuten.

R.B. Kitaj: Pictures. Edinburgh: New 57 Gallery, 18 August-12 September 1975.

The Human Clay: An Exhibition Selected by R.B. Kitaj. London: Arts Council of Great Britain, 1976, for exhibition at the Hayward Gallery, London, 5-30 August 1976.

R.B. Kitaj: Pictures/Bilder. London: Marlborough Fine Art, April-4 June 1977; Zurich: Marlborough Galerie, 14 June-22 July 1977. Introduction by Robert Creeley. Bilingual English/German edition.

R.B. Kitaj: Fifty Drawings and Pastels, Six Oil Paintings. New York: Marlborough Gallery, 31 March-28 April 1979. Introduction by Timothy Hyman.

The Artist's Eye: An Exhibition Selected by R.B. Kitaj at the National Gallery, London. London: National Gallery, 21 May-21 July 1980. Introduction by Kitaj.

R.B. Kitaj: Pastels and Drawings. London: Marlborough Fine Art, 8 October-7 November 1980. Introduction by Stephen Spender.

R.B. Kitaj. London: Marlborough Fine Art, November-December 1985. Introduction by Kitaj.

R.B. Kitaj: A Print Retrospective. London: Marlborough Graphics

Ltd, for the exhibition 'Kitaj: A Print Retrospective' at the Victoria and Albert Museum, 8 June-9 October 1994. Brochure with introduction by Rosemary Miles.

R.B. Kitaj Graphics 1974-1994. London: Marlborough Graphics Ltd, 8 June-20 August 1994.

R.B. Kitaj: Recent Pictures. London: Marlborough Fine Art, 8 June-20 August 1994.

R.B. Kitaj: Recent Pictures. New York: Marlborough Gallery, 8 February-4 March 1995.

SANDRA/Two. Paris: Marlborough Gallery, New York, and Marlborough Fine Art (London), at FIAC, 2-7 October 1996. Interview with Kitaj by Susan Shaw.

Interviews and texts by the artist

BRIGHTON, ANDREW. 'Conversations with R.B. Kitaj'. *Art in America*, June 1986, vol. 74, no. 6, pp. 98-105.

COHEN, DAVID. 'The Viennese Inspiration: In Search of Self'. *R.A.: Royal Academy Magazine*, Winter 1990, no. 29, pp. 34-6.

FAURE WALKER, JAMES. 'B.B. Kitaj interviewed by James Faure Walker'. *Artscribe*, February 1977, no. 5, pp. 4-5.

GAYFORD, MARTIN. 'A Long Lineage'. *Modern Painters*, summer 1994, vol. 7, no. 2, pp. 21-26.

HYMAN, TIMOTHY. 'R.B. Kitaj: A Return to London'. *London Magazine*, February 1980, vol. 19, no. 11, pp. 15-27.

KITAJ, R.B.'On Associating Texts with Paintings'. *Cambridge Opinion*, January 1964, no. 37, pp. 22-3.

——— . Introduction to *The Human Clay: an exhibition selected by R.B.Kitaj.* London: Arts Council of Great Britain, 1976, unpaginated (pp. 5-12).

——— . Statement in *Arte inglese oggi 1960-76.* Milan: Electa Editrice, 1976, vol. 1, p. 128.

——— . 'The Autumn of Central Paris (After Walter Benjamin), 1971'. *Art International*, March 1979, vol. 22, no. 10, pp. 19-20.

——— . Introduction to *The Artist's Eye: an exhibition selected by R.B.Kitaj at the National Gallery, London.* London: National Gallery, 21 May-21 July 1980 (no page numbers).

KITAJ, R.B., and DAVID HOCKNEY. 'R.B. Kitaj and David Hockney discuss the case for a return to the figurative'. *The new review* [London], January-February 1977, vol. 3, nos. 34-5, pp. 75-7.

MACBETH, GEORGE. 'R.B. Kitaj and George MacBeth in Dialogue'. *Art Monthly*, April 1977, no. 5, pp. 4-5.

MARLOW, TIM. 'Kitaj's true confessions'. *Tate: the art magazine*, summer 1994, issue 3, pp. 25-9.

PEPPIATT, MICHAEL. 'R.B. Kitaj: The Diaspora in London'. *Art International*, Autumn 1987, no. 1 (new series), pp. 34-8.

PLANTE, DAVID. 'Paris, 1983'. *Sulfur: a literary tri-quarterly of the whole art*, 1984, no. 9, pp. 96-110.

Articles

ASHBERY, JOHN. 'R.B. Kitaj: Hunger and Love'. *Art in America*, January 1982, pp. 130-35, reprinted as 'R.B. Kitaj' in John Ashbery, *Reported Sightings: art chronicles, 1957-1987*, edited by David Bergman. Manchester: Carcanet, 1989, pp. 299-308.

ASHTON, DORE. 'R.B. Kitaj and the Scene'. *Arts and Architecture*, April 1965, pp. 8-9, 34-5.

AUERBACH, JAKE, director. *Kitaj in the Picture.* Film, A Late Show Special, BBC2 , televised 29 June 1994. Produced by Hannah Rothschild and Robert McNab. Series editor Michael Poole.

BARO, GENE. 'The British Scene: Hockney and Kitaj'. *Arts Magazine*, May-June 1964, vol. 38, no. 9, pp. 94-101.

BARSKY, VIVIANNE. 1990. '"Home is where the Heart is": Jewish Themes in the Art of R.B. Kitaj'. In Ezra Mendelsohn, editor, *Art and its Uses: The Visual Image and Modern Jewish Society*; symposium edited by Richard I. Cohen. In *Studies in Contemporary Jewry: An Annual.* IV. New York and Oxford: Oxford University Press, for Institute of Contemporary Jewry, The Hebrew University of Jerusalem, 1990, pp. 149-185.

COHEN, DAVID. 'R.B. Kitaj and the Art of Return: "My art has turned in the shadow of our infernal history"'. *Jewish Quarterly*, 1988, vol. 35, no. 2 (no. 130), pp. 32-6.

CREELEY, ROBERT. 'Ecce Homo'. *Art International*, March 1979, vol. 22, no. 10, pp. 27-30.

DEPPNER, MARTIN ROMAN. 'Spuren geschichlicher Erfahrung: R.B. Kitajs "Reflections on Violence"'. *Idea: Jahrbuch der Hamburger Kunsthalle*, 1984, vol. 3, pp. 139-66.

——— . 'Jewish School und London Diaspora'. *Babylon: Beiträge zur jüdischen Gegenwart*, October 1993, vol. 12, pp. 37-57.

FRANCIS, RICHARD. '"The Red Banquet" by R.B.Kitaj'. *Annual Reports and Bulletin*, Walker Art Gallery, Liverpool, 1971-4 (published 1974), pp. 84-90.

GILMOUR, PAT. 'R.B. Kitaj and Chris Prater'. *Print Quarterly*, June 1994, vol. XI, no. 2, pp. 117-150.

HOCKNEY, DAVID. 'A Romantic Pessimist'. *RA: The Royal Academy Magazine*, summer 1994, no. 43, p. 55.

HYMAN, TIMOTHY. 'B.B. Kitaj: Avatar of Ezra'. *London Magazine*, August-September 1977, vol. 17, no. 3, pp. 53-61.

——— . 'R.B. Kitaj: A Prodigal Returning'. *Artscribe*, October 1980, no. 25, pp. 37-41.

——— . 'The comic high priest of diaspora'. *Times Literary Supplement*, 1 July 1994, pp. 16-17.

——— . *R.B. Kitaj: The Sensualist 1973-84.* Oslo: For Art, vol. 1, no. 1, 1991.

JOHNSON, KEN. 'R.B. Kitaj: Views of a Fractured Century'. *Art in America*, March 1995, vol. 83, pt. 3, pp. 78-85, 125-6.

KUDIELKA, ROBERT. 'R.B. Kitaj und die Schuld des Auges'. *Kunstwerk*, August-September 1967, pp. 3-12.

LIVINGSTONE, MARCO. 'Iconology as Theme in the Early Work of R.B. Kitaj'. *Burlington Magazine*, July 1980, vol. 122, no. 928, pp. 488-97.

———. 'Kitaj at Marlborough'. *Burlington Magazine*, January 1986, vol. 128, no. 994, pp. 50-53.

———. 'A Condition of Exile'. *RA: The Royal Academy Magazine*, summer 1994, no. 43, pp. 52-5.

LUBOW, ARTHUR. 'The Painter's Life is Cracking'. *New York Times Magazine*, 13 November 1994, pp. 60-65.

PEPPIATT, MICHAEL. 'R.B. Kitaj: Pictures like Novels'. *Connaissance des Arts* (English-language edition), September 1981, no. 20, pp. 28-35.

———. 'R.B. Kitaj'. *Kunst og Kultur*, vol. 66, no. 3, 1983, pp. 166-75.

PODRO, MICHAEL. 'Some Notes on Ron Kitaj'. *Art International*, March 1979, vol. 22, no. 10, pp. 18-26.

———. 'Kitaj in Retrospect'. *Burlington Magazine*, April 1995, vol. 137, no. 1105, pp. 242-7.

REICHARDT, JASIA. 'R.B. Kitaj: A Return to the Figurative? A New Direction, Indeed Unforeseen'. *Metro*, issue 6, 1962, pp. 94-7.

———. 'Kitaj's Drawings from Life'. *Connoisseur*, October 1963, vol. 154, no. 620, pp. 112-16.

ROBERTSON, BRYAN. 'R.B. Kitaj: A Fantastic Conspiracy'. *Sunday Times Colour Magazine*, 10 February 1963, pp. 23-5.

RUSSELL, JOHN. 'The Polemical Painter'. *Sunday Times*, 10 February 1963, pp. 33.

SCOTT, JAMES. *R.B. Kitaj*. Film, Arts Council of Great Britain, London, 1967, with narration by R.B. Kitaj and Christopher Finch.

TARSHIS, JEROME. 'The "Fugitive Passions" of R.B. Kitaj'. *Art News*, October 1976, vol. 75, no. 8, pp. 40-43.

TATE GALLERY, London. Entries on individual works in *Review 1953-1963 (Isaac Babel Riding with Budyonny); The Tate Gallery 1968-70 (Mahler Becomes Politics, Beisbol); Biennial Report and Illustrated Catalogue of Acquisitions 1972-74 (The Man of the Woods and the Cat of the Mountains); Acquisitions 1978-80 (The Rise of Fascism); Acquisitions 1980-82 (The Murder of Rosa Luxembourg); and Illustrated Catalogue of Acquisitions 1984-86 (Cecil Court, London W.C.2 [The Refugees]).*

Time Magazine, 19 February 1965, vol. 85, no. 8, p. 72 (no author listed). 'Painting: Literary Collage' (review of New York exhibition).

TUTEN, FREDERIC. 'Neither Fool, nor Naive, nor Poseur-saint: Fragments on R.B. Kitaj'. *Artforum*, January 1982, vol. 20, no. 5, pp. 61-9 [includes interview].

WILLETT, JOHN. 'Where to Stick it'. *Art International*, vol. 14, no. 9 November 1970, pp. 28-36.

General references

BRUN, HANS-JAKOB, and others. *Dobbel Virkelighet/Double Reality*. Exhibition catalogue, Astrup Fearnley Museet for Moderne Kunst, Oslo, 16 April-9 October 1994. Essay on Kitaj by Wenche Volle.

CALVOCORESSI, RICHARD, and others. *From London: Bacon Freud Kossoff Andrews Auerbach Kitaj*. Exhibition catalogue, The British Council, in association with the Scottish National Gallery of Modern Art, Edinburgh, 1 July-5 September 1995. Essays by David Cohen and Bruce Bernard.

HICKS, ALISTAIR. *The School of London: The Resurgence of Contemporary Painting*. Oxford: Phaidon, 1989.

LIVINGSTONE, MARCO. *Pop Art: A Continuing History*. London: Thames and Hudson, 1990.

———, editor. *Pop Art*. Exhibition catalogue, Royal Academy of Arts, London, 13 September-15 December 1991, in association with Weidenfeld and Nicolson and Rizzoli, New York. Revised versions published by the Museum Ludwig, Cologne (1992, in German), Electa España (for the showing at the Centro de Arte Reina Sofia, Madrid, 1992, in Spanish), and the Montreal Museum of Fine Arts (1992, with a substantially different selection of works, in both English and French editions).

PEPPIATT, MICHAEL, and others. *L'École de Londres de Bacon à Bevan*. Paris: Réunion des Musées Nationaux, for the exhibition at the Fondation Dina Vierny-Musée Maillol, Paris, 10 October 1998-20 January 1999.

CATALOGUE
OF WORKS

Measurements given are in inches followed by centimetres, height followed by width.

1. The First Terrorist, 1957. *Plate 19*
Oil on canvas, 6½ x 4½ (16.5 x 11.4).
Collection of the artist.

2. Tarot Variations, 1958. *Plate 4*
Oil on canvas, 44 x 34 (111.8 x 86.4).
The High Museum (J.J. Haverty Collection),
Atlanta, Georgia.

3. Erasmus Variations, 1958. *Plate 1*
Oil on canvas, 41 x 33⅛ (104.2 x 84.2).
Peter Cochrane, London.

4. Miss Ivy Cavendish (Oxford), 1958. *Plate 2*
Charcoal pencil on paper, 21 x 16⅜ (53.3 x 41.6).
Collection of the artist.

5. Ivy Cavendish, c.1958. *Fig.3*
Oil on canvas, 16 x 12 (40.6 x 30.5).
Collection of the artist.

6. Monseigneur Ungar, 1958.
Oil on canvas, 10¼ x 8 (26.1 x 20.3).
Private collection, London.

7. Knitting, c.1958–9.
Oil on canvas, 24⅛ x 20¼ (61.3 x 51.5).
Private collection.

8. Words, 1959. *Plate 7*
Oil on canvas, 30 x 24 (76.2 x 61).
Private collection, London.

9. Girl with Mauve Hair, c.1959.
Oil on board, 8¼ x 9¼ (20.6 x 23.5).
Private collection, Washington, D.C.

10. The Red Banquet, 1960. *Plate 9*
Oil on canvas, 48 x 48 (121.9 x 121.9).
Walker Art Gallery, Liverpool.

11. A Reconstitution, 1960.
Oil on canvas, 50 x 40 (127 x 101.6).
Peter Cochrane, London.

12. The Bells of Hell, 1960. *Plate 26 (detail)*
Oil on canvas, 36 x 60 (91.5 x 152.5).
Private collection.

13. The Murder of Rosa Luxemburg,
1960. *Plate 30*
Oil and collage on canvas, 60 x 60 (152.5 x 152.5).
The Tate Gallery, London.

14. Pariah, 1960. *Plate 21 (detail)*
Oil on canvas, 40 x 50 (101.6 x 127).
Silkeborg Kunstmuseum (Asger Jorn Donation),
Denmark.

15. Oh, Lemuel, 1960. *Plate 16*
Oil on canvas, 40 x 60¼ (101.6 x 153).
Private collection, Geneva.

16. The Twin Birthdates of Martin Luther,
1960. *Plate 5*
Oil on canvas, 60 x 40 (152.4 x 101.6).
Private collection.

17. Warburg's Visit to New Mexico, 1960-2.
(In collaboration with Eduardo Paolozzi).
Oil and collage on canvas, 40 x 50 (101.6 x 127).
Private collection.

18. An Untitled Romance, 1961.
Oil on canvas, 29 x 9 (73.7 x 22.9).
Private collection, London.

**19. Certain Forms of Association Neglected
Before**, 1961. *Plate 17*
Oil on canvas, 40 x 50 (101.6 x 127).
Private collection.

20. Yamhill, 1961. *Plate 11*
Oil on canvas, 40 x 50 (101.6 x 127).
James H. Grady, Atlanta, Georgia.

21. Austro-Hungarian Footsoldier, 1961.
Oil and collage on canvas, 60 x 36 (152.4 x 91.5).
Museum Ludwig, Cologne.

22. Notes towards a Definition of Nobody,
1961. *Plate 41 (detail)*
Oil on canvas, 48 x 88 (121.9 x 223.5).
The Toledo Museum of Art (Gift of Dr & Mrs
Joseph A. Gosman), Ohio.

23. Specimen Musings of a Democrat, 1961.
Plate 23.
Oil and collage on canvas, 40 x 50 (101.6 x 127).
Colin St John Wilson, London.

24. Washington Allston in Rome, 1961.
Oil on canvas, 7¼ x 6 (18.5 x 15.2).
Colin St John Wilson, London.

25. Priest, Etc., 1961. *Plate 35*
Oil on canvas, 40 x 50 (101.6 x 127).
Colin St John Wilson, London.

26. A Student of Vienna, 1961-2. *Plate 28 (detail)*
Oil and collage on canvas, 36 x 36 (91.5 x 91.5).
Private collection.

27. Warburg as Maenad, 1961-2.
Oil and collage on canvas, 76 x 36 (193 x 91.5).
Kunstmuseum, Düsseldorf.

28. Daedalus, c.1961-2.
Oil on canvas, 40 x 50 (101.6 x 127).
Museum of Art, Rhode Island.

29. Nietzsche's Moustache, 1962. *Plate 25*
Oil on canvas, 48 x 48 (121.9 x 121.9).
Private collection, London.

30. Junta, 1962. *Plate 31*
Oil and collage on canvas, 36 x 84 (91.4 x 213.4).
Colin St John Wilson, London.

31. Homage to H. Melville, 1962. *Plate 10 (detail)*
Oil on canvas, 54 x 36 (137.2 x 91.5).
The Royal College of Art, London.

32. Kennst du das Land?, 1962. *Plate 22*
Oil and collage on canvas, 48 x 48 (121.9 x 121.9).
Collection of the artist.

33. Good News for Incunabulists, 1962. *Plate 33*
Oil on canvas, 60 x 60 (152.4 x 152.4).
Private collection, Germany.

34. Reflections on Violence, 1962. *Plate 15*
Oil and collage on canvas, 60 x 60 (152.4 x 152.4).
Hamburger Kunsthalle, Hamburg.

35. Isaac Babel Riding with Budyonny, 1962.
Plate 34 (detail)
Oil on canvas, 72 x 72 (182.9 x 182.9).
The Tate Gallery, London.

36. Welcome Every Dread Delight, 1962.
Oil and collage on canvas, 60 x 48 (152.4 x 121.9).
McCrory Corporation, New York.

37. Work in Progress, 1962. *(In collaboration with
Eduardo Paolozzi).*
Mixed media on wood, 34 x 32½ (86.4 x 82.5).
Private collection.

**38. Cracks and Reforms and Bursts in the
Violet Air**, 1962.
Oil and collage on canvas, 48 x 48 (121.9 x 121.9).
Private collection.

39. Interior / Dan Chatterton's Town House,
1962. *Plate 14*
Oil and collage on canvas, 60 x 48 (152.4 x 121.9).
Private collection, London.

**40. This Train of Thought Which You Blame
is the Sole Consolation that My Life Contains**,
1962.
Oil on canvas, 30 x 30 (76.2 x 76.2).
Private collection.

41. A History of Polish Literature, 1962.
Found and assisted object, 19½ x 33½ (49.5 x 85).
Collection of the artist.

42. Rats and Roses, 1962.
Oil and collage on canvas, 60 x 48 (152.4 x 121.9).
Private collection, Switzerland.

43. How To Do It and How Not To Do It,
1962.
Found and assisted object, 9¾ x 14¼ (24.8 x 36.2).
Collection of the artist.

44. Crosses, 1962.
Oil and pencil on canvas, 36 x 36 (91.4 x 91.4).
Private collection, London.

45. Tedeum, 1963. *Plate 71*
Oil on canvas, 48 x 72 (121.9 x 182.9).
National Museum of Wales, Cardiff.

**46. Good God Where is the King? Or Where is
Count Hadik?**, 1963.
Collage, 30 x 20 (76.2 x 50.8).
Collection of the artist.

47. Value, Price and Profit, 1963. *Plate 20 (detail)*
Oil on canvas, 60 x 60 (152.4 x 152.4).
Private collection.

48. Art the Enorm, 1963.
Collage, 20 x 30 (50.8 x 76.2).
Collection of the artist.

49. The Perils of Revisionism, 1963. *Plate 45*

Oil on canvas, 60 x 60 (152.4 x 152.4).
Private collection, New York.

50. Randolph Bourne in Irving Place, 1963.
Plate 27
Oil and collage on canvas, 60 x 60 (152.4 x 152.4).
Private collection, Switzerland.

51. The Baby Tramp, 1963/4. *Plate 23*
Oil and collage on canvas, 72 x 24 (182.9 x 61).
Gemeentemuseum, The Hague.

52. Apotheosis of Groundlessness, 1964. *Plate 18*
Oil on canvas, 60 x 84 (152.4 x 213.4).
Cincinnati Art Museum, Ohio.

53. The Ohio Gang, 1964. *Plate 32*
Oil on canvas, 72 x 72 (182.9 x 182.9).
The Museum of Modern Art (Philip Johnson Fund, 1965), New York.

54. Halcyon Days, 1964.
Oil and collage on canvas, 72 x 72 (182.9 x 182.9).
Museum Boymans-van Beuningen, Rotterdam.

55. Boys and Girls!, 1964.
Collage on wood, 21 x 16 (53.4 x 40.6).
Collection of the artist.

56. Burgess Meredith as George, 1964.
Oil on canvas, 14 x 10 (35.5 x 25.4).
Marlborough Fine Art (London) Ltd.

57. Where the Railroad Leaves the Sea, 1964.
Plate 36
Oil on canvas, 48 x 60 (121.9 x 152.4).
Collection of the artist.

58. An Early Europe, 1964.
Oil on canvas, 60 x 84 (152.4 x 213.4).
Mary Moore.

59. Cover for The Times Literary Supplement
**special issue 'The Critical Moment', English
and American Criticism,** 1964.
Pencil and collage on paper, 12¼ x 10 (31 x 25.4).
The Museum of Modern Art, New York.

60. The Republic of the Southern Cross, 1964.
Collage on wood, 48 x 24 (121.9 x 61).
Colin St John Wilson, London.

**61. The Master of Sentences / Preface: Med
(Portrait of Norman Douglas),** 1964.
Oil and collage on canvas, 48 x 48 (121.9 x 121.9).
Private collection.

**62. The Nice Old Man and the Pretty Girl
(with Huskies),** 1964.
Oil on canvas, 48 x 48 (121.9 x 121.9).
Private collection.

63. A Disciple of Bernstein and Kautsky, 1964.
Oil on canvas, 60 x 48 (152.4 x 121.9).
Private collection, London.

64. The Vampire / His Kith and Kin, 1964.
Collage on wood, 13 x 10 (33 x 25.4).
Colin St John Wilson, London.

65. His Cult of the Fragment, 1964.
Oil on canvas, 10 x 8 (25.4 x 20.3).
Private collection.

66. Maria Prophetissa, 1964. *Plate 37*
Oil on canvas, 10 x 8 (25.4 x 20.3).
Private collection.

67. An Impossibilist, 1964.
Oil on canvas, 10 x 8 (25.4 x 20.3).
Private collection.

68. In the Social Memory, 1964.
Oil on canvas, 10 x 8 (25.4 x 20.3).
Private collection.

69. All I Can Say Etc., 1964.
Oil on canvas, 10 x 8 (25.4 x 20.3).
Private collection.

**70. An Urban Old Man Who Never Looked
at the Sea Except Perhaps Once,** 1964.
Oil on canvas, 50 x 40 (127 x 101.6).
Private collection.

71. Cover for The Times Literary Supplement
**'Shakespeare's Quarter Centenary
Celebrations',** 1964.
Oil and collage on canvas, 13⅜ x 10 (34 x 25.4).
Collection of the artist.

**72. The Ohio and Indiana of Anderson and
Dreiser,** 1964.
Oil on canvas, 36 x 36 (91.4 x 91.4).
The Tate Gallery Foundation, London.

73. Early Harbingers of Christ, 1964.
Oil on canvas, 35 x 36 (88.9 x 91.4).
Private collection.

74. London by Night: part I, 1964.
Oil on canvas, 57 x 73 (144.8 x 185.4).
Stedelijk Museum, Amsterdam.

75. Dismantling the Red Tent, 1964 *Plate 29*
Oil on canvas, including an original etching by
Alphonse Legros, 48 x 48 (121.9 x 121.9).
The Michael and Dorothy Blankfort Collection at
Los Angeles County Museum.

76. Aureolin, 1964. *Plate 39*
Oil on canvas, 60 x 48 (152.4 x 121.9).
Mr and Mrs Ian Stoutzker, London.

77. Dante's Every-day Wife, 1965.
Oil and collage on canvas, 10 x 14 (25.4 x 35.6).
Private collection.

78. The Sorrows of Belgium, 1965
Oil on canvas, 60 x 84 (152.4 x 213.4).
Private collection, Paris.

79. The Rival Poet, 1965.
Oil on canvas, 22½ x 15 (57.2 x 38.1).
The Graves Art Gallery, Sheffield.

80. Pogany 1, 1965.
Oil on canvas, 12 x 16 (30.5 x 40.6).
Private collection.

**81. Primer of Motives II (Intuitions of
Irregularity),** 1965. *Plate 82 (detail)*
Oil on canvas, 60 x 60 (152.4 x 152.4).
Private collection, Geneva.

82. Self-portrait, 1965.
Oil on canvas, 14 x 10 (35.6 x 25.4).

Private collection.

83. Pogany 2, 1965.
Oil on canvas, 12 x 16 (30.5 x 40.6).
Peter Blake, London.

84. Trout for Factitious Bait, 1965. *Plate 52*
Oil on canvas, 60 x 83½ (152.4 x 212.1).
The Whitworth Art Gallery, University of
Manchester.

85. They Went, 1965.
Oil on canvas, 14½ x 11½ (36.9 x 29.2).
Private collection, London.

86. Alone, 1965.
Oil on canvas, 36 x 10 (91.4 x 25.4).
Private collection.

87. Things to Come, 1965-70.
Oil and screenprint on canvas, 25 x 35 (63.5 x 89).
Private collection.

88. Walter Lippmann, 1966. *Plate 40*
Oil on canvas, 72 x 84 (182.9 x 213.4).
Albright-Knox Art Gallery (Gift of Seymour H.
Knox, 1967), Buffalo, New York.

89. Erie Shore, 1966. *Plate 43 (detail)*
Oil on canvas, 72 x 60 (182.9 x 152.4).
Nationalgalerie, Berlin, Staatliche Museen, Stiftung
Preussische Kulturbesitz.

90. Dead End Kid, 1966.
Oil on canvas, 14 x 10 (35.6 x 25.4).
Private collection, London.

91. The Harold J. Laski Field Day, 1966-7.
Oil on canvas, 60 x 60 (152.4 x 152.4).
Colin St John Wilson, London.

92. Thanksgiving, 1966-7. *Plate 70 (detail)*
Oil on canvas, 60 x 72 (152.4 x 182.9).
Colin St John Wilson, London.

93. Juan de la Cruz, 1967. *Plate 61*
Oil on canvas, 72 x 60 (182.9 x 152.4).
Private collection.

94. The Williams Shift (for Lou Boudreau),
1967. *Plate 42*
Oil on canvas, 12 x 24 (30.5 x 61).
Private collection.

95. Sisler and Schoendienst, 1967.
Oil on canvas, 10 x 14 (25.4 x 35.6).
Colin St John Wilson, London.

96. Tampa, 1967.
Oil on canvas, 8 x 10 (20.3 x 25.4).
Private collection.

97. Stanky and Berra at St Petersburg, 1967.
Oil on canvas, 14 x 10 (35.6 x 25.4).
David Hockney, Los Angeles.

98. Eddie Stanky, 1967.
Oil on canvas, 16 x 12 (40.6 x 30.5).
McCrory Corporation, New York.

99. Morton Feldman, 1967.
Oil on canvas, 12 x 12 (30.5 x 30.5).
Private collection.

100. **Tinker to Evers**, 1967.
Oil on canvas, 18 x 13¾ (45.7 x 34.9).
Private collection.

101. **Batboy**, 1967.
Oil on canvas, 12 x 15¾ (30.5 x 40).
Private collection.

102. **For Edward Dahlberg**, 1967.
Oil on canvas, 10 x 8 (25.4 x 20.3).
Private collection, London.

103. **Screenplay**, 1967.
Oil on canvas, 31½ x 33 (80 x 83.8).
Arts Council of Great Britain.

104. **Casting**, 1967-9. *Plate 38 (detail)*
Oil on canvas, 98½ x 36 (250.2 x 91.4).
Museum Ludwig, Cologne.

105. **Shanghai Gestures, 1968.**
Oil on canvas, 24 x 48 (61 x 121.9).
The Metropolitan Museum of Art, New York.

106. **Little Slum Picture**, 1968. *Plate 48*
Oil on canvas, 30 x 24 (76.2 x 61).
Stanley Seeger, Sutton Place Heritage Trust,
Guildford.

107. **Unity Mitford**, 1968. *Plate 44*
Oil on canvas, 10 x 8 (25.4 x 20.3).
Collection of the artist.

108. **Indigo**, 1968.
Oil on canvas, 20 x 20 (50.8 x 50.8).
Private collection.

109. **Robert Duncan**, 1968.
Oil on canvas, 12 x 12 (30.5 x 30.5).
Collection of the artist.

110. **David at Berkeley**, 1968.
Oil on canvas, 10 x 8 (25.4 x 20.3).
Collection of the artist.

111. **Study (Francis Bacon)**, 1968.
Oil on canvas, 11½ x 9½ (29.2 x 24.2).
Private collection, New York.

112. **Peter**, 1968.
Oil on canvas, 10 x 8 (25.4 x 20.3).
David Hockney, Los Angeles.

113. **Synchromy with F.B. – General of Hot
Desire**, 1968-9. *Plate 47 (detail)*
Oil on canvas (diptych), each panel 60 x 36 (152.4
x 91.5).
Mr and Mrs Ian Stoutzker, London.

114. **Jack London Square, Oakland**, 1969.
Plate 55
Oil on canvas, 24 x 30 (61 x 76.2)
Private collection, Belgium.

115. **Study (Michael Hamburger)**, 1969. *Plate 91*
Oil on canvas, 14 x 11 (35.6 x 28).
Private collection, England.

116. **Little Romance I**, 1969. *Plate 54*
Oil on canvas, 12 x 10 (30.5 x 25.4).
Private collection.

117. **Paul Claudel and Edwige Feuillere**, 1969.

Oil on canvas, 15 x 12 (38.1 x 30.5).
Private collection.

118. **Primo**, 1969.
Oil on canvas, 18¾ x 16 (47.6 x 40.6).
Private collection, London.

119. **Study (Kenneth Koch)** 1969.
Oil on canvas, 10 x 8 (25.4 x 20.3).
Private collection.

120. **La Pasionaria**, 1969. *Plate 51*
Oil on canvas, 16¾ x 12½ (42.5 x 31.8).
Colin St John Wilson, London.

121. **Study (Jean)**, 1969.
Pencil on paper, 22½ x 13½ (57.2 x 34.3).
Collection of the artist.

122. **Outlying London Districts (in
Camberwell)**, 1969. *Plate 69 (detail)*
Oil on canvas, 96 x 36 (243.8 x 91.5).
Private collection, Belgium.

123. **Goodbye to Europe**, 1969. *Fig. 5*
Oil on canvas, 40 x 31 (101.6 x 78.8).
Private collection.

124. **Chelsea Reach (first version) (for J.A.
MCN.W.)**, 1969.
Fabrics and wood, 96 x 180 (243.8 x 458).
Private collection.

125. **Little Suicide Picture**, 1969. *Plate 50*
Oil on canvas, 20 x 20 (50.8 x 50.8).
The Baltimore Museum of Art (Thomas Benesch
Memorial Collection), Maryland.

126. **Drawing (from: Lives of the Engineers)**,
1969.
Pastel, 23 x 16 (58.5 x 40.6).
Private collection, London.

127. **Aden-Arabie**, 1969.
Oil on canvas, 20 x 20 (50.8 x 50.8).
Private collection.

128. **His Love Affairs (Waiter)**, 1969.
Oil and crayon on canvas, 19 x 13 (48.2 x 33).
Private collection.

129. **Louis Jouvet as Anne**, 1969.
Oil on canvas, 12 x 10 (30.5 x 25.4).
Private collection, London.

130. **W.H. Auden**, 1969.
Oil on canvas board, 14 x 10 (35.6 x 25.4).
Collection of the artist.

131. **Michael McClure**, 1969.
Oil on canvas, 8 x 10 (20.3 x 25.4).
Collection of the artist.

132. **Kenneth Rexroth and John Wieners**, 1969.
Oil on canvas board, 8¾ x 18 (22.2 x 45.7).
Collection of the artist.

133. **Charles Olson**, 1969.
Oil on canvas board, 11¾ x 9⅞ (29.8 x 25.1).
Collection of the artist.

134. **Ezra Pound**, 1969.
Oil on canvas, 14 x 17 (35.6 x 43.2).

Collection of the artist.

135. **Black**, 1969.
Oil on canvas board, 9⅞ x 8 (25.2 x 20.3).
Joel Bernstein, Chicago.

136. **Outlying London Districts (English-
woman (JS) Denmark Hill)**, 1969-70.
Oil on canvas, 84 x 36 (213.4 x 91.5).
Private collection.

137. **Dashiell Hammett c.1934**, 1970.
Oil on canvas, 49 x 10 (124.5 x 25.4).
Private collection.

138. **Dashiell Hammett**, 1970.
Oil on canvas, 49 x 10 (124.5 x 25.4).
Private collection.

139. **On a Regicide Peace**, 1970. *Plate 108*
Oil and silkscreen on canvas, 38 x 21¼ (96.5 x 54).
Louisiana Museum, Humlebaek, Denmark.

140. **Piano**, 1970.
Oil on canvas, 31 x 10 (78.8 x 25.4).
Private collection, London.

141. **Girl on a Scooter**, 1970. *Plate 13 (detail)*
Oil on canvas, 36½ x 13½ (92.7 x 34.3).
Private collection, London.

142. **Desk-Murder (Formerly The Third
Department (A Teste Study)**, 1970-84. *Plate 155*
Oil on canvas, 30 x 48 (76.2 x 121.9).
Collection of the artist.

143. **As a Man Grows Older**, 1971.
Oil on canvas, 48 x 24 (121.9 x 61).
Private collection.

144. **Peer Gynt, Lunatic Asylum, Cairo**, 1971.
Pencil and collage on paper, 34⅞ x 45⅝ (88.5 x 116).
Sonja Henies og Niels Onstads Stiftelser, Norway.

145. **Clerk's Dream**, 1972.
Oil on canvas, 78 x 25 (198 x 63.5).
Marlborough Gallery Inc. New York.

146. **Profile**, 1972.
Pastel and charcoal on paper, 15½ x 22¼ (39.4 x 56.5).
Private collection.

147. **Pencil Drawing for Daybook by Robert
Creeley**, 1972.
Pencil on paper, 24½ x 16⅛ (62.2 x 41).
Private collection, London.

148. **Hugh Lane**, 1972. *Plate 56*
Oil on canvas, 96 x 30 (243.8 x 76.2).
Private collection, Switzerland.

149. **The Autumn of Central Paris (after
Walter Benjamin)**, 1972-3. *Plate 57*
Oil on canvas, 60 x 60 (152.4 x 152.4).
Mrs Susan Lloyd, New York.

150. **Arcades (after Walter Benjamin)**, 1972-4.
Plate 46
Oil on canvas, 60 x 60 (152.4 x 152.4).
I.R. Wookey, Toronto.

151. **José Vincente (unfinished study for The
Singers)**, 1972-4. *Plate 60*

Oil on charcoal on canvas, 48 x 24 (121.9 x 61).
Collection of the artist.

152. Batman, 1973. *Plate 67*
Oil on canvas, 96 x 30 (243.8 x 76.2).
Private collection, Cologne.

153. Superman, 1973. *Plates 66 and 68*
Oil on canvas, 96 x 30 (243.8 x 76.2).
Private collection, Cologne.

154. Pacific Coast Highway (Across the Pacific), 1973. *Plate 63*
Oil on canvas, left-hand panel, 96 x 60 (243.8 x 152.4), right-hand panel, 60 x 60 (152.4 x 152.4).
Colin St John Wilson, London.

155. Kenneth Anger and Michael Powell, 1973. *Plate 62*
Oil on canvas, 96 x 60 (243.8 x 152.4).
Ludwig Collection, Aix-la-Chapelle.

156. Bill at Sunset, 1973. *Plate 65*
Oil on canvas, 96 x 30 (243.8 x 76.2).
Private collection, London.

157. Still (The Other Woman), 1973. *Plate 102*
Oil on canvas, 96 x 30 (243.8 x 76.2).
Mr and Mrs Ian Stoutzker, London.

158. The Man of the Woods and the Cat of the Mountains, 1973. *Plate 53*
Oil on canvas, 60 x 60 (152.4 x 152.4).
The Tate Gallery, London.

159. To Live in Peace (The Singers), 1973-4. *Plate 73*
Oil on canvas, 84 x 30 (231.4 x 76.2).
Marlborough International Fine Art.

160. The Sensualist, 1973-84. *Plate 1a*
Oil on canvas, 97 x 30⅜ (246.4 x 77.2).
Nasjonalgalleriet, Oslo.

161. Stage-life of the Dead, 1974.
Lithographic pencil on paper, 34 x 24 (86.4 x 61).
Jan Van Lerberghe, Brussels.

162. Malta (for Chris and Rose), 1974. *Plate 49*
Oil on canvas, 60 x 96 (152.4 x 243.8).
Private collection, Belgium.

163. Sculpture, 1974.
Pastel on paper, 30 x 20 (76.2 x 50.8).
Private collection.

164. Femme du Peuple I, 1974 *Fig. 9*
Pastel on paper, 30½ x 22 (77.5 x 55.9).
Dr Eugene A. Solow, Chicago.

165. Thus to Revisit, 1974.
Pastel on paper, 22 x 30¼ (55.9 x 76.8).
Private collection, London.

166. Study for Miss Brooke, 1974. *Plate 90*
Pastel on paper, 23⅞ x 15⅛ (60.6 x 38.5).
Museum Boymans-van Beuningen, Rotterdam.

167. Frances and Geraldine, 1974.
Charcoal on paper, 15 x 17⅜ (38.1 x 44.2).
Private collection, Hamburg.

168. Study for The World's Body, 1974.

Pastel on paper, 30 x 20 (76.2 x 50.8).
Private collection, London.

169. Sunset and Sunrise, 1974.
Pastel on paper, 30¼ x 22 (76.8 x 55.9).
Private collection.

170. The Shifting of the Fire, 1974-5.
Pastel on paper, 32¼ x 30¼ (81.9 x 77.5).
Private collection.

171. His Hour, 1975. *Plate 109*
Pastel and charcoal on paper, 30½ x 22½ (77.5 x 57).
Private collection, Los Angeles.

172. Wife and World, 1975.
Pastel on paper, 30 x 22 (76.2 x 55.9).
Private collection, London.

173. Communist and Socialist, 1975. *Plate 89*
Pastel on paper, 15⅛ x 22¼ (38.5 x 56.5).
Collection of the artist.

174. Head of a Boy, 1975.
Black chalk on paper, 20 x 16 (50.8 x 40.6).
Private collection, London.

175. In Catalonia, 1975. *Plate 123*
Pastel on paper, 25½ x 15¼ (64.8 x 38.7).
Private collection, London.

176. Orgasm, 1975.
Pastel over lithograph on paper, 12 x 16⅞ (30.5 x 42.8).
Galerie Claude Bernard, Paris.

177. Sarah, 1975.
Black chalk on paper, 16 x 20 (40.6 x 50.8).
Private collection.

178. For Peter, 1975.
Pastel on paper, 20 x 30 (50.8 x 76.2).
Private collection, London.

179. The Sneeze, 1975. *Plate 120*
Charcoal and pastel on paper, 34 x 27 (86.4 x 68.6).
The Museum of Modern Art (Gift of Nancy & Jim Dine), New York.

180. Tonight the Ballet, 1975.
Pastel on paper, 19⅞ x 15 (50.5 x 38.1).
Private collection, London.

181. The Street (A Life), 1975. *Plate 136*
Pastel on paper, 30⅜ x 22 (77.2 x 55.9).
H.R. Astrup, Oslo.

182. Waiting, 1975.
Pastel on paper, 30⅞ x 22¼ (78.5 x 56.5).
Private collection, Belgium.

183. Geraldine, 1975.
Charcoal on paper, 22 x 15⅜ (55.9 x 39).
Private collection, Los Angeles.

184. This Knot of Life, 1975.
Pastel on paper, 15¼ x 22½ (38.7 x 57.2).
Collection of the artist.

185. From London (James Joll and John Golding), 1975-6. *Plate 72*
Oil on canvas, 60 x 96 (152.4 x 243.8).
Private collection, Monte Carlo.

186. If Not, Not, 1975-6. *Plate 92*
Oil on canvas, 60 x 60 (152.4 x 152.4).
Scottish National Gallery of Modern Art, Edinburgh.

187. The Arabist (formerly **Moresque**), 1975-6. *Plate 96*
Oil on canvas, 96 x 30 (243.8 x 76.2).
Museum Boymans-van Beuningen, Rotterdam.

188. The Orientalist, 1975-6. *Plate 98*
Oil on canvas, 96 x 30 (243.8 x 76.2).
The Tate Gallery, London.

189. Land of Lakes, 1975-7. *Plate 100*
Oil on canvas, 60 x 60 (152.4 x 152.4).
Private collection, London.

190. Catalan Christ (Pretending to be Dead), 1976. *Plate 64*
Oil on canvas, 30 x 96 (76.2 x 243.8).
Private collection.

191. Houseboat Days (for John Ashbery), 1976. *Plate 104*
Oil on canvas, 72 x 24 (182.9 x 61).
Private collection, London.

192. The Rash Act, 1976.
Original transfer drawing on paper, 29 x 30¾ (73.7 x 52.7).
Collection of the artist.

193. Slade Student (study for Frankfurt Brothel), 1976.
Pastel on paper, 30¼ x 22 (76.8 x 55.9).
Private collection, London.

194. Richard Wollheim (Study for Three Philosophers), 1976.
Charcoal on paper, 22 x 30¼ (55.9 x 76.8).
Private collection.

195. Marrano (The Secret Jew), 1976. *Plate 83*
Oil and charcoal on canvas, 48 x 48 (121.9 x 121.9).
Marlborough International Fine Art.

196. Femme du Peuple, 1976.
Original transfer drawing on paper, 29 x 20¾ (73.7 x 52.7). Collection of the artist.

197. David (now reworked as **422**).
Oil and charcoal on canvas, 72 x 60 (182.9 x 152.4).
Collection of the artist.

198. Smyrna Greek (Nikos), 1976-7. *Plate 122*
Oil on canvas, 96 x 30 (243.8 x 76.2).
Collection Thyssen-Bornemisza, Lugano.

199. The Jew Etc., 1976-9. *Plate 97*
Oil and charcoal on canvas, 60 x 48 (152.4 x 122).
Collection of the artist.

200. After Giotto, 1976-9. *Plate 124 (detail)*
Oil and charcoal on canvas, 36 x 36 (91.4 x 91.4).
Private collection, California.

201. My Cat and Her Husband, 1977. *Plate 74*
Pastel and charcoal on paper, 15 x 22 (38.1 x 55.9).
Dominie Lee Kitaj, London.

202. Slav Soul, 1977.
Oil on canvas, 72 x 24 (182.9 x 61).
Private collection.

203. **The Mother,** 1977. *Plate 119*
Oil and charcoal on canvas, 42 x 42 (106.7 x 106.7).
Collection of the artist.

204. **Man in an Aalto Chair (James Kirkman),**
1977.
Charcoal on canvas, 42½ x 28 (108 x 71.1).
Private collection, England.

205. **The Hispanist (Nissa Torrents),** 1977-8.
Plates 77 and 79
Oil on canvas, 96 x 30 (243.8 x 76.2).
H.R. Astrup, Oslo.

206. **A Visit to London (Robert Creeley and
Robert Duncan),** 1977-9. *Plate 99 (detail), fig.11*
Oil and charcoal on canvas, 72 x 24 (182.9 x 61).
Collection Thyssen-Bornemisza, Lugano.

207. **Frankfurt Brothel,** 1978.
Oil on canvas, 48 x 60 (121.9 x 152.4).
Private collection.

208. **Her Law School Days,** 1978.
Pastel and charcoal on paper, 22 x 15 (55.9 x 38.1).
Private collection, England.

209. **Man and Child,** 1978. *Fig.13*
Charcoal on paper, 22⅛ x 14¼ (56.2 x 36.2).
Private collection.

210. **Jim Dine in Windsor Great Park,** 1978.
Charcoal on paper, 22¼ x 30½ (56.5 x 77.5).
Collection of the artist.

211. **Thérèse,** 1978.
Charcoal on paper, 22 x 15 (55.9 x 38.1).
The Michael and Dorothy Blankfort Collection at
Los Angeles County Museum.

212. **The Dancer (Margaret),** 1978. *Plate 105*
Pencil on paper, 39⅜ x 25½ (100 x 64.8).
Edwin A. Bergman, Chicago.

213. **The Yellow Apron,** 1978.
Pastel and charcoal on paper, 30⅞ x 11⅜ (78.4 x 29).
Private collection, Spain.

214. **Beisbol,** 1978.
Charcoal and pastel on paper, 30¼ x 22 (76.8 x 56).
Private collection, New York.

215. **Emblem,** 1978.
Pastel on paper, 40⅛ x 15½ (101.9 x 39.4).
Private collection, Paris.

216. **Catalan Cap,** 1978.
Pastel and charcoal on paper, 12⅞ x 22¼ (33 x 56.5).
Private collection, New York.

217. **Dominie (Dartmouth),** 1978. *Plate 87*
Pastel and charcoal on paper, 22 x 15 (55.9 x 38.1).
Collection of the artist.

218. **Dartmouth Nude,** 1978.
Pastel and charcoal on canvas over board, 14 x 24
(35.6 x 61).
Sandra Fisher, London.

219. **Dominie (San Felíu),** 1978. *Plate 85*
Pastel and charcoal on paper, 21⅜ x 15⅜ (54.3
x 39.1).
Collection of the artist.

220. **Lem (San Felíu),** 1978. *Plate 95.*
Pastel and charcoal on paper, 30¼ x 22 (76.8 x 56).
Collection of the artist.

221. **Doctor Kohn,** 1978. *Plate 141*
Pastel and charcoal on paper, 22 x 15 (55.9 x 38.1).
Collection of the artist.

222. **Bad Faith (Chile),** 1978.
Pastel and charcoal on paper, 30¼ x 22 (76.8 x 56).
Arkansas Arts Center.

223. **Bather (Tousled Hair),** 1978. *Plate 84*
Pastel on paper, 47¾ x 22⅜ (121.3 x 56.8).
Private collection.

224. **Bather (Wading),** 1978. *Plate 78.*
Pastel on paper, 48¾ x 22⅜ (123.8 x 56.8).
Private collection.

225. **Bad Faith (Gulag),** 1978.
Pastel and charcoal on paper, 44⅝ x 22 (113.4 x 56).
Private collection.

226. **The Messiah Watcher,** 1978.
Pastel on paper, 38⅝ x 15⅛ (98.1 x 38.4).
Private collection, Connecticut.

227. **The Symbolist,** 1978.
Pastel and pencil on paper, 39⅜ x 25½ (100 x 64.8).
Private collection, London.

228. **Bather (Torsion),** 1978. *Plate 76 (detail)*
Pastel on paper, 54¼ x 22⅜ (137.8 x 56.8).
Sovereign American Arts Corporation, New York.

229. **Bather (Seated),** 1978.
Pastel on paper, 17⅝ x 22⅜ (44.8 x 56.8).
Private collection.

230. **Slovak,** 1978.
Pastel and charcoal on paper, 22⅜ x 13⅞ (56.8 x 35).
Private collection, Switzerland.

231. **The Green Blanket,** 1978. *Plate 80*
Pastel and charcoal on paper, 30¼ x 22 in, (76.8
x 56).
Private collection, Switzerland.

232. **Bad Faith (Warsaw),** 1978.
Pastel and charcoal on paper, 43¼ x 22⅜ (109.9
x 56.8).
Collection of the artist.

233. **Dying Life Model,** 1978.
Pastel on paper, 22 x 30¼ (55.9 x 76.8).
Private collection.

234. **Washing Cork (Ramón),** 1978. *Plate 59*
Pastel on paper 22 x 15 (55.9 x 38.1).
The American Can Company, Greenwich,
Connecticut.

235. **New York Nocturne,** 1978.
Pastel and charcoal on paper, 30⅝ x 11⅝ (77.8 x
29.5).
Private collection, Canada.

236. **His New Freedom,** 1978. *Plate 93*
Pastel and charcoal on paper, 30¼ x 22 (76.8 x 56).
Collection of the artist.

237. **New York Madman,** 1978.

Pastel and charcoal on paper, 22 x 15¼ (56 x 38.7).
Private collection, London.

238. **Mother and Child,** 1978.
Pastel on paper, 30¼ x 22 (76.8 x 55.9).
Private collection.

239. **The Philosopher-Queen,** 1978-9. *Plate 81*
Pastel and charcoal on paper, 30¼ x 22 (76.8 x 56).
Collection of the artist.

240. **Dominie (Ninth Street),** 1978-9.
Pastel and charcoal on paper, 16½ x 22⅝ (42 x 57.5).
Collection of the artist.

241. **Sighs from Hell,** 1979. *Plate 75*
Pastel and charcoal on paper, 38½ x 39½ (97.8
x 100.3).
Edwin A. Bergman, Chicago.

242. **Sixth Avenue Madman,** 1979.
Pastel and charcoal on paper, 30¼ x 11 (76.8 x 28).
Dr Jack E. Chachkes, New York.

243. **Richard,** 1979, *Plate 115*
Pastel and charcoal on paper, 30¼ x 22 (76.8 x 56).
Private collection, New York.

244. **Ninth Street under Snow,** 1979. *Plate 110*
Pastel and charcoal on paper, 30¼ x 44 (76.8
x 111.8).
Private collection.

245. **Manchu Decadence,** 1979. *Plate 101*
Pastel and charcoal on paper, 45¼ x 22 (115 x 56).
Private collection, Rumson, New Jersey.

246. **Two London Painters (Frank Auerbach
and Sandra Fisher),** 1979. *Plate 111*
Pastel and charcoal on paper, 22 x 30¼ (56 x 76.8).
The Michael and Dorothy Blankfort Collection at
Los Angeles County Museum.

247. **Communist and Socialist** (second version),
1979. *Plate 107 (detail)*
Pastel and charcoal on paper, 30¼ x 22 (76.8 x 56).
Collection of the artist.

248. **Sides,** 1979. *Plate 106*
Pastel and charcoal on paper, each panel of three,
30¾ x 11 (78.1 x 28).
The British Museum, London.

249. **Actor (Richard),** 1979.
Pastel and charcoal on paper, 30¼ x 19⅜ (76.8
x 49.3).
Scottish National Gallery of Modern Art, Edinburgh.

250. **Young Man by a Lake,** 1979.
Pastel on paper, 30¾ x 22¼ (78.1 x 56.5).
Private collection, Switzerland.

251. **Anabel,** 1979.
Pastel on paper, 23¾ x 22⅜ (60.3 x 56.8).
Private collection, Belgium.

252. **Fenil Hague,** 1979.
Charcoal and oil on canvas, 18¾ x 13 (47.6 x 33).
Private collection, London.

253. **Marynka,** 1979.
Pastel on paper, 22¼ x 41¾ (56.5 x 106).
Private collection, London.

254. **Quentin,** 1979. *Plate 88*
Pastel and charcoal on paper, 25¾ x 15¾ (65.4 x 40).
Collection of the artist.

255. **Form and Content (after Giulio Romano),** 1979. *Plate 131*
Pastel and charcoal on paper, 28¾ x 20½ (73 x 52).
Collection of the artist.

256. **Marynka and Janet,** 1979.
Charcoal on paper, 30⅜ x 22¼ (77.2 x 56.5).
Private collection, London.

257. **Marynka on her Stomach,** 1979.
Charcoal and pastel on paper, 30⅜ x 22¼ (77.2 x 56.5).
Collection of the artist.

258. **Self portrait fragment,** c.1979.
Oil on canvas, 16½ x 6½ (41.7 x 16.3).
Private collection.

259. **Cézanne,** c.1979.
Charcoal on paper, 20¼ x 15½ (51.4 x 39.4).
Janie C. Lee, New York.

260. **The Rise of Fascism,** 1979-80. *Plate 94*
Pastel and oil on paper, 33⅜ x 62 (84.8 x 157.5).
The Tate Gallery, London.

261. **The Sailor (David Ward),** 1979-80. *Plate 144*
Oil on canvas, 60 x 24 (152.4 x 61).
H.R. Astrup, Oslo.

262. **Examining Negatives,** 1979-81.
Oil on canvas, 60 x 24 (152.4 x 61).
Private collection.

263. **Nicky,** c.1979-81.
Pastel and charcoal on canvas, 24 x 14 (61 x 35.6).
Private collection.

264. **Susanna,** c.1979-81.
Pastel and charcoal on canvas, 24 x 14 (61 x 35.6).
Private collection, London.

265. **Goodbye to Catalonia,** 1979-83.
Oil on canvas, 60 x 24 (152.4 x 61).
Fondation Veranneman, Belgium.

266. **Degas,** 1980. *Plate 118*
Pastel and charcoal on paper, 28¾ x 20 (73 x 50.8).
Collection of the artist.

267. **Wollheim and Angela,** 1980. *Plate 134*
Charcoal on paper, 22⅛ x 30¼ (56.2 x 76.8).
Collection of the artist.

268. **Paul Blackburn,** 1980. *Plate 126*
Charcoal on paper, 15¼ x 15¾ (38.7 x 40).
Akron Institute, Ohio.

269. **Marynka Smoking,** 1980. *Plate 112*
Pastel and charcoal on paper, 35¾ x 22¼ (90.8 x 56.5).
Collection of the artist.

270. **Mary-Ann,** 1980. *Plate 121*
Pastel and charcoal on paper, 30½ x 22 (77.5 x 56).
Private collection, London.

271. **Mary-Ann on her Stomach (face right),** 1980. *Plate 130*

Pastel and charcoal on paper, 22 x 30 (55.9 x 76.2).
H.R. Astrup, Oslo.

272. **Miranda's Back,** 1980.
Pastel and charcoal on paper, 30½ x 22¼ (77.5 x 56.5).
Private collection, Monte Carlo.

273. **Anabel on her Back,** 1980.
Pastel and charcoal on paper, 22 x 30 (55.9 x 76.2).
Private collection, London.

274. **Miranda (face left),** 1980.
Pastel and charcoal on paper, 30 x 22 (76.2 x 55.9).
Private collection, Los Angeles.

275. **Red Eyes,** 1980. *Plate 157*
Pastel and charcoal on paper, 30 x 22 (76.2 x 55.9).
Private collection.

276. **The Waitress,** 1980.
Pastel and charcoal on paper, 30½ x 27½ (77.5 x 69.8).
Private collection, London.

277. **After Rodin,** 1980.
Pastel and charcoal on paper, 30½ x 22½ (77.5 x 57.2).
Private collection.

278. **Miranda,** 1980.
Charcoal on paper, 25 x 18⅞ (63.5 x 48).
Private collection, England.

279. **The Mask,** 1980.
Pastel and charcoal on paper, 30¾ x 22½ (78 x 57.2).
Private collection, Baltimore, Maryland.

280. **The Listener (Joe Singer in Hiding),** 1980. *Plate 113*
Pastel and charcoal on paper, 40⅝ x 42⅝ (103.2 x 108.2).
Private collection.

281. **Bather (Psychotic Boy),** 1980. *Plate 103*
Pastel and charcoal on paper, 52¾ x 22½ (134 x 57.2).
H.R. Astrup, Oslo.

282. **China and Russia,** 1980.
Pastel and charcoal on paper, 30¼ x 28¾ (76.8 x 73).
Private collection, New York.

283. **The Red and the Black,** 1980.
Pastel and charcoal on paper, 31 x 23 (78.7 x 58.4).
Private collection, Toronto.

284. **The Yellow Hat,** 1980. *Plate 116*
Pastel and charcoal on paper, 30½ x 22¾ (77.5 x 57.8).
Private collection, London.

285. **Bad Faith (Riga) (Joe Singer Taking Leave of his Fiancée),** 1980. *Plate 117*
Pastel, charcoal and oil on paper, 37 x 22¼ (94 x 56.5).
I.R. Wookey, Toronto.

286. **Study for The Jewish School (Joe Singer as a Boy),** 1980.
Pastel and charcoal on paper, 30½ x 22¼ (77.5 x 56.5).
Collection of the artist.

287. **Two Famous Writers,** 1980.
Charcoal on paper, 59½ x 22 (151.1 x 55.9).
Private collection.

288. **Self-portrait in Saragossa,** 1980. *Plate 132*
Charcoal and pastel on paper, 58 x 33½ (147.3 x 85.1).
The Israel Museum, Jerusalem.

289. **The Green Dress,** 1980.
Pastel and charcoal on paper, 30⅞ x 22⅝ (78.5 x 57.5).
Private collection, London.

290. **The Jewish School (Drawing a Golem),** 1980. *Plate 114*
Oil on canvas, 60 x 60 (152.4 x 152.4).
Private collection, Monte Carlo.

291. **Starting a War,** 1980-1. *Plate 153 (detail)*
Oil on canvas, 84 x 36 (213.4 x 91.5).
Private collection, Akron, Ohio.

292. **The Red Embrace,** 1980-1. *Plate 151*
Charcaol, pastel and oil on paper, 57 x 22¾ (144.7 x 57.8).
Private collection, Paris.

293. **Golem** 1980-1.
Oil on canvas, 59¼ x 20¾ (150.5 x 52.8).
Private collection, New York.

294. **Chimera,** 1980-1. *Plate 128*
Oil on canvas, 22 x 9¾ (55.9 x 24.8).
Galerie Beyeler, Basle.

295. **Marynka Pregnant,** 1981.
Charcoal and pastel on paper, 30½ x 22½ (77.5 x 57.2).
Private collection, Baltimore, Maryland.

296. **The Garden,** 1981. *Plate 125*
Oil on canvas, 48 x 48 (121.9 x 121.9).
The Cleveland Museum of Art, Ohio.

297. **Grey Girl,** 1981. *Plate 145*
Oil on canvas, 30 x 12 (76.2 x 30.5).
Collection of the artist.

298. **Maternity,** 1981.
Pastel and charcoal on paper, 30¼ x 22⅛ (76.8 x 56.2).
Private collection.

299. **Rock Garden (The Nation),** 1981 *Plate 129*
Oil on canvas, 48 x 48 (121.9 x 121.9).
Private collection.

300. **Sacha and Gabriel,** 1981. *Plate 86*
Charcoal on paper, 30⅜ x 22¼ (77.2 x 56.5).
Collection of the artist.

301. **Marynka Pregnant II,** 1981. *Plate 139*
Pastel and charcoal on paper, 22¼ x 30⅜ (56.5 x 77.2).
Collection of the artist.

302. **Winter Sun over Chelsea,** 1981.
Oil on canvas, 30 x 15 (76.2 x 38.1).
Galerie Beyeler, Basle.

303. **Garth,** 1981. *Plate 142*
Oil on canvas, 24 x 14 (61 x 35.6).
Private collection, Belgium.

304. Vert Compose Clair, 1981.
Oil on canvas, 30 x 12⅛ (76.2 x 30.8).
Private collection, London.

305. Study for The Rock Garden, 1981.
Pastel and charcoal on paper, 15⅜ x 10⅛ (39 x 25.7).
Private collection.

306. Courbet's Sister, 1981. *Plate 135*
Pencil on paper, 30 x 22½ (76.2 x 57.2).
Private collection, Switzerland.

307. Study for the Jewish School (The Last Day), 1981. *Plate 158*
Pastel and charcoal on paper, 30⅜ x 22¼ (77.2 x 56.5).
Private collection, London.

308. The White Collar, 1981.
Oil on canvas, 30⅛ x 12 (76.5 x 30.5).
Private collection

309. Fed up, 1981.
Oil on paper, 28⅛ x 24¼ (71.4 x 61.6).
Private collection, England.

310. Hockney's Mother, 1981. *Fig. 8*
Charcoal on paper, 30⅜ x 22¼ (77.2 x 56.5).
David Hockney, Los Angeles.

311. Self-portrait (San Feliu), 1982.
Charcoal and pastel on paper, 30¾ x 22¼ (78.1 x 56.5).
Collection of the artist.

312. Slav Soul (Vera), 1982.
Pastel and charcoal on paper, 30½ x 22⅛ (77.5 x 56.2).
Private collection.

313. Robert Duncan in profile (Reciting with Hands Beating Time), 1982.
Charcoal on paper, 22½ x 15½ (57.2 x 39.4).
Private collection, England.

314. Robert Duncan in profile face left, 1982.
Charcoal on paper, 15½ x 22¾ (39.4 x 57.9).
Private collection, Berkeley, California.

315. Robert Duncan with Hat leaning forward, 1982.
Pastel and charcoal on paper, 22½ x 14 (57.2 x 35.6).
Galerie Claude Bernard, Paris.

316. Robert Duncan face left (light version), 1982.
Charcoal on paper, 15½ x 22½ (39.4 x 57.2).
Private collection.

317. Robert Duncan on a Balcony, 1982.
Pastel and charcoal on paper, 29½ x 22½ (75 x 57.2).
Private collection.

318. Robert Duncan in profile with eyes closed, 1982.
Charcoal on paper, 15½ x 22½ (39.4 x 57.2).
Private collection.

319. The Poet, Eyes Closed (Robert Duncan), 1982. *Plate 138*
Charcoal on paper, 22½ x 31 (57.2 x 78.7).
Collection of the artist.

320. The Poet and Notre Dame (Robert Duncan), 1982. *Plate 127*
Pastel and charcoal on paper, 22½ x 15½ (57 x 39.4).
Private collection, Switzerland.

321. The Poet Writing (Robert Duncan), 1982.
Charcoal on paper, 31 x 22½ (78.7 x 57.2).
Private collection.

322. Paris, France, 1982.
Oil on canvas, 60 x 24 (152.4 x 61).
Private collection.

323. London, England (Bathers), 1982. *Plate 147*
Oil on canvas, 48 x 48 (121.9 x 121.9).
Private collection, Oslo.

324. In the Mountains, 1982.
Oil on canvas, 48 x 48 (121.9 x 121.9).
National Gallery, Cape Town.

325. Sailor, 1982.
Charcoal on paper, 22¾ x 15½ (57.8 x 39.4).
Private collection, Switzerland.

326. Ilan, 1982.
Pastel and charcoal on paper, 22¼ x 15⅝ (56.5 x 39.7).
Mary Moore.

327. Self-portrait (after Matteo), 1982.
Charcoal on paper, 22½ x 15⅜ (57.2 x 39).
Collection of the artist.

328. Yona in Paris, 1982. *Plate 156*
Charcoal on paper, 22½ x 15⅜ (57.2 x 39).
Collection of the artist.

329. Tim in Paris, 1982.
Charcoal on paper, 22½ x 15⅜ (57.2 x 39).
Private collection, London.

330. Man in Blue Cloak, 1982.
Pastel and charcoal on paper, 22½ x 15⅜ (57.2 x 39).
MacLaurin Art Gallery, Ayr.

331. Male Nude, 1982.
Charcoal on paper, 22⅝ x 15½ (57.5 x 39.4).
Private collection, London.

332. The Cure, 1982. *Plate 133*
Oil on canvas, 36 x 36 (91.5 x 91.5).
Private collection, London.

333. Ted in Paris, 1983.
Charcoal on paper, 22 x 14½ (56 x 36.8).
Private collection, London.

334. The Room (rue St Denis), 1982–3. *Plate 137*
Oil on canvas, 48 x 36 (121.9 x 91.5).
Private collection, Cleveland, Ohio.

335. Ellen, 1983.
Charcoal on paper, 22½ x 30¾ (57.2 x 78.1).
Private collection, New York.

336. Andropov, 1983.
Pastel and charcoal on paper, 30⅝ x 22⅝ (77.8 x 57.5).
Private collection, Italy.

337. Mother, 1983.
Charcoal and pastel on paper, 30⅞ x 22⅝ (78.4 x 57.5).
Collection of the artist.

338. Mother, 1983.
Charcoal on paper, 30¾ x 22½ (78.1 x 57.2).
Collection of the artist.

339. Mother, 1983.
Pastel and charcoal on paper, 30⅞ x 22⅝ (78.4 x 57.5).
Collection of the artist.

340. Mother, 1983.
Pastel and charcoal on paper, 30⅞ x 22⅜ (78.4 x 56.8).
Collection of the artist.

341. Sarah, 1983.
Charcoal on paper, 30½ x 22⅝ (77.5 x 57.5).
Thomas Gibson, London.

342. American in Paris (Wendy), 1983.
Charcoal on paper, 30⅝ x 22⅝ (77.8 x 57.5).
Marlborough Fine Art (London) Ltd.

343. American in Paris (Wendy's Back), 1983.
Charcoal on paper, 22½ x 15⅜ (57.2 x 39).
Galerie Claude Bernard, Paris.

344. American in Paris (Wendy Prone), 1983.
Charcoal on paper, 15¼ x 22½ (38.8 x 57.2).
Galerie Claude Bernard, Paris.

345. Self-portrait (Reading), 1983.
Charcoal on paper, 22½ x 15½ (57.2 x 39.4).
Sandra Fisher, London.

346. Self-portrait (Greta Prozor), 1983.
Charcoal on paper, 22⅝ x 15⅜ (57.5 x 39).
Collection of the artist.

347. Self-portrait (Circle), 1983.
Charcoal on paper, 22⅝ x 15¼ (57.5 x 38.8).
Collection of the artist.

348. Sandra in Paris, 1983.
Charcoal on paper, 19½ x 22½ (49.5 x 57.2).
Collection of the artist.

349. Self-portrait (Hand on Chin), 1983.
Charcoal on paper, 13¾ x 10⅝ (35 x 27).
Collection of the artist.

350. Self-portrait (Papillon), 1983.
Charcoal on paper, 13¾ x 10⅝ (35 x 27).
Collection of the artist.

351. Place de la Concorde, 1983. *Fig. 7*
Charcoal on paper, 30⅝ x 22⅝ (77.8 x 57.5).
Private collection, Paris.

352. George Orwell, 1983.
Pastel and charcoal on paper, 30½ x 22¼ (77.5 x 56.5).
Time Magazine, New York.

353. The Red Brassière, 1983. *Plate 154*
Charcoal and pastel on paper, 30⅝ x 22⅜ (77.8 x 56.8).
Private collection, Belgium.

354. Ellen (Sunlit), 1983.
Pastel and charcoal on paper, 30½ x 22⅛ (77.5 x 56.2).
Private collection, Switzerland.

355. Glen Gould (on T.V.), 1983.
Charcoal on paper, 5¾ x 7¾ (14.6 x 19.7).
Collection of the artist.

356. Ellen and Shofar, 1983-4. *Plate 140*
Pastel and charcoal on paper, 43½ x 30 (110.5 x 76.2).
Private collection, London.

357. Cecil Court, London WC2 (The Refugees), 1983-4. *Plate 143*
Oil on canvas, 72 x 72 (182.9 x 182.9).
The Tate Gallery, London.

358. Ellen's Back, 1984.
Pastel and charcoal on paper, 30¾ x 22¼ (78.1 x 56.5).
Whitney Museum of American Art, New York.
Gift of Edward L. Gardner.

359. Anna, 1984.
Charcoal and pastel on paper, 30⅝ x 22⅝ (77.8 x 57.5).
Private collection, Belgium.

360. Sarah's Back, 1984.
Charcoal and pastel on paper, 30⅝ x 22⅝ (77.8 x 57.5).
Private collection, Sydney.

361. Self-portrait as a Woman, 1984.
Plate 146
Oil on canvas, 97 x 30⅜ (246.4 x 77.2).
H.R. Astrup, Oslo.

362. Amerika (John Ford on his Death Bed), 1983-4. *Plate 148*
Oil on canvas, 60 x 60 (152.4 x 152.4).
Metropolitan Museum, New York.

363. Amerika (Baseball), 1983-4. *Plate 152*
Oil on canvas, 60 x 60 (152.4 x 152.4).
Private collection, New York.

364. Arikha Sketching, 1982.
Charcoal on paper, 7¾ x 5¾ (19.7 x 14.6).
Collection of the artist.

365. Sketch of Hockney Sketching, 1982.
Charcoal on paper, 7¾ x 5¾ (19.7 x 14.6).
Collection of the artist.

366. Isaac Stern at Chatelet 1982.
Charcoal on paper, 7¾ x 5¾ (19.7 x 14.6).
Collection of the artist.

367. Mother (Weeping), 1983.
Charcoal on paper, 7¾ x 5¾ (19.7 x 14.6).
Collection of the artist.

368. Self-portrait (Cold in Paris), 1983.
Charcoal on paper, 13¾ x 10½ (35 x 27).
Collection of the artist.

369. Grandmother Kitaj, aged 102, 1983.
Plate 149
Charcoal on paper, 7¾ x 5¾ (19.7 x 14.6).
Collection of the artist.

370. Max, 10 Minutes Old, 1984.
Charcoal on paper, 7¾ x 5¾ (19.7 x 14.6).
Collection of the artist.

371. Study for The Jewish Rider, 1984.
Pastel and charcoal on paper, 40⅞ x 30¾ (103.8 x 78.1).
Private collection, London.

372. The Cézannist, 1980-5. *Plate 159*
Oil on canvas, 60 x 24 (152.4 x 61).
Private collection, USA.

373. Painting, 1983-5. *Plate 167*
Oil on canvas, 41½ x 41½ (105.4 x 105.4).
Private collection, USA.

374. The Divinity School Address, 1983-5.
Plate 168
Oil on canvas, 36 x 48 (91.4 x 121.9).
Private collection, England.

375. The Jewish Rider, 1984-5. *Plate 164*
Oil on canvas, 60 x 60 (152.4 x 152.4).
Private collection.

376. The Gentile Conductor, 1984-5.
Oil on canvas, 84 x 11⅜ (213.4 x 28.9).
Collection of the artist.

377. The Painter (Cross and Chimney), 1984-5.
Charcoal and pastel on paper, 30¾ x 43¾ (78.1 x 111.1).
Collection of the artist.

378. Raymond Massey as Hamlet (Study for The Old Vic), 1985. *Plate 163*
Oil on canvas, 60¼ x 24⅛ (153 x 61.3).
Private collection, USA.

379. Hamlet Crouching (Study for The Old Vic), 1985.
Oil on canvas, 60 x 24 (152.4 x 61).
Private collection.

380. Hamlet Pretending Madness (Study for The Old Vic), 1985.
Oil on canvas, 60 x 24⅛ (152.4 x 61.3).
Private collection, London.

381. Hamlet's Ghost, The King of Denmark (Study for The Old Vic), 1985.
Oil on canvas, 60 x 24 (152.4 x 61).
Private collection, London.

382. Germania (The Tunnel), 1985.
Plate 169
Oil on canvas, 72⅛ x 84¼ (183.2 x 214).
Private collection, USA.

383. Lord Sieff of Brimpton, 1985.
Charcoal and pastel on paper, 22¾ x 30¾ (57.8 x 78.1).
National Portrait Gallery, London.

384. The Art Doctor, 1985.
Pastel and charcoal on paper, 30⅝ x 22½ (77.8 x 57.2).
Private collection, London.

385. Anne on Drancy Station, 1985.
Charcoal on paper, 43½ x 22½ (110.5 x 57.2).
Marlborough International Fine Art.

386. Philip Roth, 1985.
Charcoal on paper, 30⅝ x 22½ (77.8 x 57.2).
Collection of the artist.

387. Yiddish Hamlet (Y. Löwy), 1985.
Oil on canvas, 48 x 24 (122 x 61).
Marlborough International Fine Art.

388. 4 A.M. 1985. *Plate 170*
Oil on canvas, 36 x 45⅞ (91.4 x 116.5).
Private collection.

389. Arabs and Jews (Jerusalem), 1985.
Oil on canvas, 36 x 72 (91.4 x 182.9).
Collection of the artist.

390. Max, 1985.
Charcoal on paper, 8⅛ x 6¼ (20.6 x 15.9).
Collection of the artist.

391. Passion (1940-45) Cross and Chimney, 1985.
Oil on canvas, 16½ x 10⅞ (41.9 x 27.7).
Collection of the artist.

392. Bather (Frankfurt), 1985. *Plate 162*
Charcoal and pastel on paper, 50 x 22½ (127 x 57.2).
Private collection.

393. Passion (1940-45) Reading, 1985.
Oil on canvas, 18 x 20 (45.7 x 50.8).
Collection of the artist.

394. Passion (1940-45) Writing, 1985. *Plate 161*
Oil on canvas, 18 x 10½ (45.7 x 26.7).
Collection of the artist.

395. Passion (1940-45) Girl / Plume 1985.
Oil on canvas, 22 x 17 (55.9 x 43.2).
Collection of the artist.

396. Passion (1940-45) Coastline, 1985.
Oil on canvas, 8 x 10 (20.3 x 25.4).
Collection of the artist.

397. Passion (1940-45) Landscape / Chamber, 1985.
Oil on canvas, 11 x 20 (28 x 50.8).
Collection of the artist.

398. The Jewish Schoolhouse (Handshake), 1960-86.
Oil on canvas, 40½ x 35½ (102.9 x 90.2).
Private collection, USA.

399. Arabs and Jews (The Dead Sea), 1970-86.
Oil on canvas, 30⅛ x 38⅞ (76.5 x 98.8).
Collection of the artist.

400. False Messiah, 1975-86.
Oil on canvas, 24 x 16⅛ (61 x 41).
The Tate Gallery Foundation, London.

401. Messiah (Boy), 1980-6.
Oil on canvas, 20⅜ x 21¾ (51.9 x 55.2).
Private collection, USA.

402. Delacroix's Studio, 1982-6.
Pastel and charcoal on paper, 33⅛ x 22⅝ (84.1 x 57.5).
Private collection, USA.

403. Expulsion from Paradise, 1982-6.
Oil on canvas, 36⅛ x 36⅛ (91.7 x 91.7).
Collection of the artist.

404. Germania (The Engine Room), 1983-6.
Oil on canvas, 48 x 48 (122 x 122).
Private collection.

405. Paris Bather (the Art Student), 1984-6.
Pastel and charcoal on paper, 54 x 22½ (137.2 x
57.2).
Marlborough International Fine Art.

406. Drancy, 1984-6.
Pastel and charcoal on paper, 39½ x 30¾ (100.4
x 78.1).
Fondation du Judaïsme Français, Paris.

407. Notre Dame de Paris, 1984-6.
Oil on canvas, 60 x 60 (152.4 x 152.4).
Paine Webber Group Inc., New York.

408. Ophelia (study for The Old Vic),
1984-6.
Oil on canvas, 36 x 36 (91.5 x 91.5).
Private collection, USA.

409. Bather (Wanda), 1984-6.
Oil on canvas, 60 x 24¼ (152.4 x 61.6).
Royal Academy of Arts, London.

410. Fenway, 1984-6.
Oil on canvas, 28 x 45⅝ (71.1 x 45.9).
Collection of the artist.

411. Reading in Bed, 1985-6.
Oil on canvas, 72 x 36¼ (182.9 x 92.1).
Dr Jack E. Chachkes, USA.

412. The Messianist, 1985-6.
Oil on canvas, 72 x 24 (182.9 x 61).
Private collection.

**413. Passion (1940-45) Varschreibt! After
Picasso**, 1986.
Oil on canvas, 16⅝ x 9½ (42.2 x 24.1).
Collection of the artist.

414. Passion (1940-45) Two Plumes, 1986.
Oil on canvas, 12½ x 8¾ (31.8 x 22.2).
Collection of the artist.

415. After JSS, 1986.
Charcoal on paper, 58⅜ x 22½ (148.3 x 56.5).
Private collection.

**416. Hamlet and his Father's Ghost (Study for
The Old Vic)**, 1986. *Plate 166*
Oil on canvas, 48¼ x 72⅛ (122.4 x 183.2).
Private collection.

417. The Old Vic 1986.
Oil on canvas, 48 x 72 (122 x 182.9).
Private collection, Geneva.

418. Sir Ernst Gombrich, 1986.
Pastel and charcoal on paper, 26½ x 22⅜ (67.3
x 56.7).
National Portrait Gallery, London.

419. Foul Tip, 1986.
Oil on canvas, 35¾ x 27¼ (90.8 x 69.2).
Collection of the artist.

420. Catherine Gazing at Degas Poster,
1986.
Pencil on paper, 30⅜ x 22½ (77.2 x 57.2).
Private collection, Sydney.

421. Mother and Child (Tempest), 1986.
Oil on canvas, 45⅝ x 28⅛ (115.8 x 71.3).
Marlborough International Fine Art.

422. The Neo-Cubist, 1976-87. *Plate 160*
Oil on canvas, 70 x 52 (177.8 x 132.1).
Private collection.

423. The Caféist, 1980-7. *Plate 165*
Oil on canvas, 36 x 36 (91.4 x 91.4).
Private collection, London.

424. The Drivist, 1985-87.
Oil on canvas, 72¼ x 36 (183.5 x 91.4).
Saatchi Collection, London.

425. Germania (Joe Singer's Last Room),
1987.
Oil on canvas, 36 x 45¾ (91.4 x 116.2).
Collection of the artist.

426. The Sniper, 1987.
Oil on canvas, 120 x 36 (304.9 x 91.4).
Saatchi Collection, London.

427. The Londonist, 1987.
Oil on canvas, 120 x 36 (304.9 x 91.4).
Private collection.

428. Germania (To the Brothel), 1987.
Plate 175
Oil on canvas, 47¾ x 36 (121.3 x 91.4).
Laing Art Gallery, Newcastle-upon-Tyne.

429. His Last Painting, 1987. *Plate 172*
Oil on canvas, 39¼ x 24¾ (99.7 x 62.9).
Private collection, London.

430. Three Women on a Train 1987.
Oil on canvas, 32⅛ x 48⅛ (81.6 x 122.3).
Collection of the artist.

431. Man Looking Through a Keyhole, 1987.
Charcoal and coloured chalk on paper, 30⅝ x 22⅝
(77.8 x 57.5).
Private collection, London.

**432. Besht Imaginary Portrait of The Baal
Shem Tov**. 1987.
Pastel on paper, 30⅝ x 22¾ (77.8 x 57.8).
Private collection, London.

433. Moses (after Bassano), 1987.
Pastel on paper 22½ x 30⅝ (57.2 x 77.8).
Private collection.

434. After Ingres, 1987.
Charcoal on paper, 30⅝ x 22⅝ (77.8 x 57.5).
Private collection, Switzerland

435. Mother and Child and Father in Garden,
1987.
Oil on canvas, 33 x 44¾ (83.8 x 113.7).
Private collection.

436. Germania (Vienna), 1987. *Plate 174*
Oil on canvas, 47¼ x 60 (120 x 152.4).
Saatchi Collection, London.

437. The Paintist, 1987.
Oil on canvas, 28½ x 36 (72.4 x 91.4).
Private collection, USA.

438. Two Brothers, 1987.
Oil on canvas, 60⅛ x 24⅛ (152.7 x 61.3).
Private collection.

439. Degas, 1987.
Pastel and charcoal, 30½ x 22½ (77.5 x 57.2).
Private collection, London.

440. Mother and Child after Vincent,
1987.
Pastel and charcoal on paper, 30⅝ x 22⅜
(77.8 x 56.8).
Private collection, London.

441. Statue and Woman, 1980-8.
Oil on canvas, 24½ x 60¼ (61.6 x 153).
Private collection.

442. Birthday, 1988.
Oil on canvas, 50 x 60 (127 x 152.4).
Private collection, USA.

443. Lynley, 1988.
Pastel and charcoal on paper, 22¾ x 30¾ (57.8
x 78.1).
Private collection, London.

444. Lynley with Bra, 1988.
Charcoal on paper, 30¾ x 22¼ (78.1 x 56.5).
Private collection, London.

445. Two Messiahs, 1988.
Oil on canvas, 96 x 30 (243.9 x 76.2).
Private collection.

446. Messiah (Bather), 1988.
Oil on canvas, 78 x 24⅞ (198.1 x 63.2).
Private collection, USA.

447. Untitled, 1988.
Charcoal on paper, 30⅞ x 22¾ (78.4 x 57.8).
Collection of the artist.

448. The Corridor (After Sassetta), 1988.
Oil on canvas, 48¼ x 60¼ (122.5 x 153).
Saatchi Collection, London.

449. The Fulham Road, SW10 (after Bruegel),
1988.
Oil on canvas, 48¼ x 60¼ (122.6 x 153).
Private collection, London.

450. Untitled, 1988.
Charcoal on paper, 30⅝ x 22⅜ (77.7 x 56.8).
Collection of the artist.

451. After Baudelaire, 1988.
Charcoal and pastel on paper, 55 x 19⅝ (139.7
x 49.9).
Fondation Veranneman, Belgium.

452. After Hals, 1988.
Pastel on paper, 30½ x 22⅝ (77.5 x 57.5).
Private collection, USA.

**453. Robert Walser (Sculpture in a
Snowstorm)**, 1988.
Oil on canvas, 60 x 24 (152.4 x 61).
Collection of the artist.

454. **Lynley and Achille**, 1988.
Charcoal on paper, 30⅝ x 22¾ (77.8 x 57.8).
Private collection.

455. **Lynley in Corb Chaise-longue**, 1988.
Charcoal on paper, 30⅞ x 22½ (78.5 x 57.1).
Private collection, London.

456. **Fulham Road Cinema Bathers**, 1988.
Oil on canvas, 60½ x 60¾ (153.8 x 145.3).
Mr & Mrs Edward L. Gardner, Larchmont,
New York.

457. **Diasporist**, 1988.
Oil on canvas, 16 x 12 (40.6 x 30.5).
Collection of the artist.

458. **The Mountain Footpath**, 1988-9.
Oil on canvas, 36¼ x 36⅛ (92 x 91.8).
Private collection.

459. **Germania (The Audience)**, 1989.
Plate 179
Oil on canvas, 48½ x 60¼ (123.2 x 153).
Private collection.

460. **CBD Pregnant**, 1989.
Charcoal on paper, 30½ x 22½ (77.5 x 57.1).
Private collection, USA.

461. **The Heart Determines**, 1989.
Fig. 12
Oil on canvas, 48 x 48 (121.9 x 121.9).
Private collection, London.

462. **Sketch of CBD with Auerbach**,
1989.
Charcoal on paper, 22½ x 30½ (57.1 x 77.4).
Swindon Art Gallery, England.

463. **Walking in London**, 1989.
Charcoal and pastel on paper, 30½ x 22½
(77.4 x 57.1).
Janie C. Lee, New York.

464. **Melancholy**, 1989. *Plate 180*
Oil on canvas, 48¼ x 48⅛ (122.5 x 122.3).
Private collection.

465. **Melancholy after Dürer**, 1989.
Oil on canvas, 48⅝ x 48¼ (123.5 x 122.5).
British Council.

466. **Burnt Out**, 1989.
Oil on canvas, 48⅝ x 48⅜ (123.5 x 122.8).
Private collection.

467. **Joel Grey**, 1989.
Charcoal on paper, 30½ x 22½ (77.5 x 57.1).
Private collection, USA.

468. **The Man on the Ceiling**, 1989.
Oil on canvas, 48¼ x 48⅛ (122.6 x 122.2).
Private collection.

469. **Up All Night (Fulham Road)**, 1989.
Plate 181
Oil on canvas, 48 x 48 (122 x 122).
Private collection.

470. **Mirror Boxer (Self-portrait)**, 1989.
Oil on canvas, 24 x 24 (61 x 61).
Marlborough Fine Art (London) Ltd.

471. **Hotel Rembrandt**, 1989.
Oil on canvas, 65½ x 55 (166.3 x 141).
Private collection.

472. **W.S.**, 1989.
Charcoal on paper, 22½ x 14¼ (57.2 x 36.2).
Marlborough Gallery Inc., New York.

473. **Study for The Wasteland**, 1987-90.
Oil on canvas, 65⅛ x 55¼ (165.4 x 140.3).
Private collection.

474. **Heart Attack**, 1990.
Oil on canvas, 48¼ x 48¼ (122.5 x 122.5).
Private collection.

475. **The First Time (Havana, 1949)**, 1990.
Plate 177
Oil on canvas, 48⅜ x 48½ (122.8 x 123.2).
Private collection.

476. **The Second Time (Vera Cruz, 1949)**,
1990.
Oil on canvas, 60¼ x 60¼ (153 x 153).
Private collection, Connecticut.

477. **The Pursuit of Happiness**, 1990.
Oil on canvas, 48 x 36 (122 x 91.5).
Collection of the artist.

478. **Sorbonne Hotel (sw7)**, 1990.
Oil on canvas, 85½ x 23 (217.2 x 58.4).
Private collection.

479. **Rousseau**, 1990.
Oil on canvas, 60 x 60⅛ (152.4 x 153).
Private collection.

480. **Sandra (first state)**, 1990.
Charcoal on canvas, 24 x 18 (61 x 45.7).
Collection of the artist.

481. **I Married an Angel**, 1990.
Oil on canvas, 48 x 47⅞ (122 x 121.7).
Private collection.

482. **Aharon Appelfeld**, 1990.
Oil on canvas, 24½ x 24⅜ (61.6 x 61.8).
Israel Museum, Jerusalem.

483. **Julián Ríos**, 1990
Charcoal on paper, 15 x 11⅜ (38 x 29).
Private collection, Madrid.

484. **Painter (Sandra)**, 1990.
Oil on canvas, 24 x 20 (61 x 50.8).
Collection of the artist.

485. **Passion – Into the Night**,
1987-91.
Charcoal on canvas, 13¾ x 6⅜ (35 x 16.2).
Collection of the artist.

486. **A Jew in Love**, 1988-91.
Charcoal on canvas, 23⅛ x 13½ (58.7 x 34.3).
Collection of the artist.

487. **Ahad Ha-Am**, 1988-91.
Charcoal and pastel on paper, 22½ x 11½ (57.2
x 31.8).
Marlborough Gallery Inc., New York.

488. **Dr Pinsker**, 1989-91.

Pastel and charcoal on paper, 22½ x 13¼ (57.2
x 33.6).
Marlborough Gallery Inc., New York.

489. **Unpacking my Library**, 1990-1. *Fig. 14*
Oil on canvas, 48 x 48 (122 x 122).
Private collection, Los Angeles.

490. **Against Slander**, 1990-1. *Plate 171*
Oil on canvas, 60 x 60 (152.4 x 152.4).
Private collection.

491. **Lucian Freud**, 1990-91.
Charcoal and pastel on paper, 30 x 22½ (76.2
x 57.2).
Metropolitan Museum, New York.

492. **The Oak Tree**, 1991. *Plate 173*
Oil on canvas, 60⅛ x 60 (152.7 x 152.4).
Private collection.

493. **Looking at Art Books** 1991.
Oil and charcoal on canvas, 18 x 12 (45.7 x 30.5).
Private collection, Switzerland.

494. **De Morgan's House**, 1991. *Plate 178*
Oil on canvas, 48 x 48 (122 x 122).
I.R. Wookey, Toronto.

495. **De Morgan's House**, 1991.
Charcoal on canvas, 16 x 11¾ (40.6 x 29.8).
Collection of the artist.

496. **Jack My Hedgehog**, 1991.
Oil on canvas, 48 x 48 (122 x 122).
Marlborough Fine Art (London) Ltd.

497. **Sunday**, 1991. *Plate 176*
Oil on canvas, 26½ x 60⅛ (91.7 x 152.8).
Private collection.

498. **Emmanuel Levinas (after a drawing by
Avigdor Arikha)**, 1991.
Charcoal on paper, 30 x 22 (76.2 x 55.9).
Collection of the artist.

499. **The Immoralist**, 1991.
Oil on canvas, 48⅛ x 48⅛ (122.3 x 122.3).
Dr Jerry Sherman, USA.

*The following works were not listed in the
first edition*

500. **Oxford Woman**, c.1958. *Plate 3*
Charcoal pencil on paper, 14 x 12 (35.5 x 30.5).
Collection of the artist.

501. **Oxford Man**, c.1958. *Plate 6*
Oil on canvas, 15 x 8 (38.1 x 20.3).
Collection of the artist.

502. **Red Nude**, c.1960. *Plate 8*
Oil on canvas, 36 x 36 (91.5 x 91.5).
Collection of the artist.

503. **Life Study**, c.1958. *Plate 24*
Charcoal pencil on paper, 21 x 16 (53.3 x 40.6).
Collection of the artist.

504. **The Architects**, 1980-4. *Plate 150*
Oil on canvas, 48 x 48 (122 x 122).
Colin St John Wilson, London.

558. My Stepfather, 1989-94.
Oil on canvas, 36¼ x 36¼ (92 x 92).
Collection of the artist.

559. Orthodox Rabbi (Adin Steinsaltz), 1990-4.
Oil on canvas, 39⅞ x 30 (101.4 x 76.2).
Collection of the artist.

560. Reform Rabbi (Albert Friedlander),
1990-4.
Oil on canvas, 39¾ x 30 (101 x 76.2).
Private collection.

561. Amsterdam, 1991-4.
Oil on canvas, 40 x 20 (101.7 x 50.8).
Private collection.

562. Wej (after Auerbach), 1991-4.
Oil on canvas, 60 x 39½ (152.4 x 100.3).
Collection of the artist.

**563. He and She (The Spirit of the Bed
Watching),** 1991-4.
Oil on canvas, 48 x 48 (122 x 122).
Private collection.

564. Self-Portrait (Vermilion Sweater), 1992-4.
Oil on canvas, 23 x 20 (58.4 x 50.8).
Private collection.

565. Portrait of HH, 1992-4.
Oil on canvas, 30 x 24 (76.2 x 61).
Private collection.

566. Western Bathers, 1993-4. *Plate 187.*
Oil on canvas, 53¼ x 74⅞ (135.3 x 190.2).
Private collection.

567. Josephine Singer, 1993-4.
Oil on canvas, 61 x 24 (154.9 x 61).
Private collection.

568. Jeffrey Camp, 1993-4.
Charcoal on paper, 7⅞ x 5⅜ (20 x 13.7).
Collection of the artist.

569. Richard Wollheim, 1993-4.
Charcoal and pastel on paper, 30 x 20 (76.2 x 50.8).
Private collection.

570. Self-Portrait (Hockney Pillow), 1993-4.
Oil on canvas, 40 x 20 (101.6 x 50.8).
Private collection.

571. Behold the Man, 1994.
Oil on canvas, 20 x 16 (50.8 x 40.6).
Collection of the artist.

572. Father Reading Tom Sawyer to his Son,
1994. *Plate 191.*
Oil on canvas, 48 x 60 (122 x 152.4).
Private collection, Miami.

573. Leonard McComb, 1994.
Charcoal on paper, 7¾ x 5¾ (19.7 x 14.6).
Collection of the artist.

574. Lee Friedlander Photographing Me, 1994.
Charcoal on paper, 30½ x 22½ (77.5 x 57.1).
Private collection.

575. Portrait of the Artist as a Schlemiel, 1994.
Oil on canvas, 40 x 32 (101.6 x 81.3).

Collection of the artist.

576. Vincent Measuring the Sun, 1994.
Charcoal and pastel on paper, 30¾ x 22
(78.1 x 55.9).
Private collection.

577. Giotto at 70, 1994.
Charcoal and pastel on paper, 30¼ x 22
(76.8 x 55.9).
Private collection.

578. Abraham and Hagar Surprised by Sarah,
1994.
Charcoal on paper, 30¼ x 22 (76.8 x 55.9).
Ashmolean Museum, Oxford.

579. David and Goliath, 1994.
Charcoal on paper, 22¼ x 30¾ (56.5 x 78.1).
Private collection.

580. The Kiss, 1994.
Charcoal on paper, 30¾ x 22¼ (78.1 x 56.5).
Private collection.

581. Art and Literature, 1994.
Charcoal on paper, 30¾ x 22¼ (78.1 x 56.5).
Private collection.

582. On This Perfect Day, 1994.
Oil on canvas, 10 x 17⅞ (25.4 x 45.5).
Private collection.

583. NYJ, 1994.
Charcoal on paper, 7¾ x 5½ (19.7 x 14).
Collection of the artist.

584. D.I.Y. Watching (study for Bad Back),
1994.
Charcoal on paper, 7¾ x 5½ (19.7 x 14).
Collection of the artist.

585. She and He (La Vie), 1994. *Fig. 18.*
Oil on canvas, 81¼ x 52 (206.4 x 132.1).
Fonds National d'Art Contemporain, Paris.

586. He and She (The Sickness unto Death),
1994. *Plate 196.*
Oil on canvas, 25¼ x 45½ (64.2 x 115.5).
Private collection.

587. Self Portrait as a Cleveland Indian, 1994.
Charcoal and pastel on paper, 30½ x 22½
(77.5 x 57.2).
Cleveland Museum.

588. After Buñuel, 1994.
Charcoal and pastel on paper, 30½ x 22¼
(77.5 x 56.5).
Private collection.

589. Rabbi Alex Schindler, 1994.
Charcoal and pastel on paper, 22¼ x 15
(56.5 x 38.1).
Collection of the artist.

590. Farewell My Lovely, 1994.
Charcoal and pastel on paper, 30⅜ x 22¼
(77.2 x 56.5).
Private collection.

591. The Last Time, 1994.
Charcoal on paper, 22¼ x 15¼ (56.5 x 38.8).

Private collection.

592. Montaigne, 1994.
Charcoal on paper, 22¼ x 15¼ (56.5 x 38.8).
Private collection, London.

593. Weeping Soldier, 1994.
Charcoal on paper, design for Vad Yashem medal
Private collection.

594. Nell at Norton, 28 May 1995, 1995.
Charcoal on paper, 7⅝ x 5¾ (19.5 x 14.5).
Collection of the artist.

595. Finn at Norton, 28 May 1995, 1995.
Charcoal on paper, 7½ x 5¾ (19 x 14.5).
Collection of the artist.

596. The Auctioneer, 1995.
Pastel and charcoal on paper, 30½ x 22¼
(77.5 x 56.5).
Private collection.

**597. John the Baptist Jew (with Moses and
David after Dürer),** 1995.
Pastel and charcoal on paper, 30½ x 22¼
(77.5 x 56.5).
Collection of the artist.

598. Eliza, 1995.
Charcoal on paper, 30¼ x 22 (76.8 x 55.9).
Private collection.

**599. Miranda Richardson in my Own
Production of Joseph and Potiphar's Wife,**
1995-6.
Charcoal and pastel on paper, 30¾ x 22½
(78.1 x 57.1).
Private collection.

600. The Lorenzetti, 1970-96.
Oil on canvas, 10 x 12 (25.5 x 30.5).
Collection of the artist.

601. The Fascist (E.P.), 1970-96.
Oil and screenprint on canvas, 40 x 27
(101.7 x 68.6).
Collection of the artist.

602. The Typist (Typing his Novel), 1990-6.
Oil and Penguins on canvas, 29½ x 29¾ (75 x 74.5).
Private collection.

603. My First Abstract, 1990-6.
Oil on canvas, 16⅛ x 12¼ (41 x 31).
Private collection.

604. Elles, 1995-6.
Pastel on paper, 30⅜ x 52⅛ (77 x 132.5).
Private collection.

605. Walletjes, Amsterdam, 1995-6.
Oil on canvas, 60 x 24 (152.4 x 61).
Collection of the artist.

606. Clinton, 1996.
Pastel on paper, 30½ x 22¼ (77.5 x 56.5).
University College, Oxford.

**607. Isaiah Berlin and Alfred Brendel at the
Opera,** 1996.
Charcoal on paper, 7⅝ x 5⅝ (19.4 x 14.3).
Collection of the artist.

608. **UCS,** 1996.
Charcoal on paper, 7½ x 5½ (19 x 14).
Collection of the artist.

609. **IX,** 1996.
Charcoal on paper, 7⅝ x 5⅝ (19.4 x 14.3).
Collection of the artist.

610. **Ashbery,** 1996.
Charcoal on paper, 7⅝ x 5⅝ (19.4 x 14.3).
Collection of the artist.

611. **London Bus,** 1996.
Oil on canvas, 36 x 36 (61.5 x 61.5).
Collection of the artist.

612. **The Little Fourteen Year Old Model,**
1996.
Oil on canvas, 48 x 13 (122 x 33).
Private collection, London.

613. **Where We Lived in Paris,** 1996.
Oil on canvas, 24⅛ x 20⅛ (61.2 x 51.1).
Private collection, Paris.

614. **Swedish Teenager (Anna),** 1996.
Charcoal on paper, 30⅜ x 22⅛ (77.2 x 56.2).
Private collection.

615. **La Maja Vasca,** 1996.
Charcoal and pastel on paper, 21⅞ x 30¼
(55.5 x 76.8).
Private collection.

616. **The Bungee Jumper (Frances),** 1996.
Charcoal on paper, 30½ x 22 (77.5 x 56).
Collection of the artist.

617. **Heine in Paris,** 1996.
Pastel on paper, 30½ x 22¼ (77.5 x 56.5).
Private collection, Paris.

618. **Erotica Judaica (after Giotto),** 1996.
Charcoal on paper, 30½ x 21⅞ (77.5 x 55.5).
Private collection.

619. **Strife,** 1996.
Oil on Galsworthy bookcover, 6⅞ x 9⅝
(17.5 x 24.5).
Private collection.

620. **Bad Teeth,** 1996.
Oil on canvas, 24⅜ x 20⅛ (62 x 51).
Collection of the artist.

621. **Lighthouse, Andros,** 1996.
Oil on canvas, 39⅝ x 39⅞ (100 x 100.5).
Collection of the artist.

622. **When Friends Fall Out (after Duccio),**
1996.
Oil on canvas, 21⅜ x 25⅜ (54.4 x 64.5).
Private collection, San Francisco.

623. **Bad Hearing,** 1996.
Oil on canvas, 24⅜ x 20¼ (62 x 51.5).
Collection of the artist.

624. **Study for the Psalmist,** 1996.
Charcoal on canvas, 19⅞ x 18½ (50.6 x 47).
Collection of the artist.

625. **Listening to Music,** 1996.
Charcoal and pastel on paper, 30⅜ x 22⅛
(77.1 x 56.4).
Collection of the artist.

626. **Anna,** 1996.
Charcoal on paper, 30½ x 22⅛ (77.4 x 56.3).
Private collection.

627. **Lake Tahoe,** 1996.
Oil on canvas, 28 x 36 (71.1 x 91.5).
Private collection.

628. **The Artist,** 1996.
Oil on canvas, 72 x 23¾ (183 x 60).
Ho-Am Art Museum, Seoul.

629. **Gustav Mahler,** 1996.
Pastel on paper, 60½ x 48 (153.5 x 122).
The Vienna Staatsoper (Commissioned and donated
by Gilbert Kaplan).

630. **The Critic Kills**.
Oil and collage on canvas, 20⅛ x 80½ (51 x 204.2).
Collection of the artist.

631. **Emily Dickinson,** 1997.
Charcoal on paper, 30½ x 22 (77.4 x 56).
Collection of the artist.

632. **The Modernist,** 1997.
Oil on canvas, 35⅝ x 35⅝ (90.5 x 90.5).
Private collection, Toronto.

633. **The Killer-Critic Assassinated by His
Widower, Even,** 1997. *Plate 193.*
Oil and collage on canvas, 60 x 60 (152.4 x 152.4).
Astrup Fearnley Museet for Moderne Kunst, Oslo.

634. **The Violinist with the Spirit of His
Mother,** 1997. *Plate 192.*
Oil on canvas, 60 x 24 (152.4 x 61).
Private collection, Boston.

635. **Death Pitches a Curve (My First
American Picture),** 1997. *Fig. 20.*
Charcoal on paper, 15½ x 11¼ (39.4 x 28.6).
Collection of the artist.

636. **Mendelsohn House,** 1988-98. *Plate 189.*
Oil on canvas, 36 x 60 (91.4 x 152.4).
Collection of the artist.

637. **The Enemy Within,** 1990-8.
Pastel and collage on paper (reworked lithograph),
27½ x 22½ (70 x 57).
Collection of the artist.

638. **The Cleveland Indian,** 1995-8. *Plate 194.*
Oil on canvas, 72 x 24 (182.9 x 61).
Cleveland Museum.

639. **My First Ship,** 1996-8. *Plate 203.*
Oil on canvas, 35¾ x 35¾ (91.5 x 91.5).
Private collection, Nassau, Bahamas.

640. **PL (The Modernist),** 1997-8.
Charcoal on paper, 30 x 22 (76.2 x 56).
Collection of the artist.

641. **The Parist,** 1997-8. *Plate 200.*
Oil on canvas, 36 x 36 (91.5 x 91.5).
Collection of the artist.

642. **The Archaeologist,** 1997-8. *Plate 199.*
Oil on canvas, 60 x 36 (152.5 x 91.5).
Kansas City Museum

643. **Second Diasporist Manifesto,** 1997-8.
Plate 194.
Oil on canvas, 60 x 60 (152.4 x 152.4).
Collection of the artist.

644. **Moonlightist,** 1998. *Plate 198.*
Oil on canvas, 36 x 24 (91.4 x 61).
Collection of the artist.

645. **Circumcision Chair,** 1998. *Plate 197.*
Oil on canvas, 60 x 36 (152.4 x 91.4).
Collection of the artist.

646. **Bed and Sofa (After Abram Room),** 1998.
Plate 202.
Oil on canvas, 24 x 72 (61 x 182.9).
Collection of the artist.

647. **Koufax,** 1998. *Plate 201.*
Oil on canvas, 36 x 36 (91.4 x 91.4).
Los Angeles County Museum.

648. **Sandra 5,** 1999.
Oil and collage on canvas, 24 x 20 (61 x 50.8).
Collection of the artist.

649. **The Physicist (Albert Einstein),** 1999.
Oil on canvas, 60 x 24 (152.4 x 61).
Collection of the artist.

650. **The Sexist (Miss X),** 1999.
Oil on canvas, 60 x 24 (152.4 x 61).
Collection of the artist.

651. **Study for Second Diasporist Manifesto
(detail-work in progress),** 1970-.
Collage on canvas, 30¼ x 21⅞ (77 x 55.5).
Collection of the artist.

ADDENDA

652. **Jean Shrimpton,** c.1969.
Pencil on paper, 20½ x 11⅞ (52 x 30.1).
Collection of the artist.

653. **Linda,** 1975.
Oil and charcoal on canvas stretched over board,
24 x 14⅛ (61 x 36).
Collection of the artist.

654. **False Messiah,** 1986.
Oil on canvas, 30½ x 9½ (77.5 x 24.2).
Collection of the artist.

655. **Jerusalem,** 1988.
Pastel and charcoal on paper, 28¼ x 21⅛ (71.8 x
53.7).
Private collection.

656. **Abundance, Calm and Pleasure,** 1988.
Oil on canvas, 48¼ x 48¼ (122.5 x 122.5).
Collection of the artist.

INDEX OF WORKS BY KITAJ

Numbers in **bold** refer to plate numbers. *Italic* page numbers refer to figures in the text.

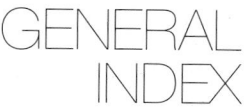

GENERAL INDEX

Page numbers in *italics*
refer to illustrations.